Sacred Interests

Sacred Interests

The United States and the Islamic World, 1821–1921

KARINE V. WALTHER

The University of North Carolina Press / Chapel Hill

Published with the assistance of the Anniversary Fund
of the University of North Carolina Press

Set in Miller by Westchester Publishing Services
Manufactured in the United States of America

The paper in this book meets the guidelines for permanence and durability
of the Committee on Production Guidelines for Book Longevity of the Council on
Library Resources. The University of North Carolina Press has been a member
of the Green Press Initiative since 2003.

Jacket illustration and frontispiece: *Jerusalem from the Mount of Olives*, 1870,
by Frederic Edwin Church, Nelson-Atkins Museum of Art

Complete cataloging information for this title is available from
the Library of Congress.

ISBN 978-1-4696-2539-3 (cloth: alk. paper)
ISBN 978-1-4696-2540-9 (cloth: alk. paper)

To Mia

"The Americans combine the notions of Christianity and of liberty so intimately in their minds, that it is impossible to make them conceive the one without the other."

—Alexis de Tocqueville, *Democracy in America*, 1835

Contents

Figures

Acknowledgments

This book has been long in the making and would have been impossible without the aid of numerous academics. Although it remains a very American story, I have tried whenever possible to frame these historical narratives within the histories of the peoples and countries with which Americans interacted. One of the most difficult challenges in writing this book has been trying to understand the various historiographical debates that have defined these diverse histories. For this reason, this work has depended heavily on the accumulated work of generations of scholars with expertise in local languages and histories. I am deeply indebted to all of them and apologize for any lack of nuance that has remained in the telling of these complex international stories. All remaining errors are mine to claim. Although space limitations preclude listing them all here, I have included their texts in my extended bibliography.

In addition to consulting these works, several scholars with expertise in Ottoman, Filipino, North African, European, Russian, and American diplomatic history have kindly read chapters and/or offered their guidance, support, and advice. I would like to thank them for their help in developing and nuancing the international aspects of this project. These include: Donald Bloxham, William Clarence-Smith, Robert Fulton, Michael Hawkins, Walter Hixson, Michael Hunt, Charles King, Lisa Leff, Catherine Lutz, Jessica Marglin, Andrew Patrick, Vijay Prashad, Aviel Roshwald, Daniel Schroeter, and Ronald Grigor Suny. I would also like to thank Julian Go and Douglas Little for their extremely helpful comments when reviewing the book. I have greatly benefited from their advice and recommendations.

In the decade that this book has been in the works, I have also received invaluable advice and encouragement from former professors, advisors, and colleagues. These include: Hisham Aidi, Abdullah Al-Arian, Lisa Anderson, Betsy Blackmar, Richard Bulliet, Heather Curtis, Eric Foner, Daniel Freund, Brendan Hill, Alice Kessler-Harris, Rashid Khalidi, Nancy Kwak, Gregory Mann, Adam McKeown, the late Ernest May, Rory Miller, JoAnn Moran Cruz, David Painter, Reza Pirbhai, Maya Primorac, Carole Sargent, Anders Stephanson, Anne Stoler, and Judith Tucker. I would particularly like to thank my colleague Edward Kolla for his ongoing support, advice and patience as a colleague, friend and intellectual, and in particular his willingness to meticulously read the entire manuscript when it was still over 500 pages long. That is true friendship.

Over the last ten years, significant parts of this book have been presented at various conferences and workshops, and I have greatly benefited from the feedback of co-panelists and commenters. These include Clara Altman, Christopher Capozzola, Anne Foster, Matthew Jacobson, Jeffrey Kimball, Martin Klimke, Paul Kramer, Adam McKeown, Andrew Patrick, Ussama Makdisi, Jay Sexton, and Heather Sharkey.

This book would not have been possible without the knowledge, advice, and help of numerous librarians and archivists. I would like to thank Susan Fahy, Elizabeth Graham, Shelley Lloyd, Ken Scott, and Frieda Wiebe. I would like to thank especially Donna Hanson and Patrick Kerwin for their tireless aid in securing me essential and difficult to obtain sources.

Several copyeditors have allowed me to transform this manuscript into a book. I would like to thank Jennifer, Anna-Lisa, Susan, and Jane for their careful attention and help. Most importantly, I would like to thank Brandon Proia, my editor at the University of North Carolina Press, for his enthusiasm and for his tireless support in turning this unwieldy and lengthy manuscript into a book.

Numerous archives and institutions have helped fund this book along the way. I would like to thank the Rockefeller Archives for granting me funding to visit their archives as I was researching this project. I am grateful to have received funding from the Organization of American Historians early in this project in the form of a La Pietra Fellowship in transnational history. I would also like to thank the Belfer Center for Science and International Relations at the Harvard Kennedy School of Government, in partnership with the Dubai Initiative and the Initiative on Religion in International Affairs, and, in particular, Monica Toft, Alex Keyssar, Ash Carter, and the late Ernest May, for offering me a postdoctoral fellowship that enabled me to work on this book. I have received several generous research grants from my home institution, Georgetown University School of Foreign Service in Qatar, that have allowed me to complete the book. I would also like to thank my students for helping me to realize why these stories matter.

The book has greatly benefited from the feedback I received at the Religion and Empire workshops, run by Tracy Leavelle and Sylvester Johnson and funded by the Kripke Center for the Study of Religion and Society at Creighton University. I would like to thank all of the workshop participants for their helpful advice during our meetings.

I would like to thank William D. Rueckert for providing me with access to the unarchived personal papers of Cleveland Dodge. I would also like to thank Patricia Herlihy for giving me access to the unarchived papers of Eugene Schuyler, which are not included in the Library of Congress.

Finally, I would like to thank my mother for her support and my husband Julien and my daughter Mia for their patience during this long process. Although I cannot fulfill my daughter's request to never write another book, I hope she will one day understand why it was so important for me to write this one.

Sacred Interests

INTRODUCTION

In 1872, Hagop Matteosian, an Armenian Ottoman subject and the civil head of the Protestant communities in the Ottoman Empire, wrote a letter from Istanbul to Nathanial Clark, corresponding secretary of the American Board of Commissioners for Foreign Missions (ABCFM), a Boston-based organization founded in 1810. In his letter, Matteosian praised the ABCFM's efforts to spread American culture and Protestant Christianity to Ottoman Christians, noting that the "most zealous advocate of American civilization could not have done half as much for his country abroad as the missionary has done."[1]

Given the ABCFM's mission to promote American Protestant civilization among Ottoman subjects, Matteosian asserted, the American people now had "a sacred interest" in the Ottoman Empire. But Matteosian went beyond just lauding the benefits the missionaries had brought to the empire's subjects. Their presence also advanced U.S. interests. Hinting at the larger political and commercial competition between Europeans and Americans, he wrote that American missionary influence could not be "overbalanced" by all of the European diplomats combined. Clark undoubtedly welcomed Matteosian's praise; the ABCFM secretary republished the letter the following month in the ABCFM's monthly journal, the *Missionary Herald*, whose readership included thousands of influential members across the country.

The primary endeavor of ABCFM missionaries was to convert Ottoman subjects to Protestant Christianity, not to serve as "advocates" to advance their own country's interests or their political and cultural values. Yet, Matteosian understood that many ABCFM missionaries did not consider these goals to be mutually exclusive. Ultimately, most American Protestant missionaries in the Ottoman Empire believed an indivisible link existed between the superiority of their faith and the superiority of their culture; thus, "conversion" meant more than just advancing religious dogma—it meant reforming the Ottoman Empire in America's image.

These goals were undoubtedly apparent to Matteosian. According to his letter, American missionary schools had not only converted Ottoman Christian subjects to Protestant Christianity, they had also inculcated in their Ottoman students a deep belief in the political, religious, material, and commercial superiority of the United States over the Ottoman Empire. If Clark were to quiz a young Ottoman schoolboy at an American missionary school about geography, he would certainly be surprised to find that "he knows more of the United States than perhaps of his own native country. Question him about social order, he will tell you all men are created equal." In addition, Clark should not be surprised to see "Yankee clocks; American chairs, tables, organs; American agricultural implements; Yankee cotton-gins, saw-mills, sewing-machines; American flowers in the very heart of Kurdistan; Yankee saddles, and a Yankee rider on the wild mountains of Asia Minor, perhaps singing, with his native companion, some familiar tune."[2] Given Matteosian's depiction of these pervasive American influences, one can easily imagine the "Yankee rider" singing "Yankee Doodle Dandy."

Matteosian's letter may have offered some comfort to American missionaries who worried about the success of their missions in the Ottoman Empire, but it could not eliminate their concerns. By 1872, when he wrote his letter, American Protestants had extended their presence throughout the empire and were able to spread their beliefs to more than 8,000 Ottoman students at hundreds of missionary schools. In this way, American Protestant missionaries far outnumbered any other American or European entity in the Ottoman Empire. Nevertheless, Matteosian broadly overstated the American missionaries' success in transforming Ottoman subjects into American Yankees. He failed to mention that Ottoman Christians, including Armenians, had been hostile toward American missionaries for decades and that they resisted missionary attempts to reform their religious practices and their culture.[3] He omitted that the Armenian patriarch had repeatedly requested that the Ottoman sultan forcibly remove the American missionaries, whom he believed challenged his authority and the overall stability of Ottoman society. The ABCFM faced similar opposition from Ottoman Christian religious leaders in other parts of the empire. Alerted by his Christian subjects to these disruptions, the Ottoman sultan had repeatedly asked the American ministers to make the missionaries leave.

But the most glaring absence in Matteosian's letter underscores the American missionaries' anxieties about their work in the Ottoman Empire. From the beginning, the ABCFM's most important missionary objective was not to convert Ottoman Christians to Protestant Christianity, but instead to convert Muslims. Ottoman legal restrictions prohibited proselytizing directly to Muslims. Thus, the ABCFM's work among Ottoman Christians constituted a strategic step toward this more important goal. As one ABCFM leader noted, these "nominal" Christians had strayed so far from "true" Christianity that they no longer served as good examples to Muslims: "Hence a wise plan for the conversion of the Mohammedans of Western Asia necessarily involved, first, a mission to the Oriental Churches."[4] Despite six decades of effort, the hopes of American missionaries that their success in spreading Protestant Christianity to Ottoman Christians would soon redound upon Muslims had thus far proved a dismal failure.

More than forty years after Matteosian sent his letter to Clark, the desire to convert Muslims and bring political and spiritual reform to Muslim lands remained a central concern for many Americans. In 1914, Josiah Strong, one of the most well-known and influential American clergymen and a strong proponent of American imperial expansion and missionary work, praised the efforts of Episcopalian bishop Charles Brent. Brent had begun working as a missionary among Filipino Muslims (or Moros) in the American colony of the Philippines shortly after the United States annexed the islands in 1898. Although Strong praised Brent's missionary efforts for their own sake, he was particularly hopeful for how Brent's success among Filipino Muslims could be expanded to Muslims around the world.

Strong was so confident in the global potential of Brent's work that he published a fund-raising pamphlet to support the cause. Entitled, "A Door into the Mohammedan World," the pamphlet highlighted the far-ranging possibilities of Brent's efforts: "To discharge our obvious duty to the nation's wards, to give a Christian civilization to a million Moros, is worth any sacrifice; but if this is done, infinitely more will have been done—we shall have demonstrated the method of approach, we shall have entered the door into the great Mohammedan world, and shall have done more in a single generation to win it to the Cross than has been done by all the diplomats and merchants and soldiers of all the centuries."[5] Strong's public support of Brent's mission acknowledged decades-long efforts by the ABCFM and other American missionary organizations to find the elusive "door into the Mohammedan world" that would allow American Protestant

Christians to convert Muslims. But what one American Protestant missionary had earlier dubbed the "Mohammedan missionary problem" continued to vex their efforts.[6]

Strong's pamphlet revealed another important facet of the American aspiration to reach Muslims. Supported by centuries of history, Strong assumed that nonmissionary actors, including "diplomats and merchants and soldiers," also wanted to convert Muslims. In Strong's imagination, these efforts united American and European Christians in a historical and global struggle against the Islamic faith and civilization. He correctly noted that American desires to spread religious and political reform abroad were not limited to American missionaries.[7] During the nineteenth and early twentieth centuries, Americans *in all segments of society* played an active role in attempting to reform the Islamic world.

Beginning in 1821, when Americans actively lobbied their government to intervene on behalf of Greek revolutionaries during the Greek War of Independence, Americans involved themselves directly in major world events that increasingly pitted Europeans and Americans against Muslim rulers. Americans helped the Greeks again during the Cretan Insurrection of 1866–69. Ten years later, American diplomats and missionaries played a central role in focusing international attention on the Ottoman repression of Bulgarian revolutionaries and then in securing the independence of Bulgaria. Beginning in 1840, American Jewish organizations concerned with the status of Jews under Muslim rule in the Ottoman Empire also lobbied the U.S. government for action and organized internationally to bring attention to the cause, further shaping American interventions in Islamic societies.

In subsequent decades, American action extended beyond the Ottoman Empire to other Islamic societies. Beliefs that Muslims were incapable of ruling themselves, much less others, fueled American support for extending French imperial rule in Morocco. Similar logic about the superiority of Euro-American civilization prompted the extension of their own empire to the Philippines, which included more than 300,000 Muslim Filipinos.

American attention focused again on the Ottoman Empire when Ottoman rulers violently suppressed revolutionary activities during the Armenian Massacres of 1894–96 and during the Armenian Genocide of 1915–17. The latter prompted calls by missionaries, diplomats, politicians, and Armenians themselves for the United States to assume a mandate over Armenia and other parts of the Ottoman Empire after World War I. Although unsuccessful in their efforts, the assertion by the Great Powers that Muslims were not yet "able to stand by themselves" prompted American and European negotiators at the Versailles Peace Conference in 1919 to ignore local demands and instead support a mandate system that extended quasi-imperial European rule over large swathes of territories that formally belonged to the Ottoman Empire.[8] Through these actions at home and abroad, American desires to convert, reform, colonize, and control Muslims in Islamic societies surfaced throughout the nineteenth and early twentieth centuries. As Hagop Matteosian had stated so suggestively, Americans' "sacred interest" in the Islamic world profoundly shaped their interactions with Muslims.

Sacred Interests tells the story of these interventions by focusing on how nonstate actors, including missionaries, religious organizations, journalists, academics, businessmen, clergymen, philanthropists, and the wider American public collaborated with diplomats, colonial officials, soldiers, and political elites in shaping foreign relations in the Islamic world. But Americans did not experience these events in isolation. These diverse global arenas became overlapping sources of both knowledge and action. Diplomatic and cultural knowledge accumulated through American participation in these events and combined to form a dominant public and diplomatic understanding about the proper way of dealing with Islam and Muslims, despite their geographic, historical, cultural, and religious differences. This happened repeatedly throughout American interactions with the Islamic world. When Americans came to the aid of Greek Christian revolutionaries fighting for independence from the Ottoman Empire, they referenced American battles with the "despotic" Barbary powers in North Africa. After the United States annexed the Philippines in 1898, the American consul in the Ottoman Empire successfully appealed to the Ottoman sultan to order Filipino Muslims to "behave" and accept American colonial rule. When discussing how to impose political reform on the Moroccan government in 1906, American policymakers drew insight from reforms imposed by European powers on the Ottoman Empire decades earlier. At the beginning of World War I, Americans feared that an Ottoman call for "holy war" might extend to its Muslim population in the Philippines. During the Versailles Peace Conference, American supporters of a U.S. League of Nations mandate over Armenia argued that the successful American administration of the Christian and Muslim populations of the Philippine Islands proved its competency to assume such a momentous task.

The tendency to rely on American experiences with Muslims in one part of the world as a knowledge base from which to draw understanding and shape policies in other Islamic societies, sometimes thousands of miles away, was driven by the beliefs of many Americans that the Islamic faith was the central and most important defining element of Islamic societies and Muslims themselves. Such interpretations also depended on the assumption that Muslims required outside intervention and the abandonment of their faith to make any civilizational advances. American beliefs about the superiority of their religious beliefs complemented their perceptions of Muslims as despotic, barbaric, intolerant of other religious faiths, and prone to violent religious fanaticism. Many Americans maintained that, because of their Islamic faith, Muslims were mired in a political past and thus incapable of forging a path to modernity—an interpretation that further rendered Muslims incapable of decently governing themselves or others.

More sympathetic treatments of Islam and Muslims did exist during this period. The Islamic "Orient" was a source of exotic fascination for some Americans. The fact that Islam, alongside Judaism and Christianity, made up part of the family of Abrahamic faiths and that the Islamic faith recognized and respected Jesus and other Abrahamic prophets also accorded the faith a higher status. This was particularly true when Americans compared Muslims with religious groups from non-Abrahamic faiths, such as Filipino animists or African "heathens." Such recognition often accorded Muslims a higher status in their hierarchies of race, religion, and civilization, albeit one doomed by its inherent decadence and despotism.[9] In the late nineteenth and early twentieth centuries, calls for religious tolerance and the right of self-determination for all peoples led some Americans working in Islamic societies to defend Muslims against European and American imperial expansion. Americans who witnessed the brutal tactics of Euro-American imperial rule throughout the world questioned the validity of these claims of civilizational superiority. Similarly, throughout the nineteenth century, some Americans who worked directly with Muslims offered more nuanced understandings, which considered the distinct histories and cultures of Islamic societies.

But despite these more positive views, a trend soon developed that profoundly shaped the *dominant* narratives about Islam and Muslims. When Americans witnessed and participated in diplomatic and global events that involved Christians and Muslims on opposing sides, negative and vociferous attacks on Islam predominated in popular and official discourse. At these moments, more tolerant interpretations of Islam were simply drowned out by belligerent rhetoric, which increasingly depicted the Islamic faith as a global problem that demanded eradication. The most ardent defenders of this view depicted these events as part of a global war of "cross against crescent." Counternarratives in which Americans and Muslims publicly and vociferously critiqued American actions or used such events to highlight domestic policies of discrimination in the United States were similarly ignored or deemed outside the purview of acceptable discourse. In other words, if a wider marketplace of ideas in the United States about Islam and Muslims in the nineteenth century did indeed exist, this marketplace was drastically reduced to a narrow and simplistic aisle of discourse during such moments.

The tendency to advance more belligerent and Manichean classifications of perceived enemies during moments of crisis has been previously acknowledged by scholars of American cultural history. Sociologists Jeffrey C. Alexander and Philip Smith have argued that it is specifically during "moments of tension, unease and crisis" that public discourse emerging from American civil society most vociferously categorizes people into "binary codes." These moments become "quasi-ritualized periods in which fundamental meanings are also at stake." As they argue, Americans drew on "a discourse of liberty" that attempted to regulate and define "actors, relationships between actors and institutions." Such a discourse could exist only by creating and depicting "antonymic" enemies that were in total opposition to the rational, egalitarian, and democratic ideals that defined American culture and government.[10] Although Alexander and Smith do not deal specifically with American foreign relations in the Islamic world, their theories are perfectly representative of the oppositional classifications that became central to American understandings of Islam and Muslims during moments of diplomatic crisis, both at home and abroad.

The predominant American view that emerged at these moments was that the religious faith of Muslims defined their identity, a belief that was only exacerbated by American perceptions regarding other aspects of their identity. Indeed, these beliefs were rarely divorced from American perceptions about race. The supposed "racial traits" that accompanied being a "Turk," "Filipino," or "Arab" infused wider American attitudes about how these historical actors would behave as Muslims. The stereotypes held by Americans about Muslims perpetuated the racialization of a broader Islamic religious identity. In contrast, for some Americans, the religious faith of Muslims trumped any other considerations, including "racial nuance," so that being "Muslim" became its own racial category, overriding competing pseudoscientific definitions of race. Such understandings helped in establishing monolithic understandings of Muslims that transcended geography.

The beliefs about religious and racial differences that drove American attitudes toward Muslims mirrored attitudes that attributed similar traits to other non-Christian groups, both at home and abroad. Indeed, Jews and Christian Arabs were not immune to such hierarchies of difference. In the United States, American attitudes about race and religious belief also merged in complex ways for American Jews, Catholics, Mormons, and other non-Protestant groups.[11] The same was also true to a certain extent for Native Americans. At various times and to various degrees, most non-Protestant groups in the United States were deemed racially and religiously inferior and identified as potential foreign threats to American society.

What is remarkable about American conceptualizations of difference in the nineteenth century, however, is how these domestic hierarchies of race and religion played out in the international sphere. Although some white, Protestant Americans deemed non-Protestants as spiritually and racially inferior and a threat to American national identity, they generally classified these religious groups as superior to Muslims in their global religious hierarchy. Protestant Americans often downplayed their domestic antipathies against Jews, Catholics, Orthodox, and other non-Protestants living in Islamic societies. They believed that these non-Protestant groups were superior to Muslims (but inferior to Protestant Christians and still in need of religious reform or conversion). In fact, they posited that these populations could mediate between American Protestants and Muslims and thus help to convert, civilize, or reform Muslims who were in greater need of such advancement.

American Jewish activists contributed to these narratives in complicated ways. Jewish organizations in the United States concerned about the status of their religious brethren abroad posited that Jews living in Muslim societies were superior to Muslims and could serve as local agents of civilizational progress. Such arguments reinforced American hierarchies of race and religion domestically and globally. For American Jewish activists, these views reflected their complicated liminal status in American society. Their fight against domestic anti-Semitism and discrimination included claiming their own equality with American Christians, while simultaneously advancing the racial and religious superiority of Jews living in Islamic lands vis-à-vis Muslim "Orientals." Part of this struggle also included advancing an ideal portrait of the United States as a secular model of religious tolerance and freedom.[12] In the process, they defended their vision of American national identity, which challenged the exclusionary narrative of the United States as a Christian Protestant nation.

Christians and Jews living in Islamic lands and Ottoman immigrants in the United States and the wider diaspora also contributed to the American understanding of Islam.[13] Revolutionaries from Greece, Crete, Bulgaria, and Armenia emphasized their religious and civilizational superiority over Muslims when petitioning for American support. Increasing numbers of Ottoman Greeks, Armenians, and Syrians migrated to the United States and lobbied for U.S. governmental intervention. These non-Protestant populations contributed to larger American narratives about the Islamic world by endorsing a hierarchy of difference with Euro-American civilization at the top, non-Protestant populations in the middle, and Islamic civilization at the bottom. This hierarchy blurred the boundaries that challenged strict divisions between East and West.[14]

Increasing political demands by these domestic and international actors also contributed to an emerging discourse of humanitarian intervention that demanded European and American intercessions into sovereign Islamic territories known to be punishing Christian subjects or thought to be mistreating religious minorities.[15] These public demands in Europe and the United States constituted coordinated transnational responses that often led to the creation of international and transnational aid organizations dedicated to aiding religious minorities under Muslim rule. These organizations cooperated to raise funds, deliver aid, and lobby their governments for action.

In conjunction with mounting demands for humanitarian intervention, calls emerged for the extension of European and American imperial rule to Muslim societies. By framing imperial expansion in the rhetoric of humanitarian intervention, Europeans and Americans justified their impingement on Muslim rulers' sovereignty as part of a broader imperial civilizing mission rather than a crude commercial or strategic grab for territory and power. For this reason, despite strong exceptionalist and anti-imperialist rhetoric in American national identity, many Americans overtly and officially supported European and American imperial expansion into Islamic lands. This moral and diplomatic endorsement made sense to Americans who believed that Muslims were incapable of advancement without the help of "civilized" outside actors.

American official and unofficial participation in these events demonstrated that there were limits to official policies of U.S. nonentanglement in global affairs outside of the Western Hemisphere. Official insistence on neutrality did not always function as a hegemonic, determinant force in governing American actions abroad. Nonstate actors, including journalists, missionaries, religious activists, immigrants, philanthropists, academics, and other Americans contributed to important transatlantic activities that directly involved these individuals in diplomatic crises in Islamic lands. Mounting frustrations over lack of U.S. action also prompted official state actors to cooperate both overtly and covertly with private American interests in Islamic lands. American foreign relations were thus complicated by messy ideological and religious sympathies that led both state and nonstate actors to circumvent official neutrality. In the process, the diverse actions of these state and nonstate actors led to discursive *exchanges* among these various groups as they worked, at times in parallel and at other times in concert, to shape American foreign relations in the Islamic world.

This global and domestic circulation of ideas about race, religious belief, empire, and humanitarian intervention throughout the nineteenth century led to the creation of several mutually reinforcing narratives that governed American interactions with the Islamic world. But the genesis of these ideas did not begin with the Greek War of Independence in 1821, when *Sacred Interests* officially begins its story. Centuries of religious and intellectual interactions with Europeans and Muslims predated this moment and forged an important ideological framework on which Americans would build their later beliefs.

Islam in the Early American Imagination

Traditional narratives of American history have often begun with the "discovery" of the New World by Columbus, largely ignoring centuries of Native American history. Columbus, however, provides an ideal beginning for articulating the transatlantic exchange of attitudes about Islam between Europe and the New World. Accounts of Columbus's journey often emphasize economic motivations or the desire to find a new trade route to the East Indies, but religious competition also played an important role. As Columbus explained in his letter to King Ferdinand and Queen Isabella of Spain in 1492, his discovery of the New World was possible only because they had financed his trip as "rulers devoted to the Holy Christian Faith and dedicated to its expansion and to combating the religion of Mahomet and all idolatries and heresies."[16]

The year 1492 also marked the success of the Spanish *Reconquista* in purging Spain of Muslim rule, after which the Spanish crown focused on continued expulsion of Muslims and Jews from its land. And just as the religious faith of Jews and Muslims precluded their right to live on Spanish land, the belief in the religious superiority of Catholicism and the papal authority that accompanied it granted Columbus the sanction to claim lands in the New World on behalf of the Spanish crown and to ignore the rights of Native Americans who had occupied the land for centuries on the partial basis that they were not Christians.[17]

This logic of territorial dispossession, not surprisingly, had its origins in the thirteenth-century Crusades to the Holy Land, when Pope Innocent III had applied the concept to Muslims.[18] As one scholar has noted, "Spanish Christianity's long history of fervently nationalistic papally sponsored warfare against the infidel Moor ensured that the Church's facilitating colonizing discourse of intolerance for normatively divergent peoples would accompany any extension of Spain's imperial aspirations beyond the Mediterranean."[19] At times, a similar logic was also enlisted to justify English colonial ventures to the New World.[20] One English promoter of colonial expansion to the New World noted in 1555 that Spanish colonization in the Americas should be praised and that Christians should be happy "to see the kingdom of God to be so far enlarged upon the face of the earth, to the confusion of the Devil and the Turkish Antichrist but also do their uttermost of their power to do the same."[21]

Europeans brought these antipathies toward Islam with them to the New World. Explorer John Smith, who helped found the first English colony of Jamestown in 1607, had inherited strong anti-Turkish sentiments from one of his mentors. These feelings encouraged his decision to fight for the Austrian Hapsburg Empire in a purported religious conflict against the Ottoman Empire.[22] After being captured and enslaved by Ottoman forces, Smith escaped by beheading his three Turkish captors, which he recounted in his memoirs: "The lamentable noise of the miserable slaughtered Turkes was most wonderful to heare."[23] Smith's coat of arms, which included the heads of three Turks wearing turbans and the Latin phrase, *Vicere est Vivere* ("To Conquer is to Live"), appeared on one of the first maps of Virginia (see figure 1).[24]

Featuring this motto on one of the first cartographic depictions of the New World illustrated the powerful, symbolic connection between Smith's experience killing Muslim Turks and English colonial attitudes toward Native American "savages."[25] Just as domestic ideas about racial and religious inferiority would later play a role in shaping American relations abroad, European ideas about Islamic and Turkish otherness would seep into American attitudes about Native Americans.

Beginning in the seventeenth century, beliefs about Islam also played a central role in some strands of American religious and eschatological thought. Prominent religious leaders and theologians identified Islam

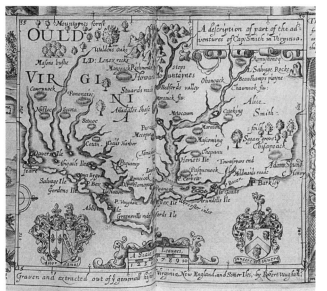

FIGURE 1. John Smith's coat of arms, included on the bottom right of his map of Virginia in 1624, contained a picture of the three turbaned Turks he beheaded during his military service fighting for the Austrian Hapsburg Empire next to the Latin phrase *Vicere est Vivere* ("To Conquer Is to Live"). (Map published in John Smith, *Generall Historie of Virginia, New-England, and the Summer Isles* [London, 1624], Virginia Historical Society)

(and sometimes Catholicism) as the Antichrist.[26] Biographical texts, often originating from Europe, vilified the Prophet Muhammad and reinforced antipathies toward the faith.[27] Influential religious leaders, including Increase Mather and Cotton Mather, maintained that only the end of the Ottoman Empire and the restoration of a Jewish state would bring about the second coming of Jesus.[28] Eschatological beliefs about the restoration of Jews to Palestine and the defeat of the Islamic faith and the Ottoman Empire as prerequisites for the second coming of Jesus and the end of days would continue to shape American attitudes toward the status of Jews in the Islamic world in the following centuries.[29]

In these early years, European political theorists also helped to forge Americans' beliefs about Islam and the detriments of Muslim rule.[30] Given the French philosopher Baron de Montesquieu's relative admiration for Protestantism, it is not surprising that he became one of the most influential Enlightenment thinkers in American political ideology.[31] But his texts also conveyed important ideas about the Islamic world. According to Montesquieu, the religion of a society often determined its political organization: Islam created despotism, Catholicism created monarchy, and Protestantism created republics. The title of one chapter in his *Spirit of Laws* is revelatory: "That a moderate Government is most agreeable to the Christian Religion and a despotic Government to the Mahometan."[32] Montesquieu's *Persian Letters*, which was translated into English in 1722—

only one year after the original French publication—advanced caricatures of Islamic despotism, albeit as a foil to critique French society.
Persian Letters influenced political thinkers and prompted imitations
by popular American authors, including Washington Irving.[33]

Similarly, in 1742, a play by Voltaire entitled *Mahomet the Imposter* portrayed Islam as a decadent religion spread through violence and tyranny.
The play, which was adapted in England and the United States, was largely
intended as a critique of the Catholic Church in Voltaire's France. In the
midst of the American Revolutionary War, the British and Americans
used the play to critique one another's alleged despotism.[34] After the
United States gained its independence, such tactics were also instrumental in partisan attacks between American political elites. In 1791, John
Quincy Adams enlisted the specter of Islamic despotism to attack Thomas
Jefferson's sympathies for French revolutionaries, accusing him of acting
"like the Arabian prophet to call upon all true believers in the Islam of
democracy, to draw their swords."[35]

By the second half of the eighteenth century, hostility toward Islam and
other non-Protestant faiths had spread, through popular literature and
church sermons, from religious and political elites to everyday Americans.
Baptist minister and defender of American religious freedom John Leland
recalled that by 1766, when he was twelve years old, his minister had
drummed the following religious injunction into the parishioners' memories: "Pity Mahomedan imposture—pagan idolatry—Jewish infidelity—
papistry and superstition: bring the downfall of anti-Christian tyranny to
a period."[36] Meanwhile, the "Muslim world" became a prevalent topic in
the swiftly growing popular press.[37] As one scholar has observed, between
1785 and 1800, a representative sample of seventeen periodicals included
more than 700 articles about the Islamic world.[38] Travel literature about
the "exotic" Orient had also become a popular genre in Europe and America
during this era.

Many of these texts, together with European and American biographies
of the Prophet Muhammad that excoriated Islam, theological literature,
and works of political philosophy on "Oriental despotism," served to so-
lidify longstanding conceptual boundaries that distinguished Muslims
from the "West," broadly understood as Europe and the United States.[39]
As Mark Mazower notes, "In the writings of travelers, pundits and phi-
losophers, powerful new polarities emerge—between civilized West and
barbarous East, between freedom-loving Europe and despotic Orient."[40]

During the early Republic, American political leaders also used the
Islamic faith to shape debates about the legal limits of American religious

liberty. As Denise Spellberg has argued in her study of the Founders' relationship to Islam, political and religious elites, including John Leland and Thomas Jefferson, used Islam, or the notion of "imaginary Muslims" who might one day be citizens of the United States, to push for complete religious freedom in both state and U.S. constitutions.[41] As she notes, these defenders of religious liberty were "able to divorce the idea of Muslim citizenship from their dislike of Islam, as they forged an 'imagined political community,' inclusive beyond all precedent."[42] Although such inclusivity was meant as an idealistic testament to religious toleration, it did not prevent the founders from expressing their deep antagonism to the Islamic faith.

Early American attitudes were also driven by direct interactions with Muslims themselves. Beginning in the late seventeenth century, Americans vilified Muslim Barbary pirates who captured American sailors and held them for ransom or used them as slave labor by attacking their religious faith.[43] In 1699, Puritan minister Cotton Mather dehumanized these Muslims and lamented the unlivable conditions faced by captured American sailors: "God hath given up several of our Sons, into the Hands of the Fierce Monsters of Africa. Mahometan Turks and Moors, and Devils are at this day oppressing many of our Sons, with a Slavery, wherein they Wish for Death, and cannot find it; a slavery from whence they cry and write unto us, it had been Good for us that we had never been Born."[44] The American captivity narratives, real and fictional, that emerged from these experiences thrilled American audiences with frightening descriptions of Muslim enslavement.[45] Authors of captivity narratives often emphasized that it was the Islamic beliefs of the captors that led them to perform such cruel and "barbarous" practices of enslavement.

Unbeknownst to many Americans at the time, from the very beginning, the Atlantic slave trade brought Muslim slaves to the American colonies. Little evidence indicates, however, that this development played any role in shaping American understandings of Islam.[46] The irony that American Christians were simultaneously enslaving African Muslims while attacking the immorality of Barbary slavery thus went unrecognized.

Public condemnation of Barbary Muslims reemerged during the early Republic. American refusal to pay tribute to the Barbary states of North Africa resulted in attacks on American ships by Barbary corsairs in the 1790s. Barbary corsairs captured more than thirty American merchant ships and ransomed approximately 700 sailors.[47] These struggles with what one American contemporary described as "merciless Mahometans" led to some of the first foreign policy debates in the new nation and inspired several new literary productions dedicated to the experiences of American Christians enslaved under Muslim rule.[48] Throughout these texts, Americans contrasted their religion, their culture, their newly formed government, and their political thought to Barbary Muslim "despots" and "fanatics." Islam thus served as a convenient foil by which Americans could advance and celebrate their own republican liberal government.[49] At this moment, as one scholar argues, Barbary Muslims ceased to be objects of exotic fascination. Instead, "the Barbary states emerged as hostile geopolitical entities" and became "monsters or buffoons to be fought and tricked."[50] The young republic had an opportunity to transform these beliefs into concrete action during the first and second Barbary Wars in 1801 and 1815, respectively.

Drawing on Orientalist tropes that emphasized a Manichean opposition between the United States and the Barbary powers allowed the young country to define itself as a leading member of the civilized Christian world through the language of political freedom, religion, and race. Racial hierarchies on the domestic front also explained how white Americans could justify African slavery on their own soil while decrying the condition of white Christians enslaved by Barbary Muslims abroad.[51] Americans were thus familiar with the trope of civilizational, religious, and racial difference and had handily adapted this language to their own domestic and foreign policy needs. Americans who had lived through the Barbary Wars and succeeding generations were thus steeped in larger transatlantic intellectual, political, and religious conceptualizations that placed the "Muslim world" in diametrical opposition to Europe and the United States.

Such beliefs were strengthened by the popular perception advanced by many Americans that the United States was above all a "Christian Nation." The religious revivalism of the Second Great Awakening that swept over Americans in the first decades of the nineteenth century further solidified this link between Christianity and American national identity. The populist religious movement also built on existing revolutionary fervor and allowed Americans to question the authority of traditional elites, both religious and secular, while simultaneously calling for greater public participation in shaping the outcome of American society. Such calls extended to publicly questioning the government's traditional diplomatic policies of nonintervention.[52] These increasingly fervent beliefs in the country's religious and political superiority drove American "manifest destiny" to extend the geographic spread of the nation westward in continental North America and beyond into the international realm. American missionary organizations such as the ABCFM were the first to translate this global manifest destiny to the Islamic world, but they were soon followed by others. As Americans experienced the momentous changes of the nineteenth century these ideas shaped not only how they saw their place in world history, but also how they understood Muslims and other non-Christians.

America and the World: International Law, the Age of Revolution, Empire, and the Christian "Family of Nations"

Negative attitudes about Islam and Muslims could be found on American soil from the arrival of the first Europeans, yet the eighteenth and nineteenth centuries witnessed important global changes that transformed and reinforced these beliefs in important ways. Alongside mounting American religious fervor and beliefs in American manifest destiny driven in part by the Second Great Awakening, American Christians increasingly identified with a wider, imagined community of global Christendom, often referred to by contemporaries as the civilized "Family of Nations." Although the historical logic that buttressed the defining parameters of this so-called family had its roots in Europe in the seventeenth and eighteenth centuries, Americans had fully adopted the concept by the late eighteenth and early nineteenth centuries and incorporated it into larger theories that divided the world into distinct civilizations. Such ideas had already found practical domestic relevance in Euro-American dealings with Native American populations.

America's self-perception as a crucial member of the Christian Family of Nations coexisted with American exceptionalist and isolationist narratives. Indeed, beliefs about U.S. national and global identity existed in a symbiotic relationship in which global identity helped define the national and in which the domestic merged with the international. As Charles Blight and David Geyer have so poignantly argued: "Both as an affair of the mind—an ideology, an imaginary, or a methodological concept—and as a manifest historical presence—as physical power—the nation-state has been, in its historical epoch, bent on bounding and capturing global forces in an effort to control them, and has thus continuously included/excluded and framed other processes in the production of U.S.-American history."[53] In ideological terms, these processes of inclusion and exclusion involved both European nation-states and Muslim societies. American beliefs about Muslim difference was one of these ideological tropes, adopted in part from European sources, but also developed and framed by the historical contingencies of the United States.

American legal, religious, and civilizational affiliations with the Christian Family of Nations functioned in a distinct yet similar way. Asserting their affiliation with this exclusive club granted the young republic legitimacy as a recognized member of the superior, civilized Christian world. A core requirement of such membership entailed an explicit exclusion of non-Christians. Membership in this club of Christian (and primarily European) powers also granted the United States an *appropriate* comparative reference against which Americans could situate their own national, political, and religious superiority. In contrast to Muslim societies, European nation-states were within the same "league" of civilization as the United States. In the nineteenth century, Americans thus "read" the world using a combination of these seemingly contradictory notions that ranked civilizations, races, and religions against each other and nation-states within their own civilizational category.

Such religious and civilizational distinctions also helped shape the development and codification of international law, which built on the existing supranational identity of a Christian Family of Nations and transformed it into a legal boundary as well.[54] The result reconfirmed the exclusion of Muslim societies while reaffirming the inclusion of the United States in this "civilized" Christian family.[55] No European thinker articulated this view more profoundly than did the German legal theorist G. F. von Martens. Martens noted in the introduction to his *Summary of the Law of Nations*, which was translated and republished in the United States in 1795: "I thought it necessary to confine my title to the *nations of Europe*; although, *in* Europe, the Turks have, in many respects, rejected the positive law of nations of which I here treat; and though, *out* of Europe, the United States of America have uniformly adopted it. It is to be understood *a potiori*, and it appears preferable to that of, *law of civilized nations*, which is too vague."[56]

These developing legal theories had important political and diplomatic repercussions for those "uncivilized" peoples who found themselves outside the bounds of international law. It reaffirmed and enshrined the sovereign rights of "civilized" states (for the most part limited to Europeans and Americans) while delegitimizing the sovereign rights for all people outside the bounds of international law, including Muslims and other non-Christian populations. By extension, this emerging logic served as a powerful justification and legal rationale for the extension of humanitarian intervention and empire into all non-Christian "uncivilized" territories.

Far from merely a European development, the codification of these legal distinctions also emerged from American sources. The influential

American international law theorist, Henry Wheaton, became a central figure in developing these theories.[57] In his work, Wheaton maintained that "Christian powers" had a distinct right to bypass Ottoman sovereignty, in part because of the empire's position outside the realm of international law.[58] In advancing the geographical boundaries of sovereignty and international law, Wheaton contributed to a developing discourse of humanitarian intervention that granted the Family of Nations the right to intervene in all non-Christian states when they believed Christians were being mistreated. In affirming this right, Wheaton's legal polemic exposed the limits of sovereign rights in Muslim lands.[59] According to Wheaton's legal and diplomatic logic, if Muslim countries were incapable of civilized behavior, then Christian powers were obligated to intervene on behalf of their religious brethren. The claims made by Wheaton, as an American, about the rights and duties of intervention only enhanced his own country's affiliation with European Christian powers, while challenging official policies of nonentanglement advanced by his own country.

The legal and civilizational repercussions of these classifications were clear and extended well beyond American relations with the Islamic world. As the attorney general of the United States and former U.S. minister to China Caleb Cushing, noted in 1862 in a wider analysis referring to both China and the Ottoman Empire: "I entered China with the formed *general* conviction that the United States ought not to concede to any foreign state, under any circumstances, jurisdiction over the life and liberty of the citizens of the United States, unless that foreign state be of our own family of nations,—in a word, a Christian state."[60] According to Cushing, because of their shared faith, Christian nations adhered to the same superior moral values that had been codified into the "law of nations." Since non-Christians were incapable of decent political rule and did not hold moral values as recognized by Christians, they could not be members of this exclusive group. For this reason, Cushing maintained that "Mohammedan or pagan states, which occupy the greater part of the globe" could not adhere to this law of nations, and in fact, it was probably easier to understand international law as "in fact, only the international law of Christendom." The fact that most of the inhabitants of the globe were excluded from this allegedly "international" club seemingly did not bother Cushing or compel him to alter the qualifier of "international." By his definition, these non-Christian states were barely worth recognizing.

Cushing's remarkable admission that the moral, religious, and legal binds that tied the Family of Nations together "impart to the states of Christendom many of the qualities of one *confederated republic*" offered proof that Americans' adherence to this supranational identity could challenge strict national affiliations.[61] Just as membership in this "confederated republic" conferred such an allegiance, what distinguished those outside of this exclusive family was their inherent barbarity and intolerance and, by extension, their mistreatment of Christians: "From the greater part of Asia and Africa, individual Christians are utterly excluded, either by the sanguinary barbarism of the inhabitants, or by their phrensied [sic] bigotry, or by the narrow-minded policy of their governments. . . . As between them and us, there is no community of ideas, no common law of nations, no interchange of good offices; and it is only during the present generation, that treaties, most of them imposed by force of arms or by terror, have begun to bring down the great Mohammedan and pagan governments into a state of inchoate peaceful association with Christendom."[62] Once again, Cushing saw no irony in critiquing the treatment of Christians in these societies while affirming an international system of law that, according to his own definition, excluded all non-Christians.

The nineteenth-century manifestation of these beliefs revealed the emergence of what Maxime Rodinson calls *homo islamicus*, a concept that defined the Muslim as "sealed off in his own specificity."[63] As one historian aptly puts it, "If one assumed that the West and Islam were fundamentally different civilizations which operated on essentially incompatible principles, it was only natural to accept that there was indeed a distinct *homo islamicus* who in his beliefs, attitudes toward life and social habits was the polar opposite of modern Western man."[64]

Similar logic shaped American understandings of imperial expansion and revolutionary nationalist movements. As historian Alexander Morrison argues, "After the American and French revolutions, the idea that government should be by consent of the populace helped accelerate the move toward the nation-state, where political, linguistic, and cultural boundaries were supposed to coincide. But the 19th century was as much, if not more, a century of empires—of large, multiethnic polities, often with varying hierarchies of political rights."[65] Both the Ottoman Empire and Morocco closely conformed to this model. During the nineteenth century, American critiques of these societies focused on the unequal religious hierarchies imposed by Muslim rulers. Yet, it was not the existence of empire or hierarchies per se that bothered Americans. In observing societies under Muslim rule, they found it galling that Christian, and to a lesser extent Jewish, subjects were placed *underneath* Muslims in imperial hierarchies, a status many Americans believed was a clear subversion of the natural religious and racial order.

These beliefs about racial and religious hierarchies and the legitimacy of imperial rule defined American attitudes toward Muslim societies and Euro-American imperial expansion. Many Americans believed that Euro-American societies were far superior to Muslim and other non-Christian, nonwhite societies. For this reason, many Americans explicitly endorsed the European notion of a "civilizing mission" to reform "uncivilized" colonial subjects. Such missions were used to justify the extension and maintenance of American and European imperial rule. This logic about imperial legitimacy led many Americans to attack the Ottoman Empire and Morocco as *illegitimate* empires and, thus, as political, historical, moral, and religious aberrations because they subverted the natural ordering of religion and race.

Such beliefs also helped shape American attitudes toward revolutionary struggles around the globe. Americans refused to recognize the newly independent Haiti in 1804 after their successful revolution, which was fought and won by black slaves against white French rulers. Indeed, U.S. recognition would not be extended until 1862. In contrast, in the first half of the nineteenth century, many Americans immediately championed the "Age of Revolution," which spread to territories in the Ottoman Empire and prompted rebellions in Greece and eventually to other areas of the Empire, including Crete, Bulgaria, and Armenia. When the Age of Revolution spread to Ottoman Christian subjects, many Americans immediately championed their cause because they viewed the rebellions as primarily a religious conflict that involved freedom-loving, white Christians attempting to free themselves from the despotic yoke of Turkish Muslim rule. These perceptions of revolution, empire, and Islamic rule became central facets of many Americans' understanding of the Eastern Question, the term European and American contemporaries employed to describe the gradual breakup of the Ottoman Empire in the nineteenth century. In supporting these revolutions, Americans also advanced strands of exceptionalism and manifest destiny that posited the United States and its own revolution as a political and religious model for these countries.

These exceptionalist facets of American identity and manifest destiny when applied globally emerged in provocative ways when Americans condemned European diplomatic inaction during the revolutionary struggles that emerged as part of the Eastern Question. When European strategic interests led politicians to retain the status quo in the Ottoman Empire by refusing to support these revolutionary movements, many Americans denounced European policies as a blatant expression of the political and religious corruption that had weakened their natural and divinely ordained allegiance to global Christendom and the civilized Family of Nations. Americans accused European rulers of propping up Muslim governments and upsetting the natural progression of history by allowing inferior Muslim rule to continue. This righteous indignation fueled both public and official demands for greater U.S. intervention in the Islamic world. At these moments, American attitudes toward Islamic societies diverged with Europeans in affirming a new, exceptional role for the United States in global affairs.

Indeed, American reactions to these revolutionary struggles were deeply shaped by their own national and imperial project. But despite the narrative that America was the consummate example of a liberal, democratic nation-state defined by civic nationalism, the United States *also* perfectly adhered to the nineteenth-century imperial model previously described by Morrison. Like the Ottoman Empire, the United States was an empire with "large, multiethnic polities" made up of "varying hierarchies of political rights."[66] For many Americans, *ethnic nationalism* and not *civic nationalism* was the glue that unified the American empire and the nation-state. In 1776, American revolutionaries had justified their independence by maintaining that all men were created equal. In practice, however, not being white legally precluded immigrants from naturalization and limited their political participation in American society. This exclusion revealed the tension between America's professed civic nationalist identity and its imperial and ethnonationalist reality.

Of course, for many nonwhites in the United States, this exclusion would have more extreme consequences. From the founding of the first American colonies through the nineteenth century, ideas about racial, religious, and civilizational difference framed Native Americans as uncivilized savages that held no rights to their land. A more extreme version of this logic continued to justify the enslavement of blacks for most of the century, positing that their alleged racial and civilizational inferiority meant they had no rights to their own labor or bodies. This logic has led many scholars to consider the enslavement of Africans and African Americans as a form of internal colonialism in which slaves became de facto imported colonial subjects.[67] Americans easily justified European imperial expansion by using the same logic that justified imperial expansion on their own continent and abroad. Such beliefs extended to the informal relations of nonstate actors with non-Christians abroad. As Edward Blum has argued, missionaries contributed in powerful ways to this logic by describing "peoples of Asia, South America, and Africa as ignorant children or subhuman demons who desperately needed American 'civilization,' which was shorthand for Protestant Christianity, consumer capitalism, and racial hierarchies."[68]

Many Americans believed that civic nationalism could function only by excluding inferior "subjects," such as blacks, Native Americans, Mexican Americans, and other racial minorities from the American polity. Thus, the American Civil War did not end political and social exclusion of African Americans. Similarly, Native American "civilization" programs continued throughout the nineteenth century. Indian removal, massacres, and forced relocation of Native Americans into reservations demonstrated that American imperial rhetoric mirrored European imperial practices. Given widespread American beliefs that Muslims were racially, religiously, and politically inferior to Christians, allowing Ottoman Christian subjects to be ruled by Muslims made as little sense as it did to afford African Americans and Native Americans the right to equal citizenship.

This logic extended to American beliefs about the *legitimate* and *morally justifiable* use of imperial violence and state power. Many Americans were blind to the inconsistencies and hypocrisies that justified African American slavery, extrajudicial lynching, and genocidal practices of settler colonialism and Indian removal. Americans were likewise oblivious in comparing their own imperial violence, practiced domestically or in their colonies abroad, or the violence of European imperialists to the practices of imperial rulers in Islamic lands. The Ottoman Empire's efforts to crush nationalist revolutions led to brutal massacres, as did the efforts by European states and the United States to extend their empires and quell colonial insurrections.[69]

Of course, religious and racial distinctions also contributed to the experiences of non-Christians in European nation states. In the nineteenth century, the rise of ethnic nationalism led to anti-Semitic discrimination throughout Europe, at times resulting in anti-Jewish pogroms and mass deportation. As Hannah Arendt noted in *The Origins of Totalitarianism*, "the representatives of the great nations knew only too well that minorities within nation-states must sooner or later be either assimilated or liquidated."[70] It should come as no surprise, therefore, that the same period that reinforced the concept of a Family of Nations also witnessed the birth of the so-called Jewish Question, which raised the issue of what role Jews should play in Euro-American nation-states.[71] Indeed, as one scholar has argued, it is no coincidence that "ideologically, both the Western quest to control foreign lands and the move to exclude Jews from Western society were grounded in the ideology of race. Whatever else one might say about them, imperialist and anti-Semitic ideologies are all unquestionably examples of racist thought."[72] As the scholar Norman Naimark has also argued, "Ethnic cleansing is a product of the most 'advanced stage' in the development of the modern state."[73]

The point of highlighting European and American practices during this time period is not to measure who trumped whom in perpetrating state-sanctioned violence against minority and colonial populations. Instead, such comparisons reveal that American condemnations of violence in Muslim societies depended on the powerful impact of expedient and con-trived religious, imperial, and civilizational distinctions that justified their own violence while condemning the violence of Muslim rulers. Such distinctions often served to elide the wider trends that linked Americans, Europeans, and Ottomans in simultaneous global processes of empire, ethnic nationalism, and the construction of the modern nation-state.

Furthermore, the dominant interpretative framework in which Americans understood conflicts in the Islamic world on purely religious grounds and as part of a global war of Islam against Christianity blinded them to centuries of peaceful and tolerant Muslim rule over religious minorities. It also blinded them to the central role of religious minorities in Islamic societies. As this early history of American attitudes about Islam has demonstrated, Americans were deeply embedded in world events that helped shape their understanding of Muslims. To ignore this early historical context elides the complex factors that helped shape American foreign relations with Islamic societies in the nineteenth and early twentieth centuries.

Sacred Interests: Theory and Approach

In examining American relations with Islamic lands, *Sacred Interests* draws significantly upon the theories that Edward Said developed in his 1978 seminal work, *Orientalism*. Said argued that a deep connection existed between cultural discourse about the "Orient," which he largely centers in the Middle East and North Africa, and the power dynamic embedded within European imperial expansion. To justify their exertions of power, Europeans created a fictive construction of the Orient as "its cultural contestant, and one of its deepest and most recurring images of the Other."[74] Said links knowledge and power in the colonial apparatus; thus, Orientalist discourse was part of "a corporate institution for dealing with the Orient—dealing with it by making statements about it, authorizing views of it, describing it, by teaching it, settling it, ruling over it: in short,

Orientalism as a Western style for dominating, restructuring, and having authority over the Orient."[75] Said effectively argues that European justifications for imperial expansion were embedded within a domestic culture that identified the Muslim world as distinct from and inferior to European civilization and thus, by extension, legitimized the extension of European imperial rule.

Although recognizing Russian and German Orientalist strands, Said's analysis of power relations exhibited through formal empire focused on Franco-British Orientalism. Because the United States lacked a formal empire in the Middle East and North Africa, Said explicates American relations with Muslims only in terms of the rise of the United States as a dominant global power after World War II. Since the publication of his book, scholars across the disciplines have extended and complicated Said's theories, focusing on other areas of the "Orient," examining how local actors actively resisted or even contributed to Orientalist tropes, and extrapolating theories of Orientalism beyond the Franco-British context to other areas, including the United States.[76]

Indeed, scholarly interest in the influence of "American Orientalism" on American relations with the Muslim world has increased since the events of 9/11. But despite the plethora of books on U.S. relations with Islam and the Middle East published after this period and the heightened focus on the impact of religion in shaping the actions of Muslim state and nonstate actors in the Middle East, with the exception of scholarly work on the Barbary Wars, the impact of religious belief on the history of *American* foreign relations with the broader Islamic world in the nineteenth and early twentieth centuries has continued to receive scant attention from historians. More recent studies have also tended to focus their attention either on official American foreign policy or on American missionary work, often discounting the broader web of interactions *between* state and nonstate actors in Islamic lands. Although these studies make strong contributions to our understanding of American foreign relations, an equally important story remains to be told. As the historian Andrew Preston argues: "The only way to capture the richness of the religious influence—and to find it where it would otherwise remain hidden—is to blend 'high' and 'low' versions of history, from the top-down perspective of policymaking elites to the bottom-up view of religious Americans who do not make policy themselves but influence it collectively, through political pressure and activism abroad."[77]

Recent studies have also tended to reaffirm Said's chronological limitations; most scholarship on U.S. foreign relations with the Islamic world has continued to focus on the period *after* World War II, either ignoring the nineteenth century completely or granting it only brief coverage.[78] Coverage of this more recent historical period helps to formulate a trajectory of sorts, with regard to how the United States has arrived at the issues policymakers face today. But these studies do not offer a full picture. Extending this history backward facilitates a deep and complex understanding of the ideological and religious foundations upon which many twentieth-century American policies were built. Extending our analysis beyond official foreign policy allows us a greater vantage point into this earlier history.

American foreign relations with the Islamic world during the nineteenth and early twentieth centuries left profound political and geographic legacies that continued to affect policy decisions taken later in the twentieth century up until today. American narratives about Islam and Muslims did not vanish when oil, Israel, and the American war on communism became the strategic foci of U.S. relations with the Middle East after World War II. Indeed, because these new strategic interests drew the United States more deeply into the Islamic world, existing American narratives about Islam and Muslims become even more relevant in understanding the background to American foreign relations in the region. Moving beyond the desire to understand history for history's sake, this narrative allows us to understand how the often-fraught relations between the United States and different Muslim peoples got to where they are today.

Meanwhile, in the past, diplomatic historians have often discounted the impact of cultural and religious beliefs on American policymakers, preferring to emphasize other more "rational" motivations, including ideologies such as realism, considerations of grand strategy, or promotion of commercial interests.[79] This approach has changed in recent years. A "cultural turn" in American diplomatic history shifted the focus to understanding how ideology affects American engagements abroad. Diplomatic historians began exploring how American ideas of gender, race, and class—and to a more limited extent, religion—have shaped American foreign relations.[80] By extension, such studies have expanded their focus to the role of nonstate actors.

Most notably, Michael Hunt's 1987 text, *Ideology and U.S. Foreign Policy*, offers a powerful analysis of the role of American cultural beliefs in shaping American foreign relations. Indeed, his definition of ideology as "an interrelated set of convictions or assumptions that reduces the complexities of a particular slice of reality to easily comprehensible terms and suggests appropriate ways of dealing with that reality" is particularly appropriate in seeking to understand American attitudes toward the Muslim world in the nineteenth and early twentieth centuries.[81]

Regardless of these new trends in American diplomatic history, the previous emphasis on "rational choice" factors in American diplomatic actions has extended to broader popular characterizations that further distinguish historical and contemporary actions, with Americans and Europeans on one side and Muslims on the other. There has been a long-standing tendency in the United States—beginning in the nineteenth century, but still active today—to overemphasize the significance of religious belief in shaping the actions of historical agents who happen to be Muslim and underemphasize that of Europeans and Americans, particularly as it concerns the decisions of political and diplomatic elites.[82]

This bias stems from ideological tropes about Muslims, which are analyzed in this book and which include the belief that an alleged fanatical piety eliminates all rational thought in Muslim actors, whereas Euro-Americans are driven above all by rational, secular, and national interests. Indeed, it is almost as if diplomatic historians have assumed that the secularist principles of the American Constitution emphasizing the separation of church and state have led American foreign policy elites to leave their religious beliefs at the policy door and become strict secularists utterly devoted to strategic national interests.[83] This assumption depends on the erroneous idea that diplomats, or any other historical agents for that matter, can compartmentalize their religious and political actions and beliefs.

Although a central focus of this book is how religious motivations shaped American actions abroad, it is obvious that these beliefs were not the sole factor in shaping American actions toward Muslim societies; nor does this book naively suggest that religious motivations were inconsequential to actors who happened to also be Muslim. Instead, we must recalibrate our analytical focus to reflect more equitably the complexity of human identity and historical causality. With this goal in mind, this book seeks to redress discrepancies—some glaring, some tacit—by magnifying the lens on American religious beliefs and widening the lens on motivations of local actors in the Ottoman Empire, North Africa, and the Philippines. This book strives, whenever possible, to offer a broader historical context to explain the agency and multifaceted motivations of local actors who played decisive roles in these events. In doing this, the book complicates and explicates American relations with the Muslim world by granting greater attention to how religious explanations informed other motivations while emphasizing that nonreligious motives *also* shaped the actions of Muslims.

Moreover, our analysis of American foreign relations in Islamic lands should also extend to other forms of American power exerted in and on Islamic societies that were intricately tied to the extension of European empire, even if American actors did not formally assume the colonial mantle. As Amy Kaplan argues, American historians have tended to view American empire "as a twentieth-century aberration, rather than as part of an expansionist continuum."[84] This "expansionist continuum" has always been intertwined with the larger global phenomenon of Euro-American imperial expansion beyond their own continents. As new studies of American empire have emerged in the last few decades, historians have proceeded to interpret American history as part of a larger global phenomenon that witnessed deep and prolonged exchanges among the American, British, French, Dutch, and other European imperial powers.[85]

To recognize the existence of the American empire and its relationship with European colonial projects is not to say that the two were identical, just as we should not portray American beliefs about Islam and Muslims as mirror images of European Orientalist discourse. Europeans and Americans have exchanged, learned, built on, and, most importantly, *supported* each other's experiences in what the scholar Andrew Rotter describes as a "morphology of imperialism."[86] We must build on this premise by analyzing *both* American imperial discourses and practices *and* the nation's occasionally tacit but usually explicit support for European imperial expansion into Islamic societies. As Paul Kramer has noted: "Far more is to be gained by exploring the imperial as a way of seeing than by arguing for or against the existence of a U.S. empire."[87] Said himself was willing to analyze Orientalism in the United States after World War II, even though the United States lacked a formal empire in the Middle East. His premise for this inclusion depends on an expanded vision of American imperial power. By extension, we must reinsert the United States within the larger global history of nineteenth-century imperial expansion and the exchange of transnational discourses about Islam and Muslims while recognizing the domestic particularities that distinguished American discourses from those of European powers.[88]

I would like to offer some caveats about what this book does *not* purport to do. Although I have sought to include local historical contingencies whenever possible, this book remains an American story. It does not presume to offer new material on the complicated historical contingencies that shaped events in the Ottoman Empire, Morocco, and the Philippines.

Scholars with necessary training in local languages have written nuanced studies that help us understand these particular histories. This book relies heavily on these studies to contrast contemporary American interpretations with these complex historical realities.

Similarly, this book does not offer a *comprehensive* narrative of American relations with Muslims between 1821 and 1921, nor does it presume to cover the entire history of American missionary work in the Islamic world. I have attempted to illustrate some of the most important and influential moments of diplomatic crisis in the history of U.S. foreign relations with Islamic societies. The extension of American missionary work to Muslims expanded well beyond areas discussed in this book, including India, Persia, and Egypt. Although not unconnected to this story, other historians have offered compelling analyses of this larger phenomenon as well as the counternarratives advanced by some American missionaries that defended Muslim interests.[89] Nor does the book offer comprehensive thematic coverage. Gender often played a central role in American narratives about Islam and Muslims. Americans, like Europeans, often maintained that Muslims mistreated women, and tales of the Oriental harem were notorious in such denouncements. This fantastical, erotic discourse has been well documented by scholars.[90] Although I recognize the importance of these factors, in the interest of conserving time and space, *Sacred Interests* does not explore this topic at length. My strong hope in identifying this lacuna is that it expresses my recognition that gender, like religion, remains a powerful category of analysis.

Furthermore, I often rely on grand narratives of American identity in analyzing American conceptualizations of Islam and Muslims. Although I focus on a range of state and nonstate actors, many of these entities enjoyed elite status in American society. As scholarly critiques of Edward Said's *Orientalism* note, by portraying only the image itself, scholars can further silence subaltern voices and perpetuate portrayals of them as passive victims of Euro-American power. *Sacred Interests* does not seek to eclipse the fact that these grand narratives were strongly contested by those populations they sought to exclude. For this reason, within the constraints of space, I try to nuance the story of American interactions with Muslims by including efforts by local actors, both domestic and international, to shape American actions.

Indeed, despite simplistic and essentialized American portrayals of these populations, local actors fought in vigorous and multifaceted ways to shape American actions that affected their political futures. Whether they were Muslim Filipinos fighting to combat American imperial expansion, Moroccan Jews attempting to influence American diplomatic interventions, or the Ottoman ambassador to Washington—who highlighted the hypocrisy of American critiques by comparing Ottoman violence to the lynching of African Americans and the waterboarding of Filipinos—these actors fought for agency in their historical realities and sought to counter simplistic American depictions of their identities. Domestic actors also sought to contest American grand narratives. African Americans at home often used these moments to advance their own civil rights by contrasting American narratives of toleration with their own circumstances. Similarly, by including Jewish American activism, I have sought to complicate historical narratives of American identity that sought to define the United States as a Christian nation.

Finally, I am also deeply aware that, whether it is the treatment of religious minorities in the Ottoman Empire and Morocco, American imperial practices in the Philippines, or the massacre of Armenian Christians culminating in the Armenian Genocide of World War I, this book inevitably covers a range of delicate and emotionally fraught topics that continue to be sources of intense historical and public debate. Current interpretations of these events have real-world consequences that resonate in our contemporary political climate.

The goal of the chapters that follow is not to minimize the brutal violence or discrimination that occurred on the ground; rather, it is to illustrate how Americans simplified the causes of this violence, generating misunderstandings that led to important diplomatic, political, and societal consequences. By emphasizing primordial religious hatred to the exclusion of all other factors, American diplomats, political elites, missionaries, religious organizations, journalists, and the American public reduced Muslims and Muslim societies to caricatures. More importantly, by failing to understand the complexity of Muslim societies, Americans offered political, diplomatic, and military solutions that did not adequately address the reality of revolutionary or imperial violence. Explanations positing Islam as the exclusive source of violence and misrule blinded Americans to the discrimination, ethnic nationalism, and imperial repression happening across the world—and in their own backyard. In telling this story, *Sacred Interests* explains the important historical legacy left by such unfortunate limited understandings of the Islamic world.

PART I

The United States and the Eastern Question

We cannot admit that in dealing with such

a people, we are bound by the laws that regulate the

intercourse of Christian nations.

—Edwin Norris Kirk, Boston speech at meeting

on Cretan relief, 1867

1

THE UNITED STATES
AND THE GREEKS, 1821–1869

Forty-five years after the United States gained its own independence and six years after the outbreak of the second Barbary War, the Greek War of Independence drew the rapt attention of Americans. They witnessed what they understood as white, civilized Christians fighting for liberation from the yoke of Ottoman Muslim rule. Between 1821 and 1832, admirers of ancient Greek culture known as *philhellenes* recruited religious organizations, journalists, academics, political leaders, and the American public to urge the U.S. government to officially intercede. One journalist coined the term "Greek Fever" in 1824 to describe the explosion of public sympathy for the Greek cause.[1] Private citizens and relief organizations raised funds, offered political and military advice, and sent arms, provisions, and even volunteers to fight alongside the Greek revolutionary army. Newspapers and journals published thousands of articles and editorials offering moral support and advertising relief requests. Yet to the dismay of the philhellenes, American officials refused to act.

Not dissuaded, philhellenes continued their push. Edward Everett, one leader of the American philhellenic movement, maintained that in this "war of the crescent against the cross," the United States had a duty to intervene: "In the great Lancastrian school of the nations, liberty is the lesson, which we are appointed to teach. Masters we claim not, we wish not, to be, but the Monitors we are of this noble doctrine."[2] Everett referred to the then-popular Lancastrian model of education, whereby advanced monitors taught less advanced students. Of course, despite his sympathy for Greece, Everett's metaphor was nonetheless patronizing, drawing on the belief that the United States should more aggressively assert its stance as a religious and political model for the world.

Four decades later, Americans again privately and publicly organized to aid the Greeks during the Cretan Insurrection of 1866–69. Still frustrated by the standing policy of nonentanglement in European affairs, Supreme Court Chief Justice Salmon P. Chase affirmed that, were he president, he would issue "a Christian doctrine" that would be "binding on the American people" to secure "the protection of the Eastern Christians."[3] Although Americans generally supported official decisions to stay out of European affairs, events such as the Greek War of Independence and the Cretan Insurrection tested the limits of this stance and led to calls for an exception to such isolationism. In the end, though unofficial, American involvement was not inconsequential.

The Myth of Ancient Greece and American Philhellenic Thought

American admiration for Greece existed long before the outbreak of war in 1821. Many wealthy educated Americans, including most of the founding fathers, were steeped in the classical traditions of ancient Greece.[4] During American debates over the Constitution, members of the Constitutional Convention had even considered adopting Greek as the country's official language.[5] Perhaps America's most explicit demonstration of its reverence for ancient Greece came in naming new towns on America's frontier after classical Greek cities, including Athens, Troy, and Sparta.[6] This phenomenon escalated in the decades surrounding the Greek War of Independence. Between 1810 and 1860, 829 American towns adopted classical names.[7] Alongside this geographic philhellenic activity arose a revival in Greek architecture throughout the United States.[8]

Literary Hellenism and the admiration of ancient Greek culture progressively transformed into political Hellenism and the desire for Greek independence from the Ottoman Empire, a trend that culminated with the outbreak of the Greek Revolution in 1821. By this time, historian William St. Clair has argued that philhellenic sentiments had coalesced into three pillars of thought: "that Ancient Greece had been a paradise inhabited by supermen; that the Modern Greeks were the true descendants of the Ancient Greeks; and that a war against the Turks could somehow 'regenerate' the Modern Greeks and restore the former glories."[9]

The influential American legal theorist Henry Wheaton, who had earlier helped write international law defining the distinctions between

Christian and non-Christian states, was also an ardent philhellene and applied his theories directly to the Greek War of Independence. His widely read study on international law was republished in 1836, only four years after the end of the war, with an ardent legal defense of military intervention in Greece: "The interference of the Christian powers of Europe in favour of the Greeks, who, after enduring ages of cruel oppression, had shaken off the Ottoman yoke, affords a further illustration of the principles of international law authorizing such an interference."[10] As Wheaton argued, "The rights of human nature, wantonly outraged by this cruel warfare, prosecuted for six years against a civilized and Christian people, to whose ancestors mankind are so largely indebted for the blessings of arts and of letters, were but tardily and imperfectly vindicated."[11] Wheaton's influence and dedication to the cause were so important that the New York and Philadelphia Greek relief committees selected him to petition Congress for recognition of Greek independence in 1823.[12]

The civilizational, racial, and religious distinctions that inspired Wheaton's theories about international law and sovereign right also had important domestic relevance. In the same decade that Greek revolutionaries fought to claim Ottoman lands for themselves, President Andrew Jackson was forcibly removing Native American Cherokees from their lands. Jackson defended the Indian Removal Act of 1830 by stating that no one could conceivably favor the uncivilized agricultural practices of "a few thousand savages" over the "blessings of liberty, civilization and religion" of white society.[13] Similar theories of exclusion applied to African Americans. Founded in 1816, the American Colonization Society sought to rid the country of free blacks by sending them to Africa. The organization received strong support from several prominent American philhellenes, including Daniel Webster, Henry Clay, James Madison, and future president James Monroe.

During the Greek War of Independence, American support for race-based discrimination at home helped to galvanize white identity while solidifying beliefs about difference and exclusion for all nonwhites.[14] During the same period, European and American racial constructions of Greek whiteness transitioned from what Athena Leoussi calls "Civic Hellenism" to "Racial Hellenism."[15] Europeans and Americans increasingly "built a sometimes tacit, sometimes explicit whiteness into this sense of shared identity between northern Europeans and their Hellenic 'ancestors.'"[16] American beliefs in the righteousness of Greek revolutionary claims to Ottoman lands at the expense of Ottoman Turkish rulers were enhanced as Greeks "became" white in the American imagination. American philhellenes also used the language of slavery to condemn the unnatural state of white Greeks "enslaved" by Ottoman rule, thus implicitly legitimating black slavery while defending a global ideal of political freedom and emancipation for whites.[17]

Although many philhellenes claimed that the American political system descended from ancient Greece, they also maintained that Greek revolutionaries were direct descendants of the American revolutionary struggle.[18] In the first two decades of the nineteenth century, the Napoleonic Wars led to new alliances between monarchical states, in part to combat the revolutionary fervor slowly spreading throughout Europe. This culminated in the monarchical Holy Alliance in Europe, which had formed only six years before the war in Greece. Many Americans understood the Greek revolution as part of this larger global political battle between republics and monarchies and found the Holy Alliance's goal of defending monarchy to be antithetical to their political values.[19] During the decade preceding the Greek Revolution, future philhellenes Henry Clay and Daniel Webster spoke out for active American support of fledgling republics in Latin America, arguing that it was America's divine role to do so in the face of European threats.

Sympathy for the Greek cause extended to religious leaders and everyday Americans. For political and religious reformers who emerged from the Second Great Awakening, the Greek struggle for independence was an ideal combination of political and religious manifest destiny. Religious fervor, joined with philhellenic sympathy, energized clergymen and their followers who sought to aid and free their Christian brethren abroad.[20] In fact, the "burned-over districts" in upstate New York, which characterized the most fervent areas of Second Great Awakening activity, were also important areas of philhellenic activity. Evangelical Christian Americans who participated in Greek relief efforts helped cement the ideological ties between the various intellectual, political, historical, and religious strands that fueled American sympathy for the Greek cause, uniting philhellenic policymaking elites with everyday Americans.

The United States' Response to the Greek War of Independence

Influenced by the deep intellectual, spiritual, and racial roots of philhellenic thought, Americans had an ingrained bias toward the Greeks. This bias was accentuated by editors and journalists who publicly supported Greek independence and who decided what stories their newspapers would cover and editorialize. Supporters included William Cullen Bryant, editor of the *New York Evening Post*; Edward Everett, editor of the *North American Review*; Colonel William L. Stone, editor of the *New York Commercial Advertiser*; Charles King, editor of the *New York American*; Hezekiah Niles, editor of the *Niles' Register*; Robert Walsh of the *Philadelphia National Gazette*; and Thomas Ritchie of the *Richmond Enquirer*.[21] Another important philhellene was the philanthropist and author Mathew Carey, who had earlier published stories about the Barbary Wars and who regularly published articles in defense of the Greek cause.

Given the sources of information and the inherent bias of press editors, unsurprisingly, American newspapers began covering the Greek revolution within weeks of its start and their coverage was predictably one-sided.[22] In a war of ongoing brutal civilian massacres perpetrated by both Ottoman Muslims and Greeks, press coverage focused almost exclusively on "Muslim" abuses. Indeed, Greek revolutionaries tortured, raped, and massacred more than 10,000 Muslim civilians, including women and children, within the first few weeks of the rebellion, but these stories were rarely, if ever, covered by the American press.[23] Neither was the fact that Greek revolutionaries massacred thousands of Jewish subjects, whom they considered allied with Muslims as enemies of the Greek cause.[24] Likewise, American reports condemned the enslavement of Christians and lamented the plight of Christian women forced into Turkish harems while ignoring the wartime practices of Greek revolutionaries who also sold Muslim women as slaves to Greek families.

These stories were often sourced from European-educated Greek revolutionaries who realized the importance of gaining international sympathy.[25] To solicit foreign aid, Greek revolutionaries needed to convince Europeans and Americans that they, too, were part of the civilized, Christian world. Greek revolutionaries corresponded directly with their American philhellenic contacts in the United States, always emphasizing the religious, historical, and political affiliations among the United States, Europe, and ancient and modern Greece. Through these exchanges, European-educated Greek revolutionaries helped turn the literary and political Hellenism that had become so important throughout Europe and the United States into a political project.[26]

Religion became the dominant explanatory lens through which Americans regarded the Ottoman government and its fighters. Ottoman rulers and soldiers became synonymous with "the followers of Mahomet," just as "Greek" and "Christian" became interchangeable terms. Philhellenic sentimentality imbued Greek fighters with political valor and Christian morality, but Ottoman Muslims were granted no such complexity. American philhellenic coverage tied Ottoman political despotism inextricably to Muslims' religious faith. This simplistic religious narrative convinced Americans that the Greek War of Independence was not solely a nationalist movement waged by a segment of the Greek population, but also a battle that pitted Christian subjects of the Ottoman Empire against its Muslim rulers.

Few stories emerged that did not rehearse the dominant narrative of Greek Christian victimization at the hands of barbaric Muslim rule. This coverage profoundly shaped the American public's perceptions of the struggle. American newspapers did not lack for brutal wartime violence to cover—reprisals for the slaughter of Muslims led to vicious massacres of tens of thousands of Greek subjects and the public hanging of the Greek patriarch in Constantinople in April 1821. Coverage of these and similar events helped persuade readers that only Ottoman Muslims were capable of brutal wartime violence against the more sympathetic Greeks.

This one-dimensional emphasis was bolstered by the statements of the Greek revolutionaries themselves. Alexander Ypsilanti, a leader of the struggle, issued a proclamation to the people of Moldavia on 7 March 1821, that made its way to American readers via dozens of American newspapers in May and June of 1821.[27] In it, Ypsilanti stated that the "civilized people of Europe" (and, by extension, the United States) were "full of gratitude for the benefits they received from our ancestors, [and] desire the liberty of Greece."[28] Ypsilanti highlighted the spiritual reasons behind the Greek cause: it was time to "deliver our country, to throw down the crescent from its height; to elevate the cross, the standard by which we may still conquer, and thus avenge our country and our holy religion, from the profanation and the mockery of barbarians."[29] Ypsilanti's address reaffirmed that Greeks were part of the civilized, Christian world and that this very affiliation morally legitimated war against uncivilized and despotic Ottoman Muslim rulers.

In contrast to his broad pronouncements about Christian unity, the reality proved more complicated. Ypsilanti's calls for participation from other freedom-loving Christians failed to entice most non-Greek Christians in Moldavia, who felt that the Greeks were potentially more oppressive than the Ottoman sultan.[30] Similarly, little support came from the eighteen thousand non-Orthodox Greek Catholics, a community that would also be excluded from Greek citizenship after the war.[31]

Moreover, although many Russians sympathized with the Greeks and supported their rebellion against Ottoman rulers, Russian tsar Alexander I refused to offer aid. Unfortunately for Ypsilanti's cause, Holy Alliance members Russia, Austria, and Prussia had convened at the Congress of Laibach in 1821, which Alexander I attended, in part to coordinate wider efforts to quell revolutionary movements in Europe. Offering military support to the Greek revolutionaries would have weakened these aims. The Austrian chancellor, Prince von Metternich, succeeded in portraying Ypsilanti's rebellion as a threat to the principles the Holy Alliance was trying to defend at the conference.[32] Despite Ypsilanti's eventual defeat, misinformation and false rumors about his success continued to appear in the American press.

Although the northern rebellion was ultimately a failure, Greek forces would find more success in Morea (the Peloponnese) and the larger islands. This continued struggle elicited a pro-Greek editorial in the *Philadelphia Democratic Press* that was republished in dozens of American newspapers throughout the summer of 1821. The author reaffirmed Ypsilanti's civilizational distinctions by asserting "that *all* the civilized world" should sympathize with the Greek cause.[33] Religion, morality, and politics united these nations together in a common struggle against "uncivilized" Muslim enemies. American sympathy for the Greeks was thus driven by their shared Christianity—the only faith, ostensibly, of which humankind could be proud: "With *modern* Greece we have bands and ties and common principles which entwine it around our hearts and connect it with our dearest wishes, our holiest hopes. They adore the same God, they acknowledge the same Redeemer. They believe in a state of future rewards and punishments founded on the same promises and the same evidence as we do, in one word they are *Christians*. They are humble believers in that system of religion and morality which is believed in by all the portion of the world which do honor to Humanity."[34] Whereas Greeks were "modern" and "Christian," their opponents were "furious, bigoted, and persecuting enemies of Christianity," the author categorically maintained.[35]

That same summer, the Messenian Senate tasked Adamantios Korais, a Parisian-based Greek scholar and revolutionary, with the important goal of gaining western European and American support for their cause.[36] Korais had numerous American philhellenic contacts, including Thomas Jefferson, classical scholar Edward Everett, and U.S. minister to France Albert Gallatin. Korais sent a copy of an appeal on behalf of the Greeks to Everett, who would eventually lead one of the most influential committees devoted to aiding Greek independence in Boston.[37]

The ideal recipient of the appeal, Everett embodied the American blend of Christian and philhellenic sentiments. As a Unitarian, Everett's influence would be augmented by his membership in the powerful "club" of

Boston "Brahmins," the religious and intellectual Boston elites who sought to merge Protestantism with rational Enlightenment values. His lifelong dedication to Greek independence began at an early age. After finishing a master's degree in theology at Harvard, Everett delivered his 1813 commencement speech entitled "On the Restoration of Greece."[38] His lecture, which explicitly praised the work of Korais, also forged connections between the "recovery" of ancient Greek as a language (which would require dropping "barbarous words") and the political freedom of the Greeks.[39] Everett's academic experiences exposed him to American, British, German, and French philhellenic works, revealing how various threads of philhellenic thought crossed national boundaries and shaped a global movement.

After resigning as pastor at the influential Brattle Street Church in Boston, Everett traveled throughout Europe from 1815 to 1819 in preparation for his new professorship in Greek literature at Harvard. During his travels, he met several times with England's most well-known philhellene, Lord Byron (to whom he presented a copy of one of the poems he had dedicated to him as an undergraduate). Everett completed his Ph.D. at Göttingen University in Germany, a center of German philhellenic thought, where he befriended Greek intellectuals supportive of Greek independence.[40] In Paris and London in 1817 and 1818, Everett interacted with other leading European philhellenes and Greek intellectuals of the time, including the Marquis de Lafayette, Benjamin Constant, Madame de Staël, Albert Gallatin, Wilhelm von Humboldt, and, most importantly perhaps, Korais himself.[41] A subsequent visit to Greece furthered his political philhellenism.[42] His trip reaffirmed his belief in the disastrous consequences of Ottoman rule for the Greek people. As he noted in his diary, "remember that it was civil liberty that made [Athens] what it was and slavery that has made it what it is."[43] Upon his return to the United States, Everett took up his post as a professor of Greek literature at Harvard, where he shared his philhellenic admiration with students. During his time there, Everett also engaged in regular correspondence with Thomas Jefferson in which the two men exchanged their mutual love for Greek culture.

As a leader of the American philhellenic community, Everett was an ideally sympathetic target for the Greek revolutionaries. He forwarded Korais's appeal to local journalists, who printed it in Boston newspapers in October 1821. Within weeks, dozens of American newspapers across the United States reprinted the story. Everett credited this moment as the beginning of what would soon be called "Greek Fever" in the United States.[44]

Greek revolutionaries had crafted their proclamation specifically to appeal to American sympathies, reminding their audience of their religious, political, and historical ties.[45] The revolutionaries claimed that Christianity helped define their mutual love of liberty, because Americans also followed "the laws of the gospel." This special understanding of freedom made it the duty of the United States to "perfect" its "glory" and help "purge Greece of barbarians who, for four centuries, had polluted it." As the moral, political, and religious leader of the Christian Family of Nations, Greeks held the United States to a higher standard: "Surely it is worthy of you to discharge the duty of all civilized nations, in expelling ignorance and barbarity from the native soil of the arts and of freedom . . . the country of Penn, of Franklin, and of Washington, cannot refuse her aid to the descendants of Phocion, Thrasybulus, Aratus, and Philopemen."[46] In reality, the Greeks' rebellion against Ottoman rule was a much more complicated affair, but Greek revolutionaries living in Europe knew that they needed to say and do whatever was necessary to garner international aid.

In the year following the publication of Korais's appeal, philhellenic activism, calls for U.S. intervention, and denouncements of European inaction increased. The *National Gazette* demanded that Congress express official American support for Greek independence and that the country send all available vessels: "An American fleet of ten, fifteen, or twenty sail . . . would destroy the Turkish navy and enable the Greeks" to "achieve their independence."[47] Since Europeans insisted on neutrality, "they could not complain of the intervention of the Americans on the side of Christianity, and civilization."[48] Hezekiah Niles, philhellene editor of the *Niles' Register*, attacked British inaction on the Greeks' behalf and accused them of prioritizing selfish commercial and strategic interests over humanitarian and Christian duties.[49]

In November 1822, philhellenes organized a public meeting in Albany, New York, to discuss American efforts on behalf of the Greek cause. One member argued that it was their moral obligation to intervene, since Greece had appealed directly to the United States "in the great work of their liberation from the fangs of a barbarian despotism, while the powers of Europe have been deaf and insensible to the voice of justice, of pity, of humanity."[50] At this meeting, the most aggressive calls for action included demands that the U.S. government intervene directly to help Greece. And should the Greeks lose their war, "then it is our duty as Christians and as men, to offer them an asylum from oppression in this happy country."[51] Subcommittees were formed to write circulars, which were then forwarded to state governors and national and local political leaders.[52]

That same month, the leader of the French philhellenic movement, the famous French officer Marquis de Lafayette, who had been so instrumental in rallying French support during the American Revolution, wrote to Speaker of the House Henry Clay and New York senator Rufus King. He too urged U.S. military intervention, noting the minimal cost of sending a small naval force, since the U.S. Navy already had a vessel in the Mediterranean.[53] That same year, George Jarvis, son of an American diplomat, offered a more personal tribute. Jarvis left his studies at a German university to join the Greek revolutionary army. He was soon promoted to lieutenant-general, leading revolutionary troops against the Ottomans.

At the end of 1822, citizens of Washington, D.C., signed a petition requesting that the government grant "two to three millions in provisions, and whatever may be necessary to the Greeks."[54] Despite such public calls for American intervention, congressmen were unwilling to risk embroiling the United States in European affairs and thus maintained a traditional and cautionary policy of neutrality. Affirmations of official American neutrality dominated congressional debates, and the motion to forward the memorial to the Committee of Foreign Relations was quickly withdrawn.[55]

Transnational ties between European and American philhellenes also bore a significant influence on American debates over intervention. In an open letter to the Earl of Liverpool, former Lord Chancellor Thomas Erskine urged British action on the Greek's behalf. Erskine's letter was reprinted in dozens of American newspapers in 1822 and initiated a public transnational conversation about the Greek cause. Erskine enumerated several justifications for intervention, including the slavery practiced by Ottoman rulers vis-à-vis Greeks, the spread of the Christian gospel that would inevitably result from British intervention, and Muslims' lack of civilized behavior. According to Erskine, a major difference existed between revolutions in European states and the Greek "resistance to the impious dominion of the Mohamedan conquerors."[56] Reprints of such European pleas for intervention united Europeans and Americans in an international humanitarian and religious cause in what may have been one of the first examples of transatlantic nonstate actors mutually organizing to push for humanitarian governmental intervention in another country.[57]

Presidential Politics, Greek Independence,
and the Monroe Doctrine

Given the rising public and media outcry, President James Monroe was forced to publicly address the events in Greece.[58] Monroe shared the public's strong sympathy for the Greek revolutionaries and his first inclination was to engage the United States directly in the struggle. Strong pressure from Secretary of State John Quincy Adams, described by one contemporary as Monroe's "master spirit in foreign affairs," forced him to temper his public commitments.[59] Adams's primary goal was to maintain American neutrality vis-à-vis the Holy Alliance, the Ottoman Empire, and Britain. He profoundly disagreed with philhellenes and maintained that official intervention would contravene the traditional American policy of nonentanglement and risked pitting the United States in a war against the Ottomans. Following Adams's guidance, Monroe kept the United States above the fray. His annual message on 3 December 1822 nonetheless expressed regret that Greece "should have been overwhelmed and so long hidden, as it were, from the world under a gloomy despotism." He also recognized that Americans had displayed "great excitement and sympathy in their favor," but he made no moves toward formal intervention.[60]

In August 1823, Monroe addressed the Greek cause again, this time during a cabinet meeting. Andreas Luriottis, the envoy of the provisional Greek government, had written Adams requesting official American diplomatic recognition of Greece and the ability to call the United States its ally in its continued battle.[61] Luriottis's emotional plea had also emphasized the two countries' shared dedication to liberty. Greece "the seat of early civilization and freedom, stretches out her hands, imploringly . . . and ventures to hope, that the youngest and most vigorous sons of liberty, will regard with no common sympathy the efforts of the descendants of the heir and the elder born."[62] At the meeting, Minister Albert Gallatin requested that the president send three navy ships to the area to help the Greeks in their battle against the Ottoman rulers.[63] Not coincidentally, Gallatin's proposal mirrored the request made by his friend Lafayette the previous year. The cabinet members also considered a proposal by Secretary of War John C. Calhoun to send an American secret agent to Greece to assess the political situation and offer private support from the United States. The cabinet's discussion about Greece occurred within a larger review of the Holy Alliance's threats to formally intervene and end revolutionary movements in South America.

With the strong exception of Adams, the cabinet members unanimously supported more aggressive American action. Secretary of the Treasury William H. Crawford believed the United States should accede to Luriottis's requests. Secretary of War John C. Calhoun agreed, believing the occasion was ideal for spreading American liberty to the world and casting the situation as proof that a war with the Holy Alliance was unavoidable.[64] Adams had no patience for Calhoun's emotional pleas on behalf of Greece, which he privately noted were based entirely in "sentiment."[65] Adams also cautioned Monroe against the cabinet members' flippant dismissal of a potential war against the Ottoman Empire. Adams also disagreed with the idea of sending a secret agent and with Calhoun's choice of Edward Everett as the agent, noting Everett's clear pro-Greek bias.[66] In the end, Monroe's deference to Adams's foreign policy expertise once again convinced the president to maintain neutrality.[67]

Adams did not have the same influence over American philhellenes. In 1823, Everett, now the editor of the popular literary magazine the *North American Review*, republished the original declaration by the Messenian Senate.[68] Everett called for American action, noting that in this war of "crescent against the cross," Greek independence constituted a blow against Islam itself.[69] If American Christian fervor could be turned toward the Greek war, Everett claimed dramatically, it was "not going too far to say, that it might be the means of giving another independent country to the church of Christ; and do more to effect the banishment of the crescent to the deserts of Tartary, than all that has yet been achieved by the counsels of Christendom."[70] Everett implored the American government to send an investigative commission to assess the progress of the Greek revolt and government. If the commission confirmed Everett's certainties, then the United States would have to recognize Greek independence and send an American minister to the area.

Everett's efforts paid off, at least with the American public. Popular fervor on behalf of the Greek cause spread across the United States. According to one newspaper, it was no longer possible to count the number of meetings that had been held on the Greeks' behalf—sympathy for their cause, the editorialist claimed, was "universal."[71] Support also came from political elites. State legislatures in Kentucky, Louisiana, Maryland, and South Carolina, as well as several governors, extended their official support for U.S. recognition of Greece.[72]

Facing this renewed public pressure to act, President Monroe again tried to extend official American support for Greek independence. A draft of his speech in which he would announce his famous Monroe Doctrine included official American recognition for Greek independence and asked Congress to authorize funds to send an American minister to the area. The majority of his cabinet members endorsed this plan, but Adams again disagreed. He warned the president that Europe would interpret such affirmations as a "summons to arms."[73] Adams vehemently petitioned the president to eliminate these commitments from his speech.[74] Again, Monroe gave in to cautious nonentanglement. He revised his speech to include a weakened declaration of hope for Greece's independence. He also pulled back from asking Congress for formal recognition.[75] Despite his unwillingness to commit the United States to formal intervention, Monroe's public statements reaffirmed that the United States joined the "whole civilized world," which had a "deep interest in their welfare" in implicit opposition to the uncivilized Ottoman Empire and expressed his hope that Greece would eventually "resume their equal station among the nations of the earth."[76]

Adams's strong disagreement with advocates of intervention did not stem from his lack of sympathy for the Greek cause. Indeed, Adams joined many philhellenes in conceptualizing the world in terms of civilized Christian powers in opposition to barbaric Islamic despotism. As he would reveal in later writings, he was deeply antagonistic to the Ottoman Empire and felt that only the eradication of Muslim rule would bring peace to the world. Much like Calhoun, Adams vehemently blamed the Holy Alliance for supporting authoritarian rule in their own political systems while simultaneously propping up Ottoman imperial rule. Adams disagreed with interventionists, however, in how he understood the role of American foreign policy in eradicating this political corruption. Whereas many philhellenes and proponents of American intervention believed that more aggressive foreign policies would spread American liberal political values abroad, Adams echoed the sentiments expressed by George Washington in his Farewell Address, delivered twenty-five years earlier, and maintained that such foreign entanglements in Europe would create the very political corruption it was trying to avoid.

As he had argued in his now famous speech of 1821, which anticipated his later authorship of the Monroe Doctrine and which was crafted in direct response to calls for U.S. intervention in Greece, the United States did not go "abroad in search of monsters to destroy."[77] Instead, the nation led by providing the world with an exemplary model of government that championed the rights of all mankind. Adams maintained that intervention in foreign wars, though their causes might be worthy, would lead the United States into a situation "of interest and intrigue, of individual avarice, envy, and ambition which assume the colors and usurp the standard of freedom."[78] Adams's strong stance on Greece also stemmed from his defense of other American interests. Unbeknownst to the public, an American agent was in the Ottoman Empire during the war trying to negotiate a commercial treaty with the empire. Any American statement on behalf of the Greek cause would endanger this commercial mission.[79]

Adams's stance appeared to be in stark opposition to the aggressive desires of interventionists, but both foreign policies revealed a fundamental belief in the United States as a benevolent global force for political freedom and liberty. Their disagreement was not over American political and moral superiority, which was taken as a veritable certainty, but over how to maintain it and spread it to the world.

Much to Adams's chagrin, Monroe's speech did not close the book on Greek fever. Six days later, Massachusetts representative Daniel Webster proposed a congressional resolution that would affirm official U.S. support for Greek independence and appoint an American commissioner to visit the area.[80] His choice for commissioner, not coincidentally, was Edward Everett. Soon after, Webster submitted his resolution and, in an effort that was undoubtedly coordinated by Everett and Webster, Congress received several memorials from philhellenic committees expressing support for the Greek cause.[81]

The Boston philhellenic committee's memorial, signed by Everett and several other local elites, expressed sympathy induced by the "oppressed and enslaved" Greeks, who were fighting as Christians for their own government and for religious liberty.[82] According to the memorial, Americans were particularly sensitive to such a struggle, given their own revolution and how American independence had affected "the whole civilized world." Thus, Americans should welcome the "momentous" opportunity offered by the "erection of a new independent Christian state." Moreover, American efforts to secure an independent Greece would have wider religious and political implications for world order. Greek independence would "add to the security of all free governments" while also contributing to the "extermination of the Turkish despotism," which was "a more worthy object of concern and coalition among civilized powers, than any which ever engaged their united attention."[83] Equating Muslim misbehavior in the Ottoman Empire and North Africa, the authors reminded Congress of the "lawless domination" exerted by the Barbary powers on the civilized world.[84] Although the Boston appeal recognized the government's policy of nonentanglement, it nonetheless suggested that it would support Congress if it deemed the Greek situation an important exception. The memorial from the New York committee mirrored these sentiments, also arguing for official recognition and noting that the Greeks were doomed under "the barbarous dominion of the Turks" and driven by the "spirit of the Mahometan superstition, presenting an insurmountable obstacle to the progress of civilization."[85]

During a week-long congressional debate over Webster's resolution in late January 1824, supporters of American intervention delivered their speeches to a packed house.[86] The ensuing debates were republished throughout the American press, with Webster's speech offering a particularly powerful fusion of Everett's knowledge and his own oratorical skills. Webster maintained that the Ottoman Empire was powered by the "ignorant and furious faith" of Islam, which was a religion whose level of fanaticism was matched only by its incapacity for change.[87] Webster cited the fact that the Turk had no more "European manners, knowledge, and arts, than when he crossed the Bosphorus." Of course, Webster assumed that change and progress could be achieved only through the adoption of European culture.

Webster was particularly appalled by the inversion of civilizational and imperial hierarchies in the Ottoman Empire. In places such as India, government was "bad enough," but it was at least a "government of barbarians over barbarians." Whereas in Greece, "millions of Christian men, not without knowledge, not without refinement, not without a strong thirst for all the pleasures of civilized life, [are] trampled into the very earth, century after century, by a pillaging, savage, relentless soldier."[88] He concluded his speech with an appeal to act. No other case merited a greater call for Christian action; the Greeks "stretch out their arms to the Christian communities of the world, beseeching them, by a generous recollection of their ancestors . . . by the common faith, and in the name, which unites all Christians."[89]

Although Webster was initially confident that his resolution would pass, Adams once again intervened. The secretary of state reached out to Representative Joel Poinsett, who had initially supported Webster's resolution. He convinced the congressman to represent the administration and speak against the resolution during the debate.[90] Poinsett's speech, broadly understood as conveying the administration's stance, doomed Webster's attempts. Nonetheless, the debate revealed the powerful interplay between government actions and public opinion. Webster's power and influence as a member of Congress demonstrated how influential politicians could shape the American public's understandings of Islam and Muslims when such debates were republished in American newspapers.

Finally, the episode exposed internal dissent over the nation's role in foreign affairs. Many Americans believed there was a moral and spiritual limit to the American policy of nonintervention; spreading political liberty and protecting Christian brethren made sense to a nation that considered its own existence as having been divinely ordained to lead Europeans on their path to progress.

But ironically, the same men who asserted the necessity of defending political liberty and Christianity abroad and lamented the tragic state of Greeks "enslaved" by Turkish Muslim rule were incapable of turning their critical lens inward. During the Greek War of Independence, most Americans could not fathom a comparison between white Greek Christians and their enslaved African American minorities at home. One of the rare occasions when Americans overtly compared the situation of black slaves with Greeks was when the French Chamber passed a law in 1826 that criminalized the African slave trade but failed to include white slaves. American editorials denounced this exclusion, reaffirming civilizational and racial distinctions between whites and blacks at home and abroad.

The author of one such editorial republished throughout several American newspapers maintained that while his goal was not to defend the African slave trade, the practice did confer some benefits for Africans: "When they tear a negro from his forests, he is transported to a civilized country; he finds chains there it is true; but religion, which can do nothing for his liberty in this world . . . at least consoles the poor negro, and assures him of that deliverance in another life." In contrast, the enslavement of Greeks defied all conceivable laws of nature, morality, and, by extension, the established racial hierarchies of humankind: "This race is civilized and Christian—To whom are they sold? To Barbary, and to Mahometanism. Here the religious crime is united to the civil and political crime, and the individual who commits it is guilty at the tribunal of the God of Christians, as well as at the tribunal of civilized nations."[91] In denouncing this "crime," the author also reaffirmed distinctions in international law between the rights of civilized versus uncivilized peoples. Similarly, newspapers in the South saw no irony in placing advertisements for meetings on behalf of the Greek cause side-by-side with notices for runaway slaves (see figure 2).[92]

Edward Everett expressed the ultimate culmination of this philhellenic racism. Elected to Congress in 1824, Everett delivered a speech in the House of Representatives defending the enslavement of African Americans at home and asserting that he would be the first to get his musket and

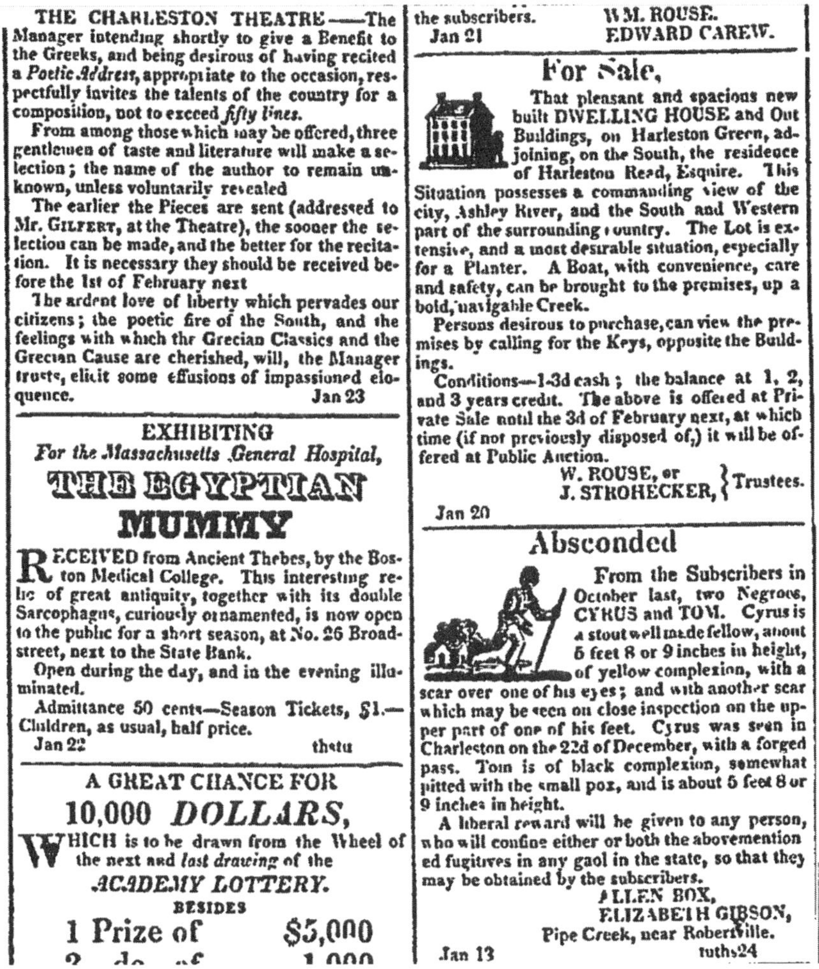

THE CHARLESTON THEATRE.—The Manager intending shortly to give a Benefit to the Greeks, and being desirous of having recited a *Poetic Address*, appropriate to the occasion, respectfully invites the talents of the country for a composition, not to exceed *fifty lines*.

From among those which may be offered, three gentlemen of taste and literature will make a selection; the name of the author to remain unknown, unless voluntarily revealed

The earlier the Pieces are sent (addressed to Mr. GILFERT, at the Theatre), the sooner the selection can be made, and the better for the recitation. It is necessary they should be received before the 1st of February next

The ardent love of liberty which pervades our citizens; the poetic fire of the South, and the feelings with which the Grecian Classics and the Grecian Cause are cherished, will, the Manager trusts, elicit some effusions of impassioned eloquence. Jan 23

EXHIBITING

For the Massachusetts General Hospital,

THE EGYPTIAN MUMMY

RECEIVED from Ancient Thebes, by the Boston Medical College. This interesting relic of great antiquity, together with its double Sarcophagus, curiously ornamented, is now open to the public for a short season, at No. 26 Broad-street, next to the State Bank.

Open during the day, and in the evening illuminated.

Admittance 50 cents—Season Tickets, $1.—Children, as usual, half price.

Jan 22 thstu

A GREAT CHANCE FOR

10,000 *DOLLARS*,

WHICH is to be drawn from the Wheel of the next and *last drawing* of the

ACADEMY LOTTERY.

BESIDES

1 Prize of $5,000

the subscribers. WM. ROUSE.

Jan 21 EDWARD CAREW.

For Sale,

That pleasant and spacious new built DWELLING HOUSE and Out Buildings, on Harleston Green, adjoining, on the South, the residence of Harleston Read, Esquire. This Situation possesses a commanding view of the city, Ashley River, and the South and Western part of the surrounding country. The Lot is extensive, and a most desirable situation, especially for a Planter. A Boat, with convenience, care and safety, can be brought to the premises, up a bold, navigable Creek.

Persons desirous to purchase, can view the premises by calling for the Keys, opposite the Buildings.

Conditions—1-3d cash; the balance at 1, 2, and 3 years credit. The above is offered at Private Sale until the 3d of February next, at which time (if not previously disposed of,) it will be offered at Public Auction.

W. ROUSE, or
J. STROHECKER, } Trustees.

Jan 20

Absconded

From the Subscribers in October last, two Negroes, CYRUS and TOM. Cyrus is a stout well made fellow, about 5 feet 8 or 9 inches in height, of yellow complexion, with a scar over one of his eyes; and with another scar which may be seen on close inspection on the upper part of one of his feet. Cyrus was seen in Charleston on the 22d of December, with a forged pass. Tom is of black complexion, somewhat pitted with the small pox, and is about 5 feet 8 or 9 inches in height.

A liberal reward will be given to any person, who will confine either or both the abovemention ed fugitives in any gaol in the state, so that they may be obtained by the subscribers.

ALLEN BOX,
ELIZABETH GIBSON,
Pipe Creek, near Robertville.

Jan 13 tuths24

FIGURE 2. American publishers saw no irony in placing an announcement for a "Benefit to the Greeks" in the upper left-hand corner next to an advertisement for a runaway slave in the bottom right corner. (*City Gazette and Daily Advertiser* [Charleston, South Carolina], 31 January 1824)

volunteer as a soldier to put down any slave rebellions, for he would rather see the United States "sunk in the bottom of the ocean" than turned into a place like Haiti where slaves had successfully thrown off white rule.[93]

In contrast to his strong antipathy for African American emancipation, Everett continued to push for American support of Greek independence. By the end of 1824, Everett's efforts had raised more than $30,000 in Greek aid.[94] Help came from religious organizations and journals and

Everett's specific appeal to American clergy. The *Christian Repository* published an address by a philhellenic committee in New Haven, Connecticut, on Greek independence, noting that the struggle "ought to make a deep and lasting impression on the heart of every Christian and every American."[95] Again, Islam was at the heart of the problem: "The despotism of the Turks is of a peculiar nature, and without a parallel in the history of man. . . . Every subject not of the Mohammedan religion, is allowed only the alternative of tribute or death."[96]

In April 1824, Sereno Edwards Dwight, the former chaplain of the Senate and the Congregationalist minister of the influential Park Street Church in Boston, also answered Everett's call to the clergy by delivering a speech full of religious imagery detailing the importance of the Greek cause for Christianity itself. The speech warned that Islam would gain in strength and that Christian churches under Muslim rule would give up hope if the Greeks failed.[97] "Freedom" itself would be defeated, a fate the Holy Alliance undoubtedly anticipated. In contrast, Greek victory would encourage other Christian subjects in the Ottoman Empire to rebel and thus assure the eventual destruction of the Ottoman government and "the bulwark of the Mohammedan faith . . . [would be] weakened or destroyed."[98] Greek success would also allow Protestant missionaries to bring the gospel to Greeks, as well as Muslims: "Missionaries loaded with Bibles will feel their way into the farthest retreats of Mohammedan darkness."[99]

As Dwight concluded, there could be no greater outcome than Greek independence to assure the advancement of Christianity among Muslims. Their success would align Jews and Christians in a common cause and bring about the end of days. What other event, Dwight asked, could "fix the attention of both Jews and Christians, as [much as] the downfall of Turkish and Mohammedan power, the recovery of Jerusalem, the liberation of the eastern churches, and the admission of the Gospel to Western Asia."[100] Dwight finished with an emotional appeal that merged Americans' patriotic and religious duty: "Are you a Christian, and do you cheerfully contribute your property to Christianize the heathen world?—what you give to Greece is to *rescue a nation of Christians* from extermination, to deliver the ancient churches, to overthrow the Mohammedan imposture, to raise up a standard for the wandering tribes of Israel, and to gather in the harvest of the world. Are you an American citizen, proud of the liberty and independence of your country? Greece, too, is struggling for these very blessings, which she taught your fathers to purchase with their blood."[101]

Pressure on political elites continued unabated. In 1825, John Quincy Adams, now president, gave in to repeated requests from philhellenes and his close friend Lafayette and dispatched a secret agent to Greece to convey American sympathies and to discreetly support its government—but the agent died from illness before he could travel to Greece. Other Americans, however, did make it all the way to Greece to offer their aid. At least a dozen American philhellenes and more than 450 volunteers from all over Europe joined George Jarvis in Greece to volunteer with the Greek revolutionary military. Among them was philhellene Samuel Gridley Howe, who left for Greece after finishing his medical degree to serve as chief surgeon in the Greek navy and establish military hospitals. At his graduation from Harvard Medical School in 1824, Howe heard a speech by the Marquis de Lafayette that praised the Greeks and asked for American support for their cause.[102] Howe's interest in Greece was also undoubtedly influenced by Edward Everett, who was Howe's minister when he was an adolescent in Boston and who would serve as Howe's benefactor and mentor throughout his lifetime.[103] Howe stayed three years in Greece, returning to the United States in 1827 only to raise more money for the cause, after which he traveled back to Greece for two more years. Thanks in part to Howe's efforts, between 1827 and 1828, American Greek relief organizations raised more than $65,000 (over $1.3 million in today's currency), which they invested in relief that filled six cargo ships.

American aid helped clothe, feed, and—to a certain extent—arm the Greek revolutionaries, but it was European military intervention that ultimately ended the protracted struggle. British, French, and Russian intervention began in 1826 and led to the infamous Battle of Navarino in 1827, which resulted in the destruction of the Ottoman and Egyptian navies. Negotiations carried out by Britain, France, and Russia with the Ottoman Empire finally led to the declaration of Greek independence in 1832.

Although waged in part as a battle for political liberty, the postwar Greeks were at the political mercy of European powers, who installed a foreign prince to rule the country. The European powers also dominated the peace process, excluding Greek revolutionaries from negotiations. Subsequently, European powers would consistently interfere in Greek domestic affairs. Moreover, the final Treaty of Constantinople, signed by Britain, France, and Russia, denied the Greeks major portions of territory inhabited by their brethren, including Crete. These frustrations would eventually prompt the *Megali Idea*, a concept of Greek nationalism that pushed for reunification of the Greek population. The treaty also stipulated the right to future intervention in areas inhabited by Greeks but under Ottoman rule, including Samos and Crete, should humanitarian motives justify it. This stipulation, which allowed for potential future European intercessions on behalf of Greek Christians, would help shape diplomatic exchanges during the Cretan Insurrection three decades later.[104]

Many Greek revolutionaries were disappointed by these concessions. In contrast, many Americans celebrated the independence of Greece and saw the Greek victory as an opportunity to effect greater change throughout the Ottoman Empire. As Samuel Gridley Howe noted in his memoirs, which he dedicated to fellow philhellenes Edward Everett and Mathew Carey, this historic moment would have a long-term impact on the empire: "The Independence of Greece is not to release her children alone from the thralldom of the Turks, but it will open the door for the advance of liberty, of civilization, and of Christianity in the East."[105] The war was about more than extending political liberty to Greeks—it was part of a consequential "war of cross against crescent" taking place throughout Muslim lands. Howe's beliefs mirrored American missionary strategies that viewed Christians in the Ottoman Empire as the conduits for American Protestant Christianity and civilization. As he wrote elsewhere, "we must make [Greeks] the pioneers of religion and civilization to Asia."[106]

Ironically, activists who maintained that the war was part of a global battle between Islam and Christianity were joined in such sentiments by an unlikely political leader. Secretary of State John Quincy Adams had adamantly opposed American intervention in Greece and had resolutely maintained the U.S. policy of neutrality. But in 1831, only two years after he left the presidency and one year before Greece officially gained its independence, Adams produced one of the most vitriolic attacks of Islam and the Ottoman Empire ever written by an American president.

Ostensibly focused on the history and politics of Russia, Adams's essay began with a history of Islam and the Prophet Mohammed, who had through "the preternatural energy of a fanatic, and the fraudulent spirit of an imposter . . . spread desolation and delusion over an extensive portion of the earth."[107] Using all capital letters to emphasize his point, he virulently denounced the Prophet Mohammed and the Islamic faith: "THE ESSENCE OF HIS DOCTRINE WAS VIOLENCE AND LUST: TO EXALT THE BRUTAL OVER THE SPIRITUAL PART OF HUMAN NATURE."[108] According to Adams, the birth of Islam had prompted a war that would continue as long the "merciless and dissolute dogmas of the false prophet shall furnish motives to human action." In the end, this was a struggle between the "dominion of matter over mind; of darkness over light; of brutal force over righteousness and truth."[109]

According to Adams, the blame also lay with European rulers who had circumvented the natural progress of history. In their efforts to maintain the status quo, Europeans had propped up "oriental despotism" and granted it "all the privileges of legitimacy."[110] Having so resolutely maintained American neutrality vis-à-vis the Greeks, Adams nonetheless decried the unfortunate consequences of delayed European action:

If ever insurrection was holy in the eyes of God, such was that of the Greeks against their Mahometan oppressors. Yet for six long years, they were suffered to be overwhelmed by the whole mass of the Ottoman power; cheered only by the sympathies of the civilized world, but without a finger raised to sustain or relieve them by the Christian governments of Europe; while the sword of extermination, instinct with the spirit of the Koran, was passing merciless horror over the classical regions of Greece, the birth-place of philosophy, of poetry, of eloquence, of all the arts that embellish, and all the sciences that dignify the human character.[111]

Still, Adams offered some hope for eventual success, promoting the Christian's duty to dominate the rest of the world, for "his superior acquirements have vested him with the privilege, and imposed upon him the obligation of becoming the teacher of his less enlightened fellow creatures."[112] Ridding the rest of Europe and ultimately the world at large from the "Koran and its Kaliph," Adams maintained, was the only solution for world peace and would be a future endeavor to which the Greeks would hopefully contribute.[113] Although the Christian powers had strayed from their ideal path, the success of Greek independence could place history on its destined course and renew the civilizational and political integrity of Christendom and the civilized Family of Nations.

Although Adams's fear of corrupting the purity of the American political project stopped him from supporting formal intervention on behalf of the Greeks, his vision of the profound civilizational differences between Muslims and Christians united him with philhellenes in shaping a powerful alternative to American national and global identity. The Monroe Doctrine may have been an essential national policy in maintaining the American national project, but it could not erase the civilizational and religious affiliations that united Americans with European Christendom in a larger global war against Islam. A little over three decades later, Adams's hopes for Greek participation in another battle in this alleged global war came true during the Cretan Insurrection of 1866, although the outcome was not what he would have liked.

The United States, Greece, and the Ottoman Empire, 1832–1866

The period between the official recognition of Greek independence in 1832 and the resurgence of Greek revolutionary activity in Crete in 1866 was not a quiet one for Americans concerned about Christian subjects under Ottoman Muslim rule. After the war, evangelicals continued to pursue their activism. American missionary organizations maintained that Greek Orthodox Christians needed American civilization, specifically in the form of Protestant Christianity and political education. With this goal in mind, during the 1830s and 1840s, American Protestant missionaries established mission stations in Greece.[114]

American Protestants' portrayal of Greek Christians changed dramatically in part to justify the extension of these missions. American missionary boards now argued that the religious practices of "Eastern" Greek Christians needed reform. Part of this effort entailed setting up schools to train young Orthodox Greeks in Protestant Christianity and to inculcate them in American values of political freedom. Although previous American discourse during the war had emphasized the Christian identity of the Greeks, American missionary Jonas King now claimed that Greeks knew less about the Bible than "an ordinary child in New England." In line with Everett's earlier exhortation, he established a Lancastrian school to train young Greek children.[115]

American missionary efforts, however, ran counter to the ethnic nationalist demands of the newly independent Greek state, which increasingly sought to reconstruct and bolster its own national identity. Maintaining loyalty to the Greek Orthodox Church was a central component of this effort. Soon, American missionaries faced a backlash from local religious and political leaders.[116] In an ironic turn of events, in 1851, Greek authorities arrested Jonas King and charged him with criticizing the Greek religion. The ABCFM covered the story alongside American newspapers. According to an article in the *Missionary Herald*, it was both deeply regrettable and a stunning betrayal to both Americans and the heritage of ancient Greece "that Greece, so long under the iron yoke of Turkish despotism, in whose struggles for liberty America so deeply sympathized, and so recently emancipated from oppression—that Greece should so soon become the oppressor."[117] Americans had accepted the Greek revolutionaries' emotional appeals professing their admiration for all things American, but they were shocked that Greeks also believed in their *own* religion and culture.

Using their political connections, the ABCFM leadership contacted Daniel Webster, who had assumed the position of secretary of state. The ABCFM argued that American missionaries such as King deserved American diplomatic protection. Webster convinced President Millard Fillmore to send the American minister to the Ottoman Empire, George Perkins Marsh, to Greece to conduct his own investigation. The minister was accompanied by a U.S. naval vessel to reinforce America's stance.[118] In the end, political changes in Greece helped to secure King's release and the betrayal felt by Americans would soon be overridden by diplomatic events in Crete that reasserted the two nations' affiliations as members of civilized Christendom.

The outbreak of the Crimean War in 1853, one year after King's trial in Greece, also helped refocus public attention on Eastern Christians in the Ottoman Empire. Russia fought the united forces of France, Britain, Sardinia, and the Ottoman Empire for control over the Empire's Christian holy places. Concern for Christian subjects of the Ottoman Empire, as well as the political influence of the Great Powers in the Eastern Question, shaped many Americans' understanding of the war. This time, Britain and France supported the Ottoman Empire against its Russian foe, reaffirming many Americans' beliefs that strategic and commercial interests, rather than humanitarian ones, dictated the foreign policies of European powers.[119]

After the war, the Ottoman Empire remained standing. Some Americans questioned whether the Franco-British alliance with the Ottomans had led them to disregard religious issues. Others blamed the European powers for buttressing what they deemed to be the despotic Ottoman government at the expense of its Christian subjects. Many Americans were particularly outraged by the peace treaty signed by the Great Powers at the Congress of Paris in 1856, which had tenuously accepted the Ottoman Empire into the "civilized" Family of Nations. The *New York Observer and Chronicle* published an editorial asking what assurances had been made to guarantee real change for the Christian subjects of the empire. Focusing once again on religious identity, the journalist asked, "Are we then to conclude that Mahometans are changed? Have they abjured their old intolerance, their contempt for Christians, their self-conceit?"[120] Similar critiques also came from Henry Wheaton. Despite the inclusion by the European powers of the Ottoman Empire into their exclusive "family" after the Congress of Paris, the 1857 edition of Wheaton's *Elements of International Law* maintained that international law "has always, and still is, limited to the civilized and Christian people of Europe or to those of European origin."[121]

Meanwhile, ongoing strife in the Ottoman Empire continued to attract American attention. In 1860, sectarian tensions between Druze and Maronites in Mt. Lebanon erupted into large-scale massacres. What began as an isolated attack by Maronite militants on a Druze village in May 1860 provoked a brutal retaliation, escalating into an all-out war that spread to the Muslim and Christian communities throughout Lebanon and Syria and resulted in the massacre of hundreds of Christians.[122] American reactions to these events included the call for the extension of formal European imperial rule to the area.

The American consul in Beirut, J. Augustus Johnson, was stationed near the events, and he worked alongside American Protestant missionaries to deliver information to the American public. Violating the consular regulations of his official position, Johnson sent privileged information, detailed reports, and personal opinions to an American newspaper, which were published anonymously. American newspapers relied on Johnson's coverage of Lebanon and Syria more than on any other source.[123] In his depiction of local events, Johnson described the conflict as purely religious in nature, while reinforcing the image of Western Christian humanity in the face of Muslim barbarity, for "wherever the American flag is seen waving on the housetop, the people flock in great numbers for admission."[124] Johnson endorsed foreign intervention as a necessary solution to the problem, noting that, because of the "shocking barbarities" against Christians, "every American would be glad to see a European occupation of the country, if by such means peace might be restored."[125]

Accounts from ABCFM missionaries reinforced Johnson's interpretations of the religious nature of the conflict and supported his view that European intervention was necessary to bring peace, justice, and safety to the Christian populations of Lebanon and Syria.[126] As the violence escalated, one missionary expressed hope that the "reign of Islamism" would quickly end and argued that the "desperate disease" of "Mohammedan fanaticism" could be cured only through European rule.[127] Affirming U.S. membership in civilized Christendom and challenging U.S. policies on nonentanglement, the *Providence Evening Press* asked, "Has Christian America no part or lot in the matter!"[128] The author was nonetheless confident that the Turks eventually would "be civilized and penetrated by the Bible," so long as the Ottoman Empire lost its despotic control.[129] Thus, the only solution was to end Muslim rule, by one means or another: "It is only in the dissolution of that empire . . . and their subjection to the effectual restraints of Christian government and the humanizing influence of Christian civilization, that can prevent the recurrence of atrocities which are prompted alike by the temper of the Turk and the bigoted fury of the Musselman."[130]

Another ABCFM missionary, Howard Bliss, argued that any foreign intervention by a Christian power would be an improvement: "Welcome to France, welcome to Russia, welcome to any Christian power which will wrench the scimitar from the hands of those whose religion makes the shedding of non-Mohammedan blood a lawful and meritorious act."[131] Much like the response in support of Greeks, religious organizations in the United States helped form relief committees and appealed to Americans to give money for the suffering Syrian Christians. By the time hostilities reemerged in 1866 between Cretan Greeks and the Ottoman government, Americans who had closely followed these events were convinced that only European or American foreign intervention would make a difference.

The United States and the Cretan Insurrection, 1866–1869

After the Greek War of Independence, Cretan Greeks continued their struggle against the Ottoman government. The Ottoman authorities had quickly repressed rebellions in 1841 and 1856, but the 1866 Cretan Insurrection drew international attention and support. The 1866 revolt began not with an attempt to seek outright independence but rather with the Cretan assembly requesting broader political, fiduciary, judicial, and infrastructural improvements.[132] The Ottoman government responded as it had before by sending in military forces to quash these demands. This time, however, funding and support from Greece prevented an easy Ottoman victory. Sympathetic activists in Europe, the United States, and the Greek diaspora quickly took the opportunity to inflate these tensions and embed Cretan Greeks into established philhellenic narratives. This entailed re-creating the familiar story of religious hatred between Cretan Muslims and Christians. As David Rodogno notes, "Contemporary accounts portrayed the Christian and Muslim communities of Crete as if they were living in two different worlds when, on the contrary, the two communities had innumerable ties."[133]

As always, domestic events also shaped American interpretations of global events. Having recently ended a civil war fought, in large part, over the status of its enslaved population, Americans were full of a newfound moral self-regard.[134] American philhellenes stirred Republican Party fervor to "emphasize their belief that the purified United States embodied the interlocking forces of freedom and progress."[135] Former abolitionists, some of whom had been philhellenic activists during the Greek War of Independence, extended their messages of political freedom to the Cretan Insurrection.[136] These included Samuel Gridley Howe, Julia Ward Howe, Wendell Philips, Henry Wadsworth Longfellow, Henry Ward Beecher, and Oliver Wendell Holmes.

Philhellenic ideas proved to be useful across the political spectrum. Whereas abolitionists and Republicans were drawn to extend their ideals abroad, former Confederates used these calls to advance political goals at home. When Americans began expressing their sympathy for Crete after the end of the Civil War, Southerners used the situation to defend their own cause, comparing the inversion of racial hierarchies that allowed Turkish Muslims to oppress white Christians to their own status under Reconstruction in which African Americans allegedly oppressed Southern whites.[137] Southern newspapers attacked Northerners for the hypocrisy of "expressing in one breath the canting, sycophantic sympathy for the poor Crete [sic]" while enabling the "arming of negroes against the whites."[138] The same newspaper reminded Northerners to "remember, occasionally, their own self-created Crete in our midst."[139]

Prominent defenders of the Cretan cause once again included political, religious, and journalistic elites. Such individuals included Edward Everett Hale, owner and editor of the *Boston Daily Advertiser*, Unitarian minister, and nephew of Edward Everett (who had passed away only one year before the outbreak of the Cretan Insurrection). Lawyer, politician, and future secretary of state William Evarts was also involved, as was Theodore Roosevelt Sr., the father of the future president. Additionally, two American diplomats joined the Cretan cause: William J. Stillman, the American consul in Crete, and Edward Joy Morris, the American minister in Istanbul. Between 1866 and 1869, both diplomats actively sought to engage the U.S. government and the public to aid the Cretan revolutionaries.

Word of the rising tensions in Crete first came through Stillman. On 18 August 1866, Stillman forwarded an appeal from Cretan revolutionaries to President Andrew Johnson, asking "our best ally, the Christian United States' Government" to intercede with the European powers on their behalf to assure "our national reunion with the kindred race of the Hellenes" and release them from the "heavy yoke of the Mussulman."[140] Much like their Greek predecessors in 1821, Cretan revolutionaries emphasized the common historical and religious ties that bound them to the

United States, assigning Americans a special role in coming to their aid: "Mr. President, if the injustice of your mother land was set right by the sacred struggle which through the Divine blessing was conducted to triumph by the ever-to-be-remembered Washington, how is ours justified! We should be happy if we had only the shadow of the benefits which your country gained in that epoch. . . . We . . . Cretan Christian people, dare to ask, Mr. President, the intercession of the Great Democracy over which you happily preside, in order that our matters may obtain attention from the cabinets of the Great European Powers."[141]

These sentiments were reinforced by the American diplomats on the scene. According to Stillman, the Cretans trusted "that free America must sympathize with the enslaved in whatever land" and had therefore chosen him as their representative to speak with the other consuls.[142] According to the consul, his sympathy for the Cretan cause stemmed from his "American instincts" that had made him "more uncompromisingly hostile to tyranny."[143] It was clear by Stillman's actions that the diplomat—and by extension the United States—were not neutral about the Cretan Insurrection.

Stillman's obvious stance in support of the Cretan struggle was largely mirrored by the American minister in Istanbul, Edward Joy Morris, albeit more discretely. Morris denounced European inaction and reaffirmed that Muslims were both incapable of progress and mired in the past. He also maintained that the United States had a central role to play in the Cretan Insurrection. Morris was proud that the suffering Cretans turned to the United States, because of their status as "true friends of liberty" with sympathy for "all who aspire to freedom, and who suffer under oppression."[144] In response to Morris and Stillman's letters, President Johnson promised he would apply "due consideration" to the Cretan petition.[145]

The diplomats' correspondences revealed the exceptionalist streak that often characterized American national identity and U.S. foreign policy rhetoric. Unlike European foreign policies, which were dominated by self-interest, the two diplomats represented the United States as the true representative of political liberty, a role reflected by its benevolent foreign policies. Unlike Stillman, however, Morris felt it was nonetheless important to work with the British and Russian ministers.[146] Secretary of State William Henry Seward authorized Morris to consult with European consuls to provide relief to the suffering Cretans.[147] Morris believed his intervention with Russian and British diplomats had obtained important results, for, after his insistence, the British had sent a naval warship to the area. Undoubtedly optimistic of American influence, he also informed

Seward that "if anything will induce the Protecting Powers to intervene on behalf of the Cretans and to obtain from them such concessions as ought to be granted them, it will be the fact that the United States has spoken on their behalf."[148]

Despite his philhellenic sympathies, Morris knew that American policies of nonentanglement limited official intervention. He warned Stillman not to let his "natural sympathies" drive his behavior, to show public restraint, and to negotiate more discretely on behalf of the Cretans, counseling him that "one must forget . . . that he is a human being or a Christian, for if he gives vent to his feelings as such he will compromise himself personally and politically."[149]

In November, Cretan revolutionaries requested that a U.S. ship be sent to transport refugees off the island for winter. In strong contrast to American actions during the Greek War of Independence, Seward accepted the Cretan plea and dispatched an American warship to the area. Despite Morris's calls for restraint, Stillman anticipated his response to a possible Ottoman complaint against the ship's arrival in a letter to the secretary of state that echoed Henry Wheaton's earlier treatise on international law: "Should the government protest on the ground of such action being contrary to international law in assisting the insurgents, I shall reply, that having violated all the laws of warfare, as recognized by civilized nations, they are not entitled to claim their observance *by civilized nations* for their exclusive benefit."[150] Unfortunately, Stillman's overt support for the Cretan cause had soured his relationship with the Ottoman authorities to such a degree that they refused permission to board any refugees.[151] That Ottoman rulers had allowed European ships to evacuate refugees during the same time period reveals the extent to which Stillman's lack of diplomatic discretion had angered the Ottoman government. However, Stillman did not give up.

Meanwhile, word of the Cretan Insurrection slowly began to reach the American public. In mid-September 1866, Greek Americans from New York City and Boston sent editorials to the *New York Times* and the *New York Herald* announcing relief efforts on behalf of the Cretans and including translated copies of Cretan pleas to the European consuls. In October 1866, Stillman sent his own editorial to the *Nation* outlining the historical struggle of Crete.[152] Three months later, the American hero of the Greek War of Independence, Samuel Gridley Howe, organized a new committee in Boston to provide aid to the Cretan Greeks. He also created a newspaper, *The Cretan*, dedicated to spreading philhellenic pleas and missionary accounts to the American public. Its first issue maintained that the circular would be "sent to every newspaper in the United States, in the hope that editors will give a generous support to the cause we advocate."[153] Howe also organized speeches by political and religious luminaries at several public meetings in Boston, New York, and Philadelphia. These speeches were republished in *The Cretan* and in hundreds of local and national newspapers, thus reaching a mass audience.

Speakers cited familiar refrains from the Greek War of Independence to make their case. In one speech, Howe maintained that the Cretan Insurrection was the "last fight between Greece and Turkey, between Christianity and Mahometanism, between freedom and despotism."[154] In the same meeting, a clergyman asked the audience to pick a side in this battle: "Are my sympathies with Islam or with Jesus, the brutal Turk or the offspring of classical Greece, now baptized in Jesus' name?" The United States was the ideal power to step in, an intervention that would not contradict "Washington's counsel against intervention" or the Monroe Doctrine, the clergyman maintained.[155]

Once again, the boundaries of international law became a central argument justifying American intervention. According to another speaker, the former missionary Edwin Norris Kirk, whereas in Christian nations, America had no right to interfere, the Ottoman Empire was a different case, as it was "outside the pale of civilization" and therefore the bounds of international law: "We cannot admit that in dealing with such a people, we are bound by the laws that regulate the intercourse of Christian nations. We draw then this line of distinction; in matters purely political, in foreign Christian nations, we have no right to go beyond the expression of opinion. But with moral questions we are bound as Christians to concern ourselves and to act as well as speak, whether they arise in our own or foreign countries. And with barbarism and brutality, we have a right to contend that wherever in God and dominion they are found."[156]

The committee passed a resolution to aid in "the last great struggle of Christianity against Mahometanism."[157] These public speeches vigorously reaffirmed American desires to move beyond the restrictions of the Monroe Doctrine while asserting that intervention was, in fact, not bound by international law, which de facto could not be applied to Muslim nations whose brutality, despotism, and religious inferiority prevented them from asserting an equal stance in the world. Newspaper coverage circulated these interpretations into the hands of thousands of American readers, relaunching the American philhellenic movement on behalf of Greeks. In subsequent months, Howe raised more than $70,000 to aid the Cretan struggle, or $1.1 million in today's currency. Howe's effort to aid the Cretans was furthered by American volunteers who once again traveled to Crete to fight alongside the revolutionaries.

In strong contrast to its inaction during the Greek War of Independence, Congress passed several resolutions expressing official American sympathy for the Cretan struggle. In July 1867, a resolution in support of the Cretan cause proposed by the well-known abolitionist Charles Sumner passed both houses of Congress. It expressed "strong sympathy" by the American people and Congress for "the suffering people of Crete."[158] Congress hoped that the resolution would "be favorably considered by the Government of Turkey in determining its policy toward Crete." Seward asked Morris to present the resolution to the Ottoman authorities. Another resolution was passed a year later, again expressing American sympathy and calling on the Ottoman Empire to recognize Cretan autonomy. It also called on the "civilized powers of the world" to convince Ottoman rulers to end the war. Finally, the resolution instructed the president to deliver a copy of the resolution to Ottoman officials via the American minister to the Ottoman Empire.[159]

Aware of this mounting influence, Ottoman rulers had engaged in their own public relations campaign to counter the pro-Greek sentiment of Europeans and Americans.[160] In 1867, the Ottoman Empire sent Blacque Bey to serve as minister to the United States. In August 1867, two months after the passage of the first congressional resolution, the *New York Times* published Blacque's critique of American bias and the hypocrisy of the United States when it came to expressing religious toleration toward their own religious minorities, notably, Mormons. Linking American intolerance toward Mormons and Muslims, the minister expressed his disappointment in the "enthusiastic sympathies felt for the Cretans and Greece in this country, and by the decided aversion to Mormon Empires, whether on the Bosphorus or on Salt Lake."[161] According to the same newspaper, American diplomats were appalled that the Ottoman minister could make such unwarranted comparisons between "the civilization of the United States and the comparative barbarism of the Empire of Turkey."[162]

In addition to drawing the anger of Ottoman rulers, Cretan appeals to the United States and the official support demonstrated for Crete by the passage of congressional resolutions succeeded in raising the ire and concern of the British Foreign Office. In May 1868, the British ambassador in Istanbul, Sir Henry Elliot, wrote his home office that the Cretans wanted "to place themselves under the protection of the United States."[163] He also maintained that the United States was on the lookout for a Mediterranean naval port and was looking to buy an island in the area.[164] Eliott was correct on both counts. Two years earlier, Stillman had recommended Crete for this very purpose and had transmitted a Cretan request that the United States annex the island.[165] While cruising the area in search of a port in 1868, Admiral Davis Glasgow Farragut stopped in Istanbul to meet with Ottoman authorities. British concerns about Greek-American rapprochement undoubtedly grew when the U.S. Congress passed an act authorizing the opening of a new American diplomatic outpost in Athens and the appointment of an American minister to Greece. Seeking to maintain the status quo, the British desperately tried to stop Russian and French efforts to intercede on the Cretans' behalf. The entry of the United States into this mix must have surely added to their annoyance. Although the American minister in Istanbul, Charles Tuckerman, reported to Secretary of State Seward in July 1868 that a Greek citizen had approached him on behalf of the Cretan provisional government to inquire about possible support for American protection, no archival evidence can be found to demonstrate any desire to follow up on this request. Nonetheless, British concerns demonstrated that American unofficial involvement on behalf of the Cretans, and American calls for greater official action, resonated beyond just the United States and the Ottoman Empire.

In the end, territorial rivalries among the British, French, and Russians yielded to fear that changes to the status quo would benefit one power over the others. These tensions mounted in 1868, when a war between Greece and the Ottoman Empire seemed unavoidable. Despite public sympathies for the Cretan cause, the American government joined with Europeans in pressuring Greece to stop supporting the Cretan Insurrection, a move that would doom their cause.

This acquiescence outraged American philhellenes, including Samuel Gridley Howe and William Stillman. In a December 1868 article published in his newspaper, the *Cretan*, Howe expressed anger and frustration at the U.S. government's inaction and called into question Secretary of State Seward's Christian morality and masculine chivalry: "How can Mr. Seward, reared by Christian parents, and whose late wife and daughter were models of womanly refinement and purity, favor the outrage upon Cretan womanhood by withholding his recognition from the Christian government? How much longer will he thus continue to encourage those Turkish revelries, which make one shudder, and which ought to shame the manhood of the world?"[166] By evoking the memories of deceased family members and insulting Seward's manhood, Howe demonstrated the boundaries he was willing to cross to advance the Cretan cause. Stillman also published his views on the abandonment of the Cretan cause by

American and European powers. In a January 1869 article in the *Nation*, he described an imaginary epitaph that blamed the failure of the Cretan revolution on the "intrigue" of its friends. Indeed, according to Stillman, "No insurrection was ever before so iniquitously excited, none before so dishonorably suppressed."[167]

Not everyone had given up, however. The strongest resolution to be considered by Congress on the subject of Crete was proposed by John Shanks, U.S. representative from Indiana. In January 1869, Shanks delivered a long, emotional plea for recognition of Cretan independence to members of the House. In advancing their cause, his speech simultaneously reaffirmed the United States as a white Christian nation by using domestic examples of non-Christian minorities to vilify Muslim Turks, unknowingly confirming the Ottoman minister's earlier denouncements of American hypocrisy in the treatment of its own domestic minorities. He noted that the cruelty of Turkish oppression had exceeded anything the world had ever seen and was "without parallel even in the annals of the Apaches." He condemned the unnatural racial and religious order that allowed Turks to "rule despotically over Christian nations who are as much its superior as the American is superior to the aboriginal Indian."[168] He moved on from there to implicate the moral failures of American Mormons alongside Ottoman Muslims. The empire was an "Asiatic Mormon dynasty of Moslems" led by a "Mormon Sultan" who, among other horrid defects, practiced polygamy.[169] Given the U.S. government's "war" against the Mormons in Utah less than a decade earlier—largely fought over this very issue of polygamy—this analogy was surely not coincidental. Indeed, associating Islam with other "theological opponents" such as Mormonism was a common tactic used by American Protestants.[170]

Clearly influenced by the recent Civil War and Southern demands for independence, Shanks also denied comparisons between American intervention on behalf of the Cretan struggle and the struggle of the North against the South. In both cases, he maintained, Americans had to fight on the side of morality. Contrary to the Cretan struggle for national liberty, the South had fought "to disrupt the unity of this great free Government, in the interest of slavery and oppression." Meanwhile, the same powers that "upheld the slaveholder's rebellion in the South . . . uphold the bondage of the Cretans and the Moslem usurpation."[171]

Shanks's speech also sought to redefine the limitations of American foreign policy and America's role in the world, building on previous themes promoted by speakers at public meetings for Cretan relief. He took the now-familiar position that the very same European powers who were too corrupt to protect the righteous cause of liberty and Christianity in the world, were trying to limit American action. The same powers that had upheld the slave south, Shanks maintained, were attempting to "expunge America from the rank of Christian nations, by making you believe that they, and they alone—they who conspired against our own and our sister republic, are the anointed guardians of Christendom."[172]

Shanks argued that Americans and Europeans misunderstood the contours of the Monroe Doctrine. Although it prevented Europeans from establishing monarchies in the Western Hemisphere and disallowed Americans from forcibly imposing republics on Europe, this policy did not prohibit American involvement on behalf of struggling nations seeking independence. Indeed, American recognition of Crete was both noble and compulsory: "[A]s we would render a service and duty to God, Christian civilization, the progress of free institutions, and to a common humanity, let me urge you to encourage the independence of Crete."[173] Although Congress preferred a weaker resolution that fell short of recognizing Cretan independence, Shanks's speech nonetheless offered a powerful testimonial supporting a radically different American foreign policy in which the United States played a central role in the world and Christian values dominated. As previously described, this view was espoused in 1868 by Chief Justice of the Supreme Court Salmon P. Chase, who proposed a "Christian doctrine" for American foreign policy that would apply to Crete but would also extend to the protection of all Eastern Christians under Ottoman rule.[174]

Despite this last call for action, European strategic interests had doomed the Cretan cause. In 1869, the Ottoman sultan acceded to a reform program proposed by Europeans that revamped the political organization of the island and imposed legal and fiduciary reforms corresponding to the initial demands of the Cretans.[175] Once again, European negotiations regarding Crete excluded any participation by the Cretans themselves. Howe denounced the "scandalous interference of the Christian despotisms of Europe. European diplomacy, not Turkish power; the pen, not the cimeter [sic]—has put a temporary stop to the bloody strife."[176] Howe further denounced the U.S. government: "Mr. Seward's policy was to favor Turkey, and suppress all movements tending to develop the independence of the Christian nationalities which she holds by the sword of subjection." According to Howe, the effort to spread American global ideals had been betrayed by its political leadership.

Howe's dismal view of American foreign policy did not overshadow his optimism that Cretan independence was a foregone conclusion; the natural and divine order of the world would inevitably result in an end to Islamic rule: "As surely as human progress is destined to go on; as surely as Christianity is to triumph over Mohammedanism—so surely will the Cretans again unfurl their flag to the breeze, and again do battle for their religion and political freedom."[177] When this divinely ordained outcome finally came to be, "a hearty cheer for them shall be heard in America."[178] The Cretan struggle for reunification with Greece did eventually succeed three decades later, when a new insurrection, prompted as much by Greeks as by Cretans, again brought international attention to their cause.

Although Howe condemned American inaction, in reality the United States had gone much further than it had during the Greek War of Independence in asserting its official support for the Cretan cause. Prompted in part by public demands, the U.S. government had taken the unlikely step of sending U.S. vessels to help Cretan refugees. On the ground, American diplomats openly sided with the Cretan cause and negotiated with European powers to try to help the revolutionaries. Public demands and diplomatic support for the cause had also helped to spur concrete action from Congress and the passage of resolutions offering official American sympathy for the cause. Finally, the struggle prompted American legislators to recognize the importance of Greece by opening an official diplomatic post in Athens. These steps established precedents and signaled an important change in American foreign relations.

Americans conceptualized Greeks as modern, civilized, Christians enslaved by barbaric Muslim despots. This imagery was deeply familiar to Americans who had used similar language to describe their own "enslavement" and ensuing freedom in their conflicts with Barbary states less than a decade before the Greek War of Independence. The language of enslavement also resonated among the citizens of a young nation having recently confronted the issue of its own domestic slavery and increasingly questioning the political viability of limiting freedom to certain members of the population. As Abraham Lincoln would famously declare only twenty-five years after the Greeks had won their independence, the United States could not endure "half slave and half free."[179] That the Cretan Insurrection broke out only one year after the end of the American Civil War, which eliminated slavery on American soil, only pushed many American philhellenes further in attacking what they perceived as the continued "enslavement" of Christians in other parts of the world.

It was no coincidence that many of the activists pushing for U.S. intervention on behalf of the Cretan Greeks were also former abolitionists. The United States now had the moral legitimacy, they felt, to spread its crusade of freedom to the world. Such language, alongside the powerful role played by nonstate actors during these events, also affirmed the fragile boundaries around American policies of nonentanglement, forcing a national conversation that challenged the limitations posed by the Monroe Doctrine. Although American responses to the Greek War of Independence and the Cretan Insurrection were uniquely defined by the existing American philhellenic mythology of Greece, these events drew Americans more deeply into the Eastern Question and the ensuing revolutionary struggles that pitted other Christian Ottoman subjects against Ottoman rulers.

In 1876, only seven years after the end of the Cretan Insurrection, the United States would become involved in a rebellion by Bulgarians against Ottoman rule. Although philhellenic interpretations would be absent in shaping American responses to this new conflict, Greek struggles nonetheless helped establish a precedent, and they served as a reference for American responses to these subsequent events. Americans would continue to posit these new conflicts as part of a larger religious war between Islam and Christianity. Instead of affirming revolutionaries' ties to ancient Greece, Americans would define these new conflicts as struggles between civilized Europeans and uncivilized Ottomans. Only independence would free these populations from centuries of oppression and allow them to resume their rightful status as part of the civilized Euro-American Family of Nations.

2

THE UNITED STATES AND

BULGARIAN INDEPENDENCE, 1876–1878

When Bulgarians began rebelling against Ottoman rule in 1876, Americans immediately sought to follow the Greek model and steer these events in favor of the Bulgarians. Their sympathies were only deepened when they learned of the Ottoman state's brutal repression of the rebellions, which resulted in the massacre of thousands of Bulgarian civilians. Described variously as the "Bulgarian massacres," "Bulgarian horrors," and "Bulgarian atrocities" by Americans, these events once again advanced religious explanations for conflict. Much like their understandings of the Greek and Cretan rebellions, Americans depicted Bulgarians as politically and religiously advanced Christians at the religious mercy of fanatical, violent, and despotic Muslim rulers.

In reality, the Ottoman Empire's violent reaction had less to do with religion and more to do with an imperial power attempting to limit territorial losses due to nationalist uprisings. After losing Greece and barely keeping Crete, they faced new rebellions in Bosnia and Herzegovina between 1866 and 1876. Instead of appeasing Bulgarians' political and economic grievances, they delivered a violent warning that they hoped would resonate throughout the empire. Ottoman rulers, however, failed to anticipate that, thanks to Americans living in the Ottoman Empire, their brutal message would reach an international audience.

American Protestant activists working in the empire had close ties to Bulgarians and quickly alerted the world to these massacres. They also worked to garner international support for the Bulgarian cause. Soon after the massacres, American journalists and diplomats joined efforts by American Protestants to spread awareness. After they had raised international awareness of the massacres, public outrage in Europe and the United States eventually forced the Great Powers to impose new reforms on the Ottoman Empire.

The refusal by Ottoman rulers to accept these reforms led to the Russo-Turkish War in 1877. During the war, American journalists, diplomats, and missionaries continued their efforts on behalf of Bulgarians. When the Ottoman Empire lost the war against Russia, European powers negotiated with Russia and the Ottoman Empire for an independent Bulgarian state. This diverse set of American actors also participated in peace negotiations between the Ottoman Empire and the Great Powers. They exerted strong pressure to secure and define a new independent Bulgarian state. Although the Bulgarian rebellion and the ensuing Ottoman repression did not attract the same level of popular American participation as that of the Greek War of Independence or the Cretan uprising, the impact of American missionaries, journalists, and diplomats nonetheless demonstrated American influence, both official and unofficial, over local events in the Ottoman Empire. In addition, their ability to raise awareness of the issue with the British public, to pressure British diplomats into action, and to use their contacts with Russian diplomats who were also eager to secure an independent Bulgaria, revealed the complex transnational web of influence Americans enlisted to advance their own goals.

American Protestants and the Eastern Question

American actions during the Greek War of Independence and the Cretan Revolt had revealed the power of public opinion and the capacity of nongovernmental actors to shape American foreign relations. American missionary organizations had been too recent in origin to influence real change in the Greek struggles for independence in 1821. Neither were they very active during the Cretan uprising in 1866, as the area was not a significant American missionary site. The same was not true ten years later.

By 1876, the political influence of the American Board of Commissioners for Foreign Missions (ABCFM) had increased dramatically.[1] In addition to corresponding regularly with the State Department, the ABCFM often played a decisive role in determining diplomatic assignments in the empire.[2] The missionaries' influence was so pronounced in the Ottoman Empire that European and American diplomats themselves sought their knowledge and assistance. The large American missionary presence in the Ottoman Empire, the missionaries' relationships with native populations, their mastery of local languages, as well as American sympathy for

Christian Ottomans, compelled the missionaries to serve as willing sources of information, advice, and action. Influential and well connected within the small American and European expatriate communities in major Ottoman cities, these diverse actors worked at times independently, more often in conjunction with one another, to play a pivotal role in determining the outcome of the Bulgarian insurrection.

In the nineteenth century, the weakening Ottoman Empire cycled between efforts to maintain power and aggravated responses to those efforts. Ottoman rulers had initiated a period of massive internal legal and political reforms to prevent future nationalist movements and to stem European encroachment, commonly referred to as the Tanzimat reforms.[3] These reforms began in 1839 with the *hatti şerif*, a political edict issued by the sultan that set out to reform tax and military conscription rules and guarantee rights to all Ottoman subjects.

Pressure to reform also came from abroad. In the 1840s, American missionaries elicited the help of British diplomats to pressure the Ottoman Empire to reform the status of Christian subjects. One of their most important early diplomatic maneuvers was the successful petition to British ambassador Stratford Canning to help the Protestant community in the empire in 1846. Canning obtained the sultan's official recognition of Protestant Ottomans as a distinct religious community through the creation of a Protestant millet.[4] This millet benefited the Protestant missionaries and their new converts by offering them legal recognition and protection. Missionaries wrote back home about these efforts, praising British diplomacy and their newfound religious freedom to spread their faith to Ottoman Christian subjects.[5]

British pressure also helped pass the 1856 *hatti hümayun*, which granted equality to all Christian subjects of the empire. The ABCFM again praised Canning, thanking him "for the great aid" he had "rendered to the cause of religious liberty . . . on behalf of our persecuted Protestant brethren in the Turkish empire."[6] The *Missionary Herald* reprinted the entire *hatti hümayun* a few months after its issuance, alongside their correspondence with Canning.[7] Such coverage informed the American public of Protestant Christian interests in the empire and demonstrated the early efforts of American missionaries to shape official diplomatic engagements with the Ottoman Empire.

As the sectarian violence in Syria and Lebanon in 1860 had demonstrated, however, one unwelcomed consequence of these British-imposed "pro-Christian" reforms was the modification of traditional power relations among various religious communities. Tensions increased as each population asserted its position within the rapidly changing society. External pressure to enact these reforms also increasingly led Ottoman rulers to view any foreign interventions on behalf of Christians with increasing skepticism.

Their fears were not unwarranted. European interventions more generally had often exacerbated existing tensions, but they were also often convenient excuses for European powers to increase their influence in the empire. Justifications for European meddling in Ottoman internal affairs had begun with the first capitulation treaties in the sixteenth century, which allowed Europe to "protect" specific Christian communities. European powers increasingly relied on these capitulatory treaties in the eighteenth and nineteenth centuries to advance their commercial and political interests in the empire. As Ottoman rulers often saw it, the more Europeans extended their influence over the empire, the more nationalist groups were prompted to rebel, further undermining the empire's coherence. The government's attempts to repress the rebellions only provoked further European intervention, as the various powers protested that their protected communities were facing Ottoman brutality. Russia, which held a capitulatory treaty over Orthodox Christians in the empire, had already relied on religious pretexts to intervene during the Crimean War and thus extend its influence. The Bulgarian massacres provided another convenient justification for intervention.

Although the United States held no similar capitulatory treaties with the Ottoman Empire, in the latter half of the nineteenth century American missionaries had actively sought to extend their work throughout the Ottoman Empire. Despite their horror at the brutal massacres that resulted from intercommunal fighting in Syria and Lebanon in the 1860s, many American missionaries believed that the Tanzimat reforms provided an ideal opening to spread their mission. As one ABCFM missionary noted in 1839, the reforms were "paving the way for the entire subversion of the Mahometan religion."[8] The extension of their work brought them into close contact with Ottoman Christian subjects, including Bulgarians.

American missionaries also saw the Crimean War and the passage of the *hatti hümayun* as an ideal moment to further their influence by opening American colleges throughout the empire. American benefactors and the American Protestant missionaries who were the beneficiaries believed that these schools would promote Protestantism and American civilization to Ottoman subjects. According to ABCFM missionary George Washburn, the moment was ideal: "Not only had the attention of the Christian world been concentrated upon the Turkish Empire by the

Crimean War, but the people of Turkey had been aroused to new life and were beginning to seek for education. It was believed that a new era of tolerance and liberty had dawned upon the East, that the government as well as the people, was desirous of encouraging progress in every form, that at last there was an open door in Turkey."[9] In 1860, ABCFM missionary Cyrus Hamlin left the organization to found Robert College in Istanbul with funding from wealthy New York merchant Christopher Robert.[10] In 1862, American Protestants in Istanbul began working with their colleagues in Syria to open the Syrian Protestant College in Beirut.

Robert College opened in September 1863, five months after the incorporation of the Syrian Protestant College in Beirut. Shortly after, Hamlin was joined by another ABCFM missionary, George Washburn, who would later become his son-in-law. Despite resigning from the ABCFM, American missionaries such as Hamlin and Washburn maintained their goal of spreading Christianity and American civilization to the Ottoman Empire.[11] The two men also continued to consult and work closely with ABCFM missionaries in the empire. In fact, Hamlin used these contacts to pressure Ottoman authorities when they resisted his project. Despite the successful incorporation of Robert College, the sultan refused to grant Hamlin permission to construct new buildings. This resistance did not originate from Ottoman rulers themselves, but rather from local Ottoman Christian leaders and consuls from Russia and France, who feared that the creation of Robert College would lead to greater American and Protestant influence over Orthodox and Maronite Catholic Christians in the empire.[12] The American and British embassies, although sympathetic to Hamlin's plight, told Hamlin they could do nothing.[13]

The issue dragged on without resolution until a wealthy New York banker named George Morgan visited Turkey in 1868. Morgan learned of the situation from Hamlin and marshaled his political contacts, including a cousin who was an Ohio congressman, his friend and future secretary of state William Evarts, and current secretary of state William H. Seward. After hearing from Morgan, Seward corresponded with the Ottoman minister, Blacque Bey, warning him of the political influence of American missionaries and their benefactors in the United States and abroad, specifically as it related to the Eastern Question: "Every grievance this class may have with the Porte is a weapon that can be used with great effect in regard to Oriental political questions."[14] Responding to Seward's demands, Blacque sent a letter to his government indicating that the Americans were concerned and the Ottoman authorities had to find a solution.

This political pressure coincided with unrelated American actions in other parts of the empire and helped change the sultan's mind. The United States had already sent a naval warship to Turkey in 1867 to rescue refugees of the Cretan uprising and the U.S. Congress was engaged in passing a congressional resolution expressing sympathy for Cretan revolutionaries. Shortly after, in August 1868, U.S. admiral David Farragut unintentionally sent a martial signal to the Ottoman authorities. As American commander of the European squadron, Farragut had been cruising the Mediterranean to find a port to serve as a naval station for the United States. When he stopped in Istanbul, Ottoman rulers assumed he did so in connection with the Cretan Insurrection. Hamlin took advantage of Farragut's visit to inform him of the difficulties he was facing with Robert College. Farragut had also been briefed by the navy to address the issue with Ottoman authorities, which he did at an official dinner that Ottoman rulers held in his honor.[15]

These unrelated events inadvertently combined to increase American pressure on the Ottoman government and had the effect of bringing about the desired results for Robert College. In December 1868, the sultan officially granted Hamlin the right to construct the new buildings. According to one account, when asked later why they had granted the Americans permission to build, an Ottoman minister responded with two simple words: "Farragut, warships."[16] William Seward proudly returned to preside over the dedication of Robert College's newly finished buildings on 4 July 1871. The shared date with America's Independence Day was surely no coincidence and illustrated the pride American Protestants felt in extending their country's religious and political values to the empire. These coordinated efforts to advance Robert College's mission also revealed the close ties among American Protestant activists, philanthropists, and political, military, and diplomatic elites.

Robert College and the Bulgarian Massacres

After twelve years as a professor and director of Robert College, former ABCFM missionary George Washburn became its president in 1872. Five years later, Robert College became a central player in the erupting conflict between Bulgarian Christians and the Ottoman government. Robert College was never intended as a strategic and influential site of American and Bulgarian revolutionary activism, but the college had many Bulgarian students.[17] By 1870, forty-one of the ninety-five enrolled students at the college were Bulgarian, and the class of 1871 was entirely Bulgarian.[18]

Throughout the 1870s, Bulgarian graduates returned to Bulgaria to occupy important political positions. Others stayed at Robert College as professors. In addition to the extensive presence of Bulgarians in Istanbul, former American missionary Dr. Albert Long also influenced Bulgarian enrollment at Robert College. Before joining the college, Long had served for twelve years in the American Methodist Bulgarian mission, where he helped translate the Bible into Bulgarian in 1864. He then moved to Istanbul to edit the monthly Bulgarian religious magazine *Zornitsa*. In 1872, he resigned as a missionary to join Robert College, serving as a professor and later as vice president. When hostilities broke out in 1876, sympathy for the Bulgarians among students and faculty was strong.

Bulgarian nationalism was reinforced by American professors at Robert College who were sympathetic to the plight of Ottoman Christians under what they perceived as despotic Ottoman Muslim rule. They educated their students about concepts of nation-states and political freedom, implicitly conveying support for ethnic and religious nationalism. George Washburn noted in his recollections that the central goals of the college became intricately linked with Bulgarian nationalism and advancing their cause in Europe and the United States: "The most important thing that we ever did for them was the educating of their young men to become leaders of their people at a time when there were very few Bulgarians who knew anything of civil government in a free state. *This was our legitimate work* and naturally and inevitably led to our doing what we could for them after they left the College, to give them the advice which they sought in their new work, *and to defend their interests where we had influence in Europe.*"[19]

By 1876, Robert College had become, in Washburn's words, "a nursery of Bulgarian statesmen" even before Bulgaria had its own state.[20] The Bulgarian students "were fitting themselves there under Christian and American influence to be leaders of their people out of the bondage of serfdom into the freedom of self-government."[21] But the beliefs of Bulgarian revolutionaries about ethnic nationalism also sought to conform to European beliefs. As in Greece, Bulgarian nationalists, who had formed the Bulgarian Revolutionary Central Committee in 1869, redefined their historical, civilizational, and "racial" narratives to elicit European sympathy and support. Bulgarian nationalist intellectuals justified their independence by defining themselves as European Christians oppressed by a despotic Islamic Turkish regime. According to one nationalist, "Twelve million Christians live in Europe under the savage rule of this bestial people."[22] Nationalists expected this depiction to help their cause. As one scholar notes, "Constructs of Europe as paragon of progress and Christendom as opposed to Turko-Muslim barbarism furthered Bulgarian expectations of European support for national liberation."[23]

Initially, the hopes of Bulgarians for European aid would be deeply disappointed as realpolitik and commercial interests trumped allegiance to Christendom's call.[24] Furthermore, although nationalist depictions may have served a political purpose, such narratives elided the larger complexity of Ottoman society. Far from constituting a homogeneous Christian population of ethnic Bulgarians, Bulgarian territories were inhabited by a complex mix of Greeks, Jews, Roma, Turks, and Pomaks (ethnic Bulgarians who had converted to Islam).[25] This multiethnic, multireligious population did not conform to western European definitions of legitimate nation-states, forcing Bulgarian nationalists to replace this reality with a narrative of ethnic and religious Bulgarian homogeneity.[26]

Complicating attempts to portray their struggle as that of European Christians fighting Turkish Islamic rule, Bulgarian nationalists employed a strategy that included the creation of a distinct Bulgarian church, one separate from the Greek Orthodox Patriarchate. This goal created deep divides and religious strife between Greek Orthodox Christians and Bulgarians. American missionaries in Bulgaria had unintentionally facilitated this process. Long's collaboration with other American missionaries in translating the Bible into Bulgarian had limited the influence of the Greek language, thus allowing the Bulgarian community to establish an independent church.[27] In 1870, Bulgarian nationalists succeeded in wresting control of their church from the Greek Patriarchate; the latter subsequently issued a proclamation in 1872 declaring the Bulgarian church schismatic and heretical, further claiming that it had become an organ dedicated to ethnic nationalism.[28] Thenceforth, Greek or Bulgarian subjects joined churches based on their professed *ethnic* identity.[29] Contrary to American perceptions of nationalist rebellions in religious terms, that is, Christians fighting against Muslims, the Bulgarian story elucidates the complex ethnic, political, and sectarian battles among various religious communities.

Motivated by rebellions in Bosnia and Herzegovina in 1875, the Bulgarian Revolutionary Central Committee accelerated its own plans for a rebellion. The committee drew on the long-term efforts of several revolutionary organizations to amass weapons and instill greater nationalism in the Bulgarian people.[30] Fifty-eight of these local revolutionary groups met to organize a rebellion in late April 1876.[31] On 2 May 1876, rebels attacked and massacred more than one thousand Muslim villagers and

Ottoman officials in what would become known as the April Uprising (so named because Bulgarians used a different date system). The revolutionaries failed to gather extensive support from local Bulgarian Christians, however. Tragically, although their efforts to mount a widespread nationalist rebellion were largely unsuccessful, it was the local Bulgarian civilians who for the most part had refused to participate in the rebellion who ended up suffering the brutal consequences.

In response to the April Uprising and the massacre of local Muslims, Ottoman officials elicited the help of local militias (*basi bozuks*), composed of Circassians and indigenous Muslims, to suppress the rebellion. Violence against Bulgarian civilians, including women and children, intensified. Death estimates ranged between 3,000 (according to the Ottoman government) and 100,000 (according to the Bulgarians). American and British sources, which were generally more sympathetic to the Bulgarians, estimated 12,000 to 15,000.[32]

The simplistic American response to these massacres that put forth a narrative of Islamic fanaticism and violence omitted the tensions rooted in history that contributed to this massacre of innocent Bulgarians by Circassians. Many Circassians who slaughtered Christians had themselves been subjected to brutal treatment not long before. During the Caucasian Wars between Russia and the Caucasian territories, fought between 1817 and 1864, Russian policies of "demographic warfare" had sought to ethnically cleanse the area through voluntary and forced deportation and to replace the inhabitants with Christian and pro-Russian settlers.[33] Between 1860 and 1864, Russian forces unleashed large-scale terror campaigns on local populations. One Russian officer involved in the killings recalled, "it was necessary to exterminate a significant portion . . . to bring the other portion to lay down its arms unconditionally."[34] By the end of the war, Russian forces had purged the territories of more than 2 million Circassians through forced displacement and the massacre of more than a quarter of their population. The Ottoman government settled between 100,000 and 250,000 of these surviving refugees in Bulgaria.[35] Resettled refugees had to compete with local Bulgarians for land and resources, which caused tension, hostility, and mistreatment. Whether out of revenge, fear, or self-protection, Circassians nonetheless became the ideal tools for Ottoman rulers to enact their brutal policies. Their complicity led to the slaughter of thousands of innocent Bulgarians.

Because of their strong connections to Bulgaria, Americans at Robert College had been well aware of mounting tensions in the area. One of Robert College's Bulgarian graduates, Stefan Panaretov, had stayed on at the college and become a professor in 1875. A year before the uprising, Pana-retov had taken Washburn on a trip to Bulgaria, where the latter was appalled by the conditions endured by Christian Bulgarian serfs. Wash-burn also had the opportunity to meet with a Bulgarian revolutionary. Although sympathetic, Washburn claimed that he discouraged him from launching a rebellion, not necessarily because he disagreed with their plight but because he was sure that it would fail.[36]

American sympathy for the Bulgarians was also enhanced from abroad. The autumn before the revolts, Washburn hosted Lady Strangford from England.[37] Her late husband had been a British expert on the region and had expressed great sympathy for Bulgarian nationalism. Lady Strangford maintained her contacts with Robert College and with ABCFM mission-aries. She would play an important role in aiding the Bulgarians the fol-lowing year, when she coordinated her efforts with American missionaries and Robert College to raise British public awareness and distribute re-lief aid to Bulgarians after the massacres.[38]

Communication between Bulgarian nationalists and American Prot-estant activists continued throughout the rebellion. The Bulgarian jour-nal *Zornitsa*, created and edited by ABCFM missionaries with the help of local Bulgarians, circulated in Istanbul and featured regular updates about Bulgaria. Information about the revolts was also transmitted se-cretly via several Bulgarian networks and eventually given to Robert Col-lege.[39] Upon receipt, Panaretov translated the material and passed it to President Washburn and Professor Long. Implicitly pointing to his coun-try's moral benevolence, Washburn maintained that it was only natural that "in their terror and helplessness the Bulgarians should have thought of us, who had no political interests at stake, as friends whom they could trust, and they found means to communicate to us the details of what was going on from week to week."[40]

Washburn worked with other American missionaries and Bulgarian students and alumnae to initiate a chain of events that would radically alter Bulgaria's future. Washburn compiled information from his Bulgar-ian sources and passed it to Sir Henry Elliot, the British ambassador to the Ottoman Empire, and to British news correspondents Antonio Ga-lenga of the *London Times* and Edwin Pears of the *London Daily News*.[41] Washburn also sent reports to his British contacts, including members of Parliament. Because of his connections and perhaps his own bias, Wash-burn relied solely on Bulgarian sources and never inquired about Muslim victims. Aware of Russian designs on Bulgaria, Elliot discounted the re-ports and told the British foreign secretary that any claims of massacre were purely Russian inventions. He refused to transmit the information to London. In contrast, Pears, who since his arrival in 1873 had been close to Washburn and Long, immediately sent the story to his newspaper, as did Galenga.[42]

The *London Daily News* published the story on 23 July 1876, provoking an immediate response. After two members raised the issue in Parliament, British prime minister Benjamin Disraeli addressed the matter publicly.[43] Seeking to quell the political and public outcry, Disraeli discounted the initial reports as "mere coffee house babble."[44] To suppress the uproar in the House of Commons, he resorted to degrading stereotypes of Oriental violence: "I doubt that torture has been practiced on a grand scale among an oriental people who seldom, I believe, resort to torture but generally terminate their connection with culprits in a more expeditious manner."[45] Disraeli's response solicited open mockery from some House members. Meanwhile, British foreign secretary Lord Derby echoed Disraeli's claims. He denied Bulgarian Christians any religious superiority and, instead, described all Ottomans as members of an "oriental basket" of racial depravity. He argued that "it was not the case of lambs and wolves but of some savage races fighting in a peculiarly savage manner."[46]

Disraeli and Derby were protecting what they perceived as Britain's strategic interests. The Crimean War had revealed Russia's eagerness to extend its reach to Istanbul, the Dardanelles, and the Mediterranean. Conceding that Christians in Bulgaria had been massacred would give Russians the excuse they needed to expand their influence in the empire. Responding to Disraeli's remarks, the editors of the *London Daily News* sent Pears a telegram requesting further explanation and proof of his initial claims. Pears returned to Robert College to gather more data and sent a second news story with detailed information. Pears also called for a formal British investigation into the matter after linking the atrocities directly to the British. The story alleged that the perpetrators of the massacres saw the British as abettors of violence and that the "Bashi-Bazouks ask the English Consul for pay, believing that England pays the Turkish army."[47] His article humiliated Disraeli and caused further outcry in Britain.

As Washburn's initial outreach flourished in the British press, Januarius MacGahan, an Irish-American journalist from Ohio who had been serving as a correspondent in St. Petersburg for the *New York Herald*, tried to interest his newspaper and the *London Times* in stories about the Bulgarian rebellion and Ottoman repression. The former rejected him for cost reasons and the latter because of MacGahan's reputation as a sensationalist journalist. He did, however, manage to convince the *London Daily*

News to send him as a special reporter to follow up on Washburn's sto-ries.[48] In this role, MacGahan would provide readers in Britain and the United States with most of their information about the massacres.

Unlike Disraeli, MacGahan had no strategic interests to protect. His pro-Russian sympathies, tendencies toward sensationalism, and antipa-thy toward the Turks, however, often colored his depictions of the events.[49] Indeed, MacGahan knew that Russia had posited itself as the defender of Bulgarian Christians in the Ottoman Empire, laying claim to a larger pan-Slavic movement to "liberate" all Slavs from Ottoman rule. MacGahan's sympathy for Russian interests had been forged during his stay there be-tween 1871 and 1873. He had socialized with elite society, including Russian nobility and generals, and forged a close friendship with Mikhail Skobelev, who later served as commanding general during the Russo-Turkish War. As a friend and fellow journalist recalled, "In the Russian army in those Bulgarian days, it was next best to being MacGahan himself to be Mac-Gahan's friend."[50] During this time, MacGahan also met his Russian wife, the daughter of an elite Russian family. He left for Istanbul in late June to speak with Pears before heading to Bulgaria.

Meanwhile, Washburn exploited his political connections to leverage the debate in the British Parliament. He forwarded reports to Lady Strang-ford who sent them on to British parliamentary leaders.[51] House mem-bers used his reports to attack Disraeli. Panaretov traveled to London to make the case for the Bulgarians, bringing letters of introduction from Washburn to all of his close contacts.[52] Panaretov was in the audience when Disraeli again took up the debate in the House on 17 July 1876.[53] The prime minister argued that, contrary to assertions made by the *London Daily News*, the conflict had no religious component. He quoted a tele-gram from Elliot, arguing that Christian subjects of the empire were allegedly so upset by the nationalist insurrection that they volunteered to enroll in the army to defend the empire: "It is proposed to give the volun-teer corps a flag, on which the crescent and the cross are displayed side by side. Nothing can be more striking in the present crisis than the almost unanimous loyalty shown by the Christians."[54]

Disraeli's attempts to allay British concerns by emphasizing that the violence was *political*, rather than *religious*, were revelatory. His empha-sis on the secular nature of the conflict and the religious unity among Ottoman Muslims and Christians was clearly an attempt to avert British public outcry about the massacre of Christians by Muslims, which inevi-tably would result in calls for Christendom to unite in the face of Muslim brutality. He understood that in Britain, as in the United States, the narrative of Muslim-on-Christian violence was a powerful emotional draw to both political elites and the British public. Religion inserted itself into the discussion in more nefarious ways. British attacks on Disraeli's inaction included claims that his lack of sympathy for Bulgarian Christians stemmed from his Jewish origins (of Jewish birth, Disraeli had converted to Anglicanism at a young age).[55]

The mounting political and public outcry over the massacres forced Disraeli's hand. He reluctantly agreed to send a delegate to investigate the massacres. Washburn protested when he discovered that Disraeli was sending his youngest secretary, Walter Baring. The young man was unfamiliar with the area's history, spoke none of the local languages, and would conduct his investigation without interpreters. Moreover, his mission was scheduled to last only two to three days.[56] Though sympathetic, the British ambassador in Istanbul told Washburn he was acting on orders from London. Washburn was convinced that Disraeli had deliberately ordered a superficial investigation that would inevitably conclude that "nothing serious had happened in Bulgaria."[57]

Having failed to obtain satisfactory diplomatic action from the British, Washburn turned to his own country. He pressured the American minister to Turkey, Horace Maynard, to act. Maynard, an active supporter of missionary endeavors and sympathetic to the Bulgarian cause, responded that he could not force anyone to go, but he would not prevent newly assigned consul-general Eugene Schuyler from accompanying the British delegate.[58] It would be up to Washburn to convince him, however. Schuyler had been serving as an American consul in Russia since 1863. Like MacGahan, he built connections among the highest echelons of Russian society and the Russian Slavophile movement, which reinforced his pro-Russian sympathies and exacerbated his existing dislike for the Ottoman Empire. During his time in Russia, Schuyler also forged a strong friendship with MacGahan. Washburn could not have hoped for a more sympathetic investigator. Alongside Washburn and MacGahan, Schuyler was crucial to the outcome of subsequent events.

Schuyler arrived in Istanbul on 6 July 1876, and met immediately with Washburn, Long, and Panaretov. The three convinced Schuyler to join the investigative committee. In a discussion that went "long into the night," Washburn provided Schuyler with evidence about events in Bulgaria and agreed to send his former graduate Peter Dimitroff as a Bulgarian interpreter.[59] Before his departure, Schuyler expressed his hostility toward the Ottoman Empire, writing to his future wife that he hoped to find evidence that would "show to the civilized world what sort of a Government is this of

England's protégé in the East."[60] He also shared hopes with his Russian friends for a positive outcome to the Eastern Question. Clearly, his trip was not intended to be an investigation; rather, it constituted a fact-finding mission to prove what he already believed to be true. This bias was obvious to the British envoy, Walter Baring. According to Baring, "Mr. Schuyler made no attempt to conceal his violent antipathy for everything Turkish, and openly expressed the hope that the Ottoman Empire would shortly fall to pieces."[61] Schuyler left on 23 July and quickly met up with MacGahan and Prince A. N. Tseretelev, second secretary of the Russian embassy, further ensuring a sympathetic Russian influence. The group caught up with Baring a few days later.

Within a week, MacGahan had sent his first dispatch to the *London Daily News*, which was published on 7 August. According to his reports, sixty to seventy villages had been destroyed and 15,000 people killed, including women and children. MacGahan explained that the reason for the violence was "simple," for "when a Mahometan has killed a certain number of infidels, he is sure of Paradise, no matter what his sins may be." Children were killed because, although "Mahomet probably intended that only armed men should count," the "ordinary Mussulman takes the precept in broader acceptation."[62] The newspaper's circulation increased as MacGahan's dispatches were printed weekly to appease the eager British public.[63]

MacGahan's coverage was not met with universal acceptance. Baring accused him of exaggerating and sensationalizing the stories, including one about Muslims dragging a cart full of Bulgarian heads through the streets. He maintained that no evidence corroborated this story. In a response that may have confirmed Baring's accusations, MacGahan argued that it was irrelevant whether the heads "were carted through the streets or not, once you admit, as Mr. Baring does, that the people who owned them had been killed."[64] Schuyler sent his "preliminary report" to Maynard on 10 August. Contravening diplomatic rules, Schuyler also shared the report with MacGahan. The latter wasted no time in forwarding it to the *London Daily News*, which published it on 29 August.

Schuyler's report prompted an unprecedented public outcry in Britain and became the key inspirational document for former prime minister Sir William Gladstone. Gladstone had lost his position two years earlier after a political defeat by Disraeli's Conservative Party. As a prominent leader of the opposition, Gladstone's political interests surely played a part in his attacks on Disraeli, his political nemesis. Gladstone was also driven by his strong Christian faith. He accused Disraeli of being a Turkophile and leaving Christian Bulgarians at the mercy of Muslim barbarians. Basing his information on MacGahan and Schuyler's reports, Gladstone published a pamphlet titled "The Bulgarian Horrors and the Question of the East," in which he thanked Schuyler and the United States for their contribution to the cause. Fifty thousand copies of the pamphlet would be sold within days.[65]

Gladstone's religious convictions and his beliefs about Turkish racial inferiority helped drive his reaction to the massacres, views he made abundantly clear in his pamphlet.[66] He maintained that the Turks' racial and religious traits distinguished them from Europeans and made for a particularly lethal combination: "It is not a question of Mahometanism simply, but of Mahometanism compounded with the peculiar character of a race. They are not the mild Mahometans of India, nor the chivalrous Saladins of Syria, nor the cultured Moors of Spain. They were, upon the whole, from the black day when they first entered Europe, the one great anti-human specimen of humanity."[67] According to Gladstone, what the Turk "had done in Bulgaria just now, he did then in Chios and in Cyprus. It is the nature of the wild beast, which cannot be driven out of him, even if you dress him up in tight-fitting clothes and teach him to talk French."[68]

The problem with the Ottoman Empire, according to Gladstone, was that it defied all natural hierarchies of religion and race. "Negro slavery . . . was a race of higher capacities ruling over lower capacities," whereas in the Ottoman Empire, it was "unfortunately a race of lower capacities which rules over a race of higher capacities."[69] Given the complex realities of Ottoman society, precisely where he would have placed Bulgarian Muslims in this racial and religious framework was unclear. In response to Gladstone's pamphlet, Disraeli commented that it was "vindictive and ill-written" and that "of all the Bulgarian horrors" Gladstone's pamphlet was "perhaps the greatest."[70]

Shortly after Gladstone issued his pamphlet, MacGahan published his own call for action in Britain, titled *The Turkish Atrocities in Bulgaria*. The book included all of his articles and writings on the Bulgarian massacres. In the introduction, MacGahan also included Schuyler's preliminary report. Gladstone's pamphlet, MacGahan's articles, and Schuyler's report prompted public meetings across Britain. According to the *London Daily News*, since MacGahan's first telegram, 262 public meetings had been announced in its paper alone.[71]

MacGahan's reports in the London newspapers and Gladstone's pamphlet crossed the Atlantic to horrify the American public as well.[72] Confirming MacGahan and Gladstone's views that Islam was central to the explanation of the events, the *New York Times* concurred that these were exceptionally zealous people: "There is a capacity of fanaticism in the Mohammedans which is almost unknown to European races and religions." Muslims' "thirst for blood" and Islam's dangerous penchant for violence, the journalist maintained, were a menace to the modern world: "The massacres in Bulgaria are only a foretaste of what the Ottoman Moslems would present to the world if this fanaticism broke loose. Few people who have not resided in the East or studied Oriental history can estimate the truly savage and barbaric spirit of Mohammedanism and how utterly unsuited it is to modern conditions."[73]

Such public depictions of Muslim violence alongside calls for protection of Americans working at Robert College prompted the involvement of the U.S. government. The U.S. Navy commander of the European Squadron was sent to Istanbul to assess the situation. Convinced of the gravity of the situation, the rear admiral called for reinforcements. Americans in the empire responded with enthusiasm when six American warships arrived in the area in June 1877. The American government also decided to relocate its squadron headquarters to Izmir and leave one of its warships permanently based in Istanbul to protect Americans at Robert College. The United States also displayed its presence by sailing the others along the shores of the Ottoman Empire.[74]

The year following the April Uprising, the American press published hundreds of articles on the massacres. In the *New York Tribune* alone, more than sixty editorials appeared on the topic.[75] According to one editorial, the Ottoman Empire had imposed itself on Europe, and this "occupancy has been preserved solely through the mutual jealousy of the Great Christian Powers."[76] Another editorial accompanied the reprint of one of MacGahan's articles, noting that Christians in Britain were finally rising against the Ottoman Empire: "The barbarities perpetrated by the Turkish authorities are equivalent to a declaration of war against all Christian mankind. By permitting them, Turkey has forfeited her right to be recognized as a nation."[77] In a letter to the *New York Tribune*, another anonymous American agreed, calling for the United States to officially express its condemnation: "Surely it would be right for the people of the United States to express through Congress, in unmistakable terms, their indignation at the course of the Turkish Government."[78] Another American wrote that it "was high time that the American people should express their indignation and abhorrence of such monstrous inhumanity."[79]

Greece, Crete, and Syria all served as historical examples upon which the American and British public responses were built. As Davide Rodogno argues, the authors of these writings successfully fabricated "a coherent and teleological history of massacre and atrocities of Ottoman Christians" to justify intervention and "went as far as to reinterpret the events of previous instances of intervention, gave massacres ex-post facto coherence, and created a narrative that distorted historical evidence to support their views."[80] A *Chicago Tribune* editorial demanded the expulsion of the Ottoman Empire from Europe: "To drive the Turks out of Europe and restore that country to its old native population, to get rid of that Asiatic nightmare which has afflicted the Sclavic [*sic*] Christians so long and exposed them for centuries to barbarity, cruelty, superstition, and fanaticism, to release twelve millions of Christians and drive back their Moslem oppressors, is a movement more important . . . than the abolition of American slavery." Whereas Americans had "only liberated four millions of slaves," this "war of religion and races promises to release twelve millions of Christians of the old Greek Empire and to expel five millions of the worst population of Europe, the deadly enemies of progress, of liberty, and of human thought."[81]

The religious press also published hundreds of articles depicting the massacres through a religious prism while also expressing hope in the efforts of American missionaries in the area. In June 1876, before reports of the brutal Ottoman repressions had even emerged, the *Christian Advocate* analyzed the area in an article titled "Bulgaria and the Oriental Question." According to the writer, although Bulgaria had "been clouded in obscurity" for centuries, American missionaries had helped assure the Bulgarians a "significant future." Ottoman rule in the last centuries, the author noted, had only demonstrated Ottoman Muslims' "selfishness, sensuality, and cruelty." Ottoman Christians "subject to the unlimited power and will of a governor who is both by race and instinct a cruel master," lived in a situation made "blacker when we take into consideration the fact that the people residing in the European provinces belong, both by their history, culture, and religious convictions to the Indo-European family of nations and [are under] the rule of an entirely different race—a race that has nothing in common with the people of Europe or America, upon which the races could effect a basis of union."[82] Race and religion had merged once again in the public imagination. And since the United States had the largest missionary presence in the area, American Christians were obligated to help. Their work would be difficult, though, because of the spiritual decadence of the "nominal" Christian subject, whose "faith has, in part, been inoculated with the spirit of Mohammedanism." Nevertheless, through American missionary work, "the slumbering embers of a former Christian civilization shall again be kindled into a flame."[83]

The ABCFM journal, the *Missionary Herald,* also took advantage of the situation to emphasize the need for a sustained missionary presence in the area. Christianity, it maintained, would help solve the Eastern Question.[84] As the Great Powers tried to maintain the status quo, American missionaries were "introducing American civilization" and ushering in profound changes. The article celebrated Robert College and American missions as forces of modernization. The ABCFM felt that American colleges could best provide the political skills and moral guidance necessary to make effective Christian statesmen for this newly independent Bulgaria.[85]

To facilitate such an outcome, however, Islam itself had to be destroyed. According to the article, "The Cross and the Crescent," published by the Reformed Church of America, the Bulgarian revolt "at bottom" was "a war of religion."[86] Additionally, Americans should support a war between Russia and the Ottoman Empire, for "if ever there was a justifiable war, one which should have the support of God's people, it is that which Russia proposes to inaugurate for the reform of these abuses." In this war of Christianity against Islam, it could only be hoped that a Russian victory would destroy Islam completely, for "history teaches us that the true religion can only prevail where the false is destroyed."[87]

Methodists also supported these views. A former missionary in the empire argued that religion, not race, was the problem. "Barbarism" was the "genuine fruit" of Islam.[88] Since the two were indistinguishable, the only logical solution was to impose European imperial rule over the entire Ottoman Empire. Providence had opened the path, and European Christians were morally obligated to follow.

With the Bulgarian massacres gaining increasing attention from the press and public, the Great Powers met in Istanbul in December 1876 to enforce reforms on the Ottoman Empire. Before the conference, British officials met with professors at Robert College to gain background information on Bulgaria.[89] Meanwhile, Schuyler continued his efforts on behalf of Bulgarians by aiding Robert College to distribute relief funds and continuing to send Gladstone information about conditions in Bulgaria.[90]

But Schuyler and MacGahan also shaped the outcome of the crisis in political ways. Before the conference, Count Nicolas Ignatiev, Russian ambassador to the Ottoman Empire, visited Schuyler to see if he would work with Prince Tserebelev to draft a constitution for Bulgaria, which would be presented at the upcoming conference. The Russian ambassador was a leading member of the pan-Slavic movement, which pushed for Slavic unity and independence under Russian guidance.[91] He had been working with Bulgarian nationalists for more than a decade and believed it was important to arrive at the conference with a concrete plan for Bulgarian independence. Schuyler accepted Ignatiev's request and began immediately working with Tserebelv. MacGahan quickly joined the group. Having two Americans participate in the writing was part of the Russian strategy to ensure some illusion of objectivity.[92] It never occurred to them that Bulgarians should have the central role in drafting their own constitution.

Schuyler and Tserebelev's draft constitution was completed by mid-November, just in time for the Constantinople Conference on 11 December. Although the United States was not officially included among the attendees, Schuyler participated unofficially in the negotiations.[93] The European powers accepted the document after requesting minor changes. In spite of unanimous support from the European delegates and the Bulgarian attendees—most of whom were former Robert College students—the American-authored constitution was not meant to be. The Ottoman foreign minister interrupted the meeting to announce a new constitution that confirmed equality for Christians. Satisfied by the promised reforms, which also conveniently allowed him to reassert British strategic interests, Disraeli reaffirmed British support for maintaining the territorial integrity of the Ottoman Empire. In the end, however, the meeting eased few international tensions and Russia declared war against the Ottoman Empire four months later on 4 April 1877.

The Russo-Turkish War, 1877–1878

Russia justified its war against the Ottoman Empire on the basis of its mistreatment of religious minorities. Given European public reactions to the Bulgarian atrocities, the other Great Powers gave Russia their moral support. Russia's conduct during the war, however, would reveal underlying hypocrisies. One major goal of the Russian army was to take control of the boundaries initially outlined in the draft constitution by Schuyler and Tserebelev. Some of these designated areas included large Muslim populations. Schuyler was aware of this thorny issue. As he later recalled, to prepare the geographic boundaries of the new Bulgarian state, a member of the Russian consulate had gathered statistics and prepared an ethnographic map of the region, identifying areas with large Muslim populations. Yet, his narrative invalidated their presence in the area. The Turks and Circassians were interlopers, for they had been "transplanted there after the Crimean war on the advice of the English embassy."[94] Meanwhile, the Bulgarian Muslims, or Pomaks, had only "adopted the Mussulman religion at the time of the Turkish conquest for the sake of preserving their lands and personal freedom."[95]

Whatever their origin, the Turks, Circassians, and other non-Bulgarian ethnic and religious groups posed a problem for Schuyler, for "it was of course impossible, in drawing the boundaries of a province, to leave small *encloves* [sic], no matter what their population might be."[96] Schuyler offered no solution to this conundrum. According to Henry Layard, the new British ambassador in Istanbul, Russia had already devised a plan to solve this thorny issue: "[T]here can be little doubt that the original design of Russia to remove the Mussulmans altogether from Bulgaria will be carried out by indirect, if not by violent, means."[97]

The belief that Muslims were "interlopers" in Bulgaria was also advanced by American journalists back home. According to the *Chicago Tribune*, Turkish Muslims in Bulgaria were a "garrison" force "with a fierceness and cruelty unparalleled in national records."[98] Given this dominant viewpoint advanced by American journalists and diplomats as well as the Russian rulers, it was not surprising that Russian and Bulgarian Christian efforts to purge the area of all Muslim inhabitants during the Russo-Turkish War found little sympathy or coverage in the United States.[99]

The British, in contrast, had important strategic reasons to address Russian atrocities. They denounced Russian brutalities by comparing them to earlier Ottoman violence against Christians, including mass rape and the burning of villages. British consuls in other parts of Bulgaria confirmed Layard's earlier suspicions, reporting more than 300,000 Muslim deaths and 1 million refugees.[100] According to scholars' recent statistical analysis, these numbers were not exaggerated.[101] One historian estimates that 17 percent of the Muslim population died during the war and another 34 percent of the Muslim population escaped to other countries.[102]

Back in Britain, Queen Victoria initially supported humanitarian intervention, but she quickly changed her mind and aligned herself with Disraeli when she realized the threat to the British Empire posed by the Russians. This led her to publicly denounce Russia: "Under the cloak of RELIGION and under the pretence of obtaining just treatment of the so-called 'Christians' of the principalities, but who are far worse than the Mussulmans, and who moreover had been *excited* to revolt by General Ignatieff, who prevented regular troops being sent out to quell the revolt, leading thereby to the so-called 'Bulgarian atrocities' as the irregular troops were sent out, this *war of extermination* (for that it is) has been iniquitously commenced!"[103]

American journalists offered a different view, in large part driven by the ongoing coverage of MacGahan. MacGahan continued to serve as correspondent for the *London Daily News* and accompanied the Russian army in battle against the Ottomans as an "embedded" journalist. In that role, he publicly discounted accusations of atrocities committed by Russian forces. His lenient depictions of Russian and Bulgarian military violence against local Muslims contrasted sharply with his earlier denunciations of Turkish Muslim violence against Bulgarian Christians. At one point, he noted that Ottoman fighters had fired shots at the Russians before hiding in the local villages and firing on them from local homes. His eyewitness testimony and the language he used to describe the events signaled his bias in support of the Russian soldiers: "The result was that we set fire to every house from which we had been fired at, and, the fire spreading, these villages were for the most part destroyed."[104] The detachment burned four or five villages, but Turkish "perversity, ignorance, and stupidity" was to blame, for according to MacGahan, if they had only fired from other areas, the troops would not have been forced to burn the villages.[105]

The British journalist, Archibald Forbes, one of MacGahan's close friends and a fellow correspondent for the *London Daily News*, also accompanied a Russian general. Unlike MacGahan's coverage, however, reporting by Forbes highlighted the atrocities committed by Bulgarian soldiers on both Muslims and Jews. Bulgarians had "begged" for arms from the Russian general, who granted their request, "then hot with the fell memories of last year, and conscious that Russians were with and for them, they fell on the Turks with the most ruthless reprisal." Forbes maintained that the Ottoman massacres of the Bulgarian Christians the previous year "is on credible evidence not one whit more barbarous than was the conduct of the Bulgarians towards the Turks. . . . The barbarian has acted like a savage in his reprisals; the Christian acted equally like a savage in what were virtually his reprisals for what happened a year previously. The one 'terror' has but followed on the other."[106] He countered Bulgarian defenders' claims in offering a powerful account of four Jewish women who had been mass raped by Bulgarians, "in sight of their own father as he lay dying murdered in his own house in Carlovo."[107] Forbes's coverage of these wartime atrocities only confirmed that brutal military violence was not a practice limited to Ottoman Muslims. MacGahan responded to Forbes's denunciations by arguing that journalists who had not seen the Ottoman atrocities against the Bulgarians the year before had no point of comparison and that, to his knowledge, the Bulgarians had not committed any atrocities.

Similarly, in the United States, public accounts in the media and full-length studies dedicated to the Russo-Turkish War assigned the worst characteristics to Ottoman Muslims, while continuing to praise the Bulgarian Christians.[108] One author went so far as to attack Turkish sexual morality in his denunciations: "Perhaps the most cogent proof that Slavonian Christians and Mohammedans can never peacefully share one country, is the fact that the former are without blame and irreproachable in the matter of chastity, while the Mussulman, and especially the Turk, allows and practices unbridled license. Among the former women are intelligent, respected, and free, and among the latter are the degraded instruments of loathsome vice. Such light and such darkness cannot dwell together."[109] The *Chicago Tribune* echoed these beliefs, arguing that "The Turk is an alien in Europe, an enemy of Western Civilization, a sanguinary fanatic by nature, a ruler whose Government is not a Government of law but of plunder."[110]

Edwin L. Godkin, an Irish-born American journalist who had previously worked as a correspondent for the *London Daily News* during the Crimean War, published an analysis of the Eastern Question for the *North American Review*. He identified Islam as the source of such atrocious Ottoman behavior. The "Mussulman aggressions" committed by the Barbary powers against the United States during the Barbary Wars were just "outposts of a system of organized oppression" by Muslim rulers against Christians. Godkin maintained that "it is probably no exaggeration to say that no single tributary to the great sea of human misery has equaled in depth and duration that which has flowed from the contact of Islam with Christianity in Europe."[111] After all, the "followers of the Prophet" viewed "the whole earth as their legitimate prey, and the sabre as the best and noblest instrument for the propagation of their creed."[112] French and British strategic interests had prevented their demise so far, but they must realize, Godkin hoped, that it was "monstrous and ignoble" to maintain "an organization so rotten as the Turkish Empire."[113] Clearly, according to Godkin, "modern society" demanded an end to all Muslim rule.[114]

Despite Godkin's hopes, British strategic interests continued to shape their approach to the Ottoman Empire. As the Russians approached the outskirts of Istanbul in early 1878, the British pressured both parties to agree to peace. Having lost more than 80,000 men, the Russians had had enough. Count Ignatiev's pan-Slavic dreams of taking Istanbul had been crushed. He engaged in a public screaming match with Grand Duke Nicolai and was soon recalled to Russia.[115] On 3 March 1878, the Ottomans and the Russians signed the Treaty of San Stefano, officially establishing Bulgaria as an autonomous principality. The borders followed Schuyler's original proposal to the Constantinople Conference. The British, however, felt that the treaty granted too many concessions to the Russians. Fearing that this imbalance would destabilize the region, London threatened war.

The Congress of Berlin and Bulgarian Independence

The Great Powers met again to negotiate a treaty more amenable to British and French interests at the Congress of Berlin in June and July 1878. The Treaty of Berlin reduced the size of the principality but kept Schuyler's constitutional framework.[116] The Great Powers also pushed the Ottoman government to fulfill its promise of equality for all non-Muslim citizens. Bulgarian officials met the following year to adopt the constitution originally written by Schuyler. The Bulgarians thanked their American advocates on the other side of the Atlantic, celebrating some and elevating one in particular to folk hero status: the journalist Januarius MacGahan.[117] They also passed resolutions thanking Dr. Long and Dr. Washburn for their help in the "elevation and independence of Bulgaria" and Eugene Schuyler and William Gladstone for their support.

Schuyler's participation in helping to deliver independence to the Bulgarians would not go unnoticed in America and the Ottoman Empire either, although the response was decidedly less adulatory. Surprisingly, however, one of the critiques of Schuyler's actions came from former Robert College president Cyrus Hamlin. In contrast to the support Schuyler received from Washburn and most American missionaries in the empire, Hamlin accused Schuyler of serving Russian interests and being "to all intents and purposes a Russian."[118] Hamlin recognized that Russian claims of religious benevolence were actually strategic tactics. He also feared that American missionary interests would be harmed if Russia gained influence over Bulgaria. Washburn and the ABCFM tried to distance themselves from Hamlin's embarrassing public assertions.

The Ottoman ambassador in Washington, D.C., also accused Schuyler of colluding with the Russians and publicly declaring that he wanted to end the Ottoman Empire, an accusation that engendered great concern in the U.S. government.[119] By November 1876, only four months into his service, Ottoman rulers had twice requested Schuyler's recall. American diplomatic officials in Washington, D.C., were caught off guard. Horace Maynard, the American minister to the Ottoman Empire, had waited until late November to inform Secretary of State Hamilton Fish of Schuyler's original investigative trip to Bulgaria and his cooperation with the Russians on the Bulgarian constitution. To his defense, Maynard likely did not know the extent of Schuyler's involvement. In late January 1877, Maynard was compelled to show Fish evidence he had himself recently obtained revealing that Schuyler had sent telegrams while in Bulgaria to newspapers in Britain and Germany detailing the massacres. Of course, Schuyler's official report had also made its way into the British press. Embarrassed by this lapse in diplomatic protocol, Fish officially reprimanded Schuyler. Shortly after issuing the reprimand, Fish learned that Gladstone had just delivered a speech with new quotes recently obtained from Schuyler.[120] Not only had Schuyler collaborated with Russians to work on a Bulgarian constitution and divulged official reports to the British press and American journalists, but he continued to send information to his British contacts months later.

Schuyler defended himself, noting to the State Department that any actions he had undertaken were done out of moral compulsion: "I had tried to keep as quiet as a man who has seen what I have seen can do," he wrote the assistant secretary of state in February 1877.[121] The real source of the problem, according to Schuyler, stemmed from British intrigue and Europeans policies that had accepted the Ottoman Empire into the "circle of civilized powers."[122] He also claimed that he had always been upfront in his actions with the Bulgarians. At the time, American and European public sympathy for the Bulgarians protected Schuyler from greater punishment. As Secretary of State Fish noted in a letter to Maynard, "The President hesitates to recall Mr. Schuyler at this time solely for fear that doing so might be misinterpreted in Europe as indicating a want of sympathy in behalf of those who are represented by Mr. Schuyler as suffering at the hands of the Turks."[123] Nonetheless, Schuyler was eventually recalled and reassigned to Birmingham, England, in the summer of 1878, just as the Great Powers were meeting at the Congress of Berlin. Despite this official sanction, Bulgarians continued to celebrate Schuyler's contributions. After Bulgaria obtained its independence, the first president of the Bulgarian National Assembly sent a telegram to Schuyler in London expressing strong appreciation for his role in the recent events: "At the time that European diplomacy was trying with all possible means to conceal the sufferings of the Bulgarian nation, in consequence of the

Turkish atrocities perpetuated two years ago, you through your famous report, brought the truth to light and helped to remedy the evil. The free Bulgarian nation hastens to thank you heartily for your great services, and to assure you that your honoured name will hold an enviable place in the history of the liberation of our nation."[124] The telegram served as a compelling testament to the role Schuyler had played both officially and unofficially in bringing about Bulgarian independence.

Such demonstrations of gratitude reinforced Schuyler's lack of contrition. In an article he wrote in 1885, after leaving diplomatic service, Schuyler proudly recalled his actions. As further support for the righteousness of his involvement, he noted that the American Civil War hero and former president Ulysses S. Grant had expressed opinions identical to his own in 1878. Grant had been staying at Schuyler's house in Istanbul when the Treaty of San Stefano was announced. According to Schuyler, Grant responded to the news by claiming that had he been at the head of the victorious Russian army, "he would have occupied Constantinople, and . . . would have issued a proclamation leaving ultimate arrangements to the European powers on one sole condition—'that the rule of the Turk in Europe was to be forever abolished.' "[125] The former president having sided with him, Schuyler felt certain that his actions were in the best interest of humanity and beyond official reproach.

The ABCFM also praised American involvement in securing Bulgarian independence, in particular the role played by American Protestants. Its 1879 annual report noted that the fact that Bulgaria had adopted a "liberal form of government" was attributable "in no small measure to the influence of the Bulgarian young men who have been educated in Robert College and thus made acquainted with a higher civilization."[126]

Ongoing concerns about the fate of the Eastern Question continued, however, and despite British reluctance to involve themselves during the recent Bulgarian conflict, American missionaries continued to praise their role in shaping future events in the Ottoman Empire. In May 1878, Henry Jessup, head of the Syrian Protestant College in Beirut, delivered a speech, "The Mohammedan Missionary Problem," before the General Assembly of the Presbyterian Church of the United States in which he argued that British intervention in the Eastern Question was crucial to solving the challenges that had thus far limited Protestant missionary success in converting Muslims to Christianity. In his book by the same name, Jessup concluded with an entire chapter devoted to the divine possibilities that would result from the extension of a British protectorate over all of "Asiatic Turkey."[127] He pictured an "Anglo-Saxon Christian

Queen [Victoria], already the ruler of forty-one millions of Mohammedans in India, stands up before the world as the protectress of the whole Turkish empire in Asia." American missionaries would serve as the spiritual partners in this great endeavor: "Let the two great branches of the christianized [sic] Anglo-Saxon race go hand in hand to the great work assigned us in evangelization of the Mohammedan World." Jessup's sermon was published for circulation to American missionaries and surely influenced American religious understanding of the area. His calls for such a united endeavor also continued to link Americans and Europeans in a larger divine plan to convert and colonize Muslims around the globe.

The Aftermath of Bulgarian Independence

Decades later, after the United States entered World War I on the side of the Allies, against the Ottoman Empire and Bulgaria, the New York Times theorized that Robert College's efforts on behalf of Bulgarian independence explained why, despite its status as an ally of the powers fighting the United States, Bulgaria had refused to cut ties with Washington.[128] Stefan Panaretov, the Bulgarian student and professor at Robert College who had played an important role working with Washburn in shaping the international response to the Bulgarian massacres, was serving as the Bulgarian minister to the United States during the war. He was the only diplomat from the Central Powers allowed to stay in the United States. As the New York Times noted, Robert College had "imbibed American ideas along with their instruction by American teachers and according to American methods." Because of this education, Bulgarians had "come to admire and respect America, to understand something of the ideals of American democracy."[129]

American diplomats, journalists, and missionaries had worked together, alongside Bulgarians, Russians, and British activists in pushing for Bulgarian independence. Simplistic beliefs about Ottoman Muslims merged with altruism to drive the American response to the massacres, but the same was not always true for Europeans. Whereas many Americans advanced an argument for religious freedom alongside their sympathy for Christian Bulgarians, Russian and Bulgarian actions were dominated by ethnic and religious nationalism. Humanitarian and religious justifications also hid strategic moves by the Great Powers. These motivations would have disastrous consequences for Christians and non-Christians. Russian atrocities during the Russo-Turkish War marked a continuation of earlier policies of demographic warfare resulting in the expulsion from Bulgaria of hundreds of thousands of Circassians, Turkish and Bulgarian Muslims, and Bulgarian Jews. Such policies inflamed ethnic hatred. Many of the Bulgarian, Turkish, and Circassian Muslims relocated to Anatolia, where Armenian-Kurdish relations were already strained. As one scholar aptly noted: "Such refugees—*muhajirs*—provided an aggressive anti-Christian constituency from which the government made appointments to local administrative posts and that went on to form part of the gendarmerie that would figure prominently in killing Armenians during World War I. They also included some of the foremost proponents of the irredentist ideology of pan-Turkism that was later adopted by some leaders of the Committee of Union and Progress, the political party of the Young Turks, many of whom themselves originated in peripheral or lost Ottoman lands."[130] Despite centuries of relatively peaceful intercommunal relations, Russian policies of ethnic and religious cleansing had succeeded in convincing their victims that Muslims and Christians could not peacefully coexist, and similar beliefs would play a central role in intercommunal strife between Armenians and Muslims in future decades.

European efforts to reform the Ottoman Empire through the Treaty of Berlin had other unintended consequences for Armenians. Ottoman paranoia resulting from their recent loss of territories to foreign encroachment and its war with Russia was exacerbated by the inclusion of British-supported reforms in the treaty. The British introduced these reforms to limit the possibility of future Russian interventions in the empire and to protect Armenians from Ottoman discrimination, thus "internationalizing the Armenian Question."[131] Russia had already fomented nationalist thought among the Armenian populations in the Ottoman Empire, to the great annoyance of both Ottoman and British rulers. Indeed, Ottoman rulers interpreted the Armenian community as yet another population challenging its authority by aligning with a foreign power. In a little over a decade, this rising paranoia would have disastrous consequences for Ottoman Armenians.

Another unintended consequence of these reforms and the Bulgarian massacres was increased American participation in Ottoman affairs. During the 1876 Congress of Constantinople, international Jewish organizations from France, Britain, and the United States joined their Christian colleagues by raising the issue of Ottoman oppression of its Jewish subjects. American Jewish leaders had previously met with their British and French counterparts in Paris to prepare two propositions for the meeting in Istanbul. The propositions asked for the inclusion of Ottoman Jewish subjects in all reforms regarding the civil and political rights of non-

Muslims in the empire and for assurance of the "emancipation of Jews in the Balkan provinces."[132]

William Seligman represented the American Board of Delegates of American Israelites, an important American Jewish organization dedicated to assisting persecuted Jews. After helping to craft the petition in Paris, Seligman secured endorsement from Minister Maynard. Ironically, Maynard noted to his secretary of state that, although he was willing to support the European and American initiative, "justice to the Turks requires me to say they have treated the Jews much better than have some of the western Powers of Europe."[133] When the Ottoman minister to the United States heard of the propositions, he also wrote the American Board, arguing that the Porte was not responsible for atrocities committed in the Balkans, but that the empire itself was "impartial and enlightened" and granted Jews both civil and religious liberties.[134]

The fears of American Jewish organizations were justified. However, the atrocities to which the Ottoman minister alluded had been committed not by Ottomans, but by Bulgarian and Russian Christians. During the Russo-Turkish war, Russian anti-Semitism combined with homegrown Bulgarian hostility to create a toxic environment for Bulgarian Jews, leading to their expulsion and exodus to Istanbul. These events countered simplistic narratives of the war that portrayed Russia as the liberators of religious minorities under barbaric and intolerant Muslim rule.[135] Although the irony of religious minorities seeking refuge from Russian and Bulgarian Christians in the Ottoman Empire may have been lost on Christian American activists who had pushed for Bulgarian independence, it demonstrated the hollowness of European claims to promoting religious tolerance. These unfortunate consequences confirmed the American Board's initial fears. Their aim was to assure the civil and political rights of Jews under Ottoman rule, but American and European Jews knew that anti-Semitism persisted among Christians in Europe. To help Jewish refugees who were forcibly displaced by Russian and Bulgarian forces, the American Board formed a relief committee and raised $7,000 to help the displaced and suffering Jews.

At the end of the Russo-Turkish War, the American Board submitted another proposal recommending that representatives from their organizations attend the Congress of Berlin to further the protection of Jewish rights. Three members of the French Jewish organization, the Alliance Israélite Universelle, attended the Congress on behalf of both the French and the American organizations. Together, they successfully lobbied the European delegates at the Congress to include the protection of Jewish civil and religious rights throughout the newly independent territories, including Bulgaria and Romania. The Russian delegate opposed the proposal for equal rights for Jews in Romania, Russia, and Serbia on the premise that Jews in these countries could not be compared to those living in western Europe. Bulgaria and Serbia inserted guarantees for Jewish equality into their constitutions, but Romania refused. In the following decades, the persecution of Jews in that country would become a major cause for activism for American Jewish organizations. Although Russians had justified their war against the Ottoman Empire in part by citing the oppression of Christian communities protected by Russian capitulatory treaties, the outcome of the Congress of Berlin revealed that the protection of religious minorities did not extend to Jews. Furthermore, the war demonstrated that such claims provided an ideal method by which Europeans could advance their imperial and strategic interests.

Amidst the diplomatic and cultural fallout of the Eastern Question, Americans in the Ottoman Empire and at home had increasingly participated in shaping diplomatic events in the Ottoman Empire. Americans helped negotiate European strategic influence with an Ottoman imperial government desperately trying to maintain its territorial integrity. A complex transnational, trans-imperial, multiethnic, and multireligious web of exchanges ensued, leading to complicated identities and affiliations beyond straightforward nationalist allegiance. American diplomats and religious organizations increasingly adopted European tactics to further their own interests, including aligning with specific religious communities, attempting to convert local populations, using diplomatic power to "protect" local subjects to their own advantage, working with European religious organizations to defend the rights of religious minorities, and attending international conferences to impose legal rights on minority populations. American missionaries, journalists, and diplomats informed the American public of important events, appealing for aid and continuing to shape American interpretations of the Eastern Question. As such, Americans in the Ottoman Empire helped craft an understanding that reified the perceived civilizational and religious "clash" between Islam and Christianity. As it gained diplomatic power, the United States relied on its accumulated experience to shape its relations with other Islamic societies. If Americans believed that the behavior of Muslims was governed by faith alone, then policies that applied to Muslims in the Ottoman Empire could logically be applied to Muslims in other areas of the world.

PART II

Jewish American Activism in the Islamic World

In the first place, the members of the human family living

in Asia and Africa under the sway of semi-barbarism, are criminally

neglected and justly claim our sympathy. . . . Therefore it appears no less

self-evident to us that we have a duty to perform to the neglected

members of the human family in the Orient.

—Rabbi Isaac M. Wise, 26 May 1865

3

JEWISH AMERICAN ACTIVISM

IN THE OTTOMAN EMPIRE AND

MOROCCO, 1840–1878

In 1833, Supreme Court Justice Joseph Storey published one of the most influential texts on American jurisprudence of the nineteenth century. Although his study was designed primarily as a treatise on the broad powers of the federal government, as laid out in the U.S. Constitution, Storey's study also maintained that the United States was, above all, a Christian nation. He argued that the Constitution's First Amendment assuring freedom of religion was intended to help regulate relations *between Christian denominations*, so as to avoid privileging one Christian denomination above the others. The First Amendment was *not*, he clearly specified, "to countenance, much less to advance Mahometanism, or Judaism, or infidelity by prostrating Christianity."[1] Couched in legal analysis, such a claim from a Supreme Court justice provided powerful validation for Christian Americans who touted their religion as a defining component of American national identity and their superiority over non-Christians at home and abroad.

As discussed in the last two chapters, many Americans believed that the country's political superiority stemmed in large part from its Christian Protestant values. During the Revolutionary War, as Americans drafted their state constitutions and debated ratification of the U.S. Constitution, a subject of contention was whether to include a religious test that would exclude Jews, Muslims, pagans, atheists, Deists, and sometimes Roman Catholics from running for office. Although ultimately not included in the U.S. Constitution, every state constitution except for those of Virginia and New York specifically excluded Jews and adherents of other non-Christian faiths from running for state office.[2] Although some states soon eliminated these restrictions, others maintained them well into the nineteenth century. Exclusionary beliefs extended into other legal and social realms, marginalizing the faiths of non-Christians in the process. As Hasia Diner has argued, "At its core, public policy privileged Christianity and made Christian practices and institutions the norm to which other religions—Judaism—had to accommodate."[3]

Throughout the nineteenth century, many American Jews actively fought against legal and political exclusion. Jewish American activists emphasized secularism and pluralism as the key values that defined the superiority of the American national project and sought to change policies that discriminated against Jews both at home and abroad. Domestically, Jewish American activists lobbied to ensure that the U.S. government treat Judaism and Christianity equally. This included having Jewish rabbis serve alongside Christian chaplains in the military and banning Christian ceremonies in public schools.[4] Jewish activists also fought for religious tolerance outside of the United States.[5] When they engaged in such pursuits, however, they frequently used the same civilizational and religious rhetoric to describe Jewish-Muslim relations in Islamic lands as American Protestant activists used to describe Christian-Muslim relations in the Ottoman Empire. They emphasized the superiority of civilized "Oriental" Jews at the mercy of uncivilized Muslims.

Such discourses adopted *and contributed* to American attitudes about Islam and Muslims in complicated but important ways. Jewish American activists attempted to bend existing discourse about the "Orient" and Muslims to their advantage. They modified negative depictions of the "Orient," which frequently denigrated Jews and Muslims as foreign, to isolate Islam as the real source of Oriental depravity. In affirming the religious and civilizational superiority of Jews over Muslims, activists inserted religious qualifications that ranked some "Orientals" above others in a hierarchy of race, religion, and civilization. In doing so, they reified a civilizational continuum with Muslims at the bottom, "Oriental" Jews and Christians in the middle, and Euro-American Jews and Christians at the pinnacle. A natural extension of such logic meant that, over the course of the nineteenth century, Jewish American activists and American diplomats and policymakers increasingly posited Jewish subjects in Islamic societies as civilizing agents through which Europeans and Americans could spread their values. The construction of such hierarchies reflected complex contemporary constructions of identity that imbricated religious belief, race, ethnic origin, empire, and civilization.[6]

Much like American connections with European philhellenism during the Greek War of Independence, Jewish American activists formulated their opinions about the Islamic world by mixing homegrown beliefs with the attitudes they adopted from Europeans. These exchanges were reinforced by developing transnational ties among American, French, and British Jewish organizations that cooperated in aiding oppressed Jews in other parts of the world. In this shared goal, American Jewish activists worked alongside Europeans to redefine Euro-American civilization as independent from Christian identity. As historian Lisa Leff has argued, "Seeing their work as leading all nations to embrace liberal values like tolerance, equality, and freedom, Jewish philanthropists viewed their solidarity as part of the progress of 'civilization' itself."[7] When Jewish activists lobbied the U.S. government to intervene on behalf of Jews living in Muslim lands, they depicted Ottoman and North African Muslims as uncivilized and intolerant. They further argued that Jews living in these societies faced fanatical discrimination.

Such discourse mirrored American Protestant assertions about the Islamic faith and affirmed American Jews' own membership in civilized, white America.[8] Jewish American organizations joined American and European governments in supporting imperial expansion to spread the ideals of religious tolerance and Euro-American civilization to "uncivilized" Islamic lands. Admittedly, given their own experience with domestic anti-Semitism and exclusion, these arguments were often fraught with ambivalence and self-protection.[9]

American Judaism and the Response to Anti-Semitism in the United States

Although in the nineteenth century American anti-Semitism never matched levels in Europe, negative depictions of Jews date back to early history and were present among the founding fathers, including George Washington and Benjamin Franklin. John Quincy Adams, whose diatribe against Islam in 1831 was unrivaled in its vitriol, unsurprisingly also held strong anti-Semitic views.[10] Like earlier discourse about Muslims, many of these early anti-Semitic beliefs were initially imported from Europe.

Despite, or perhaps because of, these anti-Semitic beliefs, the logic that posited Jews as ideal intermediaries between Christians and Muslims also helped forge a tradition of sending American Jews to occupy diplomatic positions in Islamic lands. American diplomats had also recognized from their earliest official interactions with the Barbary states that Jews played an important role in foreign diplomacy in many Islamic societies.[11]

In 1813, President James Madison and Secretary of State James Monroe appointed Mordecai Noah, one of the most prominent Jewish American leaders, as consul to the Kingdom of Tunis. Noah himself argued that his Judaism would grant him access to the wealth and connections of 40,000 Jews living in North Africa.[12] Noah was appointed consul in 1813 in the midst of continued American tensions with the Barbary states over the kidnapping of American sailors. When Noah was recalled in 1815, Monroe blamed Islamic intolerance, noting that the Tunisian bey had allegedly discovered Noah was Jewish and thereafter refused to work with him.[13]

In reality, the Tunisian bey had never opposed Noah's religion nor asked for his recall. Tunisian Jews held a great deal of influence with the Tunisian bey and occupied high positions in Tunisian society.[14] In his own writings, Noah had attempted to correct existing American beliefs that Tunisian Jews were oppressed under Muslim rule, noting that this "oppression" was "in great measure imaginary."[15] Noah's recall was instead based on his incompetence during a secret mission to rescue Americans kidnapped by Barbary pirates. The secrecy of the mission prevented Monroe from citing it as the source of the recall. In this situation, accepted tropes of Muslim intolerance offered a convenient cover.

American anti-Semitic beliefs would transform in the 1840s with the rise of what Matthew Jacobson has deemed "Anglo-supremacist exclusivity."[16] For many white, Protestant Americans, Anglo-Saxon Protestantism combined race and religion to become the norm of superiority that defined America. In these classifications, Jews and other minority groups ranked well below Anglo-Saxons.[17] Such stereotypes fused with existing American beliefs about Jews as untrustworthy, disloyal, and perpetually incompatible with American religious and political values.[18] These religious and racial biases merged in Europe and the United States, reaffirming the liminal position of Jews between "East" and "West." As one scholar has noted, "Orientalism was recast in a racial mold. The Christian West was the domain of the Indo-European races, while the Semitic 'Arabians' inhabited the Muslim Orient. The Jews, the Asiatics of Europe, straddled both worlds but were understood by everyone to stem from 'oriental stock.'"[19] Such attitudes crossed the Atlantic to inform American understandings as well.

In the decades following the Civil War, American anti-Semitism was exacerbated by mounting xenophobia that resulted from the influx of immigrants from eastern Europe, many of whom were Jewish. Just as many white Americans referred to the "Negro problem" and "Chinese problem" in the final decades of the nineteenth century, some Christian Americans increasingly wondered whether they also had a "Jewish problem." Anti-Semitic political cartoons and editorials in major journals depicted newly arrived Jewish immigrants as "Semitic barbarian[s]" and "childish semi-savages."[20] Editorials pondered whether Jews could ever become equal members of the American citizenry.

As scientific racism and xenophobia led to domestic fixations on racial classification and ranking, American Jews found themselves in the uncomfortable position of defending their racial and civilizational equality to protect their own inclusion in American society. Nativist efforts to exclude Chinese immigration to the country in the 1880s, for example, led many American Jews to adopt a defensive posture and distance themselves from these other "Orientals" by maintaining their racial and cultural superiority to Chinese immigrants.[21] When the Chinese Exclusion Act passed in 1882, an editorial in the *American Hebrew* expressed profound uneasiness toward these new policies. Perhaps fearing that anti-Chinese immigrant policies could quickly become anti-Jewish immigrant policies, the editor explicitly contrasted his community from the Chinese by arguing that "the comparison between Hebrew and Chinese will not hold on closer examination." Unlike the Chinese, American Jews had helped "build the country. . . . The Chinese are not so."[22] Affirming the superiority and loyalty of American Jews to the detriment of other groups afforded protection against popular discrimination. The same logic extended to American Jewish activists depictions of Jews living abroad.

During these years Jewish American organizations leveraged ideas about the inherent barbarity of Muslims to win foreign policy successes. Besides aiding Jews under Muslim rule, during the nineteenth and early twentieth centuries, these organizations together supported Jews in Russia, Romania, and other parts of Europe who faced state-sponsored persecution and violence. Such state-sanctioned repression was in fact the primary catalyst for Jewish people to immigrate to the United States in large numbers.[23]

There were limits to what the U.S. government was able or willing to do, however. Many Americans considered Russia and other eastern European countries as tainted by "Eastern" despotism and thus "barely" European. Nevertheless, the membership of European nation-states in the Family of Nations alongside their military, diplomatic, and commercial power granted them sovereign rights under international law. This status complicated U.S. intervention efforts in diplomatic, legal, and conceptual ways. In contrast, interference in Muslim lands steadily mounted over the course of the nineteenth century, as the French and British extended their imperial control over areas of North Africa and the former Ottoman Empire, beginning with French imperial rule over Algeria in 1830 and Tunisia in 1881 and British control over Egypt in 1882. Such examples of European breaches of sovereignty in Islamic lands facilitated calls for intervention in others. The Damascus Affair of 1840 provided an ideal opportunity for such involvement and marked the first time American Jews responded to transnational efforts by lobbying the U.S. government to intervene on behalf of their oppressed brethren abroad.

The Damascus Affair of 1840

In February 1840, a Syrian Catholic priest disappeared in Damascus, Syria. Members of the Syrian Catholic community accused Syrian Jews of kidnapping the priest to use his blood for their Passover matzo.[24] When the local Syrian Catholic community enlisted the help of the French consul, the crisis drew in other European diplomats, who tried to use the incident to advance their own country's interests in Syria. French consular pressure led to the persecution and torture of several Damascene Jews. This turn of events transformed the local dispute into an international incident that involved diplomatic officials and Jewish activists from Europe and the United States.

The French consul, Count Ulysse de Ratti-Menton, and the French consular chancellor, Jean-Baptiste Beaudin, both willing to use virulent anti-Semitic tropes to advance their country's interests, pursued the blood libel case with local Ottoman authorities.[25] The two men had strong interests in maintaining a positive relationship with Syrian Catholics. Capitulary treaties between France and the Ottoman Empire placed Syrian Catholics under French protection, but they also granted commercial and political advantages to the French over competing British interests. Shortly after the accusations surfaced, Ratti-Menton co-opted Governor Sherif Pasha of Damascus to conduct a phony investigation. They soon obtained "confessions" under torture from a Jewish barber and eight other members of the Damascus Jewish community. All were imprisoned and tortured, and one man died as a result of the abuse.

The Jewish communities in Britain and France were first to respond. The Board of Deputies of British Jews published information about the affair in local Jewish presses and called on the international Jewish community to rise in solidarity and protest. Jewish American groups organized mass protest rallies in major U.S. cities and sent petitions to the Van Buren administration voicing their concern and asking the U.S. government to formally intervene.[26]

Both the popular and the diplomatic American narrative described the Damascus Affair as yet another example of intolerant Muslim fanatics persecuting religious minorities. This narrative omitted the fact that it was largely French intercession and anti-Semitism that had led to the injustice. Many Americans assumed that, in comparison with Europe and the United States, Islamic societies were much more intolerant toward their Jewish minorities. As one scholar notes, however, "Whereas the Jews in Europe, the heartland of civilization (as they, too, usually saw it), were still hemmed in, at least east of the Rhine, by a complex array of legal and social barriers, the Jews in Damascus enjoyed a large measure of acceptance, as one among the major ethnoreligious groups that by tradition made up the city." More important, Jews in Damascus "not only ran their own communal affairs but, to a degree unimaginable in contemporary Europe, were involved in public administration and high politics."[27]

Indeed, unbeknownst to American Jews, the real story behind the accusations was far more complex. The Damascus Affair was not the result of Muslim intolerance. Rather, it was a combination of French anti-Semitism and a larger strategic power struggle among Egyptian ruler Muhammad Ali, the Ottoman Empire, the French, and the British, all of whom sought greater influence in Syria.[28] During the Greek War of Independence, the Ottoman sultan had promised Muhammad Ali control of Syria in exchange for sending his navy to help defeat Greece. After the devastating defeat of the Egyptian and Ottoman navies during the Battle of Navarino and the ensuing loss of Greece, the sultan reneged on his promise. Ali successfully fought the Ottomans to gain control over Syria in 1833, but local uprisings in 1839 allowed the Ottoman sultan to regain his lost territory, and the two powers again went to war. The French sided with Egypt against a pro-Ottoman alliance of Austria, Britain, and Russia. France sent Ratti-Menton to Damascus to support Ali's hold on Syria and maintain French influence. The British had sided with the Ottoman Empire in the hopes of countering French influence.[29] Both the French and the British attempted to increase their political and diplomatic influence in Syria by aligning themselves with local religious communities. The desire by French officials to win the allegiance of the Syrian Catholic community gained such importance that they were willing to act against the Syrian Jewish community.

The Damascus Affair provided the British a new opportunity to counter French influence. The British foreign secretary, Lord Palmerston, was aware of European machinations to exert influence over religious communities in the Ottoman Empire to their own advantage. He hoped that defending the Syrian Jews against charges of blood libel might enhance Britain's humanitarian image and extend its interests and influence.[30] British diplomats hoped to exploit French tactics and limit French influence by playing multiple angles. They knew that the French alliance with Syrian Maronites offered a more powerful entrée than a potential alliance with Syrian Jews. Only by reforming the system could the British counter the French advantage. Palmerston thus also pushed the sultan to enact reforms that would quell tensions between religious communities. According to Palmerston, if the Ottoman sultan could maintain peaceful relations between religious communities, then the French would be unable to exploit the situation to advance their own interests.[31]

Great Britain's public response to the Damascus Affair combined its strategic interests with a wider mission of extending European civilization to the Jews of Muslim lands.[32] As Abigail Green has argued, British aid to Jews in Muslim lands was motivated by "the economic community of interest that existed between Jews and British imperialism in North Africa and the Middle East" and "was dictated above all by a widespread public belief in the virtues of Commerce, Christianity and Civilization, and in the obligation of Britain to promote the cause of 'civil and religious liberty' abroad."[33] Thus, drawing the United States into the fray on the side of the Syrian Jews would only advance British interests. Undoubtedly unaware of British maneuverings, this humanitarian rhetoric resonated with an American public and political elites, who were increasingly affirming the role of the United States as a beacon for religious and political freedom.

American Jews, who were familiar with accusations of anti-Christian conspiracy, had a strong interest in defending their religious brethren from such discrimination. Indeed, such anti-Semitic claims hit close to home for some American Jewish activists. In 1837, only three years earlier, the former consul to Tunisia, Mordecai Noah, had become the editor of a newspaper in New York and faced accusations from a rival editor that he was part of "a secret conspiracy" alongside other "Jews and infidels" to "up-root" Christianity in the United States.[34] Yet, Noah responded to the Damascus Affair by discounting the existence of such domestic anti-Semitism in favor of advancing the superiority of American religious tolerance. He remarked that, although American Jews were "remote" from "such cruel-ties" and "exempt from such outrages," since divine providence had placed them in a "country of laws administered alike to Jew and Gentile," Jews across the world were nonetheless "bound together by the same destiny" and thus responsible for protesting against such violent injustice.[35] Affirm-ing the role of God and providence and the superiority of American religious toleration allowed Noah to advance an alternative version of American manifest destiny that assigned Jews living in countries like the United States a special duty to protect those less unfortunate who were living elsewhere.

As Noah's personal experiences had demonstrated, his idealized vision of American religious tolerance did not always reflect reality. Given the existence of American conspiratorial views toward Jews at home, it should come as no surprise that some American diplomatic officials initially re-sponded to the Damascus Affair by echoing the anti-Semitic views of French consular officials in Damascus. In a letter to Secretary of State John Forsyth, Jasper Chasseaud, the American consular representative in Syria, accepted the blood libel at face value and wrote that the incident confirmed long-held beliefs that Jews were secretly preying on innocent Christians. He provided Forsyth "details of a most Barbarous secret, for a long time suspected of the Jewish Nation, which at last came to light in the City of Damascus, that of serving themselves of Christian Blood in their unleavened Bread at Easter, a Secret which in these 1,840 Years must have made many unfortunate victims."[36] While endorsing the French con-sul's claims, Chasseaud identified all Jews as constituting part of a "Jew-ish Nation" that was distinct from, and inherently disloyal to, national affiliations.

Van Buren and Forsyth refused to endorse Chasseaud's version of the story. They ignored the American consul's interpretation, instead heeding the advice of London-based British officials.[37] The Lord Mayor of London had sent a letter to the American minister in Britain, Andrew Stevenson, asking that the U.S. government intervene on behalf of the Syrian Jews.[38] Stevenson immediately forwarded the request to Secretary of State Forsyth, who reacted quickly. Within a few weeks of the initial request, he had written to John Glidden, U.S. consul in Alexandria, and David Porter, U.S.

minister to the Ottoman Empire, ordering them to express American concern for these oppressed Jews and emphasizing the need to protect the Syrian Jews from these "atrocious cruelties."[39]

Although it was the French consul who transformed local accusations of blood libel into an official investigation (a course quickly endorsed by the United States' own consul in Damascus), Secretary of State Forsyth and President Van Buren blamed the incident on the absence of civilized behavior in Muslim lands. As Forsyth wrote to the American minister in Turkey: "As the scenes of these barbarities are in the Mahomedan dominions, and, as such inhuman practices are not of an infrequent occurrence in the East, the President has directed me to instruct you to do everything in your power with the government of his Imperial Highness, the Sultan, to whom you are accredited, consistent with discretion and your diplomatic character, to prevent or mitigate these horrors—the bare recital of which has caused a shudder throughout the civilized world."[40]

Although historically, most accusations of blood libel had occurred in Europe, under Christian rule rather than in the East, under "Mahomedan dominions," Forsyth was confident that such "barbarities" were typical manifestations of Muslim intolerance. Much like Noah's assertion that American Jews were "exempt" from such "cruelties," it was inconceivable to the American secretary of state that a member of the civilized, Christian Family of Nations could exhibit such intolerance. Moreover, although the French consul had been a key player in initiating the persecution, Van Buren and Forsyth maintained that only Western Christendom could discipline Ottoman Islamic fanaticism. The president welcomed the efforts "of several of the Christian Governments of Europe, to suppress or mitigate these horrors," but he also maintained the importance of American diplomatic intervention as a moral and political model for Islamic lands: "The President is of the opinion that from no one can such generous endeavors proceed with so much propriety and effect, as from the representative of a friendly power, whose institutions, political and civil, place upon the same footing, the worshippers of God, of every faith and form, acknowledging no distinction between the Mahomedan, the Jew, and the Christian."[41]

Neither President Van Buren nor Secretary of State Forsyth betrayed any awareness of the fact that, in 1840, five states in the union continued to restrict the political rights of Jews (not to mention other minorities, including more than two and half million African American slaves).[42] The motives behind President Van Buren's unprecedented attention to Jewish rights abroad stemmed not merely from support for humanitarian principles of religious equality—Van Buren was about to embark on a difficult presidential campaign against a popular opponent. His personal attention to this matter, well publicized among Jewish synagogues by the secretary of state, could only improve his chances of gaining votes among Jewish constituents.[43] Beyond this immediate concern, selling intervention to an American public, who had become convinced of Muslim barbarity toward religious minorities during the Greek War of Independence a decade earlier, could only improve Van Buren's image at home.

Although many Jewish Americans were appalled by the French consul's anti-Semitic behavior, their reaction to the Damascus Affair mirrored those of their political leaders. Their solutions did not involve reforming the French. Instead, American Jews maintained that the U.S. government had a duty to defend oppressed Jews *alongside* oppressed Christians against *Muslim* oppression.

These claims of superior American religious tolerance echoed the spiritual arguments made by American Christians during the Greek War of Independence, affirming a moral and divine duty to protect their religious brethren abroad from persecution. Indeed, references to Greek independence would be a common and reoccurring theme in American protest meetings about the Damascus Affair.[44] As the prominent Jewish leader Isaac Leeser argued in August 1840 at a Philadelphia meeting devoted to the Damascus Jews, no moral difference should exist between American actions to defend Christians during the Greek War of Independence and actions to protect oppressed Jews in Syria: "When the sons of ancient Hellas broke the chains of the Ottoman power, all Europe and America was awakened in their behalf; but have they any greater claim upon the sympathy of the world than we have?"[45] The question was not simply about protecting Christians from Muslim rule, but protecting all religious minorities who suffered at the hands of Muslim barbarity and intolerance.

Furthermore, like the Greeks, Leeser maintained that Jews had contributed to civilization: "We admit that the Greeks may have been the fathers of architecture, of painting, of sculpture, and of tragic poetry; but the world is indebted to us far more, for a gift far nobler, for the possession of the Decalogue, for the word of God, the holy and precious Bible, the book more venerable than all books, the parent of a pure belief, the foundation of true human happiness, of religion without bigotry, of liberty without licentiousness."[46] In maintaining the necessity of American actions on behalf of *both* Christians and Jews, American Jews affirmed their status as equal members of American society, while simultaneously advancing their civilizational and religious superiority over Muslims.

In the end, pressure from a French and British Jewish delegation, which included Adolphe Crémieux and Moses Montefiore, led to the release of all surviving Jewish men and to the issuance of a *firman* (decree) by the sultan to prevent future accusations of blood libel. More important, Montefiore successfully petitioned the sultan to include religious toleration for Jews in his *firman*. This inclusion was gratuitous, since Islamic law already recognized and protected Jews and Christians.[47] Jewish American activists interpreted President Van Buren and Secretary of State Forsyth's official support for the protection of Jewish minorities in the Ottoman Empire as an important precedent, demonstrating that the U.S. government was willing to intervene to protect Jews abroad.[48]

American and European Jewish communities took away a more cautionary lesson from the Damascus Affair. Their efforts had evinced a lack of coherent organization. Jewish American activists had organized most of their protests and sent the letter to President Van Buren only *after* the president and secretary of state intervened to express their support for the persecuted Jews. The Damascus Affair convinced many American and European Jews of the necessity of forging new organizations dedicated to responding to anti-Semitic persecution both at home and abroad. Only then could they organize more systematically within their respective countries to apply political pressure to their governments as cohesive entities.[49]

These efforts proceeded unevenly. In Britain, the existing Board of Deputies of British Jews expanded the organization's mission to the international sphere under the leadership of Montefiore. In the United States, however, it would take almost twenty years and another well-publicized incident of anti-Semitism in Italy—the 1858 Mortara affair—to prompt the founding of the Board of Delegates of American Israelites in 1859.[50] The board's stated mission was to strengthen the Jewish American community through education, to settle disputes, and, most important, to ensure the civil and religious rights of Jews at home and abroad, while maintaining a political organization that protected community members against violations.[51] French Jewish leaders followed the American example and founded the Alliance Israélite Universelle (French Alliance) in 1860, with the principal mission of creating an international organization to help Jews abroad. For the next twenty years, until it merged with the Union of American Hebrew Congregations, the American Board of Delegates worked closely with the French Alliance and the British Board of Deputies to pressure their governments to act on behalf of persecuted Jews.

The Board of Delegates of American Israelites and the
Spanish-Moroccan War of 1859–1860

Although language issues and miscommunication initially slowed official cooperation between the American Board and the French Alliance, the American Board interacted in important ways with the British Board from its first year. In 1859, the British Board solicited its help in aiding 3,000 Moroccan Jewish refugees of the Spanish-Moroccan War. Largely fought to extend Spain's imperial reach in Morocco, the war had targeted port towns that happened to have large Jewish populations. As the Spanish military advanced, hundreds of Jewish refugees sought refuge in Gibraltar, but the British Board needed financial assistance to guarantee their safety. The American Board quickly adopted the Morocco Relief Fund from their British sister organization and published appeals in Jewish American newspapers.

The *Jewish Messenger*, edited by American Board secretary Meyer S. Isaacs, described the situation: "The unbridled fury of the barbarous hordes now inundating the sea-ports of Morocco, [who force women to] leave their homes, their religious shrines, the graves of their sires, with the snares of death overtaking them in their perilous condition."[52] Ignoring the fact that the exodus had been largely driven by Spanish forces invading Moroccan towns, Isaacs blamed the disruptions on local Muslims, whose innate "fury," intolerance, and fanaticism naturally led them to force Jewish women to leave their religious havens and the graves of their ancestors on a path toward a certain death. Blinded by the belief that Islamic intolerance was the primary cause of Jewish suffering, Isaacs did not realize that similar repercussions frequently accompanied European imperial expansion and impacted all residents, regardless of their faith, many of whom left voluntarily believing that exile would be better than facing the consequences of war. Along with Moroccan Jews, the war had also led thousands of Muslim inhabitants to leave their homes.

Nevertheless, the perceptions held by Americans of Muslim rule in Morocco were similar to their perceptions of the Ottoman Empire in that they ignored historical realities that distinguished Moroccan culture and history from other Islamic societies. The fact that some Moroccan Jews were the descendants of refugees from the Spanish expulsion centuries earlier was only one example. Although their status as non-Muslims placed Moroccan Jews in a distinct legal category and although religious and ethnic differences played an important role in Moroccan society more generally (a factor not limited to Moroccan Jews), Moroccan Jews nonetheless played an integral role in society. Encouraged by the Moroccan sultan, Jews became the most important interlocutors with European traders in the nineteenth century and acted as diplomatic correspondents with European nations.[53] They also occupied elevated positions in the Moroccan court. Despite these factors, their legally and socially enshrined status as non-Muslims exposed Jews to persecution during periods of political tension and change.[54] Foreign interference exacerbated these existing tensions.[55] In addition, many American Jews undoubtedly overlooked the use by Europeans of Moroccan religious intolerance to advance their own interests.

During the Spanish-Moroccan War, many American Jews accepted and faithfully transmitted European accounts and pleas for aid to their local communities. In its weekly status updates about Jewish refugees and the Morocco Relief Fund, the *Jewish Messenger* published a poem dedicated to the cause. The poem affirmed that the United States was a model of religious toleration; Morocco, by contrast, was a "far distant land" both geographically and morally. The first stanzas reminded American Jews of their luck and duty living in a land that allegedly ignored all religious differences:

Our happy, free, and glorious Land
Where justice holds the balance true
Where equal rights are ever given
Alike to Christian and to Jew

The final stanzas pleaded,

Come give, with a willing hand
For on your head are blessings called
By those in that far distant land.[56]

By August 1860, the British Board had raised almost 13,000 pounds (approximately $1.5 million in today's currency), a third of which had come from Jewish Americans.[57] The French government also granted Moroccan Jewish refugees passports to resettle in its colonial outpost in Algeria. The Spanish-Moroccan War would leave an important legacy for the Moroccan government and for British-Spanish relations. Concerned by Spanish efforts to expand their reach in Morocco, British consul Sir Drummond Hay intervened at the end of the war to negotiate a peace treaty in 1860. Spanish displeasure with British intervention would lead to antagonistic competition between the two country's consuls in the following years. These inter-imperial tensions would have unfortunate consequences for some Moroccan Jews who were affiliated with the consuls. More important, the peace treaty between Spain and Morocco forced the Moroccan government to pay a large indemnity to the Spanish that it could not afford, requiring Morocco to borrow from Great Britain. The Spanish government secured the right to supervise Morocco's eight ports and to retain half of all the customs duties.[58] Morocco's weakened financial power compelled it to increase protective measures against future foreign interventions.[59] It was unable, however, to enforce these measures and thus was at the mercy of the same foreign powers against which it was trying to defend itself.

Jewish American activists sought to help Moroccan Jews, but, for reasons beyond their control, they knew little about European imperial maneuvering, the complexity of Moroccan society and history, or the important status held by Jews in Morocco. They assumed that all Islamic rulers were inherently uncivilized and intolerant toward Jews, including those in Morocco. They were also unaware that the communal and commercial ties that united Moroccan Muslims and Jews also, at times, led the former to intercede on behalf of the latter.[60] Further, they did not realize that Moroccan Jews were highly adept in navigating the Moroccan legal system and petitioning the Moroccan government to obtain redress for their claims.[61]

In their simplistic depiction of Morocco, many Americans also defined an ideal vision of America, but this vision interpreted tolerance and freedom through the eyes of Enlightenment secularism. This vision simultaneously ignored the religious and racial hierarchies of American national identity that had advanced the superiority of Anglo-Saxon Protestants. Furthermore, although Jewish American activists sought to alleviate the oppression of Moroccan Jews, much like their European counterparts, they also believed *both* Muslim and Jewish Moroccans needed Western civilization.

The Jewish American Community and the French Alliance Israélite Universelle

Because of its work in the Ottoman Empire and North Africa, the French Alliance's influence on American understandings of Muslim-Jewish relations in Muslim lands would prove to be particularly important. The French Jews who led the organization were steeped in their own country's negative visions of Islam, which were informed by French imperialist discourse of civilizational differences. Although the French Alliance's definition of aid included alleviating the legal and political oppression of Jews globally, another one of its central goals was to bring civilization and enlightenment to Asia and Africa through the establishment of French-language schools and the propagation of a larger French civilizing mission.

Alliance members considered themselves "civilized" French Jews with a duty to educate and uplift the Jews of Asia and Africa. They believed that Jews in North Africa and the Ottoman Empire were inferior in both their civilization and their religious practices. Such hierarchical attitudes toward their religious brethren in the Ottoman Empire and North Africa mirrored the attitudes of American missionaries toward "nominal" Christians in the Ottoman Empire.[62]

The French Alliance forwarded information about its organizational mission to prominent Jewish American leaders, who translated and republished the material in Jewish American newspapers. In a speech published in 1863 in the *Israelite*, one of the most influential Jewish English-language newspapers in the United States, French Alliance president Adolphe Crémieux argued that the French colonial experience in Algeria had prepared his organization to expand its work across North Africa. The necessity of reaching "Oriental Jews" was vital, Crémieux maintained, as this population was "the medium of intercommunication between the Mahometan and Christian world. It is thus that the children of Israel will pursue on the distant coasts of Africa and Asia the *civilizing mission assigned to them by Providence*."[63]

Such attitudes about the divine role of Jews living in North Africa and the Ottoman Empire in spreading civilization would surely have resonated with popular American attitudes about their own manifest destiny. Another appeal for funds for French Alliance schools noted that nothing could compare to the plight of these Jews, for their "intelligent populations" were languishing under political oppression where civilization had yet to arrive.[64] Reforming these Jews also meant reforming their religious practices, which had been similarly tarnished by years of interaction with Muslims.

In addition to publishing their appeals, the French Alliance's mission received wholehearted endorsement from Jewish American leaders. In the *Israelite*, the prominent reformer Rabbi Isaac M. Wise urged American Jews to aid "the human family in the Orient" by supporting the French Alliance. Wise's praise for the French organization's mission mirrored the arguments in Crémieux's earlier speech:

In the first place, the members of the human family living in Asia and Africa under the sway of semi-barbarism, are criminally neglected and justly claim our sympathy. We consider as self-evident that the progress of civilization is identical with the increase of our prosperity and happiness, the means to procure the comforts of life, and the opportunities to enlarge the sphere of the mind, furthermore, that it is every good man's duty to contribute to the prosperity and happiness of those who cannot acquire the necessary means for this purpose by their own exertions. Therefore it appears no less self-evident to us that we have a duty to perform to the neglected members of the human family in the Orient.[65]

By supporting the French organization, American Jews would not only help civilize their unfortunate brethren in need of spiritual and civilizational reformation, Wise maintained, but also extend European civilization to "the very hearts of Asia and Africa," because the "oriental Israelite" was the "fittest and most necessary agent to carry civilization" in the Middle East and North Africa. "His knowledge of and believe [sic] in the Bible give him a vast number of Ideas [sic] perfectly identical with those who form the basis of modern civilization." This insight provided "an advantage which the Mahometan or Pagan" did not have.[66] Additionally, unlike American Jews, French Jews had strong links with their government and, most important, had a strong influence in the Orient, presumably through the territories acquired by France in Algeria.

The resemblance between Crémieux and Wise's arguments in support of the French Alliance demonstrate how American and French beliefs about the relationship between Jews and Muslims in Islamic lands converged during these moments of transnational cooperation. Wise's claims illustrated the extent to which transnational ties between France and the United States contributed to American beliefs about the benefits of extending European civilization to Islamic lands. Willingly or not, Wise had faithfully adopted the imperial language of the French civilizing mission, conveying it in his own words to his American audience. Such attitudes would play an important role in subsequent events that again drew Jewish American involvement to Islamic lands.

The Safi Affair and the Mission to Morocco

In 1860, after the end of the Spanish-Moroccan War, competition over influence in Morocco mounted among Spain, France, and Britain. Political tensions soon extended to the consuls' Moroccan protégés, namely, Moroccan natives hired by consuls to work as their commercial agents or translators.[67] As protégés became associated with certain nations, at times, imperial rivalries led consuls to target these unfortunate proxies in their larger political battles.

Given the financial and territorial concessions the Spanish had obtained during the war and the subsequent weakness of the Moroccan government, Morocco was largely at the mercy of Spanish demands during the incident.[68] In August 1863, the Spanish vice consul in Safi accused the man's servant, a fourteen-year-old Moroccan Jewish boy named Jacob Benyuda, of poisoning and robbing the tax collector as part of a conspiracy with other Jews.[69] Although no autopsy was conducted, the young boy was tortured and then offered clemency by the Spanish vice consul if he admitted guilt and named his coconspirators. Under torture, the young boy named another Jew, an Ottoman subject and British protégé, Eliyhahu Lalouche.

Although the primary reasons for Spain's involvement stemmed from Madrid's desire to demonstrate its power by intervening in local Moroccan affairs and its own anti-Semitism, the fact that the accused was a British protégé also offered the Spanish an ideal opening to punish the British for their previous meddling. Upon the vice consul's orders, local Moroccan authorities violently "interrogated" Lalouche using a *palo*, or stake, to force a confession. Whether the idea of using a stake came from the Spanish vice consul or the Moroccan authorities, the symbolic imagery of a falsely accused Jewish man tortured via staking by Muslim authorities as the Spanish Catholic diplomat watched constituted a powerful testament to how religion, empire, and anti-Semitism merged in pernicious ways. Under torture, Lalouche named additional coconspirators, including a pregnant woman who had sold milk to the deceased Spanish official. According to Spanish minister Don Francisco Merry y Colom, she had knowingly poisoned the milk. The accused were swiftly jailed, and their family members soon gathered in protest. At one point, when Lalouche briefly escaped from jail, his own family members were jailed and beaten.

Despite initial promises of leniency if the adolescent confessed, Benyuda was publicly executed according to the wishes of the Spanish diplomats.[70] Merry further insisted that his body be dismembered in public.[71] Lalouche was also sentenced to death. The Spanish consul requested that Spain be granted the privilege of transporting the man on a Spanish ship to be executed in Tangier. As one scholar has noted, this appeal was another way of getting back at the British for their interference in Spain's most recent war with Morocco, "Now a British protégé was to be executed for the despicable murder of a Spaniard, and the Spanish would make the most of it."[72] Lalouche maintained his innocence until his execution on 13 September 1863. Two more men remained imprisoned in Safi. Much like the Damascus Affair, however, the case soon gained international attention and drew the intervention of Jewish activists and political elites in France, Britain, and the United States.

News of the Safi affair quickly traveled through a complex international circuit; the appeal originated in the Jewish Committee of Tangier and went first to the French Alliance, then to the British Board and American Board. Hoping that foreign intervention might save the two imprisoned Jews from the same fate as their unfortunate brethren, they forwarded this information to their governments. The British Board sent an appeal to U.S. secretary of state Seward, who subsequently forwarded the information back to the American consul in Morocco, Jesse McMath. Seward instructed McMath to "exert all proper influence to prevent a repetition of the barbarous cruelties to which Israelites in the Moorish Empire have, on account of their religion, been subjected."[73]

In 1863 Seward, a strong opponent of slavery, was sensitive to the brutal effects of racial discrimination against minority populations. That same year, his own country was enmeshed in a brutal civil war over the very issue. It is unknown whether Seward ever compared the persecution of Jews in Morocco to the treatment of African Americans at home, but questions of religious or racial discrimination were certainly present in his mind. Seward would also have been aware of the discriminatory anti-Jewish actions of General Ulysses S. Grant, the Union army commander. In 1862, only one year before the Safi affair, Grant had issued an order expelling all Jews from the states of Kentucky, Tennessee, and Mississippi based on the premise that several had illegally traded cotton. Grant's order gave Jewish residents of these states twenty-four hours to leave. The blanket condemnation of all American Jews residing in these states offered a powerful testimony to the continued impact of anti-Semitic beliefs on American Jews. When President Lincoln revoked the order a few weeks later, he explained that he had "no objection" to Grant's expelling traders and Jewish peddlers, but since Grant had included all Jews, including those fighting for the Union army, he felt compelled to revoke the order.[74] Perhaps not coincidentally, Lincoln announced his decision only two days after issuing the Emancipation Proclamation, which freed the slaves located in Confederate territories.

Despite his own country's fraught relationship with discrimination, Seward's assumption that the Christian powers would be moral saviors, delivering justice to Moroccan Jews, overlooked the complicated facts that helped shape the events. He failed to understand that consuls from these powers had initiated the accusations and persecution and that the Spanish demands for execution exceeded typical Moroccan punishments for murder, which generally involved the payment of blood money by the accused to the descendants of the deceased. He was also unaware that the Spanish had threatened the Moroccan government with war if it did not execute the accused.[75] Oblivious to these complexities, he wrote to McMath expressing confidence that the United States would not be alone in applying diplomatic pressure on the Moroccan government because "such a course, which is dictated by common humanity, will, no doubt, be pursued by the representatives of all the Christian powers at Tangier."[76]

In contrast to Seward's belief in the moral superiority of Euro-American Christian civilization, Consul McMath, who held greater knowledge of the political influence of the European consuls, reluctantly corrected the secretary of state. McMath acknowledged that the fault lay with the Spanish, who were behind the accusations and had initiated anti-Semitic attacks on local Jews in the past. Indeed, Spanish diplomats in Morocco were well known among Moroccan authorities, local Moroccan Jews, and other consular officials for forcing local rulers to imprison and torture Jews who showed any impertinence to Spanish officials or their protégés.[77] McMath was undoubtedly familiar with another incident that had happened just weeks after the Safi affair. A Spanish consul had two Moroccan Jews jailed after an altercation with a servant working for the Spanish consul. During the fight, the two young Jews had rhetorically asked the servant if they too would be killed like the Spanish had killed the two Moroccan Jews in Safi. Merry was not content with having a British protégé executed, so when he returned, he took them from the jail in chains and had them beaten under the windows of a British official. His actions offered tangible evidence that Moroccan subjects could fall prey to the imperial rivalries of their employers.

In contrast to Merry's known anti-Semitism, McMath maintained that the Moroccan sultan was a friend of the Jews and had no choice but to yield to Spanish demands. McMath's interpretation was later confirmed by Moroccan foreign minister Muhammad Bargash, who complained to the British that the Spanish had bullied the Moroccan government into executing the two accused murderers, telling Sir Drummond Hay of the "dark menaces made by Merry if blind compliance was not granted to their demands."[78]

A letter from the wife of one of the Moroccan prisoners who witnessed the events firsthand further challenged Americans' faulty understanding of the events. The wife's letter, republished in the *Israelite*, assigned primary blame to Minister Merry. She noted that Merry had presented certificates to the Moroccan *cadi* (judge) assigned to the case that confirmed the boy's confession—obtained under torture—and his "bad character." Based on the lack of credible evidence and the child's inability to defend himself in person, the *cadi* refused to convict. As she recalled, the *cadi* proclaimed that "both his religion and conscience did not allow him to pass sentence of death on persons whose indisputable right to defense was even denied to them."[79] The Spanish minister was furious with the *cadi*'s decision and insulted the judge in front of the entire assembly. He then appealed the decision to the sultan. Facing Spanish threats, the sultan acquiesced and ordered the boy's execution.

The letter's assessment of the situation offered a strong rebuttal to American explanations: "Now let the world see the contrast between this inhuman and barbarous Christian, Senor Merry y Colon, the Spanish Minister, and the God-fearing and conscientious Mohammedan Caddi, Mohammed Ben-abd-el-jalack, the Moorish judge. Unfortunately, brutal force prevailed over justice."[80] Much like McMath's own acknowledgments of Spanish anti-Semitism, the woman's letter challenged the premise that Europeans could offer political and civilizational advancement to Morocco. Although Moroccan Jews were certainly not exempt from discrimination or persecution at the hands of Muslims, even without pressure from foreign powers, the behavior of the Spanish consul had exceeded all bounds.

American diplomats circulated British newspaper articles that also called into question Spanish behavior.[81] One editorial accused Spain of regressing to its own barbaric past and abandoning its Enlightenment affiliations. The editor hoped that this was an isolated case and conceded that "individual fanatics, even in authority, have unfortunately existed under liberal governments even in modern times."[82] If the Damascus Affair "had its Ratti-Menton" who "lashed, racked, and tortured," why should Tangier not "be afflicted with a Merry"? Such behavior might be expected in uncivilized Morocco, for example, but the Spanish consul's actions were shocking, since he came from "a civilized nation, claiming kindred with the civilized nations of the earth."[83]

Another British journalist was less surprised by the "atrocious outrage." When Islam combined with Spanish Roman Catholicism, the journalist maintained, only the worst possible outcome could be expected.[84] He was nonetheless startled by how far the Spanish consul had gone: "Fancy him outdoing even the natural and hereditary barbarisms of Morocco!" The author concluded that the Spanish "cruelties" were undoubtedly also "copied from the Red Indian school," an absurd claim that would have nevertheless resonated with American readers.[85]

In a letter to Consul McMath, the British Board maintained that it was "scarcely conceivable that the representative of a civilized nation could have indulged in such cruelties."[86] Although he conceded Spain's central role in the affair, McMath echoed British interpretations, expressing his shock at the reversal of a "civilized" European power displaying more anti-Semitic bigotry than the Moroccan government. He could recall no other instance in modern history where people living in uncivilized domains requested protection from the abuses perpetuated by representatives of civilized powers.[87] Despite compelling evidence to the contrary, neither diplomats nor Jewish American activists believed that civilized European powers could be crueler or more intolerant than Muslims.

Although McMath was sympathetic to British views, in his correspondence with Seward he also noted that the involvement of French, British, and American Jewish organizations in Morocco had "aggravated the condition of the Jews of this country."[88] For their part, the American Board disagreed. Board secretary Meyer S. Isaacs continued regular correspondence with Moroccan Jewish communities and forwarded all relevant information to the U.S. secretary of state. Isaacs also forwarded information from the British Board and the French Alliance to American officials.

Moroccan Jewish leaders in Tangier also disagreed with McMath's assessment, continuing to enlist the help of foreign powers and French, American, and British Jewish organizations to help alleviate their oppression when the local courts would not respond to their grievances. In December 1863, Isaacs forwarded a letter sent by the Hebrew Congregation of Tangier, which thanked the American Board for its continued involvement, alongside and in conjunction with the U.S. government and European Jewish associations. The Hebrew Congregation of Tangier was undoubtedly aware of foreign influence on the Moroccan government. They appealed to American assumptions by highlighting their connections to "civilized" powers, much like the Greek revolutionaries had done previously. Jewish leaders in Tangier expressed their thanks to these "civilized nations" for defending them against the "barbarian" country of Morocco: "This we expect of you as coreligionists and inhabitants of a country of liberty and justice, and under a government full of civilization, liberal, just, and humane, that you may be seen to interest yourselves and to intervene with the honorable President of the United States that he may recommend to his representatives here, Jesse W. McMath, esq., a sincere man sympathizing with the Hebrews, to intervene under his honorable influence, and in the name of humanity, to alleviate the injustices which are sought to be committed against your brethren in Morocco. A recommendation of this sort will give us espiration [sic] and honor in this barbarian country."[89]

In their letter of gratitude, the Hebrew Congregation implicitly affirmed their affiliation with Euro-American civilized forces of progress in wider battles against Islamic intolerance. Following a fascinating international circle of transmission, the Hebrew Congregation's letter was sent from Tangier, Morocco, to New York. From there, Isaacs forwarded it to Seward in Washington, D.C., who forwarded it back to McMath in Tangier. Seward instructed McMath to offer whatever aid he could in relieving the oppressed Moroccan Jews.[90]

The Hebrew Congregation's statement, however, conflicted with the custom of Moroccan Jews to solicit foreign help only when it was likely to obtain redress. For example, as Jessica Marglin has demonstrated, Moroccan Jews found that when it came to obtaining justice against foreigners, unsurprisingly, they were more likely to obtain redress by soliciting the Moroccan government.[91] Such practices disproved European and American claims that only their intervention could bring justice to Moroccan Jews.

Such misunderstandings, however, led to the conclusion among Europeans and Americans alike that only they could bring about justice in the Safi affair. In December 1863, Montefiore traveled from Britain to Spain and finally to Morocco to plead for the release of the prisoners. Montefiore undertook the mission on behalf of the British Board, with additional support from the British foreign office, the French Alliance, and the American Board. The American Board lobbied Secretary of State Seward again, this time "to further the Mission of Sir Moses Montefiore as far as he consistently could, and exercise his influence in behalf of the oppressed Israelites of Morocco."[92] In its letter, the board reminded Seward of Van Buren's involvement in the Damascus Affair twenty-three years earlier and maintained that President Van Buren's efforts had set an important precedent for U.S. intervention and British and American cooperation in such matters.

In Madrid, Montefiore obtained pardons for the two remaining Jews from the Spanish queen. Rather than focusing on the source of the persecution, which originated with the Spanish minister, however, Montefiore instead went on to focus his attention on reforming the alleged intolerance of Moroccan law. He traveled to Morocco, where he appealed to the Moroccan sultan to follow the Ottoman Empire's lead in delivering a *zahir* (royal decree) that granted Moroccan Jews equality with Muslims under the law.[93] The sultan believed that Islamic law, as practiced in Morocco, already granted sufficient justice to Jews. Nevertheless, he willingly issued a new *zahir* stating that "all people are equal in justice."[94] Although he refused to adopt the Ottoman Empire's decrees, the sultan must have noted the irony of the situation. Forced to punish his own subjects according to the whims of a European consul and forced to discount the opinions of his own judges, who pushed for exoneration for insufficient evidence, the Europeans then asked him to reassert his commitment to the equality of his own subjects. He might have wondered from whom exactly his people really needed protection.

Unfortunately, rather than alleviating hostility between Muslim and Jewish Moroccans, foreign intervention increased tensions. Jewish subjects in Tetuan, empowered by Montefiore's intervention, thereafter refused to be governed by the local Muslim rulers. They established their own governing committee, which prompted the sultan's condemnation. Similar conflicts occurred in Essaouira, where Montefiore had stopped after his successful visit with the sultan. As one scholar has noted, "No sooner had Montefiore left Morocco than it was reported that the Jews in Essaouira—and even in some towns in the interior—were beginning to act as if they were no longer under Moroccan jurisdiction."[95] Both events prompted Montefiore to issue several circulars urging Moroccan Jews to respect "the just exercise of legally constituted [Moroccan] authority."[96] The fact that Montefiore issued a circular in this regard confirmed the very issue he hoped to solve: by "instructing" local Moroccan Jews to act in a certain way, he was usurping Moroccan authority.

Local rebellions were not the only problem. Although they continued to solicit help from local Moroccan authorities, elite Moroccan Jews, now emboldened by the prospect of foreign intervention, solicited such intervention whenever they found it more amenable than soliciting Moroccan authorities or local courts.[97] Consequently, European and American Jewish organizations assumed that crimes perpetrated on Moroccan Jews stemmed from religious hatred, even though such crimes equally affected Muslim Moroccans, who had no such recourse and whose cases did not come to their attention. One scholar has argued that, "In the long run, Montefiore's mission and European intervention encouraged Moroccan Jews to see themselves as the victims of a despotic government and 'fanatical' population—and Muslims to condemn them for collaborating with foreign powers."[98] Other scholars have downplayed these changes, emphasizing that Moroccan Jews maintained their traditional ties to Moroccan authorities despite these new avenues of protest, and they continued to rely on local legal institutions when it was convenient.[99]

Nonetheless, some of the elite Moroccan Jews continued to benefit from their status as protégés of European and American consuls. They used their contacts to forge new identities and they increasingly conceived themselves to be part of a larger international Jewish community, one that was affiliated with a "superior" Euro-American civilization. Organizations such as the American Board, the British Board, and the French Alliance, facilitated this development. The French Alliance's efforts to spread French civilization to Morocco, with the full support of its American and British counterparts, delivered a message to Moroccan Jews that civilization was achievable only by adhering to French culture and language. The French Alliance founded its first French-language school in 1862 with an enrollment of 162 students. By 1897, it had established schools throughout Morocco, including at Tangier, Essaouira, Tetuan, Fez, and Casablanca, with enrollments totaling more than 1,700 students.[100]

In Britain and the United States, the nuances of Moroccan Jewish identity and the possible disruptions of foreign interference on Moroccan society failed to prove newsworthy. Instead, as one scholar notes, Montefiore's mission was sold as "yet another triumphant British contribution to the forward march of civilization."[101] This language of benevolent humanitarian intervention also appeared in the American press. As the *Jewish Messenger* proudly noted, "As usual, we find the liberal government of Europe and America ready and generously responding to the solicitation of a portion of their people, and interceding in behalf of the oppressed."[102] Another article in the same newspaper, republished from the British newspaper the *Daily Telegraph*, praised the work of Montefiore, who had done so much to "wipe away streaming eyes and cause oppression to cease." The author went on to ask "What is Christianity, if not such deeds as his?"[103]

Despite the irony of promoting Montefiore's deeds as Christian, the author's question offered a powerful symbolic testimony to how the efforts of American and European Jewish organizations to combat persecution in "uncivilized" realms reaffirmed their own civilized status. For Jewish American activists, the Safi affair confirmed a simplistic narrative of

Euro-American superiority and the necessity of spreading its benevolent tolerance to the barbaric world of Islam. This narrative simultaneously re-affirmed their own status as civilized members of their nation.

This definition of American identity did not always match the vision of Protestant Americans back home. While lobbying for Moroccan Jews in Safi, American Jews were simultaneously struggling to defend secularism at the U.S. national level. In 1864, hundreds of Protestant activists from seven different congregations had formed the National Reform Association. Its primary goal was the passage of a so-called Christian amendment to the U.S. Constitution that would officially enshrine Christianity as the national religion of the United States. Although unsuccessful, such attempts demonstrated the precarious position of non-Christian Americans in the mid-nineteenth century.

Meanwhile, Jewish American activists continued their efforts to aid their brethren abroad. Encouraged by the success of recent efforts in Morocco, the American Board reaffirmed its endorsement of the French Alliance's mission to protect and civilize "Oriental Jews."[104] As Meyer S. Isaacs, the board's secretary, wrote to French Alliance president Crémieux in 1865: "When rights of Israelites in the still semibarbarous countries of Asia and Africa are invaded, where the interposition of the authorities of civilized nations is essential to the maintenance of their liberties, the friendly offices of the representatives of the United States can be more effectively secured through the agency of an organization like ours which, composed of American citizens, may demand our government that which a branch of the foreign [illegible], however influential abroad, could only solicit."[105]

The American Board encouraged Crémieux to continue this transnational cooperation and urged the French Alliance to communicate any information it had.[106] Isaacs's letter, however, also cautioned the French Alliance against how such cooperation should proceed, warning Crémieux to correspond only with the American Board rather than contacting members of the U.S. government directly, as they had been doing. Isaacs maintained that the board members, as American citizens, had the duty and role of lobbying their government, not foreign organizations. In reaffirming their nationalist identity as American citizens, Isaacs perhaps also hinted at another pernicious form of American anti-Semitism, one that forced American Jews to prove that their national loyalty was uncompromised by their international efforts on behalf of Jews abroad. As Edward Said had argued, "Western anti-Semitism has always included both the Jews and the Muslims. The latter have yet to be released from that ideological prison."[107] Whether such fears motivated Isaac's emphasis on American citizenship, Said's theory had not yet been proven for American Jews. In the subsequent decades, Jewish-American activists would continue to defend their American identity and their faith at home and abroad.

4

SPREADING EMPIRE AND CIVILIZATION

IN MOROCCO, 1878–1906

Jewish American communities dramatically increased in size and influence in the final decades of the nineteenth century. In 1880, the Jewish population numbered approximately 250,000. By 1900, it quadrupled to a little over 1 million. By 1920, it had reached 3.6 million. The majority of Jewish immigrants during this period were from eastern Europe, but increasingly, Jews from the Ottoman Empire joined their ranks. Meanwhile, American anti-Semitism continued to mount. In 1902, during the funeral march of an important rabbi in New York City, a riot broke out, injuring two hundred people. Police joined in the attack, and one police inspector yelled, "Kill those sheenies!"[1]

Rising anti-Semitism and xenophobia in the United States led Jewish American organizations to heighten their activism. At home, they dedicated themselves to helping newly arrived immigrants settle in, while also seeking to "Americanize" them to reduce xenophobic tensions. Abroad, they sought to end oppression in areas from which these immigrants hailed, both for altruistic purposes and in an effort to curtail immigration altogether. In 1878, American Jews worked with European organizations and lobbied the U.S. government for action in the Ottoman Empire while pushing for the newly independent territories of Bulgaria and Romania to include equality for Jews in their new constitutions. In the 1880s and 1890s, these efforts increasingly focused on Russia and Romania, where ethnic nationalism, combined with rising anti-Semitism, led to brutal pogroms and state-sanctioned discrimination.

Attempts by Jewish American activists to influence U.S. government action in these areas were hindered by the commercial, legal, and diplomatic relations between the United States and Russia. Their efforts were more successful in Morocco. In the late nineteenth century, Americans understood Morocco much like they did the Ottoman Empire, as a "dying state" in need of outside reform.[2] Morocco had not yet fallen to European imperial rule, unlike its North African neighbors Algeria (in 1830) and Tunisia (in 1882), only because of ongoing European imperial squabbles and the determined efforts of the Moroccan government to remain independent by playing France, Spain, and Britain against each other.

Although Americans had no interest in extending their empire to Morocco, they nonetheless played an important role in shaping international discussions about reform. They also participated in larger negotiations with Europeans over foreign commercial and diplomatic rights in the country and, later, which European country was best suited to extend imperial rule over Morocco. In these discussions, Jewish American activists and American consuls in Morocco pressured the American government to alleviate the alleged oppression of Moroccan Jews by Moroccan Muslims. At the local level, focusing on Jewish persecution served a more nefarious purpose, as these exaggerated claims allowed American consuls to increase their circle of protégés. At higher levels, the Board of Delegates of American Israelites coordinated with its British and French partners to defend the protégé system and insist on imposing reforms on the Moroccan government as a means to protect Moroccan Jews from Muslim oppression. At the highest levels, presidents and secretaries of state used the issue of Muslim-Jewish relations in Morocco as a wedge to insert themselves into international discussions and to garner political support and votes from the growing Jewish American community.

The Jewish American activists who lobbied for intervention based their beliefs on existing tropes about Muslim intolerance that had been reaffirmed during international events such as the Damascus affair, the Spanish-Moroccan War, and the Safi affair. American Jews were also aware of widely published calls for American intervention on behalf of Christians during the Cretan uprising and the Bulgarian Massacres. In 1894, they would be alarmed yet again by the Ottoman massacre of Christian Armenians. All of these events reinforced American perceptions that Muslims were incapable of delivering justice to religious minorities, no matter where they ruled.

The European reforms that resulted from the Bulgarian Massacres were fresh on the minds of Jewish American activists when they renewed their efforts to intervene in Morocco. As discussed in chapter 2, when European diplomats met at the Congress of Constantinople in 1876 to address the Bulgarian Massacres and impose reforms on the Ottoman Empire's treatment of Christian minorities, members of the Board of Delegates of American Israelites attended the conference and lobbied the U.S. government and European diplomats to include Jews in any such reforms and in the constitutions of any newly independent territories. Again, these efforts involved transnational cooperation and the endorsement of American diplomats. Such experiences would prove useful when Americans turned their eyes to reforming Morocco.

Europe, the United States, and the Protégé System in Morocco

Unlike the Ottoman Empire, no native Christian community existed in Morocco and thus no capitulatory treaties existed for Europeans to exploit. Instead, Europeans used the protégé system as a tool to extend their commercial and political influence throughout the country.[3] For European powers with imperial designs over Morocco, expanding their circle of protégés was a key component in their larger imperial strategy to take over Morocco. The French had included this strategy in official documents as early as 1764.[4] An added bonus for local consuls came when existing Moroccan traditions syncretized with the protégé system and established a practice of protégés delivering monetary "donations" to their consular "protectors."[5]

Protégé status granted Moroccan subjects judicial protection and tax exemption, effectively undermining the authority of the *Makhzen* (Moroccan government). The system allowed Europeans to subvert the sultan's financial and political power.[6] This protected status also gave protégés the power to solicit their consuls to imprison any unprotected Moroccans who did not reimburse their debts to the protégés on time. This authority caused great antagonism in local communities and with the Moroccan government itself.[7]

Europeans and Americans attempted to justify the protégé system in Morocco by using the same moral and religious rationales that Europeans used to justify their capitulatory treaties in the Ottoman Empire. Although many Muslims also benefited from protections in Morocco, Moroccan Jews accounted for a disproportionate number.[8] By depicting Muslim-Jewish relations in Morocco as fraught with abuse and oppression, American consuls justified extending protégé status to an increasing number of Moroccan subjects while putting money in their own pocket.

Such depictions also conflicted with reality. Although Moroccan Jews faced persecution, they had been able to work within the existing system to obtain redress. Elite Moroccan Jews who could afford the privilege increasingly sought protégé status for its financial and judicial benefits, but they also continued to seek justice by means of local courts and through the Moroccan government.[9]

Although Jewish American organizations valiantly sought to aid their Moroccan brethren who faced persecution, they unfortunately became pawns in these schemes. Ironically, given European and American protests that the system protected Jews from Muslim oppression, extending such privileges to a small percentage of elite Moroccan Jews had unfortunate consequences for Muslim-Jewish relations in Morocco. Moroccan Jews were the primary beneficiaries of the protégé system, but the system protected only an elite minority, meaning that poor and unprotected Moroccan Jews faced the brunt of local hostility when resentful Muslims lumped them together with their protected brethren.

The abuse of the protection system also impacted Moroccan Jewish subjects' traditional relations with the government. As one scholar has noted, "Jews' acquisition of protection was particularly disruptive to the social order because of its implicit challenge to the dhimma pact which had heretofore guided the relationship between the sultan (and by extension the Moroccan state) and his non-Muslim subjects."[10] Despite protests from the Moroccan government, the practice of extending protection to Moroccan Jews increased in the final decades of the nineteenth century as imperial competition intensified.

American consuls had few imperial interests in Morocco, yet their abuse of the protégé system far exceeded that of their European counterparts. For the American consuls, the protection system was a lucrative business. The 1836 Treaty of Peace and Friendship with the Moroccan government granted the United States the authority to appoint protégés.[11] When American consul George Brown arrived in Morocco in 1850, he complained that his predecessor had "greatly abused" his power while in office. By the time he left Morocco five years later, Brown's own protégés complained that he had forced them to pay for their protégé status.[12] When Felix Mathews replaced Jesse McMath as consul in 1869, he also reported that his predecessor had illegally exchanged protection for money and gifts.

In the 1870s, the expansion and abuse of the protection system faced sharp criticism. British consul Sir Drummond Hay became a key figure in the ensuing debate and scandals. The British did not wish to extend their imperial claim to Morocco, but they relied on the country as a strategic opening into the Mediterranean Sea, an entry point for travel to India, and the source for resources for their garrison in Gibraltar.[13] Much like Palmerston's strategic alliance with Syrian Jews during the Damascus affair, Hay knew that the French and the Spanish used the system to compete with the British for commercial expansion in Morocco. Thus, he would have to challenge the system itself. He began with an obvious target. In 1876, Hay publicly accused Consul Mathews of abusing the protection system for personal gain. According to Hay, Mathews was "selling protection like a tradesman sells his goods."[14] Although an American government investigation initially cleared the diplomat's name, these accusations would continue for the next ten years, until the American government eventually recognized Mathews's guilt. The true story behind Mathews's lucrative business, however, would erupt into an international scandal when major American newspapers revealed his scheme in 1887.

Mathews's downfall began in 1886 when he initiated a dispute with Ion Perdicaris, the son of Gregory Perdicaris, who was one of several Greek political refugees sent to the United States to study by ABCFM missionaries in 1826 during the Greek War of Independence.[15] The elder Perdicaris had become a U.S. citizen and married into a wealthy South Carolinian family, later returning to Greece to serve as its first American ambassador in 1837. Ion was born in Greece in 1840 and moved to the United States with his family in 1846. During the American Civil War, the pro-Confederate family's extensive real estate holdings came under threat of confiscation. In an attempt to circumvent this rule, Ion Perdicaris traveled to Greece to obtain Greek citizenship (and, presumably, to renounce his American citizenship). He eventually settled in Tangier, where he established a business and became an important member of the expatriate community in Morocco. Mathews had underestimated Perdicaris's worldly experience when he initiated a public battle with him.

In January 1886, Perdicaris asked Mathews to prosecute the case of a Moroccan woman who had accused a Moroccan subject under American protégé status of raping her. The case was referred to Mathews, because according to consular treaties, protégés could be tried in consular courts only, not local tribunals.[16] Perhaps because the accused protégé had been extended such status by his own son, whom Mathews had succeeded in appointing as vice consul a few years earlier, the American consul refused to pursue the case. His refusal angered Perdicaris, who filed an official complaint of consular misconduct with the U.S. State Department. More important to our story, Perdicaris also published his accusations in a long pamphlet entitled, "American Claims and the Protection of Native Subjects in Morocco," which he distributed throughout London.[17] The pamphlet accused the American consul of abusing the protégé system and imprisoning Moroccans at the behest of American protégés, all for personal gain.

Through Perdicaris's connections, the scandal exploded onto the pages of American newspapers in the summer and fall of 1886.[18] Given previous accusations ten years earlier by the British minister, Perdicaris's public accusations heightened Mathews's embarrassment. Mathews was furious at this public humiliation, and he had Perdicaris fined and arrested on trumped up charges.[19] The U.S. State Department had already launched an investigation into Mathews's behavior, and this last step was one too far. Mathews was relieved of his services in March 1887.

Perdicaris's pamphlet revealed a great deal about the American consul's abuse of the protection system and why he would exaggerate the abuse of Moroccan Jews at the hands of Moroccan Muslims. When Mathews's successor, William Reed Lewis, further investigated Mathews's wrongdoings, he found that, although the former consul had expressed his outrage about abuse of Moroccan Jews by "fanatical" Muslims and the imprisonment of Jews without trial, Mathews had used his influence to imprison at least forty-two Moroccan subjects "for debts due to American citizens and protégés."[20] Although this was a common and accepted practice for consular officials, Americans initially misunderstood this fact and added it to their litany of corruption charges. Less justifiable, however, was the discovery by Lewis that Mathews had placed more than eight hundred Moroccan subjects under protégé status in exchange for payment, including an entire Moroccan village of three hundred subjects.[21] When the Moroccan government came to gather owed taxes, the villagers claimed exemption because they were an "American colony" under Mathews's protection.[22] Although the United States had no imperial interests in Morocco, Mathews had personal interests in establishing his own imperial fiefdom in a Moroccan village.

Ironically, the official American reaction to Mathews's misdeeds strengthened expressions of Islamic intolerance and Jewish oppression. The U.S. State Department officially condemned his behavior by criticizing him for not fulfilling his duty as a civilized role model in "the barbarous and unhappy country in which you represent the dignity, enlightenment, and progressive spirit of the American people."[23] By imprisoning Moroccan subjects, Mathews had resorted to "the harsh measures that are characteristic of Moorish judicial procedure," but were "abhorrent to the sentiment of Christian nations." His behavior had been "so far removed from the judicial methods of civilized people that it can be accounted for only upon the supposition that the idea was borrowed from the Sultan's Minister of Justice."[24] In other words, it was so inconceivable that a "civilized" American consul would behave in such ways that he must have gotten the scheme from his uncivilized Moroccan hosts. This accusation was particularly egregious, since the Moroccan government had been pressuring consuls to stop abusing the protégé system precisely because it was disrupting Moroccan society and fomenting hostility toward Moroccan Jews.

Mathews's support for the protection system was highly motivated by personal gain: the consul benefited personally from exaggerating the poor state of Muslim-Jewish relations in Morocco. Just six years before the 1886 scandal that removed him from his consul post, Mathews had been an active player in shaping American defense of the protégé system at an international conference held in Madrid and convened precisely to deal with the abuse of the protection system by foreign powers. Knowing the motivations that led Mathews to defend the protection system so vehemently explains how Moroccan Jews had garnered such wide attention from Jewish American activists and diplomats during these years. It also provides an important context for understanding American interventions during this conference.

The Madrid Conference of 1880

Between 1877 and 1878, European nations met with the sultan's officials in unsuccessful attempts to reform the corrupt protégé system. Except for the British, who believed reforms would improve their commercial interests in Morocco, other European powers were reluctant to give up their privileges, especially given Morocco's already weakened state. According to historian Khalidi Ben-Srhir, who has analyzed Hay's involvement in these meetings, the sessions were a "struggle not between the *Makhzan* [Moroccan government] and the European countries, but between British policy which sought . . . to create a Morocco able to guarantee a market for British manufactures and the policies of the other foreign countries which wanted . . . to keep Morocco weak in order to make it easier for them to seize it at an opportune time."[25] Undeterred by this stalemate, Consul Hay proposed an international conference in Madrid to settle the issue.

By 1877, news of the reforms in Morocco had reached European and Jewish American groups, leading them to coordinate their opposition. The Board of Delegates, supported in large part by their correspondence with

Mathews, believed that the protégé system was a valuable tool in helping to protect Moroccan Jews from Muslim oppression. Eliminating the system, they maintained, would lead to greater Jewish suffering. The French Alliance Israélite Universelle (French Alliance) wrote Meyer S. Isaacs, secretary of the American Board of Delegates, and obtained the organization's signature on a letter addressed to the foreign consuls in defense of the protégé system. The French Alliance's secretary, Isidore Loeb, also asked Isaacs to pressure Consul Mathews to oppose the reforms in his correspondence with the U.S. government. Consul Mathews, heavily invested in defending the protégé system, willingly complied. In his dispatches to Secretary of State Evarts, Mathews defended the practice, arguing that the system "had had the effect for many years of protecting the Jews from violence and oppression, and of obtaining redress for injuries sustained by them from the semi-civilized races among whom they dwell."[26]

Jewish American newspapers also took up the call. The *American Hebrew* published an article in February 1880 comparing the oppression of Jews in Morocco to that of Russia and Romania. In the latter cases, the editor maintained, oppression involved commercial and political restrictions, which were bad enough; but in Morocco, the case was much worse: "brutal butcher, foul murder!" According to the author, Europe was obliged to act in Morocco because "religious fanatics—prejudiced savages have committed crimes, and the judicial authorities have refused to mete out justice to the criminals, or to grant immunity to those who yet are threatened, from future attacks. Can the duty of Europe be more plainly set before its eyes, or can aught appeal more pathetically to its heart than such sacrilege?"[27]

The editor's comparison exposed interesting distinctions between the different "levels" of persecution in Europe and Morocco. Whereas the defining features of Russian and Romanian oppression were in more "civilized" arenas, such as politics and economics, Moroccan oppression stemmed from uncivilized "barbarism" that originated in racial and religious savagery. In other words, because of the combined forces of Moroccan Muslims' religious and racial inferiority, their persecution had not yet achieved the distinct sophistication of European practices of anti-Semitic oppression.

Another article in the *Jewish Messenger* warned that recent outrages were "a sample of what may be expected, should the threatened withdrawal of European protection in Morocco be carried into effect."[28] The author nonetheless remained hopeful that American influence at the Madrid Conference would triumph, for "the generous persistence of our Consul in rescuing the otherwise friendless Hebrews of the Empire will be sup-plemented by international protection. And none of the Envoys at this remarkable Congress will be heard with more interest or respect than the Minister of our Republic."[29] The author did not elaborate on why the American delegate would have such influence. Perhaps it was the fact that the American consul had been a strong advocate on their behalf or his belief that the United States was a model of benevolent tolerance for the rest of the world. Jewish newspapers in the United States continued to follow the events closely, publishing all correspondence between Mathews, the Moroccan government, and the secretary of state.

British officials involved the U.S. government in all of these discussions and attempted to convince Washington that, in contrast to the assertions of Mathews and Jewish activists, the protégé system was detrimental to Moroccan Jews. The British minister to the United States, Sir Edward Thornton, undoubtedly aware that American diplomats faced pressure from their own Jewish groups to maintain the protégé system, noted that the Anglo-Jewish Association "entertained very erroneous ideas on the subject, which may have been produced by the misrepresentations which have been made to them or to the 'Alliance Israélite Universelle' at Paris," the source of which were "certain influential Jews who are irregularly pro-tected in Morocco by some of the representatives of foreign powers."[30]

Thornton forwarded an exchange between Hay and the Anglo-Jewish Committee on the topic in which Hay argued that the system exacerbated tensions between Muslim and Jewish subjects because it protected only the wealthiest Jews and infuriated Muslim subjects.[31] Additionally, abuse of the protection system had angered the Moroccan sultan and con-sequently diminished the influence of the foreign powers with him. Thus, only by eliminating these abuses could Europeans and Americans reestablish the sultan's trust and influence his future decisions to "use our good offices with this government on behalf of the oppressed Jews, or even to declare . . . that outrages or cruel acts of tyranny toward the oppressed race would not be tolerated by civilized powers."[32] Finally, contrary to the depictions by European and Jewish American organizations, Hay argued that Moroccan Jews were "generally in a better position than the Moham-medan population."[33] Despite this, he conceded that Morocco needed out-side influence to raise its civilization to European standards. He concluded by arguing against "too active an interference"; instead, he urged trust in the "gradual march of civilization, brought about by commerce and the presence of Europeans in this country."[34] Such methods, not coinciden-tally, conveniently played into British commercial and strategic interests.

In contrast, Consul Mathews could not admit that the system cushioned his private bank account, so instead he linked the protégé system and Jewish oppression to the larger issue of American rights in Morocco. In February of that year, Mathews had received a circular from the Moroccan government stating that Morocco would not recognize subjects who lived in Morocco but had obtained naturalization in another country.[35] Much like the protégé system, many foreign consuls naturalized Moroccan subjects (at times for profit), providing them with increased consular protection. He responded to the circular by vehemently denying the Moroccan government's right to infringe on American rights. He also linked the issue of protection and naturalization, once again, directly to the rights of religious minorities, insinuating that if Morocco did not protect its own citizens, then foreign powers had the right to interfere.

Instead of removing power from foreign consuls, Mathews insisted that Europeans and Americans exert more power against the Moroccan government, arguing that the "barbarous manner in which everything is unfortunately conducted in Morocco toward the inoffensive Jews" was serious and concerned all "governments who profess liberty and humane feelings toward their fellow human beings." Everything came down to Islam as the real source of the problem. According to Mathews, "the source of all Mohammedan law is the Koran" and for this reason, it was "hopeless to expect reforms so long as the law is administered by 'true believers.'"[36] For this reason, protecting naturalized citizens and retaining the protégé system in Morocco was crucial. Finally, undoubtedly defensive of his involvement, Mathews noted that he was just following orders; all of his efforts were in response to requests by the secretary of state and the Board of Delegates to help protect Moroccan Jews.[37]

Mathews continued to correspond regularly with Evarts and Isaacs. The latter then represented an even larger Jewish umbrella organization, the Union of American Hebrew Congregations, which had absorbed the American Board in 1878. Mathews also continued to apply direct pressure on the Moroccan government. Posing as a concerned friend, the consul warned Moroccan rulers of consequences if they did not improve their treatment of Jewish subjects. He wrote the grand vizier (chief Moroccan minister) that, because the United States had no imperial interests in Morocco, his advice was disinterested and intended purely for the "utility, benefit, and welfare of His Shereefian Majesty."[38] Claiming concern for Morocco driven by American benevolence, Mathews remarked that the recent violence against Moroccan Jews had attracted "the attention and sympathy of the foreign nations, and this state of affairs cannot continue without great prejudice and injury to the Empire of Morocco."[39] Demonstrating his keen awareness of the historical involvement of European powers in both the Ottoman Empire and Morocco, Mathews warned the vizier that international attention had resulted in disastrous consequences for the Ottoman Empire after the most recent Russo-Turkish War. Mathews concluded with a strong warning: "If you do not at once put a stop to this continued ill-treatment, God only knows how this matter will end."[40]

Mathews also attempted to influence Lucius Fairchild, the American minister to Spain and U.S. representative at the Madrid Conference. He sent Fairchild a report stating that Moroccan Jews, with the exception of those under foreign protection, were "persecuted, oppressed, hated, and degraded here more than in any other part of the world." Hoping to convince Fairchild of the necessity of preserving the status quo, Mathews argued, "Under the weight of this government . . . and within the inflexible circle of the Mussulman [sic] religion, unmoved by European influences . . . and full of savage fanaticism, everything that in other countries moves and progresses here remains motionless or falls into ruins."[41] Expressing his belief in Muslim decadence and saddened that European rivalries in the area made interference in Morocco difficult, he elicited hope that more direct European and American influence in the country might improve conditions for its Jewish population.

Fairchild was initially skeptical about American interventions on behalf of Moroccan Jews. Before attending the conference, he had investigated the matter of Moroccan Jews who had become naturalized American citizens through the consulate and who remained in Morocco to conduct business. Fairchild wrote to Secretary of State Evarts, explaining that the system was unfair in allowing these newly naturalized Moroccans to continue living in Morocco without paying taxes and enjoying protection from any criminal or financial prosecution because, as American citizens, they could not be tried in Moroccan courts.[42] He wrote several times to the secretary of state asking for reforms to the naturalization system, and offered a proposal that would rescind the citizenship of naturalized citizens who returned to Morocco after obtaining their citizenship and who stayed in Morocco for more than two years.

Secretary of State Evarts accepted Fairchild's suggestion of a two-year limit, but he suggested that the law be applied *only* to naturalized Moroccan Muslims. Naturalized Moroccan Jews would not have their citizenship revoked. In the end, nothing came of Evarts's proposal, but his willingness to discriminate between naturalized American citizens based solely on their religious affiliation was revelatory. Although Evarts offered no explanation for such a discriminatory application of the law, the belief that Moroccan Jews constituted more civilized members of Moroccan society as well as one that deserved more protection almost certainly played a role.

Such logic of religious difference was not limited to Moroccans. In the following decades, immigrants from the Ottoman Empire would face similar citizenship challenges. In the United States, laws limited naturalization only to whites. Arab, Turkish, and Armenian immigrants petitioning for American citizenship were at times denied because judges deemed that by "popular understandings" of race, such groups were not considered white. In other cases, judges and immigrants alike emphasized the Christian faith of immigrants to confirm their "whiteness." In contrast, in the rare cases that Muslims petitioned for citizenship in the nineteenth century, their faith exacerbated their racial identity as "oriental" and thus, nonwhite.[43] Such examples demonstrated how American understandings of race and religion merged in powerful ways both at home and abroad, resulting in important legal consequences.

Despite Fairchild's critique of the naturalization abuses, his analysis of Morocco also endorsed civilizational distinctions that identified Muslims as inferior to Jews and Euro-Americans more generally. The ideal solution to such inferiority should similarly have important legal ramifications for Morocco. In his dispatches to Evarts, Fairchild explicitly supported the extension of a forceful European intervention in Morocco, which he maintained was the only solution in dealing with Morocco's "persecutions and barbarous practices." If Morocco could not improve itself, it could only be hoped that the "civilized world" would eventually intercede and "send it to the wall, where sooner or later it ought to go, and the sooner, the better."[44] In the midst of ongoing imperial rivalries over Morocco, Americans had already begun expressing the benefits of transforming the country into a European colony.

Meanwhile, the French Alliance and the Union of American Hebrew Congregations continued to work together to ensure their demands at the Madrid Conference were heard, including sending their representatives directly to Spain to plead their cause.[45] In March 1880, Isaacs, who by then had assumed the presidency of the Union of American Hebrew Congregations, wrote a letter to the vice president of the French Alliance, explaining that Fairchild would attend the Madrid Conference on behalf of the United States and asking that they coordinate so that the two countries' delegates could work together: "We beg of you to exert your influence so that the Minister of France and the United States may be disposed to act in concert."[46] A few weeks later, the French Alliance wrote back thanking Isaacs for his work. It also sent him a report on the discrimination against Jews in Morocco that it had compiled for the French government. The report, which conveyed the organization's ingrained Orientalist beliefs, informed American views about the hierarchy of civilizations and religious faiths at international and local levels: French and American superiority over Morocco and Jewish superiority over Muslims. Furthermore, the report reaffirmed that removal of protection posed a direct threat to Moroccan Jews, who constituted "the only element of the native population that accept ideas of civilization, the only ones capable of spreading this civilization in the country."[47] It also warned that Europe's economic relations with Morocco would cease if the protégé system was removed.

In distinguishing Moroccan Jews from Muslims on these terms, the French Alliance depicted Moroccan Jews as imperial agents in a larger civilizing mission, for in addition to being the only civilized enclave in a barbaric Moroccan society, the organization also maintained that they were the only reliable economic connection to Europe and America. Given that markets and resources were a central interest of foreign powers, this threat was a powerful one. The French Alliance report directly challenged Hay's insistence that existing commercial relations and the "gradual march of civilization" would alleviate Jewish oppression. If the protégé system ended, the report maintained, then commerce itself would also cease.[48] The French organization encouraged Isaacs to draft a similar report, or to translate and sign its report, and send it to the American government in preparation for the conference.[49]

The issue of religious tolerance became the primary focus of American diplomats at the Madrid Conference.[50] Echoing proposals by American Jewish activists and Consul Mathews, the U.S. secretary of state supported the application of previous European-imposed reforms on the Ottoman Empire to Morocco. Evarts wrote to Fairchild, instructing him to support an Austrian proposal that aimed "to secure religious liberty and complete religious toleration for all classes in Morocco" by advancing the same reforms that Europeans had proposed for the Ottoman Empire at the Congress of Berlin in 1878 and in previous decades.[51] Fairchild extended official American support for such reforms at the Madrid Conference. The Austrian declaration was read aloud during the meeting. It asserted that "the free exercise of all worships [should] be recognized in Morocco" just as the "Emperor of the Ottomans" who in 1839, 1856, and 1878 had recognized the same principle.[52]

All foreign representatives at the conference approved the text and asked the Moroccan ruler to adopt the suggested reforms. Supporters of the reforms also maintained that the Ottoman Empire had already adopted such changes and thus such reforms were "in accord with Mohammedan law."[53] Not only were Europeans and Americans trying to impose reforms on Moroccan rulers that were copied from another conference and that addressed a situation in another Islamic society with little connection to current political or religious issues in Morocco, but delegates also felt confident enough to instruct the Moroccan government on the Islamic rectitude of a law promulgating religious equality.

The Moroccan government did not bend easily to European and American accusations. Dismissing the necessity of a proposal enacting religious equality, the Moroccan government affirmed that its subjects were already "equal before us in the matter of justice" regardless of their faith.[54] The Moroccan representative also commanded all foreign powers present to forward all grievances from Moroccan Jews not addressed by local officials. The Moroccan government's efforts to counter Euro-American manipulation of the issue for its own interests were largely in vain. For Europeans and Americans, acknowledging Moroccan religious tolerance would have removed a convenient foil justifying interference, while eliminating a system that was of financial benefit to individual consuls. In the end, the conference resulted in positive outcomes only for those countries that supported the protégé system.

The meeting was not an incidental blip in American foreign affairs. In his State of the Union address delivered in December 1880, President Hayes explicitly mentioned the Madrid Conference, noting that the United States had urged upon the "Emperor of Morocco the necessity, in accordance with the humane and enlightened spirit of the age, of putting an end to the persecutions, which have been so prevalent in that country, of persons of faith other than the Moslem, and especially of the Hebrew residents of Morocco."[55] President Hayes's reference to these issues revealed the importance of the humanitarian and strategic benefits that came with protecting Moroccan Jews. Of course, there were no native Christians in Morocco, so Hayes's reference to other "persons of faith" may have served a domestic agenda of selling American intervention to his Christian audience.

Hayes's claims to the "enlightened" religious tolerance of Europeans and Americans did not necessarily match the reality of anti-Semitic violence in Europe during that time. American diplomats were not unaware of such inconsistencies. A dispatch from Lucius Fairchild to Secretary of State

Evarts four days before the president delivered his speech noted that it was probably best if "the Sultan of Morocco is not well informed of all that is taking place in Europe; for if he should learn of the anti-Jewish agitation which now exists in Germany as stated in the newspapers of the day, he may feel encouraged to increase, rather than diminish, the oppressions of the same race in his dominions." Fairchild nonetheless condemned such displays of European anti-Semitism by reasserting civilizational distinctions that held Europeans to a higher moral standard: "We cannot expect to find a more enlightened liberality in Morocco than exists among the highly educated people of Europe."[56]

After the conference, the Jewish American press praised the attention that the U.S. government had given to Jewish rights in Morocco while reasserting claims to American exceptionalism. The *Jewish Messenger* noted the U.S. government had done "good service in publishing the facts and in pronouncing the verdict of the civilized world."[57] The United States had a special role in inflating American involvement in the events: "It is clear that the misery of the Jewish inhabitants has been assuaged because of the knowledge that the representative of the powerful American republic is the active friend of the oppressed."[58]

Meanwhile, the American experience at Madrid reinforced diplomats' perceptions of the benefits that could come from the extension of European colonial rule over Morocco. In a letter to Secretary of State James G. Blaine written on 20 April 1881, Fairchild again openly endorsed such an outcome: "All that can be done in the near future is to continue to protect the suffering people by intercession in individual cases. . . . European complications may arise which will be of vast benefit to Morocco and I look forward with pleasure to the day, which possibly we will see, when some *one or more of the European nations will have gained such ascendancy over it as to be able to compel, by force, if necessary, a more enlightened and liberal administration of affairs.* Thus the people of Morocco can be relieved, and I see at present no other hope."[59]

Although he would not live to witness this eventual outcome, only two years after the Madrid Conference, Fairchild would observe the extension of French imperial rule to one of Morocco's neighbors, Tunisia, based largely on the same premise. Fairchild's letter also revealed the degree of American involvement in the matter, noting that Americans had gathered so much information that the Department of State's files "contain all that can now be said on the subject by any one."[60] The reports, published in two volumes and entitled *Papers Relating to Foreigners in Morocco,* filled more than 1,100 pages and included a transnational range of opinions on

Morocco from the Union of American Hebrew Congregations, the French Alliance, the Council of the Anglo-Jewish Association, and the British Foreign Office.[61]

In the decade that followed the Madrid Conference, the retention of the protégé system and American embarrassment over its consul's egregious behavior in exploiting it may have discouraged American involvement in the status of Moroccan Jews. When William R. Lewis arrived in March 1887 as American consul, he initially had a different perspective of local events, going so far as to accuse elite Moroccan Jews of exaggerating cases of abuse and of using European Jewish organizations to profit from local situations.[62] To end such practices, Lewis recommended that the entire Moroccan Jewish population be placed under international protection.[63] His far-ranging proposal found no support from American diplomats.

Previous public embarrassment did not end consular misconduct. After a few months in his position, Lewis reversed course dramatically and realized the profit that could be had in the protégé system. Perhaps to protect his own behavior, he recanted his previous accusations against Mathews. He too would soon face accusations of corruption, including selling illegal protection and imprisoning Moroccans for failure to pay debts.[64] The Moroccan government asked for his recall in 1889.

In an amazing turn of events, the Moroccan government asked that Mathews return as consul. After Mathews was reinstated in 1890, he had the gall to accuse Lewis of "earning" thousands of dollars by "protecting" hundreds of Moroccans.[65] When Mathews's successor, Judson Barclay, arrived in 1894, he reported that Muslim-Jewish relations in Morocco were generally very good, but outside intervention was still needed to reform Moroccan society. He also expressed the hope in 1896 that the expected arrival of American Protestant missionaries to Morocco would "mark an important era in the history of Morocco, which it is to be hoped will begin to lose its characters as a 'terra incognita' to Americans, now that the edge of the wedge of western civilization and Christianity has entered" what he elsewhere characterized as a "stronghold of Moorish fanaticism."[66]

Continuing the pattern, Barclay too would be replaced due to corruption, including extortion and selling illegal protection. His successor took up the call for reform of the consulate, while again maintaining that "misrule, oppression, tyranny, cruelty and barbarity" would end only when a European power asserted itself to "seize and divide" Morocco—and "the sooner the better."[67] Meanwhile, Jewish American organizations had recalibrated their focus on the more urgent case of Jews in Russia and

Romania. Although American attention on Moroccan affairs diminished between 1890 and 1900, the status of Moroccan Jews would not cease to be an issue.

The Perdicaris Affair

Morocco would again explode on the pages of American newspapers in 1904, albeit for reasons unrelated to consular misconduct or the alleged oppression of Moroccan Jews. Ion Perdicaris, who helped to bring consular scandal to the American media in 1886, again took central stage. On 18 May 1904, while Perdicaris was at home having dinner with his stepson, a group of Moroccan rebels led by Mulai Ahmed Raisuli stormed into the house and kidnapped the two men, tied them atop their horses, and carried them off into the desert. Raisuli then made several demands on the Moroccan sultan, including a ransom of $70,000. Believing Perdicaris was an American citizen, the American consul, Samuel Gummere, immediately protested and asked that the American government send its naval warships. President Theodore Roosevelt immediately endorsed this plan of action. The entire South Atlantic squadron joined the Mediterranean squadron, which was already in the area, and headed to Morocco. France also offered its help in securing Perdicaris's release.

The affair soon made its way into American newspapers. On 28 May 1904, a *New York Times* headline proclaimed, "American Marines May Invade Morocco." The following week, the paper remarked sarcastically that it was a "curious coincidence" that the United States should have to police the same shores and protect its citizens from "the violence of descendants of the North African pirates," whom it had already punished a hundred years earlier during the Barbary Wars.[68] Such comparisons to the Barbary pirates led the newspaper to conclude that it was no surprise that nothing had changed in the last hundred years, for only European imperial control over Morocco, ideally in the form of a French protectorate, would bring about progress: "Our Government would be only too glad to have a strong and responsible Government set up with whom we could deal in the matters that affect us."[69]

It was later revealed, much to President Roosevelt's private embarrassment, that Perdicaris was probably not an American citizen—having given up his citizenship during the Civil War. Nonetheless, Roosevelt deemed the kidnapping an affront to the nation because Raisuli *believed* that Perdicaris was an American citizen. Undeterred by inconvenient facts, Roosevelt betrayed his own mantra of speaking softly but carrying a big stick. He ordered Secretary Hay to dispatch an ultimatum to American consul Gummere: "Perdicaris alive or Raisuli dead."[70]

That same day, the ultimatum was repeated at the Republican Party National Convention in Chicago to thundering applause, rousing the conference crowd to assert national pride in the face of a foreign threat.[71] The *New York Times* critiqued the display of overt partisan enthusiasm and jingoism, describing convention goers who were "howling, like a crowd at a prizefight, over a menace made to the ruler of a despicable little barbaric State." Indeed, why would the United States, with its unquestioned global stature and civilization, react in such a way to a "barbaric" country of no global strategic or civilizational standing?

The newspaper nonetheless praised the menacing language in the dispatch: "It is true that our Government would not have addressed a civilized, and especially a powerful, Government in the words used in the dispatch of Mr. Hay, but it would have had no occasion to do so. Civilized Governments can be approached in different form, and do not expose themselves to such claims as we were obliged to make in the case of the Sultan of Morocco."[72] Such analysis of diplomatic language was telling. American diplomacy with "uncivilized" states such as Morocco followed rules different from those practiced with respect to European powers.

In the end, Roosevelt's bluster did not impress the Moroccan kidnappers, although it may have influenced the sultan. With help from the French, the matter ended when the sultan agreed to pay the ransom and the kidnappers released Perdicaris. France's help convinced many Americans of the rightful and necessary imperial claim of France to Morocco, sentiments that were echoed by the American press alongside praise for its own country's global standing.[73] As one editor noted in *World's Work*, a periodical that championed American power abroad, the outcome perpetuated American foreign policy aims and the spread of civilization to the world: "At the beginning of the last century, it was an American fleet that exterminated the Barbary coast pirates and made the Mediterranean a sea where neutral vessels could go in safety. Now, at the beginning of this century, it looks as if, by sending our fleet and by a diplomatic combination with France, we are to be the cause of the extermination of land robbers of Morocco, and perhaps even of the establishment of a civilized rule under European supervision in the last of the old African States of the Mediterranean."[74]

Taking advantage of local unrest and American support for its imperial project, France sought to extend its foothold in Morocco by negotiating with Spain over how to divide the country between themselves and by taking control of the Tangier police force. Such assertions of French power, however, fueled imperial tensions with the other European powers.[75] Soon after, Morocco would again become the focus of an international conference at which various European powers would bicker over who would ultimately win the imperial Moroccan prize.

The Algeciras Conference of 1906

The Algeciras Conference of 1906 represented the culmination of decades-long European battles over the division and control of Morocco.[76] The conference was, in many ways, an indirect result of the Entente Cordiale, a 1904 secret agreement between Great Britain and France whereby Great Britain had given up its interests in Morocco in exchange for full control of Egypt. The Entente Cordiale empowered France to extend its empire into Morocco. By early 1905, France had taken control over Moroccan customs and sent a military representative to speak with the sultan.[77] The agreement neglected Germany, however, which was actively seeking to play a larger role in the imperialistic game.[78] The Germans demanded that their interests be heard at the Algeciras Conference, but the French and British refused.

President Roosevelt, alerted to these tensions by the German consul, feared that the growing hostilities among Germany, France, and Britain over the control of Morocco would result in a major war. Although the United States maintained an official policy of noninterference in European affairs, Roosevelt felt compelled to get involved. Having recently negotiated an end to the Russo-Japanese war, the president continued to believe that the United States (and himself in particular) should occupy a more dominant role in shaping world affairs. In partnership with Secretary of State Elihu Root, Roosevelt relied on the country's long-standing concerns for Moroccan Jews, alongside American insistence on maintaining an open-door policy in any future extension of European imperial rule in Morocco, to rationalize American participation in the conference. Although neither of these issues was the true reason for American participation, such justifications provided a credible explanation.

Defense of Moroccan Jews provided Roosevelt with another convenient solution to a vexing problem: addressing the incessant demands by Jewish American activists to protect oppressed Jews in Russia. On the eve of the Moroccan crisis, the size and influence of the Jewish American community had grown to such an extent that, much like the ABCFM, American politicians could no longer afford to ignore its demands. In 1904, Roosevelt had protested the Kishinev pogrom in Russia as part of a strategy to garner Jewish votes during the presidential election.[79] After his election, the persecution of Jews in Russia continued to be the greatest concern for Jewish American organizations.

One of the most vocal activists was the influential Jewish businessman and philanthropist Jacob Schiff, whose power often accorded him a direct line to the White House and the State Department. He lobbied Roosevelt to deliver on his promises of using "big stick" advocacy to correct humanitarian abuses abroad. Schiff also sent telegrams directly to American consuls in Russia and to the Russian government itself.

Russia's status and power continued to limit diplomatic conduct, preventing the president from imposing more concerted action by the United States on behalf of Russian Jews. Indeed, as the *New York Times* had noted so poignantly during the Perdicaris affair, American conduct regarding powerful "civilized governments" differed greatly from that toward a "despicable little Barbaric state."[80] As Roosevelt himself asserted in 1905, "We did not want to make Russia sensitive."[81] Roosevelt also offered a cautionary warning: critiquing Russia about its policy toward Jews would "be very much like the Tsar spreading his horror of our lynching Negroes."[82]

Antagonizing Russia would have other important consequences, both at home and abroad. Russia and Japan had been competing over influence in Manchuria, and, in 1902, Japan signed an alliance with Great Britain. Irish Americans, who maintained a political antipathy toward Great Britain because of its policies regarding Ireland, sympathized with Russia. As a domestic ethnic group, Irish Americans rivaled Jewish Americans in their influence, and Roosevelt risked losing their support if he attacked Russia over its oppression of Jews.[83] Americans also had interests in Manchuria that could be hindered by the Russian presence.[84] With all of these sensitivities to consider, Roosevelt found it impossible to satisfy the pleas of Schiff and the Jewish American organizations.

He could act elsewhere, however. Morocco had no such standing with or diplomatic importance to the United States, making it an ideal target to deflect the focus of Jewish American activists. This strategy was made clear during a private meeting when Roosevelt's friend and adviser, Oscar Straus, pressed the president to explain why he was not acting more aggressively toward Russia. Unable to answer himself, Roosevelt summoned Elihu Root, who literally came running from his office.[85] After regaining his breath, Root delivered a two-hour lecture on the limits of U.S. foreign policy. He also warned that Americans did not necessarily know the full truth of what was going on in Russia. He asked whether the claims to

Russian persecution had not been exaggerated, whether Russian Jews had any role in bringing the oppression on themselves, and whether it would not be more beneficial to condemn American Jews who might be fomenting the revolution in Russia, which broke out in 1905, through donations to oppressed Jews.[86] Therefore, Root concluded, nothing could be done for Russia. To compensate for such inaction, he asked Straus what he thought of the United States addressing a protest against the Moroccan oppression of its Jews instead.

In contrast to Russia, where U.S. intervention would harm American interests, Morocco's status outside the bounds of civilization and international law made it an easy target. The United States had little to lose by angering Morocco. Additionally, Root's accusation that American Jews allegedly financed Russian revolutionaries touched on a darker strand of American anti-Semitism. Many Americans had already accused Jewish immigrants of bringing radical political theories to the United States and fomenting labor unrest. Root used this perception to hint at Jewish American disloyalty and radicalism in an attempt to quiet the activists' inconvenient demands.

These threats were echoed in American newspapers. As one journal warned, American Jews should not "arouse more anti-Semitism toward themselves in America by making too much of an issue of" Russian oppression.[87] After Roosevelt's decision became public, the *New York Times* cited support for this view from an American rabbi who reiterated the legal limitations to U.S. actions in Russia, noting that although "our Government is sympathetic and feels most keenly the position in which our people are placed," there were "international laws that govern cases of this character." Just because Jews were "victims of mob violence is no reason why the Government of Russia should be held responsible for the immediate effect."[88] A similar logic did not apply to Morocco.

Conveniently, Jewish American organizations had renewed their lobbying efforts on behalf of Moroccan Jews only two years earlier. In addition to renewed pressure by the Union of American Hebrew Congregations, efforts were also undertaken by American branches of the French Alliance Israélite Universelle, which called itself the Israelite Alliance of America. By 1903, it had chapters throughout major cities in the United States. By 1905, it counted more than 6,000 members.[89] In December 1903, the president of the Israelite Alliance of America raised the issue of Moroccan oppression in a letter to Secretary of State John Hay: "It is never our purpose to see civilized governments take extreme measures for a breach of religious toleration; but our aim is to see *the three most civilized Pow-*

ers take a kindly interest in securing the fee [sic] exercise of religion in the Mohammedan countries. And this in accord with the Diplomatic policy of England, which has effectively aided the Greeks when striving for independence; and did much in support of the claims of the Armenians in the Ottoman Empire."[90]

What is most interesting about the Israelite Alliance of America's request, however, was that the author emphasized the duty of the United States, alongside France and Great Britain, to intervene on behalf of religious oppression *when this oppression occurred in Muslim countries.* Presumably, historical precedent and civilizational factors had somehow made such intervention a central pillar of the diplomatic duties of these three countries. Comparing the treatment of Moroccan Jews to the Ottoman oppression of Armenians and Greek Christians, the American Alliance again requested that the United States align with British and French efforts to reform Muslim societies. When Hay transmitted this request to Consul Samuel Gummere, however, Gummere responded that Moroccan Jews enjoyed better conditions than most Moroccan Muslims.[91] Still, the consul's analysis of local conditions did not stop Roosevelt from pressing the issue.

When imperial tensions rose between France and Germany over Morocco in 1905, Roosevelt tried to assert his power to quell the mounting hostility. Roosevelt's first success was convincing the French ambassador, Jules Jusserand, to agree to a conference in Algeciras. Roosevelt assured Jusserand that he sympathized with the French position in Morocco.[92] Roosevelt then used the alleged oppression of Moroccan Jews as justification for the United States playing a central role in mediations at the Algeciras Conference. The French agreed to the conference, and Roosevelt appointed his trusted friend, Henry White, the American ambassador to Italy, as an attendee. Meanwhile, the president continued to play a role behind the scenes.

The conference began in January 1906 and lasted four months. During this time, Roosevelt engaged in close conversations with Henry White, Secretary of State Elihu Root, and the French and German ambassadors in the United States. Although the Germans wanted American participation in the conference, because they believed Americans would be objective, Roosevelt had already decided that French imperial expansion in Morocco would be the most beneficial outcome. As the secretary of the United States delegation in Algeciras, Lewis Einstein, wrote in his memoirs, "Roosevelt's private views about the Moroccan question had already been formed. The latter liked the French and sympathized with their ambition to take up another 'White Man's Burden.'"⁹³ Indeed, Roosevelt later confirmed this sentiment. According to a letter he wrote a friend, "I desired to do anything I legitimately could for France; because I like France, and I thought her in this instance to be in the right."⁹⁴

President Roosevelt's strong support for the extension of French imperial rule into Morocco was not surprising. Although the Perdicaris affair had softened American support for the French, Roosevelt's attitudes about Euro-American imperial expansion had been forged years earlier. In a speech delivered in Boston in 1893, the president had argued that world peace would be possible only when "the civilized nations" had "expanded in some shape over the barbarous nations . . . [which] means the cooperation of the civilized people of the earth to that end, whatever the cost."⁹⁵ These "civilized people" were defined by Roosevelt elsewhere as the "white race, or, to speak more accurately, the group of peoples living in Europe, who undoubtedly have a certain kinship of blood, who profess the Christian religion, and trace back their culture to Greece and Rome."⁹⁶ In his first address to Congress, Roosevelt had similarly argued, "Wars with barbarous or semibarbarous peoples" were "a most regrettable but necessary international police duty which must be performed for the sake of the welfare of mankind."⁹⁷ According to Roosevelt's logic, the United States was obligated to support France in spreading its civilization to those in need. In the case of Morocco, this included both oppressed Jews and Moroccan Muslims, who were incapable of progress without outside interference.⁹⁸ As he would later argue in his book, *Fear God and Take Your Own Part*, published only ten years after the 1906 Algeciras Conference, the extension of European imperial rule to Muslim lands had particular importance: "The Christians of Europe possessed the warlike power to do what the Christians of Asia and Africa had failed to do—that is, to beat back the Moslem invader."⁹⁹

Many Jewish American leaders agreed with Roosevelt's assertions. Prominent Jewish leader Cyrus Adler contended that the situation in Morocco had not improved for Jews in the past twenty-five years and that the only hope for Moroccan Jews could be found in "a gradual extension of French influence to Morocco."¹⁰⁰ Other prominent American Jews pushed the United States to play a greater role in denouncing Moroccan oppression at the Algeciras Conference, maintaining that the state of Jews under Muslim rule necessitated intervention by a civilized state. Such views were only encouraged by the French Alliance.

Jacob Schiff had a private meeting with the president shortly before the Algeciras Conference, where he provided Roosevelt with a translation of a report by the French organization regarding the conditions of Moroccan Jews.[101] The report alleged that the Moroccan government forced Jews to live in ghettos (*mellah*) and to wear certain clothes that distinguished them from Muslims. Outside the *mellah*, Moroccan Jews were required to be barefooted and bareheaded; were prohibited from using horses, mules, or canes; and were exposed to "humiliating and brutal indignities" by Muslims, including the latter throwing "burning coal, broken glass, old tinware, etc., on the places where the Jews have to pass." All of this mistreatment "went unpunished." If Jews left the mellah after sundown, they were "considered as outlawed, and liable to the grossest maltreatment, for which there is no redress." Jews needed "special permission from the sheik" to travel or move. The government forbade them from building their homes above a certain level, and all Muslims considered Jews to be unclean, so they could not "drink from public fountains or spring, nor get water from there." For a similar reason, they could not use public baths and "even bathing in the ghetto is not always permitted them."[102] These restrictions were listed under "Restrictions in Lodging or Dress," but four other sections detailed restrictions in trade and commerce, money and labor, legal limitations, and other political and social restrictions. The report described a harsh existence for Jews in Morocco, but Americans would soon learn that the report was grossly inaccurate; few of the restrictions described were actually practiced in Morocco. Schiff sent the report to Secretary of State Root, noting that Muslim rule over Jews in Morocco was like Muslim rule over Christians in the Ottoman Empire—as such, the United States should push Morocco to adopt a treaty similar to the one adopted at the 1878 Berlin Conference guaranteeing Jewish rights: "While the Jew is, in Morocco, subject to particular iniquities, I am informed that Christians and all other sects are greater sufferers, in Morocco, from Mohammedan iniquities, and, as was the case in the Berlin and other Congresses when the participating powers insisted that the status of religious sects need be regulated by treaty, it appears to be most desirable that a similar course be followed in the coming international congress on Moroccan affairs."[103]

Schiff's words revealed how misled he was about the realities of Moroccan society. There *were no* native Christians residing in Morocco to suffer Muslim oppression. Moreover, just as he assumed that reforms imposed on the Ottoman Empire could be applied to Morocco, Schiff assumed that all Muslim societies could be understood in the same way. For that reason, it was obvious to him that if, as he believed, Ottoman Muslims mistreated Christians and Jews, then Moroccan Muslims must be engaging in the same behavior.

Schiff's misinformation went unnoticed. President Roosevelt explicitly backed Schiff's request in a letter to Root, noting that the "Jewish Question" was to be made an important American priority at the conference. Ironically, the so-called Jewish Question had originated not in the Ottoman Empire or Morocco, but in Europe, and it described the larger debate about the place of Jews in European societies amid rising anti-Semitism. Root conveyed Schiff and Roosevelt's information to the American delegate, Henry White, in an official letter reaffirming the importance of the issue to the United States. In a feat of rhetorical logic, Root's letter managed to link the issue of Jewish oppression to American commercial interests and the maintenance of the open door policy: "These restrictions [on Moroccan Jews] operate to contract the field of commercial intercourse by barring a notable part of the population of Morocco from the open door of equal intercourse we are so anxious to see established and by hampering the channels of barter and the opportunities of consumption and supply."[104]

In addition to these official instructions, Root sent a confidential letter to White that denounced "the suffering and humiliation which the Jews in Morocco must endure" and that described Moroccan intolerance as "a leaf from far distant ancient history of cruel and barbaric times." Root further maintained that "if such proscriptions existed among Jew or Gentile citizens in the United States, it would be impossible for the government to shut its eyes to their existence."[105] Root explicitly linked the alleviation of this alleged intolerance to American support for French imperial interests in Morocco: "You will find upon close inquiry which you will be able to make that France has legitimate interests by reason of her proximity to Morocco, quite independent of the general interests of the commercial world, and which ought to be specially safeguarded. If you find this to be so, we do not wish to oppose a provision for the protection of those interests."[106] Root also noted the importance of pandering to Jewish activist demands. He maintained that if White was successful in addressing the "Jewish Question" at the Algeciras Conference, then "it would be very opportune because our immense Jewish population is now naturally much excited over the cruelties in Russia, and it is very difficult for many of them to understand why our Government cannot interfere."[107]

In addition to Roosevelt's strong assertion emphasizing the need to address Jewish rights at the Algeciras Conference, the president ordered a special investigation into the matter. He sent Algeciras delegation secretary Lewis Einstein to Morocco to report on the conditions of Jews. Unbeknownst to Roosevelt and Root, Einstein's findings would complicate

American accusations of Moroccan Muslim barbarity. Much to the surprise of Americans, who were convinced of Moroccan intolerance, Einstein found—as had Gummere before him—that the conditions of Jewish Moroccans were better, on average, than those of their Muslim countrymen.[108] For example, Schiff's claims about unfair practices had not been in effect for some time. Moreover, contrary to European and American assumptions, Jews played an integral role in Moroccan society: "Hence it is that almost unknown to the outside world, a peaceful humanitarian reform has silently been accomplished and the Jews of Morocco are well nigh emancipated from the oppression which formerly burdened their lot." Of course, according to Einstein, Moroccan religious tolerance played only a small part in this improvement. Instead, he credited the work of "foreign representatives in Morocco, diplomatic and consular," and of an "enlightened Sultan" who had continued his father's policies.[109]

Although many American consuls in Morocco had previously affirmed Lewis's findings, Roosevelt's decision to send Einstein to Morocco indicated that he believed in the discrimination outlined by the French Alliance and Schiff. Otherwise, he would not have risked a report that challenged everything the U.S. government had publicly maintained to that point and that justified American participation in the conference. Roosevelt and Root's obstinacy in maintaining a narrative of Moroccan oppression in light of such revelations, however, testified to the fact that diplomats at the highest levels continued to believe that religious intolerance was intrinsic to the Islamic faith and its followers. Of course, such beliefs also conveniently supported Roosevelt's desires for the United States to play a role at the conference.

In fact, during Einstein's investigation Moroccan Jews asked him specifically not to raise the issue at the conference, noting that they were "fully appreciative of their present favorable situation," and preferred "no friendly intervention on their behalf."[110] This startling reversal may have confirmed that the plight of Moroccan Jews was not what Americans had assumed, but Einstein's report hinted at other possible motivations tied to the protégé issue: "Numbers of Jews are the protected subjects of European powers and as such receive the same treatment as citizens of Nations whose protection they enjoy. It would appear, however, that this benefit has frequently been obtained in an illegal way, contrary to the terms of the Madrid conference in 1880, and any too close examination into the Jewish question in Morocco might not unnaturally give rise to counter enquiries on the part of the Moors as to the legitimacy of protections enjoyed by so many native Israelites who are in reality subjects of the Sultan."[111]

A few weeks later, Einstein received a letter from the Grand Rabbi at Tangier, restating their recommendation that the United States not address the alleged oppression of Moroccan Jews at the conference.[112] Given past favors by foreign powers and the upcoming prospect of France assuming imperial rule over the country, Moroccan Jewish elites may also have wanted to downplay their affiliation with foreign powers. The latter had already drawn the ire of the Moroccan authorities—to be associated with an upcoming imperial power would have exacerbated their status in Moroccan society.

Regardless of the reasons for Einstein's favorable report, he nonetheless reasserted civilizational distinctions that placed Morocco on a historical trajectory different from the one followed by civilized societies. He remarked: "It would none the less be unfair to judge the country by Western standards. Among the most fanatical of people with whom the Koran still provides the only native law, conditions cannot be interpreted as they would appear among civilized nations."[113] Even if Moroccan Jews faced fairly good conditions, the country's Islamic rule still unequivocally justified characterizing the country as a whole as uncivilized; their Islamic faith guaranteed that Moroccans would inevitably remain irrational and barbaric Muslims in need of outside imperial intervention.

Neither did this new information about the status of Moroccan Jews change Roosevelt's belief that France should take control of Morocco. In his eyes, the country remained an uncivilized power. Only one year after the Algeciras Conference, Roosevelt wrote a friend that it was "impossible to expect moral, intellectual, and material wellbeing where Mohammedanism is supreme."[114] In the next few years, with the French taking advantage of the conference's results and assuming greater power over Morocco, clashes between French forces and local Moroccans became increasingly violent. In response to these tensions, the French sent soldiers to the area, but they failed to quell disturbances. Only six years after the Algeciras Conference, chaos in the country escalated, giving France the justification for taking over the country as a protectorate in 1912. With explicit American endorsement, French foreign "protection" over Moroccan subjects had reached its ultimate and logical end.

Roosevelt praised these developments because they reflected his views about the benefits of imperial rule in Islamic societies. Whether in Morocco, Egypt, or the Philippines, Muslims required Western imperial rule because their civilizational progress had ended with the birth of Islam itself in the seventh century.[115] Without civilizational advancement, Roosevelt maintained, political advancement could not happen. The free will of the people could be respected only when the people themselves were worthy of respect. According to this logic, French colonial rule in Morocco made sense, for as Roosevelt argued in a private letter to a friend, "At present the rule of the majority in Morocco means every variety of hideous cruelty, injustice, and social and governmental abomination. It would be enormously to the benefit of the people of Morocco if the French took hold of them and did for them what they have done in Algiers."[116] Meanwhile, although Roosevelt was willing to condemn racial and religious brutality abroad, he did virtually nothing to rectify mistreatment of racial minorities at home.

Discrimination was no less prominent in France during the period in which French Jewish organizations fought the oppression of Moroccan Jews. In 1870, Adolphe Crémieux helped pass the Crémieux Decree, which granted French citizenship to all Algerian Jews and placed them under the legal authority of French law. In contrast, Algerian Muslims were deemed inherently unfit for automatic French citizenship and had to apply individually to the French state. As part of their application, they had to agree to give up their adherence to local religious laws governing personal status, a concession that most Algerian Muslims refused to make. Algerian Jews had also resisted giving up their personal status laws, but after the Crémieux Decree, they had no choice.[117] Many French anti-Semites vehemently disagreed with the Crémieux Decree and organized an important *anti-juif* movement in Algeria and France to repeal it. As one French prefect in Algeria argued, Algerian Jews were too much like Algerian Muslims to be considered French.[118]

Meanwhile, French newspapers responded to the French Alliance's efforts on behalf of oppressed Jews by accusing the organization and Crémieux of being part of an international Jewish conspiracy to overthrow French rule.[119] Such anti-Semitic feelings extended to other realms. One of the most anti-Semitic texts of the nineteenth century, the *Protocols of the Elders of Zion*, was written in France in the late 1890s by a defender of Russian persecution of Jews. The document purported an international Jewish conspiracy to overthrow European political and commercial institutions and take over the world.[120]

Of course, one of the most notorious cases of anti-Semitic French currents was the Dreyfus affair of 1894, a case that received international attention. Captain Alfred Dreyfus, a Jewish military officer, was falsely convicted of treason and sentenced to life imprisonment for allegedly providing secrets to the German embassy in Paris. When information came out two years later that proved his innocence, French military leaders, driven in part by anti-Semitic hatred, buried the evidence. Prompted by the affair, anti-Semitic riots exploded in major French cities in 1898. Dreyfus was not exonerated until 1906—the same year France attended the Algeciras Conference and supported an American declaration urging the Moroccan sultan to continue doing what he could to grant equality to Moroccan Jews.

Perhaps because of anti-Semitism and racial discrimination in their own countries, Americans and Europeans could easily believe that Moroccans mistreated their minorities. More important, previous American experiences with the status of Christian minorities and European reforms in the Ottoman Empire shaped American policymakers' perceptions of Morocco as well. As its presence on the global stage grew, the United States played an increasingly important role in helping European powers expand their imperial control over Muslims countries—support that constituted part of a larger imperial and religious effort to bring Euro-American civilization, Christianity, and commerce to the "uncivilized" world. With their growing role in world affairs, American advocates of the extension of European imperial rule applied the same logic to themselves, simultaneously expanding their white man's burden into other areas of the world, including some inhabited by "uncivilized" Muslim subjects.

PART III

The United States and the
"Moro Problem" in the Philippines

*If you love yourselves and your country avoid
coming to blows with the Americans, because they are
like a matchbox—you strike one and they all go off.*
—Jamul-ul-Kiram II, Sultan of Sulu, 1899

*Has it ever occurred to you that
Jesus was the most imperial of the imperialists?*
—Missionary Record, December, 1899

5

UNDERSTANDING AND CLASSIFYING THE

UNITED STATES' "MOHAMMEDAN WARDS"

IN THE PHILIPPINES, 1898–1905

After its victory in the Spanish-American War, the United States annexed the Philippine Islands in 1898. In doing so, more than 6 million Roman Catholics, 300,000 Filipino Muslims, and 200,000 animists became American colonial subjects. Although Filipino Muslims, or Moros, as they were first called by the Spanish and later the Americans, constituted only a small percentage of the population, they controlled a third of the territory annexed by the United States.[1] Unlike previous interactions with Muslims around the world, this marked the first time the United States would rule over Muslim subjects as part of its own empire. This new imperial endeavor allowed Americans to apply their beliefs about Islam directly to a colonial population.

The religious identity of Filipinos played a central and determining role when Americans began to formulate their strategy for how to rule the islands. When it came to ruling over Moros, American colonial policies were primarily driven by beliefs that Muslims were uncivilized, violent, and, importantly, incapable of self-government. To be clear, Americans also looked down on the religious, political, and cultural practices of Filipino animists and Filipino Catholics, as well as the Filipino "race" more generally. American claims that Filipinos, regardless of their religious affiliation, were incapable of self-governance had served as one of the strongest justifications for annexation of the islands as a whole. Nevertheless, in comparison with Filipino non-Christians, Filipino Catholics had a more privileged status in the American colonial apparatus. If Filipino

Christians were the Americans' "little brown brothers," then the Moros were the estranged out-of-control cousins whom nobody wanted to invite to the family reunion.[2] Filipino animists, whose racial identity and religious practices were deemed so primitive that some American colonial officials believed they would eventually become extinct, were barely considered members of the family.

Americans applied their experiences with Islam and Muslims in the previous decades in formulating their opinions about Moros, but these attitudes were reinforced as colonial officials actively sought additional knowledge from European nations' imperial governance over Muslim subjects in their own empires. These transnational exchanges had an unprecedented impact on American colonial policies.[3] But Americans also drew from their own domestic imperial experiences with Native Americans to formulate their policies regarding Filipino Moros.[4]

American colonial officials also maintained that, in addition to their violent tendencies, Moros' intolerance of other faiths made them a threat not just to American colonial officials, but also to Filipino Catholics. Just as Americans deemed Greek and Bulgarian Christians and Moroccan Jews as part of the "civilized" world and at the mercy of barbaric Muslim fanaticism, they justified their continued rule over the islands in part by asserting that should they decide to give up the colonial mantle, "civilized" Filipino Catholics would fall victim to violent and intolerant Filipino Muslims.

By applying prior experiences with Muslims to the Philippines, Americans demonstrated the ideological overlaps among official and nonstate actors and across national and imperial boundaries. Policymakers used their political connections with the Ottoman Porte to try to influence and pacify the new Filipino Muslim subjects. American missionaries with experience in the Ottoman Empire offered policy advice to American colonial officials about the proper way of dealing with the "Mohammedan mind." American colonial officials openly strategized about ways to use the Philippines as a steppingstone in the wider goal of converting Muslims to Christianity globally. The American colonial project in the Philippines and, in particular, its policies with regard to its new Muslim subjects were thus embedded within Americans' larger ideas about the Islamic world.

These policies, which attempted to categorize Moros according to religious beliefs, collided with a more complicated reality. Although Filipino Muslims in the nineteenth century shared a religion, they were divided by political, linguistic, and ethnic differences. Filipino Muslims constituted thirteen different cultural-linguistic groups.[5] The various Moro

peoples were as different from each other as they were from Christian Filipinos.[6] Despite these manifold differences, Moros were alike in their
opposition to colonial rule—first, in opposing the Spanish and, later,
the Americans. The refusal of Filipino Muslims to accept Spanish domination had led to a series of "Moro Wars" during the three centuries of
Spanish rule in the islands. The Spanish were never able to fully subdue
and occupy the entire area controlled by Filipino Moros. In 1878, the sultan of Sulu, one of the most powerful rulers in the southern Philippines,
signed a peace treaty with the Spanish, making Sulu a virtual Spanish
protectorate. Despite this peace treaty with the Sulu Moros, violence
continued between other Moro groups and the Spanish until the Americans ended Spanish rule.[7] When Americans took over colonial rule from
the Spanish in 1898—in addition to adopting many of their predecessors'
biases about the Moros—they inherited an equally fraught relationship
with the various Moro peoples.

Despite seeking European guidance on colonial governance, and despite the commercial and strategic motivations that had also informed
their decision to annex the islands, which paralleled the colonial motivations of other imperial powers, many Americans, nonetheless, advanced
an exceptionalist narrative of empire. American expansionists—be they
political elites, missionaries, or colonial officials—repeatedly and vociferously contrasted the American Empire in the Philippines with the "selfish"
practices of European imperialists to themselves and to the American
public; their empire was a benevolent, humanitarian, and divine blessing that they were obligated to fulfill. Such assertions reflected the nation's
increasing confidence in assuming its stance as a unique world power.
Ironically however, much like in Europe, such claims also necessitated
heightening the rhetoric of the alleged religious, racial, and political inequality of Filipinos in order to justify such claims to imperial benevolence.
Given existing beliefs about Muslims' religious inadequacies, Moros
played a key role in such justifications. Indeed, before the United States
addressed the thorny issue of governing these new Muslim subjects, religion itself provided a powerful justification for annexing the islands.[8]

Religious Belief and American Debates over Annexation of the Philippine Islands

In 1899, in a now-infamous speech delivered before a group of Methodist
ministers, President McKinley confessed that he had "prayed Almighty
God for light and guidance" and had had the revelation that America's role

was to "take them all, and to educate the Filipinos, and uplift and civilize and Christianize them and by God's grace do the very best we could by them, as our fellow-men for whom Christ also died."[9] McKinley was not alone in believing that the Philippines offered a divine opportunity. In a speech to the president in Congress, Senator Albert J. Beveridge merged Christianity and race to justify annexation. The United States, as the self-designated embodiment of global Christian civilization, had a national prerogative to fulfill and a particularly important role to play in the world:

> God has not been preparing the English-speaking and Teutonic peoples for a thousand years for nothing but vain and idle self-contemplation and self-admiration. No! He has made us the master organizers of the world to establish system where chaos reigns. He has given us the spirit of progress to overwhelm the forces of reaction throughout the earth. He has made us adepts in government that we may administer government among savage and senile peoples. Were it not for such a force as this the world would relapse into barbarism and night. And of all our race He has marked the American people as His chosen nation to finally lead in the regeneration of the world. This is the divine mission of America, and it holds for us all the profit, all the glory, all the happiness possible to man.[10]

Given the religious rhetoric employed by these political leaders, the decision by the United States to annex the Philippines was unsurprisingly and overwhelmingly supported by American missionary groups and religious organizations. Although American missionaries, including those who worked with the American Board of Commissioners for Foreign Missions (ABCFM), had been active for several decades prior to American annexation of the islands, the explicit link between American missionary work and expansion of the American Empire—what one historian has termed "evangelical imperialism"—had been a rising force in the years immediately leading up to American annexation.[11] Religious organizations viewed American imperial expansion in the Philippines as a divine opportunity to spread their gospel alongside notions of freedom, democracy, and commerce.[12]

Evangelical imperialism was best exemplified in the work of Protestant clergyman Josiah Strong, who, as leader of the Social Gospel movement, believed that the Protestant religion was the perfect solution to cure the ills of the world. Building on ideologies that advanced the superiority of Christian civilization, Strong's Social Gospel ethics merged with Social Darwinian thought and scientific racism that classified races, nations, and peoples on an evolutionary ladder of civilization and religious belief. Imbricating the superiority of Christian civilization and imperial ideology authorized an Anglo-Saxon sense of duty. Launched in 1890 with the publication of his book, *Our Country: Its Possible Future and Its Present Crisis*, Strong's doctrine advocated a larger imperial role for the United States.[13]

Increasing American missionary efforts to convert non-Christians across the globe in the latter half of the nineteenth century fused with the desires of American expansionists to compete with European powers, which were quickly expanding their own colonial territories throughout Africa, the Middle East, and the Pacific. Just as Europeans justified their expansion through the doctrine of the "civilizing mission," evangelical imperialists such as Strong buttressed the ambitions of secular politicians by infusing religion into discussions about annexing the Philippines. They maintained that the country was obligated to follow its soldiers of war with "soldiers of Christ," a phrase itself taken from a popular Christian hymn.[14] Proponents of missionary work believed an inextricable link existed between American Empire and American Protestant missionaries and that they should work closely with the U.S. government in the Philippines. As the Presbyterian reverend Wallace Radcliffe argued, "I believe in imperialism because I believe in foreign missions. Our Foreign Mission Board can teach Congress how to deal with remote dependencies. . . . The Church must go where America goes."[15] For this clergyman, instead of being exceptional, the American imperial project was joined with that of European imperial expansion. Americans would keep expanding "until the United States of America clasps hands with the United States of Europe in spreading Christian civilization."[16] Yet another religious journal asked, "Has it ever occurred to you that Jesus was the most imperial of the imperialists?"[17]

Operating on the firm belief that only Christians could be members of the civilized world, many evangelical imperialists inextricably linked religion and political freedom while identifying these values as the sole dominion of Christian civilization. As Radcliffe noted, "The imperialism of Presbyterianism is the emancipation of humanity."[18] A Baptist journal similarly explained that the United States had an obligation: "We must give to these islands which we have delivered the Gospel whose principles are the only true foundation and guarantee of liberty. The conquest by force of arms must be followed up by the conquest for Christ."[19] Missionaries would play an increasingly active role in shaping American interactions with Moros and would contribute significantly to shaping U.S. domestic understandings of Filipino Muslims through their extensive publications in American popular magazines and missionary journals.

Support for such cooperation also came from the American government. American political elites officially advocated the separation of church and state, but, in practice, military and civilian colonial officials saw their work as intricately tied with that of American missionaries. Indeed, just as religious organizations supported extending the American Empire, government officials offered considerable private and public support for missionary work, which they believed could uplift "heathen" subjects spiritually, culturally, and politically. After McKinley's decision to annex the islands in 1898, Ida McKinley herself encouraged the president to send missionaries to the Philippines.[20] As one senator noted, Americans could "expect from the labors of the American missionary, an influence in the regeneration of the Philippines, that was the most efficient cause of the elevation of the Hawaiians to the dignity of a self-governing and educated Christian people."[21]

Of course, many Americans vehemently opposed this imperial project. The Anti-Imperialist League, the most prominent group opposed to American expansion, was formed in 1898 and included among its members such prominent leaders as industrialist Andrew Carnegie, American Federation of Labor president Samuel Gompers, and former president Grover Cleveland. By April 1899, the league claimed 30,000 members across the country.[22] The league identified the religious, pro-expansionist arguments as among the most compelling to the American public because churchgoers would hesitate to challenge their religious leaders.[23] Thus, the organization solicited writings from several important Protestant clergymen to counter religious justifications for annexation, which they published in a series of broadsides.[24]

Religious arguments extended to anti-imperialist congressmen. While affirming that the United States was a Christian nation, South Carolina senator Benjamin Tillman denounced American imperial expansion to the Philippines by comparing it to the alleged violent tendencies of Islam: "We are a Christian people and our missionaries, or those imbued with the missionary spirit, clamor for the annexation of the islands for the purpose of shedding over them the light of the gospel. We are asked to do as Mahomet did with his creed—carry the Christian religion to these people upon the point of a bayonet, as he spread Islamism over western Asia and eastern Europe and northern Africa on his scimitar."[25] Despite this organized opposition, anti-imperialists were unable to counter the mounting public and official clamor for expansion. After McKinley formally annexed the islands in 1898, the United States embarked on its first experiment in governing Muslim subjects. Americans set out to examine their new Filipino subjects to understand how they would govern them.

American military leaders, academics, missionaries, and colonial officials began the prospect of ruling the Philippines by trying to understand the varying racial, ethnic, linguistic, and religious differences that existed among Filipinos. Indeed, one of the most vexing problems Americans saw was the fact that Filipinos were not a homogenous people and until they became so, they could not become a legitimate nation-state. By extension, one of the most important anomalies of Filipino Moros was their Islamic faith, which American officials correlated directly with their lack of civilization. As historian Donna Amoroso has written, Moros' "refusal to . . . become Christian rendered the Muslims a minority and thus a problem in the mostly Christian Philippines. . . . The stubbornly Muslim Moros were thus not civilized and showed no interest in becoming so."[26] This dilemma of integrating Muslim Filipinos resonated with domestic concerns about the status of racial and religious minorities on American soil— what Americans often described as the "Indian problem," the "Negro problem," the "Chinese problem," or, increasingly, the "Jewish problem." Paralleling these domestic tensions, the status of Filipino Muslims in the American imperial state came to be popularly called the "Moro problem."

Najeeb Saleeby was a Syrian-born immigrant who had attended an American Protestant missionary school in Syria before coming to the United States. His Ottoman origins facilitated his trajectory in becoming one of the top American experts working with the Moros in the colonial administration. Saleeby summarized the "Moro problem" in a book by the same name: how could Americans govern Moros peacefully while ensuring "their gradual advancement in culture and civilization, so that in the course of a reasonable time they can be admitted into the general government of the Philippine Islands as qualified members of a republican national organization."[27] As Americans came to understand it, the heart of the "Moro problem" was how to construct a united, homogenous, civilized Christian nation given the troublesome existence of these differing religious, linguistic, and ethnic groups.

Immediately after annexation, the Moro problem generated heated public discussions. Journalists, academics, missionaries, politicians, and military officers offered advice to colonial officials via American newspapers and journals.[28] Colonel William Winthrop, a prominent military officer and former professor of law at West Point, wrote an article for the popular weekly magazine the *Outlook* in 1898 in which he identified the governance of the Moros as the "worst dilemma" facing American officials in ruling the islands: "And how are we to govern them at all, if to govern we determine? By means of a great and costly army of colored troops or sepoys, or by turning in upon them a host of Protestant missionaries such as those who vanquished the Hawaiians?"[29] Winthrop interpreted the solution to the Moro problem as either a racial or a religious one, according to which Moros should be controlled only by nonwhite soldiers, who would—presumably through some kind of racial affinity—be more adept at imposing order among the Moros than white soldiers. Alternatively, the Moros could also be "vanquished" through the Christian faith, in which case white American Protestant missionaries would do the job.

In another example of the powerful impact of domestic concerns about race, Winthrop asked if it was a good idea to extend immigration restriction "to the Chinese, who have swarmed across to the Islands as they once swarmed over to our Pacific coast," though limited entry was "consistent with our methods at home," it seemed a mistake "to discriminate injuriously against the Chinese and Chinese mestizo inhabitants, who compose at present the best element of the population."[30] Although the "Chinese problem" in the United States existed because the Chinese were allegedly inferior to white Americans, Winthrop's perceptions about their position in larger hierarchies of race meant that in the Philippines, they could become part of the solution.

Winthrop's analysis of the "Moro problem" dealt with another issue that focused on larger questions about justifications for American imperial rule, ethnic nationalism, and self-determination: "Suppose these Mussulmans should advance the claim that they 'are and have a right to be free and independent,' should we not be embarrassed in framing a satisfactory response?" Whether Winthrop meant independence from the United States or from the Philippines is unclear; in either case, his question was prescient. The dilemma of Moro independence in *both* the United States and the Philippine state would persist for decades. Thus the "Moro problem" was not simply whether Americans *should* subjugate the Moros but also whether they could ever successfully do so.

Of course, the faith of Christian Filipinos did not exempt them from racist hostility. One of the most telling examples that American beliefs about racial difference could override the benefits Filipino Christians gleaned from their religious faith was the sober admission by one editorial in *Outlook*, published in January of 1901, in which the author noted that during the Philippine-American War, American soldiers had consistently killed wounded Filipino fighters and used water torture as part of their military tactics. Ignoring the fact that Filipinos in the northern islands were in fact Christian, he noted that it was a "melancholy fact" that "soldiers of civilized nations, in dealing with an inferior race, do not observe the laws of honorable warfare as they would observe them were they dealing with their equals and fighting fellow Christians."[31] In another testament to the power of domestic concerns about race, Verena Davis, wife of the former Confederate leader Jefferson Davis, argued in an article entitled "The White Man's Problem": "I cannot see why we should add several millions of negroes to our population when we already have eight millions of negroes in the United States. The problem of how best to govern *these* and promote their welfare we have not yet solved."[32]

In contrast, others believed the Philippines presented an opportunity in solving such domestic concerns. John T. Morgan, a senator from Alabama and former Confederate general, believed the "Moro problem" might provide an ideal solution to the "Negro problem." Extending the logic of one of his earlier proposals, which was to send African Americans to Africa and replace them with white Armenian Christians victimized by the 1894 massacres, he instead proposed settling African Americans in Moro lands, where they would spread their Christian faith while ridding the United States of their complicated and unwanted presence.[33] Nobody took him up on either of his plans.

Broader concerns about the global "problem" of Islam also shaped the debate. Perhaps no advice was more indicative of the American propensity to apply beliefs about Muslims in one part of the globe to another then that offered by Henry Otis Dwight, an American missionary who had worked for the ABCFM in the Ottoman Empire for more than thirty years. Dwight claimed to possess special expertise on how the United States should proceed in governing the Moros, thanks to his experience as a missionary in Muslim lands and his historical knowledge of other imperial powers' dealings with Muslims, including the British in Egypt and India, the Russians in Central Asia, and the French in Algeria. More important, Dwight maintained, he had read the Koran. Dwight's article, "Our Mohammedan Wards," appeared in 1899 in the popular and well-respected monthly magazine the *Forum*, which focused extensively on debates over American imperial expansion.[34] He offered a long analysis of how the religious faith of the Moros was essential to shaping American colonial policy, reinforcing the view that religious values trumped all other considerations in determining Muslim behavior.

Dwight cautioned American rulers that Muslims, no matter where they lived, required tailor-made policies, because "Mohammedans differ from the rest of mankind even in regions inhabited by wild tribes alone."[35] In other words, while endorsing global categorizations that divided the world into "civilized" and "wild" realms, he maintained that when it came to Muslims, colonial officials should not understand them strictly on these terms; instead, it was their Islamic faith that truly set them apart. Indeed, Muslims around the world had an "essential peculiarity" that distinguished them from others: they could not "avoid regarding others from a religious standpoint."[36] To be successful, Americans had to understand the "Mohammedan point of view," which could be gained only by studying the Koran.[37] Muslims across the globe adhered to the central belief that all non-Muslims were enemies to be "subjugated or killed for the glory of God at the earliest convenient moment."[38] Muslim intolerance for other religious faiths extended to every level and age of society: "Babies, almost before they are weaned, lisp the word 'Blasphemer' on sight of a foreigner."[39] Dwight's analysis discounted all other influences on Muslim identity; throughout the entire world, only one "Mohammedan mind" existed, and it did not change in the context of time, place, ethnicity, culture, or historical circumstance.

But Dwight's analysis extended to warnings about the global dimensions of the problem. He warned that, although Moros "may be ignorant and imperfect Mohammedans," American annexation had attracted the attention of Muslims across the world: "For this is the age of Pan-Islamic revival; and already lineal descendants of the Prophet Mohammed have cast their lot among the people of these islands."[40] Despite the global strategic threat posed by such pan-Islamic unity, Dwight argued that it was America's duty to intervene. Americans could not relinquish their moral obligation to rule the islands, for leaving them would have disastrous results, particularly for Christian Filipinos: "If our forces were now to be withdrawn from the Philippines, Mohammedans would be at work devastating the fairest of the islands, in the name of the Lord, just so soon as they could find arms and ammunition for the purpose. . . . This fact fixes the duty of the United States to control the Moros. We may not cause, much less may we invite, the outbreak of a war so beastly and so ruinous to all concerned. We cannot escape responsibility for the control of these people."[41] In offering such warnings, Dwight implicitly recalled earlier arguments; what was at stake was a global battle between Christianity and Islam.

Given Dwight's professed "expertise" in all matters Muslim, he also offered specific policy recommendations, of which the options were few.

One was for the Americans themselves to wage war "in a way that the Moros can understand" which entailed mimicking Muslim tactics, as the Russians had successfully done in Central Asia.[42] Americans had to understand that the Moros were untamable—American military forces thus needed "to seize any trifling opportunity for the end in view, to have an overwhelming force, and then to strike without conscience; literally killing every living thing when the battle occurs, and destroying everything that cannot be carried away after the victory is won." Peace could come only through such extreme displays of violence: "The expense of such a policy will be great, the bloodshed terrible; but a few successful encounters conducted on this principle will secure abject submission and peace for a generation."[43] Such bellicose proposals, coming from an American Protestant missionary no less, reflected the degree to which American hostility toward the Islamic world shaped their everyday experiences with Muslims.

Ignoring his country's brutal history with Native Americans, Dwight conceded that the conscience of American Christians might be troubled with this resort to violence, which came so easily to Muslims. Alternatively, Americans could adopt the peaceful British model, in which officers studied Muslim law, avoided selling weapons to Moros, and offered subsidies to the sultan and his officers. No matter the approach, maintaining a large military and naval force in the area would be necessary in the short term, as would controlling the relations of Muslims with non-Muslims. In the long term, Muslims must be taught through contact with "high, manly qualities."[44] If Moros came into contact with American military officers with "sterling qualities," he maintained, they would eventually abandon their religious prejudice.

Dwight's remarks were republished in excerpts in the popular *American Monthly Review of Reviews*. In addition, his advice would gain even greater relevance when his article was referenced in a compilation by the National Library of the Philippines, which was run by the American colonial office. In sync with Dwight's suggestion, mass violence became standard practice in American governance of the Moros. More than 10,000 Moros would be killed in the next decade as Americans sought to extend their colonial rule. It is unknown how many Moros came to appreciate the "sterling qualities" of American military officers during these brutal military campaigns.

Military officers on the ground in the Philippines joined in public discussions of the Moro problem. Brigadier General George W. Davis served as commander of the Department of Mindanao and Jolo in 1902. In an article in the *Washington Post* in May of 1902, he maintained that solving the "Moro problem" involved enormous difficulties because the "savage tribes" and the climate discouraged white migration to the area: "If Anglo-Saxens [sic], Irish, Italians, Germans, Danes and Swedes could be induced to emigrate to the Moro country in tens and hundreds of thousands and take up and possess the earth as these people have done in the United States, Canada, New Zealand, and the Argentine Republic, the Moro problem would be solved, but there can never be such invasion of these tropical jungles by white men."[45] As Davis demonstrated, the race and religion of the Moros often merged, meaning that solutions to the Moro problem involved converting their faith and elevating their race. At a time when Americans increasingly perceived race as fixed in scientific terms, however, many doubted the ability of the Moros to progress. Davis's analysis of the situation offered solutions drawn from the past imperial experiences of the United States. Americans had solved the "Indian problem" with invasion, massacre, and forced removal.

Public debates about Moro slavery constituted another thorny reminder of America's past.[46] As Michael Hawkins has argued, defenders of annexation used the issue to their advantage: "For American imperialists in Mindanao, more so than any other place in the colony, slavery represented an easily identifiable and genuinely archaic practice that fundamentally legitimated the military's unique colonial project."[47] Imperialists used Moro slavery to argue for the necessity of bringing superior American practices to Moro lands. American imperialism would bring freedom and transform William McKinley into what the *Los Angeles Times* called "a second emancipator."[48]

More moderate solutions acknowledged that Moros practiced a more benevolent form of slavery that did not require immediate emancipation. Moving too quickly would be unwise, given the cultural inferiority and backwardness of the Moros. As one article argued in *Outlook*, Americans should understand the ahistorical status of Moros before shaping appropriate policies: "The Americans are living in the nineteenth century after Christ; the Moros in the tenth century before Christ. We cannot transfer them from their age into ours by any instantaneous process."[49] Regardless of the viewpoints expressed, American discussions of Moro slavery served to reinforce American superiority in the face of Islamic barbarism, confirming the necessity of American imperial rule.

THE SCHURMAN COMMISSION, 1899–1900

President McKinley signed the Treaty of Paris in December 1898, officially establishing American sovereignty over the Philippine Islands. Shortly after, he ordered the creation of the first Philippine Commission. The commission was to serve as "an advisory cabinet in the Philippines."[50] Its responsibilities included collecting information about the islands and their residents and using this data to determine suitable political arrangements and cultivate close ties "between the United States and the 8,000,000 brown men in Asia, for whom the Treaty of Paris invested us with sovereign responsibility."[51]

McKinley appointed Cornell University president Jacob Schurman, a conservative Republican who had opposed annexation, as chair.[52] McKinley persuaded him that "the peace of the world" and the future of the Philippines would be endangered without an active American sovereign to replace the Spanish.[53] The cabinet would come to be known informally as the Schurman Commission. McKinley also appointed to the commission Dean C. Worcester, a zoology professor and museum curator at the University of Michigan.[54] Worcester had spent many years in the Philippines before American annexation studying the ethnographic composition of the islands. His work included a substantial focus on the Moros. He claimed experience "among all classes, from the highest Spanish officials to the wildest savages."[55] As the only commission member with direct knowledge of Filipinos, his opinions were paramount.

Indeed, Worcester's "expertise" would prove invaluable to the commission. Based on the research he had conducted before American annexation, Worcester argued that Filipinos could be classified as either independent or subject tribes.[56] All Filipinos who were Christian could be considered "subject" to the Spanish crown—an assessment many Christian Filipino revolutionaries would have found surprising. All non-Christian Filipinos, including Moros, were classified as independent. Worcester maintained that non-Christians posed the greatest challenge to American rule. Moros in particular required firm control, sometimes by means of violence, as they were "an intractable, bloodthirsty set, quite capable of turning against those who befriend them."[57] Americans needed to "teach them a lesson," otherwise they could complicate American control of the islands in the future. This was particularly true for the Sulu Moros, whom Worcester described as the "Moros of Moros" because of their particularly heightened warlike disposition.[58]

Although Americans publicly sought to distinguish their rule from that of the "despotic" Spanish, American officials relied on Spanish information and many soon came to appreciate their methods, particularly in dealing with the Moros. Worcester had gained much information about the Moros from Spanish military officers. The best policy, Worcester maintained, was to follow the admirable example set by one of their Spanish predecessors, General Juan Arolas, who emphasized physical violence to subdue the "fanatical" Muslims. As Worcester recounted, after imprisoning the Moros and "compelling them to work in strengthening his defenses," General Arolas made "soldiers out of his slovenly native troops."[59] When Worcester and his party arrived to conduct research in the Sulu area, Arolas offered blunt advice for dealing with unruly Moros: "If they do not obey instantly, shoot them."[60] As Worcester had noted in his article, "if, by any chance, the Philippines should become part of the territory of the United States, we cannot do better, in dealing with the Malay pirates of the southern islands, than to carry out the policy which General Arolas initiated."[61] Such exchanges with Spanish military officers reinforced existing American beliefs about Muslims.[62] Thus, one imperial power transmitted its biased views to another in the American takeover of the Philippines.

American officials also actively sought information about European approaches toward governance of non-Christian subjects. Before arriving in the Philippines, American military officers engaged in "colonial tourism" in Egypt, India, Java, Borneo, and Malaysia. The U.S. government also sent detailed questionnaires to European colonial administrators. They collected and read European studies of colonial administration. Moreover, they studied the advantages to colonial rule that Europeans had found in promoting Christianity among their non-Christian subjects. As the Philippine Commission debated the applicability to Moros of various British models of colonial governance, its members maintained that only one model—the protectorate system—might work. The British had applied this system in the Malay Peninsula, an area that had similarities to the Moro-dominated Sulu Archipelago.[63]

Although American colonial officials aggressively researched European colonial methods, they attempted to publicly distance themselves from association with European empires, both privately and publicly, even if their policies built upon their example. The Schurman Commission reports recommended that Americans avoid publicly calling the Philippines a colony: "No other word in their whole political vocabulary is so ill omened, so terrible, so surcharged with wrongs, disasters, and sufferings. Merely to call it colonial would insure the emphatic and universal condemnation of the Filipinos for the most perfect system of free government which the mind and heart of man could devise for the inhabitants of that old Spanish colony of the Orient."[64] Perhaps reflecting Schurman's anti-imperialist leanings, these comments reveal that Americans were still debating their place in the global imperial context.

Nevertheless, the American government privately continued to seek European guidance. In addition to discussions of European imperial methods found in the first reports of the Philippine Commission, Oscar T. Austin, working on behalf of the Treasury Department, compiled a statistical survey and bibliography of European colonial practices entitled *Colonial Administration, 1800–1900*, which provided exhaustive information on the colonial practices of the British, Dutch, French, Danish, Belgian, German, Portuguese, and Spanish gleaned in large part from the questionnaires the U.S. government had sent to European colonial officials. The study specifically addressed American concerns about governing non-Christian subjects. Generally, the survey noted, the policy of European colonial governments was "to encourage the establishment of the Christian religion through missionary work, churches, and education."[65] Although European colonial practices encouraged the spread of Christianity, colonial powers should not interfere "with existing forms of religion whose customs are not in contravention with the accepted ideas of civilization and morals."[66] Such advice proved particularly appropriate in distinguishing between Filipino Muslims and Catholics. It would not take long for Americans to deem Islam incompatible with morality and civilization.

Colonial Administration was more than an impressive collection of information about European colonial practices; it served as a guide for American officials in determining colonial legislation and it bore testimony to a larger transnational and international framework of imperial understanding. It included a sixty-page bibliography with thousands of European texts on the "theory of colonization, government of dependencies, protectorates." Five hundred copies were distributed to members of Congress, demonstrating the text's paramount importance. Although U.S. public rhetoric distanced itself from European imperial models, American government officials demonstrated an almost compulsive desire to catalogue the colonial experiences of European nations. American efforts at empire-building were thus embedded in what the scholar Julian Go has described as a "trans-imperial and trans-colonial field, a terrain characterized by colonial states dotting the world map and by complex dynamics of intra- and inter-imperial competition, context and exchange."[67]

Meanwhile, the Schurman Commission prepared its own reports, which filled four volumes and provided a broad examination of the social, historical, political, religious, physical, and industrial conditions of the islands. The reports demonstrated the complicated ways in which Americans conceptualized Filipinos. Much like discussions of Filipinos in the

American press, the religious and racial classifications in the reports often mutually informed one another, reflecting and reinforcing American assumptions about the overlapping dimensions of religious belief, race, and civilizational status. For example, the reports maintained that Filipinos could be classified into "three sharply distinct races—the Negrito race, the Indonesian race, and the Malayan race."[68] The inherent ambiguity of racial constructions of identity, however, complicated the limitations posed by identifying these supposedly "sharply distinct races," forcing the creation of new ethnic and religious subcategories. In the reports, the authors thus identified three "subraces": the Malay Negritos, the Malay Chinese, and the Malay Mohammedans. Whereas the classifications that distinguished the "subraces" of Malay Chinese and Malay Negritos were made according to their supposed "racial" and "ethnic" intermixture, Moros were distinguished from other Malays according to their religious beliefs. In short, for Filipino Muslims, religion informed race to a greater degree than other Filipinos. More importantly, and consistent with Spanish colonial practices, the reports divided Filipinos into much broader categories, designating them as "civilized tribes" or "savage tribes," which became interchangeable with another designation: "Christian tribes" versus "non-Christian tribes." Within these broad categories were hierarchies of religious belief. Filipino animists, who did not adhere to Abrahamic faiths and were often deemed racially inferior to both Filipino Muslims and Filipino Catholics, were relegated to the lowest status.

Occasionally, an official accorded Islam and the political organization of the sultanate a degree of civilization and expressed nostalgic reverence for their "manly" qualities, particularly in comparison to Filipino Catholics. Indeed, in depicting Moros as possessing racial and religious qualities that allegedly imbued them with more violent tendencies, such depictions simultaneously and implicitly served to confirm American beliefs in the effeminacy of Filipino Catholics. The reports maintained that the "Malays of Sulu," for example, had been "modified by two distinct and *opposite foreign elements*, namely, the native of the Philippine Islands and the Arab."[69] Despite some admiration for the Moros warlike tendencies that resulted from their enhanced yet uncontrolled manliness, American colonial officials never ranked Moros as high on the civilizational ladder as Christians.[70] Instead, their uncontrollable "manly" qualities were a problem to be solved. Thus, all Moros were classified as "wild" with "suspicious character and evil disposition." Moreover, though some colonial officials recognized distinctions among the various Moro tribes, these differences typically derived from alleged racial differences, such as the belief that Sulu Moros had "racially" mixed with Arabs to a greater degree than other Moro groups and thus were the fiercest and most difficult.[71] Once again, American beliefs about Muslims in other parts of the globe informed their attitudes about Muslims in the Philippine Islands.

The authors allowed some possibility for redeeming these "ferocious" Moros, but success depended on increased contact with Christians and on eliminating slavery. Citing the advice of a Spanish Jesuit missionary, the authors indicated that the foremost goal was to first convert the animist inhabitants of Mindanao to Christianity. Unable to use these "pagans" as slaves, the Moros would be forced to work for themselves and to exchange their weapons "for the plow, and the arrogant ferocity of the warrior and pirate for the peaceablness [sic] of the man who sees himself compelled to gain his bread by the sweat of his brow."[72] Such tactics echoed the missionary policies of American Protestants in the Ottoman Empire, who hoped to "reach" Ottoman Muslims by "converting" Ottoman Christian subjects to Protestant Christianity.

This was not the only time Americans heeded the advice of Spanish Jesuit missionaries, who had been working among the Moros for more than four decades. In preparing their reports for the Philippine Commission, colonial officials interviewed them at length to obtain their guidance in ruling over the islands. Much like the opinions of Spanish colonial officials, Spanish Jesuits reinforced the American opinion that religious belief fundamentally defined Filipino identity. In contrast to Filipino Catholics, who had received the "direct influences of Spanish civilization," the Jesuits maintained that "infidel natives are still barbarous or semi-barbarous." They also identified clear divisions between Filipinos: "Catholicism is the religion, not only of the majority, *but of all civilized Filipinos.*"[73] As infidels, non-Christian Filipinos had refused to accept Christianity, but the subtext of the Jesuits' arguments was that their refusal to convert also made them disloyal subjects.[74]

The Spanish missionaries also offered policy recommendations to Americans, including limitations on religious freedom, notably the "worship of Confucius, or of Mohammed."[75] Protecting their own religious turf, they also recommended limiting the free reign of Protestant sects in the islands. One Spanish Jesuit missionary, Father Pio Pi, authored a report for American military officers in which he noted that the "principal obstacle" to civilizing Mindanao and Jolo "is the Moro." Pio Pi felt that it would be a "happy day when the Government of the United States becomes convinced of the existence of the obstacle to civilization we have here denounced and of the possibility and necessity of removing it for the common welfare of the country."[76]

Although many Americans had misgivings about Catholicism, Catholics were at least Christians, and many colonial officials applauded the benefits that accompanied the successful Spanish conversion of Filipinos.[77] This accommodation correlated with the belief that all Christians—even Catholics in this case—were part of the civilized world. With such advice in mind, American colonial officials proceeded to govern their new subjects. Filipinos, however, had other ideas about their future.

The Bates Treaty

Before dealing with the "Moro problem," Americans first had to deal with Christian Filipinos who also rejected American claims to imperial authority. Fighting broke out between American troops and pro-independence Filipino insurgents in the northern islands before the Schurman Commission had even arrived; thus, the commission's first goal was to end this anti-imperial insurrection.[78] In a letter to the people of the Philippine Islands, the commission asserted that the American government took "the solemn obligations it has assumed toward the family of nations" seriously and was deeply concerned with "the well being, the prosperity, and the happiness of the Philippine people and their elevation and advancement to a position among the most civilized people of the world."[79] Reasserting the status of the United States as a member of the Christian "family of nations," the letter posited that Filipinos for the moment were unworthy of such membership. This logic failed to convince Filipinos to surrender, given that they had based their revolutionary ideology against the Spanish largely on being civilized and capable of self-governance.

Whether the commission's letter even made it as far as Mindanao, Sulu, or the other Muslim-dominated areas of the Philippines is unclear. While trying to assume control in the northern islands, the United States sent General Elwell Otis to negotiate an entirely different peace with the Sulu Moros, the largest and most powerful group of Moros in the south. Such negotiations were based, in part, on the belief that the United States could temporarily govern Moros through indigenous religious and political leaders. In contrast, Secretary of War Elihu Root maintained that because Emilio Aguinaldo, the leader of the independence movement in the north, was not a hereditary or religious ruler, it was impossible to establish a protectorate there. Root reaffirmed the notion that the religious beliefs of

Muslims led to their unshakeable political loyalty, even though, in reality, the sultan of Sulu and other Moro leaders often struggled to maintain their rule and authority.

Americans did not seek to impose indirect rule on the Moros out of benevolence or inherent faith in the capacity of Sulu Moros to govern themselves; rather, they recognized that they lacked the military capacities to fight both powerful Moro groups in the southern islands and insurgents in the north. General John Bates, who eventually negotiated a formal treaty with the Moros, admitted that "the Government could not afford to stir up trouble with the Moros. The Treaty was made as a temporary expedient to avoid trouble."[80]

Quelling the Moro threat became even more urgent when officials realized that Sulu Moros could join forces with the northern insurgents. In January 1899, Aguinaldo had sent a letter to the sultan of Sulu requesting his support in the war for independence against the United States. He considered the sultan a potentially powerful ally in his struggle against the United States and emphasized their common history and interest in resisting imperial occupation. Despite American assertions that Muslim and Christian Filipinos were defined by mutual antagonism, Aguinaldo's letter testified to broader Filipino conceptualizations of identity and demonstrated their ability to both resist and shape the actions of American policymakers. Concerned by the prospect of an army led jointly by the sultan and Aguinaldo, American officials worked swiftly to prevent a Moro uprising.

To keep the Moros from aligning with northern insurgents, American officials looked to their studies of European colonial models. They theorized that the role of the sultan as the political leader of Muslim Filipinos might permit a functioning protectorate based on the British model. The Schurman Commission therefore recommended that an American official "should make agreements with the sultan of Sulu and his principal datos or chieftains, as well as with the other Mohammedan authorities, and the datos of the numerous semi-civilized and barbarous people who still retained their tribal organization in the less accessible parts of Mindanao."[81] Schurman visited the sultan of Sulu to discuss a potential treaty, an agreement that would enable the Americans to maintain control over one of the most important southern islands while avoiding what Schurman described as a religious war between the Americans and the Moros.[82]

In these initial talks and the subsequent treaty, Schurman sidelined the issue of Moro slaveholding, a topic that had attracted criticism from the American press.[83] Schurman believed that in future years, the impact of

Christian civilization on Moros would solve this problem. Ignoring his own country's tortured history with slavery, including the fact that pro-slavery advocates had justified the institution by using passages from the Bible, Schurman maintained that "contact with Christian civilization will undoubtedly lead to emancipation. . . . I thought the gradual abolition of slavery by peaceful methods better than the provocation of a war of Mohammedans against Christians, which an insistence on immediate emancipation would in all probability have produced."[84] The treaty had a dual aim of ensuring that the Moros understood the benefits of a relationship with a civilizing influence (the United States) and that American interests in the region were protected. As President McKinley's instructions read, "It is greatly desired by the United States, for the sake of the individual improvement and social advancement of the Moros, and for the development of trade and agriculture of the islands in their interests, also for the welfare of both the United States and Moros, that mutual friendly and well-defined relations be established."[85]

Despite Schurman's groundwork, Bates faced opposition from the sultan during negotiations, particularly regarding American sovereignty.[86] After a month of discussions, the sultan finally agreed to a treaty on 20 August 1899. The accord included fifteen points, the most important of which recognized the ultimate sovereignty of the United States over the whole archipelago of Jolo and the agreement by the United States that "the Moros shall not be interfered with on account of religion; all the religious customs shall be respected, and no one shall be persecuted on account of his religion."[87] The United States also conceded that "the government of the Sultan" would have the right to judge offenses "committed by Moros against Moros" and agreed to protect the sultan and all his subjects from attacks by a foreign nation.[88] Reflecting their military necessities, the United States would put its religious and civilizational goals on hold for the moment. The Bates Treaty ensured that the sultan of Sulu would submit to American authority, allowing the United States to focus its military attention on subduing the northern Philippines.

Building on Dwight's earlier warnings about a global "pan-Islamic" unity, some Americans believed that pressure from the sultan of the Ottoman Empire, Abdul Hamid II, might further persuade the Moros to cooperate. The American minister to the Ottoman Empire, Oscar Straus, speculated that his own positive relationship with the Ottoman sultan might lead the latter to "instruct the Mohammedans of the Philippines, who had always resisted Spain, to come willingly under our control."[89] Given their assumption that religious faith united the Muslim world,

Americans erroneously assumed that Sultan Abdul Hamid held total spiritual and political power over Filipino Muslims and that his aid in supporting American rule would make the Moros more amenable to a treaty. Thus, Straus asked the sultan for his support in dealing with the Moros, reassuring him that the United States would respect the religious beliefs of the Moros. He presented a section of a treaty between the United States and Tripoli, signed more than a hundred years earlier, which affirmed that the United States was not founded on Christianity and had no hostility toward Muslims.[90]

Clearly, the United States had considered its previous dealings with Muslim countries, even if their claims had little basis in reality. The use of the Tripoli treaty as a bargaining tool indicated that the United States was cognizant of its previous dealings with Muslims, even if American officials ignored public understandings at the time that often understood the Barbary Wars as a religious conflict between American Christians and Barbary Muslims. Furthermore, by emphasizing that Americans harbored no hostility toward Islam, Americans once again revealed both their belief that the religious faith of Muslims was the most important component of their identity and their assumption that religious issues dominated any Muslim state's negotiations with foreign powers.

The Ottoman sultan agreed to cooperate, sending a telegram "instructing [two Sulu chiefs] in the name of the Sultan that a definite understanding had been reached with the American Elchi Bey (American minister) that they would not be disturbed in the practice of their religion if they would promptly place themselves under the control of the American army."[91] He added, "Because of the Sultan's deep concern for their welfare he advised and instructed them to return at once to their people to prevent any bloodshed."[92]

Of course, the Ottoman sultan had his own agenda in cooperating with the Americans. Facing the disintegration of his empire and European and American pressures to impose reforms on his government, particularly after the Armenian Massacres that had occurred only three years before, Abdul Hamid sought to strengthen the role and power of the caliphate and develop a strong pan-Islamic identity in the empire and throughout the Muslim world. Two imperial powers had worked together to ensure that their subjects remained under their control.

The true impact of Abdul Hamid's telegram on Moros is unknown, although, in the long term, it certainly did not dissuade most of them from asserting their independence. Meanwhile, the Bates Treaty ensured, at least to a certain extent, that the Sulu Moros would not join ranks with the northern insurgents to fight American occupation. This protectorate status, however, included only Sulu Moros; other Moro groups refused to submit to American rule. In December, hostilities broke out in Mindanao. The United States sent three hundred soldiers to Zamboanga to control the uprisings.[93] This would only be the first step in shifting the brunt of American military might on the South.

Indeed, the United States had focused its military efforts in the northern, Christian-dominated areas to great effect. Officially ending in 1902, the Philippine-American War cost the lives of more than 250,000 Filipinos. After the war, the United States gradually transferred control of the northern islands to American civilian officials. The provisional Bates Treaty, which had accorded limited autonomy to Sulu Moros, now faced challenges by military rulers, who deemed even this small amount of self-governance unacceptable.

Despite the promises of the Bates Treaty, policies soon shifted to reflect the biased views of Muslims articulated by American colonial officials and reflected in the Philippine Commission reports. After successfully dominating the northern Philippines, these areas moved toward civilian rule. As a result, this allowed the American government to extend military rule in the Muslim provinces as colonial officials sought to increase their control over Moros.

THE MORO PROVINCE

On 2 March 1900 President McKinley created a second Philippine Commission to assume the duties previously held by the Schurman Commission. Headed by Governor William Howard Taft, this commission had the primary responsibility of transferring the Christian-dominated areas of the Philippines from military to civil governance. The Spooner Amendment, passed a year later, facilitated this process by ending military governance over the Christian areas of the Philippines and transferring control over the entire archipelago from the president to the Congress. In January and February 1902, the Committee on the Philippines of the United States Senate interviewed Taft to assess American rule in the Philippine Islands. In his testimony, Taft reaffirmed American distinctions between Christian and non-Christian Filipinos; indeed, pushing the argument further, Taft expressed the belief that to be Filipino, one *had* to be Christian:

> SENATOR CULBERSON. Taking the Islands as a whole, what is the difference in population between the non-Christian and the Christian people?

GOVERNOR TAFT. Of course, it is very difficult to estimate, and that is one of the reasons why the estimates of the total population are so unsatisfactory. It is very difficult to estimate what the number of non-Christian tribes is, because a great many of them live in the woods and you can not get at them. But I should suppose that the Filipinos—you understand what I mean by Filipinos—the Christians?

SENATOR CULBERSON. The Christians.[94]

Because non-Christians barely qualified as Filipinos, priority in organizing the government in the Philippines went first to the northern, Christian-dominated provinces. As the commission noted in its annual report: "For a great many years to come there will be no question of popular government in the Moro country; the Moros do not understand popular government, do not desire it and are entirely content with the control by their datos . . . it is necessary only to provide a paternal, strong but sympathetic, government for these followers of Mohammed."[95] In contrast, the commission organized thirty-three provinces in the Christian-dominated areas and visited the capital of each to appoint members of local ruling bodies or provincial boards, composed of Filipino Catholics, and to officially declare the establishment of civil government.

As was often the case in American colonial policies in the Philippines, the strict divisions they attempted to impose on Filipino Christians and non-Christians did not always conform to the reality on the ground. The commission thus faced a challenge in determining the appropriate policy for Filipino Christians living on the Moro-dominated island of Mindanao. As Governor Taft argued, Christian Filipinos would naturally have the "same desires as their brothers in other parts of the archipelago" and wish "a government not dissimilar to that established under the general laws of the Commission."[96] Of course, he did not consider that Moros might also wish for a similar government. The privilege of civil governance rather than rule through American military officers depended not only on Filipinos' religious identity, but also on their ability to "purchase" these rights through local taxation. Although they were Christian and—according to American policy—civilized enough to benefit from civilian government, many residents of the Muslim-dominated island of Mindanao could not afford this privilege. At times, Christian Filipinos chose to accept military rule rather than pay local taxes; at other times, the American government carved out Christian provinces by drawing new geographic boundary lines that separated Christian Filipinos areas from lands occupied by

Moros and other non-Christians. Although such challenges reflected the complexity of religious intermixture on the ground, these policies also increasingly encouraged Christian Filipinos to see themselves as distinct from, and superior to, their Muslim "brothers" on the island.

With the passage of the Philippine Bill, also known as the Cooper Act, on 1 July 1902, Congress enacted its first law establishing the framework to extend partial political participation to Christian Filipinos. Much like the Spooner Amendment, the Philippine Bill reaffirmed the political distinction between Christian and non-Christian Filipinos. According to the bill, the Philippines Assembly would include members from all areas not occupied "by Moros or other non-Christian tribes."[97] Its major provisions included a bill of rights, the appointment of two Filipino representatives to the U.S. Congress (although these representatives could not vote) and, most important, the establishment of the Philippine Assembly to be composed of representatives who would be elected two years after the completion of a census of the islands. Although far from granting Filipinos full political participation, the Philippine Bill granted some form of local representation. Meanwhile, the Moro-dominated areas remained under military control, with the American military governor serving as "executive authority" over all civil affairs.[98]

Meanwhile, when it came to Moros, the priority went to ensuring that Moros understood who was in charge. As Secretary of War Elihu Root wrote in his 1902 report, the military's primary obligation thereafter would be control of the Moros. In the minds of American political elites such as Root, the distinctive religious and civilizational status of the Moros made such a policy obvious: "such measures of force as are necessary to control the various Moro tribes have no more relation to the recent Philippine insurrection than our troubles with the Sioux or the Apaches had to do with the suppression of the Southern rebellion."[99] Comparing Filipino Christian insurrectionists to American Confederate rebels and Moros to Native American tribes made the civilizational, racial, and religious distinctions explicit. Much like rebellious Southerners during the Civil War, Filipino Christians might have disagreed on the political relationship between themselves and Americans, but they remained part of the body politic, whereas Moros, like Native Americans, were religious and civilizational outsiders with no valid claim to political inclusion.

Despite—or perhaps because of—distinctions that placed them above Moros, Christian Filipinos actively attempted to limit American military power in the Moro province and offered to rule the Moros themselves. American colonial officials refused, stating that Christian Filipinos were incapable of ruling over Muslim Filipinos.[100] American colonial officials publicly justified their decision by warning that, without Americans protection, Christian Filipinos would fall victim to the uncontrolled and fanatical violence of the Moros and to their hatred of Christians.

With Root's orders in mind, finding a solution to controlling the "Moro problem" became a central responsibility for military officers. General George W. Davis, who served the dual roles of local military governor and commander of the department of Mindanao and Jolo, was central to this endeavor. In his official report, Davis offered his advice on how Americans should proceed. The treatise included detailed testimony from military officers; recommendations for future policy; and copies of treaties, agreements and capitulations between the Spanish and the Moros as well as a copy of the Bates Treaty. Like Secretary of War Root, Davis claimed that the Moro problem did not entail devising new policies of political representation: "Our treatment of the Mindanao Moros and the pagan tribes is based on the same general rules that have always governed our interactions in intercourse with the Indian tribes on our Western frontiers."[101]

While American imperial precedent might provide a model of governance, Moro diversity required a nuanced approach. The most problematic Moros, according to Davis, were those living on the shoreline of Lake Lanao. Despite their "fixity of residence" and "agrarian character," attributes that implied some advancement, these Moros were the most hostile and had never been dominated by the Spanish. Moreover, their political situation complicated matters. As Davis noted, "This beehive of Mohammedan savages is governed by many score of mere hereditary chiefs, each entirely independent of every other, and there is no central authority or common head over all, but they are cemented together by a common religion and a common interest—self-preservation."[102] According to Davis, the situation was complicated for all Moros, regardless of where they lived, because their affiliation with Islam was unshakeable. He explained that the "Moro problem" had existed for more than three hundred years, since Christians had first attempted to rule Moros. Because the Moros recognized only religious law, he advised that Americans should follow the experience of other imperial powers with their Muslim subjects: "While we may refuse to recognize their rulers and even destroy them, we can not eradicate the deep-seated religious conviction, the principles of which have been cherished for more than a thousand years. They have no knowledge of, or respect for, any other law than the one which exacts an eye for an eye. It seems to me to be our duty to respect this conservatism and deeply rooted prejudice and utilize it, and to use these datos in our efforts to lead these people away from slavery, polygamy, piracy, and despotic rule, just as the Dutch have in Java and the English in India."[103]

Davis thus recommended several changes. Acknowledging that the United States had erred in signing the Bates Treaty, he first advised abrogating the treaty and imposing direct military rule over the Moros.[104] The treaty granted Moros too much autonomy. Davis noted that the treaty twice referred to the "Government of the Sultan" and conceded "to the Sultan his right to refuse consent to the purchase of land or to trade in a country over which the United States is as completely sovereign as she is over the District of Columbia."[105] Nonetheless, he did not recommend eliminating this despotic form of power too quickly, for history had shown that moving away from despotism was difficult: "How many of us have seen the failure of attempts to make self-governing citizens quickly out of the breechclouted, naked savages?"

Instead, Davis suggested that Americans replace the sultan as the new despots. He asserted that all governance over Moros be military and that Americans (instead of Moro chiefs) should be granted the power to try all crimes committed by Moros. According to Davis, Muslims responded best to force; thus, before making any changes—and to prevent ensuing hostilities—Davis advised a strong military presence within the territory and in the surrounding waters, and violent repressions of all rebellions. If the United States government wished to maintain the governance by the sultan and local *datos*, Davis proposed implementing the British and Dutch model—one in which native rulers served as puppet governors. If American officials adopted this method, then the sultan of Sulu would remain a "puppet kingling . . . robbed of all real power through measures as have been so successfully employed in the oriental lands."[106]

Based on General Davis's input, Governor Taft further codified the distinction between Filipino Moros and Filipino Christians with the passage of an act officially creating the Moro Province.[107] Under the act, passed on 1 June 1903, the civil governor of the Philippine Islands would appoint Americans to the posts of attorney, secretary, treasurer, superintendent of schools, and engineer.[108] These five members, plus the military governor of the Moro Province, would constitute the legislative assembly, otherwise called the Moro Council. At his discretion, the civil governor of the Philippine Islands could appoint a military officer as the provincial governor and engineer, an option the American colonial government exercised throughout the existence of the Moro Council.[109]

The legislative assembly, or Moro Council, also had the responsibility of collecting and codifying the customary laws of the Moros to be modified at the discretion of the council members. These new laws would regulate all civil and criminal relations among Moros. When Governor Taft drafted the legislation, he realized that governing Muslims was a "very difficult and complex problem," and, because of their religion, the Moros required a different set of laws. Thus, "it was not deemed wise or just, except to the extent absolutely necessary, to impose upon them the system of laws and of administration of justice which was well adapted to the Christian Filipinos, but which must prove burdensome and odious to them."[110] Cases between Moros and Christians or Moros and other non-Christians would be tried under a separate set of laws.[111] In organizing these new criminal and civil proceedings, Americans stripped the sultan and local *datos* of their power to regulate Christian and non-Christian relations.

American officials also believed that education was necessary if Filipinos were to have any hope of one day becoming citizens of a future homogeneous Philippines republic. The Philippine Commission passed Act 74 on 21 January 1901, creating a department of public instruction. Section 16 of the act recognized the official U.S. stance regarding the separation of church and state, specifying that teachers could not critique any religious sect, including the Islamic faith. Until the Bates Treaty was abrogated, such a policy would conform to American promises of noninterference with Moro religious practices. Those who violated this act would be dismissed from public service.[112] Such policies, however, received immediate critiques from those who blamed the Moro problem on Islam itself.

Upon learning of the law, O. J. Sweet, the military officer in command of Jolo, wrote a letter to the adjutant general of the Department of Mindanao and Jolo in May 1901, protesting this provision. Sweet believed the provision should not be applicable in the Sulu Archipelago; rather, teachers should actively teach against the Islamic faith in American schools:

> The Al Koran, a monotheism, is the most colossal forgery of the Christian religion ever perpetuated since the foundation of Christianity. It teaches that it is the duty of those of that faith to convert all peoples to become followers and believers of Mohammedanism. To make a convert means to defend the convert; to do this requires force, and the use of force means conflict to end in war with these fanatical people. The intelligent universal world does not recognize the Al Koran as true, but that its doctrines are false; and that a false doctrine may not be encouraged and fostered by being taught in the U.S. public schools in the Philippines, I have to most earnestly request early action in the case, in the premises for the manifest public good.[113]

Sanctioning Islam, he further maintained, would offset any public good established by the public schools while fomenting future fanatical violence by Moros against Americans.

Secretary of Public Instruction Bernard Moses echoed Sweet's pessimism about the capacity of Moros to progress in his first annual report, in which he noted that Moros "manifested little or no desire to place themselves under the civilizing influences which the government may exert."[114] Educating these Filipinos would be difficult because they resisted change and "they see no reason why they should be plunged into that uncomfortable stream which we call progress." Moses maintained that Moros, "like many other peoples, in the rudimentary stage of social development" entertained "an exaggerated idea of the importance of their power and popular wisdom." This belief needed to be broken before Americans would have any success in educating them. To do this, the Moro needed to be "awakened" to "an appreciation of his feebleness as contrasted with the powers of a civilized nation."[115] Again, implicit in this analysis was the belief that force seemed the most appropriate method for breaking the stubborn refusal of the Moros to advance. Such approaches would become even more entrenched in American colonial policy as officials developed new colonial institutions to officially enumerate and classify their Filipino subjects, further distinguishing Moros from Christian Filipinos.

The Bureau of Non-Christian Tribes and the Bureau of the Census, 1901–1902

In considering the prospects of increasing U.S. control over the Moro and animist areas in the southern Philippines, officials sought to gather more information about their non-Christian subjects. With this goal in mind, President McKinley approved the creation of the Bureau of Non-Christian Tribes, which was duly founded on 2 October 1901. Its role was to investigate the non-Christian tribes and gather information "with special view to determining the most practicable means for bringing about their advancement in civilization and material prosperity."[116] More important, it was "to further investigate and report upon the practical operation of all legislation with reference to non-Christian tribes." The ethnographic data collected by the bureau would help American officials to decide how best to govern and civilize these non-Christian subjects.[117]

David P. Barrows accepted the position of chief of the Bureau of Non-Christian Tribes. As an anthropologist and a bureaucrat, Barrows was well suited to straddle the worlds of ethnographic research and colonial administration. Like many anthropologists trained in the nineteenth century, Barrows saw a crucial link between racial "progress" and American imperialism.[118] Barrows acquired his expertise based on his dissertation research on some of the other non-Christian "wards" of the United States, including the Native American tribes of southern California and Colorado. Rather than spending more time in the Philippines learning about the native inhabitants, Barrows left the Philippines as soon as he was appointed chief of the bureau, and returned to the United States where he spent five months investigating Indian reservations and schools so as to study their applicability to the Philippines.[119]

Barrows concluded that the American governance of Native Americans was a poor model for governance of non-Christian Filipinos; segregating Moros on reservations would prevent them from interacting with more "civilized" Christian Filipinos. Instead, the best policy would allow for the opening of "superfluous land" to "settlement from the outside," enabling the intermixture of Moros and other non-Christians of "Malayan origin" with more advanced Filipino Christians and Americans. Furthermore, in contrast to Native American societies, which were "thoroughly democratic," Malayan society was "oppressively aristocratic"; "the entrusting authority, then, especially policy and judicial authority, should be safeguarded and restricted in every possible way."[120] Despite his focused study of non-Christians, Barrows nonetheless offered continued justification for American imperial rule in the islands as a whole. He maintained that the political and judicial characteristics of *both* Christian and non-Christian Filipinos required the guidance of American colonial officials to lead them to an "advanced" state, whereby they could eventually govern themselves.

In attempting to explain the place of non-Christians in the larger context of the islands, Barrows compiled reports for the bureau in which he presented historical background on both animists and Moros and offered a historical and religious explanation for the dominance of the Moros in the southern islands. According to Barrows, adherence to Islam had empowered Moros, allowing them to expand their territory and the Muslim faith. Following the belief that Muslims were more fanatical and violent than Christians, Barrows maintained that the religious identity of the Moros had allowed them to become dominant. Drawing on the belief that religion functioned centrally in Moro identity, bureau officials conducted additional research on Islam and established a working library on related issues, including the "Mohammedan religion, custom and law . . . primitive law and custom; and general anthropology."[121]

American officials working for the Bureau of Non-Christian Tribes also conducted their own ethnographic research; to this end, the bureau released a "Circular of Information" offering "Instructions for Volunteer Field Workers."[122] Although the fieldworkers had no formal training in ethnographic research and rarely spoke the local dialects, American officials assigned them the important task of collecting information about the cultural and spiritual customs of the numerous non-Christian peoples of the Philippines. The bureau offered suggestions "for observation" and instructed its volunteer fieldworkers to "learn carefully the names of the tribe, i.e. the name or names by which they are known to the Christianized peoples near them, the name they have for themselves, and the names they are called by other wild tribes."[123] Data gathered by these fieldworkers became institutionalized in the American bureaucracy. In stipulating identification by three names, the bureau constructed three hierarchical identities for Filipinos. The most "primitive" identities were the names that the "wild tribes" used to refer to themselves or each other. The names assigned by Christian Filipinos defined the second identity, which was of higher status than the "primitive" one defined by the "wild tribes." In the end, American officials assigned the final name, which became the most important and official one.

Much like the previous assessments of the Schurman commission, racial and physical characteristics were of great importance to the bureau in understanding non-Christian Filipinos. As an anthropologist, Barrows believed that different "races" could be ranked on a ladder of civilization. Although humans could advance on this ladder through contact with more "civilized" races, a complicated link existed between physical characteristics and degree of civilization.[124] Thus, the Circular of Information provided instructions on how to obtain a cephalic index, which it noted held "a good deal of importance in Anthropology" since it presumably revealed the intellectual capacities of the various non-Christian subjects.[125] Detailed and exhaustive questions about the physical characteristics of non-Christians included asking fieldworkers to note skin color, hair texture ("whether fine, coarse, straight, wavy, wooly, or growing in little spiral kinds peculiar to the negro,") muscular structure, and even whether women's breasts were "long and pendent or rounded and erect."[126] How the latter contributed to American classifications of non-Christians' "races" was not explained. Nonetheless, such questions revealed the continued importance of race and the extent to which physical characteristics correlated with ideas of culture and religion. Indeed, turning military officers into amateur colonial anthropologists, the Bureau of Non-Christian

Tribes institutionalized the disparate attitudes of American academics and the U.S. government with regard to its new Filipino subjects.

As part of its new colonial responsibilities, the United States followed the example of other imperial powers and set to work conducting a census. The Bureau of the Census, established by the president in 1902, had as its main objective enumerating Filipinos in preparation for their future political participation in electing a Philippines Assembly. The president would allow an election only after peace had been established and Christian Filipinos had recognized the authority of the United States. This promise of future political participation was important both for whom it did and did not include; indeed, although the census included non-Christians, the elections themselves were to be held only in territories "not inhabited by Moros or other non-Christian tribes."[127] Although American officials needed to estimate how many Moros lived in the Philippines, exact numbers were difficult to obtain and ultimately unnecessary since they would not be voting nor would they be represented in the Philippines Assembly.

The authors of the census mirrored the arguments of previous American officials in recognizing that the Moros occupied a separate, inferior place in the American colonial apparatus, while also offering a nostalgic acknowledgment of the mighty Moro warrior. Such recognition merged depictions of noble savage American Indians with stereotypes of Muslim decadence. The authors conceded that "for three centuries [Moros] defied the European and carried war with impunity into his territory" and imagined that there must have been "some barbaric splendor about these old pirate states when at the height of their power and daring" while noting "something almost melancholy about their decadence." They nonetheless had to recognize that their demise was inevitable and "a gain for civilization."[128]

More important than these sentimental reflections, because American officials limited the privilege of political participation to certain segments of the Philippine population, classifying Filipinos into distinct racial and religious categories was crucial. Accordingly, the census report data reflected the binary categorizations previously established by the Spanish and the Schurman reports: Christian tribes and non-Christian tribes. Given the lesser importance and alleged inferior status of non-Christian tribes, census officials used a simpler questionnaire for them.[129] In a powerful visual testament to the importance of distinguishing between Christians as "civilized" and non-Christians as "wild tribes," census officials codified these distinctions in official maps and tables (see figure 3 and figure 4).

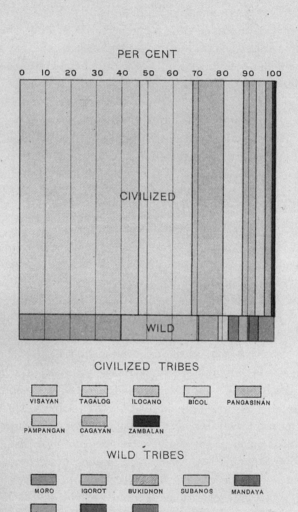

FIGURE 3. The *Census of the Philippine Islands* endeavored, among other things, to classify and enumerate the diverse Filipino populations. This included categorizing Filipinos into "civilized" or "wild" tribes, which correlated directly with the religious beliefs of Filipinos as Christian (civilized) or non-Christian (wild). (Chart: "Total Population: Distributed among the Civilized and Wild Tribes," *Census of the Philippine Islands*, 1903, vol. 2 [Washington, D.C.: Government Printing Office, 1905])

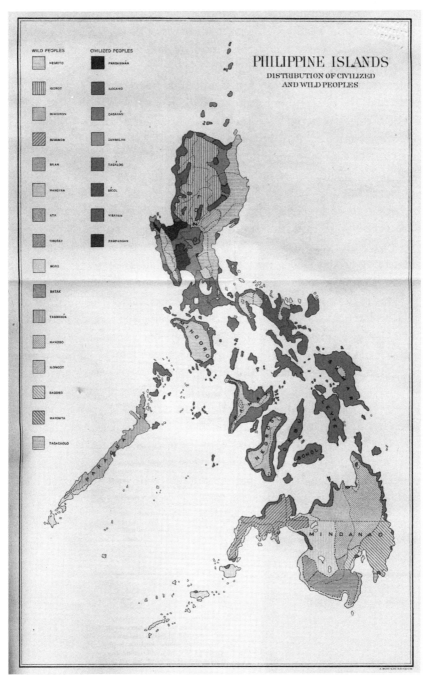

FIGURE 4. In addition to drawing up charts and tables classifying Filipinos, census officials also created maps that identified the geographic distribution of "civilized" and "wild" peoples. (Map: "Philippine Islands: Distribution of Civilized and Wild Peoples," *Census of the Philippine Islands*, 1903, vol. 2 [Washington, D.C.: Government Printing Office, 1905])

Moreover, much like the Bureau of Non-Christian Tribes, the census of the Philippine Islands reinforced the view that racial, religious, and civilizational differences among Filipinos prevented them from forming a cohesive, independent republic. Domestic ideas about ethnic nationalism and citizenship resonated in American attempts to use the census to "reconstruct" the Philippines as a homogeneous state. As Vicente Rafael has argued, the census reflected the "possibility, indeed the desirability, of molding colonial subjects into a single people."[130] Such beliefs led officials to maintain that intermingling the "uncivilized" and Christian elements of Filipino culture would uplift Moros, who were as yet unfit as Filipino subjects. Only such interactions would improve the possibility of the Philippines eventually constituting its own unified, homogeneous nation. In categorizing and ranking Filipinos in their official colonial apparatus, however, Americans succeeded only in accentuating these differences and solidifying groups that previously had little coherence, while fomenting future disagreements between Christians and non-Christians.

Unaware of these unintended consequences, American military officials had to deal with the difficult issue of forcing the Moros to adhere to the colonial framework that they had established. Imposing the American colonial framework on resistant Moros would mean applying their theoretical knowledge about Muslims on the ground, a transition military officers made quite successfully. Following the advice of missionaries, colonial officials, and military officers, brutal displays of colonial violence often became the appropriate means by which to impose American rule over the Moros. Continued Moro resistance to the imposition of American rule would result in anticolonial violence waged by Moros against Americans. The "matchbox" that the sultan of Sulu had mentioned in the first year of American annexation would soon explode.

6

EXTENDING AMERICAN

COLONIAL GOVERNANCE OVER

FILIPINO MUSLIMS, 1903–1920

In an interview in 1925, Governor General of the Philippines Leonard Wood evaluated the previous three decades of American imperial rule over the Philippine Islands and argued that Filipinos were not yet ready to assume self-governance. His assessment confirmed his deep-seated belief that Americans should continue to rule the islands for the foreseeable future. But his remarks also evinced a belief that American imperial rule in the Philippines facilitated a wider global mission. Americans could not consider the question of independence for the Philippines, he told his interviewer, "without thinking of civilization as a whole. And civilization, to us, is Christian civilization. . . . We are a stone, if not the keystone, of the arch of Christian civilization in the Pacific." For this reason, the Philippines allowed for no less than "the effective deployment of Christianity for the regeneration of the world."[1]

Much like those who had justified annexing the islands in the first place, for many high-ranking American colonial officials like Wood the continuation of American imperial rule represented more than just preparing Filipinos for self-governance or extending the nation's strategic and commercial interests. Spreading Christian civilization to the world was *also* a central mission of the American nation. This goal was a natural continuation of American manifest destiny; the Christian "regeneration of the world" had spread first through America's continental empire, then to the Pacific. In time, Wood hoped, it would extend to the rest of the non-Christian world. Wood's attitudes were revelatory. The career military officer had begun his service in the Philippines in 1903 as the first governor of the Moro Province, a position he would keep for three years before moving on to serve as the military commander of the Philippines. Wood returned to serve as governor of the Philippine Islands in 1921, a position he kept for six years, until his death in 1927.

Wood's arrival in 1903 to head the Moro Province continued the American project to transform and assimilate Moros into the larger Christian Filipino population. Before arriving in the Philippines, Wood had studied Islam in European and American texts and consulted with other policymakers, military officers, missionaries, and European colonial officials who had engaged with Islamic societies. From these diverse sources, and like the colonial officials that preceded him, Wood came to the inevitable conclusion that Muslims responded best to violence. Such views justified the continuation of military rule over Mindanao and Sulu. Colonial rulers such as Wood were so certain that the Moros required military rule that they maintained the policy in place for more than a decade.

Given his general beliefs about Muslims, Wood's use of the military term "deployment" to characterize the worldwide extension of Christian civilization to the non-Christian world was appropriate. During his tenure ruling over Filipino Muslims, Wood was notorious for deploying troops to brutally—and often controversially—"break down" Filipino Muslim uprisings. Such policies continued throughout American rule. In addition to the 10,000 deaths in the first ten years of American rule, scholars estimate that by 1936, American military confrontations with the Moros would increase the number of Moro deaths to 15,000 to 20,000, or almost 6 percent of their total population in 1898.[2]

The refusal of the Moros to relinquish control over their lands led to a drawn out conflict in the southern Philippines, the Moro Rebellion, that began shortly after annexation and would officially continue until 1913. Although many Americans explained this continued resistance as stemming from Muslim religious fanaticism and savagery, the struggles of the Moros mirrored the Filipino insurrections in the northern islands, which had led to hundreds of thousands of deaths. For the independent Moro peoples, many of whom had never been subjected to Spanish imperial rule, their lack of a unified insurrectionary force prolonged their rebellion against the United States and weakened their overall resistance. Furthermore, since the Moros were spread across a much larger territory and autonomously ruled Moro groups usually fought independently, Americans faced a greater challenge in ending the rebellions, which only increased the length and violence of their campaign of "pacification."

Of course, violent military techniques were only one tool in the American arsenal. Americans also worked in tandem with other actors to advance their shared goals of "civilizing" Filipino Muslims. For example, American missionaries, who received strong support from colonial officials, helped to shape Moro-American relations. American business leaders argued that commercial development, in addition to Christianity and American political reform, were essential to bring civilization to Filipino Muslims. Northern Filipino nationalists concurred, later seeing the gradual transfer of rule in Moro lands from Americans to Filipino Catholics as an important transition in asserting their own capacity for self-rule. Moros who had eventually and begrudgingly accepted American rule, however, also demanded to be heard by American policymakers. These diverse voices would shape American discourse about Islam and Muslims, with important consequences for both Filipinos and Americans.

Moros in the American Public Imagination

American colonial rule over Filipino Muslims would continue to garner much public interest and inform beliefs about Islam in the United States. Military officials, colonial officers, missionaries, and academics related their experiences and thoughts in accounts of their experiences in journals and newspapers accounts and even in children's stories.[3]

Americans "represented" Moros in other venues of popular culture as well. Soon after annexation, Muslim characters appeared on stage in a popular operetta entitled *The Sultan of Sulu* (see figure 5). The author conceived of the idea for the piece after learning about the Moros from an American journalist whom President McKinley had sent on a fact-finding mission to the Philippines. The opera opened on Broadway in 1902 to much success and went on to play 192 performances in Boston, Chicago, Washington, D.C., and several midwestern cities over the next five years.[4] The opera provided a humorous take on American imperial expansion in the Philippines, mocking American hubris in trying to "advance" Filipino Moros while poking fun at Moros for their religious and cultural backwardness. According to the program, the sultan of Sulu was an incompetent and immoral leader of "Mohammedans, polygamists, and slave-holders" who had "running warfare" with American rulers.[5]

Two years later, and with the help of American missionaries and colonial advisors, such as Dean Worcester and Najeeb Saleeby, the U.S. government sponsored a Philippines Exhibit at the 1904 St. Louis World Fair. Widely referred to as the "Philippine Reservation," the exhibit consisted of more

FIGURE 5. George Ade's opera *The Sultan of Sulu* opened in 1902 and played 192 performances in major American cities throughout the East Coast and the Midwest. (Author's personal copy of program)

than 1,100 Filipinos living in homes they had built themselves.[6] The American governor of the Philippines, William Howard Taft, joined the organizers in encouraging the project; they maintained that it would help Filipinos "advance" by providing them with exposure to Americans while convincing the American public of the need to transform the diverse Filipino peoples into a homogeneous nation through American tutelage.[7] For Moros in particular, officials hoped their time in the United States would convince them to stop their rebellion against American imperial rule.[8]

Anthropologists working with American colonial officials organized the "reservation" into three sections that represented a racial, religious, and temporal classification of Filipino peoples and their alleged degree of civilizational progress. After crossing the "Bridge from Spain" and entering the "Walled City," fairgoers could visit a section labeled "Indigenous Peoples," which included the non-Christian Filipinos, whom Americans deemed to be the most primitive.[9]

Even here, Americans reaffirmed hierarchies of progress. The animist Negritos occupied the lowest rungs, followed by Igorottes, and then the slightly more "advanced" Moros. Organizers urged fairgoers to see the Negritos, because this might be their only opportunity to view such primitive humans.[10] They warned that Negritos' racial, religious, and intellectual incapacities meant they were in danger of extinction.[11] Moving ahead both physically and metaphorically, fairgoers could visit a second section, labeled "Spanish Influence," which featured Christian Filipinos. Finally, fairgoers could advance through time to visit the "American Present" exhibit, which displayed the Philippines under American colonial rule. Here, the occupants were not only Christian, but also Spanish-Filipino mestizos, whose racial advancement, presumably, had been assured by Filipino intermixture with superior European stock. Of course, organizers conceptualized the Philippines Exhibit in relation to other uncivilized peoples from across the world; the fair also included exhibits of Native Americans and various "savage" peoples brought over from Africa. As Dr. W. J. McGee, the head of anthropology for the entire exhibition, informed the *New York Times*, the end goal was "to exhibit family groups of peoples still living in the stone age, others just at the beginning of metal working, others engaged in primitive pottery making, basket weaving, etc."[12] The Philippines Exhibit represented a microcosm of larger evolutionary thinking.

The extravagant cost of the Philippines exhibit at more than 1.5 million dollars (the equivalent of 30 million dollars today) was matched by its size and popularity.[13] Fairgoers were undoubtedly drawn to the thrilling depictions of the Filipino occupants in the popular press and in exhibit

FIGURE 6. A photograph of the Samal Moros, depicted here with an American flag, at the St. Louis World's Fair, 1904. Organizers hoped that traveling to the United States and attending the fair would help "Americanize" the Moros and other Filipino participants. (St. Louis Public Library)

advertisements. Igorottes attracted the most fairgoers, in part because of the well-publicized fact that their "primitive" nature included wearing only loin cloths and eating dog meat. News of the Moros' inherent propensity toward violence had also been publicized in advance of the exhibit, including accounts of armed guards on the transport ships to prevent Moros from attacking each other or others.[14] A contemporary book about the fair devoted chapters to each Filipino group and claimed that, next to the Igorottes, "the Moros attracted the most attention at the Filipino Reservation, because of the belief that they are bloodthirsty cannibals who offer up human sacrifices once a year."[15] It cast Filipino Muslims in the most violent light; they were "the most savage of the savages, and even at the world's fair were carefully watched to prevent them from murdering anybody."[16] Visitors attempting to photograph the Moros were instructed

FIGURE 7.
The exhibit included
young Moro
children—here seen
paddling a canoe as
exhibit attendees
watch overhead.
(St. Louis Public
Library)

to do so "at their own risk," because pictures were allegedly forbidden by the Muslim faith, a strange assertion given the hundreds of official pictures taken of the Moros by the exhibit organizers themselves. Moreover, Moro hostility to Christians was made explicit by fair officials, who noted: "It is characteristic of them to manifest aversion to being touched by the hand of a Christian."[17] But the exhibit was also designed as a defense of American Empire itself. Exhibit organizers made sure to suggest that American imperial rule was advancing the Moros, suggested implicitly by one picture that depicted a group of Samal Moros that included a young Moro child holding an American flag (see figure 6).

American exposure to the "savages" on display at the fair was not limited to attendees. Postcards of the exhibit reemphasized hierarchies of civilization by including pictures of fairgoers on a bridge symbolically overlooking a young "savage" Moro child on the reservation paddling his canoe in the river (see figure 7). Such representations would reach the American public in other ways. As the *New York Times* reported, the American Museum of Natural History had negotiated with the fair organizers to make life casts of "certain representatives of all primitive peoples," including Igorottes and Moros, as well as a few Native Americans. These casts would then be "distributed throughout the United States in schools and libraries as educational features."[18] American beliefs about Moro savagery were thus widely propagated to the American public. Such perceptions, of course, were driven by attitudes of U.S. colonial officials, academics, and military officers back in the Philippines; views that would have a powerful impact for policies on the ground.

Leonard Wood, First Governor of the Moro Province, 1903–1906

In 1903, when the governor of the Philippines, William Howard Taft, established the Moro Province, his first task was finding a suitable military governor. Wood was an ideal candidate. Trained as a physician at Harvard, he had joined the Army Medical Department in 1885. In 1886, the army assigned Wood to the unit of Commanding General Nelson A. Miles, whose mission was to "pacify" Native Americans and force the infamous Geronimo's surrender.[19] Later, Wood continued his military service as personal physician to President McKinley. After the outbreak of the Spanish-American War, Wood left to command Theodore Roosevelt as head of the Rough Riders.

Wood's close ties with President and Mrs. McKinley and with Roosevelt facilitated his rise through the military ranks and his ability to garner important administrative positions. Indeed, after serving with Roosevelt during the Spanish-American War, Wood's ascent was meteoric. His experience during the war earned him an appointment as military governor of Santiago de Cuba. Finally, with Roosevelt's help—and over the protestations of many competitors—Secretary of State Elihu Root appointed Wood military governor of Cuba in 1899, a position Wood kept until 1902, when Cuba became formally independent.[20] In Cuba, Wood mastered the skills of a colonial administrator, abilities that he would later apply to his governance of the Moro Province. Root and Roosevelt believed that Wood's varied experiences and training had prepared him to work among the Moros. Following Roosevelt's strong recommendation, Wood was promoted to major general, and Taft appointed him both military governor of the Moro Province and commander of the Department of Mindanao.

On his way to the Philippines in the spring of 1903, Wood prepared himself for his appointment by touring the major colonial possessions of other imperial powers. Wood's aide in Cuba, Lieutenant Frank McCoy, and another acolyte, Major Hugh Lennox Scott, joined him. Both men would

FIGURE 8. His friendship with Theodore Roosevelt served to advance Leonard Wood's professional career. The two would remain close friends throughout their lives. Pictured here in 1920. (Library of Congress)

eventually assume important positions in the Moro Province. On their way to visit European colonial outposts, the men stopped in Istanbul. For three men who were undoubtedly already steeped in American beliefs about the decadence of Ottoman Muslim rule, the visit left a strong impression. McCoy expressed his enmity for Muslims, who had "burst into this beautiful city, burning, destroying, and killing everything that was good, and it looks as though they've been camping out on the ruins ever since."[21] In an ominous sign of his future dealings with Muslims, he wrote his family, "I believe in the crusades, and feel like joining one myself against the Turk and his dogs."[22] Wood expressed a similar sentiment: "One thing impressed me above all others, and that is that the Turks have done nothing here since they captured the city. Everything has been standing still or drifting backward."[23] With such attitudes firmly entrenched, Wood and his fellow military officers headed to Egypt, where they had arranged to meet with the de facto British colonial ruler of Egypt, Evelyn Baring, the first Earl of Cromer.

Wood's visit with Cromer was long in the making. President Roosevelt had asked Cromer to come to the United States in 1902, seeking advice from him presumably about colonial issues. Cromer had responded that his colonial responsibilities prevented him from obliging the president. He nonetheless expressed the hope that Wood might be convinced to visit him, noting that he had great interest in and admiration for Wood's achievements in Cuba.[24] Roosevelt responded that he had assigned Wood "to take charge of Mindanao and its Moro problems" and that he expected Wood would stop off to see him on his way to the Philippines.[25] Four months later, the wishes of both men were fulfilled. If British colonial officers could not travel to the United States to offer their advice, American colonial officers would travel to them.

When the group arrived in Cairo, Cromer invited Wood to tour the city and meet with other British colonial officers. Wood also visited souks and spent time among the "dirt and many bad odors" emanating from the "large crowds of typical Egyptians."[26] Escaping the Egyptian street to more "civilized" occupations, Cromer invited Wood to attend a game of polo. After meeting Egyptian officers, Wood commented, "Here, as in India, the Englishmen have evidently found it necessary to retain the Egyptian in subordinate command, as a good many of them went wrong in the Arabi Pasha Affair."[27] This uprising in September 1882, almost twenty years earlier, had left an impression. It had been led by a native Egyptian, Arabi Pasha, who had attempted to usurp the current leader and regain control of Egypt by curbing French and British influence. The British had succeeded in defeating his army and capturing him. The revolt provided a convenient excuse for the British to make Egypt a de facto colony. The revolt nonetheless demonstrated the unrest caused by European imperial expansion and was obviously present in Wood's mind as he was about to embark on his own colonial adventure.

During his visit, Wood had the opportunity to speak with Cromer at length. Over several dinners, the two exchanged ideas about the necessity of imposing colonial rule to advance uncivilized populations. Wood recalled, "He said very frankly that if he and his associates withdrew he would expect an immediate retrograde movement toward old conditions; in other words, that they have not yet leavened the whole mass."[28] Indeed, Cromer believed that Egyptian Muslims would not be able to rule effectively until they had given up their religion. Echoing American imperial categorizations of Filipinos according to their religious beliefs,

Cromer would later maintain in his writings that Egyptians could be "classified as Moslems and Christians, a distinction which, being converted from terms of religious belief into those of political and social life, would differentiate the ignorant, conservative mass from the more subtle, more superficially intellectual."[29] The Islamic faith, exacerbated by local religious rulers, limited all progress, for a British colonial official "could not make the Egyptian horse drink of the waters of civilization, albeit the most limpid streams of social and juridical reform . . . if the Mufti condemned the act of drinking as impious."[30]

Much like in the United States, Cromer's beliefs about racial difference also played an important role in his analysis. In contrast to Muslims, Egyptian Christians (Copts) were not held back by their religious beliefs, he maintained, but instead by their racial identity and their unfortunate proximity to Muslims. There was a "notable difference between the stagnation of the Moslem and that of the Copt," Cromer maintained, for the lack of progress of Muslims resulted from their Islamic faith. For a Muslim, he noted: "customs which are interwoven with his religion, forbid him to change." Citing a British text on Islam, he explained, "Swathed in the bands of the Koran, the Moslem faith, unlike the Christian, is powerless to adapt itself to varying time and place, keep pace with the march of humanity, direct and purify the social life, or elevate mankind." In contrast, the Egyptian Christian had failed to progress "because he is an Oriental, and because his religion, which admits of progress, has been surrounded by associations antagonistic to progress."[31] Both religion and race, then, doomed all Egyptians.

Cromer's strong views about the inherent inadequacies of "Orientals" surely influenced Wood and his sense of the task before him. Wood drew inspiration from other European sources as well. He and the other officers left Egypt for India, where they met with other British colonial officers. Their experience in India reinforced the officers' strong associations between progress and Christianity. As McCoy noted, the British had done great work there as well, but he concluded that where the British flag waves there could be found "good government of a kind, but it only goes so far. The work of the missionary is the rest."[32] Wood, McCoy, Scott, and other American colonial officials would later encourage missionaries to work among the Moros.

The party then traveled to Java, in the Netherlands East Indies, to inspect Dutch colonial methods. McCoy noted that the most important feature of Dutch colonial administration was the idea that "the natives are the simplest of children."[33] Wood supplemented the advice and knowledge he gained from British and Dutch officers with numerous written studies. Before and during his trip, he collected hundreds of volumes on colonial administration, Islam, and the Philippines. As one friend recounted, examining the bookshelves that covered three walls of his office in Manila: "It is a fine collection. When do you expect to find time to read them?" Wood answered, "Read them? I've already read every line in every one of them. They've helped me a lot."[34] Armed with all of this information, Wood arrived in the Philippines prepared to govern with a firm hand.

Wood's perceptions about the appropriate manner of dealing with Muslim subjects were reinforced in his meetings with Governor Taft and, more important, with General Davis, whom he consulted immediately after his arrival in July 1903. These conversations further solidified his view that military force was necessary in dealing with the Moros. He soon transformed these theories into action. According to Wood, they had to begin with the "the boiling point of trouble," the rebellious Moros living in the area of Jolo on the island of Sulu.[35] As he wrote in a private letter to Roosevelt just a few weeks after his arrival, "[W]e shall have one sharp brush with the Jolo Moros, and this, I think, you can expect with reasonable promptness."[36] Wood was confident that if Americans delivered a brute message to these Moros early on, they would quickly understand who was in charge, hopefully conveying a wider message to all Filipino Muslims.

Wood assigned his trusted subordinate, Scott, to govern over the island of Sulu. He believed that Scott's "long experience with Indians has particularly fitted him for dealing with these irascible and excitable people."[37] According to Wood's understanding, Moros, like Native Americans, behaved in a typically irrational and impulsive fashion. Scott's initial perceptions perfectly matched Wood's own ideas, making him an ideal right-hand man. As Scott later recollected in his memoirs, the Spanish success in preventing the spread of Islam throughout the Philippines was to be commended, given that the Moros were "fanatical followers of the Prophet Mohammed . . . accustomed to battle and bloodshed from their earliest youth."[38] Those Filipinos who had converted to Catholicism were "one hundred years ahead of their neighbors."[39]

Although confident in Scott's ability to deal with the Moro problem in Jolo, Wood expected that American forces would quickly have the opportunity to demonstrate their force, and he wanted to be there to play a part in the action. Wood left shortly after Scott to visit Jolo and help him to enforce American rule. Immediately after his arrival, Wood addressed local Moro leaders and announced that he was both the military commander and the governor of the Moro Province and, as such, he would be responsible for devising new legal regulations. Although he expressed a wish to be informed as much as possible about their local customs, the Moros would have to accept some "disagreeable" regulations.[40] He also warned local rulers that "any resistance to the United States is simply suicide. . . . We don't want to come in here and have to kill people" as they had been forced to do in other Moro areas, but they would nonetheless "insist upon good order."[41]

Believing he had made his message clear, Wood set upon intimidating the sultan of Sulu himself. Since showing American physical supremacy was paramount, he assembled a group of "five companies of Infantry, two troops Cavalry and a section of a mountain gun battery, (two guns) in all 486 men and officers."[42] When he arrived, the sultan was absent, so Wood met with his brother, Raja Muda. As he wrote to Governor Taft and President Roosevelt, his visit convinced him that the sultan had "no real power to make an agreement nor force to carry it out" and that the United States should therefore abrogate the Bates Treaty. He had not met the sultan, but he nonetheless felt confident to assume that the leader was "degenerate, dishonest, tricky, dissipated, and absolutely devoid of principle. He has not maintained the semblance of a Government, nor could I find that he has observed, in good faith, the terms of the so called Bates treaty."[43] In a private letter to Roosevelt, he further emphasized that the sultan was a "run down, tricky little Oriental degenerate, with half a dozen wives and no children, a state of affairs of which I am sure you thoroughly disapprove!"[44] Wood recommended that the United States take over the rule of all of Sulu: "What is needed is the establishment immediately, of such simple and rather patriarchal government, as will adapt itself to their present condition."[45]

Echoing Davis's earlier recommendations, Wood's perception that Islamic rule was by nature despotic and intolerant led him to also maintain that such despotism, although undesirable in Muslims, might be ideal if adopted by American rulers. Given the fanatical faith of the Moros, Wood wrote Taft in early September 1903 that laws based on the Koran were the simplest solution and would provide a base that would be "unquestioned" by them.[46] Of course, Wood ignored the fact that Moros were not governed by religious faith alone. Local tribal affiliations, social rank, and a host of other factors contributed to the individual and community identities of the people. Nonetheless, Wood's perceptions about Islamic despotism elided such subtleties.

Having spent two weeks in Jolo, however, Wood felt he knew enough about the Islamic faith to change his approach into one of religious condescension. Indeed, having studied European and American texts on the Islamic faith, he considered himself an authority on "authentic" Islamic practices. As he wrote to Roosevelt, because Moros had been "largely cut off from their co-religionists" (presumably, those living in Arabia) they had become "retrograde" Muslims.[47] Wood's analysis was undoubtedly grounded in the perception that Muslims were identical the world over. This assumption neglected the complex and syncretic practices of the Islamic faith throughout the Islamic world. Ironically, Wood's belief that Muslims were incapable of change may have also swayed his understanding of the Islamic faith of the Moros, since he deemed as un-Islamic any practices that did not date back to the time of the Prophet Mohammed more than twelve centuries earlier. His understanding depended on an interpretation of Islamic law, practice, and culture that rendered Muslims incapable of change, while identifying those Muslims who did change as inauthentic.

Even the laws that Wood recognized as "authentically" Islamic were so abhorrent to American cultural mores that they could pose a threat to his friend's future political career. He cautioned Roosevelt: "I inclose [sic] a copy of the laws as they exist in Sulu, and I am sure you do not want this sort of thing to exist. I cannot imagine a more ugly campaign document to get into the circulation at a critical time like this."[48] Not content to limit these attacks to private correspondence with the president, Wood reinforced this point in his annual report to the Philippine Commission, castigating the Moros as "religious and moral degenerates."[49] No Islamic laws were worth maintaining, since none could rival the "humane, decent and civilized laws" of civilized societies.[50] Wood's solution, therefore, was to use laws that had already been established by the Philippine Commission. To be clear, he was not advocating integration of the Moros into the rest of the Philippines nor their equality with Christian Filipinos. He simply did not believe that Moros deserved special recognition for their defective Muslim practices. Nonetheless, he would continue to justify his brutal military techniques based on the alleged religious fanaticism of the Moros.

The religious practices of Muslim Filipinos were not the only problem. After a few months in the islands, Wood concluded that the intransigence of the Moros stemmed, in part, from the laxity of Americans. To correct such an error, only a "heavy hand" would establish a civil code among "these savages" and convince the Moros of the physical, political, and moral superiority of Americans.[51] As he noted in his official report: "Our conciliatory and good-natured policy with them resulted in their conviction that we were both cowardly and weak, and out of this conviction grew an absolute contempt for our authority. Firmness and the prompt application of disciplinary measures will maintain order. Moros for the first time must understand that the United States stands for authority, order, and government."[52]

A crucial part of this necessary demonstration of force included ending slavery, which continued to receive a great deal of public attention back home.[53] Although the Bates Treaty included a provision eliminating the practice, American officials had never enforced it.[54] In September 1903, under Wood's leadership, the Legislative Council of the Moro Province passed a law that officially reasserted slaveholding and slave hunting as crimes punishable by severe fines and imprisonment.

Wood and Governor Taft expected a clash with Moros to erupt when the antislavery legislation became public. Tensions had been mounting between Americans and Moros in Jolo during the summer of 1903, before the law was passed, when twelve slaves had escaped from the powerful Datu Hassan and received protection from American forces. This action had prompted Hassan to attack an American military party in retribution. Such rebellions demonstrated the hostility of Moros to the imposition of American imperial rule and their refusal to accept U.S. laws. Wood understood this fact and sought to counter such resistance with an iron fist. After learning of the attack, he publicized the passage of the new law throughout Moro areas, while simultaneously heading out to teach the rebellious Hassan a lesson.[55] Wood returned to Jolo in December 1903 with 1,200 infantry, cavalry, and artillery soldiers.

Upon his arrival, Wood's group was attacked by a small group of Moros. Wood blamed this outbreak of violence on *juramentados*, a term he defined as religious "fanatics sworn to die killing Christians."[56] Wood had surely read about this in Dean Worcester's study: "A juramentado is a most unpleasant sort of individual to encounter. The Moros believe that one who takes the life of a Christian thereby increases his chance of a good time in the world to come; the more Christians killed, the brighter the prospect for the future, and if one is only fortunate enough to be himself killed while slaughtering the enemies of the faithful, he is at once transported to the seventh heaven."[57]

Like Worcester, many American colonial officials believed that attacks by Moros stemmed from their supposed fanatical religious beliefs. Describing these attacks as expressions of religious fervor, rather than as general resistance to American military rule, reinforced simplistic interpretations of the behavior of Moros as governed solely by their religious faith. Such explanations mirrored those advanced by European colonialists facing anticolonial resistance in other Islamic societies. As the historian Stephan Dale has argued, Europeans often maintained that *juramentado* "attacks sprang solely from Muslim fanaticism and were quite unprovoked by Europeans, overlooking, as usual, more than two centuries of conflict."[58] Clearly, American colonial officials adopted the same interpretation.

A more nuanced analysis of *juramentados* came from Najeeb Saleeby, the Arab Christian who had been assigned as the "expert" on Filipino Muslims because of his Ottoman origins. Although denigrating Moros' religious practices as deficient, he nonetheless maintained that "there has been no greater misunderstanding by Spaniards and Americans on any one subject than on this." Instead of religious fanaticism, it was "fierce patriotism" and resistance to colonial rule that drove Moro violence.[59] Wood had openly admitted that he considered Saleeby to be an "unknown quantity," because he had "a good deal of the Oriental about his way of doing business."[60] For this reason, Saleeby's guidance held little sway, and most military officers and Americans preferred to describe *juramentados* as irrational religious actors—an explanation that refused to interpret Moro actions as driven by more "rational" desires for political independence.

Having quickly stopped the initial attack, Wood moved on to his primary objective: tracking down Hassan. Wood left orders for Scott to catch up. In the following days, American soldiers led by Wood burned Hassan's house, Wood took over his headquarters, and the troops massacred more than 1,000 Moros. As one officer who accompanied Wood on the expedition recalled, American forces were encouraged to engage in a "liberal use of ammunition" on Moro villages, a practice the officer admitted was "to be condemned in warfare with civilized foes" but that brought "very excellent results against Philippine semi-savages."[61] The conduct of American soldiers later prompted a poem written by a Moro who witnessed the massacre of a wedding party by American soldiers:

> The first place the Americans came to was Apute's
> house, where a wedding party was.
> The soldiers fired, nobody could stand against,
> people were killed like a flock of birds . . .
> The wedding took place in Saidul's house, the
> bride-groom was there, he was the guest of honor.
> The soldiers at once went up to them, the people
> were killed and smashed up like dough.[62]

Scott's party eventually captured the Moro leader, but then they lost him in a bold escape that left Scott with bullet wounds on both hands.[63] Again in pursuit, Wood and his troops chased Hassan deep into Moro territory, spreading terror alongside information about the new antislavery law.[64] Although unable to locate Hassan, Wood and his men nevertheless left a brutal impression on the Moros. Wood noted in his diary that they killed between 1,000 and 1,200 men, although in his official account and in his private correspondence with President Roosevelt, he cited only 400.[65] His private correspondence also offered a dismissive and paternalistic view of the mission's high casualty rates: "We had a little affair. . . . Nothing very serious. They have been hunting for a fight for two or three years, and started this trouble by attacking our troops . . . of course they had to be spanked afterwards."[66] A few months later, after he had recovered from his injury, Scott would lead another expedition to track Hassan down. American forces eventually found him and shot him thirty-three times. Scott took Hassan's weapons, a kris (dagger) and barong (sword), as trophies, which he sent to Wood, asking him to keep the kris but send the barong along to President Roosevelt.[67]

Hassan's rebellion provided further justification for abrogating the Bates Treaty. As soon as Wood returned to his headquarters in Zamboanga, he wrote to Roosevelt. Again he altered his telling of the expedition, noting that instead of pursuing the Moros in their homes and villages, U.S. troops had been attacked by an organized force of Moros that numbered "between 2000 and 3000 armed forces." This attack constituted "an act of treachery and rebellion" and "ample proof that the Moro no longer held to the Bates agreement."[68] His recommendations also left little doubt that Moros would continue to suffer violent repression: "We shall probably have to smash a number of these fanatical leaders from time to time, but it can be done without difficulty. . . . The Sultan of Sulu doubtless knew all about their intentions and today probably knows where Hassan is hiding. *There is one thing which is especially satisfactorily [sic] about the whole affair, and it is that the Moros themselves have given us good ground for ending the Bates treaty. There was sufficient before, but this makes more than enough.*"[69] He expressed similar sentiments in a letter to Governor Taft. Wood's arguments were apparently convincing. In March 1904, President Roosevelt officially abrogated the Bates Treaty. The sultan protested, but given recent demonstrations of American military might, he could do little to prevent the Americans from taking greater control.

Meanwhile, in Moro areas that did not fall under the purview of the Bates Treaty, the Legislative Council had passed several acts to revise the political organization of the territory. The district governors divided the Moro Province into several municipalities and "tribal wards." In an effort at demographic engineering based on religious belief, they tried to delimit the areas so that "a single race or homogeneous division thereby shall occupy as nearly as possible the territory."[70] Although using the term "race," religion was in fact how they distinguished natives and established territorial divisions. These new laws placed all Christian Filipinos living in the Moro Province into municipalities, whereas it placed all Muslims and pagans in tribal wards.[71] Echoing earlier practices put in place after the Spooner amendment, such divisions and the attempt to draw boundaries that created homogeneous groups in each category, reflected the belief that Christian Filipinos deserved a government that reflected their civilizational superiority over Moros.

In contrast, the logic fueling the creation of tribal wards for Moros was inherent in the name itself. Since most colonial officials believed that Moros could not immediately assume the political rights granted to Christian Filipinos, Moros and other non-Christians became "wards" of the American colonial state in both senses of the word. Placed into separate "wards," non-Christians were both geographically and politically disassociated from Christian Filipinos. The term "ward" also conveyed the sentiment that these populations necessitated greater paternalism and legal guardianship than did Christian Filipinos.[72] Wood confirmed such views in his "Annual Report of the Moro Province" in 1904. As his report explained, the system was meant as a continuation of "a tribal or paternal form of government" and had the added benefit of "furnishing a means of controlling the uncivilized peoples for whom it is intended."[73] In fact, Americans had succeeded in transferring their understandings of Islamic despotism into their own hands.

Of course, American imperialists had previously applied this ward mentality to other subjects of U.S. imperial rule. The concept itself drew on established legal relationships with Native American nations and American imperial territories as a whole.[74] In a set of rulings between 1901 and 1905, the Supreme Court had determined in the so-called *Insular Cases* that the civilizational and racial inferiority of Filipinos, Puerto Ricans, and other inhabitants of recently acquired American territories meant that they did not deserve the full constitutional rights of American citizens back in the United States.[75] Thus, Moros and other non-Christians in the Philippines, became wards *within* a ward who required even more American tutelage than did Filipino Christians. Neither the abrogation of the Bates Treaty nor this hierarchical system of colonial administration, however, quelled Moro rebellions. For Wood, continued resistance justified ongoing policies of annihilating Moro villages and killing Moros with little care for their guilt or innocence, resulting in thousands of Moro deaths.[76]

In addition to his belief that military violence was necessary to contain Moros' religious fanaticism, Wood may have also felt the need to prove his worth as a military officer.[77] Senate hearings over Wood's promotion to brigadier general in 1901 and, more important, his promotion to major general in early 1904 had proved embarrassing when opponents pointed to his lack of direct military experience. Fighting Moros was one way to advance his military credentials.[78]

Regardless of the rationale, the president wholeheartedly approved of his friend's conduct. In a private letter to Wood, Roosevelt quoted a soldier's letter he had recently received praising Wood's approach to Moros: "Those who have been here any length of time agree that there is only [one] way to civilize these districts containing the bad ones, that is 'clean them out' and then keep after them. However, politics will not permit of this and outrages will continue as long as politics or public feeling at home are allowed to interfere with good Government. There is only one officer in the Philippines who is feared by the bad Moros, and that is General Leonard Wood."[79]

The soldier's letter also confirmed that the casualty rates were much higher than what Wood admitted to in his official reports. Wood had claimed 1,500 Moro losses in one campaign, but a soldier noted that "5000 would come nearer the mark."[80] In another campaign, although Wood claimed that 1,000 Moros had died, the soldier remarked that his friends who had served under Wood during the battle "counted that number after two days' fighting, which was only one-fourth of the time actually fought."[81] The soldier may have been exaggerating, but the fact that he found these high casualties admirable illustrated the extent to which American soldiers and their commanding officers had dehumanized their Moro enemies.

Wood likened these violent tactics to the paternalistic hand of a civilized guardian leading rebellious savages down the proper path. As he wrote in his diary about efforts to dominate Moros in the Lake Lanao region: "The people of this valley have been so hostile and intractable for generations that I have decided to go thoroughly over the whole valley, destroying all warlike supplies, and dispersing and destroying every hostile force, and also to destroy every cota [sic] where there is the slightest resistance. *While these measures may appear harsh it is the kindest thing to do.*"[82]

Just as religion allowed Wood to shape his perception of Moro civilization, it also reinforced his belief in American benevolence. He proudly noted the expedition chaplain's endorsement of his approach during one mission. Wood had succeeded in filling his soldiers with "the crusading spirit and spoke of the troops being in service in a land of infidels where it had been impossible for the Word of God to be preached in times past."[83] With the support of military chaplains and the president himself, Wood felt he had a virtual carte blanche in dealing with the Moros and had little incentive to change his approach.

Emphasizing the obligation to dominate Moros at all costs reinforced American imperial rule in other ways. While accepting the Republican Party nomination for president in 1904, Roosevelt justified the continued U.S. presence in the Philippines, in part, by arguing that the Moros posed a major threat to civilized Christian Filipinos: "To abandon all control over the Moros would amount to releasing these Moros to prey upon the Christian Filipinos, civilized or semi-civilized, as well as upon the commerce of other peoples. . . . To abandon the Moro country, as our opponents propose in their platform, would be precisely as if twenty-five years ago we had withdrawn the army and the civil agents from within and around the Indian reservations in the West, at a time when the Sioux and the Apache were still the terror of our settlers. It would be a criminal absurdity."[84]

By justifying the eradication of Native American "terror" at home, Roosevelt also demonstrated that Americans continued to link their colonial policies with their historical practices of continental empire-building and their perceptions of other non-Christian "savages." Just as this vision of the hierarchy of civilizations justified the continued status of Native Americans as wards of the American government, Moros too had to demonstrate their progress before gaining political and civil rights. For Moros, this progress entailed understanding the legitimate use of violence and force, which in American eyes could be applied only by American forces. Christian Filipinos had unfortunately learned this lesson to gain their limited political rights. As Roosevelt maintained, "The Moros are in large part still in the stage of culture where the occupation of the bandit and the pirate are the most highly regarded; and it has not been found practical to give them self-government in the sense that we have been giving it to the Christian inhabitants."[85]

One of Roosevelt's major political opponents, William Jennings Bryan, reaffirmed American policies that distinguished between Christian and non-Christian Filipinos when he visited the Moro Province in January 1906. Although one of the most well-known anti-imperialists and a strong public supporter of independence for the Philippines, Bryan conceded that Moros were not ready for such a privilege: "The conditions existing . . . are so different from those existing in the northern islands that the two groups must be dealt with separately."[86] Roosevelt, Wood, and Bryan considered the Moros too uncivilized, too violent, and not yet Christian enough for self-government. Thus, Americans had to convince Moros to change against their will.

The Battle of Bud Dajo

Wood's brutal tactics would culminate in the Battle of Bud Dajo, fought in the last months of his tenure as governor of the Moro Province. Although Wood received the powerful endorsement of his friend Roosevelt, American officials in the Philippines had begun to question the efficacy of his tactics. Those who began to question Wood's approach included his former acolyte Scott, who continued to govern Sulu but whose five-year friendship with Wood had begun to fray largely over their differing opinions regarding the Moros.

Tensions between Americans and Moros had continued to mount throughout 1905 and had been exacerbated by a drought and severe storms, which had led to a widespread famine. Despite these hardships, Wood imposed a head tax on the Moros. Scott had pled with Wood to ease up on the Moros and, instead, engage in dialogue and negotiation, but Wood disregarded his advice. Rather, he forced Scott to engage in several deadly battles with local Moros that year. Scott's disagreements with Wood over these tactics led Wood to publicly express his doubt in Scott's leadership. Their disagreement soon went public in American newspapers in Manila, in which Scott was publicly accused of going "native" and betraying his white Anglo-Saxon roots.[87]

By January 1906 several hundred Moros who continued to resist the tax had gathered in a volcanic crater, Bud Dajo, to prepare an armed resistance. Captain Frank Langhorne, a devoted supporter of Wood, wrote to him in mid-February telling him that the Moros had congregated and ominously noting that these Moros "will probably have to be exterminated."[88] On 6 March, Wood arrived with Tasker Bliss, his successor as governor of the Moro Province. The battle began that same day. By the morning of 8 March more than 600 Moro men, women, and children were dead. There were no Moro survivors. Thirty-three American soldiers died in the battle. According to Colonel John R. White, another officer in Sulu, Moro fanaticism made the incident "unavoidable. . . . But, certainly, none of us believed that it would ever be necessary to repeat so severe a lesson."[89] His recollection of the battle concluded with a patronizing view of Moro rebellions: "Poor gallant gentlemen of Sulu, with your brilliant carmine, orange, and green jackets, your tight-fitting trousers, your wavy krises and razor barongs, your turbans and jaunty fezzes, your bastard Mohammed-anism and contempt for the unbeliever, your fairy boats on a fairy sea amid fairy isles . . . I'm afraid that you needed the lesson that even Sulu cour-age and daredeviltry could not prevail against American numbers and science."[90]

White hoped that Moros had finally learned their lesson through the application of "civilized" force. Although Americans could admire and pity Moros for their courage and quaint adherence to things past, White's analysis proudly asserted that resistance to the superiority of American progress and military might was futile. Moros were doomed by their stag-nant and retrograde ways, exemplified by their ignorant practices of Islam and their religious intolerance of "unbelievers."

American newspapers back home covered the conflict extensively, ini-tially describing Wood's actions as a justifiable response to the "fanatical Moros."[91] According to the *New York Observer and Chronicle*, the battle had offered "one of the most picturesque and thrilling fights that has taken place recently in the Philippines . . . it was a piece of slaughter demanded by the stern exigencies of government."[92] Picking up on military officers' justifications, journalists consistently pointed to the religious identity of the Moros to explain the casualties. The *New York Times*, under the sub-heading "MOROS RELIGIOUS FANATICS," quoted Ohio Republican congressman Nicolas Longworth, who had visited Jolo six months earlier: Moros were "entirely uncivilized, being Mohammedans and religious fa-natics of the most pronounced type. They have no military organization and their fights are all inspired by religious beliefs."[93] On 11 March, three days after the battle, President Roosevelt sent a cablegram to con-gratulate Wood and the officers under his command for their "brilliant feat of arms wherein you and they so well upheld the honor of the American flag."[94] His praise was republished throughout major Ameri-can newspapers.

As more information came out about the deadly battle, however, some Americans began to question the legitimacy of Wood's military tactics. The occasion also provided an opportunity for anti-imperialists to reassert their objections to annexation. Moorfield Storey, president of the Anti-Imperialist League, wrote an open letter attacking Wood's actions and comparing them to European and Ottoman acts of imperial repression that had horrified the American public: "Suppose we had heard that the

British had dealt thus with a Boer force, that the Turks had so attacked and slaughtered Armenians, that colored men had so massacred white men, or even that 600 song birds had been slaughtered for their plumage, would not our papers have been filled with protests and expressions of horror?"[95] In addition to the unflattering comparison of American tactics to the abhorrent practices of Turkish Muslims, Storey also pointed to the domestic roots of such brutality and racism, arguing that the "spirit which slaughters brown men in Jolo is the spirit which lynches black men in the South."[96]

A few days after the initial reports, the press revealed that scores of women and children had been killed. Hundreds of articles followed in major newspapers and journals. The *Washington Post* published a story entitled "NO MORO SURVIVED: Battle on Mount Dajo Was One of Extermination—Criticism of Gen. Wood—Siege of Crater, It Is Declared, Would Have Forced Surrender."[97] Another story two days later concluded that "there cannot very well have been much heroism in an encounter which resulted in the total obliteration of one of the parties while the other party incurred no losses worth mentioning." Like Storey, the newspaper compared American actions to the worst of British imperialism, which had included "massacres of helpless half-armed savages in Asia, Africa and elsewhere."[98] Such violent demonstrations of American power had destroyed the professed benevolent exceptionalism that defined American imperialism; rather, the paper depicted the United States as the British Empire's "faithful if not abject imitator."[99] These public critiques of Wood's behavior provided evidence that proponents of American imperial rule, with their narrative of American progress in the Philippines, did not completely dominate the public discourse.

In response to these critiques, military leaders tried to justify the conflict by again blaming the Moros' fanatical Islamic faith. The *New York Times*, in their ominously entitled article "Moros a Turbulent Race" cited analysis by General Henry Corbin, commander of the Division of the Philippines, who emphasized that Moros could not be compared to Filipino Christians for their only allegiance was to their religious faith: "The Moros are religious fanatics, and are not amenable to the influences of other peoples."[100] Neither did the event reflect on the larger American imperial project in the Philippines, for the religious fanaticism of the Moros represented an aberration not present among Filipino Christians.

On 13 March, Wood responded to this public criticism in a *Washington Post* article. In it, he offered contradictory explanations: he stated that the religious frenzy of mothers led them to use their children as shields, but he also stated that the women had dressed as men and thus confused the soldiers.[101] He used these gender transgressions to justify the killing, claiming that American military forces had always strived to maintain civilized decorum: "Neither in this nor any fight has an American soldier killed a woman or child except in a close action when it was impossible to distinguish sex."[102] Elsewhere, Wood deliberately misled the press. Although Scott had pleaded with Wood to negotiate with the Moros rather than use brute force, Wood claimed that, in fact, Scott had recommended the use of force and that he decided to attack only after receiving this advice and personally assessing the situation. In fact, Wood had ordered troops to the area three days before arriving and had refused to consider any other options.[103]

Despite his private disagreements with Wood, Scott publicly defended his actions. He filed a report for Taft, who was then secretary of war. Scott disingenuously argued that Wood had been a humanitarian in his conduct since his arrival and stunningly noted that "no one would take more trouble to avoid unnecessary bloodshed than he."[104] Of course, Scott's story contradicted his personal knowledge of Wood's tactics and his own attempts to mitigate his use of violence.[105] Scott's motive in defending Wood undoubtedly stemmed from a combination of military loyalty and Scott's own self-protection. He had left his position in the Philippines a few months earlier and knew that a public betrayal would have damned his future prospects. The report was subsequently released to the press to buttress the administration's defense of Wood's actions. Scott's loyalty would not go unrewarded. In later years, Wood pushed, albeit unsuccessfully, to secure Scott's promotion to governor of the Moro Province.

Wood received high-level support from other notables. In his official letter to Roosevelt, Taft offered his support for Wood's actions and corroborated his explanations, also laying the blame for the massacre on the religious fanaticism of the Moros. He argued that Moros "exhibited . . . the well-known treachery of the uncivilized Mohammedan when wounded, of attempting to kill those approaching for the purpose of giving aid and relief."[106] Of course, given that Wood's party was determined to "exterminate" these rebellious Moros, it is doubtful that any American soldiers offered the Moros "aid and relief."

Nevertheless, public critiques continued, and Wood scrambled to concoct stronger defenses. Wood convinced the governor general of the Philippines, Henry Ide, to alter the narrative explaining the deaths of women and children.[107] Instead of justifying the deaths by arguing that women were dressed as men and using their children as shields, Wood in his new explanation argued that "newspaper reports announcing wanton slaughter [of] women and children" were "extremely sensational" and the few that were killed died as a result of "preliminary shelling at a distance."[108] This account directly contradicted his previous claim that Moro women and children had been killed "in close action when it was impossible to distinguish sex."[109]

Democrats in Congress, who were sympathetic to the anti-imperialism movement, found these explanations insufficient. They continued to attack Wood and to criticize Roosevelt for excusing such conduct. William Jones, a Democratic congressman from Virginia, publicly doubted Wood's claim that Moro women used their own babies as shields. The *New York Times* published Jones's descriptions of the killings as "murder," "massacre," and "assassination." Although Jones made "allowances for the intimate personal relations between Theodore Roosevelt and Leonard Wood," he could not "understand how the President can approve this horrible massacre."[110] Democratic representative from Mississippi John Sharpe Williams read out a poem on the subject on the floor of the House. The fifty-plus lines of verse told a sad and sobering story of the massacre:

> "Forward the Wood Brigade!"
> Is there a man afraid?
> Not thou' a soldier knew
> Heathen had blundered.
> Savages can't reply,
> Heathen can't reason why
> Women and children die,
> Forced in the crater of death,
> Forced with six hundred;
>
> Cannon to right of them,
> Cannon to left of them,
> Volleyed and thundered,
> Stormed at with shot and shell.
> In the jaws of death
> Into the mouth of Hell:
> All told, six hundred.[111]

Williams's poem condemned Wood's behavior not only because he had used excessive force, but also because a civilized and superior power had used such force against childlike "heathens," whose lack of civilization and ignorance had pushed them into such desperate circumstances.

Despite the public uproar, President Roosevelt cabled Taft that he found Wood's explanation "entirely satisfactory."[112] Other newspapers also supported the officers and vehemently defended Wood's actions. The *Christian Observer* published a supportive letter, written by a soldier, which the journal hoped would "put a stop to further carping by misinformed persons." According to the soldier, Moros were "barbarians" and "Mohammedans of the most intense sort." Instead of a battle waged to assert their territorial rights in the face of American imperial rule or their refusal to pay taxes during a time of economic hardship to a government that granted them no political representation, the soldier maintained that Moros were fighting Americans as "they would fight any race or set of men, for they are fighting for their religion, and we happen to be in their way." Clearly, the concept of "no taxation without representation" did not apply to Moros. The soldier echoed Corbin's earlier analysis that Moros would never accept outside influence and concluded with an ominous warning about the only true solution to the Moro problem: "They are never conquered until dead." This draconian plan was fit for all Moros, regardless of sex, for "the women look upon Christians the same as the men."[113]

The *Los Angeles Times* echoed this sentiment in its "Pen Points" segment, which was designed to offer short, humorous commentaries on recent events: "[T]he Moro seems to be not unlike the Apache. He will not be good until he is dead," and "Now that we have taken up the brown man's burden we can't drop it just because it smears our hands with a little blood."[114] Similarly, *Life* magazine printed a caricature of four Moro heads on a stick, both men's and women's, next to an article defending Wood's actions (see figure 9).[115] The author compared Wood's actions to a similar "rat-killing," experience on the home front: "In our Indian wars . . . it was sometimes necessary to exterminate a band of Indians, as the band of Moros was exterminated."[116] A political cartoon in the *New York Times* published the same month offered a more critical analysis. Under the label "Benevolent Assimilation," it showed Uncle Sam wearing a soldier's hat and poking the "the last of the Moros" with his bayonet, as the Moro screamed "Yankee Doodle!" The Moro followed a despondent and weary-looking Native American wearing an Uncle Sam hat and holding an American flag, who looked back on the scene, seemingly recognizing his own experience (see figure 10). The *Chicago Tribune* also offered an implicit critique of American actions by publishing a political cartoon showing military officers standing next to the American flag on top of a hill. Beneath them lay rows of Moro graves. The caption read, "The only Moros from whom we may expect no uprising" (see figure 11).[117]

FIGURE 9. This political cartoon in *Life* (magazine) depicting four Moro heads on a stick was printed alongside an article defending Wood's actions. (29 March 1906, 380)

FIGURE 10. In this cartoon, Moros were represented alongside other victims of American Empire, namely, Native Americans. Neither seems happy with American plans for "Benevolent Assimilation." (*New York Times*, 18 March 1906, Proquest Historical Newspapers)

The controversy over the Battle of Bud Dajo would linger in the American press, albeit with few consequences for Wood or the other officers. In January 1907, a grisly photograph emerged in the *Philadelphia Weekly Democrat*, a newspaper edited by a member of the Anti-Imperialist League. The picture showed American soldiers standing next to piles of dead Moro bodies, including a Moro woman. According to the article, when the photographer on location showed Wood the glass plate of the photograph, he "accidentally" dropped it and then gave the photographer

THE ONLY MOROS FROM WHOM WE MAY EXPECT NO UPRISING.

FIGURE 11. Again, harkening back to American policies toward Native Americans, this political cartoon implied grimly that the only "good" Moro was a dead one. (*Chicago Daily Tribune*, 10 March 1906, Proquest Historical Newspapers)

money to excuse his "mistake."[118] The original picture shows the mark in the center where the photographer patched the two pieces together (see figure 12).[119]

Although Americans continued to maintain the exceptional status of their empire, in private, they also sympathized with other powers that faced similar critiques of excessive imperial violence. Only a few weeks before the Battle of Bud Dajo, President Roosevelt and Secretary of State Root had faced pressure by American activists and religious groups regarding the brutal treatment of Congolese colonial subjects at the hands of Belgians. The Congo was then ruled through private ownership by the Belgian king, Leopold II. Leopold's imperial practices had been so brutal

FIGURE 12. This gruesome picture of American soldiers posing next to the bodies of dead Moros on the site of the Battle of Bud Dajo appeared in one newspaper in January 1907, with little public response. (Personal Papers of John R. White, University of Oregon)

that some scholars estimate the loss of life during his rule at around 10 million Congolese.[120] Forced to react, Root maintained that ruling an empire sometimes required such violent methods, and he compared the situation in the Congo directly to American rule in the Philippines. A letter he wrote to a congressman only two weeks before the Battle of Bud Dajo offered an ominous forecast for his own government's endorsement of imperial repression: "If the United States had happened to possess in Darkest Africa a territory seven times as large and four times as populous as the Philippines, we, too, might find good government difficult and come in for our share of just or unjust criticism."[121] The fact that Root chose not to address whether the criticism was or was not "just" implicitly revealed his belief that such imperial violence was, in some cases, necessary.

Wood obviously felt the same way but was nonetheless aware of the possible political damage of such negative publicity, both for himself and for the president. Throughout his rule, he shielded his exploits, particularly from journalists. Major General Robert Bullard, district governor of

Lanao, recounted an exchange he had with Wood: "'Any newspaper correspondents up there?' came a message from [Wood] to me in the Moro country at a time when I know he had received general instructions coming from political Washington to have no fighting. 'No,' I answered. In a few days he was there conducting a punitive expedition against rebellious, marauding Moros who could be handled in no other way."[122]

Such examples of military deception were not limited to hiding his actions from journalists. According to Bullard, Wood "did not hesitate to go counter to the orders of the President of the United States if conditions of which the President was ignorant required it. He was right."[123] Indeed, despite Bud Dajo, other massacres elided the scrutiny of the American public. In the end, however, nothing came of the criticism of Wood's massacre at Bud Dajo. A few days after the battle, Wood traveled to Manila to assume his duties as commander of the Philippines Division, becoming the highest ranking military officer in the Philippines.

Soldiers of Christ: American Missionaries in the Moro Province

As the Battle of Bud Dajo had tellingly revealed, many Americans continued to believe that the Islamic faith of the Moros constituted a dire obstacle in American colonial rule. For this reason, in addition to military responses, and with the encouragement of the U.S. government, the nation's religious organizations immediately put in motion efforts to send missionaries to the Philippines.[124] As the journal *Independent* wrote in 1898, "Probably not a person directly interested in mission work has failed to recognize here an opportunity for the American churches second to none that has ever been offered."[125]

As discussed in the last chapter, secular support for extending Christianity to the Philippines had begun even before annexation, when American political and colonial elites praised the success of Spanish Jesuits in spreading Catholicism to the Philippines. Although many American Protestants viewed the Catholic faith with suspicion or outright hostility, the propagation of Roman Catholicism in the islands was often cast in a positive light. In a February 1897 article in the *North American Review*, John Barrett, the American minister to Siam, praised the ecclesiastical influence of the Spanish in the Philippines. Conceding that Catholicism was not the ideal religion, particularly given its historic ties to government, he nonetheless maintained that blending church and state in the Philippines seemed a necessary evil to prevent insurrection: "If there is evil in this ecclesiastical sway it is assuredly more than counterbalanced by the good it accomplishes for the natives or common people."[126] He also maintained that the work of the Jesuits served to engender hope for the extension of Protestant Christianity by missionaries to all parts of the Philippines, having "demonstrated that missionary work can succeed among Asiatics."[127] Like many missionaries and colonial officials, Barrett firmly believed that religious and imperial forces could and should work in tandem in these new territories.[128] Wood also expressed his support for American missionary work in the islands even before he arrived in the Philippines, identifying a direct link between Christianizing Filipinos and pacifying them; priests, he wrote in his diary, "would have a dominant influence over the people and nip incipient rebellion in the bud."[129]

Soldiers also straddled the line between military duty and missionary work. After serving as a soldier in Mindanao and Sulu beginning in 1899, Reverend John McKee became one of the first missionaries in Mindanao in April 1902. McKee had long desired to conduct missionary work and to be "sent to the heathen, and the Philippines were given as an almost immediate answer."[130] According to McKee, during his military service he had knelt after a great battle and renewed his "vow of lifelong service to my blessed Savior." Like many American soldiers, McKee believed that force and religion went hand in hand: "Our God can open doors without any help from a carnal army; but if He chooses to use the forces of this world to loose the shackles of age-long superstition from a downtrodden people, as He did use the American troops in these islands, it is no lack of faith to enter with them into the possession of the promised prize."[131]

McKee saw his service as a soldier and his service as a missionary as mutually supportive. Despite his awareness that the Bates Treaty formally prohibited him from proselytizing among the Moros, McKee nonetheless did his best to spread his faith to these people. Explaining his decision to ignore official protocol, he noted: "God has laughed at such diplomacy: for He has most blessedly flung wide open the door of opportunity to these Mohammedan hearts."[132]

McKee was not the only soldier who merged his religious faith with his military service. As was customary, Christian chaplains accompanied American troops in the Philippines. Among them, Chaplain Cephas C. Bateman served as an intelligence officer under Wood in the 28th Infantry from 1902 to 1903. Bateman had studied the Moros during his service, and he published many of his observations in both military and civilian journals. In his article, "Military Taming of the Moro," written for the *Journal of the Military Service Institution of the United States* in 1904, Bateman supported the continuation of military rule in Moro areas. He maintained that the "military instinct dominates the Moro" and cautioned his readers against trying to understand Moros through "inflexible Occidental standards of motives and morals" because "Moros reverse everything." Comparing Moros to Arab Muslims in other parts of the world, he noted that they "venerate the past and their folklore; myths and legends abound in tales not unlike those of the 'Arabian Nights Entertainment.'"[133]

Bateman also wrote for the popular and religious presses. Trying to explain to his American audience how Moros functioned, he endorsed Wood's practice of using violence to communicate with Moros. In an article for the Baptist magazine *Standard*, he professed that Wood had forced the sultan of Sulu to realize that "Moros must change their methods or disappear from the world." Equating American battles with divine rule, Bateman noted that teaching Moro chiefs a lesson has to be repeated again and again "before the 'will of God' can be perfectly understood."[134] Instruction was always backed by force. Further defending Wood's treatment of the Sulu Moros, Bateman maintained: "A knife is needed when the hour of maturity arrives. General Wood had the courage to do what was demanded by the necessities of the case. For my part, I indorse [*sic*] the heroic treatment."[135] Moros were crooks by nature and by faith, but race also played an important role: "Every Moro leader who has been largely helpful to Spaniards or Americans is a mixed breed and not a pure Malay."[136]

American missionaries who were not officially tied to the American government also worked closely with colonial leaders. Charles Brent, one of the most important missionaries working among Moros in the Philippines in the first twenty years of American rule, nurtured close ties with American government officials throughout his time there. The Episcopalian General Convention elected Brent bishop of the Philippines in 1901. As he prepared to leave for the Philippines, he traveled around the United States raising money for his work; in Washington, D.C., he met with President Roosevelt, Governor Taft, and members of Congress responsible for the Philippines. On his way to the islands, Brent traveled on the same boat as Taft.[137] During their trip, the two discussed the challenges facing the United States in governing the Philippines, and, in doing so, they launched a lifelong friendship. Brent's efforts also received the explicit support of several governors of the Moro Province, including Wood and John Pershing, both of whom would become members of his congregation in the Philippines.[138] After arriving in the Philippines, Brent would also socialize regularly with Wood, becoming his confidante and friend. He often accompanied Wood on his military expeditions in the Moro Province, where the two talked at length about the best policies for dealing with the Moros.[139] Wood felt close enough to Brent that he was willing to confide in him in a 1904 letter that he found his work among the Moros tedious. He confessed that it was "pretty unsatisfactory to have to shoot up a lot of savages."[140]

Brent's relationship with the American government in the Philippines would involve more than just close friendships with officials. In 1903, Taft appointed Brent to a government committee investigating opium in the islands. Brent, confident in the link between secular work and sacred work, no doubt saw little conflict of interest. As he wrote in his diary in 1904, "If one could only make that clear—the sacred character of the nation *as a nation*, not because the Church says so, not because the church is in the nation, but because *the nation is a divine creation*."[141] Religion and nation were intricately linked; indeed, the nation itself, he maintained, was God's creation. Such beliefs served to infuse the American imperial project in the Philippines with even greater religious meaning. American government officials agreed. President Roosevelt wrote Brent in 1904, thanking him for his upcoming service in the Philippines and letting him know, "My troubles about the Islands will be small if there are only enough Americans of your stamp to go there as officials, as laymen, and as clergymen."[142]

When Brent began his work among the Moros in 1904, he believed that medical missions, which might "soften" their attitudes toward Christianity, made a good start.[143] To facilitate this project, he created a committee in the United States responsible for raising additional money for his endeavors. Members included banker J. Pierpont Morgan, Senator Marcus Hanna, and other important financiers and political elites. A promotional pamphlet dedicated to his cause outlined the responsibilities of the Church to the nation: "The moment is ripe for action, and delay would mean the loss of an opportunity for the American nation to render an unprecedented service to Christianity, and for the Church to serve the nation."[144]

Just as Wood had done before him, Brent also sought advice from European colonialists familiar with governing Muslims. Lord Cromer, once again, was an obvious source of information. When Brent met with him in Egypt, Cromer repeated a conclusion he had previously delivered to Wood: Egyptians would never be capable of self-governance. After the meeting, Brent conceded that Cromer might be right.[145] Cromer also warned Brent of the difficulties of converting Muslims. Brent listened to Cromer's advice, but he maintained his optimistic resolve, noting: "If, some day, we are to redeem these fanatics," it would be achieved only by "gentle Christians living in contact with Moslem life."[146] Nonetheless, Brent's meeting with Cromer convinced him that Americans could learn a great deal from studying British methods.

Throughout his twelve years of service in the Philippines, Brent continued to raise financial support in the United States for missionary work among the Moros. With these funds, he created a host of institutions, including a hospital, an agricultural school for Moro boys, and a Moro Press. Brent also worked alongside the U.S. government in creating a Moro Exchange, where Moros could market their products. His work received enthusiastic coverage in American newspapers, which extended beyond praising his spread of Christian values to include the alleged benefits he brought to Moros by inculcating in them the use of America's household products. According to one journalist, the bishop had done great work, "For instance in one section families who were dwelling in tree tops two years ago now have comfortable homes in decent villages, and are cutting their grass with American lawn mowers."[147] Instilling Moros with Christian values apparently included using household goods, such as lawn mowers.

To continue funding such projects, Brent created a foundation in 1913 called The Uplifting of the Wards of the Nation. It garnered the official support of William Howard Taft and his wife Helen Herron Taft, Leonard Wood, Admiral George Dewey, Josiah Strong, and Chairman of the International YMCA, John Mott, among others. Such elites recognized that Brent's efforts in bringing Christianity to the area played an important part in eradicating the Moro problem. As Pershing wrote Brent in 1913, "Mohammedanism has been the cause of our trouble in the southern islands. Instead of encouraging Mohammedanism we should discourage it in every way."[148] Brent succeeded in convincing both Wood and Pershing to give fund-raising speeches on behalf of his work.[149]

One of Brent's most high-profile religious supporters was the famous clergyman and supporter of American Empire, Josiah Strong. As previously mentioned in the introduction, to help Brent raise additional funds, Strong published a pamphlet, entitled "A Door into the Mohammedan World," in which he maintained that Brent's work among the Moros constituted only one step in larger efforts to Christianize Muslims around the world (see figure 13). In the pamphlet, Strong concluded that if Brent was able to open the elusive "door to the Mohammedan world" it was worth any sacrifice. Furthermore, such conversion would achieve more in a generation than all past missionary, imperial, military, or diplomatic efforts

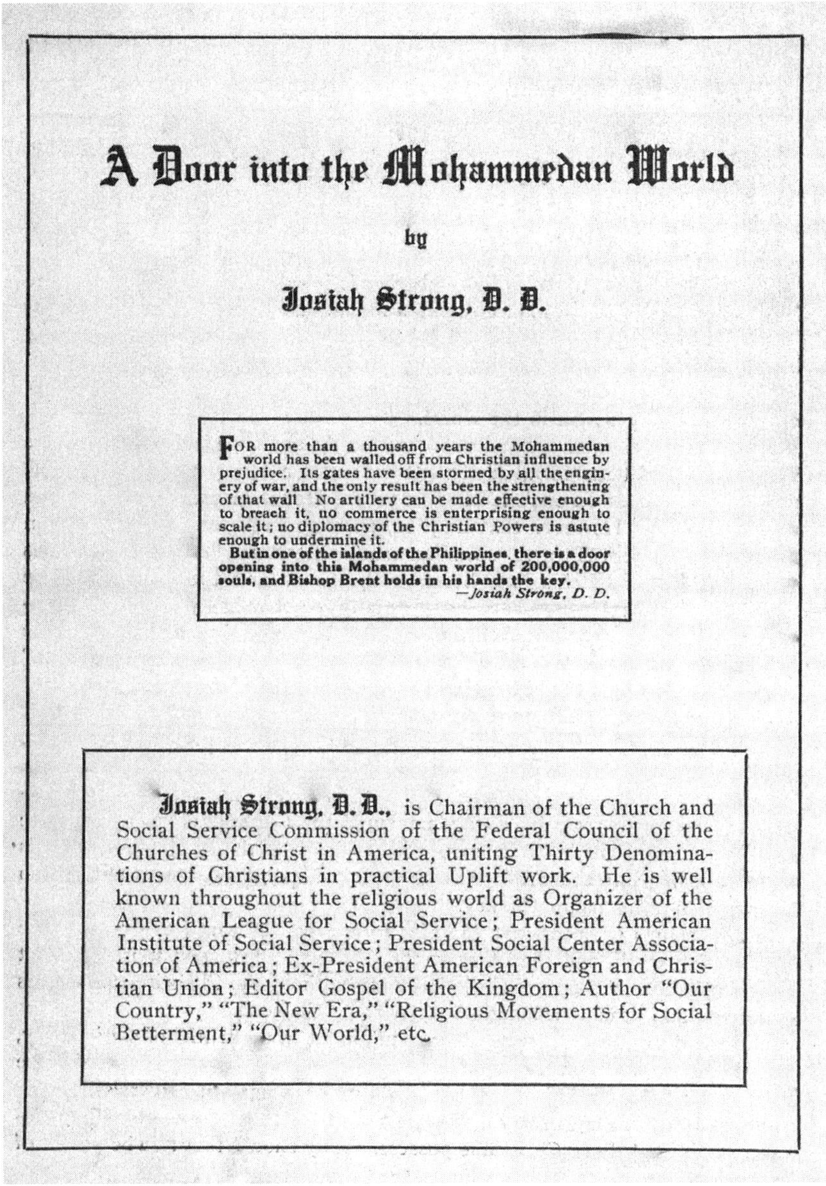

A Door into the Mohammedan World

by

Josiah Strong, D. D.

FOR more than a thousand years the Mohammedan world has been walled off from Christian influence by prejudice. Its gates have been stormed by all the enginery of war, and the only result has been the strengthening of that wall No artillery can be made effective enough to breach it, no commerce is enterprising enough to scale it; no diplomacy of the Christian Powers is astute enough to undermine it.

But in one of the islands of the Philippines there is a door opening into this Mohammedan world of 200,000,000 souls, and Bishop Brent holds in his hands the key.
—*Josiah Strong, D. D.*

Josiah Strong, D. D., is Chairman of the Church and Social Service Commission of the Federal Council of the Churches of Christ in America, uniting Thirty Denominations of Christians in practical Uplift work. He is well known throughout the religious world as Organizer of the American League for Social Service; President American Institute of Social Service; President Social Center Association of America; Ex-President American Foreign and Christian Union; Editor Gospel of the Kingdom; Author "Our Country," "The New Era," "Religious Movements for Social Betterment," "Our World," etc.

FIGURE 13. Josiah Strong published his pamphlet "A Door into the Mohammedan World" to raise funds in support of Brent's missionary work among Filipino Moros. (Yale Special Collections)

combined.[150] Strong's pamphlet reinforced American beliefs about the necessity of converting and civilizing Muslims no matter where they lived; Brent's work, in conjunction with the American imperial project, marked a first crucial step in a larger global process.

Brent strongly believed in his mission to spread American civilization and Christianity to Moros, but, like Wood, he also believed that Filipinos, no matter what their faith, could not attain the degree of civilization necessary for independence in the next few generations. In 1913, when Democrats began lobbying to grant Filipinos their independence, Brent actively opposed them by publishing his views in national newspapers and meeting privately with President Woodrow Wilson and other government officials.[151] Although Brent supported the continuation of American imperial rule over the entire Philippines, he also maintained that Moros, in particular, required prolonged American rule. He was joined by many military rulers and American business interests with a financial stake in maintaining American rule in the islands, particularly in Moro lands. They too maintained that the religious faith of the Moros made the continuation of American imperial rule a necessity. They argued that Moros should never be granted independence and that American rule should become permanent in the Moro Province.

"The Gospel of Work": Business Interests in the Moro Province

American missionaries and colonial officers believed that Christianity served as an ideal tool for civilizing the Moros. They also maintained that bringing progress to the area included bringing development through commerce and industry. As Cromer had advised Wood on his trip to Egypt, capitalism was the way to pacify Muslims: "One thing, I think, is true of all fanatical Mohammedan tribes. The only way you can get them to work with you is to interest them in trade. When you once get them interested in trade they stop going to war."[152] This advice prompted Wood to work alongside Brent in opening the Moro Exchange, whereby Moros could engage in commercial trade.[153]

In his 1904 annual report, Wood also urged the relaxation of legislation that curbed the activities of lumber companies and limited the amount of land open for settlement by non-Filipinos. He argued that the restrictive policies that limited land ownership by outside settlers to forty acres dissuaded "ambitious and industrious" Americans from settling in the "remote East." The government should increase the amount to at least 200 acres. In addition to developing the area, he maintained that encouraging American investments would also alleviate the Moro problem, since what was "needed" was a "suitable class of settlers" who would bring "knowledge of modern agricultural methods, enterprise, and some capital." If American investors were bringing civilized industrial practices to the area it would "stimulate" Moros' "ambition" and "his development would be comparatively rapid."[154] According to Wood, the practices of extending the American continental empire by taking land from the indigenous peoples should be replicated in the Philippines; with an "influx of such people as built up the West . . . the natives would be stimulated by their example and educated by their work and the possibilities of these islands would soon be apparent."[155]

Not surprisingly, American business interests supported this view and quickly began investing in Mindanao. By 1910, there were ninety-seven plantations in the Moro Province—sixty-one of them belonging to Americans and only twelve belonging to Filipino Christians and Muslims.[156] Demonstrating the close ties in the American imperial network, many of these planters were former military men. There were enough Americans living in the Moro Province by 1905 that the community founded the *Mindanao Herald*, a weekly English-language newspaper geared toward American businessmen and military personnel in the area. The newspaper advocated for American businesses, covered governmental policies of interest to agricultural and industrial development, encouraged greater American settlement in the area, and provided editorial support for extending land laws and making the Moro Province a permanent territory of the United States. The newspaper echoed Wood's argument that American commercial development of the area would benefit local Filipinos. According to the *Mindanao Herald*, Americans were in effect bringing civilization to the local population: "Villages have been laid out on these plantations and the wandering, half-savage natives have been brought from the idolatrous paths of their forefathers to learn to labor and to carry on the work that is calculated to change the waste places to well-ordered and profitable plantations."[157] The *Mindanao Herald* praised "businesslike governmental policies . . . which encourage commercial men to do their utmost in building up the community."[158] Government policies, then, should not infringe on such expansive displays of American benevolence.

In line with such self-reverence, the *Mindanao Herald* regularly published stories about successful American businessmen in Mindanao. It also encouraged new endeavors to attract more Americans to the area. One tactic was letting Americans know that Moros were available as a cheap source of labor and had "proved very satisfactory farm hands."[159]

Despite claims that American commercial development was an ideal means by which to bring civilization to native Filipinos, the newspaper implicitly reassured potential investors that providing cheap labor to American plantation owners was the glass ceiling that Moros would reach in their civilizational progress. As one editorial noted, the "Moro province is a white man's country and will remain so."[160]

Articles also reported on official promises to protect American land rights. The paper republished part of a speech that Wood had addressed to President Roosevelt in June 1905, in which he argued that "there is but one way to reclaim this unfortunate country, and this is through the medium of material prosperity, which, after all, is the only civilizer."[161] An editorial the following week pushed for the establishment of a promotion committee to encourage American investments in the province, noting that Mindanao had one-half of the tillable land of the Philippine Islands and that any American citizen could lease up to 2,500 acres at bargain prices.[162] In July, American residents of Zamboanga formed the Moro Plantation and Development Company to further facilitate American development of the area.[163]

Meanwhile, the Zamboanga Chamber of Commerce, an organization dedicated to advancing American business interests, attempted to further protect American investments by officially requesting a separate territorial status for the Moro Province, which would make the area a permanent U.S. territory. An editorial published in the *Mindanao Herald* on 29 July 1905 lent its support to this campaign. It argued that such a move was supported by several factors. First, "Moroland is in no sense a Filipino habitat," by which the editors meant that the area was not historically inhabited by Filipino Christians. Second, the island of Mindanao offered the United States an important asset since it was the only place to "maintain an American colony in a tropical country." Third, the Moro Province was so sparsely settled that the "present law is inapplicable and destructive of the most vital interests of all classes of resident here." Finally, Filipino independence movements in the northern islands threatened the stability of the area. The paper urged the government to "remove the Moro country from the bane of Filipino revolutionary agitation, and give us liberal land and forest laws, and absolutely nothing stands in the way of building up a large American colony in the Island of Mindanao."[164]

The newspaper ramped up its advocacy the following month, ahead of a planned tour of the area by more than fifty American congressmen and military officers, who were to be joined by President Roosevelt's daughter, Alice. A week before their arrival, the *Mindanao Herald* published another editorial advocating that the Moro Province become a permanent American territory.[165] It included statements of support from colonial officials, soldiers, merchants, and plantation owners. It also included a resolution, which was sponsored by the Zamboanga Chamber of Commerce and which called for the creation of an American territory south of the Straits of Surigao, an area that would have encompassed all of Mindanao and Sulu. After a year of relative quiet on the issue—a result of Taft's opposition to their demands—the Zamboanga Chamber of Commerce revived the issue after William Jennings Bryan's visit to the Moro Province. The article supported Bryan's claim, which affirmed the distinction between the North of the Philippines and the Moro-occupied South.[166] Though Bryan and the American businessmen who supported his calls had different agendas, they agreed that the Moro Province differed from other areas of the Philippines and thus required close tutelage by American interests.

Although they did not overtly preach the gospel of Protestant Christianity, American business interests did view their work as related to this divine endeavor. One *Mindanao Herald* editorial, entitled "The Gospel of Work" and published in November 1905, described how American business interests conceived of their role in the Moro Province: "If races have missions on this earth, then it may be said that the mission of the Semitic peoples was to preach the gospel of religion, while the mission of the Aryan peoples was to preach the gospel of work."[167] By demonstrating industrial and agricultural progress to Filipino non-Christians, businessmen maintained that they had brought this "gospel of work" to the Moro Province.

The newspaper also proposed to bring the "gospel of work" to Moros in more forceful ways through laws that resembled laws that had been applied decades earlier to newly freed slaves after the Civil War. The paper maintained that if Moros were unwilling to work on American "plantations," then the U.S. government could impose vagrancy laws, which benefited the "lazy, shiftless, slothful element among the native people," but also "quadruple[d] production in these Islands," and brought "relief" to "those who are more than anxious to employ labor in shop, factory, field and home."[168] Again, Americans could teach Moros by force.

In another move reminiscent of the experience of African Americans under slavery, Colonel Ralph Hoyt, commander of the Department of Mindanao, proposed that the United States separate the Moro Province from the rest of the Philippines and create what he called "The Mindanao Plantation." In his 1909 annual report, Hoyt explained that Moros had "no conception of representative government or the meaning of independence, having no word in their dialect to give it expression."[169] Hoyt believed that northern nationalist movements for independence also gave Moros bad ideas: "The constant agitation for independence, promoted by the Assembly of the northern islands and advertised in the Filipino press, soon reaches the malcontents of the southern group; meetings result; societies are formed, petitions presented, and independence of the Filipinos advocated." Hence, the continuation of a militarized government in which "the Governor controls the armed forces" was "indispensable now . . . and for generations to come."[170]

Hoyt offered other solutions that mirrored American domestic practices, this time reminiscent of the Native American experience. In addition to a civil-military government, which would easily forestall "political agitation for annexation to the northern group," Hoyt proposed that "natives might be assigned to reservations, secured in all their rights, under military policy and protection."[171] The arrangement was ideal; it provided the United States with a supply of cheap labor, encouraged trade, and established "a permanent foothold of absolute American influence in the Orient." That "ninety per cent of these people are Moros, Pagans or non-Christians, living in barbarism," who spoke neither English nor Spanish, and supposedly had no political aspirations meant they would be an "unnecessary burden upon the Filipino people, retarding their progress" and "their hopes for the future."[172] In other words, separating the Moro Province from the rest of the Philippines was an act of American imperial benevolence, one that would profit Filipino Christians, Moros, and American interests alike.

Filipino nationalists opposed calls to separate the Moro Province and make it a permanent American territory.[173] They accused American officials of inventing animosity between Moros and Christians and published articles in nationalist newspapers claiming that "Americans were deliberately perpetrating enmity between Moros and Christians as part of a Machiavellian 'divide and conquer' policy designed to annex Mindanao and Sulu to the United States."[174] Although American businessmen would not succeed in achieving their goal, their arguments reinforced the view that non-Christian Moros and animists in the Moro Province required a distinct form of governance—views they spread both in the Philippines and at home in the United States. In the next few decades, such views would continue to define American colonial policies in important ways.

The End of the Moro Rebellion, 1906–1913

After General Bliss assumed Wood's position as governor of the Moro Province in 1906, the tenor of American colonial policies vis-à-vis Moros would become less aggressive, although colonial violence would not end completely. Though American governance had become less repressive and violent under Bliss's rule, the overall goals were similar: the domination, control, and education of Filipino Moros. More peaceful relations, however, did not bring more political power for the Moros. Much to the contrary, Bliss announced in 1907: "No one dreams of now giving the Moro and pagan the powers and of imposing on them the responsibilities of self-government. The most advanced of them has no conception of what the word means."[175]

This paternalistic approach continued into 1909, when General Pershing took over the governorship. He dedicated himself to educating the Moros beginning at an early age and "aimed at training the children to be productive participants in the economic life of the region, to be clean and well disciplined and to more or less embrace American social values."[176] Though generally more pacific in his approach and more open to dialogue than Wood, Pershing nonetheless continued previous policies of coercive violence whenever necessary, and he maintained that the threat of force was an essential component in reforming Moros: "During the slow process of evolution leading up to civilization, the Moros must be kept in check by the actual application of force or by the moral effect of its presence."[177]

Pershing also expressed doubts about the possibility of integrating Moros with the Filipinos in the Christian northern islands, reinforcing existing American beliefs that the religious and civilizational distinctions between the two areas would make unification under one nation-state difficult. He worried that northern Filipinos would be responsible for ruling pagans and Moros if the United States could not make the Moro Province a separate territory: "The question involved is not one of the fitness of the Filipinos to govern themselves, but is one of their ability and fitness to dominate, justly control, and wisely guide along the pathway of civilization alien peoples, some of whom are warlike." Pershing maintained that the problem held both racial and religious components: "It is true that the Filipino, the Igorot, and the Moro are of common racial origin, but so are the Anglo-Saxon peoples, and there exists between the Filipinos on the one side and the Igorots and the Moros on the other, far greater difference than those which distinguish the Germans, the English and the Americans . . . the Moro is not only of a much later and far purer Malayan origin than the Filipino, but he is as well a Mohammedan, with all that fact implies."[178]

Under Pershing's rule, disagreements among Americans, Moros, and Filipino Christians over the future status of the Moro Province and turning it into an American territory persisted. Filipinos in the North continued to attack the idea of separating the Moro Province into an American territory. They expressed their disagreement in Filipino newspapers, petitions sent to numerous American officials, and political speeches. They maintained that the Moro Province was an essential component of the future Philippines nation.

As part of their strategy, Christian Filipinos in the Moro Province also pressured Pershing to grant them political control over Moro affairs, a request he denied. At a public event in 1910 held in honor of the visit of U.S. secretary of war Jacob Dickinson, Christian Filipinos argued their case in speeches delivered to a mixed audience of Christian Filipinos, Moros, and Americans. Moros followed with their own speeches denouncing the requests of Christian Filipinos to take over political rule from Americans. Dickinson, clearly briefed on American opposition to this policy, responded in his own speech by rebuking Christian Filipino demands. He asked them what response Filipino nationalists expected when they lobbied Congress for their independence on the basis "that government should rest upon the consent of the governed," while simultaneously asking "the American government to withdraw from the present administration and turn over 335,000 Moros to be governed by 66,000 Christians?"[179]

Pershing also disagreed with this policy and succeeded in securing the support of the governor of the Philippines, Cameron Forbes, in opposing the transfer of local leadership in the Moro Province to Filipino Christians. He could not, however, convince Forbes to pull back on his policy of transitioning the Moro Province from military to American civilian rule. To deal with these upcoming changes, and given the supposed dangerous and violent tendencies of the Moros, Pershing felt that disarming all of the Moros was necessary. He passed an executive order calling for the disarmament of all Filipino subjects in the Moro Province by 1 December 1911.

Enforcement of this new policy would prove difficult since many Moros correctly understood it as an American tactic to further reduce their power. Pershing also faced warnings from those higher up. Leonard Wood, who was then army chief of staff for the Philippines Division, recalled his experience during the Battle of Bud Dajo and warned Pershing of the political consequences should Moros respond violently to the new order. Former governor of the Philippines William Howard Taft found himself in the middle of a presidential reelection campaign. Another scandal like Bud Dajo could seriously harm his chances. Thus, upon direct orders from Washington, D.C., Pershing begrudgingly waited until after Taft had lost to Woodrow Wilson to begin enforcing the act. As soon as he began, the expected reaction came to pass.

Moros in Sulu and the Lanao region openly rebelled. Governor Forbes instructed Pershing to "absolutely smother any difficulty with an overwhelming force."[180] The Battle of Bud Bagsak in June 1912 left approximately 500 Moros dead, 50 of them women and children. Pershing personally stood on the front lines for much of the five-day battle. By October 1913, officials estimated that they had gathered almost 6,000 firearms in Sulu and 4,000 in the Lake Lanao district.[181] Although Moros would never stop asserting their demands, the battle was one of the last major attempts by overmatched Filipino Muslims to lead an organized fight against well-armed American authorities. In recognition of his leadership during the battle, Pershing earned the Distinguished Service to the Cross award in 1922. He turned down the award, believing that he had not earned the honor and that his leadership during the conflict was simply the call of duty.[182] The general finally accepted the award on his eightieth birthday in 1940, the honor delivered by President Franklin D. Roosevelt himself. By then, the American depiction of the Moros had changed little. The inscription on his medal praised Pershing "for extraordinary heroism in action against hostile, fanatical Moros."[183]

Civilian Rule and Filipinization

The show of force at the Battle of Bud Bagsak and the successful disarmament of the Moros finally convinced American policymakers that they had succeeded in pacifying the Moros to a degree that they could reward them with civilian rule. The electoral success of the Democrats in 1912 in both the Senate and the House as well as the presidency were also influential factors in bringing about this policy shift. Democrats had less sympathy for American imperial expansion and expressed more support for Filipino independence. As a result, American policy in the Philippines began to change, at least on the surface.[184] Between June and December 1913, Americans established the Department of Mindanao and Sulu and, at last, they replaced military rule with civilian rule. This shift, however, did not signify an end to American discourse advancing the necessity of continued civilizational progress of Moros to attain the level of Christian Filipinos. Instead, such attitudes led to policies that increasingly incorporated the participation of Christian Filipinos in the American imperial project in Moro lands. For their part, Christian Filipinos were not immune to American perceptions of the religious and civilizational inferiority of the Moros, and they used such views to assert their own power and authority.

In 1913, Wilson appointed Francis Burton Harrison as the new governor of the Philippines. Although a Democrat who supported the granting of independence to the Philippines, Harrison nonetheless maintained the same views about Islam as his Republican and pro-imperialist predecessors. Such attitudes became apparent in 1914, when Harrison learned about the actions of John Finley, an American district governor in the Moro Province and one of the rare American officials who did not view Islam as a negative quality of Moros. Finley had initiated a plan to contact the Ottoman sultan to reconnect Moros with their religious leader and bring back teachers to instruct the Moros in their Islamic faith. Harrison was horrified when he learned of Finley's actions and quickly stopped the plan. Pershing commended Harrison for his prudent actions, noting that any "injection of outside Mohammedan influence into the Moro problem would produce fatal results."[185] Condemnation of Finley's actions also came from the American Episcopalian missionary, Charles Brent, who deplored the idea of introducing "some religious agent of Islam" to the Moros.[186]

The inherent endorsement of a religious hierarchy that favored Christianity over Islam would have serious and irreversible consequences for Moros and for future Moro-Christian relations in the Philippines. Harrison soon altered an existing policy under which Americans had been appointed to top positions in the Department of Mindanao and Sulu; instead, he ordered that they be replaced with Filipino Christians. Previous governors felt that such a policy would hamper American power. For Democrats, who favored Filipino independence, these policies made sense. Frank Carpenter, governor of the Department of Mindanao and Sulu, gradually instituted Harrison's orders between 1914 and 1920, bringing about the "Filipinization" of all civilian posts. Given continued beliefs in the religious and civilizational inferiority of the Moros, Harrison assumed that more advanced Christian Filipinos were more appropriate political leaders for the area. Such policies also assumed that Christian Filipino leadership would facilitate Moro advancement. Having advocated for such policies for some time and aware that they advanced their own interests, Christian Filipino nationalists praised Harrison's approach.[187]

Under the Organic Act of 23 July 1914, Moros were given the same administrative status as Christian Filipinos. The legislation nonetheless reinforced the hierarchical relationship between Christian and Muslim Filipinos. According to the preamble, the act itself constituted the expression of "the desire of the people of the islands," by which they meant Christian Filipinos, "to promote the most rapid moral, social, and political development of the inhabitants of said Department in order to accomplish their complete unification with the inhabitants of other provinces of the Archipelago."[188] While continuing to be American imperial subjects, Christian Filipino nationalists used the situation to their advantage, accepting the implicit logic undergirding the American imperial civilizing mission toward Moros and their role in this complex web of imperial relations.

In 1914, using the same American imperial logic behind Filipinization, Americans encouraged Christian Filipinos in the North to populate the department by offering them cheap land. Such proposals advanced the dual goals of land development and exposing Moros to more "civilized elements." Constituting both a political and a cultural project, Americans believed that by encouraging Filipino Christians in the "overpopulated" northern islands to come establish colonies in the southern islands, their intermixture with Moros would prove the ideal solution.

To ensure the success of their demographic and social engineering endeavor, officials strategized that they would need to settle "alternately on adjacent homesteads Christian and Mohammedan or pagan colonists when the relative numbers of the two classes are approximately equal." When pagans and Muslims greatly outnumbered Christians, "the immigrant Christian colonist minority will be as widely scattered as possible throughout the non-Christian majority."[189] Such plans, they hoped, would expose non-Christians to "economic development and social betterment" and, by extension, these non-Christians would "consciously emulate the higher type of civilization."[190] Again, capitalism, religion, and the civilizing enterprise converged in American imperial discourse.

Not coincidentally and despite public declarations of noninterference, the continued official support for American missionary work, specifically the American Protestant missionaries, constituted another tactic to "civilize" the Moros. Mentioning American missionary workers Charles Brent and Lorillard Spencer by name, the same 1914 report indicated that the importance of their "organized private philanthropy" to "public service [was] second only to government in Mindanao-Sulu." It further emphasized that, far from playing a disinterested role in supporting such endeavors, American officials should provide "all assistance and courtesies which opportunities have permitted" and that "responsible Government officials" strongly condemned any efforts to end their work.[191] Given American beliefs about the inextricable ties between religion and civilization, as well as previous endorsements for American missionary work by colonial officials, diplomats, and politicians at the highest levels, such support for Christian missionaries was hardly surprising.

With these new policies in place, the burden of advancement now fell on the Moros. According to Carpenter, if Moros and pagans "do not come directly into increasing and eventual homogeneity with the highly civilized Filipino type the fault will be of the latter."[192] The answer to what would happen to those Moros who failed to advance had already been answered by more than a decade of brutal warfare and death. Christian Filipinos also had a role to play by taking up the imperial mantle. It was their duty to advance commercial, social, and political relations with Moros and pagans "until these three elements of population which for centuries have been distinct and held aloof by differences in type of civilization and religious and social customs shall have merged in one harmonious, homogeneous people."[193]

Despite Carpenter's hopes that Filipinization would lay the groundwork for the harmonious advancement of the inferior peoples of the Philippines, Moros interpreted these policies as efforts to simply replace one imperial force with another. Their lack of trust in Filipino Christians surpassed their resentment of American rule, leading many to plead for their own leadership or the continuation of American rule, even if it meant becoming a separate American territory. Although subsequent American governors eased policies of Filipinization, they would nonetheless continue to encourage Filipino Christians to move to the area. In 1919, the U.S. government passed an act that increased land grants to incoming Christian Filipino settlers from 160 acres to 240 acres. The same act, however, limited non-Christians to 100 acres.[194] The obvious reasons for the discrepancy were to encourage the migration of more civilized Christian Filipinos at the expense of Moro control over their own lands.

Moros continued to fight for sovereignty over their lands. Ironically, they would find support in the unlikely ally of Leonard Wood. After Republicans regained the White House in 1920, Wood found himself in favor again. President Warren Harding asked Wood to join former governor general of the Philippines William Cameron Forbes as members of a commission tasked with assessing the state of the Philippines. Wood reluctantly accepted and, upon their arrival, the two men found to their dismay that the changes brought about by Harrison had unfortunately resulted in encouraging Filipino independence.[195] Convinced of the need to rectify the situation, Wood accepted appointment as governor of the Philippine Islands. He subsequently reinstated Americans in several positions that had been filled by Christian Filipinos in the Department of Mindanao and Sulu. During his time as governor, he continued to oppose any efforts to grant Filipinos independence from the United States, a goal for which they would have to wait more than two decades.

In 1925, when Wood granted his interview to the American journalist and claimed that American imperial rule of the Philippine Islands should be understood as part of a wider American endeavor to spread Christianity globally, his remarks revealed one aspect of religious belief that shaped American foreign policies. American beliefs about Islam, however, also played a central role in shaping U.S. policies regarding Filipinos. As they sought to impose American colonial rule on the Moros, U.S. officials believed they were putting them on the path to higher civilization. This objective—and the tools for its accomplishment—depended on concerted and collaborative efforts by government officials, missionaries, business interests, and academics. Despite Wood's efforts, policies of Filipinization were irreversible and Americans had succeeded in imbuing many Christian Filipinos with their own attitudes about Muslim inferiority, transforming them into imperial agents who would continue to treat Filipino Muslims as inferior long after Americans had left the Philippines. Indeed, one of the arguments advanced by Filipino nationalists in favor of independence was the fact that they were Christian, and thus civilized.[196]

As the Philippines moved toward formal independence in the 1930s and 1940s, America's "Mohammedan Wards" became the de facto colonial subjects of their new Christian Filipino rulers.[197] Moreover, Moro resistance did not end with formal independence. American colonial policies had succeeded in forging a united Moro identity that had not existed prior to their arrival. This new identity would help to foment continued calls by Moros for their independence from the Philippines. The impact of American beliefs about Islam and Filipino Muslims had spread in unforeseen yet powerful ways.

PART IV

Resolving the Eastern Question

When the war will be ended, there are two lands that

will never go back to the Mohammedan apache. One is

Christian Armenia and the other is Jewish Palestine.

—Rabbi Stephen Wise quoting promise by

President Woodrow Wilson, 1920

7

THE UNITED STATES AND

THE ARMENIAN MASSACRES,

1894–1896

Between 1894 and 1896, Americans responded with horror as the Ottoman government increasingly and brutally suppressed Armenian rebellions, resulting in the deaths of between 100,000 and 200,000 Armenians. In the wake of mounting Armenian rebellions throughout the 1880s and 1890s, increasingly driven by nationalist aspirations, the first large-scale response by the Ottoman government came in the form of a massacre in August and September 1894 in Sasun, resulting in more than 10,000 Armenian deaths.[1] Armenian nationalists had encouraged local Armenians to refuse to pay their taxes to their exploitative Kurdish overlords. Local authorities declared the Armenians in rebellion, and Abdul Hamid II sent in troops to deliver a brutal message.[2]

Following international condemnation, European powers insisted on an international investigation, and they subsequently attempted to impose a reform program on Ottoman rulers in May 1895, which the latter quickly rejected almost in its entirety. Pressured by the threat of British action, Ottoman rulers begrudgingly agreed to the suggested reforms, but their failure to follow through on their promises pushed Armenians to renew demonstrations and demand their implementation. Such actions led to another massacre in September 1895. Emboldened by the previous intervention of European powers, Armenians continued to rebel. While Ottoman rulers reassured Europeans that they would implement the reforms, their policy response of massacre escalated in the ensuing months.

Europeans threatened action, but humanitarian sympathy was not enough to prompt further intervention. Russia's strategic interests no longer depended on the status of Christian minorities in the Ottoman Empire, and the country did not want revolutionary instability spreading to its own newly incorporated Armenian populations.[3] Meanwhile, in February of 1896, British prime minister Lord Salisbury publicly indicated that he was satisfied with Ottoman efforts and that the British would not intervene further. His statements crushed the hopes of Armenian nationalists, who believed that their only chance for independence would come through foreign intervention. In a final attempt to solicit foreign aid and obtain the promised reforms, Armenians occupied the Central Bank of Istanbul in August 1896. The Ottoman rulers initiated another deadly massacre, resulting in thousands more deaths. This final act of violence pushed the reluctant European powers to convene in Istanbul in January and February 1897, but competing interests resulted only in a new series of weak demands for reform.[4] Armenian hopes would again be dashed by the outbreak of the Greek-Turkish War later that year, ironically motivated in part by Armenian nationalism, which focused European attention away from their cause.[5]

Americans reacted to the massacres and European inaction with condemnation and disgust. As Roosevelt raged in 1897, on the eve of the Spanish-American War, Spain and Turkey were "the two powers I would rather smash than any in the world."[6] The ideal solution was to rid the world of Ottoman rule altogether and impose European imperial rule. In 1899, Roosevelt wrote to his friend, the British diplomat Cecil Spring-Rice, that he "always regretted that the nations of Western Europe could not themselves put an end to the rule of the Turk, and supplant it with that of some other nationality."[7] As president, Roosevelt promised that he would act on behalf of oppressed Ottoman Christians, although he would also be limited by formal policies of noninvolvement. In 1905, he admitted to a friend: "As for the Armenians in Turkey, if I could get this people to back me I really think I should be tempted to go into a crusade against the Turk."[8]

Roosevelt's reactions to the Armenian Massacres reflected what many Americans also believed: Ottoman Muslims were incapable of ruling over Christian minorities. In denouncing the Armenian Massacres, Americans drew from a long list of past examples of perceived Ottoman misrule and violent reprisals, including Bulgaria, Crete, and Greece. Roosevelt's reactions also reflected a U.S. foreign policy vision in which the United States and Europe actively promoted the advancement of Western civilization to the world, including the Ottoman Empire. This vision became particularly acute during times of violent political strife.

Americans once again became increasingly frustrated with the inability or unwillingness of the European powers to intervene. While Americans blamed the Armenian Massacres on the alleged religious "fanaticism" of Ottoman rulers—and increasingly on the racially derived violence of the Turkish "race"—many also echoed earlier accusations by arguing that Europeans had forsaken their Christian religious identity for corrupt, self-interested, and secular agendas. As an anonymous contributor to *Public Opinion* argued in 1896, if Europeans were incapable of acting as a moral power, then the United States had to step up its role in global affairs:

> The attack of the Turks on the Christian inhabitants, with the customary and incidental atrocities, the revolt of the Christians, their gallant fight for life and the safety of their families, are all typical of the struggles of Christian populations against the horrors of Mahometan supremacy. . . . The whole subject of Turkish anarchy and murder is an appalling demonstration of the heartlessness and falsity of European diplomacy. It is a demonstration that the United States has not sunk to a similar sway of selfish and cowardly motives that we urge intervention by our government in the corresponding case of Cuba.[9]

Indeed, Americans who had previously pushed for U.S. intervention in the Ottoman Empire supported U.S. military intervention in Cuba in 1898 by citing the consequences of European inaction during the Armenian Massacres three years before.[10] Intervention in Cuba was less complicated because the country was located in the Western Hemisphere and thus action did not conflict with the Monroe Doctrine. Support for U.S. intervention to stop the Armenian Massacres, however, demonstrated yet again that a significant portion of the American public wanted the United States to move beyond these limitations. They believed that the United States best represented Anglo-Saxon Christendom; thus, the nation had a divine and humanitarian duty to shape the world. Although Americans traced their identity back to what they viewed as the superiority of European civilization and, increasingly, the Anglo-Saxon race, the powerful sway of manifest destiny elevated U.S. foreign policy above both Ottoman Muslim rule *and* the corrupt European powers, neither of which was exempt from charges of barbarism and decadence. Such calls, however, ignored the fact that previous European diplomatic interventions had exacerbated existing tensions in the region.

Once again, American Protestants in the Ottoman Empire—whether serving as missionaries or working for American schools—were central actors in shaping events on the ground, conveying information to the American public and driving private and official U.S. responses to the brutalities. On the domestic front, missionary organizations such as the American Board of Commissioners for Foreign Missions (ABCFM) and the Evangelical Alliance, the largest domestic missionary organization in the United States, worked with religious and political leaders throughout the country to promote American action.

Because interpretation of the events by ABCFM missionaries dominated the explanatory narrative of the massacres, the American public and the U.S. government's understandings of Ottoman violence continued to focus on primordial religious hatred and the alleged barbarity of Muslims. Missionary accounts focused on Christian victims and omitted any mention of the many Muslims who also lost their lives at the hands of Ottoman rulers during this time of massive political unrest in the empire.

Selling intervention to the public depended on reaffirming the story that elicited the greatest sympathy and confirmed American preconceptions that imbricated race and religion. Thus, the massacres were framed as racially inferior Turkish Muslims acting on their fanatical religious hatred for Christian Armenians, who were increasingly depicted as the white "Anglo-Saxons" of the East. In emphasizing Armenian identity as "Anglo-Saxon" and Christian, American activists leveraged the mounting importance of attitudes about race to affirm the civilizational, religious, and racial divides between "white" Christians and "non-white" Muslims. In this way, American responses to the Armenian Massacres marked a new era in which ideas about race—in addition to religion—would become increasingly important for categorizing peoples of the world. Another American response to this narrative, however, dictated an equally straightforward solution that had been decades in the making: ending Ottoman Muslim rule altogether. Increasing numbers of Armenian immigrants in the United States contributed to these calls, while echoing the religious and racial language of American religious organizations.

Ironically, these public and political demands for intervention in the Ottoman Empire occurred during the presidency of Grover Cleveland, perhaps the most isolationist president since John Quincy Adams. Given the unprecedented support for increased American involvement in world affairs in the final decades of the nineteenth century, the 1892 election of Cleveland is perhaps surprising. The Democratic candidate had won due to the success of the newly created Populist Party, which split Republican voters and delivered the election to Cleveland. Historians can only guess what might have happened if expansionist Benjamin Harrison had won a second term in office, a period that coincided with the Armenian Massacres.[11] Cleveland was reluctant to act, yet pressure from the American public prompted one of the largest humanitarian responses the country had ever seen. Those who supported a greater role for the United States in world affairs directed the public and government debates, setting the stage for U.S. foreign policy in the twentieth century.

The Social Gospel, Social Darwinism, and American Protestant Missionary Work among Ottoman Armenians

After the first outbreak of violence against Ottoman Armenians in 1894, the prominent clergyman and advocate of American imperial expansion Josiah Strong became a central figure of the lobbying effort. As secretary of the Evangelical Alliance, Strong possessed an influential network of political and religious contacts, including in the ABCFM. He was thus well positioned to exert political and spiritual influence. As one of the most well-known religious leaders, Strong's ideology merged Social Gospel beliefs, which sought to reform society through Christian values, with strong support for missionary work.

Strong believed that Protestant values could solve social injustice around the world and that only Anglo-Saxon Christian civilization could provide true political and civil freedom to non-Christians. More than any other nation, Strong maintained, the combination of spiritual and political values and superior racial Anglo-Saxon stock of the United States compelled the nation to act.[12] The Armenian Massacres presented an ideal opportunity.

Such ideas resonated with American Protestant missionaries in the Ottoman Empire. The ABCFM's mission had been shifting focus in the final decades of the nineteenth century, veering from eschatological understandings of Islam and the importance of conversion toward the spread of Christian *civilization*, broadly construed. This shift brought more explicit support for general education, commercial development, political reform, and civilizational uplift. This mission was also buttressed by theories of scientific racism and Social Darwinism, which implicitly justified the European and American imperial expansion that was speedily taking place around the world.[13]

Implicit in these ideologies was a hierarchical ordering of populations and races—something that became particularly relevant in the case of the Armenians. ABCFM missionaries had tended to view "nominal" Christians and Muslims in the Ottoman Empire with condescension. Ascendant theories of racial difference, which coincided with the Social Gospel movement, bolstered preexisting ideas about difference held by many American Protestant missionaries. It also supported their belief that Anglo-Saxon Protestants should lead racial, civilization, and spiritual inferiors on their path to progress, even if they could never attain the highest rungs of the racial ladder. American Protestants continued to blame Islam for the Ottoman government's violent actions, but they increasingly assumed that such tendencies were exacerbated by the violent tendencies of the Turkish *race*. In their view, European or American foreign intervention to protect Christian minorities and offer reform to Ottoman rulers was a logical extension of missionary work on the ground.

As scientific racism grew more influential, the missionaries' racial beliefs extended beyond Arab and Turkish Muslims to include Ottoman Christian subjects. At times, scientific racism enabled American missionaries to justify discriminating against their own Protestant converts, such as when the president of the Syrian Protestant College in Beirut instituted a policy banning Christian Arabs from serving as professors in 1883. At other times, the missionaries explicitly voiced beliefs about the racial superiority of Christians in the Ottoman Empire.

Although such ideas gained ground in the final decades of the nineteenth century, they had been developing for decades. As early as 1854, ABCFM missionary Harrison Dwight had remarked that Armenians were "superior to other races" in Turkey: "In one word, they are the Anglo-Saxons of the east."[14] During the Armenian Massacres, religious and political leaders and the press repeatedly relied on this depiction of Armenians as their "Anglo-Saxon" representatives in the Ottoman Empire. As the category of whiteness narrowed with the influx of immigrants from eastern and southern Europe to the United States, identifying Armenians as Anglo-Saxons conferred membership in this club of racial privilege and enhanced their already elevated status as Christians.

The Congress of Berlin and Its Aftermath

Though ABCFM missionaries had settled on a simplistic view that assigned blame to the Ottoman Turks, the truth was that the Armenian Massacres of 1894–1896 resulted from a complex convergence of factors during the last half of the nineteenth century. The empire was reeling from territorial losses. The sultan's fears of losing more territory in the aftermath of the Russo-Turkish War and the Congress of Berlin had led him to repress any nascent nationalist movements in the empire.

As part of his strategy, Abdul Hamid II also engaged in practices of demographic engineering, relocating Muslim refugees, or *muhajirs*, from the Russo-Turkish War into areas prone to rebellion, including the eastern provinces of the empire, where the bulk of Armenian Christians resided.[15] Many *muhajirs* had been brutally expelled from lands ceded by the empire to Christian governments after the Crimean War and the Russo-Turkish War, which fueled a bitter resentment that they often took out on the Armenians.[16] Increased competition for land and resources and Ottoman rulers' increased control over the eastern provinces exacerbated tensions between Armenians and Kurds. In previous decades, Armenians had received protection from local Kurdish rulers. When the latter lost control or were disempowered as a result of increased Ottoman control in the area, the Armenians lost such protection.[17] To maintain the adherence of local Kurdish populations, in the 1890s the sultan organized Kurdish military units in eastern Anatolia, known as the *Hamidiye*, to counter and repress Armenian nationalist activity.[18]

Internally, the treaties imposed by European powers at the end of the Russo-Turkish War also increased the existing tension and violence. Russian gains from the war included territories with significant Armenian populations living in regions that were adjacent to Armenian populations under Ottoman control. As such, Armenian nationalists could openly organize resistance against the empire from within the relative safety of Russia. More important, both the Treaty of San Stefano and the Treaty of Berlin included articles that specifically addressed the Armenian Question, transforming what had previously been a domestic concern into an international issue. By internationalizing the Armenian Question, the treaties raised the possibility of future foreign intervention, further intensifying Ottoman paranoia while leaving the Armenian population unprotected.[19]

The Treaty of San Stefano initially demanded that the Porte reform the treatment of Armenians and guarantee their protection from Kurds and Circassians. It authorized the continued presence of Russian troops in the empire, incentivizing the sultan to fulfill his obligations. The Congress of Berlin, however, blunted the force of this incentive. The British sought to limit Russian gains and compel Russia to withdraw its troops, thus dividing the responsibility to protect the Armenians among several European powers. Disappointed by the weakened treaty that had failed to take into account their demands, the Armenian nationalist delegation announced that it would "return to the East carrying with it the lesson that without struggle and without insurrection nothing can be obtained. Nevertheless, the delegation will never cease addressing petitions until Europe has satisfied its just claims."[20]

Oppressed by their neighbors within the empire and divided across arbitrary borders, a new sense of disillusionment pushed Armenian nationalists to radicalize their tactics and organize more intensively, both within the Ottoman Empire and abroad. They took full advantage of their diasporic communities in Russia and, increasingly, the United States. In 1887, Russian Armenians founded the Hunchak Party, an organization dedicated to ensuring Armenian independence. Supported by revolutionary organizations, local Armenians increasingly protested the mounting threats to their legal rights and physical safety and pushed the Ottoman government to uphold the promises it had made at the Congress of Berlin.[21] Rather than respond to their legitimate grievances, the sultan resorted to violent intimidation.

Ottoman Hostility to American Influence in the Empire on the Eve of the Armenian Massacres

Although not a signatory to the Congress of Berlin, the unofficial involvement of the United States in the Armenian Question was vital. Through missionary and educational work, the number of citizens of the United States working in the empire continued to exceed those of any other country. Many worked with Armenians in territories directly affected by the massacres. Indeed, although sympathetic to the plight of all Ottoman Christians, the massacres had directly affected the communities with which the ABCFM missionaries had been working for the last eight decades. More than 10 percent of the victims were Armenians who had converted to Protestantism under ABCFM influence, prompting even greater outrage and sympathy among the missionaries and endangering their lives and work.[22]

Although ABCFM missionaries never directly encouraged Armenian nationalism, their educational curriculum could only have reinforced the developing revolutionary ideals of Armenian nationalists.[23] Suspicious of their role in fomenting nationalism among its Christian subjects, the Ottoman government began suppressing American missionary schools in the 1880s, particularly in areas prone to revolutionary activity.[24] James Barton, foreign secretary of the ABCFM, learned of the sultan's imminent threat to shut down ABCFM schools in 1893 and alerted the board leadership that the American government's help would be necessary to protect their work in the empire.[25]

As in previous decades when Americans had involved themselves in the Greek and Bulgarian rebellions, the political and media reach of American Protestants was crucial—first in protecting American schools and missionaries and later in eliciting sympathy for Armenian victims. The ABCFM had an impressive political network through which they could exercise their demands. The children of the previous generation of American missionaries had used their linguistic and cultural knowledge to gain positions in the diplomatic corps, while others were groomed as political and business leaders. They included diplomat John Hay, the cousin of George Washburn, president of Robert College. During the final decades of the nineteenth century, Hay served consecutively as assistant secretary of state, editor of the *New York Tribune*, ambassador to Great Britain, and secretary of state under Roosevelt. Indeed, the *New York Tribune* provided almost daily coverage of the Armenian Massacres during peak outbreaks.

This political influence proved beneficial in the final decades of the nineteenth century, when American missionaries faced hostility from the Ottoman government. Many ABCFM leaders felt that some American diplomats in the empire had not been responsive enough to missionary needs and that, to guarantee governmental support, they would need to handpick consuls and ministers. The first known instance of this occurred in 1887, when Reverend A. S. Barnes, a Robert College trustee and an important member of the ABCFM, recommended that Oscar Straus be appointed to the position of U.S. minister to the Ottoman Empire, the highest ranking U.S. diplomatic post. The foreign secretary of the ABCFM wrote President Cleveland directly to make his request known, and the president obliged.[26]

Given the political power of the ABCFM, newly appointed diplomats could rarely afford to be unsupportive. Chosen to deliver the commencement address at Robert College shortly after his appointment, Straus praised the institution for bringing "progress and civilization" to the Ottoman Empire not through "ships of war nor armed troops, but her most cherished institutions, a fully equipped American college."[27] Later, the ABCFM had one of its own board members, James Angell, appointed as minister. The organization would not always get its way, but its influence led to much more aggressive foreign policy actions in the empire, usually "ordered" directly by the missionaries themselves.[28]

Perhaps because of these close ties, Ottoman officials frequently accused the American government of being directly implicated in the Armenian Question. A few years before the Armenian Massacres, the Sublime Porte criticized the U.S. government's practice of naturalizing Armenians as American citizens and then allowing them to return to the empire to engage in nationalist activities under the protection of American consuls. These objections constituted part of a broader Ottoman hostility regarding abuse of the protégé system throughout the nineteenth century by European diplomats. Many Ottoman subjects became naturalized as foreign citizens to gain the same kind of protection they could obtain under the protégé system.[29] By 1869, Ottoman subjects had exploited this tactic to such an extent that naturalized citizens outnumbered citizens by birth from some countries.[30] American citizenship was particularly attractive for Ottoman subjects since the United States insisted on the full rights of its citizens, who continued to live in the empire after obtaining their American citizenship.

Beginning in the 1870s, the Porte demanded revisions to the existing 1830 commercial treaty between the Ottoman Empire and the United States that granted all Americans living in the empire—naturalized or not—full legal and criminal immunity. Believing that the naturalization system conferred additional protection to those Ottoman subjects who converted to Protestantism, many American missionaries opposed reforms. Indeed, attempts to negotiate a new naturalization treaty were unsuccessful. In 1891, just as Straus was about to present a revised treaty to the Senate for ratification, Secretary of State Blain consulted Washburn, who later met privately with Blain and two other senators to discuss the issue. Washburn's influence convinced the men to remove the treaty from consideration.[31] On the eve of the Armenian Massacres, without a new treaty limiting the activities of newly naturalized Armenians, the naturalization issue further implicated the United States in the Armenian Question.

By the 1890s, the Armenian population in the United States had begun to gain ground both in numbers and in their ability to lobby politicians and the American public on behalf of Armenian nationalism. Some Armenian Americans also maintained close ties with American missionaries. Indeed, the first Armenians to migrate to the United States in the 1830s had come as students, sent by American missionaries to pursue their spiritual and technical education in the United States.[32] Migration continued in the following decades, encouraged by men such as Cyrus Hamlin, the first president of Robert College. By the 1870s and 1880s, English-speaking Armenian students in ABCFM schools began arriving in the

United States to find work. As conditions in the Ottoman Empire worsened in the early 1890s, thousands of Armenian nationalists fled to the United States to avoid political persecution and continue their political activities. By 1893, Armenians immigrants had opened branches of Armenian nationalist and revolutionary organizations in several major U.S. cities. Activists organized political rallies, raised money, founded their own revolutionary newspapers, wrote editorials in American newspapers, and even arranged military training, all of which infuriated the Ottoman minister in Washington.[33]

In response to this domestic activism in the United States, the Ottoman minister complained that recently naturalized Armenians in New York published a newspaper that regularly contained "articles inciting the Armenians who live in Turkey to insurrection."[34] As evidence, the minister presented an editorial from the newspaper stating that it was time to use "fire and sword, which calls for soldiers and money" in their struggle for Armenian independence. The editorial encouraged Armenian revolutionaries to model their revolutionary organizations in the United States on those already created in Russia: "Just as there is an Armeno-Russian corps in the east, ready and organized, so must an Armeno-American corps, equally strong, be raised in the west."[35] Despite continued Ottoman complaints, the U.S. government refused to alter its policies. In his December 1893 First Annual Message, President Cleveland conceded that Ottoman accusations that the United States had been facilitating Armenian nationalist activities through its naturalization process were "not wholly without foundation." He nonetheless insisted that the sultan treat all naturalized Armenians as American citizens and protect Armenian Americans who returned to the empire from "unnecessary harshness of treatment."[36]

Despite their opposition to naturalization reforms, before the Armenian Massacres many American Protestant missionaries distanced themselves from Armenian nationalist activities. They realized that political associations with their cause would threaten their work in the empire.[37] This fear was particularly acute in American colleges with large Armenian populations. ABCFM missionaries and American Protestants who headed American schools actively discouraged their students from nationalist activities, while some accused the Armenian revolutionaries of trying to publicly implicate Americans in their activities as a strategy to gain international attention. The Ottoman government and the American missionaries were aware of the influence wielded by institutions such as Robert College in gaining independence for Bulgaria two decades earlier.[38]

On the eve of the Armenian Massacres, the fears of the missionaries were realized. In January 1893, the Ottoman government accused two Armenian professors at the ABCFM-run Anatolia College of printing revolutionary placards and posting them in prominent areas around town, including the college campus. Unbeknownst to the local ABCFM missionaries, the two professors were in fact members of the Hunchak Party and had been working for months to plan revolutionary activities.[39] Printed on the college's press, the placards urged locals to rebel against the government and called for the area's transfer to British rule. Ottoman officials burned down one of the college's buildings as punishment.

ABCFM leaders vehemently protested this attack, demanding that the American government force the Ottoman government to pay for the damages caused by the fire. Undoubtedly ignorant of the two professors' affiliations with nationalists, ABCFM secretary Judson Smith wrote Secretary of State Gresham denouncing the "gross insults" and "utterly groundless and calumnious charges."[40] Smith maintained that the accused professors were not nationalists, but men who had made the important and dangerous decision to accept Protestant Christianity and "Christian civilization." Of course, he ignored the fact that the two were not mutually exclusive. The importance of the two professors was without parallel, according to Smith, for they served as examples to other Ottoman subjects, both Muslim and Christian: "These men are true men," who had brought the "blessings of a Christian civilization to the peoples of the land." Smith further recommended the dispatch of American gunboats to the area and reminded the secretary of state of the political weight of the ABCFM, concluding that he was certain the board and its "constituents shall not look to the Government for instant and effective relief in vain."[41]

The American government protested the action of the Ottoman government, but President Cleveland refused to send the navy. Within weeks, the issue had garnered widespread media attention and repeated public calls for a more aggressive American foreign policy. An editorial in the popular weekly magazine *Outlook* argued that the "presence of an American squadron in the Levant would go further to secure the threatened immunities of our citizens than any quantity of mere diplomatic notes."[42] Alice Stone Blackwell, a women's rights advocate and ardent Armenophile, argued that the U.S. government should extend protection to "all the Christian subjects of the Sultan."[43] The racial, religious, and civilizational superiority of Armenians over Turks, Blackwell maintained, demanded American sympathy and it was "particularly repugnant that a nation like the Armenians—a people remarkably intelligent, with an ancient civilization and literature, and an exceptionally pure family life—should be left to perish at the hands of stupid, brutal, and ferocious Turks."[44] Blackwell urged American Christians to petition Cleveland for more aggressive action and to write to their local newspapers to publicize the oppression of Armenians.

Cyrus Hamlin, the former president of Robert College who was now based in the United States, also publicly defended American missionaries while distancing them from the Armenian revolutionary movement. In a statement published in the *Congregationalist* in December 1893, he claimed that Armenian revolutionaries pushed for Russian intervention by attacking Kurds and Turks, in turn prompting violent reactions from the Ottoman government: "The enraged Moslems will then rise and fall upon the defenseless Armenians and slaughter them with such barbarities that Russia will enter, in the name of humanity and Christian civilization and take possession."[45] Hamlin was horrified by the tactic. According to his account, an Armenian revolutionary had told him: "Europe listened to the Bulgarian horrors and made Bulgaria free. She will listen to our cry when it goes up in the shrieks and blood of millions of women and children."[46] The following spring, Hamlin nonetheless maintained that the United States had a duty, "as a Christian government," to unite with Britain to protest any violence against Christians and display its "Christian character and spirit." He chided American inaction: "Is it not disgraceful to all Christian governments that they allow their fellow Christians to be cruelly and wrongfully oppressed in the Turkish empire?"[47]

In the midst of such public discussions, the Armenian American community did not miss the opportunity to respond and lay out its broader defense for Armenian nationalism. Much like the Greeks, Cretans, and Bulgarians before them, Armenians and Armenian Americans consistently adapted their message to foster American sympathies by emphasizing the shared religious, racial, and political affiliations that united Armenians and Americans. In a letter to the *Washington Post*, an Armenian author depicted the "Armenian nation" as trying to free itself from Muslim rule and "take its place in the community of civilized Christian nations."[48] The Armenian cause could be compared directly to the battles by the American revolutionaries against tyranny and political oppression. He called for greater foreign intervention by pulling on the moral heartstrings of his readership: "All around stand the four hundred millions of Christians of Europe and America, with twenty millions of trained soldiers, all looking calmly on while their Christian brothers suffer the extreme outrage at the hands of a foe whom Christendom could crush as a man's foot crushes a worm."[49]

Other newspapers published similar pleas. A *New York Times* editorial, written by a naturalized Armenian, lambasted the American government for its weakness. According to the writer, such timid foreign policy resulted in Americans allowing themselves to be "insulted by a Government that belongs to a barbaric age" while simultaneously losing "its self-respect before the other powers."[50] The author also compared the Armenian struggle to America's own declaration of independence, when France had come to her aid during "a revolution for a cause not half so unbearable as the lot of the Armenians has been ever since the Turks conquered the land."[51] Another letter from an Armenian American in the *Washington Post* affirmed the deep racial and religious bonds between Armenians and Americans "with all the qualities which have made the Caucasian race rulers of the civilized world"[52] Furthermore, as Christians, Armenians had also served as a "buffer state," protecting Europeans from harmful contact with Islam. Sympathy for the Armenian cause—Armenia again construed as a Christian nation fighting for survival under intolerant and fanatical Muslim rule—would increase in the following months as the American public continued to witness the brutal repression of the Armenian community.

The American Missionary Response
to the Armenian Massacres

Unlike the European powers, the American missionary community acted immediately. As soon as it received word of the Sasun massacre in 1894, the ABCFM worked with Strong and the Evangelical Alliance to push for a massive public and governmental response in the United States.[53] Within a month, Strong had created a special subcommittee of the Evangelical Alliance dedicated to responding to what it called the "Turkish Outrages."[54] The committee's membership included men with significant religious, political, and corporate influence, among them William E. Dodge, who was head of the largest American coal mining company and president of the Evangelical Alliance, and Robert Burney, who was an important religious leader in the Young Men's Christian Association (YMCA). By taking over public and political lobbying on behalf of the Armenians, Strong allowed the ABCFM to protect its missionaries from Ottoman reprisals, distancing the organization from any appearance of political involvement or influence.[55]

Nonetheless, ABCFM members were central to the effort and to the new committee's work behind the scenes. The organization's foreign secretary, James Barton, who had spent ten years in the area working with Armenians, wrote privately to Secretary of State Gresham in November 1894, shortly after receiving news of the Sasun massacres. Comparing the recent violence to the Bulgarian Massacres of 1876, Barton demanded action from the American government. Intervention was a matter of "world-wide interest," Barton maintained. He had received letters, telegrams, and newspaper clippings from Americans across the country showing "how thoroughly our people are aroused at the reported outrages upon Christians."[56] He argued that the massacres were prompted by Turkish misrule and hatred of Christians and had "no connection with the 'revolutionary movement' among a few Armenians in this country, which we earnestly deprecate." He also noted that, while public outcry in Europe and the United States had led the Ottoman government to conduct an official investigation into the Sasun massacre, the U.S. government also had a duty to independently ascertain the facts, for "if such an outrage upon humanity has been committed the Christian world ought to know it."[57]

ABCFM efforts to garner public and official attention to the cause were successful. As Barton wrote a fellow clergyman in December 1894:

> I assure you that we, here, are doing everything possible to call the attention of our country, as well as the civilized world, to the facts in the case and that we have already succeeded in getting hundreds of mass meetings which express the deepest indignation at the acts of the Turkish government; and also memorializing our representatives in Congress and our government, urging them to take the matter up. Also we have visited Washington, have been in communication with the Secretary of State from the first, gave him some of the very first information which we had and caused him to reverse his action in one case at least, when he decided not to send a commission; and one of our missionaries had three conferences with Secretary of State Gresham and assistant Sec. of State—twice at their urgent request—and one of the Secretaries of our Board is now in Washington in conference with officials.[58]

With help from Barton and other ABCFM members, American newspapers immediately began covering the massacres. Between 1894 and 1896, they would publish thousands of articles on the topic, largely thanks to information from local American missionaries, though their role remained unseen. Barton proudly wrote another board member the following year:

"Most of the newspaper publications which were issued from Nov. [1894] onward came from [the American Board], although our hand did not appear."[59]

In Istanbul, George Washburn and Edwin Pears, who had both been so influential during the Bulgarian Massacres, also contributed by sending regular reports to the American and British press.[60] This involvement increased the ties between previous American actions in the Ottoman Empire and the Armenian cause. The *Chicago Tribune* published a story attempting to situate Ottoman violence against Armenians within a larger pattern of violence by other Muslims, noting: "Nothing but an Arab raid can compare with the brutality in Armenia."[61] Speeches by well-known British politicians who also had previous ties to the Bulgarians, such as William Gladstone, decried the violence against the Armenian "Anglo-Saxons of the east." Such analysis received extensive coverage in the United States.

Editorials across the country called for foreign intervention and argued that the backwardness of Turkish Muslims made their rule a historical anachronism that needed to be rectified. According to one New York daily, it was the duty of "every country worthy of being called Christian and civilized" to demand justice.[62] The *New York Recorder* denounced the "Moslem monster" who was "as insatiable as ever" and needed to be stopped, for he was "in the wrong century for this kind of business."[63] The *Philadelphia Record* called for the replacement of Turkish rule with "a government more consistent with the civilization of the nineteenth century."[64] According to the *Watchman*, the most decadent and dangerous elements of Islam were in Turkey, which had not benefited from European imperial rule. Whereas in India, British rule had assured some degree of progress among Muslims, the lack of European influence in the Ottoman Empire had made Turks "the nadir even of Moslem civilization."[65] Other editorials linked the violence to previous conflicts in the empire that had provoked similar American outrage. According to the *New York Herald* the Armenian Massacres were just a continuation of these previous events: "The massacres of Scio, where fifty thousand Christians were butchered, in 1820, led to the war of Greek Independence. Massacres in Crete preluded the great atrocities that led to the Bulgarian war in 1876. And it may be that what is being perpetrated in Armenia is only the signal for some new developments in the blood stained career of the Osmanlis Turks."[66]

In 1895, the Women's Christian Temperance Union argued in its journal, the *Union Signal*, that American Christians had a duty to act, for

American missionaries were partially responsible for instilling in the Armenians the "American spirit and example," leading to their eventual desire for independence.[67] The popular depiction of Armenians would result in other proposals by American political elites that directly addressed American domestic concerns about race. In 1895, Senator Morgan of Alabama proposed in a speech to the members of the American Colonization Society that an "ideal" solution to the "Negro Problem" would be to ship African Americans to Africa and replace them with white Christian Armenians.[68]

Armenians in the United States continued to lobby for action. The *Chicago Tribune* covered a meeting convened by Armenians in the United States protesting the violence in Sasun. According to one Armenian speaker, the United States had a special duty to intervene to pursue this "righteous cause": "The fanaticism of the Turk cannot tolerate Christian Armenia. Since the main cause of this persecution is based on religious belief, let us try to interest all the great exponents of Christianity in America and the whole world in our cause."[69] In another article, the same newspaper quoted the chairman of the Armenian Patriotic Association, G. Hagopian, who described the "fiendish lust and atrocious cruelty on unarmed Christians." According to Hagopian, the actions of the Ottoman government constituted a call for European governments to take quasi-imperial control of the empire: "The time has come to abolish in toto the existing administration of Armenia and replace it by another regime approved by Great Britain and the other signatories of the treaties of Berlin and worked under their immediate supervision."[70] By 1895, Armenian organizations in the United States were regularly corresponding with newspapers and transmitting information about Armenian demands in the empire. In October, the *New York Tribune* published a letter from the Armenian Patriotic Alliance that sought to explain to American readers why Armenians were protesting against the Ottoman government.[71]

Public attention to the atrocities did not abate. That same year, former missionary Reverend Frederick Davis Greene published a book about the massacres, entitled *Armenian Massacres or The Sword of Mohammed Containing a Complete and Thrilling Account of the Terrible Atrocities and Wholesale Murders Committed in Armenia by Mohammedan Fanatics*.[72] It received wide attention, mostly because of endorsements from prominent politicians and social reformers, including Strong, who wrote the introduction. The book also included a petition signed by prominent politicians, religious leaders, and political reformers. ABCFM president

James Barton called Greene's book the "missionary contribution to the cause" and noted that 130,000 copies had already been "sold and paid for before the first copy [was] issued from the press."[73] Missionaries such as Greene had done great work, Barton felt, in informing the world of the massacres, influencing political and religious elites both at home and abroad, and delivering a strong message to Ottoman rulers. Greene's influence would extend beyond American shores, illustrating the transnational ties that were once again developing between Europe and the United States. Indeed, Barton noted that Greene had traveled to London, where he had a "personal conference with Mr. Gladstone, Lord Kimberley, the editor of the *London Times* and many other dignitaries, and he has engagements to speak to the limit of his ability for an indefinite time in small drawing room gatherings as well as public meetings."[74] Greene's book also received rave reviews in the *Arena*. The author of the review claimed that existing situations demonstrated the necessity of extending European imperial "tutelage" to *all* Muslim countries: "Missionaries, consuls, travelers of all nations unanimously declare that no Mohammedan country, under present circumstances, can be regenerated except under European superintendence. A brief geographic survey will show this. Algeria and Tunis have been regenerated; but by whom? By the French. Marocco [*sic*], still independent, remains sunk in unspeakable barbarity. Egypt is prosperous and tranquil; why? Because she is under British administration. . . . Whenever Mohammedan governments are still in power, anarchy continues to prevail."[75]

Another prominent study soon followed. In 1896, Reverend Edwin Bliss and Cyrus Hamlin published *Turkey and the Armenian Atrocities*, which reinforced the belief that this was a battle between violent Muslims and peaceloving Christians. The book's introduction, written by Christian reformer Frances Willard, identified Armenians as exemplary Christians whose spiritual beliefs melded with their racial superiority: their "personal resemblance to the supposed physical type of our Lord is probably more striking than that of any other race."[76] According to Willard, the "cruel" and "vindictive" behavior of Muslims was solely the result of their religious faith, and "under the insane spell of this awful fanaticism," Muslims had "come down like wolves on the gentle Christian people under their sway . . . not for any wrong they have done, but only because they are Christians."[77] Such atrocities demanded action: "Where are the dastards that stand by watching the slow martyrdom of a nation whose only fault is its loyalty to the Gospel that we profess?" She responded:

And then should come the answer that Nathan uttered in the face of David: pointing to America, England, the Christian nations of the Continent of Europe, "Thou art the man!" It is you that are standing by like the traitors of old and consenting to the death of those who in an age of spiritual apathy are sealing with the blood of martyrdom their holy allegiance to "the faith once delivered to the saints." This is the situation: Armenians are the nation; the Sultan and the soldiers are the devil's scourge; the Anglo-Saxon race is the cold-hearted spectator.[78]

In contrast to such cowardice, Willard praised the work of American missionaries who had acted heroically, for their "work alone can disinfect the land of the scimitar from its awful taint, and disintegrate by means of education the public opinion that prefers the harem to the home and the Koran of Mohammed to the New Testament of Christ."[79]

Coverage of this kind prompted hundreds of Americans to write letters to editors and to the American government demanding action. As John Havemeyer asked in an open letter to President Cleveland, which was reprinted in the *New York Times*, "Has not the time come when the United States can and should be the leader in the movement to place international relations on a higher plane?"[80] The United States had a "duty of benefiting, enlightening, and influencing for good the nations of the world." Comparing Turkey to a "wild beast among the nations of the earth," Havemeyer argued that this was the moment for the United States to act, for it was "in the order of Divine Providence" that "some men and some nations must be lighthouses for the guidance and protection of others."[81]

Newspapers and journals joined in promoting relief efforts as well. One of the country's most influential and popular religious journals, the *Christian Herald*, launched a fund drive in 1895 that raised $10,000 that year alone, which it sent to ABCFM missionaries in Van, an Armenian town in the Ottoman Empire whose inhabitants had experienced particularly brutal repression. By 1898, the journal had managed to raise more than $75,000. Edward Everett Hale, the Unitarian minister and the nephew of Edward Everett, who had helped the Greeks during their war for independence, fought his own battle to help the Christians in the Ottoman Empire through his *Lend a Hand* journal, which solicited funds for suffering Armenians. As the press increasingly covered the massacres, the American public responded en masse, organizing to push for greater American intervention.

The American Public Response
to the Armenian Massacres

As they learned about the plight of Armenians in their daily newspapers and Sunday sermons, Americans increasingly joined relief commissions to raise funds and lobby the U.S. government to act. In fact, the first organization, the Friends of Armenia, had formed in reaction to Armenian revolutionary activity even before the first major massacre in Sasun. Political and religious dignitaries, including William Lloyd Garrison Jr., Henry Blackwell, Alice Stone Blackwell, Edward Everett Hale, and Julia Ward Howe, were founding members. The Friends of Armenia held its first meeting in March 1894, at which point Henry Blackwell called for Armenian Americans to vote against President Cleveland in the next election and, more drastically, to encourage Armenians to obtain what they wanted through use of arms if words were unsuccessful.[82] At another meeting, convened after the massacre at Sasun, Howe addressed the audience and passionately argued that "the spirit of civilization, the sense of Christendom, the heart of humanity . . . plead for justice, all cry out against barbarous warfare of which the victims are helpless men, tender women and children."[83]

In response to these calls, concerned Americans created local Armenian relief committees throughout the country. The New York Armenian Relief Association launched a Thanksgiving appeal in November 1895, which was published in hundreds of newspapers across the country. The appeal called for financial aid for the "quarter of a million of souls" who were "destitute and helpless through the fanatical fury of Mohammedan mobs and the soldiers of the sultan, whose constant thirst is for the blood of Christian people."[84]

With the help of the ABCFM, the New York Armenian Relief Committee expanded in December 1895 to form the National Armenian Relief Committee, which became the organizational leader for Armenian relief branches across the country. The new organization's executive board included former ABCFM missionary to the Armenians, Frederick D. Greene; Supreme Court Justice David Brewer, who was born in the Ottoman Empire to missionary parents; Spencer Trask, philanthropist, venture capitalist, and soon-to-be chairman of the *New York Times*; and Jewish philanthropist and businessman Jacob Schiff. The work of the National Armenian Relief also drew the support of major corporate donors, such as John D. Rockefeller, who immediately donated $1,000 to the cause. Relief organizations mobilized thousands of Americans in mass protests across the country. Between 1894 and 1896 they also raised an astounding $300,000 to aid suffering Armenians.

Willard also continued to involve the Women's Christian Temperance Union in the effort. Focusing on the plight of Armenian women, she injected an important gender component into the attack on Islam and the Turks by emphasizing the sexual violence committed by Muslims against Armenian women during the war. She also contrasted the sexual mores of Muslim and Christian households, excoriating Islam while reinforcing traditional domestic gender norms: "It is the old fight of the mosque against the church, the harem against the home. . . . And this is the reason why the Women of this great country should rise up en masse in behalf of the women of that downtrodden land."[85] Two months later, Willard sent a petition on behalf of its "million members" to senators and representatives in Congress. If they were devoted to the "protection of the home," Willard maintained, then the United States could "no longer remain a silent spectator of the agony and outrage inflicted by Moslem savages upon our brother and sister Christians whose only fault is their devotion to Christ and their loyalty to a pure home."[86]

As the massacres continued, the ABCFM worked alongside Armenian American leaders, Armenian relief organizations, and Secretary of State Olney to secure the intervention of the American National Red Cross. As a federally incorporated organization, the American National Red Cross straddled the worlds of relief work and government agency, and it held the benefit of constituting a member of an international organization recognized by the sultan. Clara Barton, who founded the organization, initially hesitated to engage in such a monumental task. Faced with pressure from so many organizations and religious and political leaders, she eventually consented. The organization's efforts to enter the Ottoman Empire faced immediate opposition from the sultan, who assumed that the American Red Cross would lack neutrality. Barton herself felt that the American government was becoming too politically involved in the Armenian Massacres and that the American press and relief organizations were unfairly focusing on the religious nature of the violence, thus threatening the organization's ability to provide any real relief. She was particularly incensed by an announcement made by an American relief organization, the Pro-Armenian Alliance, in the American press, whereby the organization claimed to be working "hand in glove" with the Red Cross.[87] The alliance had printed two million pamphlets to support the Armenian cause, with a title page including inflammatory phrases such as "God against Allah,"

"Christ against Mohammed," "Bible against Koran," and "Heaven against Hell."[88] As Barton noted, the Pro-Armenian Alliance's attacks on Islam and the Ottoman Empire were "only one among scores, which had led me to consider how, with these representations, we were ever to get any further."[89]

Barton met with the sultan, assuring him that the organization was nonpartisan and would not discriminate based on religion, ethnicity, or political affiliation.[90] Barton's words and actions assuaged the misgivings of the sultan but soured her relations with religious and relief organizations back home. She faced virulent critiques from the National Armenian Relief Committee, which charged that she was distributing aid to Muslims that was meant only for Armenian Christians. Although she provided aid regardless of the religious affiliation of the sufferers, Barton privately believed that the problem stemmed from the racial savagery of local tribal groups, whom she described in a letter to a friend as "uncontrollable, savage and bloodthirsty as our Indians ever are." The Ottoman government probably opposed these massacres, Barton maintained, but "I am not sure that they can quite control the situation, any more than we would be able to control our Indians on the war path."[91] Barton worked closely with American and British missionaries, but maintained strict neutrality and refusing to assign blame or to participate in political commentary. This attitude made her relations with the National Armenian Relief Committee so difficult that she eventually ended all affiliations with the group.[92]

The American Government Response to the Armenian Massacres

Pressure exerted by relief organizations extended to lobbying the U.S. government to intercede. Their calls would result in congressional action in early December 1894. Although Cleveland virtually ignored the issue in his State of the Union message on 3 December 1894, that same day, at the prompting of Senator George Hoar of Massachusetts, the Senate passed a resolution calling on the president to work with European powers to stop the massacres and to inform Congress about all diplomatic exchanges on the topic. A special delegation from the Evangelical Alliance met with Secretary of State Gresham on 20 December 1894 and presented him with a petition outlining the organization's requests. The petition opened by highlighting its political power as a religious organization that claimed to unofficially represent 15 million Americans. The organization's potential political influence was certainly not lost on the secretary of state.[93]

Discounting the historical contingencies that had determined local out-breaks of violence in the empire in the previous decades, the Evangelical Alliance maintained the now familiar explanation that the massacres con-stituted a reoccurrence of Ottoman Muslim hatred for its Christian sub-jects. It explained the violence through its accumulated understanding of these distinct events: "The destruction of Armenian villages in 1890 and 1880, the Bulgarian atrocities in 1876, when 15,000 Christians were put to the sword, two-thirds of whom were women and children, and the massacres of Lebanon and Damascus in 1860, when 12,000 Christians perished, are matters of history. The story of these atrocities renders cred-ible prior to the investigations of an authoritative commission the worst reports which have come to us of the Sassoon massacres."[94]

These recent atrocities, the petition continued, were "a crime against our common humanity," which deserved "the reprobation of every civilized people." Undoubtedly aware of President Cleveland's conservative stance on foreign policy, members of the delegation nonetheless urged the U.S. government to "exercise all the influence consistent with our foreign policy in behalf of religious liberty and personal rights in the Ottoman Empire." This pressure had to come from an outside power because there was "no hope for reform from within."[95] Finally, the delegation urged the presi-dent to accept the sultan's invitation to have an American representative accompany European powers in investigating the massacres in Sasun (a request the president had turned down two weeks earlier) and to increase the number of American consuls throughout the empire. The organiza-tion's petition was republished in major American newspapers.[96]

The Evangelical Alliance's demands clashed with President Cleveland's staunch policies of nonentanglement in foreign affairs. Cleveland had ini-tially turned down the sultan's request for American participation, main-taining that because the United States had not been a party to the Treaty of Berlin, sending a representative would be "entirely beyond the limits of justification or propriety."[97] The delegation's visit changed his mind. After receiving their reports, he authorized American consul Milo Jewett to par-ticipate in the investigation, though only to "inform this Government as to the exact truth."[98] Cleveland was not alone in wanting to keep the United States out of European and Ottoman affairs. Upon learning of the U.S. decision to send Jewett, Russia and France protested and forced the sul-tan to rescind the invitation.[99] Given the Ottoman government's hostility to American missionaries during this time—and Jewett's historical affili-ation with the ABCFM—the sultan may have felt that Jewett would not be a fair observer. Similarly, both the Russians and the French sought to keep the status quo in the Ottoman Empire. The presence of an American investigator sympathetic to the Christian Armenians could have threatened their positions of influence over the issue.[100] Throughout 1894, the American minister in Istanbul protested the sultan's change of heart, but Russian pressure proved too persuasive and he refused to change his mind.[101]

European hostility to American interference in Ottoman affairs extended to the French press. One Parisian newspaper accused the United States of violating its own foreign policy principles: "President Cleveland, who but recently had only the Monroe doctrine on his lips, now throws himself into the thick of the conflict in another hemisphere. . . . There are indications that America may become the seventh European power."[102] American newspapers republished these reproaches. The American press defended U.S. actions and took the opportunity to contrast its benevolent and Christian foreign policy to selfish European inaction. The *New York Tribune* maintained that the United States had no interest in becoming the "seventh European Power," nor did it want to meddle in European affairs. Furthermore, the United States was not interested in "territorial aggrandizement in Central Asia," but "as a civilized nation the United States" was "interested in all things that appeal to common humanity." Historical precedent demonstrated this commitment, the author noted, as when the United States had involved itself in the Damascus affair of 1840. American intervention was a humanitarian duty, and the United States had claimed its rightful membership among civilized, Christian powers: "To say that the Christians of Armenia may be outraged and butchered at the will of their oppressors, and yet this Government must not speak a word in their behalf, because it is not a party to the Berlin treaty of 1878 and has not been invited by any of the signatory Powers to interfere, is to put us outside the pale of common humanity. Would Mr. Cleveland or Mr. Gresham refuse to save a drowning man simply because he 'had not been introduced?'"[103]

By 1895, the ABCFM and the Evangelical Alliance had come to the realization that European interventions were too weak to protect Armenians from state-sponsored violence, and thus they reasserted their call for more direct American action. In October 1895, the Evangelical Alliance adopted a resolution calling upon the U.S. government to unite with Europeans in "forcibly stopping the inhuman butchery of fellow-Christians in Armenia" and "invoked the intercession of the Christian powers of Europe to unite and abate this nuisance of the civilized world."[104] The group forwarded its appeals to the U.S. government and European leadership. Its efforts were somewhat successful; the American government twice sent gunboats to the Ottoman coast, and Secretary of State Olney discussed with leaders of the American Board the possibility of sending marines to protect American missionary interests—a prospect that never came to fruition.[105]

President Cleveland was forced to deal with the issue again in his Annual Message to Congress in December 1895. He noted that the massacres had resulted from "fanatic hostility to Christian influences" and had placed American missionaries in danger. Cleveland maintained that "no effort" had been spared to protect the missionaries, though he did not discuss American efforts to help Armenians.[106] Despite the president's refusal to move beyond the protection of American lives, the ABCFM and the Evangelical Alliance nonetheless continued to push him to intervene more directly. The Evangelical Alliance's calls for greater cooperation with European powers may also have been instrumental in a British-led proposal for joint British-American action in the empire. The proposal, first offered by British diplomat Joseph Chamberlain in 1896, asked Olney if the United States would participate in a joint naval demonstration to intimidate the sultan into ending the violence.[107] Secretary of State Olney noted in his response to the British proposal: "[If] England should now seriously set about putting the Armenian charnel-house in order, there can be little doubt that the United States would consider the moment opportune for vigorous exertion on behalf of American citizens and interests in Turkey. . . . It would support such demands by all the physical force at its disposal—with the necessary result, I think, that its attitude would both morally and materially strengthen the hands of England."[108]Although British prime minister Lord Salisbury eventually backed away from the plan, Olney's initial reaction was indicative of the American government's increased openness to engage more aggressively in Ottoman affairs, under the guise of protecting its citizens.

Massive protests also exerted pressure on Congress. In late 1895, 2,000 concerned citizens gathered to hear a sermon in Brooklyn in the Central Congregational Church, where Reverend Dr. A. J. F. Behrends read a petition to Congress urging greater support for the Armenians. Although he recognized the delicate stance of the United States vis-à-vis its relations with other interested parties, he nonetheless called for the United States to pressure the Ottoman government and the European powers to act.[109] Only two weeks earlier, a mass meeting in New York City organized by the Armenian Relief Association filled Chickering Hall. Led by the president of Columbia University, Seth Low, the list of speakers boasted some of the most prominent clergymen of the time. After passionate speeches, attendees voted on a resolution firmly condemning the Ottoman Empire and calling for an end to Turkish rule over Armenians. It was resolved to immediately forward the resolution to the president.[110] Similar calls for direct American action came from the Baptist Pastors Association of New York City and from military leaders, such as Oliver Howard, a deeply religious former Union army general.

Members of Congress also called for action. In November 1895, Senator Hoar of Massachusetts organized a conference at his residence with ABCFM president Judson Smith and an important Armenian activist, Hagob Bogigian. Following the conference, Hoar sent a letter to President Cleveland letting him know that he could depend on his support "both by speech and vote, of the most vigorous action you may take to prevent further cruelties toward the Armenians in Turkey, even if you determine to treat the persons who commit them as pirates or common enemies of the human race."[111]

Six months later, the Evangelical Alliance and the ABCFM again collaborated to pressure the president and secretary of state. Strong wrote a fellow clergyman in May 1896 that the ABCFM had formed a new committee dedicated to protecting American missionary interests in the empire. Its members included influential lawyers, judges, missionaries, politicians, and businessmen, as well as Strong himself. According to Strong, "Several of the Committee are personally acquainted with the President or Mr. Olney and are believed to have a great deal of influence with him. I believe that they can do and will do all that can be done."[112] The committee met personally with the president a week later. Its objectives included convincing Cleveland to secure American consular representatives in areas with ABCFM missionary activity, defending missionaries maligned by the Ottoman government, and replacing the current American minister to the Ottoman Empire with a man more sympathetic to the ABCFM.[113]

Responding to criticism of his inaction, Cleveland again addressed the matter publicly on 9 December 1896, placing the burden on Europeans. He noted that no "decisive action [had been taken] on the part of the great nations having the right by treaty to interfere for the protection of those exposed to the rage of mad bigotry and cruel fanaticism." The United States, in contrast, had assured the protection of American missionaries who, as American citizens, deserved American diplomatic aid. He defended his stance of nonentanglement by arguing that "the deep feeling and sympathy that have been aroused among our people ought not to blind their reason and judgment as to lead them to demand impossible things." Official involvement would lead to meddling in affairs beyond the nation's reach. Yet, Cleveland remained optimistic that something could be done, that such massacres would "offend the sight of Christendom," and that it seemed impossible for the demands of "good people throughout the Christian world" to "remain unanswered."[114] Of course, his calls to Christian action were only applicable to Europe—not to the United States.

Ongoing public pressure prompted members of Congress to propose resolutions on the issue. A week after President Cleveland's State of the Union speech, Wilkinson Call, a Democratic senator from Florida, proposed that "In the name of religion, humanity, and the principles on which all civilization rests . . . the United States should use peaceful negotiations or by force of arms if necessary, to stop the cruelties inflicted on the Armenians."[115] He went so far as to support the creation of an independent Armenian state, to be guarded by "civilized powers."[116] The following month, Republican representative Elijah Morse also called for aggressive action to join Europe to "wipe the Turkish nation off the face of the earth."[117] He was joined by Representative William Hepburn of Iowa, who argued that Armenians did not want American sympathy, "they want rescue. They do not want our mere words; they want Christian people to come to their relief."[118] Another petition for action came to Congress via the Ohio legislature, which condemned the violence of "Moslem savages" who murdered Armenians "for no other reason than because of their devotion to the Christian religion."[119]

Although Congress ultimately refused to endorse resolutions calling for direct American intervention, both houses overwhelmingly passed the Cullom Resolution, named after its sponsor, Senator Shelby Cullom of Illinois. The resolution maintained that it was the "imperative duty, in the interest of humanity, to express the earnest hope that the European Concert . . . shall stay the hand of fanaticism and lawless violence."[120] Cullom maintained that the violence stemmed from religious fanaticism: "The religious leaders of those engaged in the indiscriminate slaughter which has been carried on incite the people to action by crying from the housetops, 'Woe to the Mussulman who does not kill at least one Christian and carry away some of their belongings, in the name of Mohammed and his Imperial Majesty the Sultan.'"[121] It was "a matter of some embarrassment" to the nation that it could not, "consistent with its declarations in the past, consent to send a fleet and an army to that country with orders to use whatever power may be necessary to put a stop at once to the indiscriminate murder and slaughter of all classes of Armenians who have so far offered practically no resistance." American neutrality had its limits, however: "This country of ours may be said to be a neutral Government, so far as interference with the internal affairs of any Government in Europe is concerned. It has no disposition to interfere in the affairs of European Governments, except in the cause of humanity itself. And we now appeal most earnestly, in the name of humanity, to the Governments which have contracted to protect those people that they shall carry out their obligations."[122] He further maintained that the "sympathy of America has always gone out to the oppressed and misgoverned peoples of other countries. We extended our hands and gave of our means to Greece when Turkey, years ago, strove to crush her to the earth." Moreover, he knew of no other situation "which has existed in this world for centuries which has called upon civilized nations and peoples for interference equaling the necessity of stopping the indiscriminate slaughter which has been going on in Turkish Armenia."[123]

Although the resolution passed with overwhelming support in Congress, it received little attention from President Cleveland. Cleveland's refusal to act became an issue in both presidential and state elections in 1896. The Republican Party's claim that it would act on the Armenian issue garnered the support of many religious organizations and prominent clergymen; indeed, the party platform maintained that "the United States should exercise all the influence it can properly exert to bring these atrocities to an end."[124] The election of William McKinley would ensure a new and more aggressive foreign policy.

Making the Ottoman Empire Pay: Missionary Lobbying and American Interests in the Ottoman Empire

After the Armenian revolutionary party took over the Ottoman bank in 1896, continued public outcry in Europe and the United States raised the likelihood of European intervention. With this threat in mind and with confidence that it had succeeded in teaching Armenian nationalists a lesson, the Ottoman government ended its violent campaign. Although persecution and isolated cases of violence would continue in the following decade, international attention moved away from the Armenians in early 1897 and focused again on Greece and Crete. The Greco-Turkish War began in February 1897 over Greek efforts to liberate Crete from Ottoman rule and join the island to Greece. As violence against Armenians abated, Americans transferred their sympathy and attention to the Greeks and, to a growing extent, the Cubans, whose revolutionary war against Spain was increasingly making newspaper headlines.

The end of the Armenian Massacres, however, did not end missionary lobbying to ensure American interests in the Ottoman Empire. ABCFM members successfully pressured McKinley to appoint ABCFM trustee James Angell to the position of American minister to the Ottoman Empire.[125] Barton and Strong traveled to Washington, D.C., and met personally with the president in early 1897 to ensure the appointment.[126]

Minister Angell, always attentive to missionary interests, consulted with Strong and Barton regularly. In December 1897, the three decided that a more aggressive policy would be necessary to pressure the Ottoman sultan to repay the ABCFM for buildings damaged during the massacres. Angell cabled the president requesting that he send gunboats to "rattle the Sultan's windows."[127] Strong was confident in his ability to influence the president in this regard and did not find it necessary to "bring pressure on members of Congress," for if the board decided "that a show of force is desirable, a visit to the President on the part of our Committee would doubtless lead to action—unless, indeed, the President's spinal column is a size smaller than we had reason to think."[128] President McKinley promised to send gunboats after the resolution of the Cuban issue, a promise he kept.[129] In 1900, the USS *Kentucky* arrived in the port of Smyrna, poised to launch an attack. With the governor of Smyrna warning that Americans were ready to bombard the port, the sultan acquiesced, and the ABCFM obtained its payment.

Much like American actions during the Greek War of Independence in 1821, American public pressure concerning the Armenian Massacres failed to elicit U.S. military involvement, but it did reflect the continued ability of Americans to act in unofficial ways. Nongovernmental organizations, including the American Red Cross and American missionary organizations, took up a leading role on the ground and increasingly involved the U.S. government in their endeavors. In many ways, the Armenian Massacres also prepared the way for more aggressive U.S. foreign policy on the eve of the Spanish-American War. As Strong noted in *Expansion, Under New World Conditions*, published in 1900, the selfish American policy of nonentanglement had divorced the country from its moral responsibility on the world stage, and allowed the United States to stand by "and pusillanimously watch the unspeakable Turk while, in the broad daylight of nineteenth-century civilization he butchered more Christians than suffered martyrdom during all of the 'Ten Great Persecutions' under the Roman emperors."[130] The Spanish-American War would help to erase the moral culpability many Americans felt for not having intervened during the Armenian Massacres.

The Armenian Massacres and the continued instability and violence in the following years resulted in an upsurge in Armenian migration to the United States in the first decade of the twentieth century. By World War I, more than 60,000 Armenians had come to the United States. Many became naturalized citizens shortly after their arrival, and their activism would play a central role in exhorting the United States to intervene when genocidal violence against the Armenian community broke out in 1915. This time, calls for intervention did not depend on Europe, however. By the end of the war, many Americans, urged by Armenians, called on the United States to assume a formal role, under the newly created League of Nations, as the official mandatory power to oversee an independent Armenian state.

8

THE UNITED STATES, WORLD WAR I, AND THE END OF THE OTTOMAN EMPIRE, 1908–1921

When the United States declared war on Germany in April 1917, President Woodrow Wilson justified the decision by maintaining that the war was about protecting "political liberty" and ensuring a world "made safe for democracy."[1] A few months later, in his Fourteen Points speech, Wilson further detailed American aims for an international order that many would interpret as the recognition of the legitimate right of self-determination for peoples around the world.[2] President Wilson's private views on the political rights for non-Europeans, however, were not as universal as his speeches implied. Although he opposed European-style imperialism, Wilson believed that certain groups required political and civilizational tutelage before they could achieve true independence and self-rule.

As one scholar has noted, "Wilson rejected the economic and political forms of traditional colonialism, but replaced them with a scheme equally founded upon racial hierarchy and political domination."[3] Beliefs about the racial and political inferiority of Filipinos buttressed his decision to maintain American imperial rule in the Philippines, despite continued demands for independence from Filipino nationalists and from members of his own political party.[4] Such beliefs had also helped inform his decision to occupy Haiti in 1915 and the Dominican Republic in 1916.[5] The same year the United States occupied the Dominican Republic, Wilson purchased the Virgin Islands from Denmark for $25 million, a decision he made without consulting the people of the islands and one that denied them full constitutional rights.

Neither were Wilson's beliefs about the inferiority of certain peoples limited to the foreign realm. On the home front, Wilson expanded policies of racial exclusion and discrimination against African Americans. During his presidency, he refused to address the dramatic rise in the lynching of African Americans and formal segregation was expanded into federal government offices for the first time in American history. When confronted by African American leaders about these discriminatory policies, Wilson argued that segregation reduced "friction" between the races. In Wilson's words, "The American people, as a whole, sincerely desire and wish to support, in every way they can, the advancement of the Negro race in America."[6] While meant to reassure, such statements, reinforced by discriminatory policies, implicitly conveyed Wilson's paternalistic beliefs that African Americans had not yet achieved the same degree of advancement as white Americans.

Indeed, Wilson's beliefs about the malleability of race allowed for racial progress through political, religious, and economic tutelage both at home and abroad. His liberal internationalism was suffused with the belief that so-called noncivilized populations could "advance" only by modeling themselves, by force if necessary, on modern nation-states, such as the United States. This process ideally entailed adopting Christianity, capitalism, and democracy. As one scholar argues, "this assumption—that the path followed by western European countries and by the United States was the proper path for all—was, among other things, a racial assumption. In this sense, racial hierarchy undergirded liberal developmentalism at every point."[7]

In this endeavor, Wilson's strong Christian faith played an important role. As he had remarked in a 1905 speech to the National Federation of Churches: "There is a mighty task before us and it welds us together. It is to make the United States a mighty Christian nation and to Christianize the world."[8] In 1911, as Wilson was touring the country in preparation for the launch of his presidential campaign, he delivered another speech aptly entitled "The Bible and Progress," in which he revealed the deep links between his Christian faith and his vision for American foreign policy. He stated: "there are times in the history of nations when they must take up the crude instruments of bloodshed in order to vindicate spiritual conceptions. For liberty is a spiritual conception, and when men take up arms to set other men free, there is something sacred and holy in warfare."[9]

Christianity was the key to progress itself, Wilson maintained; indeed, the United States served as an "example to the civilized world" not because of her wealth, but because of her religious and political values, which were grounded in biblical understandings of freedom and liberty. Wilson believed that the United States had a fundamental and divine role in "advancing" the rest of the world. During his presidency, the Ottoman Empire became an obvious target for such development.

Wilson was not alone in believing that only certain populations were ready for self-rule. His own secretary of state, Robert Lansing, was initially alarmed by Wilson's public commitments to self-determination. Lansing believed that such promises were unrealistic for people he deemed racially, religiously, and culturally inferior and thus incapable of self-governance. As he remarked in his diary in 1918: "The more I think about the President's declaration as to the right of 'self-determination,' the more convinced I am of the danger of putting such ideas into the minds of certain races. . . . Will it not breed discontent, disorder, and rebellion? Will not the Mohammedans of Syria and Palestine and possibly of Morocco and Tripoli rely on it? How can it be harmonized with Zionism, to which the President is practically committed? The phrase is simply loaded with dynamite. It will raise hopes which can never be realized."[10] Lansing's words revealed how race and Islam had become effectively synonymous. He feared the effect such "ideas" would have on "certain races," meaning neither Arabs nor Turks but, rather, "Mohammedans." Despite idealistic interpretations of Wilson's calls for self-determination, it was this privately expressed logic that helped drive U.S. foreign policy in the Middle East during and after World War I.

Wilson attracted other likeminded friends and advisors, many of whom had deep ties to American Protestant missionary interests in the Ottoman Empire.[11] Wilson's longest and most trusted friend, Cleveland H. Dodge, had been one of the first financiers of Robert College in Istanbul. Two of Dodge's children served as Protestant missionaries in the Ottoman Empire during World War I. Another friend, a wealthy financier of missionary endeavors and a trustee of Robert College, Charles Crane, had been one of the largest contributors to Wilson's 1912 presidential campaign. The two remained in close contact during Wilson's time in office, and Crane would serve as one of Wilson's chosen delegates to assess the future of the postwar Middle East. Crane's only son would become the personal secretary of Secretary of State Lansing, thus linking Crane even more firmly with high-level diplomats. By the end of World War I, ABCFM leader James Barton, who had played such an important role during the Armenian

Massacres in the 1890s, also became part of Wilson's inner circle through the intermediations of Crane and Dodge.

Wilson's views on the Middle East were shaped by non-Christian religious activists as well. Wilson's close friend, Louis Brandeis, whom he appointed as the first American Jew on the Supreme Court, was a leader of the American Zionist movement, as was Rabbi Stephen Wise, another close friend and advisor. It was the latter who in 1911 introduced Wilson to Henry Morgenthau, who would become a major contributor to Wilson's first presidential campaign and would be appointed U.S. ambassador to the Ottoman Empire just months before the Armenian Genocide in 1915.[12]

These advisors played an important role in shaping Wilson's policies toward the Ottoman Empire during the war, including his response to the Armenian Genocide. Crane, Barton, and Dodge had led the largest Armenian relief organization, formed in response to the genocidal violence against Ottoman Armenians. As American ambassador to the Ottoman Empire, Morgenthau had acted as information liaison between the American government and relief organizations. Together, these men prompted the largest international humanitarian effort the country had ever seen.[13]

The genocidal violence waged by Ottoman rulers against Armenians confirmed Wilson's belief that certain people, including Turkish Muslims, were incapable of civilized rule. Not surprisingly, then, by the end of the war, Wilson ignored the wishes of the people in the Middle East, who demanded political independence. Instead, Wilson supported a mandate system that assigned former Ottoman territories to the French and British. Article 22 of the League of Nations Covenant codified these views: these territories were "inhabited by peoples not yet able to stand by themselves under the strenuous conditions of the modern world," for which reason the mandatory powers would follow "the principle that the well-being and development of such peoples form a sacred trust of civilization."[14] As Wilson saw it, the professed goal of the mandate system was to turn backward people into modern citizens ready to responsibly claim their political independence. Not content in advancing European mandates alone, Wilson worked with other diplomats and activists in supporting the extension of an American mandate over Armenia, Istanbul, and other former Ottoman territories.

Likewise, Wilson's beliefs about the inherent inferiority of Muslims and Arabs, in combination with his Christian faith, helped to justify a crucial decision that would shape the political destiny of the Middle East. Partly in response to pressure from Brandeis and Wise, Wilson formally approved the 1917 Balfour Declaration, a British initiative designating a

Jewish homeland in Palestine on territory already inhabited by Arabs. Wise and Brandeis enlisted the help of Christian Zionists to appeal to Wilson's Christian faith, convincing the president that establishing a Jewish homeland would facilitate the biblical end of days and the second coming of Jesus on earth.[15] The British "gift" of land to European and American Jewish immigrants was based in part on the modern and colonial premise that the Arabs who lived there had no legitimate claim to land in an area not recognized as a nation by the international community.[16] The Balfour Declaration was also driven by British attempts to solve the larger "Jewish Question," a "problem" that resulted from the anti-Semitic exclusion of Jews from European nation-states.

Ultimately Wilson envisioned that Americans had a duty to bring Christianity, civilization, and political modernity to the world. That vision helped drive his foreign policy decisions during a war whose outcome permanently redefined the Middle East. The consequences of such beliefs bequeathed an enduring legacy to the subjects of the former Ottoman Empire, dramatically reshaping their political and national status. Ironically, although many in the Middle East and beyond had taken Wilson's promises of self-determination to heart, the imposition of mandates in the name of political reform simultaneously ignored the attempts of peoples in the region to define their status as modern citizens of the world. Furthermore, Americans failed to realize that the political modernity they sought for the Ottoman Empire, which included the powerful ideology of ethnic nationalism, had already arrived in the empire and would help drive the Armenian Genocide.

The United States and the Young Turk Revolution of 1908

Americans were not alone in wanting to bring modernity to the Ottoman Empire. A new political movement that called for modernization modeled on systems practiced in European nation-states seized power in a bloodless revolution in 1908. Known as the Young Turks, many of its members were educated in France and Germany. Their political ideology drew in part on nineteenth-century European intellectual ideas about nationhood, blending Social Darwinism with conceptions of the nation-state that identified ethnic, racial, and religious homogeneity as a crucial element of state security and national cohesion.[17] The outbreak of World War I set the stage for the most radical of the Young Turks to extend these beliefs to their most violent logical conclusion: purging more than a million Armenians from the empire.

In spite of subsequent condemnations that blamed the genocide on Muslim fanaticism, Young Turk violence against Armenian Christians did not stem from religious fervor.[18] Many Young Turks were adamant secularists, if not atheists. Rather, the violence originated in a modern worldview that sought to transform the multiethnic, religiously diverse Ottoman Empire into a Turkish state defined by Turkish identity, which included language, ethnicity, religion, and race.[19] Advancing this ideal also meant eliminating any threats to the security of the newly defined empire.[20] Ottoman subjects of other religious faiths, including Jews and Christians, and other ethnicities, including Kurdish and Arab Muslims, could remain citizens in the empire if they accepted the ideology of Turkish identity and did not challenge the regime, did not demand independence, and did not pose a security threat. Since religious identity contributed to defining what it meant to be Turkish, non-Muslims in the empire were excluded more often than were Muslim Arabs and Kurds, who could at least claim some religious affinities with Turks. Such affinities, however, would not prevent the latter from facing similar forms of Ottoman imperial violence during the war.[21]

This surge in ethnic nationalism was part of an international phenomenon that increasingly helped define modern nation-states. As one historian notes, the Young Turk movement was part of a global trend as "the basis of nationalism everywhere shifted from liberalism to authoritarianism, statism, and ethnocentrism."[22] Indeed, the United States and Europe were not exempt from such ideas, as exclusionary policies toward immigrants mounted alongside the "Jewish Question" in the first decades of the twentieth century.

Just as the Young Turks shifted toward promotion of a modern, secular, homogeneous ethnic state with exclusionary citizenship, they also abandoned many of the moral and religious safeguards that had granted non-Muslims a degree of protection under Islamic law. As historian Christopher Walker has poignantly noted, Islam had "a definite (though often obscured) place for Christian peoples" that "race-based Turkism" did not. For this reason, during the genocide, "the occasional expressions of horror by individual non-Armenians were apt to come from Muslim leaders. Religion has a place for a conscience, which racist ideologies do not."[23]

Americans who viewed the modern nation-state as the ultimate mark of progress failed to predict the inevitable consequences such ideas would have in the Ottoman Empire. When the secularist Young Turks mounted their successful opposition to the rule of Sultan Abdul Hamid in 1908, the initial reaction from many missionaries and diplomats was enthusiastic and hopeful. Having forged alliances with the Armenian Revolutionary Federation, the Young Turks' political organization, the Committee for Union and Progress (CUP), touted itself as a proponent of European-style modernity defined by a constitutional form of government, secularism, and scientific rationalism.[24] Many Americans hoped that the Young Turks had started on the path to modernity and had given up their Islamic beliefs for Western-style political liberty.[25]

Editorials in the American press offered cautious optimism and praised the Young Turks for leading the empire into the modern age. Of course, some Americans credited American missionaries for incubating this positive change. Renowned journalist Talcott Williams, who was born in Turkey to ABCFM missionaries and whose sister served as a missionary among the Armenians, reminded Americans that "for eighty years the American missionaries have been laying the foundations and preaching the doctrine which makes free government possible."[26]

Although initially supportive of the Young Turks, Armenians became swiftly disillusioned after a counterrevolutionary movement against the Young Turks prompted a massacre of Armenian Christians in the Anatolian province of Adana in 1909. Between 1878 and 1904, more than 850,000 Kurdish, Circassian, and Turcoman refugees had settled in Anatolia after fleeing Russian policies of demographic engineering.[27] More recently, new constitutional provisions allowed Armenians the right to purchase and bear arms, which they publicly celebrated. The counterrevolutionary movement exacerbated these existing tensions, fueling violence that led to the deaths of 20,000 Armenians and 2,000 Muslims. Americans in the Ottoman Empire were also included in this backlash. Two American missionaries were killed, an American missionary school was burned, and the American Singer Sewing Company factory was damaged.

The U.S. government immediately sent two warships to the area. A week after the massacres, Representative Irving Wanger of Pennsylvania sponsored a successful resolution in the House that attempted to cloak its warning to the Ottoman government behind a congratulatory statement. The resolution celebrated the new constitutional government and hoped that the Turkish people would enjoy "all the blessings of civilization," but also expressed hope that the new government would promptly restore "order" and eliminate "the appalling atrocities upon Christian missionaries and other non-Moslems which thrill the horror of the civilized world."[28]

Some Americans explained the massacres as an Islamic "hiccup" carried out by fanatical Muslims who were in their death throes. The *San Jose Evening News* noted, "Abdul Hamid, who made all things—even massacres—serve his ends is eliminated and the new administration is committed to wide *liberalis.* Better things can, at least, be hoped for the long-suffering, but not wholly innocent Armenian."[29] Eager to remain on good terms with the new government, some ABCFM missionaries blamed Armenian revolutionary activities and other Armenians who had too publicly celebrated their new freedoms. A former ABCFM secretary blamed both parties: "revolutionary Armenians" and "fanatical and reactionary Moslems."[30] Despite maintaining its faith in the Young Turk government, the *North American Review* noted with pessimism that "Young Turkey's revolutionary honeymoon" was over.[31]

Over the next few years, a painful and sometimes violent split occurred between the liberal, more tolerant wing of the Committee for Union and Progress and the extreme Turko-nationalist faction. The massacres in Adana had led more liberal members of the committee to back away from closer political alignments with Armenians, fearing the backlash of pro-Christian reforms on Muslims. Intraparty tensions were exacerbated by the Balkan Wars of 1912 and 1913, in which the Ottoman Empire lost more than 80 percent of its European territories and during which 600,000 Muslims were killed and millions more were forcibly displaced by the Greeks, Bulgarians, and Serbs.[32] Approximately 400,000 of these displaced Muslims would seek refuge in the Ottoman Empire.[33] The wars intensified Turkish nationalism among the extremist Young Turks. A 1913 coup within the Committee for Union and Progress forced out or violently eliminated its remaining liberal members.[34] The Balkan Wars had another important impact on the Young Turks: they learned about the extreme measures that nation-states used to purge ethnic minorities. As the historian Donald Bloxham argues, "Though there is no definite causal relationship between the population displacements and the coming Armenian genocide, it is beyond dispute that Muslim suffering on this scale, and the indifference of the outside world to it, heavily coloured late Ottoman perspectives, providing a model of the 'solution' of population problems and accentuating an already brutalized ethos of state demographic policy in the region."[35] Indeed, the trauma of the Balkan Wars had left a profound mark on two important CUP leaders who would later help organize the Armenian Genocide: future minister of the interior Mehmed Talaat Pasha and future minister of war Enver Pasha.[36]

The 1913 coup marked the official end to Ottoman Armenian support for the Committee for Union and Progress, leading Armenian activists to reassess their strategies to obtain political power and protection within the empire. Some sought external intervention from European powers, a strategy that corresponded particularly well with Russian interests. The Russian tsar had been facing political unrest across his empire, including from among the Armenian population. In hopes of solidifying their loyalty, the tsar reignited Russian sympathy for the Ottoman Armenian Question. In February 1914, with Russian help, the Armenian National Assembly (the official body that represented Armenians in the Ottoman Empire) convinced the Great Powers to impose a new reform program on Ottoman leaders. The reforms included provisions for two semi-independent Armenian provinces, to be governed by a supreme civil leader.[37] This push for foreign intervention was both thoroughly incompatible with and threatening to the Young Turks' nationalist program, which insisted on absolute independence from foreign influence and a stop to the security threat posed by the encroaching Russian Empire. Such reactions later pushed the Ottoman Empire to align itself with Germany against Russian, British and French forces during World War I.

The United States and the Ottoman Empire
on the Eve of War

During a period of mounting tension in 1913, a new American ambassador to the Ottoman Empire, Henry Morgenthau, arrived on the scene. Morgenthau had initially turned down Wilson's offer of the ambassadorship, which Wilson had proposed in exchange for Morgenthau's financial support during the presidential campaign. Morgenthau took offense at the appointment, complaining to the president that he had been chosen solely because he was Jewish. As one scholar has noted, "The assumption that Jews represented a natural bridge between Muslim Turks and Christian Americans merely rankled Morgenthau" who, having no diplomatic experience, felt he was more qualified for a cabinet-level position in the American government.[38] Morgenthau asked if Wilson was "aware that our people were so strongly opposed to having any position made a distinctly Jewish one or having the impression continued that Turkey was the only country where Jews would be received as our country's representative."[39] Rabbi Stephen Wise and President Wilson encouraged Morgenthau to reconsider, maintaining that his presence would be important in assuring the well-being of Palestinian Jews. Morgenthau eventually accepted the position.[40]

Shortly before Morgenthau left to assume his post, a trustee of a missionary board urged him to meet with, in his words, a "group of earnest and able men, who could speak with authority on the problems I should confront in the East."[41] Among the leaders of the Congregationalist, Presbyterian, United Presbyterian, Methodist, and Episcopal missionary boards was the omnipresent James Barton, who continued to represent the interests of the ABCFM. Morgenthau's missionary mentorship would not end with that meeting. After learning that Barton and four other men would be traveling to Europe at the same time as the ambassador on their way to a missionary conference in Europe, Morgenthau changed his ticket to travel on the same boat. During the voyage, Morgenthau recalled having a "revelation" that would forever change his outlook on American missionary work. Although he had previously stereotyped missionaries as "overzealous" and sectarian, long conversations with these men convinced him that they were, in fact, "advance agents of civilization," bringing "education, philanthropy, sanitation, medical healing, and moral uplift," to the "submerged Christians" in the Ottoman Empire.[42]

Morgenthau's enthusiasm for American Protestant missionary work increased over the following months, as he forged close contacts with the American missionary community in Istanbul. Several meetings with local American missionary leaders convinced him that "America's true mission in Turkey" was to support the "civilizing work" of the missionaries in spreading "the gospel of Americanism."[43] His praise extended to the local American schools, which demonstrated "great evidence of American idealism functioning in this remote and backward land, spreading civilization among people long submerged in ignorance."[44] Morgenthau's description of the benefits of American Protestant missionary work in the Ottoman Empire revealed the extent to which the terms *Americanism*, *Christianity*, *progress*, and *civilization* had become virtually synonymous in the American lexicon, even for diplomats of the Jewish faith.

Soon after his arrival, Morgenthau organized a trip to American missionary fields throughout the empire and the Holy Land. He traveled with several religious and diplomatic luminaries, broadening his network of American and British contacts and learning even more about missionary interests in the area and about British imperial perceptions of the Middle East. Those with whom he met included the president of Syrian Protestant College, Howard Bliss; Bliss's daughter, Mary; her husband Bayard Dodge (Cleveland Dodge's son); Presbyterian minister and chancellor of the University of Pittsburgh Samuel McKormick; and former British ambassador to the United States Viscount James Bryce, who would later become the most vocal British defender of the Armenian cause. During his trip, Morgenthau also met with important British colonial officials. In Cairo, he had a long conversation with Lord Kitchener, the

British agent and consul-general of Egypt, about the future of the Young Turks and the benefits of British colonial policy in Egypt. Only a few months later, Kitchener would assume the influential position of secretary of state for war.

Morgenthau's mounting admiration for American missionaries and British colonial officials contrasted sharply with his developing impressions of Muslims. As he wrote during his trip, he would not "soon forget the black looks of instinctive hatred upon the faces of the Arabs . . . who looked upon us as infidel intruders."[45] Walking through the winding streets of an Arab town, where the scenery reminded him of *One Thousand and One Arabian Nights*, he noted that: "Unconsciously, I could not keep from expecting genii to jump out at me from one of the little doors of the native houses."[46] His trip confirmed his belief in the necessity of bringing progress to a people unable to modernize on their own.

Within a month of Morgenthau's return to Istanbul, tensions had heated up between the Ottoman Empire and the United States. Although Morgenthau maintained that the American presence in the empire was purely altruistic, the United States had growing commercial interests in the area. Among these interests was the Singer Sewing Machine Company, which conducted millions of dollars' worth of business through hundreds of stores throughout the empire. The attack on one of the company's buildings during the Adana massacres in 1909 had earlier signaled that American companies could become targets. In June 1914, the Ottoman authorities ordered the boycott of Christian businesses and the deportation of 40,000 Greeks from Izmir, where Singer had four stores. Morgenthau felt compelled to act, both to defend American interests and to protest the deportations. Morgenthau was on good terms with Minister of the Interior Mehmed Talaat. He protested the orders, but, according to Morgenthau, Talaat responded that native populations had "conspired against Turkey," forcing it to lose "province after province." As Morgenthau recounted, "'Turkey for the Turks' was now Talaat's controlling idea."[47]

Rising tensions between Greece and the Ottoman Empire soon embroiled the United States in another matter. As relations between the two countries deteriorated, Ottoman officials expressed their fury with the United States for promising to deliver two warships to Greece, which would arrive before they would receive their own warships from Britain.[48] They accused the United States of compromising its own neutrality. According to Morgenthau, this accusation may have had some validity. He presumed that President Wilson's sympathy for the Greeks had led to his decision to sell ships to Athens for defense against a probable Ottoman attack.[49] By mid-June, after learning of massacres against the Greek population, the American consul in Izmir, George Horton, asked Morgenthau to request an American warship be sent to the area. The USS *Scorpion* arrived ten days later, further exacerbating Ottoman resentment. Again, the American press covered these recent events, thoroughly denouncing Turkish rule. Three months later, tensions between the United States and the Ottoman Empire would flare up again, this time on American soil.

Ottoman Ambassador Rustem Bey and the Debate
over Imperial Violence

By the fall of 1914, Ottoman diplomats were incensed at the extensive American press coverage of the massacres and deportation of Greek Christians. The Young Turks continued to believe that deporting non-Turks constituted part of their modern nation-building efforts and that it removed a significant national security threat. They maintained that their actions were no different from those that had been employed by the United States and by European powers, not to mention those of the Greeks themselves. In September 1914, on the eve of the Ottoman Empire's entry into World War I on the side of the Central Powers, Rustem Bey, the Ottoman ambassador in Washington, lashed out against the United States in an interview with an American newspaper, which was subsequently republished throughout the American press.[50]

Rustem attacked the U.S. decision to send an American gunboat to Izmir and the biased American press coverage of the Ottoman Empire. He maintained that Ottoman Christian subjects had been killed "not as Christians, but as political agitators engaged in undermining the Ottoman state, the while flaunting in the face of the government and dominant race the support of Russia, France and England."[51] Contrary to claims that Ottoman actions were the result of primitive Islamic fanaticism, he defended his country as a modern imperial state victimized by rebellious populations. He compared Ottoman actions to recent examples of imperial repression practiced and justified by other "civilized" countries. He reminded Americans that France had "smoked to death in caverns the Algerians fighting for the independence of their land" and that Britain's response to the "'rebels' in the Indian 'mutiny' was to blow them off [with] guns."[52] Rustem also positively compared Ottoman policies to the recent

Russian massacres of Jews, which had presented a terrible "spectacle of not one but twenty pogroms against an innocent race."[53]

Rustem's references to imperial violence did not leave the Americans unscathed. He pointed to the brutal military tactics Americans had used against Filipino colonial subjects and the extrajudicial violence regularly committed against African Americans: "The thought of the lynchings [sic] which occur daily in the United States and the memory of the 'watercures' in the Philippines should make them chary of attacking Turkey in connection with acts of savagery committed by her under provocation." He asked Americans to put themselves in the place of Turks: "Supposing . . . that the negroes were discovered to be engaged in a conspiracy with the Japanese to facilitate the invasion of the United States by the latter, how many of them would be left alive to tell the tale?"[54]

Press coverage of Rustem's critiques soon reached Secretary of State William Jennings Bryan and President Wilson. Appalled by the public denunciation of the United States by a foreign diplomat, Secretary Bryan immediately summoned Rustem to his office. Rustem doubled down on his initial attacks during the meeting and shortly after in what one historian has called "one of the most grossly insulting letters ever received by an American Secretary of State."[55] The letter attacked the American press and accused it of having over a period of years viciously maligned the Ottoman Empire: "Her religion, her nationality, her customs, her past, her present are reviled." This hateful press coverage was responsible for "poisoning public opinion" in the United States to such a degree that Turks were "seldom thought or spoken of in this country otherwise than as the 'unspeakable.'"[56] Unsurprisingly, Rustem was isolated from any future contact. Disgusted by American attitudes and unable to carry out his diplomatic duties, he resigned his position and returned home.[57]

Although Bryan and Wilson were unwilling to compare American and Ottoman practices of imperial repression, Americans with direct experience in discriminatory violence were less quick to dismiss Rustem's claims. African Americans used the ambassador's critiques of lynching to advance their own calls for civil and political equality. One African American newspaper commented that the president "could never recall the damage done by the truth that was uttered" by Rustem.[58] The National Association for the Advancement of Colored People (NAACP) newspaper, *The Crisis*, republished the ambassador's comments in full and, after the United States entered the war, joined other African American newspapers in highlighting Wilson's hypocritical calls for democracy and political freedom abroad while ignoring the fact that blacks faced deadly racial violence and political disenfranchisement at home. During the war, African Americans continued to use American critiques of Turkish atrocities to further their cause. One newspaper maintained that lynching made "the Turkish treatment of Armenians look like deeds of mercy."[59] Such critiques also found their way into the mainstream press, which questioned whether continued racial discrimination and violence at home would justify identifying the United States as a "barbarous nation" and whether such hypocrisy would weaken America's role in the world.[60]

Rustem's observations were not lost on Germany, which attempted to leverage anticolonial resentment among Muslim subjects during the war. Its alignment with the Ottoman Empire was a convenient tool for exerting this strategy. As the German ambassador to the Ottoman Empire confessed to Morgenthau, the Ottoman Empire's army was inconsequential, and the country would undoubtedly remain on the defensive throughout the war: "But the big thing is the Moslem world. If we can stir the Mohammedans up against the French, English and Russians, we can force them to make peace."[61]

Despite its secular intellectual roots, the Young Turk leadership followed German guidance and convinced a group of its highest religious leaders to call for a global jihad in November 1914.[62] The jihad required Muslims in the colonies of the Allied powers to support the Ottoman Empire and rebel against their colonial rulers.[63] According to Morgenthau, a secret pamphlet sent to Muslim subjects in the British and French colonies of India, Egypt, Tunisia, and Morocco urged Muslims to kill all Christians (except Germans) and to rid Muslim lands of colonial oppression: "India for the Indian Moslems, Algeria for the Algerian Moslems, Morocco for the Moroccan Muslims, Tunis for the Tunisian Moslems, Egypt for the Egyptian Muslims . . . and the Ottoman Empire for the Ottoman Turks and Arabs."[64] Morgenthau was alarmed by the "danger of spreading such incendiary literature among a wildly fanatical people," by whom it appears he meant all Muslims.[65]

Contrary to Morgenthau's fears, this global jihad delivered no tangible results. Nonetheless, it demonstrated that the United States was not the only country to misunderstand Muslims as defined by their religious identity above all else. Morgenthau attempted to explain away the failure of the holy war by claiming that French and British colonial subjects were happy with their current state of affairs. "Mohammedans of such countries as India, Egypt, Algiers and Morocco knew that they were getting far better treatment than they could obtain under other conceivable conditions," he wrote.[66] Given the anticolonial fervor then building in many of these countries, many of the subjects would have strongly disagreed with his analysis.[67]

Since the United States remained a neutral power in 1914, the call for "holy war" had not been explicitly extended to American colonial territories. It nonetheless provoked American security fears about a potential uprising in the Philippines and in the United States. One journalist from the *Grand Rapids Press* warned his audience that although "racial hate" between various Muslims and the fact that Germans had initiated the call had prevented the successful implementation of holy war, the threat nonetheless remained. Should Muslims decide to one day unite, the power of the holy war call could prompt "awful fanaticism of which drives Mohammedans to blood like fish to water!"[68] Furthermore, "If Ali Baku, the meek-eye acrobat in a New York vaudeville theater, suddenly charges down Broadway, killing right and left till he himself is literally cut and shot to pieces, you in America may know that the holy war is really on."[69]

Given the most recent and well-publicized battles to impose colonial rule on Filipino Moros, the same journalist who saw a lurking fanatical killer in the quiet Muslim vaudeville acrobat warned that the particularly violent character traits of Moros would combine with their religious beliefs to create a Muslim beast that "out Islams-Islam" and would put a "mad dog" to shame: "No Musselman is deadlier than the Moro. . . . Multiply this furious madman by the ten thousand and you have an idea of the bloody problem which would face Uncle Sam in case a real holy war aroused the Mohammedans of the Philippines."[70] Similar warnings filled the pages of major American newspapers. The same newspapers expressed deep relief when Moro leaders subsequently reaffirmed their allegiance to the United States.

The moment also prompted a new optimism among some American missionaries, who opined that this failed call for a global jihad displayed a fissure in the spiritual cohesion of the global Muslim community. The moment was therefore ripe for propagating Christianity and modern ideas to the Muslim world.[71] All signs pointed to the continued necessity for American involvement in the Ottoman Empire. The outbreak of new massacres against Armenian Christians in the empire only deepened such beliefs.

Ambassador Morgenthau and the Armenian Genocide

Shortly after Morgenthau arrived in the Ottoman Empire in 1913, he witnessed dramatic changes brought about by national and international events that eventually led to massive and organized campaigns of genocidal violence against Armenians. World War I changed the dynamics of the Eastern Question, allowing the Ottoman Empire to draw up new foreign alliances, in part to further nationalist goals and in part to end foreign meddling, particularly from Britain, France, and Russia.[72]

When the Young Turks signed a secret treaty aligning themselves with Germany in August 1914 and again when they officially entered the war two months later, stipulations for postwar arrangements included newly drawn territorial frontiers that would physically connect Ottoman Muslims with Russian Muslims. These war aims would have far-reaching repercussions for the Ottoman Empire's Armenian population. They erased any possibility for the consolidation and eventual independence of Armenian provinces, while also allowing the Ottoman government to end Russian and French capitulations and consequent meddling.

This new alignment pitted the Ottomans against the Russians and heightened the strategic focus of both powers on their Armenian populations, who occupied the buffer zones between them. The Young Turks increasingly viewed the Ottoman Armenian community as a potential fifth column willing to side with Russia. In reality, although some Armenian revolutionaries supported Russia, the majority remained neutral or loyal to the Ottoman government.[73] Nonetheless, as one scholar has noted, "The stereotype of Armenians as proxies of the Great Powers in peacetime was extended into a stereotype of military collaboration during warfare: the 'inner enemy' and the 'outer enemy' were now fully merged in the Ottoman mind."[74] These factors combined to shape the Young Turk's campaign of increasingly repressive policies toward their Armenian population.

Beginning in August 1914, war requisitioning led to the looting and burning of thousands of Armenian and Greek stores. Despite these provocations, the Armenian National Assembly urged Armenians to remain calm. By February 1915, Ottoman soldiers ordered all Armenians not enlisted in the army to cede their arms to the government. Efforts to fulfill these new restrictions became a convenient excuse to abuse, torture, and harass Armenian communities.[75] Massacres and deportations ensued; perpetrators forced Armenians to walk hundreds of miles into the remote desert without food, water, or clothing.[76] Entire groups were shot. By the end of 1915, Ottoman genocidal policies had led to the deaths of more than a million Armenian subjects.[77] Neither women nor children were spared. Of course, the overwhelming majority of victims were also innocent of any rebellious activities. Ottoman officials carried out this demographic engineering throughout the war, resettling Muslim refugees from the Balkan War of 1912 into emptied Armenian homes.[78]

Morgenthau's diary entries during the spring and summer of 1915 reveal a diplomat slowly piecing together the larger picture of a deliberate genocide. Morgenthau received reports of massacre, deportation, and persecution of the Armenian population from his American missionary contacts and local consuls, and he repeatedly raised the issue with Young Turk leaders. Minister of the Interior Mehmed Talaat and Minister of War Enver Pasha initially justified the deaths on military grounds, placating Morgenthau by assuring him that the massacres would soon stop.[79] When Morgenthau brought the issue up again at another meeting with Talaat in May 1915, the minister asked him if the Armenians were American, conveying the message that the ambassador to the United States should mind his own business.[80]

Not content with telling Morgenthau to stay out of Ottoman internal affairs, in a long meeting with Morgenthau in late May, Pasha explained that foreign powers, including the United States, had encouraged the Armenians to revolt, which posed a significant security threat to the empire during a time of war. Enver admitted that he personally admired the Armenians and that, were it not for external powers, the Armenians would have stayed faithful to the empire. The minister promised, nonetheless, that there would be no future massacres. Despite his assurances, missionary and consular reports continued to stream into Morgenthau's office, revealing continued deportations, persecution, and slaughter.[81]

As Morgenthau grasped the full extent of the rulers' intentions to rid the empire of Armenians, he continued to explain the purge on strictly religious terms. As he noted in his diary on 10 July 1915, after meeting with Talaat, "They are evidently determined to Islamicize the country and destroy and crush all non-Moslems. . . . When I said they would be condemned by the world, he said they would know how to defend themselves; in other words, he does not give a damn."[82] Once Morgenthau was fully aware of the extent of the problem, his close connections with American missionaries, journalists, consular agents, Ottoman officials, and the Armenian community made him a vital source of information for the U.S. government and the American people. Morgenthau forwarded a telegram that day to Secretary of State Robert Lansing. He also ensured that the information reached the American public through his friend Adolph Ochs, a publisher at the *New York Times*.[83]

As conditions for Armenians deteriorated, so did the Young Turks' veneer of truth. By 18 July, Morgenthau related that Talaat had allegedly bragged to his friends that "he had done more in three months about crushing the Armenians than Abdul Hamid could do in 37 years."[84] If true, they were hardly the words of a ruler committed to ending the violence. Meanwhile, Morgenthau received a response to his telegram from Lansing encouraging him to continue his efforts on behalf of the Armenians. On 8 August 1915, Talaat admitted to Morgenthau that they had already managed to get rid of three quarters of the Armenians and "that the hatred was so intense now that they have to finish it." When Morgenthau tried to bring up the financial costs of such a decision, Talaat responded that they did not care and they wanted "to treat the Armenians like we treat the negroes."[85]

Morgenthau noted that Talaat had probably chosen the wrong historical example in referencing America's practices of demographic engineering, writing in his diary, "I think he meant like the Indians."[86] Nonetheless, Morgenthau could not conceive of such a comparison with the United States. In a book published three years later, Morgenthau denounced "the innate attitude of the Moslem Turk to people not of his own race and religion," whom he treated not as "human beings with rights, but merely chattel." He remarked that such inequality would be incomprehensible to Americans: "Imagine a great government year in and year out maintaining this attitude toward many millions of its own subjects!"[87] Morgenthau's conviction displayed an admirable idealism. Americans had not committed genocide against African Americans. That said, the historical reality of treating millions of subjects as chattel was *not* beyond the American imagination. Indeed, in the same year that so many Americans responded with horror to the Armenian Genocide, others flocked to view the film *The Birth of a Nation*, which glorified Southern slave owners in the United States and vilified free blacks as savages and rapists whom the Civil War had unleashed on an innocent white population. President Wilson, whose own writings were cited in the film, drew the ire of African Americans in 1915 when he publicly praised the film and agreed to screen it in the White House.

Despite his idealistic sentiments about American racial and religious equality, Morgenthau himself was not immune to racial thinking vis-à-vis the Turks.[88] According to his vision, Turks were like children in their incapacity to understand notions of political liberty—albeit children who never grew up and were thus beyond reform: "After five hundred years' close contact with European civilization, the Turk remained precisely the same individual as the one who had emerged from the steppes of Asia in the Middle ages."[89]

Morgenthau's horror at Talaat's full revelations about the future status of Armenians in the empire convinced him that he could no longer remain at his post as ambassador. He resigned in 1916. Contrary to Morgenthau's harsh view of Turkish Muslims, he would not be alone in resigning out of protest at Ottoman actions. In August 1915, Morgenthau noted in his diary that the Sheik-ul-Islam, the Muslim religious authority of the Ottoman Empire, had resigned his cabinet post in part to protest the Young Turks' policies against Armenians, which he considered contrary to Islamic law.[90] Indeed, Morgenthau's simplistic reading of the Armenian Genocide ignored the fact that moral and religious outrage at the massacres extended beyond the United States and Europe to include Muslims in the Ottoman Empire.[91]

America Responds to Genocide: The American Committee for Armenian and Syrian Relief

Knowing he would not be in the territory much longer and desperate to find a solution to the Armenian issue, Morgenthau cabled the U.S. State Department on 3 September 1915, making an urgent plea for the United States to accept Armenian refugees. He also asked that a committee be formed to raise funds on behalf of the Armenians to help pay for their emigration to the United States, suggesting Cleveland Dodge and Charles Crane to lead the effort.[92] Although his proposal to donate $1 million to help 500,000 Armenians migrate to the United States never came to fruition, his request did lead to the creation of an Armenian relief organization, which would play a central role in shaping American policy toward the Ottoman Empire during World War I and afterward.[93]

Morgenthau knew that Dodge and Crane had close ties to American missionaries and that Dodge was President Wilson's oldest and closest friend. Even better, both men were wealthy philanthropists who had a history of giving to Christian causes. James Barton soon joined the group, and the three men combined their efforts to form the Committee on Armenian Atrocities, which started with a generous $60,000 donation from Dodge.[94] Dodge recommended Barton to lead the organization. By 1916, the organization merged with other groups, including a Syrian relief organization, to form the American Committee for Armenian and Syrian Relief (ACASR). The organization's membership soon drew religious and political luminaries, including Oscar Straus, former U.S. minister to the Ottoman Empire; Rabbi Stephen Wise, the Jewish leader and activist; Robert Speer, the secretary of the Presbyterian missions; John Mott, head of the international committee of the YMCA; and Talcott Williams, who presided over the School of Journalism at Columbia University. The participation of Barton, Dodge, Speer, and Mott assured that American Christian missionary interests would not be forgotten as ACASR advanced its mission in the Ottoman Empire.

When Morgenthau returned to the United States in February 1916, he met with President Wilson, Secretary of State Lansing, and the secretary of the navy. After the meeting, Morgenthau was convinced that Wilson was as committed as he was to ending the violence against Armenians, noting that Wilson "said that if necessary Americans should go to war for humanity's sake."[95] He then met with Crane and Barton and together they determined that Abraham Isaac Elkus, a Jewish lawyer, should serve as the next ambassador, a choice Wilson quickly accepted.[96] Despite his initial protest that the position was "designated" for American Jews, Morgenthau had reaffirmed the practice by suggesting yet another Jewish American for the post. Before Elkus left for the Ottoman Empire, Barton organized a banquet on his behalf, as the ABCFM had previously done for Morgenthau, in which he introduced him to the leaders of missionary organizations in the Ottoman Empire.[97]

Meanwhile, as ACASR chairman, Barton organized a massive media campaign to denounce ongoing Turkish atrocities. He was granted privileged access by government officials to all confidential reports and documents that came through official channels.[98] Support in getting ACASR stories out to the public also came directly from members of the press, including Melville Stone from the Associated Press, who helped advise ACASR, and John Finley, an editor at the *New York Times*, who served as a board trustee.[99] Barton encouraged the cooperation of journalists and newspapers in their effort: "The press of the entire country has been sympathetic, helpful, and liberal to the last degree."[100] As he later bragged, "It would be difficult to name any weekly or monthly periodical that has not published one or more special articles upon some phase of the work in the Near East."[101]

ACASR supplemented mainstream media coverage with its own news bulletins and pamphlets, which included recent missionary reports and emotional pleas to the American public. One of the first pamphlets put out by the organization was entitled *Armenia, "A Christian Nation" Her Heart-Rending Cry*, and included an address by the Episcopalian minister, Reverend James Empringham. The minister delivered a clear message to the American public that reaffirmed existing beliefs: the central cause of Turkish violence against Armenians was their Islamic faith. This problem had deep historical roots that went back to the religion's origins, the minister maintained: "As a plague of locusts sweeps over the face of the earth devouring all vegetation, leaving death and desolation behind, so the scourge of Mohammedanism blasted the East in the sixth and following centuries." According to Empringham, such expressions of violence and intolerance originated with the prophet Mohammed, who was "destined to thus butcher and exterminate whole nations of Christians." Islam was a "religion of blood" represented by the fact that today "the Moslem priest preaches each Friday, always holding a drawn sword in his hand, symbolizing the manner in which their faith must conquer the earth." In contrast to his depictions of Muslims, Armenians were true Christians responsible for the "first national church" and who for centuries had "refused to be bribed or butchered into the false faith."[102]

Another ACASR bulletin included a poem from Katherine Lee Bates, author of the famous song "America the Beautiful." Her poem compared the Armenian martyrdom to that of Jesus:

Armenia! The name is like a sword
In every Christian heart.
O martyr nation . . .
Armenia! A figure on a cross,
Pale, wasted bleeding, with imploring eyes!
Except we save her
darkness lies across
All Christendom, shamed in her sacrifice.[103]

ACASR also prepared special reports to be sent to pastors across the country to prepare their sermons for church members and Sunday schools. These publications replicated the imagery of the 1894 massacres. Islam and the Turkish "race" again became the primary focus. As one scholar has noted, "Enlarging on the idea of the terrible Turk which Americans had accepted since the 1890s, the ACASR aroused hostility against Turks as brutally inhuman, degenerate agents of German Huns; it glorified Armenians as responsible Christians victimized by Muslims. These astigmatic views portrayed religion as almost the exclusive problem in Asia minor and ignored ethnic, economic, and political factors."[104] Racial differences also played a role in these depictions. Press articles described Armenian Christians as a superior white race, hard-working and intelligent. All this led to the inevitable conclusion that Turkish Muslims were incapable of reform or civilized behavior and destined for destruction by Western powers. According to these journals, such behavior had important policy implications. As *The Independent* argued in October 1915, "We can hardly conceive of any power's favoring the perpetuation of Turkey in any form, after the ghastly exhibit of Moslem incapacity to rule alien peoples or even Mohammedans."[105]

The vocal Armenian American community joined American activists in raising awareness of the ongoing violence. After the 1894 massacres, Armenians had continued to seek exile in the United States. By 1914, more than 65,000 Armenians had come to American shores.[106] Even before the launching of the Armenian Genocide, Armenians in the United States had relied on mainstream imagery to define their public image as white, civilized Christians. Such imagery proved particularly advantageous when Armenians faced occasional legal challenges to their whiteness—and by extension, their ability to naturalize as American citizens. Armenian Americans welcomed the pronouncement of a federal judge who ruled in their favor in 1909, arguing that their Christian faith had helped cement their honorary status as white Europeans.[107] As the judge noted in his decision: "In the warfare which has raged since the beginning of history . . . between Europeans and Asiatics, the Armenians have generally, though not always, been found on the European side. . . . By reason of their Christianity, they generally ranged themselves against the Persian fire-worshippers, and against the Mohammedans, both Saracens and Turks."[108] During the Armenian Genocide, Armenians in the United States continued to assert such racial and religious logic as a reason for Americans to support their cause.[109]

By the end of 1915, ACASR had raised $177,000 in Armenian aid.[110] The organization also succeeded in rallying the American public. Numerous protests were organized throughout major American cities, parades were held on Fifth Avenue in New York, and proceeds from the 1916 Yale-Harvard football game were donated to the cause.[111] These efforts revealed the importance of the Armenian plight in the American imagination. As Herbert Hoover recalled in his memoirs, "Probably Armenia was known to the American school child in 1919 only a little less than England. The association of Mount Ararat and Noah, the staunch Christians who were massacred periodically by the Mohammedan Turks, and the Sunday School collections over fifty years for alleviating their miseries—all cumulate to impress the name Armenia on the front of the American mind."[112]

In the next few years, ACASR joined other relief organizations to raise $100 million (more than $1 billion in today's value).[113] Symbolizing the close cooperation between private organizations and official policy, the U.S. government contributed $25 million to the effort. Additionally, the State Department and the U.S. Navy helped ACASR forward the funds to American missionary organizations and the Red Cross. Local efforts also included American diplomats and missionaries, including Ambassador Elkus, other American consular officials, and Cleveland Dodge's daughter, Elizabeth Huntington.[114] ACASR propaganda efforts paid off. By the end of the war, the money it raised helped feed, clothe, shelter, and educate hundreds of thousands of Armenian refugees.[115] These private efforts merged with U.S. government support and intensified when the United States formally entered the war in 1917.

American Entry into World War I and Neutrality toward the Ottoman Empire

During 1916, President Wilson's reelection campaign promise to keep America out of war had precluded any official intervention on behalf of the Armenians.[116] This promise did not last long, however. Shortly after his reelection, he began war preparations. In April 1917, Wilson made his speech to Congress, officially declaring war. Six months later, his "Fourteen Points" speech would continue the country's international moral quest to change the world in America's image. These ideals found great support among clergymen and missionaries, who saw Wilson as an "Ambassador of God."[117] Barton and Dodge were equally supportive of Wilson's ideological commitments to spread American political values to the world, which they saw as extensions of American missionary work in the Ottoman Empire.

America's future role in Armenia was central to this project. By early 1917, even before the United States had officially declared war, Barton had begun working within ACASR and the ABCFM to ensure that the United States occupied a central political position supervising territories in the Ottoman Empire after the end of the war. Barton's strategy included reinforcing the belief among the American public and the political leadership that Turkish Muslims were incapable of ruling over others.[118] As he wrote fellow Armenophile James Bryce in England, "I want to create a sentiment that will be overwhelmingly on that side of the question."[119] The media would play an important role in advancing this strategy, as it had in informing the American public of the massacres. As Barton acknowledged in 1916, the press "will have influence in shaping thought with reference to the future of the Turkish empire."[120]

The official U.S. declaration of war against Germany in April 1917 provoked a significant political debate about whether the United States should extend its declaration of war to the Ottoman Empire. Wilson faced

pressure from both sides on this issue. The critics of Wilson's justifications for neutrality included his political rival, Republican senator Henry
Cabot Lodge, who argued in a congressional debate that American missionary interests in the Ottoman Empire should not prevent an American
declaration of war. Lamenting the Ottoman massacre of Armenians, he
"prayed" that the end of the war would bring about "the final extinction
of the Turkish Empire in Europe." He added that "as an American, as
a lover of freedom" he would regret arriving among the other powers
during postwar negotiations as "a friend of Turkey."[121] Former president
Theodore Roosevelt similarly argued that the Turkish treatment of
Armenians merited a strong American message from the United States
that could be conveyed only through a declaration of war. As Roosevelt
wrote Cleveland Dodge, with whom he had been friends since childhood,
Americans would be "guilty of a peculiarly odious form of hypocrisy
when we profess friendship for Armenia and the downtrodden races of
Turkey, but don't go to war with Turkey."[122] Roosevelt expressed similar
sentiments to James Barton.

Unbeknownst to Roosevelt, Dodge and Barton had already decided on
the issue and succeeded in convincing Wilson to remain neutral. The
ABCFM had been concerned since early 1915 about the possibility of a U.S.
declaration of war against the Ottoman Empire. Both Barton and Dodge
believed that American neutrality would protect Americans in the empire
from being identified as enemies while facilitating future work.[123] Secretary of State Robert Lansing supported their arguments, adding that in
addition to harming American missionary interests, a formal declaration
against the Ottoman Empire would lead only to more violence against
Ottoman Christians.[124]

Dodge had more personal reasons for disagreeing with Roosevelt. He
also feared the risks a declaration would pose to his two children working in American missionary colleges in the area. Dodge took advantage
of his relationship with Wilson to convey his fears. Although this was not
the first time Dodge had advised his childhood friend on policy issues, he
admitted that this case was different, writing the president that he was
conveying his strong worries on both personal and organizational grounds.
Dodge explained that he had spoken with religious leaders, missionary organizations, and Americans who worked at American Protestant colleges
in the empire as well as diplomats, including Morgenthau and Ambassador Elkus. Everyone agreed that a declaration would seriously threaten
missionary interests in the empire. Dodge also conceded that the presence
of his family members in the area had caused him "personal anxiety which

is rather disturbing."[125] Dodge nonetheless insisted that these concerns should not prevent Wilson from doing what he felt was best for the country. The president reassured Dodge: "I sympathize with every word of your letter . . . about war with Turkey and am trying to hold the Congress back from following its inclination to include all the allies of Germany in declaration of a state of war. I hope with all my heart that I can succeed."[126] Meanwhile, Barton launched a lobbying tour throughout the United States, speaking to Armenian groups, religious leaders, and missionary organizations to convince them that neutrality was the best course of action.[127] He also organized a media blitz to reaffirm public support for the position.[128]

Their efforts were successful; Wilson convinced Congress not to declare war. According to Barton, Wilson's success assured that, through its missionaries, Americans could truly make a difference in reshaping the former territories of the Ottoman Empire after the war. As Barton wrote Dodge in October 1918, "We are now in a position to do more in cleaning up that Eastern question and in getting Turkey and Bulgaria set right than we could possibly have done had we been classified among the belligerents. I think the United States is now in a position to take the lead in the reorganizing of the entire Near East and that its lead will be gladly recognized by both Bulgaria and Turkey."[129]

Americans knew that they were not alone in planning for the future "reorganization" of Ottoman territories. In November 1917, less than a year before Barton sent his letter to Dodge celebrating American neutrality with the Ottoman Empire, the Bolsheviks had released the Sykes-Picot Treaty, which was secretly negotiated between tsarist Russia, Britain, and France in 1915 and 1916. The treaty had divided Ottoman territories among the three powers as postwar spoils. The release of the embarrassing document confirmed what many war protestors already feared; that the war was in part about advancing selfish European imperialist interests. One of Wilson's goals in advancing his ideals of self-determination was to convince Americans that the United States was fighting a war to advance political freedom rather than expand European empire.[130] Similarly, men such as Dodge and Barton maintained that American desires to shape the future Ottoman territories stemmed not from selfish interests, but rather from American Christian benevolence.

The Inquiry, the American Commission to Negotiate Peace, and American Support for Armenian Independence

Given Barton and Dodge's visions for the future territories of the Ottoman Empire, a second important aspect to ACASR lobbying focused on ensuring postwar aims that included an "independent" Armenia led, ideally, by the United States as the mandatory power. The United States could then ensure the security and future development of Armenians after the war, much as it had been doing for Christian Filipinos. Moreover, Armenians would be the ideal vehicle for spreading Euro-American civilization throughout the former territories of the Ottoman Empire.

This idea had originated among some ABCFM missionaries even before the war. In 1913, ABCFM missionary Harry V. Osborne had written to President Wilson describing the advantages of an independent Armenian state. Armenians would be "the bearer of the torch of civilization in . . . Turkey" and had it not been for "his subdued humiliation by the Turk, he could have long fulfilled his mission of bringing western thought and methods in the east." Osborne had no doubt about the inevitability of Euro-American civilization taking over the region. However, he stated: "An autonomous Armenia would immensely facilitate what is eventually to come."[131]

Henry Morgenthau also supported this idea. In the summer of 1917, President Wilson had asked Morgenthau to return to the Ottoman Empire on a secret mission to convince the Young Turks to negotiate a separate peace with the Allied powers. The mission ended badly after word leaked to the international press that he was allegedly on a trip organized to ensure the future independence of Palestine for the Jews.[132] Despite this embarrassment, Morgenthau had been able to meet with Boghos Nubar, a wealthy Armenian leader who would later represent Armenians at the 1919 Paris Peace Conference. Nubar suggested to Morgenthau the idea of American tutelage over Armenia, noting that Americans "could do for the Armenians what they have done for the Philippines."[133]

Upon his return in September 1917, Morgenthau met with Wilson to discuss his findings. In preparation for the meeting, Morgenthau wrote a letter summarizing his policy advice. The letter included his vision for the future of Turkish rule: "Turkish atrocities perpetrated against Armenians, Syrians, and Arabs establish beyond doubt that the Turks should no longer be permitted to govern non-Moslems and non-Turks of any description."[134] In addition to calling for the end of Turkish rule, Morgenthau's letter revealed his awareness that Young Turk violence had extended to other rebellious subjects throughout the empire, including Arab Muslims. Such admissions conflicted with the public narrative that he and ASCAR leaders had advanced, namely, that it was Islamic intolerance for Christians alone that constituted the reason for Turkish brutality.

That same month, a group that President Wilson had assembled to prepare postwar peace plans reached an identical conclusion. Directed by Colonel House, whose close friends included George Washburn Jr., the son of the former president of Robert College, the group, labeled the Inquiry, served as an ancestor of the modern think tank. The organization would later become part of the American Commission to Negotiate Peace, whose members traveled to Paris to meet with the Allies and conduct postwar negotiations. Inquiry members solicited information from outside sources, including James Barton and other current and former missionaries, ACASR, Armenians, and Armenian Americans. In addition to placing a heavy emphasis on understanding Ottoman subjects according to their religious beliefs, reports for the Inquiry also maintained that previous American colonial policies provided a strong reference point for future actions in Ottoman territories. According to ACASR's report, Cuba and the Philippines would serve as an ideal model for Turkey.[135]

Barton's individual reports to the Inquiry repeated his ongoing mantra: Islam was the central problem of Turkish rule and the spread of Christianity was the ultimate solution. Of course, to do this entailed an end to Turkish rule. The title of one of his reports, "The Turkish Government— Analysis of Its Inherent Evil," offered a clear indication of his thoughts. He maintained that there could "be only one conclusion": that a Turkish government was by necessity a Muslim government, and a Muslim government was incapable of justice in ruling over non-Muslims.[136] In another report to the Inquiry, he claimed that he knew of no Americans in the Ottoman Empire who disagreed with him on this fact.[137] His assessment extended beyond Turkey to any society ruled by Islam for "reasons inherent to Mohammedanism itself . . . it is impossible to build up a successful Mohammedan government."[138] Because of their religious beliefs, Muslim states were "not only incompatible with, but are diametrically opposed to the principles of modern democracy, modern state-craft and modern government."[139]

In another report for the Inquiry, Barton offered advice on what kind of system should replace Ottoman rule. Following ACASR's suggestion that the Philippines would serve as a good model, Barton's proposal mirrored the organizational structure that Americans had imposed there, including the categorization of subjects according to race and religion.

Undoubtedly aware of French and British imperial designs, Barton emphasized that the territories should not become "spheres of influence" divided among foreign powers, but instead be ruled over by one benevolent power in a type of federation. The United States, of course, was the ideal power to assume this role.

Furthermore, Barton recommended that all cabinet members and all local governors, "in a word, the whole foreign administrative force sent into the country" must also come from the same ruling power. Barton's plan implicitly confirmed that no local voices would play a role in their own governance. Whatever plan foreign powers came up with, Barton advised, it should be "imposed" on the former Ottoman subjects "without submit[ting] the question to a plebiscite."[140] In its first years, this new federation could allow for "local representative assemblies" that would play an "advisory character" to the foreign rulers, and with time, play a greater role in ruling themselves "as ability was developed and as past prejudices were overcome, and as men capable of safe leadership were discovered."[141] Much like American attitudes toward the Philippines, Barton's assertions posited self-government as a privilege to be earned rather than a natural human right. Convinced of foreign altruism, Barton maintained that the local population would be willing to accept foreign rule once it understood "the benevolent character and purpose of the government."[142]

Barton's proposal also included dividing the territories into units, whereby each "race" was assigned a distinct unit. Although he recognized that "people of different races" were "scattered" across the territories, it was best that the units be drawn so as to ensure that only one race constitute the strong majority in each section. Similarly, local "prejudices" also meant that all schools should be divided according to race and religion. In one section of his report, entitled "Virile Races," he noted that the "Armenians, Georgians, Greeks, Syrians and Jews" could all be considered "virile races with great power of recuperation," also noting that none of these groups were "quarrelsome." He further remarked that the "first four races" (in other words, all except the Jews) were "intellectually strong and capable of unlimited advancement in every department in the sciences, arts and professions" and would serve as "a powerful cooperating force for law, order and progress." He offered no explanation for why Jews did not hold these latter qualities, though the fact that he also excluded Turks, Kurds, and "other kindred non Christian races" indicates his belief that Christianity was an essential element in reaching the ultimate heights of civilized behavior.[143] He conceded, though, that non-Christians could play an important role: they "would provide great numbers of unskilled laborers."[144]

Barton could not divorce missionary work and U.S. foreign policy in his strategic thinking. He undoubtedly took some of the material for his Inquiry report from a book he was about to publish, entitled *The Christian Approach to Islam*, a work intended as a guide on how Christian missionaries could more successfully spread their faith to Muslims across the world. Barton understood the war in divine terms: "What the Christian world has been unable to accomplish among the Mohammedans . . . during the last hundred years of missionary endeavor is now being achieved by the army of Christian heroes, heroines, and martyrs backed by the great Christian heart of America and England."[145] By early 1918, he had set ACASR on the task of actively promoting such goals to the press and public. These efforts went hand-in-hand with his lobbying of the U.S. government. His letter to a leading Armenian activist illustrated how much pressure he had exerted both publicly and privately to obtain his desired goals:

> In the future settlement of Turkish affairs . . . non-Moslem people must be given absolute freedom from the misrule of the Turks. That is the doctrine we are promulgating. Our [ACASR] has done much in shaping public opinion to that end. I am a member of a special American [Inquiry] Committee appointed [by] the State Department on affairs in Turkey. . . . We are taking up this matter, and I am confident we shall have influence in Washington, if any such influence is needed, to keep our own government firm to the principle above. . . . There is a sentiment gaining strength in America that Turkey is incapable of ruling even Turks. This is an increasing sentiment . . . and would be in favor of eliminating the Turkish Government absolutely. . . . *This propaganda for relief has not only furnished money to help save the starving but it has created a sentiment in favor of [Armenians that] could be done in no other way.*[146]

What Barton left out of his letter was the heavy-handed tutelage a foreign power would play in administering these new territories. The ideal plan of many American missionaries on the ground prioritized missionary interests and supported the idea of a strong American mandate that would control Armenia and large swathes of former Ottoman territories, including Anatolia and Istanbul.

By the end of the same year, Dodge and Barton joined another ABCFM missionary, William Peet, and an Armenian American activist, Vahan

Cardashian, to help launch a new organization, the American Committee for the Independence of Armenia (ACIA). Led by the former U.S. ambassador to Germany, James W. Gerard, the executive committee included Dodge, Elihu Root, Henry Cabot Lodge, Charles Evan Hughes, and Charles Eliot. Wider membership included political, military, and social elites, such as Jacob Schurman, Stephen S. Wise, Oscar Straus, Henry Jessup, Madison Grant, Samuel Gompers, Nicolas Murray Butler, Alice Stone Blackwell, and William Jennings Bryant. The list of luminaries also included twenty-one governors.[147]

In line with the policy goals of the ACIA, Barton, Dodge, and Peet sent a confidential ten-page memorandum on behalf of the committee to Secretary of State Lansing in December 1918, just as Lansing and Wilson had arrived in Paris to conduct peace negotiations.[148] The memo recommended an independent Armenian state, preferably under American tutelage. The ACIA's influence with Wilson was obvious; the memo's recommendations would be adopted almost verbatim in the final proposal Wilson put forth to Congress at the end of the war.

The memorandum maintained that Armenians deserved the right to emancipation from the Ottoman Empire for several reasons, not limited to their historical "ill-treatment" "culminating in the massacres of 1915–1916."[149] It also reaffirmed the view that Armenian Christianity was the only beacon of progress in the area and that Armenians had long served as a religious security buffer between the Islamic Ottoman Empire and Christian Europe. Armenian independence was "a matter of justice, for the sake of their own civilization and as constituting a civilizing element in the East" and "for the services they rendered Christendom since the early invasions of the Turks."[150] Armenians also deserved independence for their efforts to assist the Allied cause in refusing to help the Ottomans in their war against the Entente Powers and for fighting and sacrificing for the Allied cause during the war. Be it through religion or wartime loyalties, Armenians had made an enormous contribution to European Christian civilization and the Allied effort.

Simplistic fantasies of religious nationalism and demographic engineering also shaped the ACIA's construction of the new Armenian state. The ideal scenario, according to the same memo, was that foreign powers would encourage Armenians and "Christians of other races" to migrate to the area, resulting in combined numbers of more than 3 million Christians. This demographically engineered population—dominated by former Christian subjects of the Ottoman Empire—would "*work [its] own salvation* under the guardianship of a great and disinterested power like the

United States."[151] Relying on the biblical symbolism of "salvation" and conveying that these Christians had been literally delivered from sin (the Islamic source of which was so obvious it hardly needed mentioning), the memorandum echoed earlier American missionary narratives about saving and reforming nominal Christians and guiding them on the path of progress via American civilization. Although the strong preference was for the United States to take on this role, the memo conceded that Great Britain could also accomplish the mission.

The ACIA also formulated a plan to deal with Muslims in the area: "Any such Turks who should not wish to remain under a *Christian Government* may be given every facility to settle in that part of the Empire which will be the real Turkey."[152] Although their memo generously allowed Muslims to remain in this new Armenian state, the territory's designation as Christian, a definition that extended to the government itself, made removing Muslims from Christian areas preferable. Following similar ethnic and religious separatist logic, they recommended that Kurdish Muslims be moved to their own "homeland." Discounting the potential trauma that would result from displacing peoples who had historical ties to their lands or who had already suffered violent displacement from other territories, the authors were nonetheless confident that Muslim Kurds would adapt easily to the move for "they are used to migration through their nomadic habits."[153]

As the ACIA's policy prescriptions revealed, Americans supported demographic engineering of religious groups, as long as they or another "civilized" power enacted the policies. ACIA members were undoubtedly compelled to propose this reorganization, in part because of the extreme violence they had witnessed between Muslims and Christians. Indeed, the memo warned the secretary of state that failure to support an independent Armenian state would ensure "continued ruin and devastation" and would doom the population to "hopeless misery."[154] However, this conclusion also reasserted notions of the modern nation-state that viewed religious and ethnic plurality as a problem to be solved. Their proposals also overlooked how previous policies of demographic engineering had caused intercommunal strife in the years leading up to the Armenian Genocide. Implicit in their logic was a certainty that creating an independent Armenian state, under a superior Christian government, would align with the natural order of the world and rectify the abhorrent error of history that had placed Christians under Muslim rule. Thus, the area would "within a short time be restored to the prosperity it enjoyed before the advent of the Turk."[155]

Not content with limiting American control to an Armenian mandate, Cleveland Dodge also pushed for American influence in other parts of the Middle East. In late 1919, Dodge cabled his son-in-law, Howard Bliss, the president of Syrian Protestant College, asking him to push the negotiators for an American mandate over Syria.[156] Bliss followed his father-in-law's advice and traveled to Paris, where he met privately with Secretary of State Lansing on 28 January 1919. He urged Lansing to send investigators to gauge Syrian desires for their future political organization and leadership, confident that they would prefer an American mandate over British or French rule. President Wilson took the ACIA's advice to heart during the peace negotiations.

The Paris Peace Conference and the Birth of the Mandate System

Of course, the premise of imposing European mandates on Muslims subjects was not new. President Roosevelt and Elihu Root had proposed a similar mandate model for Morocco at the 1906 Algeciras Conference. George Beer, one of Wilson's advisors, specifically referenced the treaty reached at Algeciras in discussing the future organization of Ottoman territories. Previous American and European interactions with Muslims in one part of the globe would again serve as an ideal precedent in crafting policies for Muslims thousands of miles away.

Not coincidentally, the Algeciras agreement also served as a reference for the Smuts plan, the draft proposal put forth by South African general Jan Smuts, which would turn into the final mandate resolution put forward during the peace negotiations in Versailles. Although the original Smuts plan had included mandates for Central European territories, Wilson adamantly argued against their inclusion and maintained that the mandate system should apply only to *non-European peoples*, which included the former Ottoman territories.[157] The Council of Ten, comprised of European and American leaders who led the peacetime negotiations, adopted the final mandate resolution on 30 January 1919.[158] The council designated Syria, Armenia, Mesopotamia, Palestine, and Arabia as future mandate territories in the Middle East, though they did not settle on which powers would rule in each area.[159] Wilson nonetheless publicly stated the American interest in assuming mandates over certain territories in the Ottoman Empire.[160]

European and American support for the mandate system drew on several seemingly incompatible desires. For Wilson, the mandate system provided an ideal opportunity to merge his idealism about self-determination with his belief in the necessity of foreign tutelage over certain classes of "backward" people. For Barton, the mandate system provided an excellent means by which to advance American missionary interests and spread Christianity through Muslim lands. In contrast, for the British and French, the system would ensure that they would keep their Middle Eastern wartime spoils and allow them to impose imperial rule in all but name. As one French diplomat confided to Beer, there was "no real difference between a colony and a mandated area. . . . You will see what these mandates will develop into in ten years."[161]

The proposed mandate system engendered opposition from among the people whom it was designed to "advance." Delegations arrived from all over the world, including colonial subjects under European rule, to argue for independence. Many based their pleas on their interpretation of Wilson's promises of self-determination. The British and the French knew the risk that such opposition posed to their imperial holdings and, with few exceptions, excluded these voices from the hearings.[162] Those exceptions, however, did include Emir Faysal, the son of Hashemite Sharif Husayn. Husayn had previously secured promises from the British that Arabs would be granted independence in exchange for their military cooperation with British forces, led by the British military captain T. E. Lawrence.

With Lawrence's help, Faysal prepared two petitions for the Council of Ten. Faysal explicitly challenged the French and British positions by evoking Wilson's promises of self-determination and requesting "that the Arabic-speaking people of Asia . . . be recognized as an independent sovereign people under the guarantee of the League of Nations." He further noted his confidence that "the Powers will attach more importance to the bodies and souls of the Arabic-speaking peoples than to their own material interests."[163] Privately, Faysal remarked to Lawrence that "those that say we should be discriminated against because we, the Arabs, are a wild, unruly people incapable of self-government and not entitled to benefit by the Wilson doctrine of self-determination, should not be listened to."[164] Unfortunately, Faysal's fears would prove true, as European material interests and American perceptions of Muslims and Arabs would trump local demands for self-rule.

Other exceptions were allowed, though they were carefully chosen to reflect Great Power interests. The French allowed a Lebanese delegation to speak on behalf of a French mandate over Syria. Boghos Nubar Pasha was also allowed to speak on behalf of Armenians. His views were clear:

"Civilization must not permit non-Ottoman people to remain under the yoke of Turkish oppression. The extinction of Turkey is essential to world peace."[165]

Zionists, represented by Chaim Weizmann, also advanced demands for a Jewish homeland in a statement delivered to the Council of Ten. In contrast to Faysal, Weizmann carefully avoided any mention of democracy or self-determination, aware that such language would only weaken his stance, but he pointed out that giving Arabs power over their own lands would doom Zionist plans for a Jewish homeland. Weizmann remarked that Zionism, fueled by Jewish immigration to Palestine, would "civilize" the backward areas of the Middle East. He emphasized this aspect repeatedly, noting that Arabs had failed in this regard and that the land had been "left desolate" and was in need of "redemption" for its "present condition is a standing reproach." The solution, then, was obvious: "Two things are necessary for that redemption—a stable and enlightened government, and an addition to the present population which shall be energetic, intelligent, devoted to the country, and backed by the large financial resources that are indispensable for development. Such a population the Jews alone can supply."[166] Although not present to hear Weizmann's speech, less than a week later, President Wilson formally endorsed the Zionist request for a Jewish homeland in front of a delegation of the American Jewish Congress, which included his friend, Rabbi Stephen Wise.[167]

Howard Bliss was also allowed to address the Council of Ten. Bliss emphasized the fact that he was born in Mount Lebanon and had spent his life working there as a missionary. His sympathies lay, therefore, with the Syrians, whom he described as "intelligent, able, hospitable, lovable, but with the sure defects of a long oppressed race." Bliss used language to describe the Syrians as virtual children who required "sympathy, firmness and patience" so that they could "grow into capacity for self-determination and independence."[168] As one scholar has noted, such depictions "fit perfectly with Wilson's own attitude toward Mexicans, Haitians, and Filipinos."[169] Nonetheless, Bliss maintained that listening to the Syrian people was a necessary step in establishing future plans for the area. To achieve this, he proposed that the Council of Ten send a "neutral" commission to speak to the Syrians, allowing them "to express in a perfectly untrammeled way their political wishes and aspirations, vis: as to what form of government they desire and as to what Power, if any, should be their Mandatory Protecting Power."[170]

The British and French resisted this investigative commission. Wilson trusted Bliss's advice, however. By mid-March, he had returned to Paris and won the approval of the French and British for the proposed commission. Of the five men chosen to serve on the commission, informally called the King-Crane Commission, three were ordained Protestant clergymen, including two with missionary ties to the Ottoman Empire. In addition to Crane, Wilson chose Henry Churchill King, a Congregationalist clergyman; George Montgomery, a Protestant missionary born in Turkey; Albert Lyber, a former professor at Robert College and an ordained Presbyterian minister; and Captain William Yale, whose experience in the Middle East stemmed from his work for Standard Oil Company of New York before taking on a position as special agent in the Middle East working for the Department of State.[171] Although they had reluctantly acquiesced to the endeavor, in the end the British and French boycotted the commission and refused to appoint any members. Undaunted, the commission members set out on their appointed task of assessing the political future of the Middle East.

Back in the United States, Dodge met personally with President Wilson, continuing his push for greater American involvement in the Middle East and for an American mandate over Armenia and Syria.[172] In Paris, Crane also continued to lobby House on the same issues. Support for an American mandate over Armenia also came from the British, who believed that such a proposal would facilitate their control over other territories in the Middle East.[173] During Wilson's absence at the peace conference, British prime minister David Lloyd George and French premier Georges Clemenceau again brought up the Armenia issue.[174] House cabled Wilson immediately after the meeting, letting him know that both George and Clemenceau supported an American mandate over both Armenia and Istanbul. In May, Henry Morgenthau sent a memorandum to Wilson urging three individual mandates in Istanbul, Turkish Anatolia, and Armenia, all to be held by the United States or, should the United States decline, the British. During that period—and symbolic of its close work with the American government—ACASR was formally incorporated by Congress and renamed Near East Relief.

Meanwhile, Morgenthau also corresponded with Dodge to consider the launch of a second inquiry, modeled on the King-Crane Commission, to assess the possibility of an American mandate over Armenia. The two men convinced the president to move forward on this plan. Wilson assigned James Harbord as head of the commission. A military officer with strong colonial experience working with Filipino Moros, Harbord was an ideal choice. As an article in the *New York Times* noted, "Americans here who favor an American mandate for Armenia and Constantinople lay much stress upon Harbord's twelve years of service in the Philippines, where he had much to do with the civil as well as the military administration, and where he spent much of his time *successfully dealing with the Mohammedan elements of the population*."[175] Harbord promptly set out to complete his assigned task.

Wilson received Harbord's completed report in early October 1919. Harbord provided arguments for and against an American mandate in Armenia, but he implicitly supported the venture. According to Harbord, given the contributions of the United States in creating the League of Nations, the country was now "morally bound to accept the obligations and responsibilities of a mandatory power."[176] Harbord also cited the American colonial experience in the Philippines and Cuba to defend the mandate. Furthermore, he maintained that the United States was the first choice of the Armenians as a mandatory power; British or French rule would be exploitative; and the mandate would end the massacres and "increase the prestige of the United States abroad and inspire interest at home in the regeneration of the Near East."[177]

Harbord concluded the report with two powerful arguments. First, he invoked a trenchant biblical question: "And the Lord said unto Cain, Where is Abel, thy brother? And he said: 'I know not; am I my brother's keeper?'" Second, he called upon the country to fulfill its chivalrous duty: "Here is a man's job that the world says can be better done by America than by any other. . . . Shall it be said that our country lacks the courage to take up new and difficult duties?"[178]

Harbord's argument that the American experience in the Philippines offered support for this possible mandate was echoed in the press by other Americans who had served there. Charles Lobingier, a former American judge in the Philippines, claimed in an article entitled "America's Precedent for Mandates," that the United States had already succeeded in tackling one of the thorniest problems currently facing Turkey: negotiating the religious tensions between Christians and Muslims. Lobingier offered a dubious argument that American colonial officials had successfully ended the innate hatred between Filipino Muslims and Christians: "What American is not proud of such an achievement or would not be prouder of seeing it repeated, on a larger scale, in Turkey?"[179]

In addition to placing personal pressure on the president, Dodge, Barton, and Crane organized a massive propaganda campaign throughout the United States aimed at convincing the American public of the moral necessity of an American mandate over Armenia. The ACIA published pamphlets, articles, and a book entitled *America as Mandatory for Arme-*

nia.[180] The book compiled an impressive collection of editorials in favor of a mandate from the *New York Times* and the *New Republic*, supportive statements from university professors and presidents, poetry, petitions by clergymen, pleas by Armenian Americans, and supportive quotes from diplomats and Democratic and Republican leaders, including, ironically, Henry Cabot Lodge, the senator who would later help doom American membership in the League of Nations and the American mandate over Armenia. It also included a powerful editorial by James Gerard, president of the ACIA, which claimed that an Armenian mandate would serve the larger necessity of drastically reconfiguring American foreign policy. He denounced the "outworn policy of isolation," forwarding Kantian arguments that America had to encourage "the growth and security of institutions like our own, which relatively serve to strengthen and insure our own."[181]

By accepting the mandate and ensuring that Armenia would not be exploited, as it likely would be under a European power, the United States would serve as a role model to European mandates in the region. Gerard maintained that "by an unselfish performance of our duty in Armenia and our withdrawal at the end of the fixed period, we shall set an example to other mandataries, and thus make the mandatorial duty 'a sacred trust of civilization.'" Religious morality also dictated a response: "It is the duty of Christian America to respond to the call of Christian Armenia—the world's first Christian nation." This Christian duty would benefit America; by transforming Armenia into an "outpost of American civilization in the east. . . . Our missionaries and our educators in the Near East can carry on their work of civilization through Armenia, and our business interests can establish their branches there and thus stimulate American commerce in the Near East. Within a radius of 500 miles of the boundaries of Armenia, there are to be found over 100,000,000 who should be receptive to American ideals and methods."[182] Gerard highlighted the other potential risks of granting the mandate to another power: "if that mandatory is a non-Anglo-Saxon nation, then the Armenians will naturally drift away from Anglo-Saxon civilization, and we shall have thus lost a great opportunity for the propagation of Anglo-Saxon civilization to the Near East."[183] Armenian American activist Vahan Cardashian echoed Gerard's plea when he cited Gladstone's 1896 pronouncement that "To serve Armenia is to serve civilization." According to Cardashian, Gladstone's "prophetic words hold infinitely better today than they did in 1896."[184] Such support was also aided by Hollywood's release of a film entitled *Ravished Armenia* based on the memoirs of an Armenian girl who had escaped the massacres. The powerful and symbolic depiction

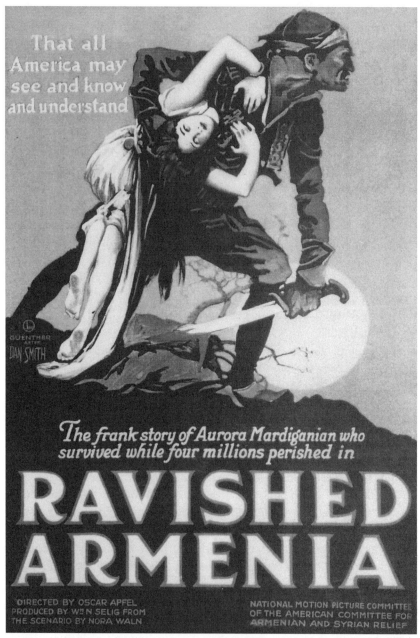

FIGURE 14. This movie poster for *Ravished Armenia* depicted Armenian Christian women at the mercy of savage Turkish Muslims. (Armenian Library and Museum of America)

FIGURE 15.
This full-page advertisement for the movie *Ravished Armenia* appeared in the *Boston Sunday Advertiser*. (12 January 1919)

in the film of young Armenian women crucified on white crosses surely contributed to the American public's existing sympathies.

Official participation in the American war effort included prominent Americans with previous experience in American foreign policy ventures in Islamic societies, including Morocco and the Philippines. In addition to the active participation of men such as James Harbord, who had worked among the Moros before heading the inquiry mission to Armenia, American military officers who had worked among the Moros found prominent roles during World War I. Of the five major generals considered to lead the American Expeditionary Force during World War I, four had served in leadership roles in the Moro Province, including Leonard Wood, Hugh Scott, Tasker Bliss, and John Pershing, who was eventually chosen.[185] Pershing would soon be joined by Charles Brent, who had worked as a

FIGURE 16. Powerful images from the film included a line of Armenian women cruci-fied by Ottoman Turks; the images were reproduced as advertisements for the movie. (*Washington Times*, 9 March 1919)

missionary among Filipino Moros and who would serve as the chaplain to the American Expeditionary Force. Bliss would go on to serve as one of the key American negotiators at the Paris Peace Conference.

Public support for the Armenians also drew the participation of former officers and diplomats with experience in Islamic societies. For example, ACASR and the ACIA included diplomats who had played active roles in Morocco and the Philippines. Members included former secretary of state Elihu Root; former governor of the Philippines William H. Taft; former ambassador to Italy Henry White, who had represented the United States at the Algeciras Conference and served as a close advisor to Wilson during the peace negotiations and later as signatory to the Treaty of Versailles; former minister to the Ottoman Empire Oscar S. Straus; and former head of the first Philippine Commission Jacob G. Schurman.

Former governor of the Moro Province Leonard Wood also played an important role in drawing attention to the Armenian cause. Wood became the spokesperson for a Near East Relief campaign to raise money for Armenian children. In his widely published plea, Wood asked the American people to act on their Christian principles: "This cry from the little children of the land where Christ gave his life for mankind cannot remain unanswered. Will you help to save this martyred people?"[186] Wood was also later designated by Armenian American organizations as an ideal choice to lead an Armenian expeditionary force and defend a new Armenian nation. The concurrent participation of Americans in these foreign policy ventures forged artificial yet influential connections by Americans in diverse parts of the Muslim world. Such wide-ranging pleas from diplomatic, religious, political, and military luminaries, when combined with Wilson's efforts, produced a powerful campaign that reached millions of Americans.

The League of Nations, the Armenian Mandate, and Congress

In September 1919, Wilson embarked on a cross-country tour in an effort to rally the public in favor of his most important contribution to the Treaty of Versailles, the League of Nations. His emotional commitment to the plan and his fervent desire for American support led him to make what became a physically exhausting trip, one that affected his health. During the tour he suffered a series of strokes that forced him to end his trip.

Although Wilson had concentrated his speeches on the League of Nations and the necessity for U.S. membership, activists refused to disassociate this goal from the effort to obtain American mandates. Ten days before Congress voted on the League of Nations resolution, the *New York Times* devoted three and a half pages to a long plea by former ambassador Henry Morgenthau. Morgenthau knew that if Congress did not vote for the League of Nations, then the Armenian mandate likely would be doomed. He outlined the benefits of the mandate, both for the United States and for the former Ottoman territories, as well as a history of the Crimean War and the Bulgarian Massacres. He contrasted European selfishness with American humanitarianism and noted the immense opportunity that had been granted by the moment to civilize the symbolic center of the Muslim world. "Only America can transform Constantinople," he wrote. "Only America can establish herself there without suspicion of bad faith and without jealousy; *only America can civilize the capital of Islam.*"[187]

Editorials defending the mandate system filled the pages of local and national newspapers. To dilute the emotional power of the Armenian cause, opponents of the treaty focused on the League itself, maintaining that it contradicted the Monroe Doctrine and traditional U.S. policies of nonentanglement abroad. One editorial in favor of a mandate countered by arguing that the higher claim of Christianity should encourage Americans to support Article 22, which "writes into the highest laws of the world the Christian doctrine." The article cited one of Wilson's speeches, noting that the United States had "nothing to fear except God and the possible failure to do our best for the rest of the world."[188]

In the end, the efforts by Wilson and his close advisors and friends to gain support for the treaty and secure a mandate over Armenia failed to convince Congress, which was driven by fears of future entanglement in foreign affairs as well as by partisanship and the deep political antagonism between Lodge and Wilson. Congress voted down U.S. membership in the League of Nations on 19 November 1919. The treaty would face two more congressional rejections in subsequent months, dooming any possibility for an American mandate over Armenia. In April of the following year, after the Treaty of San Remo had officially classified territories in need of mandatory powers, the Allies again asked the United States to take responsibility for a mandate over Armenia. This led to a renewed attempt by Wilson to lobby Congress. In his congressional address on 24 May 1920, President Wilson portrayed the American mandate over Armenia as a Christian endeavor demanded by the American people. To make his case, he relied on the language of Article 22 of the League of Nations: "The sympathy for Armenia among our people has sprung from untainted consciences, pure Christian faith and an earnest desire to see

Christian people everywhere . . . *stand upon their feet and take their place among the free nations of the world.*" In addition to this effort to rally support, Harbord's report on an American mandate in Armenia was circulated to all of the members of Congress.[189] Despite Harbord's implicit recommendation that the United States accept the mandate, Congress rejected his advice and voted against the resolution on 1 June 1920.

Meanwhile, Turkish nationalist Mustafa Kemal had begun his own movement for Turkish independence. His forces succeeded in defeating the Armenian army in 1920 and the Greek army two years later. These victories doomed any future American or European mandate over territories now part of the new Turkish state and forced the allies back to the negotiating table at the Conference of Lausanne in 1922. The resulting treaty acknowledged Kemal's political authority and granted Turkey international recognition as an independent republic.

The Turkish Republic was officially born on 23 October 1923, and with it a modern nation-state dedicated to Turkish ethnic identity. As one scholar has noted, this moment "was a watershed in the modern history of the Middle East, marking the turn of a multiethnic empire into nation-states set upon homogenizing their populations in their everlasting nationalist search for identity."[190] The process continued over the following two years as "Greece and Turkey both enjoyed international support to homogenize their countries through massive population exchange, which uprooted hundreds of thousands of people."[191] The rise of a secular Turkish Republic so soon after the emergence of the Young Turks further proved that extreme ethnic nationalism and violence did not require religious faith.

The King-Crane Commission, the Mandate System, and the Creation of a Jewish Homeland in Palestine

In the end, Wilson failed to gain American public and congressional support for the Versailles Treaty or for an American mandate over Armenia, but his earlier support for the Balfour Declaration helped secure the Council of Ten's final endorsement of a new Jewish homeland in Palestine. British pressure had initially helped convince Wilson to support the Balfour Declaration, but religion also drove his decision. Louis Brandeis had been working with Rabbi Stephen Wise and Reverend William Blackstone to pressure Wilson into supporting the declaration. Brandeis and Wise wanted a Jewish homeland in part to protect the future security of Jews, whereas Blackstone supported the idea for eschatological reasons.

Blackstone believed that enabling the "restoration" of Jews to the Holy Land would fulfill the requirements for the end of days and the return of Christ to earth. Playing on Wilson's strong religious faith, the three men convinced the president of the role he could play in shaping both world and spiritual affairs.

Race, religion, and ethnic nationalism would thus play a central role in Wilson's peacetime negotiations, directly impacting his views of the necessity of foreign mandates over former Ottoman territories and the creation of a Jewish homeland in Palestine. Indeed, the two were not disconnected. By the end of World War I, Jewish Americans had successfully secured their inclusion in American society—to such a degree that their lobbying efforts on behalf of Jewish interests abroad carried virtually as much weight as those of American missionaries. Rabbi Wise had proudly recalled in 1920 at a public meeting on behalf of Armenians that, when he had met with the president three years earlier, Wilson had promised him that "when the war will be ended, there are two lands that will never go back to the Mohammedan apache. One is Christian Armenia and the other is Jewish Palestine."[192] Whether or not Wilson used such revelatory words, Wise's recollection nonetheless offered a powerful public testimony to the links between American beliefs about race, religion, and empire. Uncivilized Muslim "apaches," be they Turkish or Arab, no more deserved to rule over their own lands than had Native Americans on the American continent. Helping to deliver this land to civilized Christians and Jews was therefore a continuation of American manifest destiny—one that now included American Jews.

While some American religious activists celebrated the future of a Jewish homeland, others offered prescient warnings that violence and hostility would accompany its creation. In late September 1919, the King-Crane Commission had finally completed its report. Although its recommendations arrived too late to influence Wilson or the peace conference, it had nonetheless concluded that Arabs vehemently opposed Balfour's project and that such a venture would require a massive military force of at least 50,000 British soldiers to maintain itself in the face of local opposition.[193] The King-Crane report further noted that the project defied the principles of self-determination that Wilson had put forward in his Fourteen Points: "To subject a people so minded to unlimited Jewish immigration, and to steady financial and social pressure to surrender the land, would be a gross violation of the principle just quoted [of free acceptance], and of the people's right, though it kept within the forms of the law." Furthermore, the legitimate use of force to enforce such an endeavor had to be based on sound moral principle, which the King-Crane report felt was not applicable to this particular situation: "Decisions, requiring armies to carry out, are sometimes necessary, but they are surely not gratuitously to be taken in the interest of a serious injustice. For the initial claim, often submitted by Zionist representatives, that they have a 'right' to Palestine, based on an occupation of 2,000 years ago, can hardly be seriously considered."[194]

The King-Crane Commission also foreshadowed resistance likely to emerge in other areas of the Middle East. Their report concluded that Syrians were adamantly opposed to a French mandate, though should a mandate be necessary, the United States would be its top choice. The Syrian rationale for an American mandate also demonstrated the powerful transnational networks of communication between Syrians and Syrian Americans across the world. Crane noted that Syrians had based their desire for American mandatory rule in part on the positive reports they had heard from Syrian Americans about U.S. rule in the Philippines. He highlighted the influence, among others, of Najeeb Saleeby, the Syrian American graduate of the Syrian Protestant College who had worked closely with Filipino Muslims as part of the American colonial apparatus. According to Crane, Saleeby had "transmitted the fine history of America's work" in the Philippines to Syrians back home.[195]

Although the King-Crane Commission had offered dire warnings about local opposition to British or French mandates and the creation of a Jewish homeland in Palestine, two members of the commission disagreed. Dr. George Montgomery's report to the King-Crane Commission argued that the "heart" of Islam was incompatible with "modern society."[196] He noted, "Mohommedan [sic] empires grew and prospered only as long as there was loot to be looted and divided. Islam contains no nucleus of unselfishness which may hold out a hope of Mohommedan [sic] reformation."[197] Thus, Montgomery maintained, Syrians could not govern themselves. The United States would have been an ideal choice, but priority for an American mandate had to go to Armenia.[198] He recommended that Lebanon and Syria be divided into separate mandates, the former to be ruled over by a French mandate and the latter by a joint French and British mandate. With regard to Palestine, he recommended a British mandate and that "the immigration of the Jews be encouraged for the benefit which it will bring to the country."[199]

The other dissenting member, William Yale, conceded that his recommendations were "entirely contrary to the wishes of the people of Palestine." Nonetheless, he believed that transforming Palestine into a Jewish homeland would bring progress and civilization to the area. Advancing his own stereotypes of Jews, he argued that "Jewish energy, Jewish genius and Jewish finances will bring many advantages to Palestine and perhaps to all of the East. Modern western methods and civilization will be brought to Palestine by the Jews."[200] This combination would lead to a "new element" in the "Orient," which would be an "Eastern race well versed in western culture and profoundly in sympathy with western ideals."[201] This belief corresponded to arguments put forth by many American Zionists that creating a Jewish homeland would constitute a civilizing mission in the Middle East.[202]

Despite the inescapable conclusion that the mandate system and the Balfour Declaration defied the direct wishes of the peoples of the Middle East, Wilson never considered the King-Crane report when formulating his policies. By the time they delivered their final report, Wilson had suffered a stroke, and the British and French had obtained their demands to divide the Middle Eastern spoils of war among themselves. The reports were not released to the American public until 1922, after Congress had rejected both the Treaty of Versailles and the American mandate over Armenia but had successfully voted in favor of a Jewish homeland.

The *New York Times* republished the report in its entirety, accompanied by an outraged introduction about what might have been possible had the report surfaced earlier.[203] According to the newspaper, the report proved "the untenability of European claims upon Turkish territory," "the unfitness of the old Ottoman Empire to rule or to continue to live," and the "doom of Zionism." The United States had let the peoples of the Middle East down, it maintained: "Turk, Greek, Arab, Armenian, Jew, Syrian and Druse" asked themselves what had happened to the American mission and did not understand "the disappearance of the Great Hope which the American Commission represented."[204]

The King-Crane Commission's report proved prescient in other ways as well. The legacy of the mandate system would help define future conflicts in the Middle East, beginning immediately after the conference itself as uprisings against mandate rule spread throughout the former Ottoman territories and in British and French colonial territories in the Middle East and Asia. Egyptians, Syrians, Lebanese, and Palestinians actively fought policies they correctly understood as the endorsement of European imperial control over their territories and resources. In British-mandated Iraq, popular revolts in 1920 led the Royal Air Force to use "air policing" for the first time, bombing entire villages to suppress insurgent populations, resulting in thousands of deaths.[205] Although Wilson had supported the mandate system, one high-level British diplomat nonetheless blamed the president for these widespread rebellions, noting that "the primary and original cause of our troubles in the East from Egypt, through Palestine, Mesopotamia, and Persia to India is President Wilson and his fourteen points, and his impossible doctrine of self determination."[206]

Despite the popular interpretation of Wilson's commitment to self-determination, his actions during World War I demonstrated a less idealistic reality. Although congressional opposition had prevented the country from accepting mandates over the territories of the former Ottoman Empire, Wilson and the other statesmen had succeeded in institutionalizing their racial and civilizational logic in an international system that would continue to limit the political and economic rights of millions across the globe. In the Middle East, such policies reflected the continuation of more than a century of American beliefs regarding the incapacity of Muslims to rule over themselves or others.

Although it resumed its noninterventionist policies after the war, the United States would find that its interests in the Middle East would nonetheless grow in the following century and extend beyond the narrow focus of American missionaries. In this regard, William Yale's dissenting reports for the King-Crane Commission were remarkably prescient. In a separate memorandum for the commission, Yale had noted an important strategic interest that the United States could not ignore. Undoubtedly aware that the chances of the United States extending a mandate throughout the Middle East were slim and drawing on his experience with Standard Oil, he recommended that all mandatory powers adopt an open-door policy with regard to petroleum interests. According to Yale, the necessity of such a policy was particularly important for the British mandate over Mesopotamia (modern-day Iraq): "Mesopotamia is regarded as one of the large potential oil fields of the future . . . it is of utmost importance to the United States Government that Americans should be interested there."[207] Yale also maintained that Americans would benefit from the creation of a Jewish homeland in the Middle East, for such a state would advance American interests. American Jews would help to turn the future Jewish state into an "outpost of Americanism."[208] In identifying the Jewish homeland and oil as central to American interests, Yale forecast what would become the two central pillars of post–World War II U.S. foreign policy in the Middle East.

In the midst of these new strategic interests, American beliefs about Islam would not disappear; perceptions of Islamic fanaticism and Muslim intolerance would continue to shape how Americans understood the Middle East and, by extension, the foreign policy of the United States in the region for years to come. World War I had left an enduring legacy in the Middle East and marked the United States as a rising new world power. For men such as Wilson, this historical trajectory was inevitable, one that was integral to the country's divinely ordained global mission. As he noted in one of his last speeches in 1923, "I am not one of those that have the least anxiety about the triumph of the principles I have stood for. I have seen fools resist Providence before and I have seen their destruction, as will come upon these again—utter destruction and contempt. That we shall prevail is as sure as that God reigns."[209] What exactly these principles would come to represent would become increasingly open to interpretation in the following century.

CONCLUSION

In 1899, two years before assuming the presidency of the United States, Theodore Roosevelt published an article entitled "Expansion and Peace" in the popular weekly political magazine the *Independent*.[1] The article's title perfectly encapsulated Roosevelt's argument that Americans and Europeans needed to work together to guarantee world peace by expanding their civilization through imperial rule. For Roosevelt, the uncivilized world extended from Africa to Asia and from the Middle East to the much diminished lands still occupied by the "red savages" in the United States. While dismissing any recognized civilization for all of these diverse peoples, Roosevelt's plan for global expansion united European and American nation-states in an imagined "civilized" community. Roosevelt's division between civilized and uncivilized extended to military tactics as well. Given the alleged natural propensities of savages, Euro-American civilization had to be delivered and enforced through violent means, "for the barbarian will yield only to force." The logical extension of such ideas led him to conclude that "Peace may only come through war."[2] Though spread through violence, Roosevelt assured his readers that "every expansion of a great civilized Power means a victory for law, order and righteousness . . . whether the expanding power were [*sic*] France or England, Russia or America."[3]

To underscore the exigency of such united action, Roosevelt offered his readers a history lesson on the benefits of Euro-American expansion to the world. Although the uncivilized realms included peoples across the globe, the Muslim world occupied the most important place in Roosevelt's global clash of civilizations. Indeed, Roosevelt cited every area of the Islamic world discussed in this book. The United States had fought wars against the Barbary powers and had paid "blood money to the

Moslem bandits," all because Algeria had not yet been occupied. French imperial expansion into Algeria had ended the ability of these barbarians to impose their savage violence on civilized powers.

Similarly, the belligerence of Turkish and Arab Muslims had "wrecked the civilization" of the Mediterranean and southeastern Europe. Roosevelt maintained that, had it not been for the Greeks fighting the Turks during their war for independence, Italian attempts to impose imperial rule on Abyssinians, and Spanish efforts to dominate Morocco, the "Mediterranean coasts would be overrun either by the Turks or by the Sudan Mahdists." Roosevelt also applauded the results of the Russo-Turkish war, in which Russia had delivered independence to Bulgaria, Serbia, and Bosnia and Herzegovina and saved them from Ottoman barbarians: "This expansion of the domain of civilization at the expense of barbarism has been simply incalculable." Other notable examples of the extension of civilization included the British domination of Egypt, the Sudan, and India; Russian expansion into Asia; and, of course, American imperial expansion into the Philippines. At these moments, Roosevelt maintained, civilized powers had suppressed their peaceful tendencies in the interest of dominating, and thus advancing, uncivilized peoples.

Roosevelt nonetheless lamented the fact that European powers had at times shamefully placated uncivilized powers. In such instances, maintaining peace had tragic consequences: "The great blot upon European international morality in the closing decades of this century has been not war, but the infamous peace kept by the joint action of the great powers, while Turkey inflicted the last horrors of butchery, torture and outrage upon the men, women and children of despairing Armenia." To bolster his argument, Roosevelt cited the opinions of his friend Alfred Mahan, the well-respected navy officer, military strategist, and fellow supporter of American imperial expansion. Describing Mahan as "a Christian gentleman who is incapable of advocating wrongdoing of any kind," Roosevelt noted that even Mahan had lambasted European inaction: "Witness Armenia and witness Crete. War has been avoided; but what of the national consciences that beheld such iniquity and withheld the hand?" According to Roosevelt, Mahan's opinion on the matter represented the "feeling of the great majority of manly and thoughtful men."[4]

Roosevelt was a man defined by the beliefs of his era. Like many Americans at the turn of the twentieth century, he drew sharp distinctions between the civilized Christian Family of Nations and the non-Christian world. Though less vitriolic than John Quincy Adams's attack more than half a century earlier, Roosevelt's implicit denunciation of Islamic societies nevertheless implicated Muslims as the villains in a larger global story. By involving the United States in the global effort to eradicate Muslim rule, Roosevelt offered a new paradigm for American foreign policy that directly challenged traditional American pronouncements of nonentanglement in world affairs outside of the Western Hemisphere. As president, Roosevelt would have the opportunity to convert his beliefs into action.

During the nineteenth and early twentieth centuries, Americans codified such beliefs in both theory and action. Although strategic motivations and commercial interests often dictated American foreign relations, American beliefs about Muslim barbarity were also an important ideological incentive to expand the country's national interests beyond the limited boundaries of the nation-state. Despite the rhetoric of nonentanglement, many Americans believed their country should help shape the "proper" trajectory of global history.

Beliefs in the cultural, religious, and civilizational inferiority of Islamic societies played a central role in constructing this historical narrative. Like European nation-states, American attitudes toward the Muslim world were uniquely defined by its history—including domestic attitudes about religious difference, American manifest destiny, empire, and hierarchies of race, religion, and civilization. Such perceptions justified discrimination against domestic minorities, including American Jews, Mormons, and Catholics, as well as Asians, Native Americans, African Americans and other groups that did not conform to hegemonic narratives of American ethnic, racial, and religious nationalism. But such beliefs were also shaped by transnational exchanges. During the nineteenth and early twentieth centuries, global interactions between people, nongovernmental organizations, nations, and empires embedded American attitudes within larger transnational conceptualizations of the Islamic world. Increasing calls by these diverse groups for humanitarian intervention also implicated Americans and Europeans in wider global affairs. During the same period, Euro-American conceptualizations of international law sanctioned Western imperial expansion and the right to intervene in the sovereignty of Muslim societies in North Africa, Asia, and the Middle East. American beliefs about Islam and Muslims thus emerged within wider national and international discussions about what it meant to be an American, beliefs that would have important consequences both at home and in American foreign relations.

Writing in 1899, Roosevelt's belief that civilized nation-states were less prone to go to war with each other had not yet been disproven. Fifteen years later, the "civilized" peoples of Europe, whose independence and civilization his article celebrated, would wage a war, in part, over competition for imperial territory. Given his belief in the inherently peaceful nature of civilized societies and his fear that civilized men had lost their "strenuous manhood," Roosevelt could not have predicted that this war would result in so much bloodshed and brutality that many Europeans and Americans would question the so-called civilized status of their own societies. Yet, this doubt did not necessarily stop them from continuing to brandish anti-Muslim discourses to justify the imposition of Euro-American civilization onto large portions of the Middle East after the war.

Although Roosevelt's views reflected the beliefs of many contemporary Americans and Europeans, they did not go unchallenged, either at home or abroad. Throughout the nineteenth and twentieth centuries, Muslims fought against European and American attempts to challenge their sovereignty or demean their religious beliefs. At home, African Americans challenged claims of American civilizational superiority over "intolerant" Muslim societies by pointing to the ongoing discrimination and violent oppression they faced at the very hands of those professing the superiority of American political ideals. Jewish Americans sought to redefine the United States as a secular beacon of religious tolerance rather than a "Christian nation." American anti-imperialists denounced the extension of American power abroad and questioned the legitimacy of using violence against colonial subjects fighting for independence and self-rule. After World War I, colonized peoples around the globe appropriated Wilson's language of self-determination to challenge the continuation and extension of European and American imperial rule.[5] After World War II, such demands became even more forceful during the global anticolonial movements that swept across Africa, Asia, and the Middle East. Alongside these mounting demands came increased links between African Americans in the American Civil Rights movement and anticolonialists across the world.[6]

Historical events after World War I, however, would prove the hollowness of American and European claims to religious and racial tolerance in other ways. During his presidency, Roosevelt's support for French imperial rule in Morocco had facilitated the establishment of an official French protectorate in 1912, which would leave France in power for the next half century. Roosevelt and other policymakers justified the expansion of French imperial rule in Morocco in part by arguing that France would help assure tolerance for Moroccan Jews. During World War II, however, the French Vichy government and many French citizens were complicit in aiding the Nazi genocide of millions of Jews and other vilified minorities—policies the French tried to extend to their colonial territories in Morocco, Tunisia, and Algeria.[7] Such historical events demonstrated the tragic fulfillment of ethnic nationalism and the "Jewish Question" in Europe and the irony of France's earlier claims of spreading religious tolerance to Morocco.

Similarly, during World War II, Henry Morgenthau Sr.'s son, Henry Morgenthau Jr., pleaded with President Franklin Roosevelt to allow Jewish refugees fleeing the genocidal policies of Nazi Germany to enter the United States. The American public's anti-Semitism and popular nativist sentiments against further immigration thwarted any official action to save European Jews.[8] Morgenthau Sr. had condemned the inaction of Europe and the United States during the genocide of Armenians in 1915, only to have his son fail in prompting American domestic relief for European Jews during yet another genocide less than three decades later.

This repetition of historical atrocities, however, was not disconnected from the past and from the use of historical memory, or lack thereof. As historians have often noted, in August 1939, as Adolf Hitler was launching his plans for Jewish extermination in Poland, he told a group of Axis officers: "Who, after all, speaks today of the annihilation of the Armenians?"[9] But Hitler's references to ethnic cleansing were not limited to the Armenians. Hitler also referenced American manifest destiny and the ethnic cleansing of Native Americans as a model on which he could base German colonial expansion into the Soviet Union.[10] As the historian Timothy Snyder has noted regarding Hitler's plans: "Colonization would make Germany a continental empire fit to rival the United States, another hard frontier state based upon exterminatory colonialism and slave labor. The East was the Nazi Manifest Destiny. In Hitler's view, 'in the East a similar process will repeat itself for a second time as in the conquest of America.' As Hitler imagined the future, Germany would deal with the Slavs much as the North Americans had dealt with the Indians. The Volga River, he once proclaimed, will be Germany's Mississippi."[11]

After World War II, immigration restrictions and domestic expressions of anti-Semitism continued to limit the migration of Jewish refugees to the United States. Some Americans were so eager to have Jews migrate elsewhere that policymakers worked with Filipino leaders on the "Mindanao Plan," a proposal to relocate Jewish refugees to Moro-dominated areas of Mindanao.[12] American support for the creation of an Israeli state in 1948, at the expense of Palestinian rights, would also lead to yet another example of state-sponsored demographic engineering as thousands of

Palestinians were violently expelled from their lands.[13] The results of such policies left a legacy that remains one of the most contentious political issues facing the Middle East and the world today.

American involvement in the Middle East would not be limited to its support for Israel. American missionaries had discounted ongoing calls for U.S. policies of nonentanglement after World War I; they saw the end of the war as a momentous opportunity to continue spreading Christian civilization to Muslims in the Middle East. Thus, converting Muslims to Christianity gained in importance after the war. In 1919, the journal the *Moslem World*, created by American Protestant missionaries in 1911 to address the difficulty of converting Muslims, published several articles on how to take advantage of the new political and social changes brought about in the Middle East as a result of the war and ensuing peace negotiations. As one missionary noted, "Old things have passed away," and the "new world" was defined by hope, life, and freedom as Euro-American civilization was "sweeping over the East."[14]

Imbuing a Christian element into Wilson's infamous war claims, Samuel Zwemer, a missionary and editor of the *Moslem World*, maintained in the same issue that American war aims derived from a higher power, for "only God can make His world safe for Democracy and only His kind of Democracy is safe for the world."[15] For this reason, the "Evangelization of the Moslem world" was a "supra-national" task that should unite "all the forces of Christianity in the conflict with Islam."[16] Another missionary maintained that American missionaries should approach the conversion of Islam using the strategic model of the victorious Allied forces, one that had taught the world the "absolute necessity of watching for the least sign of weakening anywhere along the enemy's line, and then driving home the attack at the vulnerable point." He added, "Islam has developed a weak point," and it was time to act.[17] The bloodshed and brutality of World War I had apparently not dissuaded this missionary from applying the language of war and violence to the conversion of Muslims.

Transnational support by Protestant missionaries outside of the United States also encouraged continued efforts to convert Muslims. In an article published in the same journal, Arthur French, a British missionary based in India who worked for the Society for the Propagation of the Gospel, advised a line of attack similar to that of his American colleague. He suggested that Christians adapt Allied military strategies to defeat Islam.[18] One such tool was already in place. Eerily foreshadowing the British tactic of bombing rebellious Iraqi villages, which it would apply only a year after French wrote his article, the British missionary maintained that "Our 'Air Force' (the Holy Scriptures) is everywhere flying over enemy lines and lands and literally 'bombing' places formerly unattackable." The author posited a veritable military takeover by Christian missions, just as the Allied forces had advanced from Mesopotamia to Baghdad: "The Frontier Missions of India must move forward into Afghanistan and Persia, and the Missions along the North African coast use the coast towns merely as 'bases.' We would, similarly, like to see Khartoum the Headquarters of the Nile Mission. The Malay Peninsula is another strategic point to be occupied—Singapore to be the base. The whole stretches of the Tigris up to Mosul from Baghdad as a centre; the Baghdad Railway with Aleppo as a base and Damascus for Syria; Arabia is the only exception, but Mecca is 'our Mecca.'"[19]

Another important tool of attack, according to French, was the League of Nations. Missionaries needed to use their representatives in the League to advance their cause by demonstrating "that the protagonists of Christianity are the best friends of the League of Nations. In other words we have to convince the founders of the League that we are out to help; to propagate peace and good will amongst men, that the weapons of our warfare are not carnal but spiritual and mighty through God to the throwing down of the strongholds of unrighteousness."[20] Part of this effort required moving away from secular foreign policies that focused on strategic interests to the detriment of moral and spiritual advancement. The only solution, according to this same calculation, was that the League join with missionaries in their efforts to convert Muslims by having Christianity serve as the driving force for world relations: "We have to prove to the Founders of the League of Nations that Islamic lands can only become vital parts of the League by coming into the 'Christian Family.'" In a remarkable reference to American imperial rule over Muslims thousands of miles away, French then noted that "as ex-President Taft said of the Moslems of the Philippines 'they will never understand democracy until they accept Christianity.'"[21] The British missionary's reference to Taft and American imperial policies toward Filipino Muslims offered a powerful testament to the transnational connections that existed between Americans and Europeans regarding the extension of imperial rule and the spread of Christianity to the Muslim world.

French was not alone in including the Philippines in the postwar global plan to spread Protestant Christianity to the world. In 1919, the same year the *Moslem World* published its articles about missionary plans for the Middle East, it also published several articles about Filipino Muslims that echoed these sentiments.[22] Robert McCutchen, who had worked alongside

Charles Brent in the Episcopalian mission to Filipino Muslims, praised the work of American missionaries who had brought progress and civilization to the area through their missions.[23] Indeed, missionary concerns over advancing "Orientals" was a problem that would require great effort, whether in the Middle East or in Asia. As McCutchen maintained, the project of transforming the Moros from the "Mohammedan of intolerance" to the "more liberal minded, tolerant and receptive stage" required patience, for "progress among any Oriental people is slow as considered in comparison with Occidental movements." Nonetheless, the project to civilize and Christianize Filipino Muslims presented "the world's first and greatest experiment among Eastern Orientals under a Democratic form of government."[24] As the *Moslem World* articles predicted, Protestant missionaries would have their hands full in the following decades in attempting to solve the racial and religious obstacles posed by the Muslims of the "Orient."

This attention did not stem solely from benevolent concern. Echoing Roosevelt's earlier admonitions, other prominent Americans warned of the dire consequences if Christians were unsuccessful in converting Muslims. Such ideas were best exemplified by the influential American scholar, journalist, and eugenicist Lothrop Stoddard. Stoddard's book, *The Rising Tide of Color against White World Supremacy*, became a bestseller in the United States when it was released in 1920. As demonstrated by the title, Stoddard's fears extended beyond Muslims in the Middle East to encompass the spread of Islam to all of Africa and Asia. He argued that "Islam is, in fact, the intimate link between the brown and black worlds."[25] He further cautioned his readers about what might occur if the Islamic faith continued to spread to these areas: "Islam is militant by nature, and the Arab is a restless and warlike breed. Pan-Islamism once possessed of the Dark Continent and fired by militant zealots, might forge black Africa into a sword of wrath, the executor of sinister adventures."[26] The successful propagation of the faith had already prompted insurrections throughout North Africa, India, and the Middle East, "prompting a rebellion against European civilization."[27] To avoid such a calamity, he maintained, Africa had to remain a "white man's country" dominated by French and British imperial rule.[28] Despite the popular rhetoric of self-determination, in the minds of many Americans, empire remained a solution rather than a problem.

In practice, the legacies of empire would forever alter the political and religious identities of colonial subjects. In the Philippines, American colonial policies that had distinguished Muslims from Christian Filipinos had already helped in establishing a virtual colony within a colony. During World War I, Americans gradually began to transfer positions of leadership to Filipino Christians, including in Mindanao and other areas where majority populations were Muslim. Most often, American colonial rulers deemed Moros unworthy of leadership positions. After the war, American policymakers, missionaries, and, later, Filipino Christians continued to maintain that the solution to the Moro problem entailed greater contact between Moros and Christian civilization. In addition to American missionary work, the solution also entailed encouraging Filipino Christians to migrate to Moro lands.

The American colonial apparatus helped perpetuate attitudes about Moros' religious and civilizational inferiority to Christian Filipinos. In 1934, the U.S. Congress voted to establish a commonwealth in the Philippines and initiated a ten-year transition period toward full independence. When Manual Quezon was elected president of the commonwealth the following year, he adopted the paternalism of American colonial attitudes to Filipino Muslims. In a speech delivered shortly after his election, he remarked that "the Moro Problem is a thing of the past. We are giving our Mohammedan brethren the best government they have ever had and we are showing them our devoted interest in their welfare and advancement."[29] Just as Filipinos had become America's "little brown brothers" in 1898, Moros would continue to be assigned the role of younger, inferior siblings to the more advanced Christian Filipinos. As Quezon argued—in language reminiscent of justifications for American policies regarding Native Americans and American expansion on the western frontier: "Let us reserve for [Moros] in their respective localities such land of the public domain as they may need for their well-being. Let us at the same time, place in the unoccupied lands of that region industrious Filipinos from other provinces of the Archipelago, so that they may live together in perfect harmony and brotherhood." Indeed, "the time has come," Quezon maintained, to "bring about the colonization and economic development of Mindanao." Quezon specified that this colonization would be "by Filipinos themselves," by which he meant, of course, Christian Filipinos.[30] Such sentiments confirmed that the colonial mantle had been passed from Americans to Christian Filipinos, as Moro lands became colonial territories for Christian Filipino occupation.

American colonial policies that had codified Moro inferiority also found support among other Filipino political elites. In 1938, the Philippine Council, the advisory body of Christian Filipinos that helped guide the country's president, confirmed the necessity of Christian Filipino colonization policies during a meeting to discuss the "development of Mindanao and the future of the Non-Christians."[31] During the meeting, the council specifically referenced American colonial policies and the reports of the Bureau of Non-Christian Tribes in crafting its future plans for Filipino Muslims, illustrating the continued impact of American views on Filipino ruling elites. The council recommended launching a major project to build roads, an infrastructural endeavor that would ease the Christian penetration of Mindanao and facilitate the colonization process by Filipino Christians. In addition to aiding the "social, commercial and educational intercourse" between Mindanao and areas to the north, the project would also maintain peace "in the provinces where the rebellious elements still constitute a deterrent factor to the uninterrupted flow of immigration from the Christian provinces."[32] This language implied that submerging the Moros in a sea of Christian Filipino migrants was the only way that the area could be fully integrated into an independent Philippine state.

The council continued to echo the empire-building tactics inherent in American manifest destiny. As council member Eulogio Rodriguez noted, the agricultural potential of the area meant that "Mindanao is Providence's gift." Much like American manifest destiny had necessitated the removal of Native Americans, God's gift to Filipino Christians did not come without challenges. As Rodriguez conceded, the larger project of "empire-building in the Pacific" was complicated by the presence of "different peoples," a euphemistic reference to the Moros and other non-Christian Filipinos. For this reason, Mindanao was thus "both a treasure and a problem."[33] The solution, however, had already been found. Both American colonial officials and Filipino Christians simply replicated previous American policies of empire by assigning Moros limited parcels of land while appropriating the majority of the remaining lands for Christian Filipinos.

Muslim Filipinos' opposition to these policies united them in a way that had never existed before American colonial rule. As the Philippines moved toward formal independence, Filipino Muslims adamantly rejected attempts by Filipino Christians to treat them as second-class citizens. Such tensions would lead to the development of a Moro independence movement that united what had previously been diverse groups of Moros into a movement largely defined under the banner of a newly constructed Islamic identity. The movement for Moro independence continues to vex the Philippines to the present day.

Outside the Philippines and around the world, American influence continued to spread. By 1941, when Henry Luce published his famous essay calling for an "American Century" defined by American dominance in global affairs, the rhetoric of nonentanglement was all but dead.[34] Luce, the son of American missionaries, had grown up with the belief that the United States had a divine role to play in spreading Protestant Christianity and American civilization to the world.[35] After World War II, American involvement in Islamic lands increased as the nation emerged as a dominant foreign power and as oil and Israel became crucial, strategic pillars of American foreign policy. The Cold War heightened this involvement, as the Middle East became a key battleground between the United States and the Soviet Union. The Manichean logic that posited Christianity and Islam as religious forces engaged in a zero-sum game for survival offered an obvious ideological stepping stone to Cold War ideology.[36]

During and after the Cold War, American attitudes about Islam would remain crucial in defining American attitudes toward the Muslim world. However, it would be a mistake to trace an unbroken trajectory from the nineteenth century to the post–Cold War period and, more importantly, to the post-9/11 era. As *Sacred Interests* has demonstrated, American attitudes about Islam and Muslims have been shaped by specific historical contingencies. Yet it would be equally erroneous to discount the ways in which American discourses about Islam have persisted in the recent relations of the United States with the Muslim world, albeit in varied forms.[37]

Indeed, negative imagery of Islam never fully vanished from American discourse; it reappeared during the ideological and foreign policy vacuum that emerged after the Cold War. Whereas some political scientists advanced the notion that the end of the Cold War had brought about the "end of history" and the ideological victory of liberal, secular democracies, other scholars theorized powerful alternative visions of the world, in which a simplistically defined "Islamic Civilization" would play a central role in opposing an equally simplistic construction of the "West," broadly understood as Euro-American civilization.[38] The most influential—if controversial—assertion of such views was advanced by Samuel Huntington in his 1993 essay, "The Clash of Civilizations," which he later expanding into a full-length book. His particular focus on religion as the "most important" of the "objective elements which define civilization" led to his theory that such religious affiliations would result in an inevitable "clash" between Islam and the West.[39] In many ways, Huntington's arguments drew on the pre–Cold War logic of American discourse that divided the world into distinct realms of civilization. Indeed, he argued that such intra-civilizational conflict had been the *defining historical norm* for centuries; by extension, the end of the Cold War would bring about a logical *return* to civilizational conflict.[40]

Huntington's theory drew criticism from many scholars, who rightfully traced his theories to essentialized distinctions that had emerged from nineteenth-century Orientalism.[41] Although Huntington must be understood as a product of his time, one cannot fully discount the historical continuities that allowed him to develop his theories. Huntington's civilizational distinctions, after all, were largely an extension of existing notions put forth by the early-twentieth-century British policymaker and historian Arnold J. Toynbee. Toynbee's scholarship advanced the idea of Western Christendom as the dominant, superior civilization that pressured other, declining civilizations, whose moral failures precluded them from truly competing with the West.[42] Although Toynbee's theories were largely discounted by historians after the 1960s, Huntington's extension of Toynbee's earlier civilizational classifications offered a clear link to earlier visions of the world that highlighted religion as the defining element in an imagined community of clashing Islamic and Christian civilizations.

Huntington's arguments had important consequences for American foreign policy.[43] His theories appeared particularly prophetic after the events of 9/11. Indeed, less than a decade after the publication of "The Clash of Civilizations," the George W. Bush administration's "Global War on Terror" borrowed Huntington's theory to explain its emerging ideological conceptualizations.[44] As President Bush noted days after the 9/11 attacks, the United States had not seen "this kind of barbarism in a long period of time. . . . And the American people are beginning to understand. This crusade, this war on terrorism is going to take a while."[45] Huntington's theory resonated with Americans after 9/11, not because it was accurate but because this particular kind of discourse has a long history of shaping how Americans identified with the world. Huntington's theories demonstrated, above all, the continued power of ideological notions of difference that embedded religion within overarching paradigms of global identity, particularly regarding the Muslim world.

When Theodore Roosevelt published his essay in 1899, his central argument was that spreading Euro-American civilization to the world was the only way to assure world peace. More than a century later, when President George W. Bush led the United States into its second war in Iraq, he was inspired by a neoconservative movement that believed spreading democracy to the Middle East was the best way to ensure world peace. Similarly, the war in Iraq, formally titled "Operation Iraqi Freedom," prompted some policymakers and scholars to question whether American Empire should be the new paradigm for American foreign policy.[46] Perhaps moved by such an idea, on his way to Iraq during the second Gulf

War, Bush stopped in the Philippines, where he addressed the Philippine Congress: "Some say the culture of the Middle East will not sustain the institutions of democracy." He affirmed: "The same doubts were once expressed about the culture of Asia. Those doubts were proven wrong nearly six decades ago."[47] As such examples demonstrate, America's efforts to spread its values to the Muslim world have remained integral to American foreign policy aims in the twenty-first century.

Similarly, simplistic understandings of Islam and Muslims have continued to drive the actions of American policymakers and military officers during engagements in the Middle East. As several journalists have noted during and after the 2003 war in Iraq, military rulers and policymakers at the highest levels relied on the book *The Arab Mind*, a widely discredited study by Raphael Patai, originally published in 1973. The book purported to explain the shared (and identical) "mentality" of Arabs living in the diverse areas of the Middle East and North Africa, noting that people in the West did not realize how much Arabs hated them.[48] Furthermore, as one journalist noted, Patai's book helped convince conservative policymakers in Washington "that Arabs only understand force."[49] The book became "required reading" for many soldiers and officers on their way to Iraq.[50] As the *New York Times* reported in 2003, such beliefs were publicly expressed by American military officers: "'You have to understand the Arab mind,' Captain Todd Brown, a company commander with the Fourth Infantry Division, said as he stood outside the gates of Abu Hishma. 'The only thing they understand is force—force, pride and saving face.'"[51] Not limited to Arab Muslims, American policies during the Global War on Terror extended to the surveillance of Filipino Muslims in its previous imperial territories, the so-called Operation Enduring Freedom-Philippines. Accompanied by U.S. funding and military training of Filipino soldiers, the operation conveniently also supported the attempts by the Philippines government to repress both Moro political demands and Moro insurgencies.[52]

The repercussions of such dehumanizing beliefs about Muslims on American policies both at home and abroad appear obvious, particularly after the release in December 2014 of the Senate Intelligence Committee's report on the use of torture by American CIA agents between 2001 and 2006. Similarly, the dramatic rise in hate crimes against American Muslims in the years following 9/11 has demonstrated that American Islamophobia has not limited itself to foreign shores alone.[53] Such examples reveal a continued and unfortunate practice of simplifying the identities of peoples around the world—and in the United States—who happen to be Muslim, at times with brutal consequences. As these most recent examples demonstrate, American "sacred interests" in the Muslim world remain a powerful force in shaping domestic and foreign policies that impact the lives of Muslims both in the United States and abroad. As this book has demonstrated, far from a recent phenomenon, such attitudes have a long history in American foreign relations. Hopefully, by analyzing this history, fraught with unfortunate consequences, future U.S. policymakers will not repeat the same mistakes.

Notes

INTRODUCTION

1. "Protestantism in Turkey," *Missionary Herald* 68 (February 1872): 46–47.

2. Ibid., 47.

3. For a historical account of these tensions, see Makdisi, *Artillery of Heaven* and Erhan, "Ottoman Official Attitudes towards American Missionaries."

4. Anderson, *History of the Missions of the American Board of Commissioners for Foreign Missions to the Oriental Churches*, 1. "Mohammedan" was the most common term used to describe Muslims in the nineteenth century and up to the mid-twentieth century. It was, and remains, a term that is offensive to Muslims, since it conflicted with one of the most central tenets of Islam by implying that the Prophet Muhammad (like Jesus Christ) was the source of veneration as a divine figure. In this book, I maintain the use of the term, including its alternate spellings Musselman, Mohametan, and others in contemporary sources. Despite its offensive nature, the term exemplifies the degree to which Americans misunderstood the Islamic faith.

5. Strong, "A Door into the Mohammedan World," Yale University Library Archives, n.d. (pamphlet certainly published during Charles Brent's fund-raising visit to the United States in 1914).

6. Jessup, *The Mohammedan Missionary Problem*.

7. Throughout *Sacred Interests*, I use the term "Islamic" to describe geographic areas ruled by peoples of the Muslim faith and/or where Islam was often declared as the official "state" religion. I am cognizant of the limitations posed by this term, which elides the plurality of religious groups and the central contributions of non-Muslims in shaping and defining these societies. The term "Islamicate" was first coined by the scholar of Islam, Marshall Hodgson, to address these limitations and to describe practices and beliefs that emerged from areas where Muslims were culturally dominant but not necessarily linked to the Islamic religion. He differentiated this term from the term "Islamic," which he used to describe purely religious beliefs. Unfortunately, his term has not gained wide usage. Thus, to avoid confusion, I use the term "Islamic" throughout the book. See Hodgson, *The Venture of Islam*, 57–60.

8. Ellis, "Annex A: The Covenant," in *The Origin, Structure and Working of the League of Nations*, 493.

9. For the analysis of the impact of "hierarchies of race" on American foreign relations more broadly, see Hunt, *Ideology and U.S. Foreign Policy*, chapter 3.

10. Alexander and Smith, "The Discourse of American Civil Society," 161–66.

11. See, for example, Kalmar and Penslar, *Orientalism and the Jews*; Talbot, "'Turkey Is in Our Midst': Orientalism and Contagion in Nineteenth Century Anti-Mormonism"; Givens, *The Viper on the Hearth*, 130–31.

12. For the European angle, see Leff, *Sacred Bonds of Solidarity*, 2.

13. For a larger discussion of how Arab immigrants used and challenged American Orientalist tropes, see Berman, *American Arabesque*, 179–210; Gualtieri, *Between Arab and White*; and Tehranian, *Whitewashed*, 53–54.

14. Kalmar and Penslar, "Orientalism and the Jews: An Introduction," xix.

15. For recent literature on the history of humanitarian intervention, see Simms and Trim, *Humanitarian Intervention*. For its application to the Ottoman Empire, see Rodogno, *Against Massacre*. For lack of a better term, I use the term minorities—but I recognize that the term is problematic when describing the various religious communities in the Ottoman Empire. For a scholarly discussion of this usage, see Nancy Reynolds's interview of Aron Rodrigue in "Difference and Tolerance in the Ottoman Empire."

16. Cited in Cummins, *The Voyage of Columbus*, 81.

17. Williams, *The American Indian in Western Legal Thought*, 13–15.

18. Ibid., 14.

19. Ibid., 75.

20. Ibid., 162.

21. Cited in Read, *Temperate Conquests*, 114.

22. Hindley, "Soldier of Fortune," 12–16.

23. Cited in Marr, *The Cultural Roots of American Islamicism*, 2–3.

24. Ibid.

25. Ibid.

26. Kidd, *American Christians and Islam*, 8, 11.

27. Ibid., 6–8.

28. See Cogley, "The Fall of the Ottoman Empire and the Restoration of Israel in the 'Judeo-centric' Strand of Puritan Millenarianism."

29. For a historical analysis of this interpretation, see Kidd, *American Christians and Islam*, 27–36.

30. For an excellent overview of this influence, see Spellberg, *Thomas Jefferson's Qur'an*, 13–40.

31. See Cirakman, "From the 'Terror of the World' to the 'Sick Man of Europe,'" 109, 125; and Lutz, "The Relative Influence of European Writers on Late Eighteenth Century American Political Thought," 190–92.

32. Montesquieu (baron de), *The Spirit of Laws*, 408.

33. As one literary critic has noted, "His Persians are thus unquestionably more French than Persian, and the society imaged in their letters is ridden with clichés obviously derived from Galland's translation of *The Thousand and One Nights* and Chardin's *Voyage en Perse*." Healy, "Introduction," *The Persian Letters*, xi.

34. Spellberg, *Jefferson's Qur'an*, 28–33.

35. Allison, *Crescent Obscured*, 40.

36. Cited in Leland, "Extracts from Number Two: A Little Sermon, Sixteen Minutes Long," in *The Writings of the Late Elder John Leland*, 410. Leland was an adamant defender of religious liberties in the United States, including for Muslims. See Spellberg, *Jefferson's Qur'an*, 240–63.

37. Battistini, "Glimpses of the Other before Orientalism," 447.

38. Ibid.

39. For a study of this influence, see Sha'ban, *Islam and Arabs in Early American Thought*; and Marr, *The Cultural Roots of American Islamicism*.

40. Mazower, *The Balkans*, xxxiv.

41. Spellberg, *Jefferson's Qur'an*, 10–11.

42. Ibid., 8–9.

43. Friedman, "Christian Captives at 'Hard Labor' in Algiers," 616–32.

44. Mather, *Decennium Luctuosum*, 231–32. Mather was well acquainted with Islam and wrote about it regularly. See Isani, "Cotton Mather and the Orient," 46–58.

45. These narratives paralleled those written by British colonists captured by Native Americans at the same period. See Matar, *Turks, Moors and Englishmen in the Age of Discovery*, 83–107.

46. See Diouf, *Servants of Allah*; and Gomez, "Muslims in Early America," 671–710.

47. Marr, *The Cultural Roots of American Islamicism*, 110.

48. Cited in Baepler, *White Slaves, African Masters*, 95.

49. Marr, *The Cultural Roots of American Islamicism*, 21.

50. Battistini, "Glimpses of the Other before Orientalism," 460, 461.

51. Ibid. There were, however, some exceptions to this in the popular literature. See Kidd, *American Christians and Islam*, 25–26.

52. Hatch, *The Democratization of American Christianity*, 14.

53. Blight and Geyer, "Where in the World Is America?" 66.

54. Anghie, *Imperialism, Sovereignty and the Making of International Law*, chapter 2; Kayaoglu, *Legal Imperialism*, 106–14; Armitage, "The Declaration of Independence and International Law," 39–64.

55. Pitts, "Empire and Legal Universalism in the Eighteenth Century," 92–121.

56. Emphasis in original. Martens, *Summary of the Law of Nations*, 5; Pitts, "Empire and Legal Universalism in the Eighteenth Century," 103.

57. Wheaton and Lawrence, *Elements of International Law*, 91. Emphasis mine.

58. Ibid., 93.

59. This belief was not limited to the Ottoman Empire and later formed a key justification for European imperial expansion. See Anghie, *Imperialism, Sovereignty and the Making of International Law*, chapter 2.

60. Cushing, "Opinion of the Attorney General Concerning the Judicial Powers of the Commissioner or Minister and of Consuls of the United States in Turkey and China," 96. Emphasis in original.

61. Ibid. Emphasis mine.

62. Ibid.

63. Rodinson, *Europe and the Mystique of Islam*, 60.

64. Lockman, *Contending Visions of the Middle East*, 89.

65. Morrison, "Metropole, Colony, and Imperial Citizenship in the Russian Empire," 332.

66. Ibid.

67. See McLaughlin, "Black Women, Identity, and the Quest for Humanhood and Wholeness," 167–74. See also discussion between Paul Gilroy and bell hooks in Gilroy, *Small Acts*, 217–23.

68. Blum, *Reforging the White Republic*, 212.

69. See Bellamy, *Massacres and Morality*, chapter 2.

70. Arendt, *The Origins of Totalitarianism*, 273.

71. For the American context, see Steinberg, *The Academic Melting Pot: Catholics and Jews in American Higher Education*, 8–9.

72. Kalmar and Penslar, *Orientalism and the Jews*, xxxii.

73. Naimark, *Fires of Hatred*, 8.

74. Said, *Orientalism*, 1.

75. Ibid., 3.

76. For an overview of critiques and reactions to Said's work, see Burke and Prochaska, *Genealogies of Orientalism*. For the application of Orientalist theories to the United States and to areas outside of the Middle East, see Schueller, *U.S. Orientalisms*; Leong, *The China Mystique*; Iwamura, *Virtual Orientalism*; Klein, *Cold War Orientalism*; and Sha'ban, *Islam and Arabs in Early American Thought*. For ways in which scholars have reframed Orientalism as a dialogue, see Celik, "Speaking Back to Orientalist Discourse," 19–42. For the contribution of local actors to Orientalist thought, see Makdisi, "Ottoman Orientalism."

77. Preston, *Sword of the Spirit, Shield of Faith*, 6.

78. Examples include the following excellent studies: McAlister, *Epic Encounters*; Little, *American Orientalism*; Gerges, *America and Political Islam*.

79. Preston, *Sword of the Spirit, Shield of Faith*, 5. See also Hunt, *Ideology and U.S. Foreign Policy*, 8.

80. For more on this topic, see Manela, "America and the World"; and Glickman, "The 'Cultural Turn,'" 201–41.

81. Hunt, *Ideology and U.S. Foreign Policy*, xi.

82. For an excellent analysis of this trend, see Sen, *Identity and Violence*; and Mamdani, *Good Muslim, Bad Muslim*.

83. Preston, "Bridging the Gap," 788.

84. Kaplan, "'Left Alone with America,'" 17.

85. See, for example, Kramer, "Empires, Exceptions, and Anglo-Saxons," 1315–53; and Schumacher "The American Way of Empire," 35–50.

86. Rotter, "Saidism without Said," 1215.

87. Kramer, "Power and Connection," 1350.

88. See, for example, Bender, *A Nation among Nations*; Iriye, *Cultural Internationalism and World Order*; Iriye, *Global Community*.

89. See, for example, Makdisi, *Artillery of Heaven*; Sharkey, *American Evangelicals in Egypt*; Dogan and Sharkey, eds., *American Missionaries and the Middle East*; Tejirian and Simon, *Conflict, Conquest and Conversion*; Murre-van den Berg, ed., *New Faith in Ancient Lands*.

90. See, for example, Yoshihara, *Embracing the East*.

CHAPTER 1

1. "The Greek Fever," *Salem Gazette*, 20 January 1824.

2. Everett, "The Ethics of Aristotle to Nicomachus," *North American Review* 17 (October 1823): 420, 423.

3. Julius Bing to John Andrew, Washington, 14 August 1867, Andrews Papers.

4. A long debate exists on this topic. For a broad synthesis, see Bailyn, *The Ideological Origins of the American Revolution*; and Lutz, "The Relative Influence of European Writers on Late Eighteenth-Century American Political Thought," 189–97; and Richard, *The Founders and the Classics*.

5. Mayers, *Dissenting Voices in America's Rise to Power*, 59.

6. Ibid.

7. Zelinsky, "Classical Town Names in the United States," 472. See also Kennedy, *Greek Revival America*; Reinhold, *Classica Americana*; Dyson, *Ancient Marbles to American Shores*, 20.

8. Kennedy, *Greek Revival America*, 194–95.

9. Although St. Clair described these attitude vis-à-vis European philhellenes, his overall argument also maintained that the United States was "a cultural colony of the movement in Britain," which allows us to extend his depictions to the American philhellenic movement. See St. Clair, *That Greece Might Still Be Free*, 19, 298.

10. Wheaton and Lawrence, *Elements of International Law*, 91.

11. Ibid., 93.

12. For newspaper coverage of the Philadelphia Greek Committee meeting assigning Wheaton to this influential position, see "Philadelphia, 4 Dec. 1823," *American Mercury*, 17 December 1823.

13. Cited in Mayers, *Dissenting Voices*, 84.

14. On the creation of a more cohesive white identity in the first half of the nineteenth century, see Roediger, *Wages of Whiteness*, 39–64.

15. Leoussi, "Nationalism and Racial Hellenism in Nineteenth Century England and France," 42–68.

16. Tanner, "Introduction to the New Edition Race and Representation in Ancient Art," 7. Although Tanner describes "racial hellenism" as an American phenomenon, Leoussi's article limits this phenomenon to England and France.

17. As Eric Foner's groundbreaking study has shown, the language of slavery was later used for domestic purposes as well. See Foner, *Free Soil, Free Labor, Free Men*.

18. For the American side, see Nelson, *The Greek Tradition in Republican Thought*.

19. Sexton, *The Monroe Doctrine*, 11.

20. For the ties between the Second Great Awakening and American philhellenism, see Repousis, "'The Cause of the Greeks,'" 345–46.

21. Curti, *American Philanthropy Abroad*, 21, 24.

22. Cline, "American Attitude toward the Greek War of Independence, 1821–1828," 19.

23. Earle, "American Interest in the Greek Cause, 1821–1827," 62. For a more detailed historical account of the Greek massacres, see Rodogno, *Against Massacre*, 65–66.

24. Rodogno, *Against Massacre*, 65.

25. St. Clair, *That Greece Might Still Be Free*, 23.

26. Ibid., 19.

27. See, for example, the *Baltimore Patriot and Mercantile Advisor*, the *City Gazette and Daily Advertiser* (Charleston, S.C.), the *Niles' Register*, the *New Hampshire Sentinel*, the *Vermont Gazette*, the *Pennsylvania Washington Reporter*, and the *St. Louis Enquirer*.

28. "Address to the Greeks," *Niles' Register*, 26 May 1821, 207.

29. Ibid.

30. Dakin, *The Greek Struggle for Independence*, 54–55; and St. Clair, *That Greece Might Still Be Free*, 3.

31. Carabott, "State, Society and the Religious Other," 9–10.

32. Dakin, *British and American Philhellenes during the Greek War for Independence*, 22. Metternich had no doubt of Ypsilanti's revolutionary guilt. After Ypsilanti escaped Moldovia, he was imprisoned in Austria for the next six years and died shortly after his release.

33. "The Greeks and the Turks," *American Mercury*, 31 July 1821. Emphasis in original.

34. Ibid. Emphasis in original.

35. Ibid.

36. Everett, *Mount Vernon Papers*, 266.

37. Pappas, *The United States and the Greek War for Independence*, 34.

38. Everett (published anonymously), "On the Literature and Language of Modern Greece," *General Repository and Review*, 80–95. Everett had studied under Daniel Webster's brother, Ezekiel. Everett met Webster when he came to teach for a few months at the school, and the two forged a close relationship, one that would become important when Webster and Everett later worked together to pressure the United States government to act on behalf of Greek revolutionaries. See the biographical article written on Everett in 1833, "Hon. Edward Everett," *New England Magazine* 5 September 1833.

39. Everett, "On the Literature and Language of Modern Greece," *General Repository and Review*, 82, 86–87.

40. See Dyson, *Ancient Marbles to American Shores*, 20.

41. Hatzidimitriou, *Founded on Freedom and Virtue*, xxviii.

42. Everett, *Mount Vernon Papers*, 262–67.

43. "Trip through Greece," Everett Papers.

44. Everett, *Mount Vernon Papers*, 266.

45. Originally published in the *Boston Daily Advertiser*, 15 October 1821, 2. In a later translation, which Everett republished in the *North American Review* a few years later, he made religion even more explicit, replacing "gospel" with "Christian": "just because free, *generous and liberal because Christian*." See Everett, "The Ethics of Aristotle to Nicomachus," 415–16.

46. *Boston Daily Advertiser*, 2.

47. *American Repertory*, 10 October 1822. The newspaper republished the editorial from the *National Gazette*, 22 September 1822.

48. Ibid.

49. "Rights of Things—Greece," *Niles' Register* 23, 28 September 1822, 50–51.

50. *Albany Argus*, 26 November 1822. Cited in Cline, "American Attitude," 23.

51. Ibid.

52. Curti, *American Philanthropy Abroad*, 23.

53. Pappas, "Lafayette's Efforts to Send American Aid to Revolutionary Greece," 107.

54. U.S. Congress, *Annals of Congress of the United States*, 17th Cong., 2nd sess., 24 December 1822, 458.

55. Ibid., 460.

56. For the full letter, see "Miscellany: A Letter to the Earl of Liverpool, on the Subject of the Greeks by Thomas Lord Erskine," *Massachusetts Spy*, 6 November 1822.

57. Although the language of humanitarian intervention existed before the Greek War of Independence, American and European actions in Greece would prove a powerful precedent for advocates of humanitarian intervention in future conflicts. For a wider history of humanitarian intervention, see Simms, *Humanitarian Intervention*.

58. For an excellent discussion of how the Greek Question influenced American foreign policy, see May, *The Making of the Monroe Doctrine*, 9–11, 63–64, 185.

59. Schurz, *Life of Henry Clay*, 210. Cited in Mayers, *Dissenting Voices in America's Rise to Power*, 61.

60. Monroe, *1822 State of the Union Address*, 22 December 1822.

61. "Andreas Luriottis, Envoy of the Provisional Government of Greece, to the Honorable John Quincy Adams, Secretary of State to the United States of America," 24 February 1823, in *Message from the President of the United States Transmitting a Report of the Secretary of State, upon the Subject of the Present Condition and Future Prospects of the Greeks*, 15.

62. Ibid.

63. Adams, *Memoirs of John Quincy Adams*, 172–73.

64. Coit, *John C. Calhoun*, 126–27.

65. Adams, *Memoirs of John Quincy Adams*, 173.

66. Ibid.

67. "Mr. Adams to Mr. Luriottis," 18 August 1823, in *Message from the President*, 17. See also Pappas, "Lafayette and Revolutionary Greece," 107. The three men's conflicting views stemmed from more than just disagreements over the future path of American foreign policy. They were also expecting to be competing presidential candidates in the next election. Adams believed that Crawford and Calhoun were taking this stance only to benefit their future candidacies. See May's analysis of this political gesturing in *The Making of the Monroe Doctrine*, 9–11, 63–64, 185.

68. Everett, "The Ethics of Aristotle to Nicomachus," 413–16.

69. Ibid., 420.

70. Ibid.

71. "The Greeks," *Zion's Herald*, 1 January 1824. Article republished from the *Providence Gazette*.

72. Pappas, *United States and the Greek War*, 61.

73. Parsons, *John Quincy Adams*, 152.

74. Ibid.

75. Monroe, *1823 State of the Union Address*, 2 December 1823; Pappas, "Lafayette and Revolutionary Greece," 109.

76. Monroe, Seventh Annual Message to Congress, 2 December 1823.

77. Coffman, *American Umpire*, 153.

78. Seward, *Life and Public Services of John Quincy Adams*, 132–33.

79. Field, *America and the Mediterranean World, 1776–1882*, 125.

80. Webster, "The Revolution in Greece," 62–64.

81. U.S. House, *Journal of the House of Representatives of the United States, Being the First Session of the Eighteenth Congress begun and Held at the City of Washington*, 97, 115, 156.

82. "Memorial of a Committee Appointed at a Public Meeting of the Citizens of New York to Take into Consideration the Situation of the Greeks," 18th Cong., 1st sess., 3.

83. Ibid.

84. Ibid., 4.

85. Ibid., 3–4.

86. "Mr. Webster's Speech, On His Resolution in Favor of the Greeks," *New Hampshire Observer*, 2 February 1824.

87. Webster, "The Revolution in Greece," 68.

88. Ibid., 69.

89. Ibid., 76. Some who opposed the resolution, such as John Randolph of Virginia, accused supporters of using the issue to attack slavery in the United States. See Pappas, *The United States and the Greek War for Independence*, 71.

90. Varg, *Edward Everett*, 33.

91. "Greek Slaves," *Essex Register*, 27 April 1826.

92. *Commercial Advertiser*, 26 May 1826.

93. "Speech of the Hon. Edward Everett, in the House of Representative of the United States, March 9, 1826," 15–16.

94. In addition to sending money, Americans also donated guns and swords. For newspaper articles covering the amount of money raised by Americans in support of the Greek cause, see "Greek Fund," *Newport Mercury*, 8 May 1824; and "The Greeks," *Salem Gazette*, 11 May 1824. For the speeches presented during Greek committee meetings appealing to the American public, see Winthrop and Everett, *Address of the Committee Appointed at a Public Meeting Held in Boston, December 19, 1823, for the Relief of the Greeks, to Their Fellow Citizens*; and the New York Committee, *Address of the Committee of the Greek Fund, of the City of New York, to Their Fellow-Citizens Throughout the United States*.

95. "The Greeks," *Christian Repository*, 13 February 1824, 97.

96. Ibid.

97. Dwight, "Address on the Greek Revolution," 370.

98. Ibid., 375.

99. Ibid., 376.

100. Ibid., 377.

101. Ibid.

102. Ibid., 382. Emphasis in original.

103. Trent, *The Manliest Man*, 10.

104. Rodogno, *Against Massacre*, 124.

105. Howe, *An Historical Sketch of the Greek Revolution*, 24. See also Roessel, *In Byron's Shadow*, 285 fn. 3.

106. "The Experiment," *American Ladies' Magazine* 7, no. 10 (October 1834): 460.

107. "Russia," *American Annual Register for the Years 1827-8-9*, 269. Proof that Adams was the author of this essay can be found in Adams, *Memoirs of John Quincy Adams*, 207. For correspondence between John Quincy Adams and Joseph Blunt, the editor of the *American Annual Register*, see Adams Family Papers MSS, 9 January 1830, box 1, folder: "Correspondence, 1830." Adams asked Blunt to send him a copy of the Koran at one point to help him write his article. See "Adams to Blunt, 9 January 1830" in the same folder.

108. "Russia," 269.

109. Ibid.

110. Ibid., 277.

111. Ibid., 278.

112. Ibid., 273.

113. Ibid., 425.

114. The best account of American philhellenism and American missionary work can be found in Repousis, *Greek-American Foreign Relations from Monroe to Truman*, 86–117.

115. Cited in Haines, *Jonas King*, 249.

116. Ibid., 154. See also Frazee, *The Orthodox Church and Independent Greece*, 184.

117. "Report of the Prudential Committee," 295. Originally cited in Repousis, *Greek-American Foreign Relations from Monroe to Truman*, 165.

118. The background to this story is well-documented by Repousis, *Greek-American Foreign Relations from Monroe to Truman*, 164–70.

119. American commercial relationships with Russia during this time also complicated the U.S. position vis-à-vis both Britain and the Ottoman Empire. For a detailed study of American interests in the Crimean War, see Dowty, *The Limits of American Isolation*.

120. "Chronicles of the East," *New York Observer and Chronicle*, 18 September 1856.

121. Wheaton and Lawrence, *Elements of International Law*.

122. Makdisi, *The Culture of Sectarianism*, 118.

123. Identical reports are present in the articles and journal excerpts from Johnson's own memoirs. See Johnson, *The Life of a Citizen at Home and in Foreign Service*, 109.

124. Ibid.

125. "General Intelligence. Massacre of Christians in Syria," *Boston Recorder*, 19 July 1860. Republished from the *Boston Traveller*, 2 July 1860.

126. Numerous articles appeared throughout the American press, often quoting letters from American missionaries in Syria. See, for example, "Massacre of Christians at Sidon," *Independent*, 12 July 1860, 2–3; "The Syrian Massacre," *New York Observer and Chronicle*, 19 July 1860; "The Civil War in Syria," *New York Times*, 21 July 1860;

"Letter from Mr. Jessup, June 1–6, 1860," *Missionary Herald* 56 (August 1860): 241–44.

127. "French Occupation of Syria," *New York Observer and Herald*, 27 September 1860.

128. "The Slaughter of Christians by the Druses," *Providence Evening Press*, 4 August 1860.

129. Ibid.

130. Ibid.

131. Bliss, "A Letter from Mount Lebanon," *New York Observer and Chronicle*, 20 December 1860.

132. Rodogno, *Against Massacre*, 119.

133. Ibid.

134. An excellent analysis of how domestic issues shaped American interpretations of the Cretan Insurrection can be found in Prior, "Crete the Opening Wedge."

135. Ibid., 863.

136. Cumbler, *From Abolition to Rights for All*, 143.

137. Prior, "Crete the Opening Wedge," 861–87.

138. "Canting Sympathies," *Constitution*, 31 July 1868, 2. Cited in Prior, "Crete the Opening Wedge," 875.

139. "Foreign versus Home Philanthropy," *Constitution*, 19 June 1868, ibid., 876.

140. The full document can be found in Stillman, *Articles and Despatches from Crete*, appendix B, 128.

141. Ibid., 187.

142. Ibid., 35.

143. Ibid., 36.

144. "Mr. Morris to Mr. Seward, 28 August 1866," in Johnson, *Message from the President of the United States, in Answer to a Resolution of the House of the 17th ultimo, Relative to the Revolution in Candia*, 8.

145. Stillman, *Articles and Despatches from Crete*, 34.

146. Ibid.

147. "Mr. Seward to Mr. Morris, 25 September 1866," in Johnson, *Message from the President of the United States, in Answer to a Resolution of the House of the 17th ultimo, Relative to the Revolution in Candia*, 9.

148. "Morris to Seward," 15 November 1866, *Turkey Despatches*, XIX. Cited in Kerner, "Turko-American Diplomatic Relations," 189.

149. "Mr. Morris to Mr. Seward," 28 August 1866, ibid., 188.

150. "Mr. Stillman to Mr. Seward," 19 November 1866, ibid., 14.

151. Thomas Bryson, *Tars, Turks and Tankers*, 28–29.

152. W. J. S., "War in Candia," *Nation* 4 (October 1866): 275–77.

153. "To the American Press," *Cretan* 1 (April 1868): 1.

154. "Cretan Relief," *Boston Journal*, 15 January 1867.

155. Ibid.

156. Ibid.

157. Ibid.

158. Sanger, *The Statutes at Large, Treaties, and Proclamations of the United States of America from December 1867, to March 1869*, 31.

159. Ibid., 263.

160. Davison, "Ottoman Public Relations in the Nineteenth Century," in *Histoire Économique et Social de l'Empire Ottoman de la Turquie (1326–1960)*, ed. D. Panzac, 594.

161. "Washington: Affairs at the National Capital," *New York Times*, 22 August 1867.

162. "Washington: Affairs at the National Capital," *New York Times*, 24 August 1867.

163. Elliot to Stanley, 19 May 1868, and 21 May 1868, London Public Records Office, cited in May, "Crete and the United States, 1866–1869," 286.

164. Ibid., 287.

165. Despatch No. 21, "Stillman to Seward," 14 May 1866, in Stillman, *Articles and Despatches from Crete*, 30–31.

166. "Crete and Spain," *Cretan* 1 (December 1868): 2.

167. Stillman, "The Farce in the Levant," *Nation* 8 (21 January 1869): 48.

168. "Recognition of Crete," *Congressional Globe*, Session 40-3, 7 January 1869, 244–45.

169. Ibid.

170. Kidd, *American Christians and Islam*, 26.

171. "Recognition of Crete," *Congressional Globe*, Session 40-3, 7 January 1869, 244.

172. Ibid.

173. Ibid., 247.

174. "Julius Bing to John Andrew," Washington, 14 August 1867, Andrews Papers.

175. Rodogno, *Against Massacre*, 137.

176. "The Close of Act First," *Cretan* 1 (June 1869): 1.

177. Ibid.

178. Ibid.

179. Lincoln's 16 June 1858 speech "A House Divided" can be found in Lincoln, *The Language of Liberty*, 223–31.

CHAPTER 2

1. Reed, "American Foreign Policy, the Politics of Missions and Josiah Strong, 1890–1900," 232.

2. At times, Americans assigned to the Ottoman Empire as ministers and consuls came from within the organization, as when James B. Angell, president of the ABCFM in 1893 and 1894, was appointed to serve as minister to Turkey. Angell had also served previously as American minister to China in 1880 and 1881, another area of important American missionary work.

3. Makdisi, "Reclaiming the Land of the Bible," 683–84.

4. A millet, stemming from the Arabic "millah" is a confessional community that, under Ottoman rule, allowed religious groups to have their own courts and legal

system for personal law. This gave various non-Muslim communities the right to limited self-governance under Ottoman rule.

5. "American Board of Commissioners for Foreign Missions, Thirty-Seventh Annual Meeting," 332.

6. Ibid., 343.

7. See "Miscellanies: Important Concessions by the Sultan," *Missionary Herald* 52 (June 1856): 181.

8. Temple, *Life and Letters of Rev. Daniel Temple*, 246.

9. Washburn, *Fifty Years in Constantinople*, 2.

10. Field, *America and the Mediterranean World, 1776–1882*, 354.

11. The ABCFM's decision not to participate in the college and instead concentrate on more formal means of spreading the gospel stemmed from the influential views of ABCFM foreign secretary Rufus Anderson, who maintained that American missionaries should distance themselves from efforts to instill "Christian civilization," which necessitated several generations of work and succeeded best in the vernacular. Many American missionaries strongly disagreed with Anderson's vision, prompting some to leave the organization and join American Protestant colleges opening throughout the Ottoman Empire.

12. See Washburn, *Fifty Years in Constantinople*, 10; and Hamlin, *My Life and Times*, 431–32.

13. According to Hamlin, British minister Sir Henry had received a bribe from the khedive of Egypt "to settle a quarrel he had with the sultan. The grand vizier agreed to settle the quarrel if Sir Henry would abandon three questions—the Bulgarian, the Servian, and the American College." Hamlin, *My Life and Times*, 439.

14. "Seward to Blacque Bey," 1 July 1868. Cited in Kerner, "Turko-American Diplomatic Relations, 1860–1880," 176.

15. For an account of this story, see "Debt of Bulgaria to Robert College," *New York Times*, 13 October 1918. On Farragut's mission, see Bryson, *Tars, Turks and Tankers*, 29.

16. This account was widely publicized in several newspapers in 1896 as Clara Barton, president of the Red Cross, was about to embark on a trip to address the Armenian massacres. See "Brave Clara Barton's Task." *Los Angeles Herald*, 23 February 1896.

17. For accounts of this, see Hamlin, *My Life and Times*, 445–50; and Washburn, *Fifty Years in Constantinople*, 12–13.

18. Washburn, *Fifty Years in Constantinople*, 40, 49. Emphasis mine.

19. Ibid., 298–99.

20. Washburn, "American Influence in Bulgaria," *Amherst Graduates' Quarterly* 2 (1913): 206.

21. Ibid.

22. Cited in Neuberger, *The Orient Within*, 25.

23. Ibid.

24. Ibid.

25. Bulgarian nationalist fervor would later impose harsh consequences on these populations, many of whom were deemed unfit as Bulgarian citizens and forced to leave after Bulgaria gained its independence.

26. For the larger manifestation of this tendency, see Todorova, *Imagining the Balkans.*

27. Washburn, *Fifty Years in Constantinople*, 65.

28. Roudometof, *Nationalism, Globalization, and Orthodoxy*, 139.

29. Ibid., 139.

30. See Crampton, *A Short History of Modern Bulgaria*, 18.

31. Ibid., 19.

32. Jelavich, *History of the Balkans*, 348.

33. See Holquist, "To Count, to Extract, and to Exterminate," 117–18.

34. Ibid., 118.

35. Jelavich, *History of the Balkans*, 348.

36. Washburn, *Fifty Years in Constantinople*, 90.

37. Ibid., 102.

38. Todorova, *Imagining the Balkans*, 99.

39. Clarke, *The Pen and the Sword*, 395.

40. Washburn, *Fifty Years in Constantinople*, 103–4. Bulgarians also conveyed the information to Russian newspapers. See Walker, *Januarius MacGahan*, 168.

41. Sympathy for the Bulgarian plight colored Washburn and Long's accounts. Although many historians identify the massacres as claiming between 3,000 and 15,000 lives, Washburn wrote in his recollections that "fifty or sixty thousand men, women and children were massacred in cold blood, sold as slaves or judiciously murdered." See Washburn, *Fifty Years in Constantinople*, 103–4.

42. Elliot was also supplied information from the Turkish authorities, who assured him that nothing serious had taken place. See Shannon, *Gladstone and the Bulgarian Agitation, 1876*, 39.

43. For the British reaction, see Harris, *Britain and the Bulgarian Horrors of 1876.*

44. Washburn, *Fifty Years in Constantinople*, 108. In his study of Turkey, Pears wrote that the Bulgarian massacres were caused by Muslim jealousy of Christian prosperity. Linking Christianity with industrial, commercial, intellectual, and moral advancement, he wrote, "For, in spite of centuries of oppression and blunder, Christian industry and Christian morality everywhere makes for national wealth and intelligence." See Pears, *Turkey and Its People*, 214.

45. Cited in Harris, *Britain and the Bulgarian Horrors of 1876*, 53.

46. *London Times*, 15 July 1876. Cited in Harris, ibid., 55.

47. *London Daily News*, 19 July 1876. Cited in Harris, ibid., 154.

48. Walker, *Januarius MacGahan*, 170.

49. Millman, "The Bulgarian Massacres Reconsidered," 228.

50. Cited in Walker, *Januarius MacGahan*, 225.

51. Saab, *Reluctant Icon*, 84.

52. Pundeff, *Bulgaria in American Perspective*, 245.

53. Clarke, *The Pen and the Sword*, 396.

54. Hansard, *Parliamentary Debates*, 1495.

55. Saab, *Reluctant Icon*, 85.

56. Washburn, *Fifty Years in Constantinople*, 108.

57. Ibid., 109.

58. Washburn, "American Influence in Bulgaria," 206. For Maynard's sympathies, see Herlihy, "Eugene Schuyler and the Bulgarian Constitution," 168. See also Field, *From the Lakes of Killarney to the Golden Horn*, 318–19.

59. Cited in Pundeff, *Bulgaria in American Perspective*, 219.

60. Schaeffer, *Eugene Schuyler Selected Essays*, 64.

61. Gillard, Doc. 456, "Mr. Baring to Sir H. Elliot, Sept. 5, 1876," in *British Documents on Foreign Affairs*, 2:374.

62. Cited in Walker, *Januarius MacGahan*, 179.

63. Ibid., 176.

64. MacGahan, *The Turkish Atrocities in Bulgaria*, 156.

65. Harris, *Britain and the Bulgarian Horrors*, 234.

66. For a detailed description of British reactions to the massacres, including Mac-Gahan's role, see Marsh, "Lord Salisbury and the Ottoman Massacres." See also Hollander, "Januarius MacGahan and the British Reaction to the Bulgarian Massacres of 1876."

67. Gladstone, *Bulgarian Horrors and the Question of the East*, 10.

68. Ibid.

69. Gladstone, *The Sclavonic Provinces of the Ottoman Empire*, 10.

70. Cited in Jenkins, *Gladstone*, 399–403.

71. Harris, *Britain and the Bulgarian Horrors of 1876*, 253.

72. For the republication of MacGahan's accounts in the *London Daily News*, see "Atrocities in the East: Turkish Murders in Bulgaria," *New York Times*, 3 September 1876, and another article published one week later in the same newspaper, "Turkish Atrocities," *New York Times*, 10 September 1876.

73. "The Eastern War," *New York Times*, 27 October 1876.

74. All information in this paragraph taken from Bryson, *Tars, Turks and Tankers*, 30–31.

75. Shasko, "From the Other Shore," 4.

76. "The Sick Man," *New York Tribune*, 15 May 1876. Cited in Shashko, "From the Other Shore," 4.

77. "Europe Aroused against Turkey," *New York Tribune*, 6 September 1876. Ibid.

78. "Letter by 'An American,'" *New York Tribune*, 9 September 1876. Ibid., 9.

79. Buck, "The Bulgarian Massacres," *New York Tribune*, 16 September 1876. Ibid.

80. Rodogno, *Against Massacre*, 159.

81. "The European War," *Chicago Tribune*, 29 June 1876.

82. "Bulgaria and the Oriental Question," *Christian Advocate*, 22 June 1876.

83. Ibid.

84. Salter, "The Solution to the Eastern Question," *Missionary Herald* 72 (December 1876): 392–93.

85. Ibid.

86. "The Cross and the Crescent," *Messenger* 45 (6 December 1876): 4.

87. Ibid.

88. Van-Lessep, "Turkish Barbarity," *New York Evangelist*, 28 September 1876.

89. Field, *America and the Mediterranean World, 1776–1882*, 368.

90. Jensen, "Eugene Schuyler and the Balkan Crisis," 33. In an interesting turn of events, although Schuyler worked well with Washburn and Long at Robert College, he criticized ABCFM missionaries in Bulgaria for mixing relief with proselytism.

91. Roudometof, *Nationalism, Globalization and Orthodoxy*, 138–39. See also Strakhovsky, "General Count N. P. Ignatiev and the Pan-Slav Movement," 223–35.

92. Herlihy, "Eugene Schuyler and the Bulgarian Constitution of 1876," 171–72.

93. Ibid., 175.

94. Schuyler, "United Bulgaria," *North American Review* 141 (November 1885): 468.

95. Ibid.

96. Ibid. Emphasis in original.

97. Cited in Karpat, *Studies in Ottoman Social and Political History*, 764.

98. No Title. *Chicago Tribune*, 7 August 1877, 4.

99. For the rare exceptions, see McCarthy, *The Turk in America*, 100.

100. For more on this, see Turan, *The Turkish Minority in Bulgaria*, 119–33; and Avtorkhanov et al., *The North Caucasus Barrier*, 62–111.

101. Ibid., 763.

102. For more details on population figures, see Crampton, "The Turks in Bulgaria," 42–77; and Mojzes, *Balkan Genocides*, 11–12.

103. Cited in Bass, *Freedom's Battle*, 301, emphasis in original.

104. Walker, *Januarius MacGahan*, 269.

105. Ibid., 270. Despite the burning of villages, MacGahan maintained in the same letter that no Turks were killed or raped during the Russian campaign, which contradicts reports from British consuls in the area.

106. Forbes, "The Russians, the Turks, and the Bulgarians," *Eclectic Magazine*, January 1878.

107. Ibid.

108. For the general sympathy expressed by American journalists toward Russia, see Saul, *Concord and Conflict*, 120.

109. Barnwell, *The Russo-Turkish War*, 367.

110. "The Cause of the Russo-Turkish War," *Chicago Tribune*, 7 August 1877.

111. Godkin, "Article VI: The Eastern Question," *North American Review* 124 (January 1877): 108.

112. Ibid., 119.

113. Ibid., 125.

114. Ibid., 126.

115. Ignatief, *The Russian Album*, 51. A notorious anti-Semite, when Ignatief became minister of the interior in 1881 he used his political power to sponsor the infamous May Laws, which imposed harsh restrictions on Russia's Jewish population.

116. Herlihy, "Eugene Schuyler and the Bulgarian Constitution of 1876," 177–78.

117. Field, *America and the Mediterranean World, 1776-1882*, 373. In New Lexington, Ohio, where MacGahan was buried, the MacGahan American-Bulgarian Foundation still holds an annual festival celebrating MacGahan's journalistic coverage of the Bulgarian massacres, designating him as the "liberator of Bulgaria." See Walker, *Januarius MacGahan*, 316.

118. Cited in Jensen, "Eugene Schuyler and the Balkan Crisis," 35.

119. Ibid. See also Herlihy, "Eugene Schuyler and the Bulgarian Constitution of 1876," 178–79.

120. Jensen, "Eugene Schuyler and the Balkan Crisis," 37.

121. Eugene Schuyler Letter Book, 6 February 1877. Schuyler Papers.

122. Ibid.

123. Fish to Maynard, "Diplomatic Instructions, Turkey," 1 February 1877, Microcopy 77 roll 164, NA. Cited in Jensen, "Eugene Schuyler and the Balkan Crisis," 37, note 38.

124. Schuyler, *Eugene Schuyler*, 133.

125. Schuyler, "United Bulgaria," *North American Review* 141 (November 1885): 470.

126. *Sixty-Ninth Annual Report of the American Board of Commissioners for Foreign Missions*, 19.

127. Jessup, *The Mohammedan Missionary Problem*, 107–38.

128. "Debt of Bulgaria to Robert College," *New York Times*, 13 October 1918.

129. Ibid.

130. Bloxham, "Internal Colonization, Inter-imperial Conflict and the Armenian Genocide," 330.

131. Ibid.

132. Kohler and Wolf, *Jewish Disabilities in the Balkan States*, 30.

133. U.S. Department of State, "Mr. Maynard to Mr. Evarts," *Papers Relating to the Foreign Relations of the United States*, 1877, 593 (hereafter cited as *FRUS*).

134. Cited in Kohler and Wolf, *Jewish Disabilities in the Balkan States*, 31.

135. For a detailed study of these atrocities, see Neuberger, "The Russo-Turkish War and the 'Eastern Jewish Question,'" 53–66.

CHAPTER 3

1. Storey, *Commentaries on the Constitution of the United States*, 701.

2. This included the state constitutions of New York, Delaware, New Jersey, Massachusetts, New Hampshire, Maryland, Rhode Island, Connecticut, North Carolina, and Pennsylvania. For an excellent analysis of these debates, see Spellberg, *Thomas Jefferson's Qur'an*, 158–96.

3. Diner, *The Jews of the United States*, 166. See also Foster, *Moral Reconstruction*.

4. Diner, *The Jews of the United States*, 168.

5. Ibid., 164.

6. For an excellent analysis of this phenomenon in Europe, see Schroeter, "From Sephardi to Oriental," 141.

7. Leff, *Sacred Bonds of Solidarity*, 2.

8. Scholars have noted that in the late nineteenth and early twentieth centuries, some Jewish Americans adopted similar tactics with regards to African Americans. See Rogin, *Blackface, White Noise*.

9. Goldstein, *The Price of Whiteness*, 3. See also Glanz, "Jews and Chinese in America," 219–34.

10. Jaher, *A Scapegoat in the New Wilderness*, 135; and Pencak, "Anti-Semitism, Toleration, and Appreciation," 260.

11. Cited in Spellberg, *Thomas Jefferson's Qur'an*, 142.

12. Sarna, *Jacksonian Jew*, 15.

13. Cited in ibid., 26.

14. Ibid., 23.

15. Ibid.

16. Jacobson, *Whiteness of a Different Color*, 183. For a history of the racial construction of Jews in American social scientific thinking, see 178–84.

17. For the application of scientific racist theories to Jews in the United States, see Jaher, *The Jews and the Nation*, 225.

18. See Michael, *A Concise History of American Antisemitism*, chapter 3. Of course, Jews were not the only religious group to face such suspicions.

19. Kalmar and Penslar, *Orientalism and the Jews*, xxix. See also Hart, *Social Science and the Politics of Modern Jewish Identity*, 148–50.

20. Cited in Jacobson, *Whiteness of a Different Color*, 184.

21. For the background to this story, see Eisenberg, *First to Cry Down Injustice*, 17–18 and Glanz, "Jews and Chinese in America," 228–29.

22. *American Hebrew*, 24 March 1882, 61.

23. For one of the best primary sources discussing American Jewish activism abroad, see Adler, "Jews in the Diplomatic Correspondence of the United States."

24. Syrian Maronites are in communion with Rome and therefore fall under the authority of the Roman Catholic Church. Throughout this text, I use Catholic and Maronite interchangeably.

25. See Wilson, "The Damascus Affair and the Beginnings of France's Empire in the Middle East," 69–71. For accounts of Beaudin's anti-Semitism, see Frankel, *The Damascus Affair*, 59–60.

26. Diner, *A Time for Gathering*, 153–54.

27. Frankel, *The Damascus Affair*, 34–35.

28. For a more in depth analysis of European strategic interests and the Damascus Affair, see Frankel, *The Damascus Affair*, 10, 18–19.

29. Ibid., 19.

30. Ibid., 126.

31. See "Palmerston to Ponsonby," No. 147, 15 June 1841, cited in Rodkey, "Lord Palmerston and the Rejuvenation of Turkey, Part II, 1839–1841," 218.

32. Green, "The British Empire and the Jews," 188.

33. Ibid., 203.

34. Cited in Jaher, *Scapegoat*, 137.

35. Cited in Frankel, *The Damascus Affair*, 225. See also Noah, *The Selected Writings of Mordecai Noah*, 74–75.

36. "Jasper Chasseaud to John Forsyth, Beyrout, 24 March 1840." Cited in Blau and Baron, *The Jews of the United States, 1790–1840*, 924.

37. Marcus, *United States Jewry, 1776–1985*, 656.

38. Frankel, *The Damascus Affair*, 226.

39. "John Forsyth, Secretary of State, to David Porter, U.S. Minister to Turkey, 17 August 1840." For a copy of the dispatch, see Doc. 325 in Blau and Baron, *The Jews of the United States*, 924.

40. Ibid.

41. Ibid.

42. Jews continued to face political exclusion in New Jersey, North Carolina, New Hampshire, Connecticut, and Rhode Island. See Chyet, "The Political Rights of Jews in the United States," 235–62.

43. Marcus, *United States Jewry, 1776-1985*, 656.

44. Monaco, *Rise of Modern Jewish Politics*, 77.

45. *Persecution of the Jews in the East*, 17.

46. Ibid.

47. Green, "Intervening in the Jewish Question," 145.

48. Adler, *With Firmness in the Right*, 20.

49. Grinstein, *The Rise of the Jewish Community of New York*, 420. For the temporary unity this caused in the American Jewish community, see also Blau and Baron, *The Jews of the United States*, 933.

50. This case, in which a young Jewish child in Italy was kidnapped from his parents and secretly baptized by the Catholic Church, demonstrated that the persecution of Jews was not limited to those living under Islamic rule.

51. Board of Delegates of American Israelites, *Constitution and By-Laws of the Board of Delegates of American Israelites*, 2–3. See also Tarshish, "Board of Delegates of American Israelites (1859–1878)," 11.

52. "The Cry for Help from Gibraltar," *Jewish Messenger*, 9 December 1859.

53. Ibid.

54. The exact nature of Jewish-Muslim relations in Morocco is an enduring subject of debate among historians. As Schroeter has qualified the debate, scholars have focused on two positions: "(1) that relations between Jews and Muslims were essentially good until foreign intervention disturbed the harmony and (2) that Muslim-Jewish relations were generally poor, though pressures from the foreign powers led to an improvement in Jewish status." For a broad overview of the debate and how politics have shaped historical interpretations, see Schroeter, *The Sultan's Jew*, 4–7; and "Trade as a Mediator in Muslim-Jewish Relations," 113. For the influence of politics on historical writing about Jews in Arab lands, see Cohen, "The Neo-lachrymose Conception of Jewish-Arab History," 55–64; and a response by Stillman, "Myth, Counter-myth and Distortion."

55. Schroeter, *The Sultan's Jew*, 10.

56. "An Appeal in Behalf of the Moroccan Jews," *Jewish Messenger*, 13 January 1860.

57. Marcus, *United States Jewry, 1776-1985*, 317. See also Schroeter, "Anglo-Jewry and Essaouira (Mogador), 1860–1900," 63.

58. Schroeter, *Merchants of Essaouira*, 133.

59. Ibid., 134.

60. For an example of this, see Marglin, "In the Courts of the Nations: Jews, Muslims and Legal Pluralism in Nineteenth-Century Morocco," 271.

61. For an excellent and detailed analysis of Moroccan Jews' navigation of the legal system in the nineteenth century, see ibid.

62. Voldoire, "The Transnational Politics of French and American Jews, 1860–1920," 65. See also Rodrigue, *Jews and Muslims*, 71–72.

63. "Speech of the President of the Universal Israelitish Alliance," *Israelite*, 21 August 1863. Emphasis mine.

64. "L'oeuvre des écoles," *Bulletin de l'Alliance Israélite Universelle*, January 1865, 3.

65. Wise, "The Alliance," *Israelite*, 26 May 1865.

66. Ibid.

67. Burke, *Prelude to Protectorate in Morocco*, 25.

68. Kenbib, *Juifs et Musulmans au Maroc*, 124–47.

69. The most detailed historical account of the Safi Affair is Littman, "Mission to Morocco, 1863–1864," 171–229. Unless otherwise cited, all subsequent details on the affair in this paragraph are taken from that text.

70. "Dispatch No. 12, Jesse McMath to William H. Seward, September 24, 1863," cited in Landenberger, "United States Diplomatic Efforts on Behalf of Moroccan Jews, 1880–1906," 23.

71. Green, *Moses Montefiore*, 303.

72. Parfitt, "*Dhimma* versus Protection in Nineteenth Century Morocco," 147.

73. "Seward to McMath, 9 December 1863," *FRUS*, 1864, 410–11.

74. Cited in Neely, *The Fate of Liberty*, 108.

75. Marglin, "In the Courts of the Nations," 350; and Kenbib, *Juifs et Musulmans*, 126.

76. "Seward to McMath, 9 December 1863," *FRUS*, 1864, 410–11.

77. Littman, "Mission to Morocco," 182–83.

78. Ibid., 182. See also Parfitt, "*Dhimma* versus Protection in Nineteenth Century Morocco," 147.

79. "Atrocities on the Coast of Morocco," *Jewish Messenger*, 27 November 1863.

80. Ibid.

81. "Cruelties by Spanish Officials," *Jewish Chronicle and Hebrew Observer*, 16 October 1863, 422–25.

82. Ibid., 423.

83. Ibid.

84. Ibid.

85. Ibid., 439.

86. "Board of Deputies—Atrocities in Morocco," *FRUS*, 1864, 418.

87. Hall, *The United States and Morocco*, 134.

88. "Mr. McMath to Mr. Seward, 5 November 1863," *FRUS*, 1864, 414.

89. "Moses Pariente to Board of Delegates of American Israelites," quoted and translated by Meyer S. Isaacs in "Isaacs to Seward," 1 December 1863, *FRUS*, 1864, 411–12.

90. "Seward to Josephs," ibid., 411.

91. See Marglin, "In the Courts of the Nations," chapter 9.

92. "Henry Josephs, Chairman, and Myer S. Isaacs, Secretary to Mr. Seward, 25 November 1863," *FRUS*, 1864, 411.

93. Loewe, *Diaries of Sir Moses and Lady Montefiore*, 153. Montefiore was referring to the passage of the 1838 *Hatti Şerif of Gulhane* and the 1856 *hatti hümayun* in the Ottoman Empire, largely adopted through British pressure. See chapter 2 in this book.

94. Cited in Marglin, "In the Courts of the Nation," 353–54. See also Green, *Moses Montefiore*, 312.

95. Schroeter, "Anglo-Jewry and Essaouira (Mogador)," 67.

96. "Montefiore to the Rabbis, Elders and Congregational Authorities of the Jews of Morocco, 7 September 1864 (6 Ellul 5624): PRO, FO 99/126." Cited in Green, "The British Empire and the Jews," 203.

97. Ibid., 69.

98. Green, *Moses Montefiore*, 319.

99. See Marglin, "In the Courts of the Nation."

100. Pennell, *Morocco since 1830*, 83. See also Green, "British Empire and the Jews," 203.

101. Ibid., 203.

102. "Success of Sir Moses Montefior's [*sic*] Mission," *Jewish Messenger*, 15 January 1864.

103. "The Mission to Morocco," *Jewish Messenger*, 8 April 1864.

104. Tarshish, "Board of Delegates of American Israelites (1859–1878)," 9.

105. "Meyer S. Isaacs, Secretary and Albert Cardoza, President, Board of Delegates of American Israelites to Adolphe Crémieux, President of the Universal Israelite Alliance," 10 July 1865, in "États-Unis IC," Alliance Israélite Universelle archives.

106. Ibid.

107. Cited in Kalmar and Penslar, *Orientalism and the Jews*, xxxv.

CHAPTER 4

1. For a full analysis of this episode, see Dinnerstein, *Uneasy at Home*, 149–78.

2. Hollingsworth Miller, "The Maghrib through French Eyes," in *Through Foreign Eyes*, ed. Alf Andrew Hegoy et al., 84.

3. Kenbib, "Structures Traditionelles et Protection Etrangère au Maroc au XIXe siècle," 79.

4. Ibid., 80, and footnote 1 *bis*. The title of the 1764 document left little up to the imagination: "Projet de conquête de l'Empire du Maroc" ("The Project of Conquest of the Moroccan Empire," translation mine).

5. Ibid., 83.

6. See Hall, *The United States and Morocco, 1776–1956*, 205. For a detailed study of how Europeans and Americans used protection status to gain power in Morocco and how this conduct destabilized Muslim-Jewish relations, see Kenbib, *Les Protégés: Contribution à l'histoire Contemporaine du Maroc*; and Bowie, "An Aspect of Muslim-Jewish Relations in Late Nineteenth-Century Morocco."

7. See Marglin, "In the Courts of the Nations," 275.

8. Ibid., 277.

9. Ibid.

10. Ibid.

11. Landenberger, "United States Diplomatic Efforts on Behalf of Moroccan Jews: 1880–1906," 7.

12. Ibid., 9. Although Brown was ultimately cleared of wrongdoing, his subsequent actions cast doubt on his innocence.

13. Miller, *A History of Modern Morocco*, 22.

14. Cited in Cruickshank, "Morocco at the Parting of the Ways," 42.

15. Anderson, *History of the Missions of the American Board of Commissioners for Foreign Missions to the Oriental Churches*, 143. See also "George J. Leber's History of the 1821 Greek War of Independence," in U.S. Congress, *Proceedings and Debates of the United States Congress*, vol. 117, part 6, 8802.

16. As Jessica Marglin has demonstrated, however, despite these consular treaties, which were supposed to determine legal options for Moroccans, in practice Moroccans often "shopped" for the legal forum they thought would be to their best advantage. See Marglin, "In the Courts of the Nations," chapter 7.

17. Perdicaris, *American Claims and the Protection of Native Subjects in Morocco*.

18. Hall, *The United States and Morocco, 1776–1956*, 239, 280, n. 147. The scandal even made its way into local newspapers. See "The Extortionate Consul: The American Consul at Tangiers Accused," *Macon Telegraph* (Macon, Ga.), 16 September 1886. Articles appeared in other major presses, including the *New York Tribune*, the *New York Times*, and the *Chicago Tribune*, throughout 1887. See, for example, "The Tangier Consulate: What Caused the Removal of Col. Mathews," *New York Times*, 5 August 1887.

19. Hall, *The United States and Morocco, 1776–1956*, 238–39.

20. "W. R. Lewis to J. D. Porter, Tangiers, September 12, 1887." Cited in Cruickshank, "Morocco at the Parting of the Ways," 198.

21. Hall, *The United States and Morocco, 1776–1956*, 243.

22. Stuart, *The International City of Tangier*, 19–20.

23. "Porter to Mathews, December 9, 1886," *Diplomatic Instructions, Barbary Powers*, RG 59. National Archives.

24. Ibid. Portions of correspondence between the State Department and Mathews were republished in the press. See "Our Flag in Morocco," *New York Times*, 5 August 1887.

25. Ben-Srhir, *Britain and Morocco during the Embassy of John Drummond Hay*, 183.

26. "Dispatch no. 258, Felix Mathews to William M. Evarts, November 9, 1877," *Dispatches from U.S. Consuls at Tangier*, vol. 11, General Records of the Department of State, RG 59, NA, Washington, D.C. Cited in Landenberger, "United States Diplomatic Efforts on Behalf of Moroccan Jews," 41.

27. "The Massacre in Morocco," *American Hebrew*, 27 February 1880.

28. "Outrages upon Jews in Morocco," *American Hebrew*, 27 February 1880.

29. "Morocco," *Jewish Messenger*, 16 April 1880.

30. "Edward Thornton to Secretary of State Evarts, 13 December 1879," *FRUS*, 1880, 499–500.

31. "Memorandum of the language held to Sir J. H. Drummond Hay by the Rev. A. Lowy, Secretary of the Anglo-Jewish Association, and of Sir J. H. Drummond Hay's replies," ibid., 500. See also Ben-Srhir, *Britain and Morocco*.

32. "Thornton to Evarts, 13 December 1879," *FRUS*, 1880, 499–501.

33. Ibid.

34. Ibid.

35. "Translation of a circular note addressed by the Moorish minister of foreign affairs to the foreign representatives, dates 26 Saffar, 1297 (18 February 1880)," enclosed with "Mathews to Evarts," *FRUS*, 1880, 791.

36. "Mathews to Evarts, 28 February 1880," *FRUS*, 1880, 794.

37. "Mathews to Evarts, 8 March 1880," *FRUS*, 1880, 794–95.

38. "Mathews to Dehami, 21 February 1880," *FRUS*, 1880, 796.

39. Ibid.

40. Ibid.

41. "Mathews to Fairchild, 11 April 1880," *FRUS*, 1880, 799.

42. "Dispatch, No. 10, Lucius Fairchild to William M. Evarts, 13 April 1880," *Dispatches from Foreign Ministers in Spain*. Cited in Landenberger, "United States Efforts on Behalf of Moroccan Jews," 79.

43. For more on this phenomenon, see Hoogland, *Crossing the Waters;* and Gualtieri, *Between Arab and White*.

44. "Dispatch No. 27, Lucius Fairchild to William M. Evarts, 2 May, 180, Dispatches from U.S. Ministers in Spain." Cited in Landenberger, "United States Efforts on Behalf of Moroccan Jews," 79.

45. Ibid., 55. See also Hall, *The United States and Morocco, 1776–1956*, 223.

46. "Isaacs to Goldschmidt, 14 April 1880," États-Unis, IC, archives of the Alliance Israélite Universelle.

47. My translation. Original reads: "Les Juifs sont le seul élément de la population indigène qui accept les idées de la civilisation, le seul qui puisse le répandre dans le pays." *Memoire en Faveur des Israélites Marocains*, 3, archives of the Alliance Israélite Universelle.

48. Ibid.

49. "Letter from Alliance [exact author illegible] to Myer S. Issacs," Translation mine. Myer S. Isaacs papers.

50. Hall, *The United States and Morocco, 1776–1956*, 224.

51. "Evarts to Fairchild," 15 June 1880, *FRUS*, 1880–81, 897.

52. "Question of Religious Toleration," *FRUS*, 1880–81, 916.

53. For the full report on the conference, see: "Question of Religious Toleration. Lucius Fairchild, 1880–1881, Spain," *FRUS*, 1880–81, 897–920.

54. Ibid., 912.

55. Hayes, *State of the Union*.

56. "Fairchild to Evarts, 2 December 1880," *FRUS*, 1880–81, 1044.

57. "Religious Liberty in Morocco," *Jewish Messenger*, 9 July 1880.

58. "Morocco," *Jewish Messenger*, 18 March 1881.

59. "Fairchild to Secretary of State Blaine, April 20 1881," *FRUS*, 1880–81, 1054–56. Emphasis mine.

60. Ibid., 1055.

61. See National Archives, *Papers Relating to Foreigners in Morocco*, vols. 425 and 426.

62. Hall, *The United States and Morocco, 1776–1956*, 238–39.

63. Ibid., 247.

64. Such accusations combined with claims that Lewis had murdered his wife. Ibid., 248–50.

65. *Papers Relating to Foreigners in Morocco*, 143.

66. "Missionaries in Morocco," Bureau of Statistics, Department of State, *Consular Reports*, serial vol. 3419, session 52, serial set 3419 H. doc. 132. Barclay's comments were also republished in local American newspapers. See "Missionaries in Morocco," *San Francisco Call*, 23 February 1896.

67. Cited in Hall, *The United States and Morocco, 1776–1956*, 313.

68. "Our Task at Morocco," *New York Times*, 1 June 1904.

69. Ibid.

70. "Hay to Gummere, 2 June 1904," *FRUS*, 1904, 503.

71. Hall, *The United States and Morocco, 1776–1956*, 341.

72. "The Threat to Morocco," *New York Times*, 26 June 1904.

73. Hall, *The United States and Morocco, 1776–1956*, 342.

74. "Mr. Hay's Opportunity in Morocco," *World's Work*, 8 July 1904, 495. Cited in Hall, *The United States and Morocco, 1776–1956*, 348.

75. The Perdicaris affair, as it was later called, became such a popular historical event it was later canonized in a 1975 Hollywood film, *The Wind and the Lion*.

76. See Anderson, *The First Moroccan Crisis, 1904–1906*, 1.

77. Hall, *The United States and Morocco, 1776–1956*, 394.

78. Ibid., 289.

79. Thompson, *The Uncertain Crusade*, 115.

80. "The Threat to Morocco," *New York Times*, 26 June 1904.

81. Cited in Thompson, *Uncertain Crusade*, 115.

82. Cited in Morris, *The Rise of Theodore Roosevelt*, 243.

83. Ward, "Immigrant Minority 'Diplomacy,'" 8.

84. Ibid.

85. Ibid.

86. Ibid. This was not the first time such accusations had been made. The Russian ambassador to the United States had defended his country's actions in 1903 by maintaining that Jewish "money lenders" had "destroyed" local Russian peasants through their corrupt practices and their refusal to assimilate into Russian society. His views were republished in "Cause of the Massacres," *New York Times*, 19 May 1903.

87. Originally published in *Vogue* and republished by the *Literary Digest*, 25 November 1905. Cited in Thompson, *Uncertain Crusade*, 109.

88. "Mr. Roosevelt Unable to Aid Russian Jews," *New York Times*, 7 November 1905.

89. *Brooklyn Daily Eagle Almanac, 1906*, 235.

90. Emphasis mine. "Joseph Baum, President, Israelite Alliance of America to Secretary of State John Hay, 11 December 1903," archives of the Alliance Israélite Universelle.

91. "Samuel Gummere to France B. Loomis, 24 March 1904," *Dispatches from U.S. Consuls at Tangier*, Vol. 27, General Records of the Department of State, Record Group 59.

92. Kostandarithes, "The Diplomatic Career of Henry White," 93.

93. Emphasis mine. Einstein, *A Diplomat Looks Back*, 7.

94. Bishop, *Theodore Roosevelt and His Time Shown in His Own Letters*, 475.

95. Cited in Beale, *Theodore Roosevelt and the Rise of America to World Power*, 32.

96. Ibid., 27. For full speech, see "Biological Analogies," in Roosevelt, *History as Literature and Other Essays*, 76.

97. Roosevelt, "First Annual Message," State of the Union Address, 3 December 1901.

98. Mowry, *The Era of Theodore Roosevelt*, 144.

99. Roosevelt, *Fear God and Take Your Own Part*, 71.

100. Adler, "Jews in American Diplomatic Correspondence," 47.

101. Although Schiff noted only that the report was "from Europe," the following year the American Jewish Committee (founded that year by Jacob Schiff) thanked the French Alliance for sending detailed information regarding the Moroccan Jews. See "Herbert Friedenwald, Secretary, the American Jewish Committee to M. J. Bigart, Secretary," 22 October 1907, "États-Unis—IC," Alliance Israélite Universelle archives.

102. Adler, "Jews in American Diplomatic Correspondence," 47.

103. For the full letter and a copy of the report, see "The Government of the United States and Affairs of Interest to the Jews, 1905–1906," *American Jewish Year Book, 1905/1906*, 92–98.

104. "Elihu Root to Henry White, 28 November 1905," *FRUS*, 1905, 680.

105. Confidential letter, "Elihu Root to Henry White," 28 November 1905, in Letterbooks, vol. 187, part 1, Elihu Root Papers.

106. Ibid.

107. Ibid.

108. Einstein, *A Diplomat Looks Back*, 10.

109. "A Report on the Restrictions Suffered by the Jews in Morocco," box 9, folder 6, no date. Lewis Einstein Papers. The report can also be found in *FRUS*, 1906, 1472–76.

110. Ibid.

111. Ibid.

112. Larsen, "Theodore Roosevelt and the Moroccan Crisis," 172.

113. Ibid.

114. "Theodore Roosevelt to Spring Rice, 1 July 1907," in Morison, *The Letters of Theodore Roosevelt*, vol. 5, 698–99.

115. Ibid., vol. 7, 349.

116. Ibid., 256.

117. For more on this, see Lorcin, *Imperial Identities*, 171–73; and Smith, *Colonial Memory and Postcolonial Europe*, 106–7.

118. Leff, *Sacred Bonds of Solidarity*, 210–11.

119. Ibid., 204.

120. The book would also have a wide impact in the United States, when Henry Ford had segments widely republished in the 1920s. See Segal, *A Lie and a Libel*, 25–27.

CHAPTER 5

1. The spread of Islam in Southeast Asia began in the ninth century when Arab Muslim traders dominated commercial activities in the area. In 1380, a Muslim missionary spread Islam to the Sulu Archipelago and Mindanao in the Philippines. Subsequent missionaries reinforced the faith. One of these missionaries, Abu Bakr, established a government in Sulu based on the Arab sultanate, and he became the first sultan of Sulu in 1450. Bakr and his descendants spread their political power and faith to other parts of the Philippines in the fifteenth and sixteenth centuries, until the arrival of the Spanish in 1565 halted their efforts. See Saleeby, *The History of Sulu*; and Majul, *Muslims in the Philippines.*

2. The term "little brown brothers" has been attributed to William Howard Taft, who served as the president of the second Philippine Commission and, later, governor general of the Philippine Islands.

3. The only exception to this statement would be American imperial rule over Native Americans. For a more detailed study of American imperial exchanges with other powers, see Kramer, "Empires, Exceptions, and Anglo-Saxons."

4. Williams, "United States Indian Policy and the Debate over Philippine Annexation," 810.

5. The four largest groups included the Maguindanaos in North Cotabato, the Maranao-Ilanun in the Lanao provinces, and the Tausug and Samal, in Sulu. See Gowing, *Muslim Filipinos*, 1.

6. Ibid., 4.

7. By 1895, the sultan of Sulu, Jamal ul-Kiram II, held very little power over his subjects. See Majul, *Muslims in the Philippines*, 298–304.

8. For a wider analysis of the role of religious rhetoric in shaping American justifications for annexation, see Harris, *God's Arbiters.*

9. Rusling, "Interview with President McKinley," *Christian Advocate*, 22 January 1903, 810.

10. U.S. Congress, *Congressional Record*, vol. 33, 56th Cong., 1st sess., 705, 711.

11. "Evangelical Imperialism" was coined by Tompkins, *Anti-Imperialism in the United States*, 10.

12. Pratt, *Expansionists of 1898*, 291. See also Clymer, *Protestant Missionaries in the Philippines, 1898–1916*, 3–5; and Miller, "Benevolent Assimilation," 17–18.

13. Strong, *Our Country*, 159–79.

14. "The Call to the Philippines," *Christian and Missionary Alliance*, 100.

15. Cited in Miller, "Benevolent Assimilation," 18.

16. "Dr. Radcliffe's Response," *Reading Times* (Reading, Pa.), 8 December 1898.

17. Cited in Miller, "Benevolent Assimilation," 17–18.

18. Ibid.

19. *Baptist Union*, vol. 3, 27 August 1898, 631. Cited in Pratt, *Expansionists of 1898*, 292.

20. Gould, "McKinley, Ida Saxton," *American National Biography Online.*

21. Morgan, "What Shall We Do with the Conquered Islands?" *North American Review* 166 (June 1898): 645.

22. "Anti-Imperialist Broadsides," Washington, D.C., 13 April 1899, Microfilm S4104, Lamont Library, Harvard University. Microfilm entitled *Anti-Imperialist Broadsides*, but film includes correspondence and other documents written by the Anti-Imperialist League, in addition to "Broadsides."

23. Tompkins, *Anti-Imperialism in the United States*, 11.

24. Ibid.

25. U.S. Congress, Senate, 55th Cong., 3rd sess., 1532. See also Harris, *God's Arbiters*, 28.

26. Amoroso, "Inheriting the 'Moro Problem,'" in *The American Colonial State in the Philippines*, ed. Go and Foster, 122.

27. Saleeby, *The Moro Problem*, 122.

28. For other examples of articles that discuss the implications of the "Moro problem," see Benjamin, "Our Mohammedan Wards in Sulu," *Outlook*, 18 November 1899; "Slavery in Philippines," *Chicago Tribune*, 5 March 1899; "A Moro Cannibal of the Philippine Islands," *Atlanta Constitution*, 19 March 1899; Carpenter, "The Sultan of Mindanao," *Atlanta Constitution*, 3 June 1900; "Butchered by Moros," *Boston Daily Advertiser*, 10 June 1900; Whitmarsh, "The Sulu Archipelago," *Outlook*, 26 January 1901; and Miller, "The Semi-Civilized Tribes of the Philippine Islands," *Annals of the American Academy of Political and Social Science* (July 1901).

29. Winthrop, "The Problem of the Philippines: Racial, Commercial, Religious, Political, and Social Conditions," *Outlook*, 11 June 1898, 382–83.

30. Ibid.

31. Kennan, "The Philippines," *Outlook*, 9 March 1901, 583.

32. Davis, "The White Man's Problem," *Arena*, January–June 1900, 2.

33. Baylen, "Senator John Tyler Morgan and Negro Colonization in the Philippines," 65. For an interesting contemporary discussion of this issue, see Holly et al., "The Race Problem: A Symposium," *Arena*, April 1899, 421.

34. Dwight, "Our Mohammedan Wards," *Forum*, March 1900, 15–31.

35. Ibid., 16.

36. Ibid.

37. Ibid., 17.

38. Ibid., 20–21.

39. Ibid., 22.

40. Ibid., 26.

41. Ibid., 27.

42. Ibid.

43. Ibid., 27–28.

44. Ibid., 29.

45. Quoted in "Rule of Blood and Iron: Gen. Davis' Recipe for Controlling Moros in the Philippines," *Washington Post*, 10 May 1902, 4.

46. See Salman, *The Embarrassment of Slavery*; and Hawkins, *Making Moros*, 64–71.

47. Hawkins, *Making Moros*, 65.

48. "Philippine Slaves: President M'Kinley Will Be a Second Emancipator," *Los Angeles Times*, 5 March 1899. See also "Conditions in Sulu Islands," *New York Times*, 26 May 1901, which noted that American imperial rule would bring about a second emancipation proclamation. Cited in Hawkins, *Making Moros*, 64.

49. "Slavery in the Sulu Archipelago," *Outlook*, 2 December 1899, 765.

50. Schurman, *Philippine Affairs: A Retrospect and Outlook*, 3; and "Instructions of the President to the Commission," in Report of the Philippine Commission to the President, 1900, I, Exhibit II, 3. Hereafter cited as RPC.

51. RPC, Ibid.

52. Many conservative Republicans opposed imperial expansion, which created a split within the Republican Party. For more on this, see Tompkins, *Anti-Imperialism in the United States*, 73–74; Schurman, *Philippine Affairs*, 3; and Hendrickson Jr., "Reluctant Expansionist," 407.

53. Schurman, *Philippine Affairs*, 3.

54. Before creating a commission of five members, McKinley had asked Worcester to go to the Philippines as his personal representative. Pier, *American Apostles to the Philippines*, 71–74.

55. Worcester, *The Philippine Islands and Their People*, 1898, x. For more on this relationship, see Kramer, "The Pragmatic Empire."

56. Worcester, "Knotty Problems of the Philippines," *Century Illustrated Magazine*, October 1898, 876.

57. Ibid.

58. See Worcester, "The Malay Pirates of the Philippines," *Century Illustrated*, September 1898, 693.

59. Ibid., 695.

60. Ibid.

61. Ibid., 702.

62. War Department, *Annual Reports of the War Department*, 1903, vol. 3, appendix 6, 378.

63. RPC, vol. 1, 1900, 101. For a greater analysis of the influence of British Malay on the governance of Moros, see Amoroso, "Inheriting the Moro Problem."

64. RPC, vol. 1, 1900, 106.

65. Austin, *Colonial Administration*, 1329.

66. Ibid., 1,329.

67. Go, "Introduction," in *The American Colonial State in the Philippines*, ed. Go and Foster, 16.

68. RPC, 1900, "Part II—The Native Peoples of the Philippines," vol. 1, 11.

69. RPC, 1900, vol. 3, 363. Emphasis mine.

70. For example, in the introductory segment of the report, Moros were classified as one of the "more important civilized tribes." Moros were the only non-Christian group among the "civilized tribes." A few paragraphs later, however, it noted: "A considerable number of the wild tribes not only practice polygamy but take and keep slaves." These were both practices American officials accused Moros of committing. See RPC, 1900, "Part II—The Native Peoples of the Philippines," vol. 1, 15–16.

71. Ibid., 363. Jolo and Sulu are interchangeable terms. According to the authors of the census, Jolo was a corruption of the term "Sulu," a term used to describe both the island and the people living there. See U.S. Bureau of the Census, *Census of the Philippine Islands, 1903*, vols. 1 and 2, 463.

72. Ibid., vol. 3, 364.

73. RPC, 1900, vol. 4, 109. Emphasis mine.

74. As the historian Cesar Majul has written, "Although during the last decade of Spanish rule in the Philippines, the official policy was to make the Muslims loyal subjects of Spain rather than Christians, the Spanish clergy tried to impress government officials that such loyalty was possible only if the Muslims became Christians." Majul, *Muslims in the Philippines*, 345.

75. RPC, 1900, vol. 4, 111.

76. *Annual Reports of the War Department*, 1903, vol. 3, appendix 6, 378.

77. For more on this, see Kramer, *Blood of Government*, 211.

78. RPC, 1900, vols. 1, 3.

79. Ibid., 3–4. The full letter was translated into native dialects and "25,000 copies [were] . . . affixed throughout the city and suburbs of Manila, carried to the provinces, and disseminated in the interior wherever possible." Ibid., 5–6.

80. Cited in Tarling, *Imperialism and Southeast Asia*, 194.

81. Ibid.

82. See General Davis's report on Moro affairs in *Annual Reports of the War Department*, 1903, 151.

83. For a full account of this controversy, see Salman, *The Embarrassment of Slavery*.

84. *Annual Reports of the War Department*, 1903, 17–18.

85. Ibid.

86. Gowing, *Mandate in Moroland*, 33.

87. For the original text of the Bates document, see "Report of John C. Bates on Agreement with Sultan of Sulu," Senate document 136, 56th Cong., 1st sess., 1 February 1900.

88. Although at the time, Americans believed that the sultan had agreed to American sovereignty, it was later revealed that the interpreter of the treaty had mistranslated the American document into the Sulu language, Tao Sug. The American version read, "The sovereignty of the United States over the whole Archipelago of Jolo and its dependencies is declared and acknowledged." The translator, who was later charged with purposely changing the meaning of the text, had translated this portion as, "The support, aid, and protection of the Jolo Island and Archipelago are in the American nation." Gowing, *Mandate in Moroland*, 122, footnote 28.

89. Straus, *Under Four Administrations*, 143.

90. Article XI of treaty signed between United States and Tripoli, negotiated by Joel Barlow in 1796. Quoted in Straus, *Under Four Administrations*, 145.

91. Ibid.

92. Ibid.

93. Tan, "Sulu under American Military Rule," 39.

94. U. S. Congress, *Affairs in the Philippine Islands*, part 1, 39.

95. RPC, 1902, part 1, 15.

96. RPC, 1901, part 1, 91–92.

97. The Philippines Bill of 1902. For full text of the bill, see Bernas, *A Historical and Juridical Study of the Philippine Bill of Rights*, appendix.

98. Ibid., 15.

99. Root, *Military and Colonial Policy of the United States*, 321–22.

100. Gowing, *Mandate in Moroland*, 203.

101. U.S. Congress, *Affairs in the Philippine Islands*, part 2, 123.

102. Ibid., 124.

103. Ibid., 127.

104. Ibid., 122–29.

105. Ibid., 126.

106. Ibid.

107. RPC, 1904, part 1, 8. As the report noted, "In drafting this act Governor Taft and his colleagues had the benefit of the advice and assistance of Maj. Gen. Geo. W. Davis, who for nearly two years had been in command of the troops stationed in the Moro Province and had given much thought and study to the conditions there prevailing." Meanwhile, American colonial officials would create the "Mountain Province" to rule over animists in 1908.

108. "An Act Providing for the Organization and Government of the Moro Province," No. 787, in folder "Dept. of Mindanao and Sulu: Legislation and Government," box 650, Record Group 350, National Archives.

109. For a detailed explanation of the military rule of the Moro Province, see "Annual Report of the Governor of the Department of Mindanao and Sulu," in Philippines Commission, Manuscript Reports of the Philippines Commission (hereafter cited as MRPC), 1914, 504, National Archives.

110. RPC, 1904, part 1, 18.

111. Ibid., 19.

112. RPC, 1901, part 1, 133–35.

113. RPC, 1901, part 2, 275.

114. RPC, 1902, vol. 2, part 2, 37. See the document: "First Annual Report of the Secretary of Public Instruction to the Philippine Commission for the Year Ending October 15, 1902."

115. Ibid.

116. "An Act Creating a Bureau of Non-Christian Tribes for the Philippine Islands," No. 253, 2 October 1901. Folder: "Non-Christian Tribes and Provinces," box 368, n. 3833, Record Group 350, National Archives.

117. As Worcester noted, once bureau officials had completed their work in northern Luzon, "it is purposed to transfer the entire field force of the Bureau to the island of Mindanao, with a view to the gathering of data which may be useful in the solution of the serious problem presented by the numerous Mohammedan and pagan tribes of that island." See RPC, 1902, vol. 1, part 2, 632.

118. As the President of the American Anthropological Society, W. J. McGee, had stated in a speech before the National Geographic Society in 1899, it was an American

duty to uplift "the darker fellows to liberty's plane." Cited in Haller Jr., *Outcasts from Evolution*, 106.

119. "Report of the Chief of the Bureau of Non-Christian Tribes for the Year Ending August 31, 1902," RPC, 1902, vol. 1, part 3, appendix Q, 15.

120. Ibid., 18.

121. Ibid., 682.

122. Barrows, *The Bureau of Non-Christian Tribes for the Philippine Islands*.

123. Ibid., 9.

124. One of the leading anthropologists of his time, W. J. McGee had written in 1899: "the records show that cranial capacity is correlated with culture-grade so closely that the relative status of the peoples and nations of the earth may be stated as justly in terms of brain-size as in any other way." McGee, "The Trend of Human Progress," 410. During his lifetime, McGee led the Bureau of American Ethnology and served as head anthropologist of the St. Louis exhibition, which included an exhibit of "live Moros." For more on the relationship between anthropology and the physical measurements associated with race, see Stanton, *The Leopard's Spots*; and Smedley, *Race in North America*.

125. Barrows, *The Bureau of Non-Christian Tribes for the Philippine Islands*, 11.

126. Ibid., 10.

127. U.S. Bureau of the Census, *Census of Philippine Islands*, vol. 1, 11.

128. Ibid., 467.

129. U.S. Bureau of the Census, *Census of Philippine Islands*, vol. 2, 9.

130. Rafael, *White Love and Other Events in Filipino History*, 33.

CHAPTER 6

1. Edward Price Bell interview of Leonard Wood. Cited in Bell, "Future of the Philippines," 23.

2. Rodil, *The Minoritization of the Indigenous Communities of Mindanao and the Sulu Archipelago*, 49.

3. See, for example, Cloman and Freeman, *A Soldier in the Philippines*; and Austin, *Uncle Sam's Children*. For articles by military officials in popular journals, see Sweet, "American Rule in the Sulus," *Independent*, 3 October 1901; and Bonsal, "The Moros and Their Country," *Outlook*, 10 May 1902.

4. The opera was again staged in 2004 in Canton, Ohio, site of the William McKinley presidential library.

5. Description from the program of *The Sultan of Sulu*.

6. Most of the information in this paragraph is taken from Parezo and Fowler, *Anthropology Goes to the Fair*, 166, 170.

7. Ibid., 165.

8. Ibid., 185.

9. Ibid., 166–67.

10. Ibid., 168.

11. Ibid.

12. "Ancient Types at St. Louis," *New York Times*, 6 September 1903.

13. Parezo and Fowler, *Anthropology Goes to the Fair*, 165.

14. Ibid., 169–70.

15. Everett, M., *The Book of the Fair*, 318.

16. Ibid.

17. Cited in Parezo and Fowler, *Anthropology Goes to the Fair*, 185.

18. "Casts of Primitive Races," *New York Times*, 26 July 1904.

19. Lane, "Introduction," in Wood, *Chasing Geronimo*, 8–9.

20. For the background to Leonard Wood's Cuban experience, see Lane, *Armed Progressive*, chapter 6.

21. Cited in Bacevich, *Diplomat in Khaki*, 26.

22. Ibid.

23. Diary, 5 May 1903, Leonard Wood Papers.

24. "Earl of Cromer to Theodore Roosevelt," 25 December 1902, Theodore Roosevelt Papers.

25. "Theodore Roosevelt to Lord Cromer," 15 January 1903, box 32, Leonard Wood Papers. Roosevelt later sent Wood a copy of the letter.

26. Diary, 10 May 1903, Leonard Wood Papers.

27. Ibid.

28. Diary, 16 May 1903, Leonard Wood Papers.

29. Baring, *Modern Egypt*, 168–69.

30. Ibid., 97.

31. Ibid., 203. Baring also cites from Muir, *The Caliphate*, in this excerpt.

32. "McCoy to family," undated [June 1903], box 3, McCoy Papers. Cited in Bacevich, *Diplomat in Khaki*, 26.

33. Ibid., "McCoy to family," 24 June 1903.

34. Cited in Murray, "The Pacifier of the Philippines," *World's Work*, October 1908, 10774. See also Holme, *The Life of Leonard Wood*, 139; and Laubach, *The People of the Philippines*, 65–66, who notes that many of the books were on Islam and Moros.

35. "Leonard Wood to Secretary of War Elihu Root," 23 July 1903, box 32, Leonard Wood Papers.

36. "Leonard Wood to Theodore Roosevelt," 3 August 1903, box 32, Leonard Wood Papers.

37. Ibid.

38. Scott, *Some Memories of a Soldier*, 274.

39. Ibid.

40. "Conference between General Wood and Hadji Butu, at Jolo," 24 August 1903, box 32, Leonard Wood Papers.

41. Ibid.

42. "Leonard Wood to Theodore Roosevelt," 20 September 1903, ibid.

43. "Leonard Wood to William Howard Taft," 5 September 1903, ibid.

44. "Leonard Wood to Theodore Roosevelt," 20 September 1903, ibid.

45. "Leonard Wood to William Howard Taft," 5 September 1903, ibid.

46. Ibid.

47. "Leonard Wood to Theodore Roosevelt," 20 September 1903, ibid.

48. Ibid.

49. RPC, 1904, Part 2, 577.

50. Ibid.

51. Diary, 18 November 1903, Leonard Wood Papers.

52. Cited in Hagedorn, *Leonard Wood*, 45.

53. "An Act Providing for the Organization and Government of the Moro Province," box 650, in folder "Dept. of Mindanao and Sulu: Legislation and Government," RG 350, National Archives.

54. For more on this, see Salman, *The Embarrassment of Slavery*.

55. Salman, *The Embarrassment of Slavery*, 102.

56. "Leonard Wood to Theodore Roosevelt," 7 December 1903," box 33, Leonard Wood Papers.

57. Worcester, *The Philippine Islands and Their People*, 175–76.

58. Dale, "Religious Suicide in Islamic Asia," 49.

59. Saleeby, *The Moro Problem*, 24.

60. Cited in Fulton, *Moroland, 1899–1906*, 201, footnote 27.

61. "R. L. Bullard to Adj., Inf. Force, Jolo Expedition, 23 November 1903," Bullard Papers, Cited in Thompson, "Governors of the Moro Province: Wood, Bliss, and Pershing in the Southern Philippines, 1903–1913," 56. See also Fulton, *Moroland*, 206.

62. Cited in Fulton, *Moroland*, 206. The veracity of the poet's story was later confirmed by another American military officer who had witnessed the events firsthand.

63. Diary, 25 November 1903, Leonard Wood Papers. As Jack McCallum has written in his biography of Wood, "As time went on, the numbers continued to drift about and the story changed with the audience." McCallum, *Leonard Wood*, 218.

64. Salman, *The Embarrassment of Slavery*, 106–7.

65. 25 November 1903, Diary. For Wood's private account to Roosevelt, see "Wood to Roosevelt," 7 December 1903, box 33, Leonard Wood Papers.

66. "Leonard Wood to Horace Fletcher," 26 December 1903, box 32. See also Linn, *Guardians of Empire*, 38.

67. Thompson, "Governors of the Moro Province," 58.

68. Cited in Bacevich, *Diplomat in Khaki*, 33.

69. "Leonard Wood to Theodore Roosevelt," 12 December 1903, box 32, Leonard Wood Papers.

70. RPC, 1904, Part 2, 634–35.

71. Gowing, *Mandate in Moroland*, 114.

72. RPC, 1904, Part 2, 575. For the official act, see "An Act Temporarily to Provide for the Government of the Moros and Other Non-Christian Tribes," ibid., 633–38.

73. Ibid., 575.

74. See W. Williams, "United States Indian Policy and the Debate over Philippine Annexation"; and Baldoz, *The Third Asiatic Invasion*, 32–33.

75. The rulings specified that such rights only extended to "incorporated" territories, which included Alaska and Hawaii. For a greater analysis of the legal justifications behind the *Insular Cases*, see Monge, "Injustice According to Law," 228.

76. Lane, *Armed Progressive*, 115, 125–27.

77. Ibid.

78. Ibid.

79. "Theodore Roosevelt to Leonard Wood," 2 August 1904, box 35, Leonard Wood Papers.

80. Ibid.

81. Ibid.

82. "4 April 1904" and "7 April 1904," Diary, Leonard Wood Papers. *Cottas* were fortifications set up for self-defense.

83. "3 April 1904," ibid.

84. "Theodore Roosevelt to Joseph Gurney Cannon, accepting the nomination for the Presidency of the Republican National Convention," 12 September 1904. Cited in Morison, *The Letters of Theodore Roosevelt*, vol. 4, 940.

85. Ibid.

86. Cited in Abinales, *Making Mindanao*, 21–22.

87. Fulton, *Honor for the Flag*, 62.

88. Cited in Fulton, *Moroland*, 265.

89. White, *Bullets and Bolos*, 312.

90. Ibid.

91. "Secular and Religious," *New York Observer and Chronicle* 84 (15 March 1906): 326.

92. White, *Bullets and Bolos*, 312.

93. "War Department Gets News—Taft Says Wood Had No Idea of What Was Going to Happen," *New York Times*, 10 March 1906.

94. "No Moro Survived," *Washington Post*, 11 March 1906; and "Congratulated by Roosevelt," *The Sun*, 11 March 1906. Roosevelt's praise was also cited in the *New York Times*, the *Chicago Tribune*, and other newspapers.

95. Storey, *The Moro Massacre*.

96. Ibid.

97. "No Moro Survived," *Washington Post*, 11 March 1906.

98. "Our Exploit in the Philippines," *Washington Post*, 13 March 1906.

99. Ibid.

100. "Moros a Turbulent Race: Corbin Thinks They Will Make Trouble Till They Become Extinct," *New York Times*, 10 March 1906.

101. "Women in Battle: Stood Beside Moros and Fought Like Demons," *Washington Post*, 14 March 1906.

102. Ibid. For full report, see Leonard Wood Papers. See also Leonard Wood's diary on the same date and U.S. Congress, "Wood to the Military Secretary," 12 March 1906, in William H. Taft, Secretary of War, *Attack by United States Troops on Mount Dajo*, Senate Document 289, 59th Cong., 1st sess.

103. McCallum, *Leonard Wood*, 230.

104. Emphasis mine. U.S. Congress, *Attack by United States Troops on Mount Dajo*, 20 March 1906, 9. In addition to contributing to the official report, Scott's defense also made its way into the popular press. See "Cablegram Says Reports Are False," *Los Angeles Herald*, 21 March 1906.

105. Thompson, "Governors of the Moro Province," 94.

106. "William H. Taft to Theodore Roosevelt," in U.S. Congress, *Attack by United States Troops on Mount Dajo*, 13 March 1906, 4.

107. Ibid., 89.

108. "Henry Ide to Sec. of War," in U.S. Congress, *Attack by United States Troops on Mount Dajo*, 20 March 1906, 9.

109. "Women in Battle: Stood Beside Moros and Fought Like Demons," *Washington Post*, 14 March 1906.

110. "Wood's Battle Called Murder in Congress," *New York Times*, 16 March 1906.

111. Quoted in the *New York Times*, 16 March 1906. The poem was based on an earlier poem, "The Charge of the Light Brigade," written by Alfred, Lord Tennyson on the charge made by British troops in the Crimean War.

112. See "No Wanton Slaughter of Moros, Wood Cables," *New York Times*, 15 March 1906.

113. "The Moros," *Christian Observer*, 18 April 1906.

114. "Pen Points," *Los Angeles Times*, 11 March 1906.

115. *Life* 47, 29 March 1906, 380.

116. Ibid.

117. See *New York Times* and *Chicago Daily Tribune*, 15 March 1906.

118. Fulton, *Honor the Flag*, 51. Fulton also cites the original article published in 1907 that explains this story.

119. Ibid.

120. Hochschild, *King Leopold's Ghost*, 233.

121. "Elihu Root to Hon. Edwin Denby, 20 February 1906," in *FRUS*, 1906, 88–89.

122. Bullard, *Personalities and Reminiscences of the War*, 12.

123. Ibid.

124. For the most comprehensive study on the subject, see Clymer, *Protestant Missionaries in the Philippines*.

125. "The Missionary Problem in the Philippines," *Independent* 50 (16 June 1898): 12.

126. Barrett, "The Cuba of the Far East," *North American Review* 164 (February 1897): 176.

127. Ibid.

128. Ibid.

129. "8 December 1902," Diary, Leonard Wood Papers.

130. "Alliance Missions Mr. McKee," *Christian and Missionary Alliance*, 31 October 1903, 303.

131. Ibid.

132. McKee, "Shall the Moros Be Evangelized; Or Shall an Unwise American Treaty Succeed in Shutting Out the Gospel?" *Christian and Missionary Alliance*, 2 August 1902; and "News and Notes from Wide Fields," *Christian and Missionary Alliance*, 31 October 1903.

133. Bateman, "Taming the Moro," *Journal of the Military Service Institution of the United States* 34 (March–April 1904): 261.

134. Bateman, "Moro Priests," *The Standard*, 8–9.

135. Ibid., 9.

136. Ibid., 9. For other articles on the Moros by Bateman, see "The Rise of a Sultan: A Tale of Moro Reconstruction," *Overland Monthly and Out West*, March 1905.

137. See, "Theodore Roosevelt to Charles Brent," 10 November 1904; and "Charles Brent to William Taft," 6 February 1904, Charles Brent Papers.

138. Thompson, "Governors of the Moro Province," 265.

139. "11 May 1904," Charles Brent Papers.

140. "Leonard Wood to Charles Brent," 12 December 1904, Leonard Wood Papers.

141. "11 May 1904," Diary, Charles Brent Paper. Emphasis in original text.

142. "Theodore Roosevelt to Charles Brent," 10 November 1904, container 6, Charles Brent Papers.

143. "Religious Conditions in the Philippine Islands," Charles Brent Papers.

144. Ibid., pamphlet, no date, but included in correspondence around late 1904.

145. "Charles Brent to George W. Pepper," 30 March 1905, Charles Brent Papers.

146. Ibid.

147. "A Bigger Slice of Civilization for the Filipinos," *Florida Times Union*, December 1913. Clipping originally found in "Missionary Work of Protestants," box 170, n. 1158, RG59, National Archives.

148. "Pershing to Brent," 9 August 1913, Gen. Correspondence, Pershing Papers, cited in Thompson, "Governors of the Moro Province," 265.

149. Ibid., 267.

150. Strong, "A Door into the Mohammedan World," no date, but given information on the pamphlet, the author estimates it was published in 1914. Yale Library.

151. Clymer, *Protestant Missionaries in the Philippines*, 142–45.

152. Cited in Hagedorn, *Leonard Wood*, vol. 2, 49–50.

153. For a description of the Moro Exchange, see *Third Annual Report of the Governor of the Moro Province*, 1905, 4.

154. Philippines Commission, *Manuscript Report of the Philippines Commission*, 1904, part 2, vol. 2, 38, National Archives.

155. Ibid.

156. Gowing, *Mandate in Moroland*, 222.

157. Ibid.

158. *Mindanao Herald*, 29 April 1905.

159. Ibid.

160. *Mindanao Herald*, 8 April 1905.

161. "Editorial Comment," *Mindanao Herald*, 10 June 1905.

162. *Mindanao Herald*, 22 July 1905.

163. Ibid.

164. "The Moro Territory," *Mindanao Herald*, 20 July 1905.

165. "Give Us Territorial Form of Government," *Mindanao Herald*, 12 August 1905.

166. "Governor-General of Philippines, Frank McIntyre to Secretary of War, William Taft, 23 August 1906," folder "Moros: Suggestions for Government," RG 350, National Archives.

167. "The Gospel of Work," *Mindanao Herald*, 11 November 1905.

168. Ibid.

169. Philippines Commission, *Manuscript Report of the Philippines Commission*, "Annual Report of the Moro Province," vol. 2, 2, National Archives.

170. Ibid. See also Kramer, *Blood of Government*, 341.

171. Philippines Commission, *Manuscript Report of the Philippines Commission*, "Annual Report of the Moro Province," vol. 2, 2, National Archives.

172. Ibid., 6.

173. According to Gowing, this idea never became an official American policy. In 1926, Senator Robert L. Bacon raised the issue again, but it never succeeded. See Gowing, *Mandate in Moroland*, 250, footnote 111. See also Kramer, *Blood of Government*, 342–46. For a more detailed analysis of Filipino Christian elites' opposition to such propositions, see Suzuki, "Upholding Filipino Nationhood."

174. Cited in Gowing, *Mandate in Moroland*, 252.

175. Philippines Commission, *Manuscript Report of the Philippines Commission*, 1910, 39, National Archives.

176. Gowing, *Mandate in Moroland*, 218.

177. Philippines Commission, *Manuscript Report of the Philippines Commission*, 1910, vol. 1, 141–42.

178. Ibid.

179. Cited in Thompson, "Governors of the Moro Province," 199–200.

180. Ibid., 207.

181. Gowing, *Mandate in Moroland*, 242. See also Pershing, "Annual Report of the Moro Province," 1912; and Philippines Commission, *Manuscript Report of the Philippines Commission*, 1912, vol. 1, 500.

182. Lacely, *Pershing*, 72–73.

183. Arnold, *The Moro War*, 269.

184. Gowing, *Mandate in Moroland*, 258.

185. Ibid., 241.

186. Cited in Thompson, "Governors of the Moro Province," 266.

187. Gowing, *Mandate in Moroland*, 275.

188. Philippines Commission, *Manuscript Report of the Philippines Commission*, Carpenter, "Annual Report of the Governor of the Department of Mindanao and Sulu," 17–18, National Archives.

189. Ibid., 119.

190. Ibid.

191. Ibid., 146.

192. Ibid.

193. Ibid.

194. See Public Land Act No. 926 and No. 2874 in Rodil, *The Minoritization of the Indigenous Communities of Mindanao and the Sulu Archipelago*, 30.

195. Thompson, "Governor of the Moro Province," 275–76.

196. Kramer, *Blood of Government*, 372.

197. Ibid., 6.

CHAPTER 7

1. Bloxham, *The Great Game of Genocide*, 16. See also Hovanissian, "The Armenian Question in the Ottoman Empire," in *Armenian People from Ancient to Modern Times*, vol. 2, ed. R. Hovanissian, 218.

2. For more on this, see Hovanissian, "The Armenian Question in the Ottoman Empire," in *Armenian People from Ancient to Modern Times*, vol. 2, ed. R. Hovanissian, 218–21.

3. Kirakossian further argues that Russia had changed its policies "shifting its expansion efforts from the Near East to the Far East. . . . The Russian policies coincided with the Turkish interests, and, despite the noisy rhetoric from Russia, the Czarist government chose not to intervene on behalf of the Armenian Christians, although Russia, in concert with the European powers, had demanded from the Porte reforms to guarantee the safety of the Christian population of the Ottoman Empire." See Kirakossian, *The Armenian Massacres, 1894–1896*, 24–25. See also Suny, *Looking toward Ararat*, chapter 5. *Union Signal*, 12 December 1895. Cited in Tyrell, *America in the World: Moral Reform and the Networks of American Empire*, 104. See also Suny, *Looking toward Ararat*, chapter 5.

4. See Walker, *Armenia*, 169–70.

5. Bloxham, *The Great Game of Genocide*, 54.

6. "Theodore Roosevelt to William Sewell, 4 May 1898," Morison, *Letters of Theodore Roosevelt*, vol. 2, 823.

7. "Theodore Roosevelt to Cecil Spring-Rice, 11 April 1899," in Brands, *The Selected Letters of Theodore Roosevelt*, 230.

8. "Theodore Roosevelt to George Otto Trevelyan, 13 May 1905," in Morison, *The Letters of Theodore Roosevelt*, vol. 4, 1175; Holmes, *Theodore Roosevelt and World Order*, 73.

9. "Pittsburgh Dispatch," *Public Opinion*, 16 July 1896.

10. See Pérez, *Cuba in the American Imagination*, 62–65.

11. Despite his loss to Cleveland, Harrison's aggressive foreign policy influenced future president Theodore Roosevelt.

12. Strong's understanding of the "Anglo-Saxon race" was different from that of some of his contemporaries. Strong believed that American Anglo-Saxons had been strengthened by the racial mixture with other white races. Although Americans needed to be careful in allowing too many white immigrants to arrive, these new white "sub-races" would add value to the American racial stock, resulting in an improved "new Anglo-Saxon race of the New World." Strong's ideas about race were informed by the father of social Darwinism, Herbert Spencer, whom he quoted at length to support his own ideas. See Strong, *Our Country*, 172.

13. See Hutchison, *Errand to the World*, 91–124.

14. Dwight, *Christianity in Turkey*, 14.

15. Bloxham, *The Great Game of Genocide*, 47–48.

16. Ibid., 42.

17. Astourian, "The Silence of the Land: Agrarian Relations, Ethnicity, and Power," 64.

18. For a broader study of this, see Klein, *The Margins of Empire*; and Suny, *Looking toward Ararat*, 103–5.

19. Hovanissian, "The Armenian Question in the Ottoman Empire, 1876–1914," in *Armenian People from Ancient to Modern Times*, vol. 2, ed. R. Hovanissian, 210.

20. Cited in Vratzian, *Armenia and the Armenian Question*, 12.

21. Theriault, "Rethinking Dehumanization in Genocide," 36.

22. Grabill, *Protestant Diplomacy*, 41.

23. See Moranian, "The American Missionaries and the Armenian Question," 79–83.

24. See Carpenter, "A Worldly Errand," 247. See also Wilson, "In the Name of God, Civilization and Humanity," 31.

25. Carpenter, "A Worldly Errand," 247.

26. "Clark to Barnes, 16 February 1897," vol. 123, 249–50, American Board of Commissioners for Foreign Missions Archives. This information is confirmed in Straus, *Under Four Administrations*, 45.

27. Straus, *Under Four Administrations*, 67.

28. For more on this, see Gordon, *American Relations with Turkey*, 235.

29. Ibid., 327.

30. DeNovo, *American Interests and Policies in the Middle East*, 24.

31. See Washburn, *Fifty Years in Constantinople*, 211–12; and Straus, *Under Four Administrations*, 87–92.

32. For more on Armenian migration to the United States, see Mirak, *Torn between Two Lands*, 35–59.

33. Ibid., 210.

34. "Mevroyeni Bey to Secretary of State Gresham, 26 October 1893," in *FRUS*, 1894, 712.

35. Extracts of *Haik* translated by Turkish officials included with "Bey to Gresham, 26 October 1893," in *FRUS*, 1894. Although these are Turkish translations, it is clear from scholarly work that Armenian nationalists did organize in the United States. See Mirak, *Torn between Two Lands*, 43.

36. Grover Cleveland, First Annual Message, December 1893.

37. See Wilson, "In the Name of God, Civilization, and Humanity," 31–32.

38. Salt, *Imperialism, Evangelism and the Ottoman Armenians, 1878-1896*, 63–67, 111–12.

39. Nalbandian, *The Armenian Revolutionary Movement of the Nineteenth Century*, 120. See also Daniel, *American Philanthropy in the Near East*, 116.

40. "Judson Smith, Foreign Secretary ABCFM to Secretary of State W. Q. Gresham," 30 March 1893, ABC 1.1, vol. 159, 559, American Board of Commissioners for Foreign Missions Archives.

41. Ibid.

42. "The Missionary Crisis in Turkey," *Outlook*, 7 October 1893.

43. Blackwell, "The Armenian Question," *Outlook*, 28 October 1893, 779.

44. Ibid.

45. Hamlin, "A Dangerous Movement among the Armenians," republished in *FRUS*, 1895, Part 2, 1415. See also Washburn, *Fifty Years in Constantinople*, 201. This interpretation was also made by Bliss in *Turkey and the Armenian Atrocities*, 337–38. In many ways, Hamlin and Washburn's attitude corresponds to the "provocation thesis" that many historians have used to explain the Armenian Massacres. Scholars of Armenian and Ottoman history disagree about this so-called provocation thesis, the idea that Armenians provoked Ottomans to react to solicit European sympathy and support. Scholars sympathetic to the Armenian cause argue that the provocation thesis makes Armenians "the agents of their own destruction," blaming them for Ottoman violence. See Melson, "A Theoretical Inquiry into the Armenian Massacres of 1894–1896," 485–86. Other scholars argue that blaming the Ottomans vilifies Islam and ignores the thousands of Muslims massacred by Christians during the nationalist uprisings. See McCarthy, *Death and Exile*; and Salt, *Imperialism, Evangelism and the Ottoman Armenians, 1878–1896*. Lewy offers a convincing argument that reactions against the provocation thesis have been "needlessly defensive. To take note of the tactical designs of the Armenian revolutionaries does not mean to ignore or excuse the malevolent intentions and deeds of the Turkish authorities. Given the weakness of the Armenian side, the need for great power intervention (especially on the part of Britain and Russia) was always an essential part of Armenian thinking." See Lewy, *The Armenian Massacres in Ottoman Turkey*, 17.

46. Hamlin, "A Dangerous Movement among the Armenians," *Congregationalist*, 28 December 1893. For a more detailed analysis of revolutionary accounts, see Lewy, *The Armenian Massacres in Ottoman Turkey*, 16–19.

47. Hamlin, "The Armenians," *Boston Journal*, 14 April 1894.

48. "Turkey and Armenia," *Washington Post*, 19 December 1893, 12.

49. Ibid.

50. "The Armenian Question," *New York Times*, 11 March 1894.

51. Ibid.

52. "Under Turkish Rule: A Hard Master to Serve Is the 'Sick Man of the East,'" *Washington Post*, 11 March 1894.

53. Strong, *Our Country*, 210.

54. Wilson, "In the Name of God and Humanity," 33.

55. Ibid. See also Reed, "American Foreign Policy, the Politics of Missions and Josiah Strong, 1890–1900," 236.

56. "Barton to Gresham, 30 November 1894," ABC 1.1, vol. 171, 249–53, American Board of Commissioners for Foreign Missions Archives.

57. Ibid.

58. "James Barton to Reverend T. Melbourne May, 20 December 1894," ABC 1.1, vol. 171, 556, American Board of Commissioners for Foreign Missions Archives.

59. "James Barton to E. W. Blatchford, 22 April 1895," ABC 1.1, vol. 175, 129, American Board of Commissioners for Foreign Missions Archives. See also Reed, "American Foreign Policy," 235.

60. Kirakossian, *The Armenian Massacres*, 24–25.

61. "Porte Should Be Brought to Book," *Chicago Tribune*, 18 November 1894.

62. Taken from "Armenian Horrors," an article summarizing the reactions of the press in the East to the massacres published in the *Chicago Tribune*, 20 November 1894.

63. Ibid.

64. Ibid.

65. "The Pitiable Dilemma in Armenia," *Watchman*, 14 March 1895.

66. "The Armenian Massacre," *New York Herald*, 22 November 1894.

67. *Union Signal*, 12 December 1895, Cited in Tyrell, *America in the World*, 104.

68. See "The Negro's Natural Home: Senator Morgan's Plan for Sending the Race Back to Africa," *Greensboro Patriot*, 23 January 1895.

69. "Shed Tears of Woe: Armenians Weep over the Tale of a People's Wrong," *Chicago Tribune*, 19 November 1894.

70. "News from Abroad: Thousands of Armenians Slaughtered by Cruel Kurds," *Chicago Tribune*, 17 November 1894. The same letter was reprinted in numerous newspapers connected through the Associated Press.

71. "Turkey Coming to Terms," *New York Tribune*, 18 October 1895.

72. Greene, *Armenian Massacres*.

73. "Barton to Blatchford, 22 April 1895," ABC 1.1, vol. 175, 127–28, American Board of Commissioners for Foreign Missions Archives.

74. Ibid.

75. Stein, "Armenia Must Have a European Governor," *Arena*, May, 1895, 368.

76. Willard, "Introduction," in *Turkey and the Armenian Atrocities*, by E. Bliss, 1–2.

77. Ibid., 2–3.

78. Ibid.

79. Ibid., 4.

80. Havemeyer, "Reprint of Communication Addressed to President Cleveland in 1896, on the Subject of Armenian Complications." Pamphlet, 10 January 1896, Missionary Research Library Collection. Also reprinted in "The United States and Armenia," *New York Times*, 12 January 1896.

81. Ibid.

82. "Friends of Armenia," *Boston Daily Advertiser*, 22 March 1894.

83. Richard and Elliott, *Julia Ward Howe*, vol. 2, 190.

84. For examples of the appeal republished throughout the United States, see "An Appeal for Armenians," *State*, 25 November 1895; "Give Aid to Armenia," *Daily Inter Ocean* (Chicago), 18 November 1895; and "Turks Must Stop," *Boston Herald*, 25 November 1895.

85. "Give Aid to Armenia," *Daily Inter Ocean* (Chicago), 18 November 1895.

86. Cited in Gordon, *The Beautiful Life of Frances E. Willard*. For more on this, see also Tyrell, *Reforming the World*, 104–6.

87. Cited in C. Barton, *The Red Cross in Peace and War*, 283.

88. "Pro-Armenian Alliance," *Boston Herald*, 9 May 1896. See also C. Barton, *The Red Cross*, 283–84; and C. Barton, "The Red Cross in Turkey," *Methodist Magazine and Review*, April 1897, 301.

89. C. Barton, *The Red Cross*, 283.

90. Curti, *American Philanthropy Abroad*, 127.

91. Cited in Jones, *The American Red Cross from Clara Barton to the New Deal*, 77.

92. Pryor, *Clara Barton*, 294.

93. "Josiah Strong to Dr. C. H. Daniels, 18 September 1894," ABC 10, vol. 92, letter 455, American Board of Commissioners for Foreign Missions Archives.

94. See "An Appeal for Armenians," *New York Herald*, 21 November 1894.

95. All quotes in this paragraph taken from "The Armenian Agitation," *New York Times*, 21 December 1894. Original petition also included in Greene, *Armenian Massacres or the Sword of Mohammed*, Appendix B, 176–78.

96. See, for example, "The Armenian Agitation," *New York Times*, 21 December 1894. "Fears for Its Friends: Evangelical Alliance Appeals to Secretary Gresham," *Washington Post*, 21 December 1894.

97. *FRUS*, 1894, 715–16.

98. Ibid., 716.

99. See Gordon, *American Relations with Turkey*, 24–25.

100. For more on how the strategic interests of the Great Powers shaped their reactions to the Sasun massacre, see Kirkossian, *The Armenian Massacres*, 24–27.

101. See Cook, "The United States and the Armenian Question, 1894–1924," 49–50.

102. "The United States and Armenia," *New York Times*, 10 December 1894. The article republished excerpts from the article in the Paris newspaper *Le Temps*.

103. "America and Armenia," *New York Tribune*, 13 December 1894.

104. Resolutions republished in "Evangelists against Turkey: Resolutions Calling upon the United States to Aid the Armenians," *New York Times*, 1 October 1895.

105. See *FRUS*, 1895, 1256–65; and Erhan, "Ottoman Official Attitudes towards American Missionaries," 332–33.

106. Cleveland, "Third Annual Message of the President," 2 December 1895, in Richardson, *A Compilation of the Messages and Papers of the Presidents, 1789-1897*, vol. 9, 637. See also Grabill, *Protestant Diplomacy*, 41; and *FRUS*, 1893, 633. British and American diplomatic pressure eventually resulted in the release and exculpation of the prisoners. After repeated demands, the sultan indemnified the American Board for the destroyed buildings in 1895.

107. See May, *Imperial Democracy*, 59–60.

108. Cited in Dennis, *Adventures in American Diplomacy*, 450.

109. For coverage of this meeting, see "To Save the Armenians, a Mass Meeting to Be Held: Clergymen and Others Express Condemnation without Reserve—Turkey Must Be Taught a Lesson," *New York Times*, 17 November 1895; and "Call of 2,000 for Armenia," *New York Times*, 9 December 1895. Other mass meetings were held at Columbia College (presided by Seth Low). See "Sympathy for the Armenians," *New York Times*, 20 November 1895.

110. For coverage of meeting see "In Behalf of Armenians: Big Mass Meeting Protests Against Turkish Outrages," *New York Times*, 22 November 1895.

111. "Mr. Hoar for Vigorous Action," *New York Times*, 25 November 1895.

112. "Josiah Strong to Reverend C. H. Daniels, 5 May 1896," ABC 10, vol. 92, letter 461, American Board of Commissioners for Foreign Missions Archives.

113. Ibid., letter 462.

114. Cleveland, "Fourth Annual Message (second term)," 7 December 1896. Reprinted in *New York Times*, 8 December 1896.

115. U.S. Congress, *Congressional Record*, 54th Cong., 1st sess., 1896, vol. 28, pr. 1, 108, 959–65. For public coverage of the speech, see "Call Talks about Armenia," *New York Times*, 13 December 1895.

116. Curti, *American Philanthropy Abroad*, 130–33.

117. Cited in Tyrell, *America in the World*, 110.

118. Cited in Mirak, *Torn between Two Lands*, 220–21.

119. Ibid., 220.

120. U.S. Congress, *Congressional Record*, 54th Cong., 1896, vol. 28, 22 January 1896, 854.

121. Ibid., 960.

122. Ibid.

123. Ibid. Cullom's entire speech was reprinted that same year in *Story of Turkey and Armenia*, ed. Rev. James Wilson Pierce.

124. Peters and Wooley, "Republican Party Platform of 1896." http://www .presidency.ucsb.edu/ws/?pid=29629?

125. See Angell, *The Reminiscences of James B. Angell*, 188.

126. For a detailed description of Strong's lobbying efforts, see "Strong to Smith, 19 February 1897," ABC 10, vol. 92, letter 474, American Board of Commissioners for Foreign Missions Archives.

127. See Reed, "American Foreign Policy," 230–31.

128. "Strong to Barton, 13 December 1897," ABC 10, vol. 92, letter 495, American Board of Commissioners for Foreign Missions Archives.

129. Reed, "American Foreign Policy," 240; and Bryson, *Tars, Turks and Tankers*, 37–38.

130. For this analysis, see Reed, "American Foreign Policy," 242. Citation from Josiah Strong, *Expansion: Under New World Conditions*, 248.

CHAPTER 8

1. Wilson, "Address to a Joint Session of Congress Calling for a Declaration of War," in *Woodrow Wilson*, ed. M. R. Dinunzio, 402.

2. Stivers, "Woodrow Wilson and the Arab World," 118.

3. Renda, *Taking Haiti*, 113.

4. For more on Wilson's attitudes toward Philippines independence, see Kramer, *Blood of Government*, 344–45, 360–61.

5. For an excellent analysis of how Wilson's beliefs about self-determination overlapped with his views of African Americans, American imperial rule in the Philippines, and Haiti, see Manela, *The Wilsonian Moment*, 25–33. On Wilson's views of the Middle East, see Stivers, "Woodrow Wilson and the Arab World"; and Christison, *Perceptions of Palestine*, 26–44.

6. Cited in Renda, *Taking Haiti*, 110.

7. Ibid., 114.

8. "Dr. Wilson Hits at Excluded Faiths," 230. Reprinted in *New York Herald*, 20 November 1905.

9. Wilson, *The Bible and Progress*.

10. Lansing, *The Peace Negotiations*, 97.

11. For more on this, see Moranian, "The Armenian Genocide and American Missionary Relief Efforts," 203.

12. In contrast to Brandeis and Wise, Morgenthau opposed Zionism.

13. Balakian, "From Ezra Pound to Theodore Roosevelt," 253.

14. Ellis, "Annex A: The Covenant," 493.

15. For more on this, see Ariel, "An Unexpected Alliance," 77–80; and Merkley, *The Politics of Christian Zionism, 1891–1948*, 87–92.

16. See Christison, *Perceptions of Palestine*, 43.

17. For the influence of European thought on the Young Turks, see Hanioğlu, "The Ideological Roots of the Young Turks," 7–32.

18. For the historiographical debate on causality and the Armenian Genocide, see Suny "Writing Genocide," in *A Question of Genocide*, ed. R. G. Suny, F. M. Göçek, and N. M. Naimark, 15–54.

19. Ibid., 34, footnote 14. Although Suny argues that Ottoman rulers "were primarily state imperialists, empire preservers, rather than fully committed ethno-nationalists."

20. Scholars disagree on the degree that ethic nationalism contributed to the Armenian Genocide. Donald Bloxham argues that this process helped shape the decision to massacre the Armenians. See Bloxham, *The Great Game of Genocide*, 59. Suny, in contrast, sees ethnic nationalism as a process not fully developed until later. As he argues, "While they did not have a nation-building project in mind, by carrying out the deportations and genocidal murders, the Young Turks engaged in a national-building process, the founding crime on which the empire's successor, the present republic of Turkey, would be built." See Suny, "Writing Genocide," 34–35.

21. For the Ottoman manifestation of such ideas in 1913, see Aksakal, *The Ottoman Road to War in 1914*, 25–29.

22. Bloxham, *The Great Game of Genocide*, 59.

23. C. Walker, *Armenia*, 243.

24. See Hanioğlu, *Young Turks in Opposition*, 8–13.

25. J. Barton, "Turkey and the Constitution," *Outlook*, 19 September 1908.

26. Williams, in an address at Brooklyn, New York, 15 October 1908. Cited in J. Barton, *Daybreak in Turkey*, 274.

27. Bloxham, *The Great Game of Genocide*, 60–61. See also Akçam, *From Empire to Republic*, 93.

28. U.S. Congress, *Congressional Record*, 61st Cong., 1st sess., vol. 44, pt. 2, 29 April 1909, 1615.

29. "Hope for the Armenians," *Evening News* (San Jose, Calif.), 7 May 1909.

30. "The Peril of Being a Christian in the East," *Duluth News-Tribune* (Duluth, Minn.), 23 May 1909.

31. "Constantinople, June, 1909," *North American Review* 90 (July 1909): 132.

32. Scholars differ on the exact numbers, but most recognize the numbers in the hundreds of thousands. See Despot, *The Balkan Wars in the Eyes of the Warring Parties*, 191.

33. Aksakal, *The Ottoman Road to War in 1914*, 23.

34. See Bloxham, *The Great Game of Genocide*, 62–63.

35. Ibid., 63.

36. For the wider influence of the Balkan Wars on Ottoman society and its political rulers, see Aksakal, *The Ottoman Road to War in 1914*, chapters 1–2.

37. For a broad overview of these negotiations, see Hovanissian, *Armenian People from Ancient to Modern Times*, vol. 2, 233–38.

38. Oren, *Power, Faith and Fantasy*, 333.

39. Cited in "Epilogue," in Morgenthau, *Ambassador Morgenthau's Story*, 282–83.

40. Ibid.

41. Morgenthau, *All in a Life-Time*, 175.

42. Ibid., 176.

43. Ibid., 203–4.

44. Ibid., 206.

45. Ibid., 217.

46. Ibid., 233.

47. Morgenthau, *Ambassador Morgenthau's Story*, 35.

48. See Payaslian, *United States Policy toward the Armenian Question and the Armenian Genocide*, 45.

49. Morgenthau, *Ambassador Morgenthau's Story*, 38.

50. See "Statement by the Turkish Ambassador (Rustem) as Published in the Washington, D.C. 'Evening Star,'" 8 September 1914, Lansing Papers, vol. 1, 70.

51. Ibid.

52. Ibid.

53. Ibid.

54. Ibid.

55. Link, *Wilson*, 68.

56. All quotes in this paragraph from Lansing Papers, "The Turkish Ambassador (Rustem) to the Secretary of State," 12 September 1914, vol. 1, 68.

57. Ibid., "The Counselor for the Department of State (Lansing) to the Secretary of State," 14 September 1914, 71.

58. Cited in W. G. Jordan, *Black Newspapers and America's War for Democracy*, 46.

59. Ibid., 42.

60. Ibid., 46.

61. "Untitled memorandum," box 1, folder 19, series 1, 35–36. Cornellius van H. Engert Papers. Morgenthau prepared a memorandum for President Woodrow Wilson in 1917 after returning from an aborted secret mission to negotiation a separate peace with the Young Turks.

62. For the larger historical background to the call to jihad, see Aksakal, "'Holy War Made in Germany?'"

63. For the larger story behind this call for global jihad, see McMeekin, *The Berlin-Baghdad Express*.

64. Morgenthau, "Untitled memorandum," 40–41. Document found in box 1, folder 19, "Morgenthau, Henry (1917?)," series 1, Cornellius van H. Engert Papers.

65. Ibid., 44.

66. Ibid., 45.

67. Egypt was a case in point. For an analysis of Egyptian demands for independence from British rule, see Manela, *The Wilsonian Moment*, chapter 3.

68. "Holy War Hangs Fire Because Islam Won't Stand for German Christians as Allies—Would Kill Unbelievers," *Daily Illinois State Journal*, 5 February 1915.

69. Merrill, "Hitch in Holy War Due to Racial Hate," *Grand Rapids Press*, 4 February 1915.

70. Ibid.

71. "A Missionary Opening," *Omaha World Herald* (Omaha, Nebr.), 28 September 1913.

72. For a more detailed analysis, see Bloxham, *The Great Game of Genocide*, 66–68.

73. C. Walker, *Armenia*, 245.

74. Bloxham, *The Great Game of Genocide*, 68. For greater analysis of the Armenian Genocide, see also Kevorkian, *The Armenian Genocide*.

75. C. Walker, *Armenia*, 246.

76. Ibid., 247.

77. Scholars disagree on estimates of the number of Armenians killed during the genocide. For the range of numbers offered by various scholars see Mann, *The Dark Side of Democracy*, 140 (footnote 1).

78. C. Walker, *Armenia*, 203, 249.

79. Morgenthau, *Diary*, 28 April 1915, 1 May 1915, and 6 May 1915, Henry Morgenthau Papers.

80. Ibid., 10 May 1915.

81. Ibid., 19 June 1915.

82. Ibid., 10 July 1915.

83. Oren, *Power, Faith and Fantasy*, 336.

84. Morgenthau, *Diary*, 18 July 1915.

85. Ibid., 8 August 1915.

86. Ibid.

87. All citations in this paragraph taken from Morgenthau, *Ambassador Morgenthau's Story*, 195.

88. For an analysis of Morgenthau's views of the Turkish "race" see Suny, "Writing Genocide: The Fate of the Ottoman Armenians," 17–18.

89. Morgenthau, *Ambassador Morgenthau's Story*, 196.

90. See Morgenthau, *Diary*, 23 August 1915; and "Defense Committee Corners Supplies," *New York Times*, 14 September 1915.

91. Of course, the Sheik-ul-Islam was not alone in condemning these massacres. Many Ottoman Muslims sought to protect Armenians during the massacres as well. See Hovanissian, *Armenian People from Ancient to Modern Times*, vol. 2, 173–207.

92. Ibid., 70.

93. For Morgenthau's proposal to support Armenian refugees, see Oren, *Power, Faith and Fantasy*, 336, 655 (endnote 12).

94. Grabill, *Protestant Diplomacy*, 70.

95. Cited in Payaslian, *United States Policy toward the Armenian Question and the Armenian Genocide*, 104.

96. Grabill, *Protestant Diplomacy*, 74.

97. Ibid.

98. J. Barton, *Story of Near East Relief*, 38–40. See also Moranian, "The Armenian Genocide and American Missionary Relief Efforts," 211.

99. Peterson, "Starving Armenians," 53 and J. Barton, *Story of Near East Relief*, 14.

100. J. Barton, *Story of the Near East Relief*, 14.

101. Ibid., 389.

102. *Armenia*, "A Christian Nation," reprinted in Robert George Koolakian, *Struggle for Justice*, 31.

103. Cited in Peterson, "Starving Armenians," 58–59.

104. Grabill, *Protestant Diplomacy*, 76. See also Morananian, "The Armenian Genocide and American Missionary Relief Efforts," 210.

105. *The Independent*, 18 October 1915. Cited in Grabill, *Protestant Diplomacy*, 77.

106. Mirak, *Torn between Two Lands*, 290.

107. For more on how Christianity helped Armenians assert their whiteness both legally and culturally, see Spickard, *Almost All Aliens*, 259; and Tehranian, *Whitewashed*, 53–54.

108. Cited in Bayoumi, "Racing Religion," 282.

109. See Coulson, "Persecutory Agency in Racial Prerequisite Cases."

110. Moranian, "The Armenian Genocide and American Missionary Relief Efforts," 194.

111. Malkasian, "The Disintegration of the Armenian Cause in the United States, 1918–1927," 350.

112. Hoover, *The Memoirs of Herbert Hoover*, vols. v–vi, 385.

113. Oren, *Power, Faith and Fantasy*, 336.

114. Grabill, *Protestant Diplomacy*, 78.

115. Moranian, "The Armenian Genocide and American Missionary Relief Efforts," 206.

116. See Payaslian, *United States Policy toward the Armenian Question and the Armenian Genocide*, chapter 8.

117. Grabill, *Protestant Diplomacy*, 120.

118. Ibid., 101.

119. "Barton to Bryce, January 25, 1917," ABC 3.2. Cited in Grabil, *Protestant Diplomacy*, 100.

120. "Barton to William W. Rockwell, 11 March 1916," ABC 3.2. Cited in Carpenter, "James L. Barton's American Mission to the Near East," 313.

121. *Congressional Record*, 65th Cong., 2nd sess., vol. LVI, part 1, 7 December 1917, 64–65.

122. For full letter, see "Roosevelt to Dodge," 11 May 1918, *Letters of Theodore Roosevelt*, vol. 8, 1316–18.

123. See Moranian, "The American Missionaries and the Armenian Question," 247–49.

124. Lansing to Stone, 6 December 1917, *FRUS*, 1917, supplement 2, vol. 1, *The World War*, 448–50.

125. Cleveland H. Dodge Foundation, "Dodge to Wilson, 2 December 1917." Draft of letter in Cleveland Dodge personal papers (private collection), New York City. Access to papers provided by Bill Rueckert, president.

126. Cited in Grabill, *Protestant Diplomacy*, 93.

127. Ibid., 250.

128. Ibid., 253.

129. Ibid., 121.

130. Stivers, "Woodrow Wilson and the Arab World," 108.

131. Osborne, "The Near East and World Peace," 1–7. Cited in Koolakian, *Struggle for Justice*, 26.

132. See DeNovo, *American Interests and Policies in the Middle East*, 107; and Brecher, "Revising Ambassador Morgenthau's Turkish Peace Mission of 1917."

133. Cited in Peterson, *"Starving Armenians,"* 68.

134. Morgenthau spoke to Wilson instead of writing him, but he included a draft of the letter in his book. See Morgenthau, *All in a Life-Time*, 274.

135. Hall, *The Reconstruction of Turkey*, 183–84. See also Grabill, *Protestant Diplomacy*, 125.

136. J. Barton, "The Turkish Government: Analysis of Its Inherent Evil," 1. Undated, but surely delivered in 1918. Found in box 38, records of U.S. American Commission to Negotiate Peace Papers.

137. See Barton's letter outlining reasons for and against a U.S. declaration of war against Bulgaria and Turkey accompanying Barton, "Suggested Possible Forms of Government for the Areas Covered by the Ottoman Empire at the Outbreak of the War, Exclusive of Arabia but Inclusive of the Trans-Caucasus May 21," 3, box 38, records of U.S. American Commission to Negotiate Peace Papers.

138. J. Barton, "The Turkish Government: Analysis of Its Inherent Evil," 1.

139. Ibid., 6.

140. Ibid.

141. Ibid.

142. Ibid., 7.

143. Ibid., 9. At the time, the label Syrian was most often attributed to Syrian Christians, whereas Syrian Muslims were generally referred to as Arabs.

144. Ibid.

145. J. Barton, "The War and the Mohammedan World," 43, ibid.

146. Cited in Carpenter, "James L. Barton's American Mission to the Near East," 321.

147. See Fig. 26, "The first official roster of the American Committee for the Independence of Armenia (ACIA), December 1918," in Koolakian, *Struggle for Justice*, 97.

148. All quotes in this paragraph and the next taken from "Confidential Memorandum by James L. Barton, Cleveland H. Dodge and W. W. Peet to Secretary of State

Lansing, 23 December 1918," box 1, folder 38: "Reports, Oct.–Dec. 1918," Cornellius van H. Engert Papers.

149. Ibid., 3.

150. Ibid.

151. Ibid., 6. Emphasis mine.

152. Ibid. Emphasis mine.

153. Ibid., 6–7.

154. Ibid., 8.

155. Ibid.

156. See Grabill, *Protestant Diplomacy*, 156–57.

157. Anghie, *Imperialism, Sovereignty, and the Making of International Law*, 119–20. Former Ottoman territories were not the only ones to face mandate supervision. Other areas that fell under similar mandate treaties included territories in Africa and the Pacific. For an excellent analysis of how General Smuts sought to maintain British imperial rule and his influence on Wilson, see Mazower, *No Enchanted Palace*, chapter 1. See also Curry, "Woodrow Wilson, Jan Smuts, and the Versailles Settlement," 968–86.

158. Potter, "Origin of the System of Mandates under the League of Nations," 580–81; Mitchell, *Carbon Democracy*, 83–84.

159. Grabill, *Protestant Diplomacy*, 159.

160. Ibid.

161. Cited in Andrew and Kanya-Forstner, *The Climax of French Imperial Expansion, 1914–1924*, 182. On the scholarly debate over the extent to which the mandate system represented a continuation of European imperial rule, see Sluglett, "An Improvement on Colonialism? The 'A' Mandates and Their Legacy in the Middle East."

162. Makdisi, *Faith Misplaced*, 132.

163. Cited in Makdisi, *Faith Misplaced*, 133.

164. Cited in the published accounts of Stephen Bonsal who attended the peace negotiations, *Suitors and Suppliants*, 41.

165. Ibid., 190.

166. "Zionist Organization, Statement Regarding Palestine Presented to the Paris Peace Conference (With Proposed Map of Zionist Borders), 3 February 1919," in *Palestine: Documents*, ed. Abdul Hadi, 47. See also Makdisi, *Faith Misplaced*, 135.

167. See "President Gives Hope to Zionism," *New York Times*, 3 March 1919.

168. *FRUS, The Paris Peace Conference, 1919*, 3: 1016.

169. Makdisi, *Faith Misplaced*, 137.

170. *FRUS, The Paris Peace Conference, 1919*, 3: 1016. See also Makdisi, *Faith Misplaced*, 137.

171. Gidney, *A Mandate for Armenia*, 146–47.

172. Grabill, *Protestant Diplomacy*, 162.

173. Fromkin, *A Peace to End All Peace*, 398.

174. Bonsal, *Suitors and Suppliants*, 193.

175. Selden, "Counting upon Us to Save Armenia," *New York Times*, 14 August 1919. Emphasis mine.

176. Harbord, *Conditions in the Near East*, 25.

177. Ibid., 27.

178. Ibid., 27–28.

179. Lobingier, "America's Precedent for Mandates," *American Review of Reviews* 61 (January 1920): 60–62. Lobingier had published the same article in the *Christian Century* (36 [30 October 1919]: 11–13) three months earlier, assuring a wide audience for his views.

180. American Committee for the Independence of Armenia, *America as a Mandatory for Armenia*.

181. Ibid., 3–10.

182. Ibid.

183. Ibid. For Gerard's editorial in the *New York Times*, see "Why America Should Accept Mandate for Armenia," *New York Times*, 6 July 1919.

184. Cardashian, "Should America Accept a Mandate for Armenia?" in American Committee for the Independence of Armenia, *America as a Mandatory for Armenia*, 36.

185. Arnold, *The Moro War*, 268.

186. "General Wood's Stirring Appeal for Armenia," *Philadelphia Inquirer*, 4 March 1921. Wood's plea was published throughout the American press.

187. Morgenthau, "Mandates or War: World Peace Held to Be Menaced Unless the United States Assumes Control of the Sultan's Former Dominions," *New York Times*, 9 November 1919. Emphasis mine.

188. "The Covenant and Its Interpretations," *Macon Telegraph* (Macon, Ga.), 9 April 1920.

189. Gidney, *A Mandate for Armenia*, 163.

190. Üngör, "'Turkey for the Turks,'" 290.

191. Ibid., 300.

192. "American Mandate Urged," *New York Times*, 3 May 1920.

193. Howard, *The King-Crane Commission*, 225.

194. King-Crane Commission Report. Cited in Makdisi, *Faith Misplaced*, 143.

195. Crane's discussion of this can be found in "Memorandum by Charles R. Crane about the Syrian Mandate," 24 November 1925, Oberlin College Digital Archives.

196. "Report by George Montgomery on Syria," 1 August 1919, 2, Oberlin Digital Archives. For a larger analysis of Montgomery and Yale's viewpoints, see Howard, *The King-Crane Commission*, 196.

197. "Report by George Montgomery on Syria," 1 August 1919, 2, Oberlin Digital Archives.

198. Ibid., 9.

199. Ibid., 3, 10.

200. "Report by William Yale," 1 August 1919, 35–36, Oberlin Digital Archives. See also Howard, *The King-Crane Commission*, 205.

201. "Report by William Yale," 1 August 1919, 35–36, Oberlin Digital Archives.

202. See MacDonald, "'A Land without a People for a People without a Land.'" See also Christison, *Perceptions of Palestine*, 39.

203. "Crane and King's Long-Hid Report on the Near East," *New York Times*, 3 December 1922.

204. Ibid.

205. See Satia, "The Defense of Inhumanity," 16. Satia further argues that British Orientalist ideas about Arabs pushed them to adopt such brutal tactics. See also Tanaka, "British 'Humane Bombing' in Iraq during the Interwar Era," in Young and Tanaka, *Bombing Civilians*, 8–29.

206. Cited in Jeffrey, *The British Army and the Crisis of Empire, 1918–22*, 161.

207. "Memorandum by William Yale Concerning Oil," 1 May 1919, 1, Oberlin Digital Archives.

208. Makdisi, *Faith Misplaced*, 144.

209. Link, ed., *Papers of Woodrow Wilson*, vol. 68, 469.

CONCLUSION

1. Roosevelt, "Expansion and Peace," *Independent*, 21 December 1899.

2. Ibid., 402.

3. Ibid., 403.

4. Ibid.

5. See Manela, *The Wilsonian Moment*.

6. See von Eschen, *Race against Empire*.

7. Curtis, *Verdict on Vichy*, 167–68.

8. See Wyman, *The Abandonment of the Jews: America and the Holocaust, 1941–1945*.

9. Cited in Nelson, "Sins of Commission, Sins of Omission," 318.

10. Snyder, *Bloodlands*, 160. See also Barder, *Empire Within*, chapter 2.

11. Ibid.

12. For more on this project see Ehraim, "The Mindanao Plan."

13. For scholarship on this topic, see Esber, *Under the Cover of War*; Pappé, *The Ethnic Cleansing of Palestine*; and Morris, *The Birth of the Palestinian Refugee Problem, 1947–1949*.

14. Macdonald, "Anno Domini 1919," 2.

15. Zwemer, "Supernational because Supernatural," 4.

16. Ibid., 6.

17. Riggs, "The Waning Crescent in Turkey," 75.

18. French, "Wanted—A More Vigorous Policy," 247.

19. Ibid.

20. Ibid., 250.

21. Ibid., 251.

22. Vol. IX of the *Moslem World*, which included all of the issues published in 1919, had four different entries on Filipino Muslims.

23. McCutchen "Islam in the Philippine Islands," 238.

24. Ibid., 239.

25. Stoddard, *The Rising Tide of Color against White World Supremacy*, 86.

26. Ibid., 102.

27. Ibid., 77.

28. Ibid., 102–3.

29. Quezon, "First State of the Nation Address."

30. Ibid.

31. Philippine Council, Institute of Pacific Relations, "The Development of Mindanao and the Future of the Non-Christians."

32. Ibid., 18.

33. Ibid., 8.

34. Henry R. Luce, "The American Century," *Life* (magazine), 17 February 1941.

35. Herzstein, *Henry R. Luce, Time, and the American Crusade in Asia*, 1.

36. For an excellent analysis of this phenomenon, see Pietz, "The 'Post-colonialism' of Cold War Discourse," 55–75.

37. Such analysis has garnered considerable attention from historians in the last few decades. A few notable examples include Mamdani, *Good Muslim, Bad Muslim: America, the Cold War, and the Roots of Terror*; Said, *Covering Islam: How the Media and the Experts Determine How We See the Rest of the World*; and McAlister, *Epic Encounters: Culture, Media, and U.S. Interests in the Middle East since 1945*.

38. See Fukuyama, "The End of History?"

39. Huntington, *The Clash of Civilizations*, 42.

40. Huntington, "The Clash of Civilizations," 25; Henderson and Tucker, "Clear and Present Strangers: The Clash of Civilizations and International Conflict," 321–22.

41. See Said, "A Clash of Ignorance"; and Sen, "What Clash of Civilizations?" For a wider study, see Sajjad, "A 'Non Western' Reading of the 'Clash of Civilizations' Theory."

42. See Toynbee's massive twelve-volume work, *A Study of History*.

43. Huntington, *The Clash of Civilizations*, 42. The publication of Huntington's article in *Foreign Affairs*, a journal that targets policymakers and scholars of international relations, further assured his influence in the policymaking world.

44. In the concluding chapter of *The Clash of Civilizations*, Huntington predicted that a major global war between civilizations would "most likely involve Muslims on one side and non-Muslims on the other." See Huntington, 312. For an analysis of the cultural constructions of the Global War on Terror and its links to Huntington's theories, see Bonney, *False Prophets: The "Clash of Civilizations" and the Global War on Terror*.

45. Bush, "Remarks by the President upon Arrival: The South Lawn."

46. See Daalder and Lindsay, "American Empire, Not 'If' but 'What Kind,'" *New York Times*, 10 May 2003.

47. Sanger, "Bush Cites Philippines as Model in Rebuilding Iraq."

48. Patai, *The Arab Mind*, originally published in 1973. For journalistic critiques, see Hersch, "The Grey Zone: Annals of National Security"; and Whitaker, "Its Best Use Is a Doorstop." For scholarly analysis of this phenomenon, see Hasso, "'Culture Knowledge' and the Violence of Imperialism: Revisiting *The Arab Mind*," 24–40; Little, *American Orientalism: The United States and the Middle East since 1945*, 335.

49. Hersch, "The Grey Zone."

50. Other scholars who were highly influential with American policymakers included Bernard Lewis, the primary target of Edward Said's examples of contempo-

rary Orientalist writings on the Middle East and the scholar who originally coined the term "Clash of Civilizations." As Lewis stated after the beginning of the war, "The Islamic world is now at the beginning of the 15th century," and they needed a new "Ataturk" to bring it to modernity. Cited in Little, *American Orientalism*, 335–36.

51. Filkins, "A Region Inflamed," *New York Times*, 7 December 2003.

52. See Abinales and Quimpo, eds., *The U.S. and the War on Terror in the Philippines*.

53. For more on this phenomenon, see Peek, *Behind the Backlash*, and Kundnani, *The Muslims Are Coming!*

Bibliography

ARCHIVAL SOURCES

Boston, Mass. Massachusetts Historical Society
    John A. Andrews Papers
    Edward Everett Papers
Carlisle, Pa. U.S. Military History Institute
    John P. Finley Papers
Cambridge, Mass. Houghton Library, Harvard University
    American Board of Commissioners for Foreign Missions Archives
College Park, Md. National Archives and Records Administration
    Bureau of Insular Affairs, Record Group 350
    General Records of the Department of State, Record Group 59
        Despatches from Foreign Ministers in Spain, Vol. 89
        Despatches from United States Ministers to Turkey, 1818–1906
        Despatches from U.S. Consuls at Tangier, Vol. 27
        Diplomatic Instructions, Barbary Powers
        Papers Relating to Foreigners in Morocco, 1877–1880. Vols. 425–26
    Records of the Foreign Service Posts of the Department of State, Record
        Group 84
Dickinson, N.D. Dickinson State University, Theodore Roosevelt Center
    Roosevelt Digital Library. www.theodorerooseveltcenter.org
Eugene Schuyler Papers, Private Collection. Held with Patricia Herhily
Kew, Richmond, U.K. National Archives
    Public Records Office
Laramie, Wy. American Heritage Center, University of Wyoming
    Lewis Einstein Papers
New York, N.Y. American Jewish Historical Society
    Board of Delegates of American Israelites Records
    Myer S. Isaacs Papers
New York, N.Y. Burke Library, Union Theological Seminar
    Missionary Research Library Collection
    Near East Relief Committee Records
New York, N.Y. Cleveland H. Dodge Foundation
    Cleveland H. Dodge Papers, private collection
Oberlin, Ohio. Oberlin College Digital Archives
    King-Crane Commission Digital Collection
Paris, France. Alliance Israélite Universelle
    Archives of the Alliance Israélite Universelle

Princeton, N.J. Princeton University, Rare Books and Special Collections,
      Manuscripts Collections, Firestone Memorial Library
   Armenia Collection
Theodore Roosevelt Digital Library, Manuscript Division
   Theodore Roosevelt Papers. *http://www.theodorerooseveltcenter.org/Research
      /Digital-Library/Record.aspx?libID=039931*
Washington, D.C. Georgetown University Special Collections, Lauinger
      Library
   Cornellius van H. Engert Papers
Washington, D.C. Library of Congress
   Adams Family Papers
   American Board of Commissioners for Foreign Missions Archives
   Charles Brent Papers
   Clara Barton Papers
   Elihu Root Papers
   Eugene Schuyler Papers
   Frank Carpenter Papers
   Henry Morgenthau Papers
   Henry White Papers
   Hugh Lenox Scott Papers
   John J. Pershing Papers
   Joseph H. Choate Papers
   Leonard Wood Papers
   Robert Lee Bullard Papers
   Theodore Roosevelt Papers
   U.S. American Commission to Negotiate Peace Papers
   Woodrow Wilson Papers

NEWSPAPERS AND PERIODICALS

Albany Argus
American Annual Register
American Hebrew
American Jewish Year Book
American Ladies' Magazine
American Mercury
American Repertory
American Review of Reviews
Arena
Atlanta Constitution
*Baltimore Patriot and Mercantile
   Advisor*
Boston Daily Advertiser
Boston Herald

Boston Journal
Boston Recorder
Boston Traveller
Brooklyn Daily Eagle Almanac
*Bulletin de l'Alliance Israélite
   Universelle*
Century Illustrated Magazine
Chicago Daily News
Chicago Times
Chicago Tribune
Christian Advocate
Christian and Missionary Alliance
Christian Observer
Christian Repository

Christian Union
City Gazette and Daily Advertiser
   (Charleston, S.C.)
Congregationalist
Congressional Globe
Constitution
Cretan
Crisis
Daily Illinois State Journal
Daily Inter Ocean (Chicago)
Daily Telegraph
Duluth News-Tribune (Duluth, Minn.)
Eclectic Magazine
Essex Register
Florida Times Union
Foreign Affairs
Forum
General Repository and Review
Geographical Review
Grand Rapids Press (Grand Rapids,
   Mich.)
Harper's Weekly
Independent
Israelite
Jewish Chronicle and Hebrew Observer
Jewish Messenger
Jewish Social Studies
Journal of the Military Service
   Institution of the United States
Lend a Hand
Life
London Daily News
London Times
Los Angeles Herald
Los Angeles Times
Macon Telegraph (Macon, Ga.)
Massachusetts Spy
Messenger
Mindanao Herald
Missionary Herald
Moslem World
Nation
National Gazette
National Interest

New England Magazine
New England Quarterly
New Hampshire Observer
Newport Mercury
New Republic
New York American
New-York Commercial Advertiser
New York Evangelist
New York Evening Post
New York Herald
New York Observer and Chronicle
New York Observer and Herald
New York Recorder
New York Times
New York Tribune
Newport Mercury
Niles' Register
North American Review
Omaha World Herald
Outlook
Overland Monthly and Out West
   Magazine
Pacific Historical Review
Pennsylvania Magazine of History
   and Biography
Pennsylvania Washington Reporter
Philadelphia Democratic Press
Philadelphia Inquirer
Philadelphia Record
Philadelphia Weekly Democrat
Phylon
Providence Evening Press
Providence Gazette
Public Opinion
Reading Times (Reading, Pa.)
Richmond Enquirer
Salem Gazette
San Francisco Call
San Jose Evening News (San Jose, Calif.)
Slate
Slavonic and East European Review
Social Text
Stanford Electronic Humanities Review
State (Columbia, S.C.)

St. Louis Enquirer
Sun
Turkish Yearbook
Union Signal
Vermont Gazette

Washington Post
Washington Times
William and Mary Quarterly
World's Work
Zion's Herald

GOVERNMENT PUBLICATIONS

Austin, Oscar P. *Colonial Administration, 1800–1900: Methods of Government and Development Adopted by the Principal Colonizing Nations in Their Control of Tropical and Other Colonies and Dependencies.* Washington, D.C.: Government Printing Office, 1901.

Gillard, David, ed. *British Documents on Foreign Affairs—Reports and Papers from the Foreign Office Confidential Print, Part I, From the Mid-Nineteenth Century to the First World War,* Series B, *The Near and Middle East.* Vol. 2. Frederick, Md.: University Publications of America, 1984.

Hansard Parliamentary Debates. 17 July 1876. http://hansard.millbanksystems .com/.

Johnson, Andrew. *Message from the President of the United States, in Answer to a Resolution of the House of the 17th ultimo, Relative to the Revolution in Candia.* Washington, D.C.: Government Printing Office, 1867.

Monroe, James. *Message from the President of the United States Transmitting a Report of the Secretary of State, Upon the Subject of the Present Condition and Future Prospects of the Greeks.* Washington, D.C.: [s.n.], 1823.

Philippines Commission. *Report of the Philippines Commission to the Secretary of War.* Washington, D.C.: Government Printing Office, 1900–16.

U.S. Bureau of the Census, *Census of the Philippine Islands: 1903.* 4 vols. Washington, D.C.: Government Printing Office, 1905.

U.S. Congress. *Congressional Record.* Vol. 28. 54th Cong., 22 January 1896.

———. Cleveland, Grover. "Fourth Annual Message (second term)." Vol. 28, pr. 1, 108. 54th Cong., 1st sess., 7 December 1896.

———. *Proceedings and Debates of the United States Congress.* Vol. 117, part 6, 8802.

———. Senate, 55th Cong., 3rd sess., Tuesday, 7 February 1899.

———. Vol. 3. 56th Congress, 1st sess.

———. Vol. 44. 61st Cong., 1st sess.

U.S. Congress. House of Representatives. *Annals of Congress of the United States,* 17th Cong., 2nd sess., 24 December 1822. Washington, D.C.: Government Printing Office, 1823.

———. *Journal of the House of Representatives of the United States, Being the First Session of the Eighteenth Congress Begun and Held at the City of Washington.* Washington, D.C.: Government Printing Office, 1823.

———. *Memorial of a Committee Appointed at a Public Meeting of the Citizens of New York to Take into Consideration the Situation of the Greeks.* 18th Cong., 1st sess. Washington, D.C.: Gale and Seaton, 1823.

U.S. Congress. Senate Committee on the Philippines. *Affairs in the Philippine Islands: Hearings before the Committee of the Philippines of the United States Senate.* 57th Cong., 1st sess., 1902. S. Doc. 331.

———. *Attack by United States Troops on Mount Dajo,* 59th Cong., 1st sess., 1906. Doc. 289.

———. *Report of John C. Bates on Agreement with Sultan of Sulu.* 56th Cong., 1st sess., 1 February 1900. Doc. 136.

U.S. Department of State. *Papers Relating to the Foreign Relations of the United States.* Washington, D.C.: Government Printing Office, 1861–1922.

———. *Papers Relating to the Foreign Relations of the United States: The Lansing Papers, 1914–1920.* 2 vols. Washington, D.C.: Government Printing Office, 1939–40.

U.S. Department of State, Bureau of Statistics. "Missionaries in Morocco." *Consular Reports,* Serial Vol. 3419, sess. 52, Serial Set 3419 H. doc. 132.

War Department. *Annual Reports of the War Department.* Washington, D.C.: Government Printing Office, 1903.

PUBLISHED PRIMARY SOURCES

Adams, Charles Francis, ed. *Memoirs of John Quincy Adams: Comprising Portions of His Diary from 1795 to 1848.* 12 vols. Philadelphia: J. B. Lippincott, 1874–77.

Adams, John Quincy. *Writings of John Quincy Adams.* 7 vols. New York: MacMillan, 1913–17.

Ade, George. *The Sultan of Sulu.* New York: M. Witmark, 1902.

Adler, Cyrus. "Jews in American Diplomatic Correspondence." *Publications of the American Jewish Historical Society* 15 (1906).

American Board of Commissioners for Foreign Missions. *Sixty-Ninth Annual Report of the American Board of Commissioners for Foreign Missions.* Boston: Riverside Press, 1879.

American Committee for the Independence of Armenia. *America as a Mandatory for Armenia.* New York: American Committee for the Independence of Armenia, 1919.

Anderson, Rufus. *History of the Missions of the American Board of Commissioners for Foreign Missions to the Oriental Churches.* Vol. 1. Boston: Congregational Publishing Company, 1872.

———. *To Advance the Gospel: Selections from the Writings of Rufus Anderson.* Edited by R. Pierce Beaver. Grand Rapids, Mich.: W.B. Eerdmans, 1967.

Angell, James. *The Reminiscences of James B. Angell.* New York: Longmans, Green, 1912.

Armenian Assembly of America. *The Armenian Genocide and America's Outcry: A Compilation of U.S. Documents, 1890–1923.* Washington, D.C.: Armenian Assembly of America, 1985.

Atkinson, Tacy. *"The German, the Turk and the Devil Made a Triple Alliance": Harpoot Diaries, 1908–1917.* Princeton, N.J.: Gomidas Institute, 2000.

Austin, Oscar P. *Uncle Sam's Children: A Story of Life in the Philippines.* New York: D. Appleton, 1906.

Badeau, John S. *Bread from Stones: Fifty Years of Technical Assistance*. Englewood Cliffs, N.J.: Prentice Hall, 1966.

Baring, Evelyn. *Modern Egypt*. Vol. 2. New York: Macmillan, 1908.

Barnwell, R. Grant. *The Russo-Turkish War*. Toledo, Ohio: I. D. Cartright, 1878.

Barrett, John. "The Cuba of the Far East." *North American Review* 164 (February 1897): 176.

Barrows, David P. *The Bureau of Non-Christian Tribes for the Philippine Islands: Circular of Information Instructions for Volunteer Field Workers*. Manila: n.p., 1901.

Barrows, John Henry. *The World's Parliament of Religions: An Illustrated and Popular Story of the World's First Parliament of Religions, Held in Chicago in Connection with the Columbian Exposition of 1893*. Vol. 1. Chicago: Parliament Publishing Company, 1893.

Barton, Clara. *The Red Cross*. Washington D.C.: American National Red Cross, 1898.

———. *The Red Cross in Peace and War*. Washington, D.C.: American Historical Press, 1906.

———. "The Red Cross in Turkey." *Methodist Magazine and Review*, April 1897, 301.

Barton, James. *Daybreak in Turkey*. Boston: Pilgrim Press, 1908.

———. *Story of Near East Relief, 1915–1930: An Interpretation*. New York: Macmillan, 1930.

———. "Turkey and the Constitution." *Outlook*, 19 September 1908.

———. "The War and the Mohammedan World." *Biblical Review* (January 1919): 43.

Bateman, Cephus. "Moro Priests." *The Standard* 52 (25 March 1905): 8–9.

———. "The Rise of a Sultan: A Tale of Moro Reconstruction." *Overland Monthly and Out West Magazine*, March 1905.

———. "Taming the Moro." *Journal of the Military Service Institution of the United States* 34 (March–April 1904): 261.

Bell, Edward Price. *Future of the Philippines: Interviews with Manuel Quezon*. *Chicago:* Chicago Daily News, 1925.

Benjamin, Anna Northend. "Our Mohammedan Wards in Sulu." *Outlook*, 18 November 1899.

Bishop, Joseph. *Theodore Roosevelt and His Time Shown in His Own Letters*. Vol. 1. New York: Charles Scribner's Sons, 1920.

Blackwell, Alice Stone. "The Armenian Question." *Outlook*, 28 October 1893, 779.

Blau, Joseph, and Salo Baron, eds. *The Jews of the United States, 1790–1840: A Documentary History. Vol. 3*. New York: Columbia University Press, 1963.

Bliss, Edwin. *Turkey and the Armenian Atrocities: A Reign of Terror*. Philadelphia: Hubbard, 1896.

Bliss, Reverend Howard. "A Letter from Mount Lebanon." *New York Observer and Chronicle*, 20 December 1860.

Blount, James H. *The American Occupation of the Philippines, 1898–1912*. New York: G. P. Putnam's Sons, 1912.

Board of Delegates of American Israelites. *Constitution and By-Laws of the Board of Delegates of American Israelites*. New York: Joseph Davis Printer, 1860.

Bonsal, Stephen. "The Moros and Their Country." *Outlook*, 10 May 1902.

———. *Suitors and Suppliants: The Little Nations at Versailles*. New York: Prentice Hall, 1946.

Brands, H. W., ed. *The Selected Letters of Theodore Roosevelt*. Lanham, Md.: Rowman and Littlefield, 2007.

Brookes, Francis. *Barbarian Cruelty: Being a True History of the Distressed Condition of the Christian Capitol under the Tyranny of Mully Ishmael Emperor of Morocco, and King of Fez and Macqueness in Barbary: In which Is Likewise Given a Particular Account of His Late Wars with the Algerines*. Boston: Reprinted for S. Phillips, 1700.

Bryan, William Jennings. *Bryan on Imperialism*. New York: Arno Press, 1970. Reprint. Originally published under title: *Imperialism: Extracts from Speeches, Interviews and Articles*. S.l.: s.n., 1900.

———. *The Memoirs of William Jennings Bryan, by Himself and His Wife Mary Baird Bryan*. New York: Haskell House, 1971.

Bryce, James, and Arnold Toynbee. *The Treatment of Armenians in the Ottoman Empire, 1915–1916: Documents Presented to Viscount Grey of Fallodon by Viscount Bryce: Uncensored Edition*. Edited by Ara Sarafian. Princeton, N.J.: Gomidas Institute, 2005.

Bullard, Robert Lee. *Personalities and Reminiscences of the War*. New York: Doubleday, Page, 1925.

Bush, George W. "Remarks by the President upon Arrival: The South Lawn," 16 September 2001. http://georgewbush-whitehouse.archives.gov/news/releases /2001/09/20010916-2.html. Accessed 1 June 2013.

"The Call to the Philippines." *Christian and Missionary Alliance* 21 (3 August 1898): 98–100.

Cardashian, Vahan. "Should America Accept a Mandate for Armenia?" In American Committee for the Independence of Armenia, *America as a Mandatory for Armenia: Notes and Opinions*, edited by Armenian Committee for the Independence of Armenia, 25–36. New York: Armenian Committee for the Independence of Armenia, 1919.

Carey, Mathew. *Mathew Carey Autobiography*. Brooklyn, N.Y.: E. L. Schwaab, 1942.

Carpenter, Frank G. "A Moro Cannibal of the Philippine Islands." *Atlanta Constitution*, 19 March 1899.

Clay, Henry. *The Works of Henry Clay, Comprising His Life, Correspondence and Speeches*. Edited by Calvin Colton. 10 vols. New York: J. P. Putnam's Sons, 1904.

Cleveland, Grover. "The Annual Message of the President," 2 December 1895.

Cloman, Sydney, and N. N. Freeman. *Myself and a Few Moros*. Garden City, N.Y.: Doubleday, Page, 1923.

———. *A Soldier in the Philippines*. New York: F. Tennyson Neely, 1901.

Columbus, Christopher. *The Voyage of Christopher Columbus: Columbus's Own Journal of Discovery*. Newly restored and translated by John Cummins. New York: St. Martin's, 1992.

Comstock, John Lee. *History of the Greek Revolution: Compiled from Official Documents of the Greek Government*. New York: William W. Reed, 1828.

Cullom, Shelby M. *Fifty Years of Public Service: Personal Recollections of Shelby M. Cullom, Senior United States Senator from Illinois*. Chicago: A. C. McClurg, 1911.

Cushing, Caleb. "Opinion of the Attorney General Concerning the Judicial Powers of the Commissioner or Minister and of Consuls of the United States in Turkey and China." In *Treaties between the United States of America and China, Japan, Lewchew and Siam, Acts of Congress, and the Attorney-General's Opinion, with the Decrees and Regulations Issued for the Guidance of the U.S. Consular Courts in China*. 95:112. Hong Kong: n.p., 1862.

d'Anghiera, Pietry Martire. "The decades of the newe worlde or West India (1555)." In *Race in Early Modern England: A Documentary Companion*, edited by Ania Loomba and Jonathan Burton, 83–86. New York: Palgrave Macmillan, 2007.

Davis, Mrs. Jefferson. "The White Man's Problem." *Arena*, January–June 1900, 2.

Dwight, Harrison O. *Christianity in Turkey: A Narrative of the Protestant Reformation in the Armenian Church*. London: J. Nisbet, 1854.

Dwight, Henry Otis. "Our Mohammedan Wards." *Forum*, March 1900, 15–31.

———. *Turkish Life in War Time*. New York: Scribner's, 1881.

Dwight, William T. D. D. *Selected Discourses of Sereno Edwards Dwight with a Memoir of his Life*. Boston: Crocker & Brewster, 1851.

Einstein, Lewis. *A Diplomat Looks Back*. New Haven, Conn.: Yale University Press, 1968.

———. *Inside Constantinople: A Diplomatist's Diary during the Dardanelles Expedition, April–September, 1915*. London: John Murray, 1917.

———. *Roosevelt: His Mind in Action*. Boston: Houghton Mifflin, 1930.

Everett, Edward. "The Ethics of Aristotle to Nicomachus." *North American Review* 36 (October 1823).

———. *Mount Vernon Papers*. New York: D. Appleton, 1860.

———[published anonymously]. "On the Literature and Language of Modern Greece." *General Repository and Review* 3 (January 1813): 80–94.

———. *Orations and Speeches on Various Occasions*. Vol. 1. 2nd ed. Boston: C. Little & J. Brown, 1850.

———. *Speech of the Hon. Edward Everett, in the House of Representative of the United States, March 9, 1826*. Boston: Dutton & Wentworth, 1826.

Everett, Marshall. *The Book of the Fair*. Philadelphia: P. W. Zeigler, 1904.

Field, Henry Martin. *From the Lakes of Killarney to the Golden Horn*. New York: Scribner, Armstrong, 1877.

Filkins, Dexter. "A Region Inflamed: Strategy; Tough New Tactics by U.S. Tighten Grip on Iraq Towns." *New York Times*, 7 December 2003.

Forbes, Archibald. "The Russians, the Turks, and the Bulgarians." *Eclectic Magazine*, January 1878.

Forbes, William Cameron. *The Philippine Islands*. New York: Houghton Mifflin, 1928.

French, Arthur J. P. "Wanted—a More Vigorous Policy." *Moslem World* 9 (July 1919): 247.

Gallatin, Albert. *The Writings of Albert Gallatin*. Vol. 2. Edited by Henry Adams. New York: Antiquarian Press, 1960.

Gates, Caleb F. *Not to Me Only*. Princeton, N.J.: Princeton University Press, 1940.

Gerard, James W. *My First Eighty-Three Years in America: The Memoirs of James W. Gerard*. Garden City, N.Y.: Doubleday, 1951.

———. "Why America Should Accept Mandate for Armenia." *New York Times*, 6 July 1919.

Gladstone, William E. *Bulgarian Horrors and the Question of the East*. New York: Lovell, Adam, Wesson, 1876.

———. *The Slavonic Provinces of the Ottoman Empire: Address at Hawarden*. London: Eastern Question Association, 1877.

Godkin, Edwin L. "Article VI: The Eastern Question." *North American Review* 124 (January 1877): 108.

Gordon, Anna Adams. *The Beautiful Life of Frances E. Willard: A Memorial Volume*. Chicago: Women's Temperance Publishing Association, 1898.

Greene, Frederick Davis. *Armenian Massacres or the Sword of Mohammed, Containing a Complete and Thrilling Account of the Terrible Atrocities and Wholesale Murders Committed in Armenia by Mohammedan Fanatics, Including a Full Account of the Turkish People, Their History, Government, Manners, Customs and Strange Religious Belief*. New York: Oxford, 1896.

Hadi, Mahdi F. Abdul, ed. *Palestine: Documents*. Jerusalem: Passia, 1997.

Haines, F .E. H. *Jonas King: Missionary to Syria and Greece*. New York: American Tract Society, 1879.

Hall, William H. *The Reconstruction of Turkey: A Series of Reports Compiled for the American Committee for Armenian and Syrian Relief*. New York: n.p., 1918.

Hamlin, Cyrus. "The Armenians." *Boston Journal*, 14 April 1894.

———. "Cross and Crescent." *Christian Union*, 4 October 1876.

———. "A Dangerous Movement among the Armenians." *Congregationalist*, 28 December 1893.

———. *My Life and Times*. Boston: Congregational Sunday-School and Publishing Society, 1893.

Harbord, James G. *America in the World War*. New York: Houghton Mifflin, 1933.

———. *Conditions in the Near East: Report of the American Military Mission to Armenia*. Washington, D.C.: Government Printing Office, 1920.

———. *Leaves from a War Diary*. New York: Dodd, Mead, 1925.

Harrison, Francis Burton. *Origins of the Philippine Republic: Extracts from the Diaries and Records of Francis Burton Harrison*. Ithaca, N.Y.: Southeast Asia Program, Dept. of Asian Studies, Cornell University, 1974.

Hayes, Rutherford B. "State of the Union" (speech), 6 December 1880.

Holly, James Theodore, W. H. Council, J. Montgomery McGovern, W. S. McCurley, and Booker T. Washington. "The Race Problem: A Symposium." *Arena* 21 (April 1899): 422–46.

Hoover, Herbert. *The Memoirs of Herbert Hoover: Years of Adventure, 1874–1920*. New York: MacMillan, 1951.

Horton, George. *The Blight of Asia: An Account of the Systematic Extermination of Christian Populations by Mohammedans and of the Culpability of Certain Great*

Powers: With a True Story of the Burning of Smyrna. Indianapolis: Bobbs-Merrill, 1926.

House, Edward Mandell, and Charles Seymour. *What Really Happened at Paris: The Story of the Peace Conference, 1918–1919.* New York: Scribner's Sons, 1921.

Howe, Samuel Gridley. *An Historical Sketch of the Greek Revolution.* New York: White Gallaher & White, 1828.

Jessup, Henry. *The Mohammedan Missionary Problem.* Philadelphia: Presbyterian Board of Publication, 1879.

Johnson, J. Augustus. *The Life of a Citizen at Home and in Foreign Service.* New York: Vail Ballou Press, 1915.

Kennan, George. "The Philippines: Present Conditions and Possible Courses of Action—III." *Outlook* 67 (9 March 1901): 576–84.

Kohler, Max J., and Simon Wolf. *Jewish Disabilities in the Balkan States.* New York: American Jewish Committee, 1916.

Lansing, Robert. *The Peace Negotiations: A Personal Narrative.* Boston: Houghton Mifflin, 1921.

———. *War Memoirs of Robert Lansing, Secretary of State.* New York: Bobbs-Merrill, 1935.

Laubach, Frank. *The People of the Philippines.* New York: George Doran, 1925.

Leland, John. "Extracts from Number Two: A Little Sermon, Sixteen Minutes Long." In *The Writings of the Late Elder John Leland, Including Some Events in His Life, Written by Himself, with Additional Sketches, & c,* edited by L. F. Greene, 408–12. New York: G. W. Wood, 1845.

Lincoln, Abraham. *The Language of Liberty: The Political Speeches and Writings of Abraham Lincoln.* Edited by Joseph R. Fournier. Washington D.C.: Regnery, 2003.

Link, Arthur S., ed. *The Papers of Woodrow Wilson.* 69 vols. Princeton, N.J.: Princeton University Press, 1966.

Lobingier, Charles Sumner. "America's Precedent for Mandates." *American Review of Reviews* 61 (January 1920): 60–62.

Loewe, L., ed. *Diaries of Sir Moses and Lady Montefiore.* Vol. 2. London: Griffith Farran, Okeden & Walsh, 1890.

Macdonald, D. B. "Anno Domini 1919." *Moslem World* 9 (January 1919): 2.

MacGahan, Januarius. *The Turkish Atrocities in Bulgaria, Letters of the Special Commissioner of the "Daily News," J. A. MacGahan Asq., with an Introduction and Mr. Schuyler's Preliminary Report.* London: Bradbury, Agnew, 1876.

Mahan, Albert Thayer. *The Problem of Asia and Its Effect upon International Policies.* Boston: Little Brown, 1900.

Malcolm, M. Vartan. *The Armenians in America.* Boston: Pilgrim Press, 1919.

Martens, G. F. de. *Summary of the Law of Nations, Founded on the Treaties and Customs of the Modern Nations of Europe: With a List of the Principal Treaties.* Translated by William Cobbett. Philadelphia: Thomas Bradford, 1795.

Mather, Cotton. *Decennium Luctuosum: An History of Remarkable Occurrences, in the Long War, Which New-England Hath Had with the Indian Salvages, from the*

Year, 1688 to the Year 1698. Boston: Printed by B. Green and J. Allen for Samuel
  Phillips, 1699.
Mayer, H. Y. "Some Impressions of the Passing Show." *New York Times*,
  18 March 1906.
McCutchen, Robert T. "Islam in the Philippine Islands." *Moslem World* 9
  (July 1919): 239.
McGee, W. J. "The Trend of Human Progress." *American Anthropologist*, July
  1899.
McKee, John. "News and Notes from Wide Fields." *Christian and Missionary
  Alliance*, 31 October 1903.
——. "Shall the Moros Be Evangelized; Or Shall an Unwise American Treaty
  Succeed in Shutting Out the Gospel?" *Christian and Missionary Alliance*,
  2 August 1902.
Merrill, M. R. "Hitch in Holy War Due to Racial Hate." *Grand Rapids Press*,
  4 February 1915.
Miller, Donald E., and Lorna Touryan Miller. *Survivors: An Oral History of the
  Armenian Genocide*. Berkeley: University of California Press, 1993.
Miller, Oliver C. "The Semi-civilized Tribes of the Philippine Islands." *Annals of the
  American Academy of Political and Social Science*, July 1901, 43–63.
Monroe, James. "1822 State of the Union Address," 22 December 1822.
——. *The Writings of James Monroe, Including a Collection of His Public and
  Private Papers and Correspondence Now for the First Time Printed*. Edited by
  Stanislaus Murray Hamilton. 7 vols. New York: G. P. Putnam's Sons, 1898–1903.
Montesquieu, Charles de Secondat. *The Spirit of Laws*. Vol. 2. Translated by Thomas
  Nugent. New York: Cosimo, 2011.
Morgan, John T. "What Shall We Do with the Conquered Islands?" *North American
  Review* 166 (June 1898): 645.
Morgenthau, Henry. *All in a Life-Time*. Garden City, N.Y.: Doubleday, Page, 1922.
——. *Ambassador Morgenthau's Story*. Detroit: Wayne State University Press,
  2003.
——. "Mandates or War: World Peace Held to Be Menaced unless the United States
  Assumes Control of the Sultan's Former Dominions." *New York Times*,
  9 November 1919.
——. *United States Diplomacy on the Bosphorus: The Diaries of Henry
  Morgenthau, 1913–1916*. Princeton, N.J.: Gomidas Institute, 2004
Morison, Elting E., et al. *The Letters of Theodore Roosevelt*. 8 vols. Cambridge,
  Mass.: Harvard University Press, 1951–54.
Murray, Robert Hammond. "The Pacifier of the Philippines: The Strenuous and
  Adventurous Career of General Leonard Wood." *World's Work*, October 1908,
  10774.
New York Committee. *Address of the Committee of the Greek Fund, of the City of
  New York, to their Fellow-citizens Throughout the United States*. New York:
  J. W. Palmer, 1823.
Noah, Mordecai. *The Selected Writings of Mordecai Noah*. Edited by Michael
  Schuldiner and Daniel J. Kleinfeld. Westport, Conn.: Greenwood, 1999.

Pears, Sir Edwin. *Turkey and Its People*. London: Methuen, 1911.

Perdicaris, Ion. *American Claims and the Protection of Native Subjects in Morocco*. London: Printed for Ion Perdicaris by W. P. Griffith & Sons, 1886.

Persecution of the Jews in the East, Containing the Proceedings of a Meeting Held at Mikveh Israel, Philadelphia, on Thursday Evening, the 28th of Ab, 5600, Corresponding with the 27th of August, 1840. Philadelphia, 1840.

Peters, Carolyn, and John T. Wooley. "Republican Party Platform of 1896." The American Presidency Project. http://www.presidency.ucsb.edu/ws/?pid=29629. Accessed 4 October 2014.

Philippine Council, Institute of Pacific Relations. "The Development of Mindanao and the Future of the Non-Christians." Manila: Philippine Council, Institute of Pacific Relations, 1938.

Pierce, Rev. James Wilson., ed. *Story of Turkey and Armenia*. Baltimore: R. H. Woodward Company, 1896.

Post, Henry A. V. *A Visit to Greece and Constantinople, in the Year 1827-1828, by Henry A. V. Post, One of the Agents of the New York Greek Committee*. New York: Carey & Hart, 1830.

Quezon, Manuel L. "First State of the Nation Address," 16 June 1936. In Philippines Commonwealth Anniversary Committee, *White Book of the Commonwealth of the Philippines: An Authentic Record of the Celebration of the First Anniversary of the Commonwealth of the Philippines on November 15, 1936*. Manila: Bureau of Printing, 1937.

Richardson, James D. *A Compilation of the Messages and Papers of the Presidents, 1789-1897*. Washington. D.C.: Government Printing Office, 1898.

Riggs, Charles Trowbridge. "The Waning Crescent in Turkey." *Moslem World* 9 (January 1919): 68–79.

Riggs, Henry H. *Days of Tragedy in Armenia: Personal Experiences in Harpoot, 1915-1917*. Ann Arbor, Mich.: Gomidas Institute, 1997.

Rodgers, James B. *Forty Years in the Philippines: A History of the Philippine Mission of the Presbyterian Church in the United States of America, 1899-1939*. New York: Board of Foreign Missions of the Presbyterian Church in the United States of America, 1940.

Roosevelt, Theodore. *The Autobiography of Theodore Roosevelt*. Edited by Wayne Andrews. New York: Scribner, 1958.

———. "Expansion and Peace." *Independent*, 21 December 1899.

———. *Fear God and Take Your Own Part*. New York: George H. Doran, 1916.

———. "First Annual Message." State of the Union Address, 3 December 1901. The American Presidency Project. http://www.presidency.ucsb.edu/ws/?pid=29542. Accessed 29 March 2015.

———. "The Strenuous Life." In *The Strenuous Life: Essays and Addresses*. By Theodore Roosevelt, 1–24. New York: Cosimo, 2006.

———. *Theodore Roosevelt, History as Literature and Other Essays*. New York: Charles Scribner's Sons, 1913.

———. *Theodore Roosevelt's Diaries of Boyhood and Youth*. New York: Charles Scribner's Sons, 1928.

Root, Elihu. *Military and Colonial Policy of the United States: Addresses and Reports by Elihu Root.* Cambridge, Mass.: Harvard University Press, 1916.

Rusling, James F. "Interview with President McKinley." *Christian Advocate,* 22 January 1903, 810.

Saleeby, Najeeb M. *The History of Sulu.* Manila: Filipiniana Book Guild, 1963.

———. *The Moro Problem: An Academic Discussion of the History and Solution of the Problem of the Government of the Moros of the Philippine Islands.* Manila: Press of E. C. McCullough, 1913.

Salter, C. C. "The Solution to the Eastern Question." *Missionary Herald* 72 (December 1876): 392–93.

Sarafian, Ara, ed. *British Parliamentary Debates on the Armenian Genocide, 1915–1918.* Princeton, N.J.: Gomidas Institute, 2003.

———. *United States Official Documents on the Armenian Genocide: Compiled and Introduced by Ara Sarafian.* 3 vols. Watertown, Mass.: Armenian Review, 1993.

Schaeffer, Evelyn Schuyler. *Eugene Schuyler Selected Essays, with a Memoir by Evelyn Schuyler Schaeffer.* New York: Charles Scribner's Sons, 1901.

Schiff, Jacob H. *Jacob H. Schiff: His Life and Letters.* Edited by Cyrus Adler. Grosse Pointe, Mich.: Scholarly Press, 1968.

Schurman, Jacob Gould. *Philippine Affairs: A Retrospect and Outlook.* New York: Charles Scribner's Sons, 1902.

Schuyler, Eugene. "United Bulgaria." *North American Review* 141 (November 1885): 468.

Scott, Hugh Lenox. *Some Memories of a Soldier.* New York: Century, 1928.

Selden, Charles. "Counting upon Us to Save Armenia." *New York Times,* 14 August 1919.

Seward, William Henry. *Life and Public Services of John Quincy Adams, Sixth President of the United States, with the Eulogy Delivered before the Legislature of New York.* Port Auburn, N.Y.: Derby, Miller, 1849.

Smith, John. *The True Travels, Adventures and Observations of Captaine John Smith.* London: Printed by John Haviland for Thomas Slater at the Blew Bible in Greene Arbour, 1630.

Snow, Alpheus Henry. *The Administration of Dependencies: A Study of the Evolution of the Federal Empire, with Special Reference to American Colonial Problems.* New York: G. P. Putnam's Sons, 1902.

Stein, Robert. "Armenia Must Have a European Governor." *Arena,* May 1895, 368.

Stillman, William. *Articles and Despatches from Crete.* Austin, Tex.: Center for Neo-Hellenic Studies, 1976.

———. *The Autobiography of a Journalist.* 2 vols. New York: Houghton Mifflin, 1901.

———. "The Farce in the Levant." *Nation* 8 (21 January 1869): 48.

———. "War in Candia." *Nation* 4 (October 1866): 275–77.

Stoddard, Lothrop. *The New World of Islam.* London: Chapman and Hall, 1922.

———. *The Rising Tide of Color against White World Supremacy.* New York: Charles Scribner's Sons, 1921.

Storey, Joseph. *Commentaries on the Constitution of the United States with a Preliminary Review of the Constitutional History of the Colonies and States, before the Adoption of the Constitution.* Boston: Hilliard Gray, 1833.

Storey, Moorfield. *The Moro Massacre.* Boston: Anti-Imperialist League, 1906.

Straus, Oscar S. *Under Four Administrations: From Cleveland to Taft.* Boston: Houghton Mifflin, 1922.

Strong, Josiah. "A Door into the Mohammedan World." New Haven, Conn.: Yale University Library Archives, n.d.

———. *Expansion: Under New World Conditions.* New York: Baker & Taylor, 1900.

———. *Our Country: Its Possible Future and Its Present Crisis.* New York: Baker & Taylor, 1885.

Sweet, O. J. "American Rule in the Sulus." *Independent,* 3 October 1901.

Taft, William H. *The Collected Works of William Howard Taft.* Vol. 1. Edited by David H. Burton. Athens: Ohio University Press, 2001.

Tan, Samuel K. *Filipino Muslim Perceptions of Their History and Culture as Seen through Indigenous Written Sources.* Zamboanga City, Philippines: SKT Publications, 2003.

———. *Surat Sug: Letters of the Sultanate of Sulu.* 2 vols. Compiled by Samuel K. Tan. Manila: National Historical Institute, 2005.

Temple, Daniel H. *Life and Letters of Rev. Daniel Temple, for Twenty-Three Years a Missionary of the A. B. C. F. M. in Western Asia.* Boston: Congregational Board of Publication, 1855.

Tocqueville, Alexis de. *Democracy in America.* Vol. 1. New York: George Dearborn, 1838.

Toynbee, Arnold J. *Armenian Atrocities, the Murder of a Nation.* New York: Hodder & Stoughton, 1915.

———. *Christianity among the Religions of the World.* New York: Scribner, 1957.

———. *A Study of History.* 12 vols. London: Oxford University Press, 1939–61.

———. *The Western Question in Greece and Turkey: A Study in the Contact of Civilisations.* London: Constable, 1922.

Van-Lessep, H. J. D. D. "Turkish Barbarity." *New York Evangelist,* 28 September 1876.

Washburn, George. "American Influence in Bulgaria." *Amherst Graduates' Quarterly* 2 (1913): 206.

———. *Fifty Years in Constantinople and Recollections of Robert College.* Boston: Houghton Mifflin, 1911.

Webster, Daniel. *Daniel Webster, "The Completest Man."* Edited by Kenneth E. Shewmaker. Hanover, N.H.: University Press of New England, 1990.

———. *The Papers of Daniel Webster.* Series 1. Vol. 1. Hanover, N.H.: University Press of New England, 1974–89.

———. "The Revolution in Greece: A Speech Delivered in the House of Representatives of the United States, on the 19th of January, 1824." In *The Great Speeches and Orations of Daniel Webster.* 57–76. Boston: Little Brown, 1919.

Wheaton, Henry, and William Beach Lawrence. *Elements of International Law.* Boston: Little, 1857.

White, John R. *Bullets and Bolos: Fifteen Years in the Philippine Islands*. New York: Century, 1928.

Whitmarsh, Phelps. "The Sulu Archipelago." *Outlook*, 26 January 1901.

Willard, Frances. "Introduction." In Edwin Bliss, *Turkey and the Armenian Atrocities: A Reign of Terror*, 1–4. Philadelphia: Hubbard Publishing, 1896.

Wilson, Woodrow. "Address to a Joint Session of Congress Calling for a Declaration of War." In *Woodrow Wilson: Essential Writings and Speeches of the Scholar-President*, edited by Mario R. Dinunzio, 397–402. New York: New York University Press, 2006.

———. *The Bible as Progress*. New York: Globe Litho, 1911.

Winthrop, Thomas, Edward Everett, and Members of the Boston Committee for the Relief of the Greeks. *Address of the Committee Appointed at a Public Meeting Held in Boston, December 19, 1823, for the Relief of the Greeks, to Their Fellow Citizens*. Boston: Press of the North American Review, 1823.

Winthrop, W. Colonel. "The Problem of the Philippines: Racial, Commercial, Religious, Political, and Social Conditions." *Outlook*, 11 June 1898, 382–83.

Wise, Isaac M. "The Alliance." *Israelite*, 26 May 1865.

Wood, Leonard. *Chasing Geronimo: The Journal of Leonard Wood, May–September 1886*. Edited by Jack C. Lane. Lincoln: University of Nebraska Press, 2006.

Worcester, Dean. "Knotty Problems of the Philippines." *Century Illustrated Magazine*, October 1898, 876.

———. "The Malay Pirates of the Philippines: With Observations from Personal Experience." *Century Illustrated Magazine*, September 1898, 876.

———. *The Philippine Islands and Their People*. New York: Macmillan, 1898.

Zwemer, Samuel. "Supernational Because Supernatural." *Moslem World* 9 (January 1919): 4–6.

Zwemer, Samuel, E. M. Wherry, and James Barton, eds. *The Mohammedan World of To-Day: Being Papers Read at the First Missionary Conference on Behalf of the Mohammed World, Held at Cairo, April 4th–9th, 1906*. New York: Fleming H. Revell, 1906.

SECONDARY SOURCES

Abinales, Patricio N. *Making Mindanao: Cotabato and Davao in the Formation of the Philippine Nation-State*. Quezon City, Philippines: Ateneo de Manila University Press, 2002.

———. *Orthodoxy and History in the Muslim-Mindanao Narrative*. Quezon City, Philippines: Ateneo de Manila University Press, 2010.

Abinales, Patricio N., and Donna J. Amoroso. *State and Society in the Philippines*. Lanham, Md.: Rowman & Littlefield, 2005.

Abinales, Patricio N., and Nathan Gilbert Quimpo, eds. *The U.S. and the War on Terror in the Philippines*. Manila: Anvil, 2008.

Abitbol, Michel. *Les Juifs d'Afrique du Nord sous Vichy*. Paris: G. P. Maisonneuve & Larose, 1983.

Abrams, Elliott, ed. *The Influence of Faith: Religious Groups and U.S. Foreign Policy*. Lanham, Md.: Rowman & Littlefield, 2001.

Abu-Ghazaleh, Adnan. *American Missions in Syria: A Study of American Missionary Contributions to Arab Nationalism in 19th Century Syria*. Brattleboro, Vt.: Amana, 1990.

Adas, Michael. *Islamic and European Expansion: The Forging of a Global Order*. Philadelphia: Temple University Press, 1993.

Adelson, Roger. *London and the Invention of the Middle East: Money, Power, and War, 1902–1922*. New Haven, Conn.: Yale University Press, 1995.

Adib-Moghaddam, Arshin. *A Metahistory of the Clash of Civilisations: Us and Them beyond Orientalism*. New York: Columbia University Press, 2011.

Adler, Cyrus. *With Firmness in the Right: American Diplomatic Action Affecting Jews, 1840–1945*. New York: Arno, 1977.

Aftandilian, Gregory L. *Armenia, Vision of a Republic: The Independence Lobby in America, 1918–1927*. Boston: Charles River Books, 1981.

Akçam, Taner. *From Empire to Republic: Turkish Nationalism and the Armenian Genocide*. New York: Palgrave Macmillan, 2004.

———. *The Young Turks' Crime against Humanity*. Princeton, N.J.: Princeton University Press. 2012.

Aksakal, Mustafa. " 'Holy War Made in Germany'? Ottoman Origins of the 1915 Jihad." *War in History* 18, no. 2 (2011): 184–99.

———. *The Ottoman Road to War in 1914: The Ottoman Empire and the First World War*. New York: Cambridge University Press, 2008.

Al-Djazairi, Salah Eddine. *The Myth of Muslim Barbarism and its Aims*. Manchester, U.K.: Bayt Al-Hikma, 2007.

Alexander, Jeffrey C., and Philip Smith, "The Discourse of American Civil Society: A New Proposal for Cultural Studies." *Theory and Society* 22 (April 1993): 151–207.

Allison, Robert. *Crescent Obscured: The United States and the Muslim World, 1776–1815*. Chicago: University of Chicago Press, 1995.

Ammon, Harry. *James Monroe: The Quest for National Identity*. New York: McGraw-Hill, 1971.

Amoroso, Donna J. "Inheriting the 'Moro Problem': Muslim Authority and Colonial Rule in British Malaya and the Philippines." In *The American Colonial State in the Philippines: Global Perspectives*, edited by Julian Go and Anne L. Foster, 118–47. Durham, N.C.: Duke University Press, 2003.

Anagnostou, Yiorgos. *Contours of White Ethnicity: Popular Ethnography and the Making of Usable Pasts in Greek America*. Athens: Ohio University Press, 2009.

Anderson, Dorothy. *The Balkan Volunteers*. London: Hutchinson, 1968.

Anderson, Eugene. *The First Moroccan Crisis, 1904–1906*. Chicago: University of Chicago Press, 1930.

Anderson, Matthew Smith. *The Great Powers and the Near East, 1774–1923*. London: Edward Arnold, 1970.

Andrew, Christopher M., and Alexander Sydney Kanya-Forstner. *The Climax of French Imperial Expansion, 1914–1924*. Stanford, Calif.: Stanford University Press, 1981.

Anghie, Anthony. *Imperialism, Sovereignty and the Making of International Law.* Cambridge, U.K.: Cambridge University Press, 2005.

Antelyes, Peter. *Tales of Adventurous Enterprise: Washington Irving and the Poetics of Western Expansion.* New York: Columbia University Press, 1990.

Arendt, Hannah. *The Origins of Totalitarianism.* New York: Schocken, 2004.

Ariel, Yaakov. "An Unexpected Alliance: Christian Zionism and Its Historical Significance." *Modern Judaism* 26 (February 2006): 74–100.

Armitage, David. *The Declaration of Independence: A Global History.* Cambridge, Mass.: Harvard University Press, 2007.

———. "The Declaration of Independence and International Law." *William and Mary Quarterly* 59 (January 2002): 38–64.

Armitage, David, and Sanjay Subrahmanyam, eds. *The Age of Revolutions in a Global Context, c. 1760–1840.* New York: Palgrave Macmillan, 2010.

Arnakis, George Georgiades. *American Consul in a Cretan War: William J. Stillman.* Austin, Tex.: Center for Neo-Hellenic Studies, 1966.

———, ed. *George Jarvis: His Journal and Related Documents.* Thessaloniki, Greece: Institute for Balkan Studies, 1965.

Arnold, James. *The Moro War: How America Battled a Muslim Insurgency in the Philippine Jungle, 1902–1913.* New York: Bloomsbury, 2011.

Assaraf, Robert. *Une Certaine Histoire des Juifs du Maroc.* Paris: Jean-Claude Gawsewitch, 2005.

Astourian, Stephan H. "The Silence of the Land: Agrarian Relations, Ethnicity, and Power." In *A Question of Genocide: Armenians and Turks at the End of the Ottoman Empire*, edited by Ronald Grigor Suny and Fatma Muge Göçek, 55–81. New York: Oxford University Press, 2011.

Ataöv, Türkkaya, ed. *The Armenians in the Late Ottoman Period.* Ankara: Turkish Historical Society, 2001.

Avtorkhanov, Abdulrahman, et al., eds. *The North Caucasus Barrier: The Russian Advance towards the Muslim World.* New York: St. Martin's, 1992.

Aydin, Mustafa, and Çağri Erhan, eds. *Turkish-American Relations: Past, Present and Future.* New York: Routledge, 2004.

Bacevich, Andrew J. *Diplomat in Khaki: Major General Frank Ross McCoy and American Foreign Policy, 1898–1949.* Lawrence: University Press of Kansas, 1989.

Badem, Candan. *The Ottoman Crimean War, 1853–1856.* Boston: Brill, 2010.

Baepler, Paul Michel. *White Slaves, African Masters: An Anthology of American Barbary Captivity.* Chicago: University of Chicago Press, 1999.

Baer, Marc David. *The Dönme: Jewish Converts, Muslim Revolutionaries, and Secular Turks.* Stanford, Calif.: Stanford University Press, 2010.

Bailyn, Bernard. *The Ideological Origins of the American Revolution.* Cambridge, Mass.: Belknap Press of Harvard University Press, 1965.

Balakian, Peter. *The Burning Tigris: The Armenian Genocide and America's Response.* New York: Perennial, 2003.

———. "From Ezra Pound to Theodore Roosevelt: American Intellectual and Cultural Responses to the Armenian Genocide." In *America and the Armenian*

Genocide, edited by Jay Winter, 240–55. Cambridge, UK: Cambridge University Press, 2003.

Baldoz, Rick. *The Third Asiatic Invasion: Migration and Empire in Filipino America, 1898–1946*. New York: New York University Press, 2011.

Barder, Alexander D. *Empire Within: International Hierarchy and Its Imperial Laboratories of Governance*. New York: Routledge, 2015.

Bartov, Omer, and Phyllis Mack, eds. *In God's Name: Genocide and Religion in the Twentieth Century*. New York: Berghahn, 2001.

Bass, Gary J. *Freedom's Battle: The Origins of Humanitarian Intervention*. New York: Alfred A. Knopf, 2008.

Battistini, Robert. "Glimpses of the Other before Orientalism: The Muslim World in Early American Periodicals, 1785–1800." *Early American Studies* 8 (Spring 2010): 446–74.

Bauzon, Kenneth España. "Islamic Nationalism in the Philippines: Reflections in Socio-political Analysis." Ph.D. diss., Duke University, 1981.

Baylen, Joseph O. "Senator John Tyler Morgan and Negro Colonization in the Philippines, 1901 to 1902." *Phylon* (1st Quarter 1968): 65–75.

Baymoumi, Moustafa. "Racing Religion." *New Centennial Review* 6 (Fall 2006): 267–93.

Beale, Howard K. *Theodore Roosevelt and the Rise of America to World Power*. Baltimore: Johns Hopkins University Press, 1956.

Beaton, Roderick, and David Ricks, eds. *The Making of Modern Greece: Nationalism, Romanticism, and the Uses of the Past, 1797–1896*. Burlington, Vt.: Ashgate, 2009.

Bellamy, Alex J. *Massacres and Morality: Mass Atrocities in an Age of Civilian Immunity*. Oxford: Oxford University Press, 2012.

Bemis, Samuel Flagg. *John Quincy Adams and the Foundations of American Foreign Policy*. New York: Alfred A. Knopf, 1949.

———. *John Quincy Adams and the Union*. New York: Alfred A. Knopf, 1956.

———, ed. *The American Secretaries of State and Their Diplomacy*. Vols. 1–10. New York: Alfred A. Knopf, 1928–59.

Benbassa, Esther, and Aron Rodrigue. *Sephardi Jewry: A History of the Judeo-Spanish Community, 14th–20th Centuries*. Berkeley: University of California Press, 2000.

Bender, Thomas. *A Nation among Nations: America's Place in World History*. New York: Hill & Wang, 2006.

Benjamin, Russell, and Gregory O. Hall, eds. *Eternal Colonialism*. Lanham, Md.: University Press of America, 2010.

Ben-Srhir, Khalidi. *Britain and Morocco during the Embassy of John Drummond Hay, 1845–1886*. New York: Routledge, 2005.

Berman, Jacob Rama. *American Arabesque: Arabs, Islam, and the 19th-Century Imaginary*. New York: New York University Press, 2012.

Bernas, Joaquin. *A Historical and Juridical Study of the Philippine Bill of Rights*. Manila: Ateneo University Press, 1971.

Berramdane, Abdelkhaleq. *Le Maroc et l'Occident, 1800–1974*. Paris: Karthala, 1987.

Blight, Charles, and David Geyer. "Where in the World Is America? The History of the United States in the Global Age." In *Rethinking American History in a Global Age*, edited by Thomas Bender, 63–100. Berkeley: University of California Press, 2002.

Bloxham, Donald. *The Great Game of Genocide: Imperialism, Nationalism, and the Destruction of the Ottoman Armenians*. New York: Oxford University Press, 2005.

———. "Internal Colonization, Inter-imperial Conflict and the Armenian Genocide." In *Empire, Colony, Genocide: Conquest, Occupation, and Subaltern Resistance in World History*, edited by A. Dirk Moses, 325–42. New York: Berghahn, 2008.

Blum, Edward. *Reforging the White Republic: Race, Religion and American Nationalism, 1865–1898*. Baton Rouge: Louisiana State University Press, 2005.

Blumi, Isa. *Ottoman Refugees, 1878–1939: Migration in a Post-imperial World*. London: Bloomsbury Academic, 2013.

Bobelian, Michael. *Children of Armenia: A Forgotten Genocide and the Century-Long Struggle for Justice*. New York: Simon & Schuster, 2009.

Bonney, Richard. *False Prophets: The "Clash of Civilizations" and the Global War on Terror*. Oxford: Peter Lang, 2008.

Bowden, Brett. *The Empire of Civilization: The Evolution of an Imperial Idea*. Chicago: University of Chicago Press, 2009.

Bowie, Leland. "An Aspect of Muslim-Jewish Relations in Late Nineteenth-Century Morocco: A European Diplomatic View." *International Journal of Middle East Studies* 7 (January 1976): 3–19.

Braude, Benjamin, and Bernard Lews, eds. *Christians and Jews in the Ottoman Empire: The Functioning of a Plural Society*. New York: Holmes & Meier, 1982.

Brecher, Frank. "Revisiting Ambassador Morgenthau's Turkish Peace Mission of 1917." *Middle Eastern Studies* 24 (July 1988): 413–27.

Brewer, David. *Greece, the Hidden Centuries: Turkish Rule from the Fall of Constantinople to Greek Independence*. London: I. B. Tauris, 2010.

———. *The Greek War of Independence: The Struggle for Freedom from Ottoman Oppression*. New York: Duckworth, 2011.

Bridge, F. R., and Roger Bullen. *The Great Powers and the European States System, 1814–1914*. 2nd ed. Harlow, U.K.: Pearson Education, 2005.

Bryson, Thomas A. *Tars, Turks and Tankers: The Role of the United States Navy in the Middle East, 1800–1979*. Metuchen, N.J.: Scarecrow Press, 1980.

Bull, Hedley, and Adam Watson, eds. *The Expansion of International Society*. New York: Oxford University Press, 1984.

Burke, Edmund. *Prelude to Protectorate in Morocco: Precolonial Protest and Resistance, 1860–1912*. Chicago: University of Chicago Press, 1976.

Burke, Edmund, and David Prochaska. *Genealogies of Orientalism: History, Theory, Politics*. Lincoln: University of Nebraska Press, 2008.

Burris, John P. *Exhibiting Religion: Colonialism and Spectacle at International Expositions, 1851–1893*. Charlottesville: University of Virginia Press, 2001.

Calhoun, Craig, Frederick Cooper, and Kevin W. Moore, eds. *Lessons of Empire: Imperial Histories and American Power*. New York: The New Press, 2006.

Calotychos, Vangelis. *Modern Greece: A Cultural Poetics*. New York: Berg, 2003.

Carabott, Philip. "State, Society and the Religious 'Other' in Nineteenth-Century Greece." *Kambos: Cambridge Papers in Modern Greek* 18 (2011): 1–24.

Carey, Hilary M. *God's Empire: Religion and Colonialism in the British World, c. 1801–1908*. New York: Cambridge University Press, 2011.

Carmichael, Cathie. *Ethnic Cleansing in the Balkans: Nationalism and the Destruction of Tradition*. New York: Routledge, 2002.

Carpenter, Kaley. "A Worldly Errand: James L. Barton's American Mission to the Near East." Ph.D. diss., Princeton Theological Seminary, 2009.

Carpenter, Teresa. *The Miss Stone Affair: America's First Modern Hostage Crisis*. New York: Simon & Schuster, 2003.

Carwadine, Richard. *Evangelicals and Politics in Antebellum America*. New Haven, Conn.: Yale University Press, 1993.

Celik, Zeynep. "Speaking Back to Orientalist Discourse." In *Orientalism's Interlocutors: Painting, Architecture, Photography*, edited by Jill Beaulieu and Mary Roberts. Durham, N.C.: Duke University Press, 2002.

Chang, Derek. *Citizens of a Christian Nation: Evangelical Missions and the Problem of Race in the Nineteenth Century*. Philadelphia: University of Pennsylvania Press, 2010.

Chaplin, Jonathan, and Robert Joustra, eds. *God and Global Order: The Power of Religion in American Foreign Policy*. Waco, Tex.: Baylor University Press, 2010.

Chatty, Dawn. *Displacement and Dispossession in the Modern Middle East*. New York: Cambridge University Press, 2010.

Cherry, Conrad, ed. *God's New Israel: Religious Interpretations of American Destiny*. Rev. ed. Chapel Hill: University of North Carolina Press, 1998.

Chester, Edward W. *Africa and U.S. Foreign Policy*. Maryknoll, N.Y.: Orbis, 1974.

Christison, Kathleen. *Perceptions of Palestine: Their Influence on U.S. Middle East Policy*. Berkeley: University of California Press, 1999.

Chyet, Stanley F. "The Political Rights of Jews in the United States: 1776–1841." In *Critical Studies in American Jewish History: Selected Articles from American Jewish Archives*, edited by Jacob R. Marcus, 27–88. Cincinnati: American Jewish Archives, 1971.

Cirakman, Asli. *From the "Terror of the World" to the "Sick Man of Europe": European Images of the Ottoman Empire and Society from the Sixteenth Century to the Nineteenth*. New York: Peter Lang, 2002.

Clark, Victoria. *Allies for Armageddon: The Rise of Christian Zionism*. New Haven, Conn.: Yale University Press, 2007.

Clarke, James F. *Bible Societies, American Missionaries, and the National Revival of Bulgaria*. New York: Arno, 1971.

———. *The Pen and the Sword: Studies in Bulgarian History*. Boulder, Colo.: East European Monographs, 1988.

Clarke, James F., and George A. Tabakov, eds. *MacGahan and Bulgaria, 1878–1978: A Centennial Commemoration, New Lexington, June 3, 1978*. Akron, Ohio: MacGahan American-Bulgarian Foundation, 1979.

Cline, Myrtle. "American Attitude toward the Greek War of Independence, 1821–1828." Ph.D. diss., Columbia University, 1930.

Clogg, Richard, ed. *Balkan Society in the Age of Greek Independence*. London: Macmillan, 1981.

———. *The Movement for Greek Independence, 1770–1821: A Collection of Documents*. London: Macmillan, 1976.

———. *The Struggle for Greek Independence: Essays to Mark the 150th Anniversary of the Greek War of Independence*. London: Macmillan, 1973.

Clymer, Kenton J. *Protestant Missionaries in the Philippines, 1898–1916: An Inquiry into the American Colonial Mentality*. Urbana: University of Illinois Press, 1986.

Coffman, Elizabeth Hobbs. *American Umpire*. Cambridge, Mass.: Harvard University Press, 2013.

Cogley, Richard. "The Fall of the Ottoman Empire and the Restoration of Israel in the 'Judeo-centric' Strand of Puritan Millenarianism." *Church History* 72 (June 2003): 304–32.

Cohen, Marc. "The Neo-lachrymose Conception of Jewish-Arab History." *Tikkun* 6 (May–June 1991): 55–64.

Cohen, Naomi. *Jews in Christian America: The Pursuit of Religious Equality*. New York: Oxford University Press, 1992.

Cohler, Anne M. *Montesquieu's Comparative Politics and the Spirit of American Constitutionalism*. Lawrence: University Press of Kansas, 1988.

Coit, Margaret L. *John C. Calhoun: American Portrait*. Boston: Houghton Mifflin, 1950.

Colley, Linda. *Captives*. New York: Pantheon, 2002.

Cook, Ralph Elliott. "The United States and the Armenian Question, 1894–1924." Ph.D. diss., Fletcher School of Law and Diplomacy, 1957.

Cooper, Frederick and Ann Laura Stoler. *Tensions of Empire: Colonial Cultures in a Bourgeois World*. Berkeley: University of California Press, 1997.

Coulson, Douglas. "Persecutory Agency in Racial Prerequisite Cases: Islam, Christianity and Martyrdom in *United States v. Cartozian*." *University of Miami Race and Social Justice Law Review* 2 (2012): 117–88.

Cragg, Kenneth. *The Arab Christian: A History in the Middle East*. Louisville, Ky.: Westminster/John Knox Press, 1991.

Crampton, Richard J. *Bulgaria, 1878–1918: A History*. New York: East European Monographs, 1983.

———. *A Short History of Modern Bulgaria*. Cambridge, U.K.: Cambridge University Press, 1987.

———. "The Turks in Bulgaria, 1878–1944." *International Journal of Turkish Studies* 4, no. 2 (1989): 42–77.

Crawley, Charles William. *The Question of Greek Independence: A Study of British Policy in the Near East, 1821–1833*. Cambridge, U.K.: Cambridge University Press, 1930.

Cruickshank, Earl Fee. "Morocco at the Parting of the Ways." Ph.D. diss., University of Pennsylvania, 1935.

Cumbler, John T. *From Abolition to Rights for All: The Making of a Reform Community in the Nineteenth Century*. Philadelphia: University of Pennsylvania Press, 2008.

Curry, George. "Woodrow Wilson, Jan Smuts, and the Versailles Settlement." *American Historical Review* 66 (July 1961): 968–86.

Curti, Merle. *American Philanthropy Abroad*. New Brunswick, N.J.: Rutgers University Press, 1963.

———. *Prelude to Point Four: American Technical Missions Overseas, 1838–1939*. Madison: University of Wisconsin Press, 1954.

Curtis, Edward E. *Muslims in America: A Short History*. New York: Oxford University Press, 2009.

Curtis, Michael. *Verdict on Vichy: Power and Prejudice in the Vichy France Regime*. New York: Arcade, 2002.

Daalder Ivo H., and James M. Lindsay. "American Empire, Not 'If' but 'What Kind.'" *New York Times*, 10 May 2003.

Dadrian, Vahakn N. *The History of the Armenian Genocide: Ethnic Conflict from the Balkans to Anatolia to the Caucasus*. Providence, R.I.: Berghahn, 1995.

Dain, Bruce R. *A Hideous Monster of the Mind: American Race Theory in the Early Republic*. Cambridge, Mass.: Harvard University Press, 2002.

Dakin, Douglas. *British and American Philhellenes during the Greek War for Independence*. Thessaloniki, Greece: Institute for Balkan Studies, 1955.

———. *The Greek Struggle for Independence, 1821–1833*. Berkeley: University of California Press, 1973.

Dale, Stephan Frederic. "Religious Suicide in Islamic Asia: Anticolonial Terrorism in India, Indonesia, and the Philippines." *Journal of Conflict Resolution* 32 (March 1988): 37–59.

Daniel, Robert. *American Philanthropy in the Near East, 1820–1960*. Athens: Ohio University Press, 1970.

Daskalov, Rumen. *The Making of a Nation in the Balkans: Historiography of the Bulgarian Revival*. New York: Central European University Press, 2004.

David-Fox, Michael, Peter Holquist, and Alexander Martins, eds. *Orientalism and Empire in Russia*. Bloomington, Ind.: Slavica, 2006.

Davidson, Lawrence. *America's Palestine: Popular and Official Perceptions from Balfour to Israeli Statehood*. Gainesville: University Press of Florida, 2001.

Davis, John. *The Landscape of Belief: Encountering the Holy Land in Nineteenth-Century American Art and Culture*. Princeton, N.J.: Princeton University Press, 1996.

Davison, Roderic H. "Ottoman Public Relations in the Nineteenth Century: How the Sublime Porte Tried to Influence European Public Opinion." In *Histoire Économique et Social de l'Empire Ottoman de la Turquie, 1326–1960*, edited by Daniel Panzac, 593–603. Paris: Peeters, 1995.

Dennis, Alfred Lewis. *Adventures in American Diplomacy*. New York: E. P. Dutton, 1928.

DeNovo, John A. *American Interests and Policies in the Middle East, 1900–1939*. Minneapolis: University of Minnesota Press, 1969.

Dent, David W. *The Legacy of the Monroe Doctrine: A Reference Guide to U.S. Involvement in Latin America and the Caribbean.* Westport, Conn.: Greenwood, 1999.

Despot, Igor. *The Balkan Wars in the Eyes of the Warring Parties: Perceptions and Interpretations.* Bloomington, Ind.: IUniverse, 2012.

Deutsch, Nathaniel. *Inventing America's "Worst" Family: Eugenics, Islam, and the Fall and Rise of the Tribe of Ishmael.* Berkeley: University of California Press, 2009.

Diner, Hasia R. *The Jews of the United States, 1654–2000.* Berkeley: University of California Press, 2004.

———. *A Time for Gathering: The Second Migration, 1820–1880.* Baltimore: Johns Hopkins University Press, 1992.

Dinnerstein, Leonard. *Uneasy at Home: Antisemitism and the American Jewish Experience.* New York: Columbia University Press, 1987.

Diouf, Sylviane. *Servants of Allah: African Muslims Enslaved in the Americas.* New York: New York University Press, 1998.

Dirks, Jerald. *Muslims in American History: A Forgotten Legacy.* Beltsville, Md.: Amana, 2006.

Doğan, Mehmet Ali, and Heather Sharkey, eds. *American Missionaries and the Middle East: Foundational Encounters.* Salt Lake City: University of Utah Press, 2011.

Doolen, Andy. *Fugitive Empire: Locating Early American Imperialism.* Minneapolis: University of Minnesota Press, 2005.

Doty, Roxanne Lynn. *Imperial Encounters: The Politics of Representation in North-South Relations.* Minneapolis: University of Minnesota Press, 1996.

Doumanis, Nicolas. *Before the Nation: Muslim-Christian Coexistence and Its Destruction in Late Ottoman Anatolia.* Oxford: Oxford University Press, 2013.

Dowty, Alan. *The Limits of American Isolation: The United States and the Crimean War.* New York: New York University Press, 1971.

Doyle, Don H., ed. *Secession as an International Phenomenon: From America's Civil War to Contemporary Separatist Movements.* Athens: University of Georgia Press, 2010.

Drake, James D. *The Nation's Nature: How Continental Presumptions Gave Rise to the United States of America.* Charlottesville: University of Virginia Press, 2011.

Drinnon, Richard. *Facing West: The Metaphysics of Indian-Hating and Empire-Building.* Minneapolis: University of Minnesota Press, 1980.

Dunbar, Elizabeth. *Talcott Williams: Gentleman of the Fourth Estate.* Brooklyn, N.Y.: Robert E. Simpson & Son, 1936.

Dyson, Stephen. *Ancient Marbles to American Shores: Classical Archaeology in the United States.* Philadelphia: University of Pennsylvania Press, 1998.

Earle, E. M. "American Interest in the Greek Cause, 1821–1827." *American Historical Review* 33 (October 1927): 44–63.

Edgerton, Ronald King. *People of the Middle Ground: A Century of Conflict and Accommodation in Central Mindanao, 1880s–1980s.* Quezon City, Philippines: Ateneo de Manila University Press, 2008.

Ehraim, Frank. "The Mindanao Plan: Political Obstacles to Jewish Refugee Settlement." *Holocaust Genocide Studies* 20 (Winter 2006): 410–36.

Eisenberg, Ellen. *First to Cry down Injustice: Western Jews and Japanese Internment during World War II*. Lanham, Md.: Lexington, 2008.

Eisenhower, John S. D. *Teddy Roosevelt and Leonard Wood: Partners in Command*. Columbia: University of Missouri Press, 2014.

Ellis, Charles Howard. "Annex A: The Covenant." In *The Origin, Structure and Working of the League of Nations*, edited by Charles Howard Ellis, 487–95. Boston: Houghton Mifflin, 1928.

Erhan, Cagri. "Ottoman Official Attitudes towards American Missionaries." *Turkish Yearbook* 30 (2000): 196–201.

Esber, Rosemarie. *Under the Cover of War: The Zionist Expulsion of the Palestinians*. Alexandria, Va.: Arabicus Books & Media, 2008.

Etherington, Norman, ed. *Missions and Empire*. New York: Oxford University Press, 2005.

Farah, Caesar E. *The Politics of Interventionism in Ottoman Lebanon, 1830–1861*. New York: I. B. Tauris, 2000.

Fawaz, Leila Tarazi. *An Occasion for War: Civil Conflict in Lebanon and Damascus in 1860*. New York: I. B. Tauris, 1994.

Ferguson, Robert A. *The American Enlightenment, 1750–1820*. Cambridge, Mass.: Harvard University Press, 1997.

Field, James A. *America and the Mediterranean World, 1776–1882*. Princeton, N.J.: Princeton University Press, 1969.

Fields, Karen E., and Barbara J. Fields. *Racecraft: The Soul of Inequality in American Life*. New York: Verso, 2012.

Figes, Orlando. *Crimea: The Last Crusade*. New York: Allen Lane, 2010.

Findley, Carter V. *Turkey, Islam, Nationalism, and Modernity: A History, 1789–2007*. New Haven, Conn.: Yale University Press, 2010.

Fink, Carole. *Defending the Rights of Others: The Great Powers, the Jews, and International Minority Protection, 1878–1938*. New York: Cambridge University Press, 2004.

Finnie, David H. *Pioneers East: The Early American Experience in the Middle East*. Cambridge, Mass.: Harvard University Press, 1967.

Flournoy, Francis R. *British Policy towards Morocco in the Age of Palmerston, 1830–1865*. London: P. S. King & Son, 1935.

Foner, Eric. *Free Soil, Free Labor, Free Men: The Ideology of the Republican Party before the Civil War*. Oxford: Oxford University Press, 1995.

Fortna, Benjamin C., Stefanos Katsikas, Dimitris Kamouzis, and Paraskevas Konortas, eds. *State-Nationalisms in the Ottoman Empire, Greece and Turkey: Orthodox and Muslims, 1830–1945*. New York: Routledge, 2013.

Foster, Anne L. *Projections of Power: The United States and Europe in Colonial Southeast Asia, 1919–1941*. Durham, N.C.: Duke University Press, 2010.

Foster, Gaines M. *Moral Reconstruction: Christian Lobbyists and the Federal Legislation of Morality, 1865–1920*. Chapel Hill: University of North Carolina Press, 2002.

Frankel, Jonathan. *The Damascus Affair: "Ritual Murder," Politics and the Jews in 1840.* Cambridge, U.K.: Cambridge University Press, 1997.

Frazee, Charles. *The Orthodox Church and Independent Greece, 1821–1852.* Cambridge, U.K.: Cambridge University Press, 1969.

Friedman, Ellen G. "Christian Captives at 'Hard Labor' in Algiers, 16th–18th Centuries." *International Journal of African Historical Studies* 13, no. 4 (1980): 616–32.

Fromkin, David. *A Peace to End All Peace: The Fall of the Ottoman Empire and the Creation of the Modern Middle East.* London: Phoenix, 2000.

Frothingham, Paule Revere. *Edward Everett, Orator and Statesman.* New York: Houghton Mifflin, 1925.

Fukuyama, Francis. "The End of History?" *National Interest*, Summer 1989, 3–18.

Fulton, Robert. *Honor for the Flag: The Battle of Bud Dajo—1906 and the Moro Massacre.* Bend, Ore.: Tumalo Creek Press, 2011.

——. *Moroland, 1899–1906: America's First Attempt to Transform an Islamic Society.* Bend, Ore.: Tumalo Creek Press, 2007.

Gale, Robert L. *John Hay.* Boston: Twayne, 1978.

Gaunt, David. *Massacres, Resistance, Protectors: Muslim-Christian Relations in Eastern Anatolia during World War I.* Piscataway, N.J.: Gorgias, 2006.

Gelfand, Lawrence E. *The Inquiry: American Preparations for Peace, 1917–1919.* New Haven, Conn.: Yale University Press, 1963.

George, Thayil J. S. *Revolt in Mindanao: The Rise of Islam in Philippine Politics.* New York: Oxford University Press, 1980.

Gerber, David A., ed. *Anti-Semitism in American History.* Urbana: University of Illinois Press, 1986.

Gerges, Fawaz. *America and Political Islam: Clash of Cultures or Clash of Interests?* New York: Cambridge University Press, 1999.

Gershovich, Moshe. *French Military Rule in Morocco: Colonialism and Its Consequences.* Portland, Ore.: F. Cass, 2000.

Gerstle, Gary. *American Crucible: Race and Nation in the Twentieth Century.* Princeton, N.J.: Princeton University Press, 2001.

GhaneaBassiri, Kambiz. *A History of Islam in America.* New York: Cambridge University Press, 2010.

Gidney, James B. *A Mandate for Armenia.* Oberlin, Ohio: Kent State University Press, 1967.

Gilroy, Paul. *Small Acts: Thoughts on the Politics of Black Culture.* London: Serpent's Tail, 1993.

Givens, Terryl L. *The Viper on the Hearth: Mormons, Myths, and the Construction of Heresy.* Oxford: Oxford University Press, 1997.

Glanz, Rudolf. "Jews and Chinese in America." *Jewish Social Studies* 16 (July 1954): 219–34.

Gleek, Lewis E., Jr. *American Institutions in the Philippines, 1898–1941.* Quezon City, Philippines: R. P. Garcia, 1976.

——. *Americans on the Philippine Frontiers.* Manila: Carmelo & Bauermann, 1974.

Glickman, Lawrence. "The 'Cultural Turn.' " In *American History Now*, edited by Eric Foner and Lisa McGirr, 221–43. Philadelphia: Temple University Press, 2011.

Go, Julian. *American Empire and the Politics of Meaning: Elite Political Cultures in the Philippines and Puerto Rico during U.S. Colonialism*. Durham, N.C.: Duke University Press, 2008.

———. *Patterns of Empire: The British and American Empires, 1688 to the Present*. New York: Cambridge University Press, 2011.

Go, Julian, and Anne L. Foster, eds. *The American Colonial State in the Philippines*. Durham, N.C.: Duke University Press, 2003.

Göçek, Fatma Müge. *Rise of the Bourgeoisie, Demise of Empire: Ottoman Westernization and Social Change*. New York: Oxford University Press, 1996.

———, ed. *Social Constructions of Nationalism in the Middle East*. Albany: State University of New York Press, 2002.

Goldschmidt, Henry, and Elizabeth McAlister. *Race, Nation and Religion in the Americas*. New York: Oxford University Press, 2004.

Goldstein, Eric. *The Price of Whiteness: Jews, Race and American Identity*. Princeton, N.J.: Princeton University Press, 2006.

Gomez, Michael A. "Muslims in Early America." *Journal of Southern History* 60 (1994): 671–710.

Gordon, Leland James. *American Relations with Turkey, 1830–1930: An Economic Interpretation*. Philadelphia: University of Pennsylvania Press, 1932.

Gould, Lewis L. "McKinley, Ida Saxton." *American National Biography Online*. http://www.anb.org/articles/20/20-01377.html. Accessed 13 March 2012.

Gould, Philip. *Barbaric Traffic: Commerce and Antislavery in the Eighteenth-Century Atlantic World*. Cambridge, Mass.: Harvard University Press, 2003.

Gould, Stephen Jay. *The Mismeasure of Man*. New York: W. W. Norton, 1981.

Gourgouris, Stathis. *Dream Nation: Enlightenment, Colonization, and the Institution of Modern Greece*. Stanford, Calif.: Stanford University Press, 1996.

Gowing, Peter. *Mandate in Moroland: The American Government of Muslim Filipinos, 1899–1920*. Quezon City, Philippines: Philippine Center for Advanced Studies, 1977.

———. *Mosque and Moro: A Study of Muslims in the Philippines*. Manila: Philippine Federation of Christian Churches, 1964.

———. *Muslim Filipinos: Heritage and Horizon*. Quezon City, Philippines: New Day Publishers, 1979.

Grabill, Joseph L. *Protestant Diplomacy and the Near East: Missionary Influence on American Policy, 1810–1927*. Minneapolis: University of Minnesota Press, 1971.

Graebner, Norman A., ed. *Ideas and Diplomacy: Readings in the Intellectual Tradition of American Foreign Policy*. New York: Oxford University Press, 1964.

Grandits, Hannes, Nathalie Clayer, and Robert Pichier, eds. *Conflicting Loyalties in the Balkans: The Great Powers, the Ottoman Empire and Nation-Building*. New York: I. B. Tauris, 2011.

Green, Abigail. "The British Empire and the Jews: An Imperialism of Human Rights?" *Past and Present* 199 (May 2008): 75–105.

——. "Intervening in the Jewish Question, 1840–1878." In *Humanitarian Intervention: A History*, edited by Brendan Simms and D. J. B. Trim, 139–58. Cambridge, U.K.: Cambridge University Press, 2011.

——. *Moses Montefiore: Jewish Liberator, Imperial Hero.* Cambridge, Mass.: Belknap Press of Harvard University Press, 2010.

Greenberg, Amy S. *Manifest Manhood and the Antebellum American Empire.* New York: Cambridge University Press, 2005.

Greene, Jack P. *The Intellectual Construction of America: Exceptionalism and Identity from 1492–1800.* Chapel Hill: University of North Carolina Press, 1993.

Gregory, Derek. *The Colonial Present: Afghanistan, Palestine, and Iraq.* Malden, Mass.: Blackwell, 2004.

Grinstein, Hyman B. *The Rise of the Jewish Community of New York.* Philadelphia: Jewish Publication Society of America, 1942.

Gualtieri, Sarah M. *Between Arab and White: Race and Ethnicity in the Early Syrian American Diaspora.* Berkeley: University of California Press, 2009.

Gunter, Michael M. *Armenian History and the Question of Genocide.* New York: Palgrave Macmillan, 2011.

Hagedorn, Hermann. *Leonard Wood: A Biography.* Vol. 2. New York: Harper & Brothers, 1931.

Hall, Luella J. *The United States and Morocco, 1776–1956.* Metuchen, N.J.: Scarecrow Press, 1971.

Hall, William Webster. *Puritans in the Balkans: The American Board Mission in Bulgaria, 1878–1918: A Study in Purpose and Procedure.* Sofia: Cultura Printing House, 1938.

Haller, John S., Jr. *Outcasts from Evolution: Scientific Attitudes of Racial Inferiority, 1859–1900.* Urbana: University of Illinois Press, 1971.

Hamilton, Michael P. ed. *American Character and Foreign Policy.* Grand Rapids, Mich.: W. B. Eerdmans, 1986.

Handy, Robert T., ed. *The Social Gospel in America, 1870–1920.* New York: Oxford University Press, 1966.

Hanioğlu, Şükrü. *The Young Turks in Opposition.* New York: Oxford University Press, 1995.

Harbaugh, William H. *Power and Responsibility: The Life and Times of Theodore Roosevelt.* New York: Farrar, Straus & Cudahy, 1961.

Harris, David. *Britain and the Bulgarian Horrors of 1876.* Chicago: University of Chicago Press, 1939.

Harris, Susan K. *God's Arbiters: Americans and the Philippines, 1898–1902.* New York: Oxford University Press, 2011.

Hart, Mitchell Bryan. *Social Science and the Politics of Modern Jewish Identity.* Stanford, Calif.: Stanford University Press, 2000.

Harvey, Bruce A. *American Geographies: U.S. National Narratives and the Representation of the Non-European World, 1830–1865.* Stanford, Calif.: Stanford University Press, 2001.

Hassan, Waïl S. *Immigrant Narratives: Orientalism and Cultural Translation in Arab American and Arab British Literature.* Oxford: Oxford University Press, 2011.

Hasso, F. S. "'Culture Knowledge' and the Violence of Imperialism: Revisiting *The Arab Mind.*" *MIT Electronic Journal of Middle East Studies* 7 (Spring 2007): 24–40.

Hatch, Nathan O. *The Democratization of American Christianity.* New Haven, Conn.: Yale University Press, 1989.

Hatzidimitriou, Constantine G. *Founded on Freedom and Virtue: Documents Illustrating the Impact in the United States of the Greek War of Independence, 1821–1829.* New York: Aristide C. Caratzas, 2002.

Hawkins, Michael. *Making Moros: Imperial Historicism and American Military Rule in the Philippines' Muslim South.* De Kalb: Northern Illinois University Press, 2013.

Hayase, Shinzo. *Mindanao Ethnohistory beyond Nations: Maguindanao, Sangir, and Bagobo Societies in East Maritime Southeast Asia.* Quezon City, Philippines: Ateneo de Manila University Press, 2007.

Healy, George, trans. "Introduction." In *Persian Letters*, by Charles de Secondat Montesquieu. Indianapolis: Hacket, 1999.

Heggoy, Alf Andrew, Aurie H. Miller, James J. Cooke, and Paul J. Zingg, eds. *Through Foreign Eyes: Western Attitudes toward North Africa.* Washington, D.C.: University Press of America, 1982.

Helmreich, Paul C. *From Paris to Sèvres: The Partition of the Ottoman Empire at the Peace Conference of 1919–1920.* Columbia: Ohio State University Press, 1974.

Henderson, Eroll, and Richard Tucker. "Clear and Present Strangers: The Clash of Civilizations and International Conflict." *International Studies Quarterly* 45 (June 2001): 317–38.

Hendrickson, David C. *Union, Nation, or Empire: The American Debate over International Relations, 1789–1941.* Lawrence: University Press of Kansas, 2009.

Hendrickson, Kenneth E., Jr. "Reluctant Expansionist: Jacob Gould Schurman and the Philippine Question." *Pacific Historical Review* 36 (1967): 405–21.

Hentsch, Thierry. *Imagining the Middle East.* Translated by Fred A. Reed. New York: Black Rose Books, 1992.

Herlihy, Patricia. "Eugene Schuyler and the Bulgarian Constitution." In *Russia, Europe, and the Rule of Law*, edited by F. J. Ferdinand et al., 165–84. Boston: Martinus Nijhoff, 2007.

Hersch, Seymour. "The Gray Zone: Annals of National Security." *New Yorker,* 24 May 2004, 38–44.

Herzfeld, Michael. *Ours Once More: Folklore, Ideology and the Making of Modern Greece.* New York: Pella, 1986.

Herzstein, Robert Edwin. *Henry R. Luce, Time, and the American Crusade in Asia.* New York: Cambridge University Press, 2005.

Hietala, Thomas R. *Manifest Design: American Exceptionalism and Empire.* Rev. ed. Ithaca, N.Y.: Cornell University Press, 2003.

Hilderbrand, Robert C. *Power and the People: Executive Management of Public Opinion in Foreign Affairs, 1897–1921.* Chapel Hill: University of North Carolina Press, 1981.

Hindley, Meredith. "Soldier of Fortune: John Smith before Jamestown." *Humanities* 28 (January–February 2007): 12–16.

Hirschberg, H. Z. (J. W.). *A History of the Jews in North Africa*. Vol. 2. Leiden, The Netherlands: E. J. Brill, 1981.

Hirschman, Elizabeth Caldwell, and Donald Yates. *Jews and Muslims in British Colonial America: A Genealogical History*. Jefferson, N.C.: McFarland, 2012.

Hixson, Walter L. *American Settler Colonialism: A History*. New York: Palgrave Macmillan, 2013.

———. *The Myth of American Diplomacy: National Identity and U.S. Foreign Policy*. New Haven, Conn.: Yale University Press, 2008.

Hobsbawm, Eric. *The Age of Revolution, 1789–1848*. New York: Vintage Books, 1996.

Hochschild, Adam. *King Leopold's Ghost: A Story of Greed, Terror, and Heroism in Colonial Africa*. New York: Houghton Mifflin, 1999.

Hodgson, Marshall. *The Venture of Islam: Conscience and History in World Civilization*. Chicago: University of Chicago Press, 1974.

Hollander, Edith Portier. "Januarius MacGahan and the British Reaction to the Bulgarian Massacres of 1876: A Study of Influence." M.A. thesis, University of Florida, 1989.

Hollingsworth Miller, Aurie. "One Man's View: William Shaler and Algiers." In *Through Foreign Eyes: Western Attitudes toward North Africa*, edited by Alf Heggoy Andrew, Aurie H. Miller, James J. Cooke, and Paul J. Zingg, 7–56. Washington, D.C.: University Press of America, 1982.

Holme, John G. *The Life of Leonard Wood*. Garden City, N.Y.: Doubleday, Page, 1920.

Holmes, David L. *The Faiths of the Founding Fathers*. New York: Oxford University Press, 2006.

Holmes, James R. *Theodore Roosevelt and World Order: Police Power in International Relations*. Washington, D.C.: Potomac, 2006.

Holquist, Peter. "To Count, to Extract, and to Exterminate: Population Statistics and Population Politics in Late Imperial and Soviet Russia." In *A State of Nations: Empire and Nation-Making in the Age of Lenin and Stalin*, edited by Martin Terry and Ronald Grigor Suny, 111–44. New York: Oxford University Press, 2001.

Hoogland, Eric, ed. *Crossing the Waters: Arabic-Speaking Immigrants to the United States before 1940*. Washington, D.C.: Smithsonian Institute Press, 1987.

Horsman, Reginald. *Race and Manifest Destiny: The Origins of American Racial Anglo-Saxonism*. Cambridge, Mass.: Harvard University Press, 1981.

Hovanissian, Richard, ed. *The Armenian Genocide: Cultural and Ethical Legacies*. New Brunswick, N.J.: Transaction Publishers, 2007.

———. *The Armenian Genocide in Perspective*. New Brunswick, N.J.: Transaction Publishers, 1986.

———. *The Armenian People from Ancient to Modern Times*. Vol. 2. New York: St. Martin's, 1997.

———. *Remembrance and Denial: The Case of the Armenian Genocide*. Detroit: Wayne State University Press, 1998.

Howard, Harry N. *The King-Crane Commission: An American Inquiry in the Middle East.* Beirut: Khayats, 1963.

Hudson, Winthrop S. *Nationalism and Religion in America: Concepts of American Identity and Mission.* New York: Harper & Row, 1970.

Hunt, Michael. *The American Ascendancy: How the United States Gained and Wielded Global Dominance.* Chapel Hill: University of North Carolina Press, 2007.

———. *Ideology and U.S. Foreign Policy.* 2nd ed. New Haven, Conn.: Yale University Press, 2009.

Huntington, Samuel. "The Clash of Civilizations." *Foreign Affairs* 72 (Summer 1993): 22–49.

———. *The Clash of Civilizations and the Remaking of World Order.* New York: Simon & Schuster, 2006.

Hurley, Victor. *Malay Pirates: The Story of the Moros.* Bangkok: Orchid Press, 2009.

———. *Men in Sun Helmets.* New York: E. P. Dutton, 1936.

———. *Swish of the Kris: The Story of the Moros.* New York: E. P. Dutton, 1936.

Hutchison, William. *Errand to the World: American Protestant Thought and Foreign Missions.* Chicago: University of Chicago Press, 1987.

Hutchison, William, and Hartmut Lehmann, eds. *Many Are Chosen: Divine Election and Western Nationalism.* Harvard Theological Studies no. 38. Minneapolis: Fortress Press, 1994.

Hyman, Paula. *The Jews of Modern France.* Berkeley: University of California Press, 1998.

Ignatief, Michael. *The Russian Album.* New York: Viking, 1987.

Immerman, Richard H. *Empire for Liberty: A History of American Imperialism from Benjamin Franklin to Paul Wolfowitz.* Princeton, N.J.: Princeton University Press, 2010.

Iriye, Akira. *Cultural Internationalism and World Order.* Baltimore: Johns Hopkins University Press, 1997.

———. *Global Community: The Role of International Organizations in the Making of the Contemporary World.* Berkeley: University of California Press, 2002.

Isani, Mukhtar Ali. "Cotton Mather and the Orient." *New England Quarterly* 43 (March 1970): 46–58.

Iwamura, Jane Naomi. *Virtual Orientalism: Asian Religions and American Popular Culture.* New York: Oxford University Press, 2011.

Jackson, Carl T. *The Oriental Religions and American Thought: Nineteenth-Century Explorations.* Contributions in American Studies 55. Westport, Conn.: Greenwood, 1981.

Jacobs, Matthew F. *Imagining the Middle East: The Building of an American Foreign Policy, 1918–1967.* Chapel Hill: University of North Carolina Press, 2011.

Jacobson, Matthew Frye. *Barbarian Virtues: The United States Encounters Foreign Peoples at Home and Abroad.* New York: Hill & Wang, 2001.

———. *Whiteness of a Different Color: European Immigrants and the Alchemy of Race.* Cambridge, Mass.: Harvard University Press, 1999.

Jaher, Frederic Cople. *The Jews and the Nation: Revolution, Emancipation, State Formation and the Liberal Paradigm in America and France*. Princeton, N.J.: Princeton University Press, 2003.

——. *A Scapegoat in the New Wilderness: The Origins and Rise of Anti-Semitism in America*. Cambridge, Mass.: Harvard University Press, 1994.

Janis, Mark W., and Carolyn Evans, eds. *Religion and International Law*. Boston: Martinus Nijhoff, 2004.

Jeffrey, Keith. *The British Army and the Crisis of Empire, 1918–22*. Manchester, U.K.: Manchester University Press, 1984.

Jelavich, Barbara. *History of the Balkans: Eighteenth and Nineteenth Centuries*. Vol. 1. Cambridge, U.K.: Cambridge University Press, 1983.

Jenkins, Philip. *The Great and Holy War: How World War I Became a Religious Crusade*. New York: HarperCollins, 2014.

Jenkins, Roy. *Gladstone*. London: Macmillan, 1995.

Jensen, Ronald. "Eugene Schuyler and the Balkan Crisis." *Diplomatic History* 5 (June 2007): 23–37.

Jessup, Philip C. *Elihu Root*. 2 vols. New York: Dodd, Mead, 1938.

Jonassohn, Kurt, with Karin Solveig Björnson. *Genocide and Gross Human Rights Violations in Comparative Perspective*. New Brunswick, N.J.: Transaction Publishers, 1998.

Jones, Arun W. *Christian Missions in the American Empire: Episcopalians in Northern Luzon, the Philippines, 1902–1946*. New York: P. Lang, 2003.

Jones, Marian Moser. *The American Red Cross from Clara Barton to the New Deal*. Baltimore: Johns Hopkins University Press, 2014.

Jordan, Philip D. *The Evangelical Alliance for the United States of America, 1847–1900: Ecumenism, Identity and the Religion of the Republic*. Studies in American Religion 7. New York: Edwin Mellen, 1982.

Jordan, William G. *Black Newspapers and America's War for Democracy, 1914–1920*. Chapel Hill: University of North Carolina Press, 2001.

Kafadar, Cemal. *Between Two Worlds: The Construction of the Ottoman State*. Berkeley: University of California Press, 1995.

Kaiser, Hilmar. *Imperialism, Racism, and Development Theories: The Construction of a Dominant Paradigm on Ottoman Armenians*. Ann Arbor, Mich.: Gomidas Institute, 1997.

Kalmar, Ivan Davidson, and Derek J. Penslar, "Orientalism and the Jews: An Introduction." In *Orientalism and the Jews*, edited by Ivan Davidson Kalmar and Derek J. Penslar, xiii–xl. Waltham, Mass.: Brandeis University Press, 2002.

Kaplan, Amy. "'Left Alone with America': The Absence of Empire in the Study of American Culture." In *Cultures of United States Imperialism*, edited by Amy Kaplan and Donald Pease, 3–21. Durham, N.C.: Duke University Press, 1993.

Kark, Ruth. *American Consuls in the Holy Land, 1832–1914*. Detroit: Wayne State University Press, 1994.

Karpat, Kemal. *Studies in Ottoman Social and Political History: Selected Articles and Essays*. Boston: Brill, 2002.

———, ed. *The Turks of Bulgaria: The History, Culture and Political Fate of a Minority.* Istanbul: Isis, 1990.

Kayaoglu, Turan. *Legal Imperialism: Sovereignty and Extraterritoriality in Japan, the Ottoman Empire, and China.* New York: Cambridge University Press, 2010.

Kedourie, Elie. *England and the Middle East: The Destruction of the Ottoman Empire, 1914–1921.* Boulder, Colo.: Westview, 1987.

———, ed. *Nationalism in Asia and Africa.* New York: World Publishing, 1970.

Keiser, Hans-Lukas. *Nearest East: American Millennialism and Mission to the Middle East.* Philadelphia: Temple University Press, 2010.

Kenbib, Mohamed. *Juifs et Musulmans au Maroc, 1859–1948.* Rabat, Morocco: Publications de Faculté des Lettres et des Sciences Humaines, 1994.

———. *Les Protégés: Contribution à l'histoire Contemporaine du Maroc.* Rabat, Morocco: Publications de la Faculté des Lettres et des Sciences Humaines, 1996.

———. "Structures traditionnelles et protection etrangère au Maroc au XIXe siècle." *Hésperis-Tamuda* 22 (1984): 79–101.

Kennedy, Roger G. *Greek Revival America.* New York: Stuart, Tabori, & Chang, 1989.

Kerner, Howard Joseph. "Turko-American Diplomatic Relations, 1860–1880." Ph.D. diss., Georgetown University, 1949.

Kevorkian, Raymond. *The Armenian Genocide: A Complete History.* New York: Palgrave Macmillan, 2011.

Khala, Samir. *Civil and Uncivil Violence in Lebanon: A History of the Internationalization of Communal Conflict.* New York: Columbia University Press, 2002.

———. *Cultural Resistance: Global and Local Encounters in the Middle East.* London: Saqi Books, 2001.

———. *Protestant Missionaries in the Levant: Ungodly Puritans, 1820–1860.* New York: Routledge, 2012.

Kidd, Thomas. *American Christians and Islam: Evangelical Culture and Muslims from the Colonial Age to the Present.* Princeton, N.J.: Princeton University Press, 2009.

———. "Is It Worse to Follow Mahomet Than the Devil? Early American Uses of Islam." *Church History* 72 (December 2003): 766–90.

Kiefer, Thomas M. *The Tausug: Violence and Law in a Philippine Moslem Society.* Prospect Heights, Ill.: Waverland Press, 1986.

Kirakossian, Arman J. *The Armenian Massacres, 1894–1896: U.S. Media Testimony.* Detroit: Wayne State University, 2004.

———. *British Diplomacy and the Armenian Question: From the 1830s to 1914.* Princeton, N.J.: Gomidas Institute, 2003.

Klein, Christina. *Cold War Orientalism: Asia in the Middlebrow Imagination, 1945–1961.* Berkeley: University of California Press, 2006.

Klein, Janet. *The Margins of Empire: Kurdish Militias in the Ottoman Tribal Zone.* Stanford, Calif.: Stanford University Press, 2011.

Kloian, Richard Diran, ed. *The Armenian Genocide: News Accounts from the American Press, 1915–1922.* Richmond, Calif.: Heritage, 2007.

Koolakian, Robert George. *Struggle for Justice: The Story of the American Committee for the Independence of Armenia, 1915–1920.* Dearborn: Armenian Research Center, University of Michigan-Dearborn, 2008.

Kostandarithes, Danton Prescott. "The Diplomatic Career of Henry White, 1883–1919." Ph.D. diss., Tulane University, 1992.

Kramer, Lloyd S. *Lafayette in Two Worlds: Public Cultures and Personal Identities in an Age of Revolutions.* Chapel Hill: University of North Carolina Press, 1996.

Kramer, Paul A. *The Blood of Government: Race, Empire, the United States and the Philippines.* Chapel Hill: University of North Carolina Press, 2006.

———. "Empires, Exceptions, and Anglo-Saxons: Race and Rule between the British and United States Empires, 1880–1910." *Journal of American History* 88 (March 2002): 1315–53.

———. "Power and Connection: Imperial History of the United States and the World." *American Historical Review* (December 2011): 1348–91.

———. "The Pragmatic Empire: U.S. Anthropology and Colonial Politics in the Occupied Philippines, 1898–1916." Ph.D. diss., Princeton University, 1998.

Krenn, Michael L. *The Color of Empire: Race and American Foreign Relations.* Washington, D.C.: Potomac Books, 2006.

Kundnani, Arun. *The Muslims are Coming!: Islamophobia, Extremism, and the Domestic War on Terror.* Brooklyn: Verso Books, 2014.

Kyle, Richard G. *Evangelicalism: An Americanized Christianity.* New Brunswick, N.J.: Transaction Publishers, 2006.

Lacely, Jim. *Pershing.* New York: Palgrave Macmillan, 2008.

Lake, Marilyn, and Henry Reynolds. *Drawing the Global Colour Line: White Men's Countries and the International Challenge of Racial Equality.* New York: Cambridge University Press, 2008.

Lambert, Frank. *The Barbary Wars: American Independence in the Atlantic World.* New York: Hill & Wang, 2005.

———. *The Founding Fathers and the Place of Religion in America.* Princeton, N.J.: Princeton University Press, 2003.

Landenberger, Margaret. "United States Diplomatic Efforts on Behalf of Moroccan Jews, 1880–1906." Ph.D. diss., St. John's University, 1981.

Lane, Jack C. *Armed Progressive: General Leonard Wood.* San Rafael, Calif.: Presidio Press, 1978.

Larrabee, Stephen A. *Hellas Observed: The American Experience of Greece, 1775–1865.* New York: New York University Press, 1957.

Larsen, Peter. "Theodore Roosevelt and the Moroccan Crisis, 1904–1906." Ph.D. diss., Princeton University, 1984.

Laskier, Michael M. *The Alliance Israélite Universelle and the Jewish Communities of Morocco, 1862–1962.* Publications of the Diaspora Research Institute 45. Albany: State University of New York Press, 1983.

———. *North African Jewry in the Twentieth Century: The Jews of Morocco, Tunisia, and Algeria.* New York: New York University Press, 1994.

Laycock, Jo. *Imagining Armenia: Orientalism, Ambiguity and Intervention.* Manchester, U.K.: Manchester University Press, 2009.

Leff, Lisa Moses. *Sacred Bonds of Solidarity: The Rise of Jewish Internationalism in Nineteenth Century France*. Stanford, Calif.: Stanford University Press, 2006.

Leong, Karen J. *The China Mystique: Pearl S. Buck, Anna May Wong, Mayling Soong, and the Transformation of American Orientalism*. Berkeley: University of California Press, 2005.

Leoussi, Athena. "Nationalism and Racial Hellenism in Nineteenth Century England and France." *Ethnic and Racial Studies* 20 (January 1997): 42–68.

Lewis, James E. *The American Union and the Problem of Neighborhood: The United States and the Collapse of the Spanish Empire, 1783-1829*. Chapel Hill: University of North Carolina Press, 1998.

——. *John Quincy Adams: Policymaker for the Union*. Wilmington, Del.: SR Books, 2001.

Lewis, Martin W., and Kären E. Wigen, eds. *The Myth of Continents: A Critique of Metageography*. Berkeley: University of California Press, 1997.

Lewis, Mary D. *Divided Rule: Sovereignty and Empire in French Tunisia, 1881-1938*. Berkeley: University of California Press, 2013.

Lewy, Guenter. *The Armenian Massacres in Ottoman Turkey: A Disputed Genocide*. Salt Lake City: University of Utah Press, 2005.

Lieberman, Benjamin. *Terrible Fate: Ethnic Cleansing in the Making of Modern Europe*. Chicago: Ivan R. Dee, 2006.

Liebler, William F. "The United States and the Crimean War, 1853–1856." Ph.D. diss., University of Massachusetts, 1972.

Link, Arthur S. *Wilson: The Struggle for Neutrality*. Princeton, N.J.: Princeton University Press, 1960.

Linn, Brian McAllister. *Guardians of Empire: The U.S. Army and the Pacific, 1902-1940*. Chapel Hill: University of North Carolina Press, 1997.

Lipsky, George A. *John Quincy Adams: His Theory and Ideas*. New York: Crowell, 1950.

Little, Douglas. *American Orientalism: The United States and the Middle East since 1945*. Chapel Hill: University of North Carolina Press, 2002.

Littman, David. "Mission to Morocco, 1863–1864." In *The Century of Moses Montefiore*, edited by Sondia and V. D. Lipman, 171–229. Oxford: Oxford University Press, 1985.

Lockman, Zachary. *Contending Visions of the Middle East: The History and Politics of Orientalism*. New York: Cambridge University Press, 2004.

Logan, Rayford W. *The Senate and the Versailles Mandate System*. Washington, D.C.: Minorities Publishers, 1945.

Lorcin, Patricia. *Imperial Identities: Stereotyping, Prejudice and Race in Colonial Algeria*. New York: I. B. Tauris, 1995.

Love, Eric T. *Race over Empire: Racism and U.S. Imperialism 1865-1900*. Chapel Hill, N.C.: University of North Carolina Press, 2004.

Lowe, Lisa. *Critical Terrains: French and British Orientalisms*. Ithaca, N.Y.: Cornell University Press, 1991.

Lowry, Heath W. *The Story behind Ambassador Morgenthau's Story*. Istanbul: Isis, 1990.

Lutz, Donald. "The Relative Influence of European Writers on Late Eighteenth-Century American Political Thought." *American Political Science Review* 78 (March 1984): 189–97.

Macartney, C. A. *National States and National Minorities*. London: Oxford University Press, 1934.

MacDonald, Robert. "A Land without a People for a People without a Land": Civilizing Mission and American Support for Zionism, 1880s–1929." Ph.D. diss., Bowling Green State University, 2012.

Macfie, A. L. *The Eastern Question, 1774–1923*. New York: Longman, 1996.

———. *Orientalism*. New York: Longman, 2002.

MacKenzie, Kenneth M. *The Robe and the Sword: The Methodist Church and the Rise of American Imperialism*. Washington, D.C.: Public Affairs Press, 1961.

Majul, Cesar Adib. *Muslims in the Philippines*. Quezon City: University of the Philippines Press, 1973.

Makdisi, Ussama. *Artillery of Heaven: American Missionaries and the Failed Conversion of the Middle East*. Ithaca, N.Y.: Cornell University Press, 2008.

———. *The Culture of Sectarianism: Community, History, and Violence in Nineteenth-Century Ottoman Lebanon*. Berkeley: University of California Press, 2000.

———. *Faith Misplaced: The Broken Promise of U.S.-Arab Relations, 1820–2001*. New York: Public Affairs Press, 2010.

———. "Ottoman Orientalism." *American Historical Review* 107 (June 2002): 768–96.

———. "Reclaiming the Land of the Bible: Missionaries, Secularism, and Evangelical Modernity." *American Historical Review* 102 (June 1997): 683–84.

Malkasian, Mark. "The Disintegration of the Armenian Cause in the United States, 1918–1927." *International Journal of Middle East Studies* 16 (August 1984): 349–65.

Mamdani, Mahmood. *Good Muslim, Bad Muslim: America, the Cold War, and the Roots of Terror*. New York: Pantheon, 2004.

Manela, Erez. "The United States in the World." In *American History Now*, edited by Eric Foner and Lisa McGirr, 201–20. Philadelphia: Temple University Press, 2011.

———. *The Wilsonian Moment: Self-Determination and the International Origins of Anticolonial Nationalism*. New York: Oxford University Press, 2007.

Mann, Michael. *The Dark Side of Democracy: Explaining Ethnic Cleansing*. New York: Cambridge University Press, 2005.

Manuel, Frank E. *The Realities of American-Palestine Relations*. Westport, Conn.: Greenwood, 1949.

Marcus, Jacob Rader. *United States Jewry, 1776–1985*. 2 vols. Detroit: Wayne State University Press, 1989.

Marglin, Jessica M. "In the Courts of the Nations: Jews, Muslims and Legal Pluralism in Nineteenth-Century Morocco." Ph.D. diss., Princeton University, 2013.

Marr, Timothy. *The Cultural Roots of American Islamicism*. New York: Cambridge University Press, 2006.

Marsh, Peter. "Lord Salisbury and the Ottoman Massacres." *Journal of British Studies* 11 (May 1972): 63–83.

Marty, Martin E. *Righteous Empire: The Protestant Experience in America.* New York: Dial, 1970.

Marx, Anthony W. *Faith in Nation: Exclusionary Origins of Nationalism.* New York: Oxford University Press, 2003.

Masters, Bruce A. *Christians and Jews in the Ottoman Arab World: The Roots of Sectarianism.* New York: Cambridge University Press, 2001.

Masuzawa, Tomoko. *The Invention of World Religions, or, How European Universalism was Preserved in the Language of Pluralism.* Chicago: University of Chicago Press, 2005.

Matar, Nabil. *Turks, Moors and Englishmen in the Age of Discovery.* New York: Columbia University Press, 1999.

Mathews, Basil. *John R. Mott, World Citizen.* London: Student Christian Movement Press, 1934.

Matthew, Henry C. G. *Gladstone, 1875–1898.* New York: Oxford University Press, 1995.

Matthewson, Tim. *A Proslavery Foreign Policy: Haitian-American Relations during the Early Republic.* Westport, Conn.: Praeger, 2003.

May, Arthur J. "Crete and the United States, 1866–1869." *Journal of Modern History* 16 (December 1944): 286–93.

May, Ernest. *American Imperialism: A Speculative Essay.* New York: Atheneum, 1968.

———. *Imperial Democracy: The Emergence of America as a Great Power.* New York: Harcourt, Brace & World, 1961.

———. *The Making of the Monroe Doctrine.* Cambridge, Mass.: Belknap Press of Harvard University Press, 1975.

May, Glenn A. *Social Engineering in the Philippines: The Aims, Execution, and Impact of American Colonial Policy, 1900–1913.* Westport, Conn.: Greenwood, 1980.

Mayers, David. *Dissenting Voices in America's Rise to Power.* New York: Cambridge University Press, 2007.

Mayo, Louise A. *The Ambivalent Image: Nineteenth-Century America's Perception of the Jew.* Cranbury, N.J.: Associated University Presses, 1988.

Mazower, Mark. *The Balkans: A Short History.* New York: Modern Library, 2002.

———. *No Enchanted Palace: The End of Empire and the Ideological Origins of the United Nations.* Princeton, N.J.: Princeton University Press, 2009.

McAlister, Melani. *Epic Encounters: Culture, Media, and U.S. Interests in the Middle East since 1945.* Berkeley: University of California Press, 2001.

McCallum, Jack. *Leonard Wood: Rough Rider, Surgeon, Architect of American Empire.* New York: New York University Press, 2005.

McCarthy, Justin. *Death and Exile: The Ethnic Cleansing of Ottoman Muslims, 1821–1922.* Ann Arbor: University of Michigan Press, 1995.

———. *Muslims and Minorities: The Population of Ottoman Anatolia and the End of the Empire.* New York: New York University Press, 1983.

———. *The Turk in America: The Creation of an Enduring Prejudice.* Salt Lake City: Utah University Press, 2010.

McCarthy, Thomas. *Race, Empire, and the Idea of Human Development*. New York: Cambridge University Press, 2009.

McCoy, Alfred W. *Policing America's Empire: The United States, the Philippines, and the Rise of the Surveillance State*. Madison: University of Wisconsin Press, 2009.

McDougall, Walter A. *Promised Land, Crusader State: The American Encounter with the World since 1776*. New York: Houghton Mifflin Company, 1997.

McKenna, Thomas W. *Muslim Rulers and Rebels: Everyday Politics and Armed Separatism in the Southern Philippines*. Berkeley: University of California Press, 1998.

McLaughlin, Andrea Nicola. "Black Women, Identity, and the Quest for Humanhood and Wholeness: Wild Women in the Whirlwind." In *Wild Women in the Whirlwind: Afra-American Culture and the Contemporary Literary Renaissance*, edited by Joanne M. Braxton and Andrea Nicola McLaughlin, 147–80. New Brunswick, N.J.: Rutgers University Press, 1990.

McMeekin, Sean. *The Berlin-Baghdad Express: The Ottoman Empire and Germany's Bid for World Power*. Cambridge, Mass.: Belknap Press of Harvard University Press, 2010.

Meininger, Thomas A. *Ignatiev and the Establishment of the Bulgarian Exarchate, 1864–1872: A Study in Personal Diplomacy*. Madison: State Historical Society for the Department of History, University of Wisconsin, 1970.

Melson, Robert. "A Theoretical Inquiry into the Armenian Massacres of 1894–1896." *Comparative Studies in Society and History* 24 (July 1982): 481–509.

Merkley, Paul C. *The Politics of Christian Zionism, 1891–1948*. London: Routledge, 1998.

Mesrobian, Arpena S. *Like One Family: The Armenians of Syracuse*. Ann Arbor, Mich.: Gomidas Institute, 2000.

Michael, Robert. *A Concise History of American Antisemitism*. New York: Rowman & Littlefield, 2005.

Michie, Helena, and Ronald R. Thomas, eds. *Nineteenth-Century Geographies: The Transformation of Space from the Victorian Age to the American Century*. New Brunswick, N.J.: Rutgers University Press, 2003.

Milius, John, dir. *The Wind and the Lion*. Beverley Hills, Calif.: Herb Jaffe Productions, 1975.

Miller, Stuart Creighton. *"Benevolent Assimilation": The American Conquest of the Philippines, 1899–1903*. New Haven, Conn.: Yale University Press, 1982.

Miller, Susan. *A History of Modern Morocco*. New York: Cambridge University Press, 2012.

Millman, Richard. "The Bulgarian Massacres Reconsidered." *Slavonic and East European Review* 58 (April 1980): 218–31.

Mintz, Steven, and John Stauffer, eds. *The Problem of Evil: Slavery, Freedom, and the Ambiguities of American Reform*. Amherst: University of Massachusetts Press, 2007.

Mirak, Robert. *Torn between Two Lands: Armenians in America, 1890 to World War I*. Cambridge, Mass.: Harvard University Press, 1983.

Mitchell, Timothy. *Carbon Democracy: Political Power in the Age of Oil*. New York: Verso, 2011.

Mojzes, Paul. *Balkan Genocides: Holocaust and Ethnic Cleansings in the Twentieth Century*. Lanham, Md.: Rowman & Littlefield, 2011.

Monaco, C. S. *Rise of Modern Jewish Politics: Extraordinary Movement*. New York: Routledge, 2013.

Monge, José Trías. "Injustice According to Law: The *Insular Cases* and Other Oddities." In *Foreign in a Domestic Sense: Puerto Rico, American Expansion and the Constitution*, edited by Christina Duffy Burnett and Burke Marshall, 226–40. Durham, N.C.: Duke University Press, 2001.

Moranian, Suzanne. "The American Missionaries and the Armenian Question, 1915–1927." Ph.D. diss., University of Wisconsin, Madison, 1994.

———. "The Armenian Genocide and American Missionary Relief Efforts." In *America and the Armenian Genocide of 1915*, edited by Jay Winter, 185–213. Cambridge, U.K.: Cambridge University Press, 2003.

Morris, Benny. *The Birth of the Palestinian Refugee Problem, 1947–1949*. New York: Cambridge University Press, 1987.

Morris, Edmund. *The Rise of Theodore Roosevelt*. New York: Modern Library, 2001.

Morris, Ian, ed. *Classical Greece: Ancient Histories and Modern Archaeologies*. New York: Cambridge University Press, 1994.

Morrison, Alexander. "Metropole, Colony, and Imperial Citizenship in the Russian Empire." *Kritika: Explorations in Russian and Eurasian History* 13 (Spring 2012): 327–64.

Moses, A. Dirk, ed. *Empire, Colony, Genocide: Conquest, Occupation, and Subaltern Resistance in World History*. New York: Berghahn, 2008.

Mostashari, Firouzeh. *On the Religious Frontier: Tsarist Russia and Islam in the Caucasus*. International Library of Historical Studies 32. New York: I. B. Tauris, 2006.

Motadel, David, ed. *Islam and the European Empires*. Oxford: Oxford University Press, 2014.

Mowry, George. *The Era of Theodore Roosevelt, 1900–1912*. New York: Harper, 1958.

Murphy, Gretchen. *Hemispheric Imaginings: The Monroe Doctrine and Narratives of U.S. Empire*. Durham, N.C.: Duke University Press, 2005.

Murre-van den Berg, Heleen, ed. *New Faith in Ancient Lands: Western Missions in the Middle East in the Nineteenth and Early Twentieth Centuries*. Boston: Brill, 2006.

Musa, Bala A. *Framing Genocide: Media, Diplomacy, and Conflict Transformation*. Bethesda, Md.: Academica Press, 2007.

Naimark, Norman M. *Fires of Hatred: Ethnic Cleansing in Twentieth-Century Europe*. Cambridge, Mass.: Harvard University Press, 2001.

Nalbandian, Louise. *The Armenian Revolutionary Movement of the Nineteenth Century: The Origins and Development of Armenian Political Parties*. Berkeley: University of California Press, 1963.

Nassibian, Akaby. *Britain and the Armenian Questions, 1915–1923*. New York: St. Martin's, 1984.

Neely, Mark E., Jr. *The Fate of Liberty: Abraham Lincoln and Civil Liberties.*
New York: Oxford University Press, 1991.

Nelson, Derek. "Sins of Commission, Sins of Omission: Girard, Ricoeur, and the
Armenian Genocide." In *The Evolution of Evil*, edited by Gaymond Bennet,
Martinez J. Hewlitt, Ted Peters, and Robert John Russell, 318–33. Göttingen,
Germany: Vandenhoeck & Ruprecht, 2008.

Nelson, Eric. *The Greek Tradition in Republican Thought.* Cambridge, U.K.:
Cambridge University Press, 2004.

Nestorova-Matejic, Tatyana K. *American Missionaries among the Bulgarians,
1858–1912.* Boulder, Colo.: East European Monographs, 1987.

Neuberger, Mary. *The Orient Within: Muslim Minorities and the Negotiation of
Nationhood in Modern Bulgaria.* Ithaca, N.Y.: Cornell University Press, 2004.

———. "The Russo-Turkish War and the 'Eastern Jewish Question': Encounters
between Victims and Victors in Ottoman Bulgaria, 1877–8." *East European
Jewish Affairs* 26, no. 2 (1996): 53–66.

Neuman, Iver B. *Uses of the Other: "The East" in European Identity Formation.*
Minneapolis: University of Minnesota Press, 1999.

Nevins, Allan. *Henry White: Thirty Years of American Diplomacy.* New York:
Harper & Brothers, 1930.

Ninkovich, Frank A. *Global Dawn: The Cultural Foundation of American
Internationalism, 1865–1890.* Cambridge, Mass.: Harvard University Press, 2009.

Noll, Mark, David W. Bebbington, and George A. Rawlyk, eds. *Evangelicalism:
Comparative Studies of Popular Protestantism in North America, the British
Isles, and Beyond, 1700–1990.* New York: Oxford University Press, 1994.

Norris, Jacob. *Land of Progress: Palestine in the Age of Colonial Development,
1905–1948.* Oxford: Oxford University Press, 2013.

Nugent, Walter. *Habits of Empire: A History of American Expansion.* New York:
Vintage Books, 2009.

Nye, Russel B. *This Almost Chosen People: Essays in the History of American Ideas.*
East Lansing: Michigan State University Press, 1966.

Obenzinger, Hilton. *American Palestine: Melville, Twain, and the Holy Land
Mania.* Princeton, N.J.: Princeton University Press, 1999.

Offner, John L. *An Unwanted War: The Diplomacy of the United States and Spain
over Cuba, 1895–1898.* Chapel Hill: University of North Carolina Press, 1992.

Oren, Michael. *Power, Faith and Fantasy: America in the Middle East, 1776 to the
Present.* New York: W. W. Norton, 2007.

Orosa, Sixto Y. *The Sulu Archipelago and Its People.* Yonkers-on-Hudson, N.Y.:
World Book, 1923.

Pappas, Paul C. "Lafayette's Efforts to Send American Aid to Revolutionary Greece."
Journal of Modern Greek Studies 2 (May 1984): 105–16.

———. *The United States and the Greek War for Independence, 1821–1828.* New York:
Columbia University Press, 1978.

Pappé, Ilan. *The Ethnic Cleansing of Palestine.* Oxford: Oneworld, 2006.

Parezo, Nancy J., and Don D. Fowler. *Anthropology Goes to the Fair: The 1904
Louisiana Purchase Exposition.* Lincoln: University of Nebraska Press, 2007.

Parfitt, Tudor. "*Dhimma* versus Protection in Nineteenth Century Morocco." In *Israel and Ishmael: Studies in Muslim-Jewish Relations*, edited by Tudor Parfitt, 142–66. New York: St. Martin's, 2000.

Parsons, Lynn Hudson. *John Quincy Adams*. Madison, Wis.: Madison House, 1998.

———. *John Quincy Adams: A Bibliography*. Westport, Conn.: Greenwood, 1993.

Patai, Raphael. *The Arab Mind*. New York: Hatherleigh Press, 2002.

Payaslian, Simon. *United States Policy toward the Armenian Question and the Armenian Genocide*. New York: Palgrave Macmillan, 2005.

Peckham, Robert Shannan. *National Histories, Natural States: Nationalism and Politics of Place in Greece*. New York: I. B. Tauris, 2001.

Peek, Lori. *Behind the Backlash: Muslim Americans after 9/11*. Philadelphia: Temple University Press, 2011.

Pencak, William. "Anti-Semitism, Toleration, and Appreciation: The Changing Relations of Jews and Gentiles in Earl America." In *The First Prejudice: Religious Tolerance and Intolerance in Early America*, edited by Chris Beneke and Christopher Grenda, 241–63. Philadelphia: University of Pennsylvania Press, 2011.

Pennell, C. R. *Morocco since 1830: A History*. New York: New York University Press, 2000.

Penrose, Stephen B. L. *That They May Have Life: The Story of the American University of Beirut, 1866–1941*. New York: Trustees of the American University of Beirut, 1941.

Pérez, Louis A. *Cuba in the American Imagination: Metaphor and the Imperial Ethos*. Chapel Hill: University of North Carolina Press, 2008.

Perkins, Bradford. *The Creation of a Republic Empire*. Vol. 1 of *The Cambridge History of American Foreign Relations*. New York: Cambridge University Press, 1993.

Perkins, Dexter. *Hands Off: A History of the Monroe Doctrine*. Boston: Little Brown, 1941.

———. *A History of the Monroe Doctrine*. Boston: Little Brown, 1963.

Peskin, Lawrence A. *Captives and Countrymen: Barbary Slavery and the American Public, 1785–1816*. Baltimore: Johns Hopkins University Press, 2009.

Peterson, Merrill D. *"Starving Armenians": America and the Armenian Genocide, 1915–1930 and After*. Charlottesville: University of Virginia Press, 2004.

Philips, Clifton Jackson. *Protestant America and the Pagan World: The First Half Century of the American Board of Commissioners for Foreign Missions, 1810–1860*. Harvard East Asian Monographs 32. Cambridge, Mass.: Harvard University Press, 1969.

Philliou, Christine May. *Biography of an Empire: Governing Ottomans in an Age of Revolution*. Berkeley: University of California Press, 2011.

Pier, Arthur S. *American Apostles to the Philippines*. Boston: Beacon, 1950.

Pietz, William. "The 'Post-colonialism' of Cold War Discourse." *Social Text* 19–20 (Autumn 1988): 55–75.

Pitts, Jennifer. "Empire and Legal Universalisms in the Eighteenth Century." *American Historical Review* 117 (February 2012): 287–313.

Pizanias, Petros, ed. *The Greek Revolution of 1821: A European Event.* Istanbul: Isis, 2011.

Pope, Nicole, and Hugh Pope. *Turkey Unveiled: A History of Modern Turkey, Revised and Updated.* New York: Overlook Press, 2011.

Potter, Pitman. "Origin of the System of Mandates under the League of Nations." *American Political Science Review* 16 (November 1922): 563–83.

Pratt, Julius. *Expansionists of 1898: The Acquisition of Hawaii and the Spanish Islands.* Baltimore: Johns Hopkins University Press, 1934.

Preston, Andrew. "Bridging the Gap between the Sacred and the Secular in History of American Foreign Relations." *Diplomatic History* 30 (November 2006): 783–812.

———. *Sword of the Spirit, Shield of Faith: Religion in American War and Diplomacy.* New York: Alfred A. Knopf, 2012.

Prior, David. "Crete the Opening Wedge: Nationalism and International Affairs in Postbellum America." *Journal of Social History* 42 (Summer 2009): 861–87.

Prongas, Harry. "United States Recognition of Greek Independence." M.A. thesis, Washington, D.C., The American University, 1961.

Pryor, Elizabeth Brown. *Clara Barton: Professional Angel.* Philadelphia: University of Pennsylvania Press, 1987.

Pundeff, Marin V. *Bulgaria in American Perspective: Political and Cultural Issues.* Boulder, Colo.: East European Monographs, 1994.

Putney, Clifford, and Paul T. Burlin, eds. *Role of the American Board in the World: Bicentennial Reflections on the Organization's Missionary Work, 1810–2010.* Eugene: Ore.: Wipf & Stock, 2012.

Qureshi, Emran, and Michael A. Sells, eds. *The New Crusades: Constructing the Muslim Enemy.* New York: Columbia University Press, 2003.

Rae, Heather. *State Identities and the Homogenisation of Peoples.* Cambridge Studies in International Relations 84. Cambridge, U.K.: Cambridge University Press, 2002.

Rafael, Vicente L. *White Love and Other Events in Filipino History.* Durham, N.C.: Duke University Press, 2000.

Raizis, M. Byron, ed. *Greek Revolution and the American Muse: A Collection of Philhellenic Poetry, 1821–1828.* Thessaloniki, Greece: Institute for Balkan Studies, 1972.

Rambo, David Lloyd. "The Christian and Missionary Alliance in the Philippines, 1901–1970." Ph.D. diss., New York University, 1975.

Rana, Aziz. *The Two Faces of American Freedom.* Cambridge, Mass.: Harvard University Press, 2010.

Read, David. *Temperate Conquests: Spenser and the Spanish New World.* Detroit: Wayne State University Press, 2000.

Reed, James Eldin. "American Foreign Policy, the Politics of Missions and Josiah Strong, 1890–1900." *Church History: Studies in Christianity and Culture* 41 (June 1972): 230–45.

Reeves-Ellington, Barbara, Kathryn Kish Sklar, and Connie A. Shemio, eds. *Competing Kingdoms: Women, Mission, Nation, and the American Protestant Empire, 1812–1960.* Durham, N.C.: Duke University Press, 2010.

Reid, James J. *Crisis of the Ottoman Empire: Prelude to Collapse, 1839–1878.* Stuttgart: F. Steiner, 2000.

Reinhold, Meyer. *Classica Americana: The Greek and Roman Heritage in the United States.* Detroit: Wayne State University Press, 1984.

Reisser, Wesley J. *The Black Book: Woodrow Wilson's Secret Plan for Peace.* Lanham, Md.: Lexington, 2012.

Renda, Mary. *Taking Haiti: Military Occupation and the Culture of U.S. Imperialism, 1915–1940.* Chapel Hill: University of North Carolina Press, 2001.

Repousis, Angelo. "'The Cause of the Greeks': Philadelphia and the Greek War for Independence, 1821–1828." *Pennsylvania Magazine of History and Biography* 123 (October 1999): 333–63.

———. *Greek-American Relations from Monroe to Truman.* Kent, Ohio: Kent State University Press. 2013.

Reuter, Frank T. *Catholic Influence on American Colonial Policies, 1898–1904.* Austin: University of Texas Press, 1967.

Reynolds, Michael A. *Shattering Empires: The Clash and Collapse of the Ottoman and Russian Empires, 1908–1918.* New York: Cambridge University Press, 2011.

Richard, Carl J. *The Founders and the Classics: Greece, Rome and the American Enlightenment.* Cambridge, Mass.: Harvard University Press, 1995.

———. *The Golden Age of the Classics in America: Greece, Rome, and the Antebellum United States.* Cambridge, Mass.: Harvard University Press, 2009.

Richard, Laura E., and Maud Howe Elliott. *Julia Ward Howe, 1819–1910.* Vol. 2. Boston: Houghton Mifflin, 1916.

Richmond, Walter. *The Circassian Genocide.* New Brunswick, N.J.: Rutgers University Press, 2013.

Robinson, David M. *America in Greece: A Traditional Policy.* New York: Anatolia Press, 1948.

Rodil, B. R. *The Minoritization of the Indigenous Communities of Mindanao and the Sulu Archipelago.* Davao City, Philippines: Alternate Forum for Research in Mindanao, 1994.

Rodinson, Maxime. *Europe and the Mystique of Islam.* London: I. B. Tauris, 2002.

Rodkey, Frederick Stanley. "Lord Palmerston and the Rejuvenation of Turkey, Part II, 1839–1841." *Journal of Modern History* 2 (June 1930): 193–225.

Rodogno, Davide. *Against Massacre: Humanitarian Interventions in the Ottoman Empire, 1815–1914: The Emergence of a European Concept and International Practice.* Princeton, N.J.: Princeton University Press, 2012.

Rodrigue, Aron. "Difference and Tolerance in the Ottoman Empire: Interview by Nancy Reynolds." *Stanford Electronic Humanities Review* 5, no. 1 (1996).

———. *French Jews, Turkish Jews: The Alliance Israélite Universelle and the Politics of Jewish Schooling in Turkey, 1860–1925.* Bloomington: Indiana State University, 1990.

———. *Jews and Muslims: Images of Sephardi and Eastern Jewries in Modern Times.* Seattle: University of Washington Press, 2003.

Roediger, David. *Wages of Whiteness: Race and the Makings of the American Working Class*. New York: Verso, 1999.

Roessel, David. *In Byron's Shadow: Modern Greece in the England and American Imagination*. New York: Oxford University Press, 2001.

Rogin, Michael. *Blackface, White Noise: Jewish Immigrants in the Hollywood Melting Pot*. Berkeley: University of California Press, 1998.

Rotberg, Robert I., and Thomas G. Weiss, eds. *From Massacres to Genocide: The Media, Public Policy, and Humanitarian Crises*. Washington, D.C.: Brookings Institution, 1996.

Rotter, Andrew. "Saidism without Said: Orientalism and U.S. Diplomatic History." *American Historical Review* 105 (October 2000): 1205–17.

Rouard de Card, Edgard. *Les États-Unis d'Amérique et le Protectorat de la France au Maroc*. Paris: A. Pedone, 1930.

Roudometof, Victor. *Nationalism, Globalization, and Orthodoxy: The Social Origins of Ethnic Conflict in the Balkans*. Westport, Conn.: Greenwood, 2001.

Rowe, Kenneth Wyer. *Mathew Carey: A Study in American Economic Development*. Baltimore: Johns Hopkins University Press, 1922.

Rubinstein, William D., and Hilary L. Rubinstein. *Philosemitism: Admiration and Support in the English-Speaking World for Jews, 1840–1939*. New York: St. Martin's, 1999.

Ruether, Rosemary Radford. *America, Amerikkka: Elect Nation and Imperial Violence*. Oakville, Conn.: Equinox, 2007.

Rushdy, Ashraf H. A. *American Lynching*. New Haven, Conn.: Yale University Press, 2012.

Russell, Greg. *John Quincy Adams and the Public Virtues of Diplomacy*. Columbia: University of Missouri Press, 1995.

Ryan, David. *U.S. Foreign Policy in World History*. New York: Routledge, 2000.

Saab, Ann. *Reluctant Icon: Gladstone, Bulgaria and the Working Classes*. Harvard Historical Studies 109. Cambridge, Mass.: Harvard University Press, 1991.

Said, Edward. "A Clash of Ignorance." *Nation*, 21 October 2001.

——. *Covering Islam: How the Media and the Experts Determine How We See the Rest of the World*. New York: Pantheon Books, 1981.

——. *Orientalism*. New York: Vintage Books, 1978.

St. Clair, William. *That Greece Might Still Be Free: The Philhellenes in the War for Independence*. Cambridge, U.K.: Open Book, 2008.

Sajjad, Memoona. "A 'Non Western' Reading of the 'Clash of Civilizations' Theory: Through the Eyes of 'The Rest.'" *International Journal of Political Science and Development* 1 (October 2013): 42–104.

Salman, Michael. *The Embarrassment of Slavery: Controversies over Bondage and Nationalism in the American Colonial Philippines*. Berkeley: University of California Press, 2001.

Salt, Jeremy. *Imperialism, Evangelism and the Ottoman Armenians, 1878–1896*. London: Frank Cass, 1993.

Sanger, David. "Bush Cites Philippines as Model in Rebuilding Iraq." *New York Times*, 19 October 2003.

Sanger, George P., ed. *The Statutes at Large, Treaties, and Proclamations of the United States of America from December 1867, to March 1869*. Vol. 10. Boston: Little Brown, 1869.

Sarna, Jonathan D. *Jacksonian Jew: The Two Worlds of Mordecai Noah*. New York: Holmes & Meier, 1981.

Sarna, Jonathan D., and David G. Dalin. *Religion and the State in the American Jewish Experience*. Notre Dame, Ind.: University of Notre Dame Press, 1997.

Satia, Priya. "The Defense of Inhumanity: Air Control and the British Idea of Arabia." *American Historical Review* 111 (February 2006): 16–51.

Saul, Norman E. *Concord and Conflict: The United States and Russia, 1867–1914*. Lawrence: University Press of Kansas, 1996.

Saxton, Alexander. *The Rise and Fall of the White Republic: Class Politics and Mass Culture in Nineteenth-Century America*. New York: Verso, 1990.

Schreurs, Peter. *Angry Days in Mindanao: The Philippine Revolution and the War against the U.S. in East and Northeast Mindanao, 1897–1908*. Manila: National Commission for Culture and the Arts, National Historical Institute, 2000.

Schroeter, Daniel J. "Anglo-Jewry and Essaouira (Mogador), 1860–1900: The Social Implications of Philanthropy." *Jewish Historical Society of England* 28 (1981–82): 60–88.

———. "From Sephardi to Oriental: The 'Decline' Theory of Jewish Civilization in Middle East and North Africa." In *The Jewish Contribution to Civilization: Reassessing an Idea*, edited by Jeremy Cohen and Richard I. Cohen, 125–48. Portland, Ore.: Littman Library of Jewish Civilization, 2008.

———. *Merchants of Essaouira: Urban Society and Imperialism in Southwestern Morocco, 1844–1886*. Cambridge, U.K.: Cambridge University Press, 1988.

———. *The Sultan's Jew: Morocco and the Sephardi World*. Stanford, Calif.: Stanford University Press, 2002.

———. "Trade as a Mediator in Muslim-Jewish Relations: Southwestern Morocco in the Nineteenth Century." In *Jews among Arabs: Contacts and Boundaries*, edited by Marc Cohen and Abraham Udovitch, 113–40. Princeton, N.J.: Darwin Press, 1989.

Schueller, Malini Johar. *U.S. Orientalisms: Race, Nation, and Gender in Literature, 1790–1890*. Ann Arbor: University of Michigan Press, 1998.

Schumacher, Frank. "The American Way of Empire: National Tradition and Transatlantic Adaptation in America's Search for Imperial Identity, 1898–1910." *GHI Bulletin* 31 (Fall 2002): 35–50.

Schurz, Carl. *Life of Henry Clay*. Vol. 1. New York: AMS Press, 1972.

Segel, Binjamin W. *A Lie and a Libel: The History of the Protocols of the Elders of Zion*. Lincoln: University of Nebraska Press, 1995.

Sekulow, Jay A. *Witnessing Their Faith: Religious Influence on Supreme Court Justices and Their Opinions*. Lanham, Md.: Rowman & Littlefield, 2006.

Sen, Amartya. *Identity and Violence: The Illusion of Destiny*. New York: W. W. Norton, 2006.

———. "What Clash of Civilizations?" *Slate*, 29 March 2006.

Seton-Watson, Robert W. *Disraeli, Gladstone and the Eastern Question: A Study in Diplomacy and Party Politics*. London: F. Cass, 1971.

Setton, Kenneth Meyer. *Western Hostility to Islam and Prophecies of Turkish Doom*. Philadelphia: American Philosophical Society, 1992.

Sexton, Jay. *The Monroe Doctrine: Empire and Nation in Nineteenth-Century America*. New York: Hill & Wang, 2011.

Sha'ban, Fuad. *Islam and Arabs in Early American Thought: The Roots of Orientalism in America*. Durham, N.C.: Acorn University Press, 1991.

Shaffer, Brenda, ed. *The Limits of Culture: Islam and Foreign Policy*. Cambridge, Mass.: MIT Press, 2006.

Shannon, R. T. *Gladstone and the Bulgarian Agitation, 1876*. London: Thomas Nelson & Sons, 1963.

Sharkey, Heather. *American Evangelicals in Egypt: Missionary Encounters in an Age of Empire*. Princeton, N.J.: Princeton University Press, 2008.

Shasko, Philip. "From the Other Shore: The American Perspective of the Eastern Question and the Bulgarian Crisis of 1876." *Bulgarian Historical Review* 4 (1990): 3–21.

Shaw, Angel Velasco, and Luis H. Francia, eds. *Vestiges of War: The Philippine-American War and the Aftermath of an Imperial Dream, 1899–1999*. New York: New York University Press, 2002.

Silbey, David J. *A War of Frontier and Empire: The Philippine-American War, 1899–1902*. New York: Hill & Wang, 2007.

Simms, Brendan, and D. J. B. Trim, eds. *Humanitarian Intervention: A History*. Cambridge, U.K.: Cambridge University Press, 2011.

Skinner, Elliott P. *African Americans and U.S. Policy toward Africa, 1850–1924: In Defense of Black Nationality*. Washington, D.C.: Howard University Press, 1992.

Sluglett, Peter. "An Improvement on Colonialism? The 'A' Mandates and Their Legacy in the Middle East." *International Affairs* 90, no. 2 (2014): 413–27.

Smedley, Audrey. *Race in North America: Origin and Evolution of a World View*. Oxford: Westview Press, 1993.

Smith, Andrea. *Colonial Memory and Postcolonial Europe: Maltese Settlers in Algeria and France*. Bloomington: Indiana University Press, 2006.

Smith, Anthony D. *Chosen Peoples: Sacred Sources of National Identity*. Oxford: Oxford University Press, 2003.

———. *Theories of Nationalism*. New York: Harper & Row, 1971.

Smith, Gary Scott. *Faith and the Presidency: From George Washington to George W. Bush*. New York: Oxford University Press, 2006.

Smith, Neil. *American Empire: Roosevelt's Geographer and the Prelude to Globalization*. Berkeley: University of California Press, 2004.

Smythe, Donald. *Guerrilla Warrior: The Early Life of John J. Pershing*. New York: Scribner, 1973.

Snyder, Timothy. *Bloodlands: Europe between Hitler and Stalin*. New York: Basic Books, 2010.

Spellberg, Denise. *Thomas Jefferson's Qur'an: Islam and the Founders.* New York: Alfred A. Knopf, 2013.

Spickard, Paul. *Almost All Aliens: Immigration, Race, and Colonialism in American History and Identity.* New York: Routledge, 2007.

Stanley, Peter W. ed. *Reappraising an Empire: New Perspectives on Philippine-American History.* Cambridge, Mass.: Committee on American-East Asian Relations of the Department of History/Council on East Asian Studies, Harvard University, 1984.

Stanton, William. *The Leopard's Spots: Scientific Attitudes toward Race in America, 1815–59.* Chicago: University of Chicago Press, 1982.

Steinberg, Stephen. *The Academic Melting Pot: Catholics and Jews in American Higher Education.* New York: McGraw-Hill, 1974.

Stephanson, Anders. *Manifest Destiny: American Expansion and the Empire of Right.* New York: Hill & Wang, 1995.

Still, William N., Jr. *American Sea Power in the Old World: The United States Navy in European and Near Eastern Waters, 1865–1917.* Westport, Conn.: Greenwood, 1980.

Stillman, Norman. "Myth, Countermyth and Distortion." *Tikkun* 6 (May–June 1991): 55–64.

Stivers, William. "Woodrow Wilson and the Arab World: The Liberal Dilemma." In *The Prospects of Liberalism: Nine Essays,* edited by Timothy Fuller, 106–23. Colorado Springs: Colorado College, 1984.

Stojanović, Mihailo D. *The Great Powers and the Balkans, 1875–1878.* Cambridge, U.K.: Cambridge University Press, 1939.

Stoler, Ann Laura. *Carnal Knowledge and Imperial Power: Race and the Intimate in Colonial Rule.* Berkeley: University of California Press, 2002.

———. *Haunted by Empire: Geographies of Intimacy in North American History.* Durham, N.C.: Duke University Press, 2006.

Stoler, Ann Laura, and Frederick Cooper, eds. *Tensions of Empire: Colonial Cultures in a Bourgeois World.* Berkeley: University of California Press, 1997.

Strakhovsky, Leonid I. "General Count N. P. Ignatiev and the Pan-Slav Movement." *Journal of Central European Affairs* 17 (October 1957): 223–36.

Strong, William Ellsworth. *The Story of the American Board.* New York: Arno Press, 1969.

Stuart, Graham H. *The International City of Tangier.* Stanford, Calif.: Stanford University Press, 1931.

Sturtevant, David Reeves. *Popular Uprisings in the Philippines, 1840–1940.* Ithaca, N.Y.: Cornell University Press, 1976.

Sullivan, Rodney J. *Exemplar of Americanism: The Philippine Career of Dean C. Worcester.* Ann Arbor: Center for South and Southeast Asian Studies, University of Michigan, 1991.

Sumner, Benedict H. *Russia and the Balkans, 1870–1880.* Hamden, Conn.: Archon, 1962.

Suny, Ronald G. *Looking toward Ararat: Armenia in Modern History.* Bloomington: Indiana University Press, 1993.

——. "Writing Genocide: The Fate of the Ottoman Armenians." In *A Question of Genocide: Armenians and Turks at the End of the Ottoman Empire*, edited by Ronald Grigor Suny, Fatma Muge Gōçek, and Naiman M. Naimark, 15–41. New York: Oxford University Press, 2011.

Sutton, Robert K. *Americans Interpret the Parthenon: The Progression of Greek Revival Architecture from the East Coast to Oregon, 1800–1860*. Niwot: University Press of Colorado, 1992.

Suzuki, Nobutaka. "Upholding Filipino Nationhood: The Debate over Mindanao in the Philippine Legislature, 1907–1913." *Journal of Southeast Asian Studies* 44 (June 2013): 266–91.

Taïeb, Jacques. *Être Juif au Maghreb à la Veille de la Colonisation*. Paris: Éditions Albin Michel, 1994.

Talbot, Christine. "'Turkey Is in Our Midst': Orientalism and Contagion in Nineteenth Century Anti-Mormonism." *Journal of Law and Family Studies* 8 (Summer 2006): 363–88.

Tamarkin, Elisa. *Anglophilia: Deference, Devotion, and Antebellum America*. Chicago: University of Chicago Press, 2008.

——. *A History of the Philippines*. Quezon City: University of the Philippines Press, 1987.

Tan, Samuel K. *Sulu under American Military Rule*. Quezon City: University of the Philippines Press, 1968.

Tanaka, Yuki, and Marily B. Young, eds. *Bombing Civilians: A Twentieth Century History*. New York: New Press, 2009.

Tanner, Jeremy. "Introduction to the New Edition Race and Representation in Ancient Art: Black Athena and After." In *From the Pharaohs to the Fall of the Roman Empire*. Vol. 1 of *The Image of the Black in Western Art*, edited by David Bindman, Henry Louis Gates Jr., and Karen C. Dalton, 1–40. Cambridge, Mass.: Harvard University Press, 2010.

Tarling, Nicolas. *Imperialism and Southeast Asia: "A Fleeting, Passing Phase."* New York: Routledge, 2001.

Tarshish, Allan. "Board of Delegates of American Israelites (1859–1878)." Rabbinical thesis, Hebrew Union College, Jewish Institute of Religion, 1932.

Teed, Paul E. *John Quincy Adams: Yankee Nationalist*. New York: Nova Science, 2011.

Tehranian, John. *Whitewashed: America's Invisible Middle Eastern Minority*. New York: New York University Press, 2009.

Tejirian, Eleanor H., and Reeva Spector Simon, eds. *Altruism and Imperialism: Western Cultural and Religious Missions in the Middle East*. New York: Middle East Institute, Columbia University, 2002.

——. *Conflict, Conquest and Conversion: Two Thousand Years of Christian Missions in the Middle East*. New York: Columbia University Press, 2012.

Theriault, Henry C. "Rethinking Dehumanization in Genocide." In *The Armenian Genocide: Cultural and Ethical Legacies*, edited by Richard Hovannisian, 27–40. New Brunswick, N.J.: Transaction Publishers, 2007.

Thistlethwaite, Frank. *The Anglo-American Connection in the Early Nineteenth Century*. Philadelphia: University of Pennsylvania Press, 1959.

Thompson, Arthur William. *The Uncertain Crusade: America and the Russian Revolution of 1905.* Amherst: University of Massachusetts Press, 1970.

Thompson, Wayne Wray. "Governors of the Moro Province: Wood, Bliss, and Pershing in the Southern Philippines, 1903–1913." Ph.D. diss., University of California, 1975.

Tirman, John. *The Deaths of Others: The Fate of Civilians in America's Wars.* New York: Oxford University Press, 2011.

Todorova, Maria. *Imagining the Balkans.* New York: Oxford University Press, 1997.

Tompkins, E. Berkeley. *Anti-Imperialism in the United States: The Great Debate, 1890–1920.* Philadelphia: University of Pennsylvania Press, 1970.

Trent, James W., Jr. *The Manliest Man: Samuel Howe and the Contours of Nineteenth-Century America Reform.* Amherst: University of Massachusetts Press, 2012.

Turan, Ömer. *The Turkish Minority in Bulgaria.* Ankara: Türk Tarih Kurumu Basimevi, 1998.

Tuveson, Ernest Lee. *Redeemer Nation: The Idea of America's Millennial Role.* Chicago: University of Chicago Press, 1968.

Trask, Roger R. *The United States Response to Turkish Nationalism and Reform, 1914–1939.* Minneapolis: University of Minnesota Press, 1971.

Tyrell, Ian. *Reforming the World: The Creation of America's Moral Empire.* Princeton, N.J.: Princeton University Press, 2011.

———. *Transnational Nation: United States History in Global Perspective since 1789.* Basingstoke, U.K.: Palgrave Macmillan, 2007.

Üngör, Uğur Ümit. "Turkey for the Turks: Demographic Engineering in Eastern Anatolia, 1914–1945." In *A Question of Genocide: Armenians and Turks at the End of the Ottoman Empire*, edited by Ronald Grigor Suny and Fatma Muge Göçek, 287–305. New York: Oxford University Press, 2011.

van der Veer, Peter and Hartmut Lehmann, eds. *Nation and Religion: Perspectives on Europe and Asia.* Princeton, N.J.: Princeton University Press, 1999.

van Seteen, Gonda Aline Hector. *Liberating Hellenism from the Ottoman Empire: Comte de Marcellus and the Last of the Classics.* New York: Palgrave Macmillan, 2010.

Varg, Paul A. *Edward Everett: The Intellectual in the Turmoil of Politics.* Selinsgrove, Pa.: Susquehanna University Press, 1992.

Vergara, Benito M., Jr. *Displaying Filipinos: Photography and Colonialism in Early 20th Century Philippines.* Quezon City: University of the Philippines Press, 1995.

Vogel, Lester I. *To See a Promised Land: Americans and the Holy Land in the Nineteenth Century.* University Park: Pennsylvania State University Press, 1993.

Voldoire, Aline. "The Transnational Politics of French and American Jews, 1860–1920." Ph.D. diss., Columbia University, 2007.

von Eschen, Penny M. *Race against Empire: Black Americans and Anticolonialism, 1937–1957.* Ithaca, N.Y.: Cornell University Press, 1997.

Vratzian, Simon. *Armenia and the Armenian Question.* Boston: Hairenik, 1943.

Walker, Christopher. *Armenia: The Survival of a Nation.* New York: St. Martin's, 1980.

Walker, Dale L. *Januarius MacGahan: The Life and Campaigns of an American War Correspondent.* Athens: Ohio University Press, 1988.

Ward, Alan J. "Immigrant Minority 'Diplomacy': American Jews and Russia, 1901–1912." *Bulletin of the British Association for American Studies* 9 (December 1964): 8.

Warren, James Francis. *The Sulu Zone, 1768–1898: The Dynamics of External Trade, Slavery and Ethnicity in the Transformation of a Southeast Asian Maritime State.* Singapore: Singapore University Press, 1981.

Weeks, William Earl. *John Quincy Adams and American Global Empire.* Lexington: University Press of Kentucky, 1992.

Weill, Georges. *Émancipation et Progrès: L'Alliance Israélite Universelle et les Droits de l'homme.* Paris: Éditions du Nadir, 2000.

Weiner, Myron, and Michael S. Teitelbaum. *Political Demography, Demographic Engineering.* New York: Berghahn, 2001.

Wesling, Meg. *Empire's Proxy: American Literature and U.S. Imperialism in the Philippines.* New York: New York University Press, 2011.

Wheelan, Joseph. *Jefferson's War: America's First War on Terror, 1801–1805.* New York: Carroll & Graf, 2003.

Whitaker, Brian. "Its Best Use Is a Doorstop." *Guardian,* 24 May 2004.

White, Ronald, Jr., and C. Howard Hopkins. *The Social Gospel: Religion and Reform in Changing America.* Philadelphia: Temple University Press, 1976.

Williams, Robert A. *The American Indian in Western Legal Thought: The Discourses of Conquest.* New York: Oxford University Press, 1990.

Williams, Walter L. "United States Indian Policy and the Debate over Philippine Annexation: Implications for the Origins of American Imperialism." *Journal of American History* 66 (March 1980): 810–31.

Wilson, Ann. "In the Name of God, Civilization and Humanity: The United States and the Armenian Massacres of the 1890s." *Le Mouvement Social* 227 (April 2009): 27–44.

Wilson, Mary C. "The Damascus Affair and the Beginnings of France's Empire in the Middle East." In *Histories of the Modern Middle East: New Directions,* edited by Israel Gershoni, Hakan Erdem, and Ursala Wökock. Boulder, Colo.: Lynne Rienner Publishers, 2002.

Winter, Jay, ed. *America and the Armenian Genocide of 1915.* Cambridge, U.K.: Cambridge University Press, 2003.

Winterer, Caroline. *The Culture of Classicism: Ancient Greece and Rome in American Intellectual Life, 1780–1910.* Baltimore: Johns Hopkins University Press, 2002.

Woodhouse, C. M. *The Philhellenes.* London: Hodder & Stoughton, 1969.

Wyman, David S. *The Abandonment of the Jews: America and the Holocaust, 1941–1945.* New York: Pantheon, 1984.

Yokota, Kariann Akemi. *Unbecoming British: How Revolutionary America Became a Postcolonial Nation.* New York: Oxford University Press, 2011.

Yoshihara, Mari. *Embracing the East: White Women and American Orientalism.* New York: Oxford University Press, 2003.

Yothers, Brian. *The Romance of the Holy Land in American Travel Writing, 1790–1876.* Burlington, Vt.: Ashgate, 2007.

Young, Robert J. *An American by Degrees: The Extraordinary Lives of the French Ambassador Jules Jusserand.* Montreal: McGill-Queen's University Press, 2009.

Zacks, Richard. *Thomas Jefferson, the First Marines, and the Secret Mission of 1805.* New York: Hyperion, 2005.

Zafrani, Haïm. *Le Judaïsme Maghrébin: Le Maroc, Terre de Rencontres des Cultures et des Civilisations.* Rabat, Morocco: Marsam, 2003.

Zein, M. Faruk. *Christianity, Islam and Orientalism.* London: Saqi, 2003.

Zelinsky, Wilber. "Classical Town Names in the United States: The Historical Geography of an American Idea." *Geographical Review* 57 (October 1967): 463–95.

Index

ABCFM. *See* American Board of
Commissioners for Foreign Missions
Abdul Hamid II (Ottoman sultan),
176–77, 241, 247, 276, 277–78
abolitionism, 58, 66–67, 117, 340 (n. 89)
Abrahamic faiths, 6
Abu Bakr (sultan of Sulu), 357 (n. 1)
ACASR (American Committee for
Armenian and Syrian Relief),
289–93, 297, 305
ACIA (American Committee for the
Independence of Armenia), 300–301,
306–7
Adams, John Quincy: and American
domestic politics, 339 (n. 67);
and American Revolution, 13;
anti-Semitism, 101; denunciation of
Islam, 52–53, 320, 341 (n. 107); and
Greek War of Independence, 43, 44,
45–46, 47, 50–51, 339 (n. 67)
Adana massacres (1909), 277, 281
Ade, George, 193, 194 (ill.)
Adler, Cyrus, 148
African Americans, 14, 283–84. *See also*
American racism; slavery
Aguinaldo, Emilio, 174, 175
Alexander, Jeffrey C., 7
Alexander I (tsar of Russia), 38–39
Algeciras Conference (1906), 144–52;
and Dreyfus affair, 154; Einstein
mission, 150–52; and Jewish
American activism, 146–47, 148–49,
356 (n. 101); and mandate system,
302; origins of, 144–47
Algeria, 104, 114, 153
Alliance Israélite Universelle (France):
and Algeciras Conference, 148–49,
356 (n. 101); and Bulgarian national-

ism, 95–96; founding of, 110; and
imperialism/colonialism, 113–14;
Jewish American coordination with,
114–15; and Jews as civilizing/
mediating agents, 114; and Moroccan
protégé system, 123, 133, 137–38;
and Safi Affair, 124; and Spanish-
Moroccan War, 111
America as Mandatory for Armenia
(ACIA), 306–7
American Anthropological Society,
361–62 (n. 118)
American anti-imperialism, 6, 162,
212–13, 215, 322, 366 (n. 111)
American anti-Semitism: and Damascus
Affair, 106–7, 108; and ethnic
nationalism, 276; and Holocaust, 323;
and immigration, 103, 126, 276; and
Jewish American activism, 8, 101, 103,
117, 124–25, 126; and Mindanao Plan,
323; and mistrust, 102, 146; and *The
Protocols of the Elders of Zion*, 357
(n. 120); and racial/religious hierarchies, 8, 102, 103; and Safi Affair,
117; and United States as Christian
nation, 99–100, 124, 348 (n. 2)
American Board of Commissioners for
Foreign Missions (ABCFM), 1–3; and
Bulgarian nationalism, 85, 90, 92, 347
(n. 90); and Druze-Maronite conflict,
56; and Ottoman reforms, 70, 71;
political influence, 69, 249, 343 (n. 2);
and postwar Greece, 54; and Robert
College, 72, 344 (n. 11); and U.S.
annexation of the Philippines, 160; and
World War I, 294; and Young Turks,
278. *See also* Protestant missionaries
and Armenian Massacres

435

American Board of Delegates of
American Israelites. *See* Board of
Delegates of American Israelites
American Civil War: and American
racism, 22; and American treatment
of Moros, 180; and Cretan Insurrec-
tion, 57–58, 63, 64, 66; and Jewish
American activism, 117; and Perdicaris, 130
American colonial era, 10–13
American Colonization Society, 35
American Committee for Armenian and
Syrian Relief (ACASR), 289–93, 297,
305. *See also* Near East Relief
American Committee for the Independence of Armenia (ACIA), 300–301,
306–7
American domestic politics: and
American treatment of Moros,
232–33, 359 (n. 52); and Armenian
mandate proposals, 312; and
Armenian Massacres, 244–45, 260,
268; and Damascus Affair, 108–9;
and Greek War of Independence, 339
(n. 67); and Russian anti-Semitism,
144–45
American exceptionalism, 23; and
American treatment of Moros, 159,
209–10; and Armenian mandate
proposals, 301, 307, 312; and
Barbary pirates, 15; and Bulgarian
nationalism, 77; and Cretan Insurrection, 58–60; and Damascus
Affair, 106; and European policies,
20–21; and Family of Nations
concept, 16; and imperialism/
colonialism, 159; and isolationism,
45–46, 48; and Jewish American
activism, 8, 107, 112, 113, 322; and
Madrid Conference, 134, 140; and
mandate system, 316; and Moroccan
protégé system, 131–32; and United
States as Christian nation, 99–100;
and Wilson's foreign policy, 272–73,
275, 293, 318; and World War I, 318

American imperialism/colonialism:
ambivalence about, 170; American
opposition to, 6, 162, 212–13, 215,
322, 366 (n. 111); Christianity as
justification for, 159–61, 191–92
(*see also* Family of Nations concept);
and conversion goals, 161; and ethnic
nationalism, 21; and exceptionalism,
159; and force, 22, 23, 184, 218–19,
319; historiography, 27; Insular
Cases, 208, 364 (n. 75); and Iraq War,
330–31; and Jewish American
activism, 101; legacies of, 326–27;
and mandate system, 305; and
Muslims as incapable of civilized
rule, 21–22; and Native Americans,
21, 22, 158, 210, 357 (n. 3); and Nazi
Germany, 323; Philippines annexation, 159–63, 169, 359 (n. 52); and
Protestant missionaries, 21–22, 161,
245; Theodore Roosevelt on, 319–21;
and Wilson's foreign policy, 271–72;
and Young Turk global jihad, 285. *See
also* American treatment of Moros;
manifest destiny
American isolationism, 9–10; and
Armenian mandate proposals, 312;
and Armenian Massacres, 244–45,
263–64, 266–68, 269–70; and
Cretan Insurrection, 34, 60, 67; end
of, 328–29; and exceptionalism,
45–46, 48; and Family of Nations
concept, 16; and Greek War of
Independence, 33, 41–42, 43–46, 48;
and Manichean discourse, 45, 321;
and Second Great Awakening, 15.
See also Monroe Doctrine
American Jewish activism. *See* Jewish
American activism
American Jewish Committee, 356
(n. 101)
American Museum of Natural History,
197–98
American National Red Cross, 261–62,
269, 293, 344 (n. 16)

American racism: and African-American colonization proposals, 35, 165; and American treatment of Moros, 163, 165, 229; and anti-imperialism, 213; and Armenian Genocide, 284, 288; and Armenian Massacres, 245, 257; and Cretan Insurrection, 58; and Family of Nations concept, 322; and imperialism/colonialism, 21, 22; and Jewish American activism, 348 (n. 8); and philhellenic movement, 35; and Protestant missionaries, 245, 246, 369 (n. 12); Rustem Bey accusations, 283–84; scientific racism, 103, 160–61, 168, 245, 246; and social Darwinism, 369 (n. 12); and Woodrow Wilson, 272, 288. *See also* racial/religious hierarchies; slavery

American Revolution, 13, 21, 36, 46. *See also* early Republic

American treatment of Moros: and American exceptionalism, 159, 209–10; and animism, 172, 173, 195, 361 (n. 107); and Armenian mandate proposals, 309, 311; Bates treaty, 174–78, 182, 183, 203, 205, 207, 221, 360 (n. 88); Battle of Bud Bagsak, 233; Bureau of Non-Christian Tribes, 184–87, 328, 361–62 (nn. 117, 118); Bureau of the Census, 187, 188 (ill.), 189 (ill.), 190; and Catholicism, 158, 172, 173–74, 220–21; civilian rule, 233–34; and commercial interests, 226–30; and conversion goals, 3–4, 158, 173, 174, 183–84, 191–92, 360 (n. 74); disarmament order, 232–33; European colonialist models, 170–71, 175, 198–202, 223–24, 363 (n. 25); and Filipino diversity, 190; and Filipino nationalism, 174, 178, 230, 236–37; and Global War on Terror, 331; and humanitarian intervention rhetoric, 158, 210; and Islamic society equivalence assumptions, 3–4, 158, 165–66, 173, 176–77, 204; and Jesuit missionaries, 173–74, 220–21; and League of Nations, 325; Mindanao Plan, 323; and Moro diversity, 158–59, 181, 203, 357 (n. 5); Moro origins, 357 (n. 1); "Moro problem" debate, 163–68; Moro Province establishment, 178–84, 361 (n. 107); Moro resistance, 159, 192, 195, 205–7, 208–9; and Muslims as incapable of civilized rule, 157, 201, 208–9, 210–11, 229–30; and Native Americans, 167, 168, 180, 181, 185, 187, 202, 210, 216, 217 (ill.), 230; permanent territory proposals, 230, 368 (n. 173); Pershing governorship, 231–33; and political organization of Moro territory, 207–8; and popular culture, 193, 194 (ill.), 195–98, 196 (ill.), 197 (ill.); and popular press, 211, 212, 213, 216–18, 217 (ill.), 218 (ill.), 219 (ill.), 222, 365 (n. 104); and Protestant missionaries, 3, 164, 173, 193, 201, 220–26, 225 (ill.), 235–36, 325–26; and race, 164–65, 168, 172, 186–87, 362 (n. 124); Schurman commission, 168–74, 175; and slavery, 168, 175–76, 205, 359 (n. 48); and U.S. annexation of the Philippines, 159–63, 169, 359 (n. 52); and Young Turk global jihad, 285. *See also* Battle of Bud Dajo; force and American treatment of Moros; Moro identity as defined by religion; racial/religious hierarchies in American treatment of Moros

Amoroso, Donna, 163

Anderson, Rufus, 344 (n. 11)

Angell, James B., 249, 269, 343 (n. 2)

Anglo-Jewish Committee, 134

animism among Filipinos, 172, 173, 195, 361 (n. 107)

anthropology, 184–85, 186–87, 196, 361–62 (nn. 118, 124)

chies, 81, 82; and Robert College, 73–74, 76–77, 83, 85, 86, 92, 93; and Russo-Turkish War, 86–90; Schuyler's role, 80–81, 85–86, 87, 90–92, 347 (n. 90)

Bullard, Robert, 219–20

Bureau of Non-Christian Tribes, 184–87, 328, 361–62 (nn. 117, 118)

Bureau of the Census, 187, 188 (ill.), 189 (ill.), 190

Burney, Robert, 254

Bush, George W., 330

business interests. *See* commercial interests

Butler, Nicolas Murray, 300

Byron, Lord (George Gordon Byron), 40

Calhoun, John C., 43, 44, 339 (n. 67)

Call, Wilkinson, 267

Canning, Stratford, 70

captivity narratives, 14, 335 (n. 45)

Cardashian, Vahan, 299–300, 307

Carey, Mathew, 37, 52

Carnegie, Andrew, 162

Carpenter, Frank, 234, 236

Catholicism: and American treatment of Moros, 158, 172, 173–74, 220–21; European political theory on, 12, 13; and Greek War of Independence, 38; and imperialism/colonialism, 10–11; and Manichean discourse, 12; Syria, 349 (n. 24). *See also* Damascus Affair; racial/religious hierarchies

Caucasian Wars, 76

Chamberlain, Joseph, 265

"The Charge of the Light Brigade" (Tennyson), 366 (n. 111)

Chase, Salmon P., 34, 65

Chasseaud, Jasper, 107

China, 18

Chinese Exclusion Act (1882), 103

Chinese immigration to the United States and Philippines, 103, 164

The Christian Approach to Islam (Barton), 299

Christianity as justification for American imperialism/colonialism, 159–61, 191–92. *See also* Family of Nations concept

civic nationalism, 21, 22

civilized nations. *See* Family of Nations concept

Clark, Nathanial, 1

The Clash of Civilizations (Huntington), 329, 383 (nn. 43, 44)

Clay, Henry, 35, 36, 42

Clemenceau, Georges, 305

Cleveland, Grover: and American government responses to Armenian Massacres, 262, 263, 264, 266–67, 268; anti-imperialism, 162; and Armenian Massacres, 244–45, 260; and naturalization system, 251; and Protestant missionaries, 249

Cold War, 328

colonial administration, 1800–1900 (Austin), 171

colonialism. *See* imperialism/ colonialism

Columbus, Christopher, 10–11

commercial interests: and American treatment of Moros, 226–30; and capitulatory treaties, 71; and Crimean War, 341 (n. 119); and Greek War of Independence, 46; and Madrid Conference, 132, 134; and Morgenthau ambassadorship, 281; and Moroccan protégé system, 129–32, 141, 353 (n. 12)

Committee of Union and Progress (CUP). *See* Young Turks

Conference of Lausanne (1922), 313

Congress of Berlin (1878), 90, 95–96, 149, 247–48. *See also* Treaty of Berlin

Congress of Laibach (1821), 39

Congress of Paris (1856), 55

Constant, Benjamin, 40

Constantinople, Treaty of (1832), 51–52

Constantinople Conference (1876–77), 85–86, 94–95, 127–28

conversion goals: and American imperialism/colonialism, 161; and American treatment of Moros, 3–4, 158, 173, 174, 183–84, 191–92, 360 (n. 74); and Greek War of Independence, 50; post-World War I, 324–25. *See also* Protestant missionaries

Cooper Act (Philippine Bill) (1902), 180

Corbin, Henry, 213

counternarratives, 6, 7, 28

Crane, Charles, 273, 289, 290, 305, 306, 315

Crawford, William H., 44, 339 (n. 67)

Crémieux, Adolphe, 110, 114, 124, 153

Crémieux Decree, 153

Cretan Insurrection (1866–69), 57–67; and American exceptionalism, 58–60; American fundraising, 61–62; and American isolationism, 34, 60, 67; Cretan revolutionary appeals, 58–59; and philhellenic movement, 57–58, 66; Shanks speech, 64–65; and Treaty of Constantinople, 52; U.S. official abandonment, 63–64; U.S. official support, 60, 61, 66

Crete. *See* Cretan Insurrection; Greco-Turkish War

Crimean War, 55, 71, 78, 341 (n. 119)

Cromer, Lord (Eveyln Baring), 200–201, 223–24, 226, 363 (n. 25)

Crusades, 11, 199

Cuba, 198, 200, 269, 305. *See also* Spanish-American War

Cullom, Shelby, 267

cultural influences on policy, 25–26

CUP (Committee of Union and Progress). *See* Young Turks

Cushing, Caleb, 18–19

Dale, Stephan, 206

Damascus Affair (1840), 104–10; and American anti-Semitism, 106–7, 108; and American domestic politics, 108–9; British response, 105–6; and

humanitarian intervention rhetoric, 106, 109, 264; and Jewish American activism, 105, 106–7, 109–10, 119, 121; as precedent for American intervention, 121

Davis, George W., 167–68, 181–82, 202, 361 (n. 107)

Davis, Verena, 165

demographic engineering: and American treatment of Moros, 168, 208, 235, 327, 328; and Armenian mandate proposals, 300–301; and Bulgarian nationalism, 76, 93–94; and Jewish homeland, 323–24; and *muhajirs*, 94, 247; and Native Americans, 288; Russian Empire, 277

Derby, Lord (Edward Stanley), 78

Dewey, George, 224

Dickinson, Jacob, 232

Dimitroff, Peter, 80

Diner, Hasia, 100

Disraeli, Benjamin, 78, 79–80, 81, 82, 86, 87

Dodge, Bayard, 280

Dodge, Cleveland H., 273, 289, 294–95, 296, 300, 302, 305, 306

Dodge, Mary, 280

Dodge, William E., 254

Dominican Republic, 271

"A Door Into the Mohammedan World" (Strong), 3–4, 224, 225 (ill.), 226

Dreyfus affair (1894), 153–54

Druze-Maronite conflict (1860), 56–57, 70, 341 (n. 126)

Dwight, Harrison, 246

Dwight, Henry Otis, 165–67, 176

Dwight, Sereno Edwards, 50

early Republic, 13–15; and Family of Nations concept, 17; philhellenic movement, 34; racial/religious hierarchies, 15, 335 (n. 51); religious liberty ideal, 13–14; and United States as Christian nation, 15, 99–100, 348 (n. 2)

Eastern Question, 68; and American exceptionalism, 20–21; European policies toward, 20–21, 38–39; and Family of Nations concept, 21; and force, 22; Jessup speech, 92–93; and Protestant missionaries, 92–93. *See also* Armenian Genocide; Armenian Massacres; Bulgarian nationalism; Cretan Insurrection; Greek War of Independence; mandate system; World War I

Egypt, 377 (n. 67); and Battle of Navarino, 51; British imperial rule, 104, 144, 199–201, 223; and Damascus Affair, 105

Einstein, Lewis, 147–48, 150–51

Elements of International Law (Wheaton), 18, 34–35, 55–56, 60

Eliot, Charles, 300

Elkus, Abraham Isaac, 290, 293

Elliot, Henry, 62–63, 77–78, 79, 345 (n. 42)

Emancipation Proclamation, 117

Empringham, James, 290–91

Enlightenment, 12, 40, 113, 119

Entente Cordiale, 144

Enver Pasha, Ismail, 278, 287

Erskine, Thomas, 42

eschatology, 12, 275, 313–14

ethnic cleansing, 23, 76, 93–94. *See also* demographic engineering

ethnic nationalism: and Armenian Genocide, 276, 375 (nn. 19, 20); and Bulgarian nationalism, 74–75, 93; and European anti-Semitism, 22–23; and Philippines, 190; and Turkish Republic, 313; and the United States, 21–22

European anti-Semitism: and American anti-Semitism, 101; and Bulgarian nationalism, 95; and Crémieux Decree, 153; Damascus Affair, 104–10, 119, 121, 264; Dreyfus affair, 153–54; and ethnic nationalism, 22–23, 276; and Family of Nations

concept, 22, 103–4; and Holocaust, 322–23; and Jewish American activism, 103–4, 107–8, 126–27; and Jewish homeland, 275; and Madrid Conference, 133, 139–40; and race, 22–23; Russian Empire, 95, 126–27, 133, 144–46, 347 (n. 115), 355 (n. 86); and Treaty of Berlin, 96

European policies: and American exceptionalism, 20–21; and Armenian Massacres, 242, 243, 263–64, 369 (n. 3), 373 (n. 106); and Bulgarian nationalism, 78, 79–80, 81–82, 85–86; and Cretan Insurrection, 59–60, 62–63, 64–65; and Crimean War, 55; and Damascus Affair, 105–6; and Eastern Question, 20–21, 38–39; and Greek War of Independence, 38–39, 41, 51, 53, 338 (n. 32); Holy Alliance, 38–39, 43, 44, 45, 50; and Jewish homeland, 274–75, 313, 314; Theodore Roosevelt on, 320; and Spanish-Moroccan War, 112–13, 115–16, 117. *See also* imperialism/ colonialism

European thought: and Bulgarian nationalism, 74–75; and Family of Nations concept, 16, 17; and international law, 17; and Jewish American activism, 101; philhellenic movement, 35, 40, 42, 337 (n. 9); political theory, 12–13, 334 (n. 33); and Young Turks, 275. *See also* European anti-Semitism

Evangelical Alliance, 244, 254, 262–63, 264–66

Evarts, William, 58, 72, 133, 135, 136–37, 138

Everett, Edward, 37; and American isolationism, 44; background of, 39–40, 338 (n. 38); and Greek revolutionary appeals, 40–41, 338 (n. 45); and Greek War of Independence fundraising, 49–50; and Howe, 51, 52; on Lancastrian model of education, 33–34, 54; on slavery, 48–49; and Webster resolution, 46

Expansion, Under New World Conditions (Strong), 269–70

"Expansion and Peace" (Roosevelt), 319–21

Fairchild, Lucius, 136, 137, 138, 139–40

Family of Nations concept, 16–19, 21; and Algeciras Conference, 146; and American treatment of Moros, 161, 174; and Armenian Massacres, 264; and Cretan Insurrection, 61; and Crimean War, 55; and Druze-Maronite conflict, 56; and European anti-Semitism, 22, 103–4; and European policies, 20–21; and Greek War of Independence, 38, 39, 41, 338 (n. 45); and League of Nations, 325; Theodore Roosevelt on, 319–20, 321–22; and Safi Affair, 119; and World War I, 321–22

Farragut, Davis Glasgow, 63, 73

Faysal, Emir, 303

Fear God and Take Your Own Part (Roosevelt), 148

Filipino Christians. *See* Catholicism; racial/religious hierarchies in American treatment of Moros

Fillmore, Millard, 55

Finley, John, 234

Fish, Hamilton, 91

Foner, Eric, 337 (n. 17)

Forbes, Archibald, 88–89

Forbes, Cameron, 232, 233, 236–37

force: and Global War on Terror, 331; and imperialism/colonialism, 22, 23, 184, 218–19, 283–84, 319; and Jewish homeland, 314–15; and mandate system, 316, 382 (n. 205); and Protestant missionaries, 221, 222, 324–25. *See also* force and American treatment of Moros; *specific wars*

force and American treatment of Moros: Battle of Bud Bagsak, 233; and commercial interests, 229; and European imperialism/colonialism, 170; "Moro problem" debate, 167; and Moro Province establishment, 182, 183, 184; Pershing governorship, 231; and Protestant missionaries, 221, 222; Root on, 218–19; Wood on, 192, 202–3, 204–5, 206–7, 208–9, 364 (nn. 62, 63). *See also* Battle of Bud Dajo

Ford, Henry, 357 (n. 120)

Forsyth, John, 107, 108, 110

France: anti-Semitism, 153; and Armenian Massacres, 263–64; Damascus Affair, 104–10, 119, 121, 264; French Revolution, 13; and mandate system, 303, 316; and Moroccan protégé system, 128, 352 (n. 4); Morocco imperialism, 144, 145, 148, 152–53, 322–23; Sykes-Picot Treaty, 295. *See also* Alliance Israélite Universelle; European thought; imperialism/colonialism

Franklin, Benjamin, 101

French, Arthur, 324–25

French Alliance Israélite Universelle. *See* Alliance Israélite Universelle

French Revolution, 13

Friends of Armenia, 260

Galenga, Antonio, 77, 78

Gallatin, Albert, 39, 40, 43

Garrison, William Lloyd, Jr., 260

Gascoyne-Cecil, Robert (Lord Salisbury), 242, 265

gender rhetoric, 28; and American treatment of Moros, 172, 214; and Armenian mandate proposals, 307, 308 (ill.), 309, 309 (ill.); and Armenian Massacres, 261; and Cretan Insurrection, 63; and Russo-Turkish War, 89

George, David Lloyd, 305

hatti şerif (1839) (Ottoman Empire), 70, 352 (n. 93)

Havemeyer, John, 259

Hawkins, Michael, 168

Hay, Drummond, 112, 118–19, 129, 130, 134, 147

Hay, John, 249

Hayes, Rutherford, 139

Hebrew Congregation of Tangier, 120–21

Hellenism. *See* philhellenic movement

Hepburn, William, 267

historiography, 25–27

Hitler, Adolf, 323

Hoar, George, 262, 266

Hodgson, Marshall, 333 (n. 7)

Holmes, Oliver Wendell, 58

Holocaust, 323

Holy Alliance, 38–39, 43, 44, 45, 50

homo islamicus, 19

Hoover, Herbert, 292

Horton, George, 282

House, Edward M., 297, 305

Howard, Oliver, 266

Howe, Julia Ward, 58, 260

Howe, Samuel Gridley, 51, 52, 58, 60–62, 63, 65–66

Hoyt, Ralph, 229–30

Hughes, Charles Evan, 300

humanitarian intervention rhetoric, 9; and Algeciras Conference, 149–50; and American treatment of Moros, 158, 210; and Armenian Genocide, 290–91; and Armenian mandate proposals, 301; and Armenian Massacres, 242–43, 252–53, 254, 258–59, 263; and Barbary pirates, 14–15; and Bulgarian nationalism, 74, 79–80; and capitulatory treaties, 71; and Cretan Insurrection, 64; and Crimean War, 55; and Damascus Affair, 106, 109, 264; and Druze-Maronite conflict (1860), 56; and Family of Nations concept, 17, 18–19; Greek War of Independence as origin

of, 42, 339 (n. 57); and imperialism/colonialism, 9, 18, 19, 101, 104, 335 (n. 59); and international law, 17; and Jewish American activism, 94–96, 101, 127; and Moroccan protégé system, 131–32, 133, 139, 353 (n. 24); and Russo-Turkish War, 86; and slavery, 36, 37, 337 (n. 17); terminology, 334 (n. 15); transnational nature of, 42; and Treaty of Constantinople, 51–52. *See also* Greek War of Independence; imaginary nature of religious minority oppression; Muslims as incapable of civilized rule

Humboldt, Wilhelm von, 40

Hunchak Party (Russia), 248, 252

Hunt, Michael, 25–26

Huntington, Elizabeth, 293

Huntington, Samuel, 329, 383 (nn. 43, 44)

Ide, Henry, 214–15

ideal vision of America. *See* American exceptionalism

ideology, 25–26

Ideology and U.S. Foreign Policy (Hunt), 25–26

Ignatiev, Nicolas (count), 85–86, 87–88, 90, 347 (n. 115)

imaginary nature of religious minority oppression, 23; and Algeciras Conference, 147, 149, 150–52; and Bulgarian nationalism, 95; and Damascus Affair, 105, 110; and mandate system, 296–97; and Moroccan protégé system, 128–29, 134; and Safi Affair, 121, 122; and Spanish-Moroccan War, 111–12, 113; and Tunisian Jews, 102

immigration to the United States: and American anti-Semitism, 103, 126, 276; and American imperialism/colonialism, 21; Armenian, 250–51, 270; and "Moro problem" debate, 164; and racial/religious hierarchies, 137, 164

Bulgarian nationalism, 94–96, 127–28; and Damascus Affair, 105, 106–7, 109–10, 119, 121; and European anti-Semitism, 103–4, 107–8, 126–27; and humanitarian intervention rhetoric, 94–96, 101, 127; and immigration, 126; and Jewish homeland, 314; and Jews as civilizing/mediating agents, 100, 114, 138; and Madrid Conference, 132–34, 137–38, 140; and manifest destiny, 114; and Moroccan protégé system, 123, 127, 128–29, 132–34; and Mortara Affair, 110, 350 (n. 50); and racial/religious hierarchies, 8, 100–101, 103, 109, 123–24, 348 (n. 8); and Russian Empire, 126–27, 144–46; and Safi Affair, 116–24; transnational nature of, 101, 110, 111, 113–15, 123, 124, 128, 137–38; and United States as Christian nation, 99–100; and Wilson's foreign policy, 274

Jewish homeland, 313–16; Balfour Declaration, 274–75, 313, 314; and demographic engineering, 323–24; and force, 314–15; and Jews as civilizing/mediating agents, 304, 315–16; King-Crane Commission on, 317; and Protestant eschatology, 12, 275, 313–14; and Wilson, 239, 304, 314–15

Jewish Question. *See* European anti-Semitism

Jews: as civilizing/mediating agents, 100, 101–2, 114, 138, 279, 304, 315–16; and Greek War of Independence, 37; and mandate system, 298; position in Morocco, 111–12, 121, 122–23, 350 (n. 54). *See also* American anti-Semitism; European anti-Semitism; humanitarian intervention rhetoric; Jewish American activism; religious minorities in the Ottoman Empire

Johnson, Andrew, 58, 59
Johnson, J. Augustus, 56, 341 (n. 123)
Jones, William, 215
journalism. *See* popular press
juramentados, 205–6
Jusserand, Jules, 147

Kaplan, Amy, 27
Kemal, Mustafa, 313
King, Charles, 37
King, Henry Churchill, 305
King, Jonas, 54, 55
King, Rufus, 42
King-Crane Commission, 304–5, 314–16, 317
Kirakossian, Arman J., 369 (n. 3)
Kirk, Edwin Norris, 31, 60
Kitchener, Herbert (Lord Kitchener), 280–81
Korais, Adamantios, 39, 40–41, 338 (n. 45)
Kramer, Paul, 27

Lafayette, Marquis de (Gilbert du Motier), 40, 42, 51
Laibach, Congress of (1821), 39
Lalouche, Eliyhahu. *See* Safi Affair
Lancastrian model of education, 33–34, 54
Langhorne, Frank, 211
Lansing, Robert, 273, 287, 288, 290, 294, 302
Latin American revolutionary movements, 36, 43
Lausanne, Conference of (1922), 313
Lawrence, T. E., 303
Layard, Henry, 87
League of Nations, 274, 311–12, 325. *See also* mandate system
Lebanon, 56–57, 70, 341 (n. 126)
Leeser, Isaac, 109
Leff, Lisa, 101
legal theories. *See* international law
Leland, John, 13, 14, 334 (n. 36)
Leopold II (king of Belgium), 218–19

Leoussi, Athena, 35, 337 (n. 16)
Lewis, William Reed, 131, 141, 355 (n. 64)
Lewy, Guenter, 371 (n. 45)
Lincoln, Abraham, 66, 117
Lobingier, Charles, 306, 381 (n. 179)
local actors, 26–27, 28–29. *See also*
   specific events and groups
Lodge, Henry Cabot, 294, 300, 307, 312
Loeb, Isidore, 133
Long, Albert, 74, 77, 80, 90, 345 (n. 41)
Longfellow, Henry Wadsworth, 58
Longworth, Nicolas, 212
Low, Seth, 373 (n. 109)
Luce, Henry, 328–29
Luriottis, Andreas, 43, 44
Lyber, Albert, 305

MacGahan, Januarius: and Constantinople Conference, 86; as folk hero,
   90, 347 (n. 117); and Muslim identity
   as defined by religion, 82–83; and
   Russo-Turkish War, 88–89, 347
   (n. 105); and Schuyler mission, 80,
   81; special reporter role, 78–79
Madison, James, 35, 102
Madrid Conference (1880), 132–41; and
   imperialism/colonialism, 137, 140;
   and Jewish American activism,
   132–34, 137–38, 140; Mathews
   responses, 135–36; and naturalization system, 136–37; and religious
   tolerance, 138–40
Mahan, Alfred, 320
Mahomet the Imposter (Voltaire), 13
Majul, Cesar, 360 (n. 74)
mandate system, 296–311; and Algeciras Conference, 302; and force, 316,
   382 (n. 205); and the Inquiry,
   297–99; King-Crane Commission on,
   304–5, 315, 316; and Muslims as
   incapable of civilized rule, 5, 274,
   293, 295, 297, 315, 317; non-
   Ottoman territories, 380 (n. 157);
   and Protestant missionaries, 296, 299,
   303; and racial/religious hierarchies,

298–99, 379 (n. 143); resistance
   against, 303, 316–17, 322; Wilson on,
   274, 275, 296, 300, 302–3, 304–6,
   316, 379 (n. 134). *See also* Armenian
   mandate proposals
Manichean discourse, 6–7; Adams
   essay, 52–53, 320, 341 (n. 107);
   American colonial era, 11–12, 12 (ill.);
   and American exceptionalism, 15;
   and American isolationism, 45, 321;
   and American treatment of Moros,
   166, 199; and Armenian Massacres,
   261–62; and Bulgarian nationalism,
   85; and Cold War, 328; and Columbus, 10; and Cretan Insurrection, 60,
   61; early Republic, 13; and Family of
   Nations concept, 19; Huntington on,
   329–30, 383 (nn. 43, 44); and
   Protestant missionaries, 4; Theodore
   Roosevelt on, 320–21
manifest destiny, 20; and American
   treatment of Moros, 191; and
   Armenian Massacres, 243; and
   Greek War of Independence, 36;
   and Jewish American activism, 114;
   and Nazi Germany, 323; and Second
   Great Awakening, 15–16, 36
Marglin, Jessica, 121, 353 (n. 16)
Maronite. *See* Catholicism
Marsh, George Perkins, 55
Mather, Cotton, 12, 14, 335 (n. 44)
Mather, Increase, 12
Mathews, Felix, 129, 130–33, 135–36,
   141, 353 (n. 24)
Matteosian, Hagop, 1, 5
Maynard, Horace, 80, 91, 95
Mazower, Mark, 13
McCoy, Frank, 198–99, 201–2
McCutchen, Robert, 325–26
McGhee, William J., 195, 361–62
   (nn. 118, 124)
McKee, John, 221
McKinley, Ida, 162
McKinley, William: and American
   treatment of Moros, 176, 178, 184,

193, 359 (n. 54); and Armenian Massacres, 268, 269; and U.S. annexation of the Philippines, 159–60, 162, 168–69; and Wood, 198

McKormick, Samuel, 280

McMath, Jesse, 117, 118, 120, 121, 129

Megali Idea, 51

Merry y Colom, Don Francisco, 116, 118, 119

Metternich, Klemens von, 39, 338 (n. 32)

Miles, Nelson A., 198

"Military Taming of the Moro" (Bateman), 221–22

Mindanao Plan, 323

Monroe, James, 35, 43, 44–45, 102

Monroe Doctrine, 44–45, 53, 60, 61, 65, 67, 243, 312

Montefiore, Moses, 110, 121, 122, 123

Montesquieu, 12–13

Montgomery, George, 305, 315

Morgan, George, 72

Morgan, John T., 165, 257

Morgan, J. Pierpont, 223

Morgenthau, Henry, Jr., 323

Morgenthau, Henry, Sr.: and Armenian Genocide, 285–89, 290; and Armenian mandate proposals, 312; and Greek warship incident (1914), 281–82; and mandate system, 296, 305, 379 (n. 134); Ottoman Empire ambassadorship, 279–81; and Wilson, 274; and World War I, 284, 376 (n. 61)

Mormons, 8, 62, 63, 64

Moroccan protégé system, 353 (n. 16); American abuses of, 129–32, 141, 353 (n. 12); and imperialism/colonialism, 115–16, 128, 130, 131, 132, 134, 352 (n. 4); and Jewish American activism, 123, 127, 128–29, 132–34; and naturalization system, 136–37; and popular press, 131, 353 (nn. 18, 24); and Safi Affair, 116, 118. *See also* Madrid Conference

Morocco, 126–54; French imperialism, 144, 145, 148, 152–53, 322–23; as illegitimate empire, 19, 20; Jewish position in, 111–12, 121, 122–23, 350 (n. 54); naturalization system, 136–37, 151–52; Perdicaris Affair, 142–44, 148, 355 (n. 75); and Protestant missionaries, 141, 355 (n. 66); Safi Affair, 116–24; Spanish-Moroccan War, 111–13, 115–16, 117. *See also* Algeciras Conference; Madrid Conference; Moroccan protégé system

Moro identity as defined by religion: and Bates treaty, 174–75; and Bureau of Non-Christian Tribes, 185; and European colonialist models, 201; and Islamic society equivalence assumptions, 165–66, 176–77; and Moro Province establishment, 181; and Moro resistance, 205–6, 212, 213, 216; Schurman commission on, 173; Wood on, 203–4. *See also* racial/religious hierarchies in American treatment of Moros

Moro independence movement, 328, 331

Moro Rebellion, 159, 192, 195, 205–7, 208–9, 233. *See also* Battle of Bud Dajo

Moros. *See* American treatment of Moros

Morris, Edward Joy, 58, 59–60, 62

Morrison, Alexander, 19, 21

Morse, Elijah, 267

Mortara Affair (1858), 110, 350 (n. 50)

Moses, Bernard, 184

Mott, John, 224, 289–90

muhajirs, 94, 247

Muhammad Ali Pasha (khedive of Egypt), 105

Muslim identity as defined by religion, 6; and American treatment of Moros, 166; and Armenian Genocide, 287, 290–91; and Armenian Massacres, 244; and Bulgarian nationalism,

82–83; and European colonialist models, 201; and Greek War of Independence, 37–38; and historiographical trends, 26–27; and mandate system, 297; and race, 7; and Russo-Turkish War, 89; and Young Turks, 284–85. *See also* Islamic society equivalence assumptions

Muslims as incapable of civilized rule, 6; and American treatment of Moros, 157, 201, 208–9, 210–11, 229–30; and Armenian Genocide, 274, 288, 291–92; and Armenian Massacres, 242; and Damascus Affair, 108; and European political theory, 12–13; and Family of Nations concept, 18; and humanitarian intervention rhetoric, 18; and imperialism/colonialism, 9, 21–22; and mandate system, 5, 274, 293, 295, 297, 315, 317; and Morgenthau ambassadorship, 281; and Wilson's foreign policy, 273, 274; and World War I, 293. *See also* Family of Nations concept; humanitarian intervention rhetoric

Naimark, Norman, 23
Napoleonic Wars, 36
National Armenian Relief Committee, 260–61, 262
National Association for the Advancement of Colored People (NAACP), 283–84
National Reform Association, 124
Native Americans, treatment of: and American imperialism/colonialism, 21, 22, 158, 210, 357 (n. 3); and American treatment of Moros, 167, 168, 180, 181, 185, 187, 202, 210, 216, 217 (ill.), 230; and Armenian Genocide, 288; and captivity narratives, 335 (n. 45); and Catholic imperialism/colonialism, 10–11; and demographic engineering, 288; and

Family of Nations concept, 16; and Manichean discourse, 11; and Nazi Germany, 323; and philhellenic movement, 35; and racial/religious hierarchies, 8, 21, 210; and Safi Affair, 120; and St. Louis World's Fair, 195, 197; and ward mentality, 208; and Wood, 198

naturalization: in Morocco, 135, 136–37; in the Ottoman Empire, 250, 251; in the United States, 21, 270, 292

Navarino, Battle of (1827), 51, 105
Near East Relief, 305, 311. *See also* American Committee for Armenian and Syrian Relief
"Negro Problem". *See* American racism
Netherlands, 201–2
neutrality policies. *See* American isolationism
newspapers. *See* popular press
Niles, Hezekiah, 37, 41
Noah, Mordecai, 102, 106–7, 108
nonintervention. *See* American isolationism
non-Protestant groups in Western societies: and Cretan Insurrection, 63, 64; and racial/religious hierarchies, 8; stereotypes of, 102, 349 (n. 18). *See also* American anti-Semitism; European anti-Semitism; Jewish American activism
Nubar Pasha, Boghos, 296, 303–4

Ochs, Adolph, 287
oil interests, 317, 328
Olney, Richard, 261, 265, 266
"On the Restoration of Greece" (Everett), 40
open door policy, 150
oppositional classifications. *See* Manichean discourse
Orientalism, 23–24, 27, 28, 100, 102, 330
Orientalism (Said), 23–24, 27, 28

Osborne, Harry V., 296
Otis, Elwell, 174
Ottoman Empire: Adana massacres
(1909), 277, 281; American commercial interests in, 46, 281; and
American National Red Cross,
261–62; and American treatment of
Moros, 176–77, 199, 234; Crimean
War, 55, 71, 78, 341 (n. 119); Damascus Affair, 104–10, 119, 121, 264;
Druze-Maronite conflict (1860),
56–57, 341 (n. 126); and Family of
Nations concept, 18, 55; Greek
warship incident, 281–82; as
illegitimate empire, 19, 20, 22; and
international law, 18; Morgenthau
ambassadorship, 279–81; naturalization system, 250, 251; post-World
War I dismantling (*see* mandate
system); Russo-Turkish War, 86–90,
93–94, 136, 247–48; Rustem Bey
accusations, 282–84; Tanzimat
reforms, 70–71, 352 (n. 93); and
World War I, 279, 286; Young Turks,
94, 275–79, 282, 284, 286, 375
(nn. 19, 20), 376 (n. 61). *See also*
Armenian Genocide; Armenian
Massacres; Bulgarian nationalism;
Eastern Question; Greek War of
Independence; humanitarian
intervention rhetoric; religious
minorities in the Ottoman Empire
*Our Country: Its Possible Future and Its
Present Crisis* (Strong), 161
"Our Mohammedan Wards" (Dwight),
165–67

Palmerston, Lord (Henry John Temple),
106
Panaretov, Stefan, 76–77, 79, 80, 93
pan-Islamic unity, 166, 176, 177
pan-Turkism, 94
*Papers Relating to Foreigners in
Morocco* (U.S. Department of State),
140–41

Paris, Congress of (1856), 55
Paris, Treaty of (1898), 168–69
Patai, Raphael, 331
Pears, Edwin, 77, 78, 79, 256, 345 (n. 44)
Peet, William, 299–300
Perdicaris, Gregory, 130
Perdicaris, Ion, 130–31, 142. *See also*
Perdicaris Affair
Perdicaris Affair, 142–44, 148, 355 (n.
75)
Pershing, John J., 222, 224, 231–32,
234, 309
Persian Letters (Montesqieu), 12–13
philhellenic movement, 33–36, 39–42;
and American isolationism, 44;
beliefs of, 34–35; and Cretan
Insurrection, 57–58, 63–64, 66;
European, 35, 40, 42, 337 (n. 9); and
Greek revolutionary appeals, 40–41;
and Muslim identity as defined by
religion, 37–38; and popular press,
37; and race, 35–36, 337 (n. 16); and
Second Great Awakening, 36; and
Webster resolution, 46
Philippine-American War (1899–1902),
174, 178
Philippine Bill (Cooper Act) (1902), 180
Philippine Reservation (St. Louis
World's Fair, 1904), 193, 195–98, 196
(ill.), 197 (ill.)
Philippines: animism, 172, 173, 195, 361
(n. 107); and Armenian mandate
proposals, 297, 305–6, 309, 381
(n. 179); Philippine-American War,
174, 178; and Syrian mandate
proposals, 315; U.S. annexation of,
159–63, 169, 359 (n. 52); and
Wilson's foreign policy, 271. *See also*
American treatment of Moros
Philips, Wendell, 58
Pio Pi, Father, 173–74
Poinsett, Joel, 47
popular culture: and American
treatment of Moros, 193, 194 (ill.),
195–98, 196 (ill.), 197 (ill.); and

Armenian mandate proposals, 307, 308 (ill.), 309, 309 (ill.), 310 (ill.)

popular press: and American treatment of Moros, 211, 212, 213, 216–18, 217 (ill.), 218 (ill.), 219 (ill.), 222, 365 (n. 104); and Armenian Genocide, 290; and Armenian mandate proposals, 312; and Armenian Massacres, 249, 255–56, 259, 264; and Bulgarian nationalism, 77–79, 81, 82–83, 84, 345 (nn. 40, 41); and Cretan Insurrection, 60–61; and Druze-Maronite conflict (1860), 56–57; early Republic, 13; and Greek War of Independence, 36–38, 40; and Moroccan protégé system, 131, 353 (nn. 18, 24); and Ottoman reforms, 70; and Robert College, 73, 344 (n. 16); and Russo-Turkish War, 87, 88–89, 347 (n. 105)

Populist Party, 245

Porter, David, 107–8

Preston, Andrew, 24

protégé system, 250. *See also* Moroccan protégé system

Protestantism: eschatology, 12, 275, 313–14; Second Great Awakening, 15, 16, 36. *See also* Protestant missionaries; racial/religious hierarchies

Protestant missionaries, 1–4; and American imperialism/colonialism, 21–22, 161, 245; and American treatment of Moros, 3, 164, 173, 193, 201, 220–26, 225 (ill.), 235–36, 325–26; and Armenian Genocide, 290; and Bulgarian nationalism, 69–70, 75, 77, 84–85, 90, 92, 347 (n. 90); and Druze-Maronite conflict (1860), 56, 57; and Eastern Question, 92–93; and force, 221, 222, 324–25; and Greek War of Independence, 50, 52; and mandate system, 296, 299, 303; and manifest destiny, 15–16; and Morgenthau ambassadorship, 280; and Morocco, 141, 355 (n. 66);

and Ottoman reforms, 70, 71; political influence of, 69–70, 72, 249–50, 262, 343 (n. 2); postwar Greece, 54–55; post-World War I, 324–25; and Protestant colleges, 71–73, 344 (n. 11); and racism, 245, 246, 369 (n. 12); and U.S. annexation of the Philippines, 160–61; and Wilson's foreign policy, 273–74; and World War I, 294–95; and Young Turks, 277, 278. *See also* conversion goals; Protestant missionaries and Armenian Massacres

Protestant missionaries and Armenian Massacres: and American government responses, 262–63, 264–66; and Armenian-American activism, 250–51, 253; Greene's book, 257–58; immediate response, 154–56; and Muslim identity as defined by religion, 244; Ottoman hostility towards, 248–49, 251–52; Ottoman repayment, 269, 373 (n. 106); and race, 244, 245–46

The Protocols of the Elders of Zion, 153, 357 (n. 120)

Quezon, Manual, 327

race: and American treatment of Moros, 164–65, 168, 172, 186–87, 362 (n. 124); and Armenian Massacres, 244, 245–46; and imperialism/colonialism, 22–23; and Muslim identity as defined by religion, 7; and philhellenic movement, 35–36, 337 (n. 16); and social Darwinism, 369 (n. 12). *See also* American racism; racial/religious hierarchies

racial Hellenism, 35–36, 337 (n. 16)

racial/religious hierarchies: and American anti-Semitism, 8, 102, 103; and American exceptionalism, 272; and anti-Semitism, 8, 22–23, 102, 103; and Armenian-American activism, 292; and Armenian Massacres, 246; and Bulgarian nationalism, 81, 82; and civilizing/mediating agents, 8; and Cretan Insurrection, 58, 64; early Republic, 15, 335 (n. 51); European political theory on, 12; and Greek War of Independence, 47; and immigration to the United States, 137, 164; and imperialism/colonialism, 19–20; and Jewish American activism, 8, 100–101, 103, 109, 123–24, 348 (n. 8); Jews as civilizing/mediating agents, 100, 101–2, 114, 138, 279; and mandate system, 298–99, 379 (n. 143); and "Moro problem" debate, 164–65, 168; and non-Protestant groups in Western societies, 8; and revolutionary appeals, 9; and scientific racism, 160–61; and slavery, 15, 48, 335 (n. 51); and sympathetic treatment of Islamic societies, 6; and treatment of Native Americans, 8, 21, 210; and Wilson's foreign policy, 272, 273. *See also* American racism; race; racial/religious hierarchies in American treatment of Moros

racial/religious hierarchies in American treatment of Moros, 157–58; and British colonialist model, 200–201; and Bureau of Non-Christian Tribes, 186; and Bureau of the Census, 187, 188 (ill.), 189 (ill.), 190; and Cooper Act, 180; and Filipinization, 234–36, 237; legacies of, 190, 326–28; and Moro Province establishment, 179–81; Pershing governorship, 231–32; and Philippine Reservation, 195; and political organization of Moro territory, 208; Schurman commission on, 172–73, 359 (n. 70); Taft on, 178–79, 357 (n. 2); terminology, 360 (n. 71)

Radcliffe, Wallace, 161

Rafael, Vicente, 190

Raisuli, Mulai Ahmed, 142–44

Randolph, John, 340 (n. 89)

rational choice approaches, 25, 26

Ratti-Menton, Ulysse de, 104, 105, 119

Ravished Armenia, 307, 308 (ill.), 309, 309 (ill.), 310 (ill.)

Reconquista, 10

Reconstruction, 58

refugee resettlement. *See* demographic engineering

religious hierarchies. *See* racial/religious hierarchies

religious liberty ideal, 13–14. *See also* American exceptionalism

religious minorities in the Ottoman Empire: capitulatory treaties, 71, 104, 128; Constantinople Conference (1876–77), 85–86, 94–95, 127–28; millet system, 70, 343–44 (n. 4); and Young Turks, 276. *See also* humanitarian intervention rhetoric; imaginary nature of religious minority oppression

revolutionary appeals: and Armenian Massacres, 253–54; and Cretan Insurrection, 58–59; and Greek War of Independence, 37–39, 40–41, 43, 44, 338 (n. 32); and racial/religious hierarchies, 9

revolutionary struggles. *See* Eastern Question

The Rising Tide of Color against White World Supremacy (Stoddard), 326

Ritchie, Thomas, 37

Robert, Christopher, 72

Robert College (Beirut), 72–74, 76–77, 83, 85, 86, 92, 93, 344 (nn. 11, 16)

Rockefeller, John D., 260

Rodinson, Maxime, 19

Rodogno, David, 57, 83–84

Rodriguez, Eulogio, 328

Romania, 96, 126, 133

Roosevelt, Alice, 228

Roosevelt, Franklin D., 233, 323

Roosevelt, Theodore, Jr.: and Algeciras
Conference, 144–46, 147–50, 151;
and Armenian Massacres, 242; and
Bates Treaty, 203, 207; and Battle of
Bud Dajo, 212, 216, 365 (n. 94); and
British advice on imperialism/
colonialism, 200, 363 (n. 25); on
Family of Nations concept, 319–20,
321–22; on force, 209; and Benjamin
Harrison, 369 (n. 11); and humanitarian intervention rhetoric, 210; on
imperialism/colonialism, 147–48,
152–53, 319–21; and Muslim identity
as defined by religion, 204; and
Perdicaris Affair, 142–43; and
Protestant missionaries, 223;
and Wood's background, 198, 199
(ill.); and World War I, 294
Roosevelt, Theodore, Sr., 58
Root, Elihu: and Algeciras Conference,
144, 145–46, 147, 151; and American
treatment of Moros, 174–75, 180, 181,
218–19; and Armenian mandate
proposals, 300, 311; and Wood, 198
Rotter, Andrew, 27
Russian Empire: anti-Semitism, 95,
126–27, 133, 144–46, 347 (n. 115),
355 (n. 86); and Armenian Genocide,
277, 286; and Armenian Massacres,
242, 263–64, 369 (n. 3); and Bulgarian nationalism, 76, 77–78, 79, 85–86,
345 (n. 40); Caucasian Wars, 76;
Crimean War, 55, 71, 78, 341 (n. 119);
and Greek War of Independence,
38–39; and humanitarian intervention rhetoric, 74, 79; Russo-Turkish
War, 86–90, 93–94, 136, 247–48;
Sykes-Picot Treaty, 295; and Young
Turks, 279
Russo-Turkish War (1877–78), 86–90,
93–94, 136, 247–48
Rustem Bey, 282–84

Safi Affair (1863), 116–24; British
responses, 119–20; and imperialism/

colonialism, 116–17, 118; Montefiore
mission, 121–24; and Moroccan
Jewish activism, 120–21, 122;
Seward's role, 117–18; and Spanish
anti-Semitism, 118–19
Said, Edward, 8, 23–24, 27, 28, 124–25
St. Clair, William, 34, 337 (n. 9)
St. Louis World's Fair (1904), 193,
195–98, 196 (ill.), 197 (ill.)
Saleeby, Najeeb, 163, 193, 206, 315
Salisbury, Lord (Robert Gascoyne-
Cecil), 242, 265
San Remo, Treaty of (1920), 312
San Stefano, Treaty of (1878), 90,
247–48
Satia, Priya, 382 (n. 205)
Schiff, Jacob, 145, 148–50, 151, 260, 356
(n. 101)
Schroeter, Daniel J., 350 (n. 54)
Schurman, Jacob, 169, 175–76, 300, 311.
See also Schurman commission
Schurman commission, 168–74, 175
Schuyler, Eugene, 80–81, 85–86, 87,
90–92, 347 (n. 90)
scientific racism, 103, 160–61, 168, 245,
246
Scott, Hugh Lennox, 198–99, 201, 202,
206, 207, 211, 214, 309
Second Great Awakening, 15, 16, 36
self-determination: and anticolonial
resistance, 322; and Bulgarian
nationalism, 74; and counternarratives, 6; and Jewish homeland, 314;
and mandate system, 275; and
Muslims as incapable of civilized
rule, 273; and resistance against
mandate system, 316–17; and World
War I, 271, 295
Seligman, William, 95
September 11, 2001 terrorist attacks, 24,
330
Seward, William Henry, 59–60, 62, 63,
72, 117, 118, 121
sexuality. *See* gender rhetoric
Shanks, John, 64

Skobelev, Mikhail, 79

slavery: abolitionism, 58, 66–67, 117, 340 (n. 89); and American imperialism/colonialism, 21; and American treatment of Moros, 168, 175–76, 205, 359 (n. 48); and Cretan Insurrection, 64, 65, 66–67; and Greek War of Independence, 36, 37, 48–49, 49 (ill.), 340 (n. 89); and humanitarian intervention rhetoric, 36, 37, 337 (n. 17); and Jewish American activism, 117; and racial/religious hierarchies, 15, 48, 335 (n. 51)

slave trade, 14

Smith, John, 11, 12 (ill.)

Smith, Judson, 252, 266

Smith, Philip, 7

Smuts, Jan, 302

Snyder, Timothy, 323

Social Darwinism, 160–61, 245, 275, 369 (n. 12)

Social Gospel movement, 160–61, 245, 246

Spain: advice on American treatment of Moros, 170; Philippines colonialism, 159, 169–70, 173, 174, 360 (n. 74); Safi Affair, 116–24; Spanish-American War, 157, 198, 242, 269, 270; Spanish-Moroccan War, 111–13, 115–16, 117

Spanish-American War (1898), 157, 198, 242, 269, 270

Spanish-Moroccan War (1860), 111–13, 115–16, 117

Speer, Robert, 289

Spellberg, Denise, 14

Spencer, Herbert, 369 (n. 12)

Spencer, Lorillard, 235

Spooner Amendment (1899), 178

Spring-Rice, Cecil, 242

Staël, Germaine de (Madame de Staël), 40

Stanley, Edward (Lord Derby), 78

Stevenson, Andrew, 107–8

Stillman, William J., 58–59, 60, 63–64

Stoddard, Lothrop, 326

Stone, Melville, 290

Stone, William L., 37

Storey, Joseph, 99

Storey, Moorfield, 212–13

Strangford, Lady (Emily Ann Beaufort), 77, 79

Straus, Oscar: and Armenian Genocide, 289; and Armenian mandate proposals, 300, 311; and Bates treaty, 176; and missionary political influence, 249; and naturalization system, 250; and Russian anti-Semitism, 145, 146

Strong, Josiah: and American treatment of Moros, 3–4, 224, 225 (ill.), 226; and Armenian Massacres, 245, 254, 257, 269–70; and U.S. annexation of the Philippines, 160–61

The Sultan of Sulu (Ade), 193, 194 (ill.)

Summary of the Law of Nations (von Martens), 17

Sumner, Charles, 62

Suny, Ronald G., 375 (n. 20)

Sweet, O. J., 183–84

Sykes-Picot Treaty (1917), 295

Syria: Catholicism, 349 (n. 24); Damascus Affair, 104–10, 119, 121, 264; Druze-Maronite conflict (1860), 56–57, 70, 341 (n. 126); King-Crane Commission, 304–5; and mandate system, 302, 304, 315

Taft, Helen Herron, 224

Taft, William Howard: and Armenian mandate proposals, 311; and Battle of Bud Dajo, 214; and commercial interests, 229; and Moro disarmament order, 232–33; and Moro Province establishment, 179, 182, 183, 198, 361 (n. 107); and Philippine Reservation, 195; and Protestant missionaries, 222, 223, 224; and racial/religious hierarchies, 178–79, 357 (n. 2); and Wood governorship, 202, 203, 207

Talaat Pasha, Mehmed, 278, 281, 287–88
Tanner, Jeremy, 337 (n. 16)
Tanzimat reforms, 70–71, 352 (n. 93)
Temple, Henry John (Lord Palmerston),
   106
Tennyson, Alfred, Lord, 366 (n. 111)
terminology, 333 (nn. 4, 7), 334 (n. 15),
   360 (n. 71)
Thornton, Edward, 134
Tillman, Benjamin, 162
Toynbee, Arnold J., 330
Trask, Spencer, 260
travel literature, 13
Treaty of Berlin (1878), 90, 94, 247, 263,
   264
Treaty of Constantinople (1832), 51–52
Treaty of Paris (1898), 168–69
Treaty of San Remo (1920), 312
Treaty of San Stefano (1878), 90,
   247–48
Tseretelev, A. N. (Russian prince), 81,
   85–86
Tuckerman, Charles, 63
Tunisia, 102, 104, 140–41
Turkey and the Armenian Atrocities
   (Bliss & Hamlin), 258–59
The Turkish Atrocities in Bulgaria
   (MacGahan), 82
Turkish Republic, 313
Turks. *See* Ottoman Empire

Union of American Hebrew Congrega-
   tions, 135, 137–38, 146
Unitarianism, 39–40
United States as Christian nation:
   Christian amendment movement
   (1864), 124; and early republic, 15,
   99–100, 348 (n. 2); and Second Great
   Awakening, 15; Storey treatise, 99.
   See also Family of Nations concept

Van Buren, Martin, 107, 108–9, 110, 121
Versailles Peace Conference. *See*
   mandate system
Victoria (queen of England), 87–88

violence. *See* force
Virgin Islands, 272
Voltaire, 13
von Martens, G. F., 17

Walker, Christopher, 276
Walsh, Robert, 37
Wanger, Irving, 277
Washburn, George, Jr., 297
Washburn, George, Sr.: and Armenian
   Massacres, 256, 371 (n. 45); and
   Bulgarian nationalism, 74, 77–78, 79,
   345 (n. 41); and naturalization
   system, 250; and Protestant colleges
   establishment, 71–72; Robert College
   presidency, 73; thanked by Bulgar-
   ians, 90
Washington, George, 45, 101
Webster, Daniel, 35, 36, 46–48, 55, 338
   (n. 38)
Weizmann, Chaim, 304
Wheaton, Henry, 18, 34–35, 55–56, 60
White, Henry, 147, 150, 311
White, John R., 211–12
Willard, Frances, 258–59, 261
Williams, John Sharpe, 215
Williams, Talcott, 277, 290
Wilson, Woodrow, 271–75; and
   American exceptionalism, 272–73,
   275, 293, 318; and American racism,
   272, 288; and American treatment
   of Moros, 226, 233; and Armenian
   Genocide, 290; and Armenian
   mandate proposals, 300, 312–13;
   Greek warship incident (1914),
   281–82; and imperialism/colonialism,
   271–72; and Jewish homeland, 239,
   304, 314–15; and League of Nations,
   311–12; and mandate system, 274,
   296, 300, 302–3, 304–6, 316, 379 (n.
   134); and Morgenthau ambassadorship, 279; and Rustem Bey accusations, 283; and self-determination,
   271, 273, 316–17; and World War I,
   293–95, 376 (n. 61)